Privacy Preservation
of Genomic and Medical Data

Scrivener Publishing
100 Cummings Center, Suite 541J
Beverly, MA 01915-6106

Publishers at Scrivener
Martin Scrivener (martin@scrivenerpublishing.com)
Phillip Carmical (pcarmical@scrivenerpublishing.com)

Privacy Preservation
of Genomic and Medical Data

Edited by
Amit Kumar Tyagi
National Institute of Fashion Technology, New Delhi, India

Scrivener
Publishing

This edition first published 2024 by John Wiley & Sons, Inc., 111 River Street, Hoboken, NJ 07030, USA and Scrivener Publishing LLC, 100 Cummings Center, Suite 541J, Beverly, MA 01915, USA
© 2024 Scrivener Publishing LLC
For more information about Scrivener publications please visit www.scrivenerpublishing.com.

Wiley Global Headquarters
111 River Street, Hoboken, NJ 07030, USA

For details of our global editorial offices, customer services, and more information about Wiley products visit us at www.wiley.com.

Limit of Liability/Disclaimer of Warranty
While the publisher and authors have used their best efforts in preparing this work, they make no representations or warranties with respect to the accuracy or completeness of the contents of this work and specifically disclaim all warranties, including without limitation any implied warranties of merchantability or fitness for a particular purpose. No warranty may be created or extended by sales representatives, written sales materials, or promotional statements for this work. The fact that an organization, website, or product is referred to in this work as a citation and/or potential source of further information does not mean that the publisher and authors endorse the information or services the organization, website, or product may provide or recommendations it may make. This work is sold with the understanding that the publisher is not engaged in rendering professional services. The advice and strategies contained herein may not be suitable for your situation. You should consult with a specialist where appropriate. Neither the publisher nor authors shall be liable for any loss of profit or any other commercial damages, including but not limited to special, incidental, consequential, or other damages. Further, readers should be aware that websites listed in this work may have changed or disappeared between when this work was written and when it is read.

Library of Congress Cataloging-in-Publication Data

ISBN 978-1-394-21262-0

Cover image: Pixabay.Com
Cover design by Russell Richardson

Set in size of 11pt and Minion Pro by Manila Typesetting Company, Makati, Philippines

Printed in the USA

10 9 8 7 6 5 4 3 2 1

Contents

Part 4: Issues and Challenges 383

Preface

Data science is a broad field encompassing some of the fastest-growing subjects in interdisciplinary statistics, mathematics and computer science. It encompasses a process of inspecting, cleaning, transforming, and modeling data with the goal of discovering useful information, suggesting conclusions, and supporting decision making. Data analysis has multiple facets and approaches, including diverse techniques under a variety of names, in different business, science, and social science domains. Similarly, data analytics is now required in the medial field for analyzing genomic and genetic data.

Genomics is a branch of genetics coined by Tom Roderick in 1986. Genetics is the study of a single gene, whereas genomics refers to the study of a group of genes called genomes. Genomes can be considered an instruction manual for human life. Originally the analysis of genomic data was very costly. However, due to the advancements in technology, the sequencing cost has come down significantly, so that genomic analysis can even be included in daily medical routines. The more we explore our genomes, the easier it will be to make medical decisions and cure diseases.

Genomic data does not only include personal information, but also the family ancestors' data. Any leakage of this type of information could cause very serious issues, so data-protection is critical. Privacy laws such as GINA (Genetic Information Non-discrimination Act), HIPAA (Health Insurance Portability and Accountability Act of 1996) and GDPR (General Data Protection Regulation) help users protect their privacy by restricting the sharing of patients' sensitive information. However, we must focus on privacy issues in an era of such rapid developments in the healthcare sectors. The main categories of privacy in healthcare include data, location, identity, and genomic privacy. Existing tools are insufficient to handle genomic data because of the large size of the datasets.

This book focuses on genomic data sources, analytical tools, and the importance of privacy preservation. Topics discussed include tensor flow and Bio-Weka, privacy laws, HIPAA, and other emerging technologies like

Internet of Things, IoT-based cloud environments, cloud computing, edge computing, and blockchain technology for smart applications. The book starts with a basic introduction to genomes, genomics, genetics, transcriptomes, proteomes, and other basic concepts of modern molecular biology. It concludes with future predictions for genomic and genomic privacy, emerging technologies, and applications.

Amit Kumar Tyagi

Acknowledgements

First, we extend our gratitude to our family members, friends, and supervisors who stood by us as advisors during the completion of this book. Also, we thank our almighty God who inspired us to write this book. Furthermore, we thank Wiley and Scrivener Publishing, who have provided continuous support; and our colleagues with whom we have worked inside the college and university system, as well as those outside of academia who have provided their endless support toward completing this book.

Finally, we wish to thank our Respected Madam, Prof. G Aghila, Prof. Siva Sathya, our Respected Sir Prof. N Sreenath, and Prof. Aswani Kumar Cherukuri, for their valuable input and help in completing this book.

Amit Kumar Tyagi

Part 1
FUNDAMENTALS

Introduction to Genomics and Genetics

Mahreen Fatima[1], Sana Zia[2], Maheen Murtaza[3], Asyia Shafique[4],
Afshan Muneer[3], Junaid Sattar[5], Muhammad Ashir Nabeel[6]
and Amjad Islam Aqib[7]*

*[1]Faculty of Biosciences, Cholistan University of Veterinary and Animal Sciences,
Bahawalpur, Pakistan*
*[2]Department of Zoology, Government Sadiq College Women, University,
Bahawalpur, Pakistan*
*[3]Department of Zoology, Cholistan University of Veterinary and Animal Sciences
Bahawalpur, Pakistan*
*[4]Department of Clinical Medicine and Surgery, University of Agriculture,
Faisalabad, Pakistan*
*[5]Faculty of Veterinary Sciences, Choliatan University of Veterinary and Animal
Sciences, Bahawalpur, Pakistan*
*[6]Animal Sciences, University of Illinois Urbana Champaign, Urbana,
United States of America*
*[7]Department of Medicine, Cholistan University of Veterinary and Animal Sciences,
Bahawalpur, Pakistan*

Abstract

Genomic research is a relatively new field in biotechnology, with DNA sequencing as its essential technology. Genomic research is progressing quickly due to the accessibility of advanced technologies, which enables genome-wide sequencing to address biological questions. During the last decade, genomic studies have evolved into potential tools for understanding human disease genetics. It was essential to organize a sequence of 3 billion letter codes in a cost-effective manner after the evolution of the human project. By producing large amounts of sequencing data at a low cost, this breakthrough enabled the emergence of a wide variety of biomedical applications after the completion of the project. For the interpretation of the human genome, these technological advancements have enabled the sequencing of various vertebrate genomes. In addition to allowing the study of vertebrate genome evolution, this sequencing will also benefit human medicine

Corresponding author: amjadislamaqib@cuvas.edu.pk

Amit Kumar Tyagi (ed.) Privacy Preservation of Genomic and Medical Data, (3–18) © 2024
Scrivener Publishing LLC

and comparative genomics. The focus of this chapter is to introduce and review the basic aspects of genomics, as well as its role in the pharmaceutical industry.

Keywords: Genomic, genetic, technology, biomedical application, pharmaceutical industry

1.1   Introduction

There are slightly more than 20,000 human protein-coding genes, but every one of these classifications typically codes for numerous proteins thanks to mechanisms like uncommon concerning, differing strand transcripts, and others. There may be up to five determined transcripts per gene sequence, giving some confirmation. Two percent part of the human genome's DNA balance contains the real protein-encoding orders. It is now generally acknowledged that there are tens of thousands of genomic areas that encode "noncoding RNA transcripts." These RNAs display a role in the control of messenger RNA translation and gene entrance (mRNAs) [1]. Given how the chromatin state moves gene appearance, it is strong that epigenomic cause changes to histone chemistry and DNA methylation levels can have a significant impact on transcription. Once more, this is a cutting-edge field of cellular biology where the potential position of activity and inactivity needs to be widely explored. If genomics is the study of the assets of the genome, genetics is the study of how characters or phenotypes are approved down through groups [2]. The identification of genetic differences related to neuropsychiatric disorders and treatment significances has thus amplified self-assurance that these findings will rapidly be functional in the clinic to improve diagnosis, disease risk forecast, and patient reply to drug therapy. Slower DNA segments can be sequenced using the shotgun method, clone by clone, whole genome, Maxam Gilbert, and Sanger sequencing methods. Sanger chemistry, the "original" sequencing method, reads through a DNA template shaped during DNA synthesis using specially branded nucleotides [3]. The Sanger method is used read 1000 to 1200 base pairs (bp) thanks to a number of practical developments, but it is still imperfect to the 2-kilo base pair (kbps) [4]. In this book chapter focus, the hub of genomics, Genome Sequencing Methods, Variation of Genome Sequencing, Diseases and Disorders, and Future Prospects.

1.2   Hub of Genomics

There are slightly more than 20,000 human protein-coding genes. Still, every one of these classifications typically codes for numerous proteins thanks to mechanisms like uncommon concerning, differing strand transcripts, and others. There may be up to five determined transcripts per gene sequence, giving some confirmation. Two percent of the human genome's DNA balance contains the real protein-encoding orders. It is now generally acknowledged that tens of thousands of genomic areas encode "noncoding RNA transcripts." These RNAs display a role in controlling messenger RNA translation and gene entrance (mRNAs) [5]. Given how the chromatin state moves gene appearance, it is strong that epigenomic cause changes to histone chemistry and DNA methylation levels can significantly impact transcription. Once more, this is a cutting-edge field of cellular biology where the potential position of activity and inactivity needs to be widely explored. If genomics is the study of the assets of the genome, genetics is the study of how characters or phenotypes are approved down through groups [6]. Identifying genetic differences related to neuropsychiatric disorders and treatment significance has thus amplified self-assurance that these findings will rapidly be functional in the clinic to improve diagnosis, disease risk forecast, and patient reply to drug therapy. Slower DNA segments can be sequenced using the shotgun method, clone by clone, whole genome, Maxam Gilbert, and Sanger sequencing methods. Sanger chemistry, the "original" sequencing method, reads through a DNA template shaped during DNA synthesis using specially branded nucleotides [7]. The Sanger method is used 1000 to 1200 base pairs (bp) thanks to some practical developments, but it is still imperfect to the 2 kbps [8]. The chapter aims to review some hubs of genomics, genome sequencing methods, variations of genome sequencing, diseases and disorders, and prospects.

A. Phenotype

The hypothetical molecular phenotypes comprise organism-level phenotypes like diseases and some molecular variations. For example, these include the over- or under-expression of specific genes [9]. So, one of the first steps is classifying the molecular phenotypes that go sideways with them. In the past 10 years, gene appearance has advanced a molecular-level trait used as a molecular phenotype to classify diseases, classify drug targets, and infer gene-gene exchanges [10].

The consequences are typically more consistent and humbler when gene appearance variations are carefully examined under various circumstances. Furthermore, it can be difficult to identify a gene's function outside its context when its function is obscure [11]. The amplified statistical power of a module-based method also makes it credible to identify a disturbed module even when individual genes within the module may not have suffered statistically significant perturbation [12].

B. Genotype

The sympathetic of phenotype models—whose fluctuations are linked in expression with changes in phenotype—was enclosed in the section before this one. This section focuses on the gene foundations of suffering and the substitute networks that these supports define. According to new studies, genomic changes vary greatly in complex diseases like cancer and neurological disorders. Theoretically, the changed or mutant genes may be part of the same pathways, collectively dysregulating those pathways. For example, O'Roak *et al.* [30] discovered that 39% (49 of 126) of the most severe or disordered *de novo* mutations map to a highly organized network of the proteins—catenin and chromatin remodeling in sporadic autism [33]. These strategies focus on identifying genotypic modules, or subnetworks, that are enriched with genes having genetic changes linked to disease. This mindset is common in the research of somatic cell mutations in cancer, which are the primary causes of the disease [13].

C. Gene Environmental Interaction

The environment may assist (or prevent) prospects for the entrance of genotype-guided social penchants in the most open and perhaps most overall sense. For case, some examples of dormant variable G-E interactions previously mentioned imply this. There, the inspiration of religion, public features (such as urban/rural), peer substance use, or parental guideline on smoking or drinking varied. Furthermore, it has been recognized that some of these environmental factors can decrease the social properties of specific polymorphisms [14]. Other environmental issues that play a vital role in G-E interactions include shocking events like child exploitation that cause penetrating delicate and physical responses. New data proposes that these replies affect the organic paths that collaborate with genetic effects, maybe uniformly varying how the genes are expressed. These properties can last for the mainstream or all of a person's lifespan due to specific genomic variations, or they can be passed and linked with environmental contact [15].

D. Epigenetics

DNA sequence differences are not compound in epigenetic changes. Although, throughout mitosis, they regularly pass from one cell to its daughter cells. It has also been documented that some epigenetic changes can be approved down the germ lines from one group to the next. It is extensively accepted that exposure to nutrients, cellular insults, stress, etc., can lead to epigenetic alterations at any age [16].

A chromosome's double-stranded DNA is packed very firmly, as previously stated. Each nucleosome is related to the one after it by a piece of free DNA that has been thankful by the linker histone, H1. The histone of nucleosomes can experience a diversity of chemical alterations, such as acetylation, methylation, and phosphorylation. The patterns of histone modifications can affect how chromatin is arranged, potentially affecting transcription activity. Methylating a cytosine base in the 5' positions can also change DNA [15].

1.3   Genome Sequencing Methods

A. Clone by Clone

Smaller pieces of the genome must be duplicated and put into bacteria using this technique. The deliberate genome's desirable 150,000 base pairs can be invented in identical duplicates, or "clones," created by growing the bacteria. The injected DNA is then further fragmented into 500 base pair portions that overlay in each clone. These more flattened supplements have a sequence. After sequencing, the overlying sections are used to put the clone back calmly. Using Sanger sequencing, this method was used to order the first human genome. While it takes a lot of time and money, this method works [17].

B. Maxam-Gilbert Sequencing

The Maxam-Gilbert method, this is genuine by subcloning. The five consecutive steps—base-specific alteration, resting the reactions, ethanol rainfall and centrifugation in arrangement, piperidine cleavage, and recurrent reduced-pressure evaporation—are exceptionally laborious, though. The option of losing the DNA pellet during the ethanol precipitation and centrifuging is additional issue. Additionally, during the ethanol precipitation, hydrazine might co-precipitate with DNA and affect the reactions' specificity [18].

Advantages and Disadvantages

The DNA template utilized in the Maxim-Gilbert sequencing method can be single-stranded or double-stranded, which is its chief draw. At one point, the Maxam-Gilbert approach was selected over the Sanger method since the later wanted to clone the single-stranded DNA for each read start. Moreover, DNA protein connections and epigenetic DNA alterations can be studied using the Maxam-Gilbert approach. Maxam-Gilbert sequencing was primarily forced by the use of dangerous substances and methods like radiolabeling and X-rays. The method was disapproved since it obligatory the use of hydrazine, a known neurotoxin, and was hard to scale up and manage [1].

C. Sanger Sequencing Method
The Sanger technique for genetic or DNA sequencing has been found main request in the field of veterinary diagnostics.

Outdated Sanger sequencing lasts to be the most popular sequencing approach utilized in VDLs for sequence verification, assay watching, and as the foundation for many phylogenetic analyses. It not only helps as the basis for fresher and automatic procedures. In this method, complementary DNA that had previously been prolonged by the DNA polymerase enzyme using any combination of the four deoxynucleotide triphosphates (dNTPs: dATP, dGTP, dCTP, and dTTP) or chain-terminating dideoxynucleotide triphosphates is annealed using an oligonucleotide primer. When rate-limiting amounts of the ddNTPs are added, the elongation synthesis becomes stationary and produces distinct DNA fragments of different lengths. Sanger sequencing technology can currently produce widely used NA sequences up to 800 to 1,000 bp. The method's most significant disadvantages characteristically include primer binding-induced lowermost quality sequence from 15 to 40 bp and the incapability to notice single base pair variations in longer segments. Seeing these limits, both commercial and open-source sequence analysis software is emerging to contribution users in automatically classifying and eliminating low-quality data. The capillary gel electrophoresis method used in Sanger sequencing is the focus of the VDL rules described here [19].

Advantages and Disadvantages
Researchers were able to find mutations and the fundamental cause of genetic illnesses with the aid of Sanger sequencing. It is the most actual technique for locating brief tandem repeats and sequencing a single gene. However, this method's major drawback is the length of time it takes, which results in a low throughput. Short DNA sequences (between 300 and 1000 base pairs) can only be processed using this method one at a time [19].

Principle of Genome Sequencing and Assembly
Currently, a shotgun sequencing approach is used for the majority of genome projects. Genomic DNA is first cut into a variety of tiny, random fragments. These are independently sequenced to a specific length, depending on the technology. The resulting sequence reads are then put back together into longer uninterrupted sequence stretches (contigs) using

potent computer algorithms, a procedure known as *de novo* assembly. High sequencing coverage is necessary to ensure that the sequence reads at each position in the genome overlap sufficiently for proper assembly (or read depth). Naturally, more overlap can be anticipated for longer sequence reads, which lowers the necessary raw read depth. Longer fragments (a few hundred base pairs) are typically sequenced from both ends (paired-end sequencing) to provide more details on where the reads should be placed in the assembled sequence [20]. The library's anticipated fragment length tells us how far apart the two contigs are physically, and the blank space is filled with the meaningless base-pair character "N." The missing base-pair information is filled in by later gap-closing techniques, ideally using long reads that read across repetitive sequences. The final step frequently involves joining the scaffolds into linkage groups or putting them on chromosomes. Unquestionably, the best method for arranging and orienting scaffolds into longer sequence blocks is to create genetic maps from crosses or pedigree data [21].

1.4   Variation of Genome Sequencing

A. Single Nucleotide Polymorphism
In single nucleotide polymorphisms, a specific nucleotide site differs from others [22]. DNA molecules may have different nucleotide pairings at the same sites in different populations, such as a T-A base pair at one nucleotide site and a C-G base pair at another. Statistically, significant differences are referred to as SNPs. There are two alleles associated with the SNP, for which the population may have three genotypes: homozygous or heterozygous chromosomes, T-A on one chromosome, and C-G on the homologous chromosome [23]. Alleles are enclosed in quotation marks because they do not need to be in coding arrangements or even genes [24]. Genetic variations that affect less than 1% of DNA molecules in a population are excluded from the SNP definition because they differ at a nucleotide site. A genetic variant that occurs too rarely in a population is not as useful for genetic analysis as a variant that occurs more frequently in a population [25].

B. INDELs (Insertion and Deletion)
SNPs, on the other hand, have received extensive research compared to other forms of genetic variation in humans [36]. The discovery of INDELs has lagged far behind the discovery of SNPs, and only a small number of them have been found. INDELs can be classified into five major categories:

(1) insertions and deletions of a single base pair, (2) monomeric expansions of two to five base pairs, (3) multiple expansions of a repeat unit between two and fifteen bases, (4) transposon insertions and (5) INDELs with random DNA sequences [23].

C. Copy Number Variation
Genetic association studies often evaluate SNPs, which are differences between individuals of the same species at a particular genomic location. Copy number variations (CNVs) in DNA sequences are common in naturally occurring organisms and have functional significance, their full significance has not yet been fully understood. Recombination and replication processes, as well as a higher rate of *de novo* locus-specific mutations than SNPs, all contribute to the production of CNVs. Through chromosomal segment deletions and duplications, Hastings *et al.* [13] described the mechanisms of change that result in CNV evolution in humans.

1.5   Diseases and Disorders

A. Multiple Sclerosis
A non-traumatic disabling disease most commonly affecting young adults is multiple sclerosis (MS). Both developed and developing countries are experiencing an increase in MS incidence and prevalence, with no clear cause identified. Ascherio A [26] describes MS as a complex disease caused by many genes, as well as several well-described environmental factors, including vitamin D exposure. In recent years, however, B-cell targeted therapies have challenged the conventional dogma about T-cell autoimmune disease. Traditionally, MS has been considered a two-stage disease involving relapsing–remitting disease and secondary or primary progressive disease caused by delayed neurodegeneration [27]. In addition to providing neural insulation and saltatory conduction of neurodegeneration and conduction failure. Several genes have been identified as responsible for CMT, which is a form of inherited peripheral neuropathy. A component of the age-related progression of MS can be explained by comorbid diseases, such as smoking and vascular disease. The comorbid disease makes patients more likely to progress more rapidly [28].

B. Klinefelter Syndrome
A common sex chromosome disorder and genetic irregularity, (KS) are chromosome disorders [29]. The traditional phenotype of the syndrome, defined as tall stature, small testes, gynecomastia, gynoid hips, sparse body

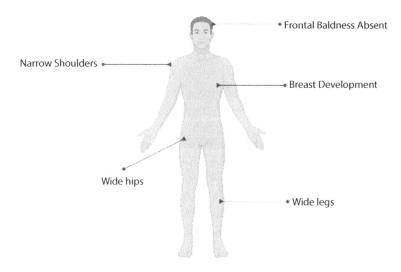

Figure 1.5.1 Signs and symptoms of Klinefelter's syndrome [30].

hair, primary hypogonadism, mental retardation, and sparse body hair, has been shown to be rarely observed in the clinical setting (refer Figure 1.5.1).

It may be due to a combination of the severity of genetic defects that the final KS phenotype develops. There are a variety of phenotypes, ranging from hypogonadotropic hypogonadism, infertility, neurocognitive deficits, as well as severe comorbidities [30].

C. Down Syndrome

Around 1 in every 600 to 700 live births has Down syndrome (DS) or trisomy 21, which reasons to basic bright incapability. Chromosome 21 trisomy is the reason for DS, which is produced by a total or partial trisomy of the autosomal chromosome 21. DS population life expectation has increased evocatively over the past numerous periods. In difference to other populations, individuals with DS still experience higher mortality rates. Characteristics present in all DS populations are craniofacial irregularities, and hypotonia in early beginning, there are numerous other preserved [31]. A DS baby have a big toe, irregular fingerprint pattern, and short fingers. Moreover, Robertson Ian translocations and is chromosomal or ring chromosomal disorders can cause the condition. In the process of developing an egg sperm, an chromosome refers to two long arms of the chromosome unraveling collected rather than the long arm and the short arm unravelling together. A mosaic is a mis division of cells after fertilization that happens at a sure point during cell division. In mosaic DS, two lineages of cells donate to tissues and organs; one lineage has usual chromosomes, while the other has 21 extra chromosomes [32].

D. Polycystic Ovarian Syndrome

There is an extremely high incidence and prevalence of polycystic ovary syndrome. Women in early to late-night reproductive phases universally are pretentious by it, but its prevalence varies extensively according to race and society. For example, South Asians are more likely to hurt from it than Caucasians. Asian women have a higher polycystic ovarian syndrome (PCOS) incidence (52% versus 20%–25%) than Western Caucasian women. As informed by the World Health Organization (WHO), PCOS affected 116 million women globally in 2012 (4%–12%) and was predictable to reach 26% by 2020 [33]. Rather than being a disease, PCOS is a disorder characterized by engorged ovaries and cysts more than ten in number. It is supposed that these cysts are the residues of follicles that have not advanced. An increase in thickening of the ovary wall happens as the disorder develops, and checks ripened follicles from being free. ANOVA, infertility, and disturbances in the menstrual cycle are all considered symptoms of PCOS [34].

PCOS produced by insulin confrontation (refer Figure 1.5.2): (1) High insulin levels are the important cause of PCOS. (2) Adrenal PCOS: This condition is shaped by adrenal excretions being inspired during puberty; patients with this disorder usually experience more stress due to extra levels of DHEAS. (3) Inflammatory PCOS: PCOS patients tend to have smaller chronic inflammation. (4) Post-pill PCOS: e.g., as a result of hormonal inequalities and contraceptive pills. Presently, PCOS can be achieved with

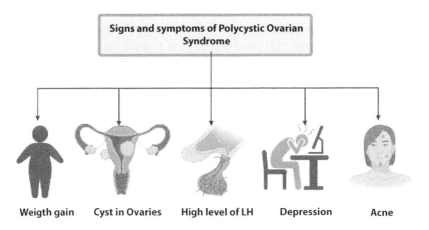

Weigth gain   **Cyst in Ovaries**   **High level of LH**   **Depression**   **Acne**

Figure 1.5.2 Classification of polycystic ovarian syndrome (PCOS) based different factors [35].

Allopathic therapy, herbal therapy, lifestyle variations, and dietary alterations [35].

1.6   Future Prospects

One reference genome cannot accurately reflect the diversity of human genetics, given the complexity of genetic variation. Normal genomes from diverse human populations, but especially those of African origin, who have the most genetic variety, must be sequenced and assembled [36].

Several new reference genomes are being produced with the help of long-read DNA sequencing in combination with short-read error correction. According to our current discovery rate, sequencing 300 human genomes in this manner will lead to a double number of structural variants that have been identified (at the DNA sequence level), identifying, in theory, the majority of common structural variants [37]. In millions of Illumina genomes that have already been generated, structural variation sequence resolution allows better genotyping of such alleles, allowing the discovery of new relationships [38].

A number of pathogenic variations are located outside of coding regions, which can have a negative effect on gene expression and translation. Despite the fact that exome sequencing is less expensive and provides greater sample sizes and power, it provides little information on regulatory modifications and hampers the discovery of minor structural variants even within coding sequences [39]. It is challenging to identify harmful variants linked with noncoding mutations. It may, however, be possible to understand noncoding regulatory mutations and their contribution to common and rare genetic diseases if structural variants are detected on a systematic basis as they are more likely than SNVs to be dysfunctional and alter gene expression [40]. In order to detect structural variations, whole genome sequencing is crucial. Fully phased long-read genome sequences are expected to yield 2.8 times as many structural variations as Illumina whole-genome sequencing, plus a 30% boost over long-read callers that do not phase. In other words, rather than a 3-Gbps genome, we should consider a 6-Gbps genome, where both parental haplotypes are perfectly sequenced and assembled [41].

It is essential to understand the genetic basis of *de novo* mutations, DNA sequence conservation between species, and selection at a given locus before one can interpret variants. Methods that utilize these factors have been successful in identifying potential pathogenic variants by adopting specific methods [42]. They require, however, that variation both within and between species be equally described. Non-human primate, mammalian, and vertebrate genomes must be sequenced with the same rigor as extrahuman genomes because orthologous DNA sequences are historically poorly aligned and have rates of mutation that differ by orders of magnitude [43].

Conventional human genome analysis utilizing short-read sequencing data catches only around 85% of the genome and ignores some of the most variable areas, excluding them from association testing [44, 45]. To describe all human chromosomes, including acrocentric, telomeric, centromeric, and segmentally duplicated DNA, from telomere to telomere is a simple goal. Sequencing platforms for long reads and ultralong reads [46].

1.7   Conclusion

This chapter gives a detailed review on genomics and genetics. This chapter describes the perpetuity of genomics to genetics in the practice of treatment diagnosis of disease. In the future, by using genetic information, a disease can be diagnosed at very early stages, and it can also be cured. Researchers need to become very active and savvy in interpreting genetic information that could be used for in medical and public health. Researcher, professional academia, and organization should communicate collectively to conduct the necessary research.

References

1. Jain, M., Olsen, H.E., Turner, D.J., Stoddart, D., Bulazel, K.V., Paten, B., Miga, K.H., Linear assembly of a human centromere on the Y chromosome. *Nat. Biotechnol.*, 36, 4, 321–323, 2018.
2. Vollger, M.R., Dishuck, P.C., Sorensen, M., Welch, A.E., Dang, V., Dougherty, M.L., Eichler, E.E., Long-read sequence and assembly of segmental duplications. *Nat. Methods*, 16, 1, 88–94, 2019.
3. Kronenberg, Z.N., Fiddes, I.T., Gordon, D., Murali, S., Cantsilieris, S., Meyerson, O.S., Eichler, E.E., High-resolution comparative analysis of great ape genomes. *Science*, 360, 6393, eaar6343, 2018.
4. Kircher, M., Witten, D.M., Jain, P., O'roak, B.J., Cooper, G.M., Shendure, J., A general framework for estimating the relative pathogenicity of human genetic variants. *Nat. Genet.*, 46, 3, 310–315, 2014.
5. Ebert, P., Audano, P.A., Zhu, Q., Rodriguez-Martin, B., Porubsky, D., Bonder, M.J., Eichler, E.E., Haplotype-resolved diverse human genomes and integrated analysis of structural variation. *Science*, 372, 6537, eabf7117, 2021.

6. Koren, S., Rhie, A., Walenz, B.P., Dilthey, A.T., Bickhart, D.M., Kingan, S.B., Phillippy, A.M., De novo assembly of haplotype-resolved genomes with trio binning. *Nat. Biotechnol.*, 36, 12, 1174–1182, 2018.

7. Turner, T.N., Coe, B.P., Dickel, D.E., Hoekzema, K., Nelson, B.J., Zody, M.C., Eichler, E.E., Genomic patterns of de novo mutation in simplex autism. *Cell*, 171, 3, 710–722, 2017.

8. Audano, P.A., Sulovari, A., Graves-Lindsay, T.A., Cantsilieris, S., Sorensen, M., Welch, A.E., Eichler, E.E., Characterizing the major structural variant alleles of the human genome. *Cell*, 176, 3, 663–675, 2019.

9. McClellan, J.M., Lehner, T., King, M.C., Gene discovery for complex traits: Lessons from Africa. *Cell*, 171, 2, 261–264, 2017.

10. Huddleston, J., Chaisson, M.J., Steinberg, K.M., Warren, W., Hoekzema, K., Gordon, D., Eichler, E.E., Discovery and genotyping of structural variation from long-read haploid genome sequence data. *Genome Res.*, 27, 5, 677–685, 2017.

11. Conrad, D.F., Pinto, D., Redon, R., Feuk, L., Gokcumen, O., Zhang, Y., Hurles, M.E., Origins and functional impact of copy number variation in the human genome. *Nature*, 464, 7289, 704–712, 2010.

12. Stankiewicz, P. and Lupski, J.R., Structural variation in the human genome and its role in disease. *Annu. Rev. Med.*, 61, 437–455, 2010.

13. Hastings, P.J., Lupski, J.R., Rosenberg, S.M., Ira, G., Mechanisms of change in gene copy number. *Nat. Rev. Genet.*, 10, 8, 551–564, 2009.

14. Belsky, D.W., Moffitt, T.E., Corcoran, D.L., Domingue, B., Harrington, H., Hogan, S., Caspi, A., The genetics of success: How single-nucleotide polymorphisms associated with educational attainment relate to life-course development. *Psychol. Sci.*, 27, 7, 957–972, 2016.

15. Belsky, D.W., Moffitt, T.E., Corcoran, D.L., Domingue, B., Harrington, H., Hogan, S., Caspi, A., The genetics of success: How single-nucleotide polymorphisms associated with educational attainment relate to life-course development. *Psychol. Sci.*, 27, 7, 957–972, 2016.

16. Michailidou, K., Lindström, S., Dennis, J., Beesley, J., Hui, S., Kar, S., Humphreys, K., Association analysis identifies 65 new breast cancer risk loci. *Nature*, 551, 7678, 92–94, 2017.

17. Berger, J., Suzuki, T., Senti, K.A., Stubbs, J., Schaffner, G., Dickson, B.J., Genetic mapping with SNP markers in Drosophila. *Nat. Gen.*, 29, 4, 475–481, 2001.

18. Wicks, S.R., Yeh, R.T., Gish, W.R., Waterston, R.H., Plasterk, R.H., Rapid gene mapping in Caenorhabditis elegans using a high density polymorphism map. *Nat. Gen.*, 28, 2, 160–164, 2001.

19. Dawson, E., Chen, Y., Hunt, S., Smink, L.J., Hunt, A., Rice, K., Dunham, I., A SNP resource for human chromosome 22: Extracting dense clusters of SNPs from the genomic sequence. *Genome Res.*, 11, 1, 170–178, 2001.

20. Hendriksen, R.S., Bortolaia, V., Tate, H., Tyson, G.H., Aarestrup, F.M., McDermott, P.F., Using genomics to track global antimicrobial resistance. *Front. Public Health*, 7, 242, 2019.
21. Malla, M.A., Dubey, A., Kumar, A., Yadav, S., Hashem, A., Abd_Allah, E.F., Exploring the human microbiome: The potential future role of next-generation sequencing in disease diagnosis and treatment. *Front. Immunol.*, 9, 2868, 2019.
22. Shokralla, S., Spall, J.L., Gibson, J.F., Hajibabaei, M., Next-generation sequencing technologies for environmental DNA research. *Mol. Ecol.*, 21, 8, 1794–1805, 2012.
23. Mahmoud, A.M., An overview of epigenetics in obesity: The role of lifestyle and therapeutic interventions. *Int. J. Mol. Sci.*, 23, 3, 1341, 2022.
24. Agustí, A., Melén, E., DeMeo, D.L., Breyer-Kohansal, R., Faner, R., Pathogenesis of chronic obstructive pulmonary disease: Understanding the contributions of gene–environment interactions across the lifespan. *Lancet Respir. Med.*, 10, 512–524, 2022.
25. Chaste, P. and Leboyer, M., Autism risk factors: Genes, environment, and gene-environment interactions. *Dialogues Clin. Neurosci.*, 14, 281–292, 2022.
26. Ascherio, A., Environmental factors in multiple sclerosis. *Expert Review of Neurotherapeutics*, 13(sup2), 3–9, 2013
27. Zahid, G., Aka Kaçar, Y., Dönmez, D., Küden, A., Giordani, T., Perspectives and recent progress of genome-wide association studies (GWAS) in fruits. *Mol. Biol. Rep.*, 49, 6, 5341–5352, 2022.
28. McArthur, E., Rinker, D.C., Gilbertson, E.N., Fudenberg, G., Pittman, M., Keough, ... K., Capra, J.A., *Reconstructing the 3D genome organization of Neanderthals reveals that chromatin folding shaped phenotypic and sequence divergence*, Biorxiv, 2022, 2022-02.
29. Pudlo, N.A., Urs, K., Crawford, R., Pirani, A., Atherly, T., Jimenez, R., Martens, E.C., Phenotypic and genomic diversification in complex carbohydrate-degrading human gut bacteria. *Msystems*, 7, 1, e00947–21, 2022.
30. O'Roak, B.J., Vives, L., Girirajan, S., Karakoc, E., Krumm, N., Coe, B.P., Eichler, E.E., Sporadic autism exomes reveal a highly interconnected protein network of de novo mutations. *Nature*, 485, 7397, 246–250, 2012.
31. Hendriksen, R.S., Bortolaia, V., Tate, H., Tyson, G.H., Aarestrup, F.M., McDermott, P.F., Using genomics to track global antimicrobial resistance. *Front. Public Health*, 7, 242, 2019.
32. Koren, S., Rhie, A., Walenz, B.P. *et al.*, De novo assembly of haplotype-resolved ge nomes with trio binning. *Nat. Biotechnol.*, 36, 12, 1174–1182, 2018.
33. Gilman, S.R., Iossifov, I., Levy, D., Ronemus, M., Wigler, M., Vitkup, D., Rare de novo variants associated with autism implicate a large functional network of genes involved in formation and function of synapses. *Neuron*, 70, 5, 898–907, 2011.

34. Greenfield, A.L. and Hauser, S.L., B-cell therapy for multiple sclerosis: Entering an era. *Ann. Neurol.*, 83, 1, 13–26, 2018.
35. Coles, A.J., Cox, A., Le Page, E. *et al.*, The window of therapeutic opportunity in multiple sclerosis: Evidence from monoclonal antibody therapy. *J. Neurol.*, 253, 98–108, 2006.
36. Handel, A.E., Williamson, A.J., Disanto, G., Dobson, R., Giovannoni, G., Ramagopalan, S.V., Smoking and multiple sclerosis: An updated meta-analysis. *PLoS One*, 6, 1, e16149, 2011.
37. Gravholt, C.H., Chang, S., Wallentin, M., Fedder, J., Moore, P., Skakkebaek, A., Klinefelter syndrome - integrating genetics, neuropsychology and endocrinology. *Endocr. Rev.*, 39, 389– 423, 2018.
38. Bonomi, M., Rochira, V., Pasquali, D., Balercia, G., Jannini, E.A., Ferlin, A., Klinefelter syndrome (KS): Genetics, clinical phenotype and hypogonadism. *J. Endocrinol. Invest.*, 40, 123–134, 2017.
39. De Graaf, G., Buckley, F., Skotko, B.G., Estimation of the number of people with down syndrome in the United States. *Genet. Med.*, 19, 4, 439–447, 2017.
40. Ellegren, H., Smeds, L., Burri, R., Olason, P.I., Backström, N., Kawakami, T., Wolf, J.B., The genomic landscape of species divergence in Ficedula flycatchers. *Nature*, 491, 7426, 756–760, 2012.
41. Ellegren, H., Genome sequencing and population genomics in non-model organisms. *Trends Ecol. Evol.*, 29, 1, 51–63, 2014.
42. Correale, J. and Gaitan, M.I., Multiple sclerosis and environmental factors: The role of vitamin D, parasites, and Epstein–barr virus infection. *Acta Neurol. Scand.*, 132, 46–55, 2015.
43. Santos, F., Gómez-Manzo, S., Sierra-Palacios, E., González-Valdez, A., Castillo Villanueva, A., Reyes-Vivas, H., Marcial-Quino, J., Purification, concentration and recovery of small fragments of DNA from Giardia lamblia and their use for other molecular techniques. *MethodsX*, 4, 289–296, 2017.
44. Vandin, F., Upfal, E., Raphael, B.J., Algorithms for detecting significantly mutated pathways in cancer. *J. Comput. Biol.*, 18, 507–522, 2011.
45. Crossley, B.M., Bai, J., Glaser, A., Maes, R., Porter, E., Killian, M.L., Clement, T., Toohey-Kurth, K., Guidelines for sanger sequencing and molecular assay monitoring. *J. Vet. Diagn. Invest.: Off. Publ. Am. Assoc. Veterinary Lab. Diagnosticians Inc.*, 32, 6, 767–775, 2020. https://doi.org/10.1177/1040638720905833.
46. Hoehe, M.R. and Morris-Rosendahl, D.J., The role of genetics and genomics in clinical psychiatry. *Dialogues Clin. Neurosci.*, 20, 169–177, 2022.

An Overview of Genomics and Frontiers in Genetics for Smart Era

Saagar Bafna[1], Akash Shedage[1], Amber Agarwal[1], Somya Rakesh Goyal[1]*
and Istiaque Ahmed[2]

[1]Manipal University Jaipur, Jaipur, Rajasthan, India
[2]Gwangju Institute of Science and Technology (GIST), Gwangju, Korea

Abstract

The genome is a complete set of genetic information contained in an organism's DNA that encodes all its traits and properties. Understanding genomes is crucial in fields such as genetics, biotechnology, and medicine as it allows the study of heredity and the manipulation of genes for various purposes such as diagnosis and treatment of diseases. This chapter explains dedicatedly the applications of genomics in our real day-to-day life. It covers all broad categories of application areas ranging from Agriculture to Biomed. Further, two application areas are discussed in detail named, genomes in the military and genomes in personalized medicines. The issues, challenges, and sub-application areas are identified. Later, Human Genome Project and All of Us project are discussed. Few case studies are added to put light on the methods to decipher the meanings hidden in genomic sequences in humans. The major contribution of this study is to bring awareness about the cruciality of the concept of genomics in the evolving world of new technology for medical and technical aspects.

Keywords: Genome, personalized medicine, genomic counseling, human genome project (HGP), cancer therapy, diabetes type 2

2.1 Introduction

Genomics is the branch of molecular biology concerned with the structure, function, evolution, and mapping of genomes. In a broad sense, it

---

*Corresponding author: somyagoyal1988@gmail.com

Amit Kumar Tyagi (ed.) *Privacy Preservation of Genomic and Medical Data*, (19–44) © 2024 Scrivener Publishing LLC

is also referred to as functional genomics, which aims to characterize the function of every genomic element of an organism by using genome-scale assays, such as genome sequencing, transcriptome profiling, and proteomics. There is various application of genomics such as finding relation or association between genotypes and phenotypes, discovering biomarkers for separating patient based on gender, ethnicity, risk, disease state, etc., predicting the function of genes, and charting the biochemically activated genomics region, such as transcriptional enhancer [1, 2].

Proteomics is the study of proteins and their function within cells, tissues, and organisms. Proteins are essential for cell structure and function and play a central role in many biological processes, including metabolism, growth and responses to stimuli. Proteomics aims to identify, quantify, and analyze all of the proteins expressed by an organism, and to understand the relationships between proteins, their functions, and their interactions with other cellular components. Genes reside within chromosomes and are responsible for traits of humans. Figure 2.1 gives a snapshot for understanding the positions of genes and proteins [3].

The goal of proteomics is to provide a comprehensive understanding of the molecular mechanisms underlying cellular processes and to provide insights into the molecular basis of diseases, including cancer, neurological disorders, and infectious diseases. Proteomics can be used to identify new drug targets, monitor the effectiveness of treatments, and develop new diagnostic tools and treatments [1].

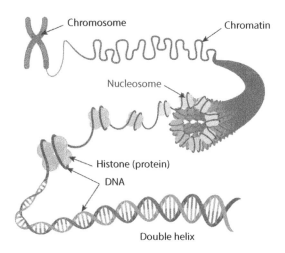

Figure 2.1 Insight into DNA: gene and protein.

Proteomics is a rapidly growing field, and advances in technology have enabled researchers to identify and analyze an increasing number of proteins and to understand their roles in health and disease. The integration of proteomics with other omics disciplines, such as genomics and transcriptomics, is expected to provide a more comprehensive understanding of the cellular function and disease, and to drive further advances in the fields of medicine, drug development, and biotechnology.

2.1.1 Organization of Chapter

The chapter is organized as follows- Section 2.2 discusses the application areas and the key role of genomics in the respective application area. Section 2.3 discusses the military applications of genomics along with the issues, and challenges. Section 2.4 brings the applications of genomics in medicines. Section 2.5 discusses two international projects namely- the human genome project and All of Us project. The case studies are given under Section 2.6 for better understanding of concepts and applications. The study is concluded in Section 2.7.

2.2 Application of Genomes—The Frontiers in Genetics

This section brings into notice the diverse areas where genomics is playing a crucial role. The study of genes allows an understanding of the hidden meaning and aspects of the human body. The behavior that we observe is just the reflection of gene properties [4]. Hence, the clarity about genomics allows understanding the reasons behind a particular behavior or condition. Here are the major application areas as shown in Figure 2.2 and explained as follows.

2.2.1 Personalized Medicine

Using genome sequencing to understand a person's unique genetic makeup and how it affects their health. Personalized medicine utilizes a patient's genetic data in order to take medical decisions that are customized as per the individual's need and can help improve their health outcomes [4, 5]. Some of the key applications of personalized medicine include the following:

- Diagnosis: By analyzing a patient's genetic makeup, doctors can make more accurate diagnoses and identify conditions that may have been previously overlooked.

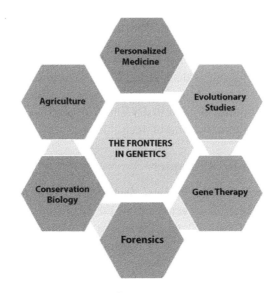

Figure 2.2 Major application arenas of genomics.

- Treatment selection: Using genetic information to determine which medications or treatments are most likely to be effective for a particular patient.
- Predictive testing: The goal is to identify genetic mutations that may mean a person's chances of getting certain diseases can be increased by certain factors. so that an earlier diagnosis and intervention can be made.
- Precision oncology: Targeting the specific genetic mutations that are causing the cancer.
- Genetic counseling: Using genetic information to advise patients and families on their risk of inherited diseases and disorders.

Personalized medicine is helping to revolutionize healthcare by improving diagnoses, informing treatment decisions, and ultimately leading to better health outcomes for patients.

2.2.2 Agriculture

Genomic studies are used to improve crop yield, drought tolerance, and disease resistance. Agriculture is using genomic studies to improve crops for better yield, disease resistance, and environmental adaptability. Some key applications of genomics in agriculture include:

- Crop improvement: identifying and selecting desirable genetic traits in crops to improve yield, nutrient content, and disease resistance.
- Plant breeding: using genomic information to guide plant breeding programs and create new, improved crop varieties.
- Pest and disease management: identifying the genomic basis of pest and disease resistance in crops, and using this information to develop more effective control strategies.
- Climate change adaptation: the aim is to use genomic data to create plants that are more resilient to changing environmental conditions, such as B. higher temperatures, lower precipitation and saltier soils.
- Sustainable agriculture: using genomic tools to promote sustainable agriculture practices, such as reducing the use of chemical pesticides and increasing the use of beneficial insects.

Genomics is playing an increasingly important role in agriculture, helping to improve crop production, protect against disease and pests, and ensure a more sustainable food supply for a growing global population.

2.2.3   Conservation Biology

Studying the genomes of endangered species to better understand their evolution and improve conservation efforts.

2.2.4   Forensics

DNA analysis for criminal investigations and identification of missing persons. Forensic genomics is the use of genomic data in criminal investigations and legal proceedings [6]. Some key applications of forensic genomics include:

- DNA analysis: using DNA analysis to identify suspects and victims in criminal investigations, or to establish biological relationships in paternity or immigration cases.
- Databanks: building and maintaining DNA databases to store and compare the genomic profiles of known offenders, or to track the spread of infectious diseases.
- Cold cases: using advanced genomic techniques to re-analyze old DNA evidence and solve cold cases.

- Mass disasters: genomic data can be used to help identify victims of mass tragedies, such as plane crashes, natural disasters, or mass shootings.
- Human rights: using genomic data to investigate human rights abuses, such as war crimes, genocide, or forced disappearance.

Forensic genomics has revolutionized the field of forensic science, providing powerful tools for solving crimes, and bringing justice to victims and their families.

2.2.5   Evolutionary Studies

Understanding the evolutionary history of species and how genomes have changed over time. Evolutionary studies use genomic data to understand the evolution of species and how genomes have changed over time. Some key applications of evolutionary studies include:

- Phylogenetic: reconstructing the evolutionary relationships between species and understanding the evolutionary history of life on Earth.
- Comparative genomics: comparing the genomes of different species to identify similarities and differences, and to understand how genomes have evolved over time.
- Adaptive evolution: identifying the genetic changes that have allowed species to adapt to changing environments, such as increased resistance to diseases, or the ability to survive in extreme conditions.
- Speciation: studying the genomic changes that lead to the formation of new species and the mechanisms that drive speciation.
- Conservation genetics: using genomic data to inform conservation efforts and to better understand the genetic diversity and health of endangered species.

Evolutionary studies provide a window into the past, and give us a deeper understanding of the complex processes that have shaped the diversity of life on Earth, and how species are likely to evolve in response to environmental change.

2.2.6   Biotechnology

Using genetic information to develop new drugs, vaccines, and other biotechnology products. Biotechnology is the use of biological systems, living organisms, or their components to develop new products and technologies [7]. Some key applications of biotechnology include:

- Pharmaceuticals: developing new drugs and vaccines using biotechnology methods, such as recombinant DNA technology and monoclonal antibody production.
- Agricultural biotechnology: improving crops through genetic engineering, such as creating crops with increased resistance to pests and diseases, and improved yield and nutritional content.
- Medical devices: developing new medical devices using biotechnology, such as implantable devices for drug delivery or artificial organs.
- Diagnostics: developing new diagnostic tests using biotechnology, such as genetic tests for diseases or cancers.
- Bioremediation: using microorganisms to clean up environmental pollution, such as oil spills or toxic waste sites.
- Industrial biotechnology: using biotechnology in industrial processes, such as the production of biofuels, biodegradable plastics, and other sustainable products.

Biotechnology has had a profound impact on many aspects of our lives and has the potential to revolutionize the way we approach a wide range of challenges, from healthcare to the environment.

2.2.7   Gene Therapy

Using genes or genetic material to treat diseases and disorders. Gene therapy is a medical approach that uses genetic material, such as DNA or RNA, to treat diseases and disorders [8]. Key applications of gene therapy include:

- Genetic disorders: using healthy genes to replace or repair disease-causing genes in patients with genetic disorders such as cystic fibrosis and hemophilia.
- Cancer treatment: using gene therapy to enhance the body's immune response to cancer, or to deliver therapeutic genes directly to cancer cells to trigger cell death.
- Neurological disorders: use of gene therapy to treat a variety of neurological disorders such as Parkinson's and Alzheimer's by delivering therapeutic genes to affected areas of the brain.

- Cardiovascular diseases: using gene therapy to treat cardiovascular diseases by delivering therapeutic genes to repair or
  replace damaged heart tissue.
- Inherited blindness: using gene therapy to restore vision in
  patients with inherited forms of blindness by introducing a
  functioning copy of a missing or malfunctioning gene into
  the affected cells.

Gene therapy is a rapidly advancing field with the potential to provide
new treatment options for a range of diseases and disorders, offering hope
for patients with conditions that have no cure. The process is depicted in
Figure 2.3. It shows how specific cells are killed under gene therapy to cure
the diseases.

These abovementioned are some key areas where is being applied to
improve the condition of humans and support them in having a better
lifestyle.

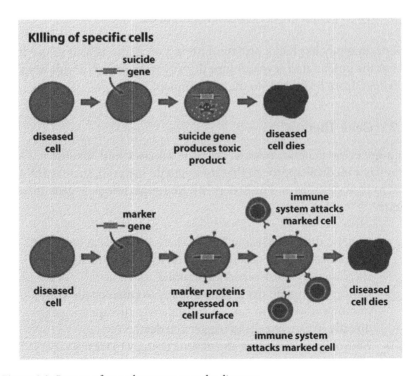

Figure 2.3 Process of gene therapy to cure the diseases.

Next, we discuss the specific application of genomics in the military area along with the achievements made to date and the challenges, we are facing in this key area.

2.3   Genomics in Military

On January 30, 2015, US President Obama announced the precision medicine initiative, as this initiative is a multimillion-dollar initiative, this initiative also aims to improve the traditional method to treat and prevent diseases by focusing on the genetics of human beings, as every human is different from each other on the genetic level, the medicine will differ from each other. In this way, we can target people with special conditions and make medicine for them. The Precision Medicine Initiative (PMI) is a national research effort launched by the National Institutes of Health (NIH) in 2015, with the goal of developing individualized, or "precision," approaches to the prevention and treatment of disease. The PMI aims to create a large, diverse cohort of one million or more participants who will provide data and samples to enable researchers to study how individual differences in genetic, environmental, and lifestyle factors contribute to health and disease [21].

The PMI is a multi-disciplinary effort that involves collaboration between researchers, healthcare providers, patient organizations, and other stakeholders, and involves the use of advanced technologies, such as genomics, proteomics, and imaging, to collect and analyze large amounts of data. The goal of the PMI is to develop a new model of healthcare that is based on individualized information and tailored treatments, and to advance our understanding of the underlying causes of disease.

The PMI is expected to have a significant impact on healthcare and medical research, by enabling the development of new treatments and therapies that are based on an individual's unique genetic and environmental profile, and by improving our understanding of how health and disease are influenced by multiple factors [9]. The PMI is also expected to provide important insights into the development and progression of diseases, and to improve the accuracy of diagnoses and treatments. Overall, the PMI represents a major step forward in the development of precision medicine, and is expected to have far-reaching benefits for patients, healthcare providers, and the broader scientific community.

In the near future, molecular signatures of tumors could lead to the identification of more effective drug candidates for the treatment of cancer, while a better understanding of the disease mechanism could facilitate tailored therapies for a variety of illnesses.

2.3.1   Potential Career Impact Due to Genetic Variation

The potential career impact of genetic variation for service members can depend on several factors, including their specific military specialty, the requirements of their job, and the type of genetic variation they possess. However, here are a few ways in which genetic variation can impact careers for service members:

Medical disqualification: Depending on the type of genetic variation and its potential impact on a service member's health and performance, they may be disqualified from certain military specialties or from serving in certain environments. Some of the examples are malignant hyperthermia, arrhytmogenic right ventricular cardiomyopathy/dysplasia.

- Impact on promotions: Depending on the type of genetic variation and its potential impact on a service member's health and performance, it may impact their ability to be promoted or to advance in their career.
- Impact on deployment: Depending on the type of genetic variation and its potential impact on a service member's health and performance, it may impact their ability to deploy to certain locations or to participate in certain missions.
- Impact on benefits: Depending on the type of genetic variation and its potential impact on a service member's health and performance, it may impact their eligibility for certain benefits, such as disability compensation or access to medical care.
- Impact on retirement: Depending on the type of genetic variation and its potential impact on a service member's health and performance, it may impact their eligibility for retirement benefits or their ability to continue to serve.

It is important to note that the potential impact of genetic variation on a service member's career can vary greatly depending on the specific situation, and service members should seek guidance from their chain of command and medical personnel if they have concerns about the potential impact of genetic variation on their career [10].

2.3.2   Challenges Remain

There are several challenges that remain in the field of genetic variation and its impact on various industries and careers [11]. Some of the key challenges include:

- Lack of understanding: there is still a lack of understanding among the general public and many professionals about the implications of genetic variation and its impact on various aspects of life, including health, career, and personal relationships.
- Inadequate data: despite advances in genetics and genomics, there is still a limited amount of data available on the impact of specific genetic variations on health, performance, and other factors that may impact careers and other aspects of life.
- Ethical concerns: there are several ethical concerns associated with the use of genetic information, including privacy, discrimination, and the potential for unintended consequences.
- Technical limitations: despite advances in the field of genetics and genomics, there remain technical challenges in accurately predicting the effects of particular genetic alterations on health, performance, and other aspects.
- Interpreting results: there is often a lack of consensus among experts on how to interpret genetic results and their implications for various aspects of life, including health and career.

In summary, while there have been significant advances in the field of genetics and genomics, there are still many challenges that need to be addressed in order to fully understand and effectively use genetic information to benefit individuals, industries, and society as a whole.

2.4   Genomics in Medicine

Genomes play a key role in the medical sector, as they are the source of genetic information which can be used to diagnose, predict, and treat various medical conditions. Genomic medicine is an emerging field involving genomic information to tailor treatments and improve health outcomes [15]. For example, genomic testing can be used to identify genetic markers associated with a particular disease, which can then be used to inform treatment decisions and provide more personalized care. Additionally, genomic data can be used to identify potential drug targets and to develop new drugs and treatments tailored to the individual's genetic makeup [12].

Genomics will have a major impact on the future of medicine and health. Genomic data can be used to better diagnose, predict, and treat diseases, and to develop new drugs and treatments tailored to the individual's genetic makeup. Additionally, genomics can be utilized to gain insight into the root causes of various diseases and create treatments that are tailored to the individual, resulting in more effective treatments with fewer side effects. Genomics can also be used to understand how the environment affects health and well-being, allowing for better prevention and management of diseases.

The study of genomes has revolutionized medicine and has led to new approaches to diagnosis, treatment, and prevention of disease. The use of genomic data in medicine has many applications, including:

- Personalized medicine: genomic data can be used to predict how an individual will respond to drugs or other forms of therapy, allowing for the creation of customized treatment plans.
- Predictive diagnostics: genomic data can be utilized to evaluate an individual's risk of contracting certain diseases, allowing for early intervention and prevention.
- Gene therapy: genomic data can be used to identify genetic mutations that cause disease, and to develop new therapies that target these mutations, such as gene editing.
- Cancer genomics: genomic data can be used to understand the genomic changes that drive the development and progression of cancer, leading to the development of new treatments and therapies.
- Pharmacogenomics: genomic data can be used to anticipate an individual's reaction to medications, facilitating the creation of safer and more effective treatments.
- Genetic counseling: genomic data can be used to provide genetic counseling and support to individuals and families affected by genetic disease.

The utilization of genomic data in healthcare is anticipated to expand, resulting in novel understandings of the fundamental mechanisms of disease and the emergence of more efficacious and personalized treatments.

2.4.1   Cancer Genomics

Cancer genomics involves investigating the genetic alterations that are responsible for the initiation and progression of cancer [13]. The main objectives of cancer genomics are to:

- Identify the genomic changes that drive cancer: Cancer genomics aims to identify the genomic mutations and changes that are responsible for the development and progression of cancer, including changes in DNA sequence, copy number changes, and epigenetic changes.
- Develop new treatments: Cancer genomics aims to develop new treatments and therapies that target the genomic changes that drive cancer, including drugs that target specific mutations, immunotherapies, and gene editing.
- Improve diagnosis and prognosis: Cancer genomics aims to improve the medical diagnosis and condition of cancer by using genomic data to classify cancers based on their genomic changes and to predict patient outcomes.
- Personalized medicine: Cancer genomics aims to develop personalized treatments for cancer patients based on the genomic changes in their tumors, leading to more effective and safer treatments.

Cancer genomics is an interdisciplinary field that involves collaboration between researchers from different disciplines, including genetics, biology, computer science, and medicine. The study of cancer genomics has led to many important advances in our understanding of cancer and has the potential to improve the lives of cancer patients worldwide.

2.4.2   Counseling in Genetics

Genetic counseling is the process of helping individuals and families understand and manage the risk of inherited diseases [14]. Genetic counseling typically involves:

- Assessment of family and medical history: Genetic counselors will assess an individual's family and medical history to determine their risk of inherited diseases.
- Discussion of genetic testing options: Genetic counselors will discuss the options for genetic testing, including the type of test, the risk of disease, and the potential benefits and limitations of testing.
- Interpretation of test results: Genetic counselors will interpret the results of genetic tests and explain the results to individuals and families.
- Discussion of risk management options: Genetic counselors will discuss risk management options for individuals

and families who are at risk of inherited diseases, including lifestyle changes, medical surveillance, and prophylactic surgeries.
- Support and resources: Genetic counselors will provide emotional support and connect individuals and families with resources and support services.

Genetic counseling is an important part of genetic medicine, as it helps individuals and families understand and manage their risk of inherited diseases. Genetic counselors are trained professionals who have specialized knowledge in genetics, biology, and counseling, and are an essential resource for individuals and families affected by genetic disease.

2.4.3   Personalized Medicine

Personalized medicine is a medical approach that uses genomic and other patient-specific data to inform the diagnosis, treatment, and prevention of disease. The main objectives of personalized medicine are to:

- Improve patient outcomes: Personalized medicine aims to improve patient outcomes by using patient-specific data to tailor treatments and therapies to individual patients, leading to more effective and safer treatments.
- Increase efficiency: Personalized medicine aims to increase the efficiency of the healthcare system by reducing the use of ineffective or harmful treatments and by streamlining the development of new treatments.
- Reduce healthcare costs: Personalized medicine aims to reduce healthcare costs by reducing the use of ineffective or harmful treatments and by improving patient outcomes, leading to reduced hospitalization and fewer follow-up appointments.
- Empower patients: Personalized medicine aims to empower patients by giving them more control over their health and by providing them with personalized information and advice on how to manage their health.

Personalized medicine is an interdisciplinary field that involves collaboration between researchers from different disciplines, including genetics, biology, computer science, and medicine [16]. The study of personalized medicine has led to many important advances in our understanding of disease and has the potential to improve the lives of patients worldwide.

2.5   International Projects

This section summarizes the key points about two international projects namely Human Genome Project and All of Us project that have been carried out in the domain of genomics.

2.5.1   Human Genome Project

The Human Genome Project (HGP) was an international research that is trying to make an effort to sequence and map the entire human genome, which is the complete set of genetic protocols or coding for a human being [17, 19]. The project was launched in 1990 and was completed in 2003 [20]. The main objectives of the HGP were to:

- The Human Genome Project (HGP) sought to uncover the order of the three billion chemical pairs that compose the base of human genome.
- Map the human genome: the HGP aimed to create a detailed map of the human genome, which would identify the location of all its genes and other important genomic features (as shown in Figure 2.4).
- Improve genetic understanding: the HGP aimed to increase understanding of the human genomes and how it influences our body and how it affects to a disease.
- Develop new tools and technologies: the HGP aimed to develop new tools and technologies for genomic research, including high-throughput sequencing, bioinformatics, and computational biology.
- Promote ethical and legal considerations: the HGP aimed to promote discussions about the ethical, legal, and social implications of genomic research and its applications.

The HGP was a massive scientific effort that involved hundreds of scientists from around the world and required the development of new technologies and methods. The project has had a profound impact on medicine and biology, leading to new insights into the underlying mechanisms of disease and the development of new treatments and therapies [18]. The Human Genome Project (HGP), responsible for producing the 2001 human genome, was an incredible scientific feat that marked a pivotal moment in human genetics and laid the groundwork for human genomics.

2.5.2   The All of Us Research Program

The All of Us Research Program is a large-scale research initiative that aims to improve health outcomes and advance precision medicine. The National Institutes of Health (NIH) launched the program in 2018 with the goal of collecting data from one million or even more citizens who reside in the United States.

- The All of Us Research Program is a voluntary program that encourages participants to share their health information, including their electronic health records, genetic data, and lifestyle information, such as diet and exercise habits. The program aims to create a diverse database of health information, including information about individuals from different racial and ethnic groups, geographic regions, and socioeconomic backgrounds.
- Researchers can use the data collected by the All of Us Research Program to better understand the factors that contribute to health and disease, and to develop new strategies for preventing and treating diseases. The program also aims to improve health outcomes for individual participants by providing them with personalized health information and recommendations based on their data.
- The All of Us Research Program has a strong emphasis on privacy and data security, and participants have control over how their data are used and shared. The program also includes a diverse community engagement and outreach effort to ensure that all individuals, including those who are historically underrepresented in biomedical research, have the opportunity to participate and benefit from the program.

In summary, the All of Us Research Program is a promising initiative that has the potential to accelerate the pace of medical research and improve health outcomes for individuals and communities across the United States.

2.5.3   The Transformation of Genomics

The transformation from medical genomics to systems medicine involves the integration of genomic data with other data types, such as clinical data, lifestyle data, and environmental data, to create a more comprehensive understanding of human health [22]. The goal of systems medicine is to

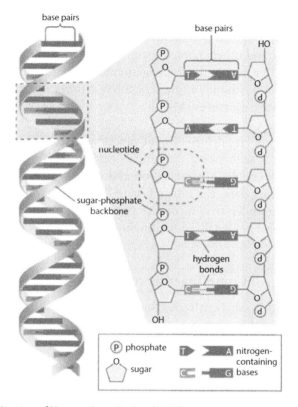

Figure 2.4 Mapping of Human Gene Project (HGP)

move beyond a purely genetic view of disease, to a holistic view that considers the complex interplay between genetics, environment, and lifestyle factors.

Key aspects of this transition include:

- Big Data Integration: the integration of large, diverse datasets from multiple sources, in order to obtain a more complete picture of human health [23].
- Multi-Omics: the integration of genomic data with other data types, such as proteomic, metabolomic, and epigenetic data, to create a more comprehensive understanding of human biology and disease.
- Personalized medicine: the use of genomic and other data to develop personalized treatment plans and predict individual responses to drugs and other therapies.

- Precision medicine: the use of genomic and other data to develop targeted treatments that are tailored to the specific genetic and other characteristics of individual patients [24].
- Predictive health: the use of genomic and other data to predict the likelihood of future health outcomes and to inform preventive measures [25].

This transition is driven by advances in technology, including high-throughput sequencing, machine learning, and cloud computing, which have enabled the collection and analysis of large amounts of genomic and other data. The integration of these data types is expected to result in a better understanding of disease mechanisms and the creation of more efficient and personalized treatments.

2.5.4   When All Come Together to Develop Systems Medicine

When East and West, North and South collaborate to develop systems medicine, the goal is to bring together the best minds, resources, and expertise from around the world to advance the field of medicine. Such collaboration can bring many benefits, including:

- Sharing of expertise: collaboration between different regions can allow the sharing of expertise, knowledge, and best practices.
- Access to diverse data sets: by collaborating, different regions can access larger and more diverse data sets, allowing for a more comprehensive understanding of human health and disease.
- Integration of different perspectives: collaboration can bring together different cultural, political, and scientific perspectives, leading to a more holistic and inclusive approach to healthcare.
- Advancements in technology: by pooling resources, different regions can invest in the development of new technologies, such as high-throughput sequencing, machine learning, and cloud computing, to advance the field of medicine.
- Improved global health outcomes: by collaborating, different regions can work towards improving global health outcomes and reducing health disparities, leading to a more equitable and sustainable healthcare system for all.

Such collaboration can play a crucial role in advancing the field of systems medicine and in creating a more comprehensive and effective approach to healthcare that benefits everyone.

2.5.5   Interaction Between Genetic and Environmental Factors

The interaction between these factors is complex and not fully understood, but it is clear that both genetic and environmental factors play important roles in the development of the disease.

For example, obesity is a major risk factor for type 2 diabetes, and it is known that both genetic and environmental factors can contribute to the development of obesity. In some cases, genetic variants may make a person more susceptible to developing obesity, while in other cases environmental factors such as a high-calorie diet and sedentary lifestyle may be the primary drivers.

Overall, the interaction between genetic and environmental factors in the development of type 2 diabetes is complex and multifactorial. Understanding these interactions is important for the prevention and treatment of the disease, as it allows for the identification of individuals who may be at increased risk and the development of targeted interventions to reduce that risk.

2.6   Case Study

2.6.1   Target Therapies for Cancer

Targeted therapies for cancer are a type of precision medicine that is tailored to the specific genetic profile of a patient's cancer. These therapies are more effective and less carcinogenic than conventional chemotherapy because they identify particular molecules involved in the growth and spread of cancer cells. Here are a few examples of targeted therapies for cancer:

- Imatinib (Gleevec): This drug is used to treat chronic myeloid leukemia (CML) and certain types of gastrointestinal stromal tumors (GISTs). It works by blocking the activity of BCR-ABL, which is produced by a specific genetic mutation that is present in many patients with CML and GISTs.
- Trastuzumab (Herceptin): This drug is used to treat certain types of breast cancer that overproduce a protein called HER2. Trastuzumab works by binding to the HER2 protein

and blocking its activity, which can slow or stop the growth of cancer cells.

- Vemurafenib (Zelboraf): This drug is used to treat certain types of melanoma that have a specific genetic mutation in the BRAF gene. Vemurafenib works by blocking the activity of the mutated BRAF protein, which can slow or stop the growth of cancer cells.
- Bevacizumab (Avastin): This medication is used to treat cancers such as colorectal, lung, and kidney cancer. Bevacizumab inhibits the activity of a protein known as vascular endothelial growth factor (VEGF), which is implicated in the formation of new blood vessels that supply nutrients to cancer cells.

Targeted therapies for cancer are often used in combination with other treatments, such as chemotherapy or radiation therapy, and can improve outcomes for many cancer patients. However, targeted therapies are not effective for all types of cancer, and more research is needed to develop new therapies and improve existing ones.

2.6.2   Pharmacogenomics and Drug Dosing

Pharmacogenomics is the study of how a person's genes can influence their response to drugs. By analyzing a patient's genetic information, doctors can determine the most effective drug and dosage for that patient, based on their unique genetic makeup. This approach is known as pharmacogenetic dosing or precision dosing.

One example of pharmacogenetic dosing is the drug warfarin, which is commonly used to prevent blood clots. Warfarin has a narrow therapeutic window, which means that the dose must be carefully monitored to avoid bleeding or blood clots. A patient's response to warfarin can be affected by genetic difference in the genes that control its metabolism and clearance from the body. By analyzing a patient's genetic information, doctors can predict how the patient is likely to respond to warfarin and adjust the dose accordingly.

Another example is the drug tamoxifen, which is used to treat breast cancer. Tamoxifen is a prodrug that is converted into its active form by enzymes in the liver. However, some patients have genetic variations that can reduce the activity of these enzymes, leading to reduced effectiveness of the drug. By analyzing a patient's genetic information, doctors can determine whether the patient is likely to respond well to tamoxifen, and adjust the dose or consider alternative treatments if necessary.

Pharmacogenetic dosing is an important tool for optimizing drug therapy and minimizing the risk of adverse reactions or treatment failure. As genetic testing becomes more widely available and affordable, it has the potential to transform the way drugs are prescribed and personalized to individual patients.

2.6.3   Precision Medicine in Cardiology

Precision medicine has the potential to improve outcomes for patients with cardiovascular disease by tailoring treatment to the individual patient's unique genetic and clinical characteristics. Here are some examples of precision medicine in cardiology:

- Genetic testing: genetic testing can help identify inherited risk factors for cardiovascular disease, such as familial hypercholesterolemia (FH), a genetic condition that leads to high levels of cholesterol in the blood. By identifying patients with FH, doctors can recommend early interventions such as medication and lifestyle changes to reduce their risk of heart disease.
- Pharmacogenomics: pharmacogenomic testing can help determine the most effective and safe drug therapy for individual patients. For example, some patients with heart disease may have genetic variations that affect their response to certain drugs, such as antiplatelet agents or statins. By tailoring drug therapy to the patient's genetic profile, doctors can improve the effectiveness and safety of the treatment.
- Biomarkers: biomarkers are measurable indicators of disease that can help diagnose and monitor cardiovascular disease. By using biomarkers to identify patients at high risk, doctors can recommend early interventions to prevent or treat cardiovascular disease [26].
- Cardiovascular imaging: advanced imaging techniques, such as coronary CT angiography (CTA) or cardiac magnetic resonance imaging (MRI), can provide more impactful information about the structure and function of the heart and blood vessels. By using imaging to diagnose and monitor cardiovascular disease, doctors can tailor treatment to

the individual patient's needs and monitor the response to treatment over time.

Overall, precision medicine has the potential to transform the way cardiovascular disease is diagnosed and treated, leading to better outcomes for patients.

2.6.4 Personalized Treatment for Cystic Fibrosis

Personalized treatment for cystic fibrosis involves the use of drugs that are tailored to the specific genetic mutations that cause the disease in individual patients. One example of a personalized treatment for cystic fibrosis is the drug ivacaftor (Kalydeco).

- Ivacaftor is a targeted therapy that is used to treat patients with cystic fibrosis who have a specific genetic mutation in the cystic fibrosis transmembrane conductance regulator (CFTR) gene. The drug works by correcting the function of a specific protein that is affected by the mutation and has been shown to improve lung function in patients.
- Ivacaftor is not effective for all types of cystic fibrosis, as it only works for patients with certain genetic mutations. However, for patients who are eligible for treatment with ivacaftor, the drug can be life-changing, improving lung function, reducing hospitalizations, and increasing quality of life.

Other personalized treatments for cystic fibrosis are currently being developed, including other drugs that target different genetic mutations that cause the disease. Personalized treatments for cystic fibrosis are a promising area of research and have the potential to significantly improve outcomes for patients with this debilitating disease.

2.6.5 Diabetic Type 2 in Genomes

Type 2 diabetes is a complex condition that is affected by both genetic and environmental factors. While there is no single "diabetes gene," there are many genetic variants that have been identified as increasing the risk of developing type 2 diabetes [27].

Some of these genetic variants are involved in the regulation of insulin secretion and glucose metabolism, which are key processes that are disrupted in type 2 diabetes. For example, variants in the TCF7L2 gene have been strongly associated with an increased risk of developing type 2 diabetes in many populations.

It is likely that the interaction between genetic and environmental factors is what ultimately leads to the development of type 2 diabetes in most cases.

It is also important to note that having a genetic variant associated with an increased risk of type 2 diabetes does not necessarily mean that a person will develop the condition. Many other factors, including lifestyle choices and other genetic variations, can modify the risk and ultimately determine whether a person develops diabetes or not.

2.7   Conclusion

We have a duty to humanity to speed up the adoption of genomic medicine and ensure that the advantages of genomics are realized promptly for individuals, families, and healthcare systems. Finally, genomics can be used to improve public health by providing more accurate and comprehensive data about population-level health outcomes, allowing for better policy decisions. In the last 5 years, we have made significant advances in our understanding of the nature of copy number variation in the human genome.

At present, genomic medicine is widely used in the medical sector to diagnose, predict, and treat various medical conditions. Genomic testing can be used to identify genetic markers associated with a particular disease, which can then be used to inform treatment decisions and provide more personalized care. Additionally, genomic data can be used to identify potential drug targets and to develop new drugs and treatments tailored to the individual's genetic makeup. Furthermore, genomic data can be used to better understand the underlying causes of diseases and to develop personalized and precision treatments that are more effective and have fewer side effects. Finally, genomics can also be used to improve public health by providing more accurate and comprehensive data about population-level health outcomes, allowing for better policy decisions.

References

1. Ideker, T., Galitski, T., Hood, L., A new approach to decoding life: Systems biology. *Annu. Rev. Genom. Hum. Genet.*, 2, 1, 343–372, 2001.
2. Kitano, H., Systems biology: A brief overview. *Science*, 295, 5560, 1662–1664, 2002.

3. Gromov, P.S., Østergaard, M., Gromova, I., Celis, J.E., Human proteomic databases: A powerful resource for functional genomics in health and disease. *Prog. Biophys. Mol. Biol.*, *80*, 1-2, 3–22, 2002.

4. Gray, M.W., Evolution of organellar genomes. *Curr. Opin. Genet. Dev.*, *9*, 6, 678–687, 1999.

5. Drysdale, R.A., FlyBase Consortium, Crosby, M.A., FlyBase: Genes and gene models. *Nucleic Acids Res.*, *33*, suppl_1, D390–D395, 2005.

6. Moran, N.A. and Bennett, G.M., The tiniest tiny genomes. *Annu. Rev. Microbiol.*, *68*, 195–215, 2014.

7. Darling, A.E., Jospin, G., Lowe, E., Matsen IV, F.A., Bik, H.M., Eisen, J.A., PhyloSift: Phylogenetic analysis of genomes and metagenomes. *PeerJ*, *2*, e243, 2014.

8. Nielsen, C.B., Cantor, M., Dubchak, I., Gordon, D., Wang, T., Visualizing genomes: Techniques and challenges. *Nat. Methods*, *7*, Suppl 3, S5–S15, 2010.

9. Burger, G., Gray, M.W., Lang, B.F., Mitochondrial genomes: Anything goes. *Trends Gent.*, *19*, 12, 709–716, 2003.

10. Stratton, M.R., Exploring the genomes of cancer cells: Progress and promise. *Science*, *331*, 6024, 1553–1558, 2011.

11. Mira, A., Ochman, H., Moran, N.A., Deletional bias and the evolution of bacterial genomes. *Trends Gent.*, *17*, 10, 589–596, 2001.

12. Mewes, H.W., Heumann, K., Kaps, A., Mayer, K., Pfeiffer, F., Stocker, S., Frishman, D., MIPS: A database for genomes and protein sequences. *Nucleic Acids Res.*, *27*, 1, 44–48, 1999.

13. Pedersen, B.S. and Quinlan, A.R., Mosdepth: Quick coverage calculation for genomes and exomes. *Bioinformatics*, *34*, 5, 867–868, 2018.

14. Bork, P., Dandekar, T., Diaz-Lazcoz, Y., Eisenhaber, F., Huynen, M., Yuan, Y., Predicting function: From genes to genomes and back. *J. Mol. Biol.*, *283*, 4, 707–725, 1998.

15. Lan, R. and Reeves, P.R., Intraspecies variation in bacterial genomes: The need for a species genome concept. *Trends Microbiol.*, *8*, 9, 396–401, 2000.

16. Karlin, S., Ladunga, I., Blaisdell, B.E., Heterogeneity of genomes: Measures and values. *Proc. Nat. Acad. Sci.*, *91*, 26, 12837–12841, 1994.

17. Galardini, M., Biondi, E.G., Bazzicalupo, M., Mengoni, A., CONTIGuator: A bacterial genomes finishing tool for structural insights on draft genomes. *Source Code Biol. Med.*, *6*, 1–5, 2011.

18. Silby, M.W., Winstanley, C., Godfrey, S.A., Levy, S.B., Jackson, R.W., and Pseudomonas genomes: Diverse and adaptable. *FEMS Microbiol. Rev.*, *35*, 4, 652–680, 2011.

19. Collins, F.S., Patrinos, A., Jordan, E., Chakravarti, A., Gesteland, R., Walters, L., members of the DOE and NIH planning groups, New goals for the US human genome project: 1998-2003. *Science*, *282*, 5389, 682–689, 1998.

20. https://www.ncbi.nlm.nih.gov/projects/genome/guide/human/index.shtml. [Accessed on 01.02.2023].

21. De Castro, M., Biesecker, L.G., Turner, C., Brenner, R., Witkop, C., Mehlman, M., Bradburne, C., Green, R.C., Genomic medicine in the military. *NPJ Genom. Med.*, *1*, 1, 1–4, 2016.

22. Goyal, S., Predicting the heart disease using machine learning techniques, in: *ICT Analysis and Applications,* Lecture Notes in Networks and Systems, vol. 517, pp. 191–199, Springer, Singapore, 2023, https://doi.org/10.1007/978-981-19-5224-1_21.

23. Goyal, S., Software fault prediction using evolving populations with mathematical diversification. *Soft Comput.*, 26, 13999–14020, 2022. https://doi.org/10.1007/s00500-022-07445-6.

24. Goyal, S., Genetic evolution-based feature selection for software defect prediction using SVMs. *J. Circuits, Syst. Comput.*, 31, 11, 2250161, 2022. https://doi.org/10.1142/S0218126622501614.

25. Goyal, S., 3PcGE: 3-parent child-based genetic evolution for software defect prediction. *Innov. Syst. Softw. Eng*, 9, 197–216, 2022. https://doi.org/10.1007/s11334-021-00427-1.

26. Miao, L., Deng, G.X., Yin, R.X., Nie, R.J., Yang, S., Wang, Y., Li, H., No causal effects of plasma homocysteine levels on the risk of coronary heart disease or acute myocardial infarction: A Mendelian randomization study. *Eur. J. Prev. Cardiol.*, 28, 2, 227–234, 2021.

27. Floyd, J.S. and Psaty, B.M., The application of genomics in diabetes: Barriers to discovery and implementation. *Diabetes Care*, 39, 11, 1858–1869, 2016.

3

Technical Trends in Public Healthcare and Medical Engineering

Asha Rani Mishra[1]*, Amrita Rai[2], Mohd Dayem Ansari[1] and Ritesh Pratap Singh[3]

[1]Department of Computer Science Engineering, GL Bajaj Institute of Technology & Management, Noida, India
[2]Department of Electronics and Comunication Engineering GL Bajaj Institute of Technology & Management, Noida, India
[3]School of Electrical and Computer Engineering, Harmaya Institute of Technology, Harmaya University, Dire Dawa, Ethiopia

Abstract

Healthcare is a sizable sector of the economy with outdated systems, which can result in inefficiencies. For healthcare and associated purposes, use computing platforms, networking, software, and sensors as digital health technologies. When new technologies develop and rules change as a result of pooled expertise, this has led to a significant movement in the areas of interest within the field of digital health. Technology can help with trainings, supervision, and the delivery of healthcare in remote areas through telemedicine, m-health, and digital platforms or apps. For unbreakable and infinite connection between medical personnel and patients, present hospitals require online healthcare management and control using different types of sensors, and recent tools and technology that can be used in the medical domain. This chapter discusses health system-related difficulties and looks for appropriate solutions using technologies from the Internet of Things (IoT), clouds, sensors, and soft computing. It also elaborates how several AI-based technologies are creating effective decision assistance for medical applications.

Keywords: Digital healthcare, medical engineering, e-health, artificial intelligence, Internet of medical things

---

*Corresponding author: asha.mishra@glbitm.ac.in

Amit Kumar Tyagi (ed.) *Privacy Preservation of Genomic and Medical Data*, (45–72) © 2024 Scrivener Publishing LLC

3.1 Introduction

Medical engineering applications of machine learning, deep learning, and other cognitive technologies are better understood when artificial intelligence (AI) is used in the field. AI in healthcare is the use of machines to analyses and act on medical information, usually with the target of envisioning a particular outcome. By using patient health data and other related information, AI can help the doctors and health professionals to remit more accurate and precise diagnoses and medicament plans [1]. Artificial intelligence can help us to make healthcare more precise and proactive by analyzing big data technologies to develop an enhanced preventive care guidance system for patients. Artificial intelligence can upgrade preventive care and quality of life, produce more predictable diagnoses and medicament plans, and can lead to better patient health. Artificial intelligence can also envision and keep track of the spread of infectious and contagious diseases by analyzing the data from the government, healthcare, and other sources. Artificial intelligence (AI) technology has the potential to revolutionize the healthcare industry. AI can enhance medical outcomes and streamline workflows by analyzing vast volumes of data and making predictions. In this research, we will discuss some of the ways in which AI is currently being used in healthcare and the potential benefits and challenges of this technology.

The role of AI in healthcare is rapidly growing and has the potential to revolutionize the way healthcare is delivered. AI can be used for tasks such as image analysis, diagnostics, drug discovery, and even patient monitoring. It can help to improve the accuracy and efficiency of healthcare, as well as provide more personalized treatment options. However, it is important to note that AI is not a replacement for human healthcare professionals, but rather a tool to assist them in their work. Additionally, there are ethical concerns that need to be addressed in the development and implementation of AI in healthcare. Overall, AI has the potential to greatly benefit the healthcare industry, but it must be implemented responsibly and with proper oversight.

In addition to the applications mentioned above, AI can also be used in areas such as population health management, precision medicine, and virtual care. In population health management, AI can help to identify and track population-level health trends, and in precision medicine, it can assist in identifying the best treatment options for individual patients based on their genetic and other personal information. Virtual care, which includes telemedicine and virtual consultations, can also benefit from AI, as it can be used to improve the accuracy of diagnoses, triage patients, and provide remote monitoring.

It is also worth mentioning that AI in healthcare is a rapidly evolving field, with new technologies and applications being developed all the time. This is why it is crucial for healthcare professionals, researchers, and policymakers to stay informed about the latest developments in AI and how they can be used to improve healthcare.

However, it is important that its development and implementation is done responsibly, with proper oversight and consideration of ethical concerns. The healthcare industry must also stay informed about the latest developments in AI to ensure that they are able to take full advantage of its potential benefits.

The rest of the chapter is outlined as follow. Section 3.2 discusses the background detail by highlighting use of recent technologies and advancements in healthcare and medical engineering. Section 3.3 presents current situation of Medical Engineering and Public Healthcare System; section 3.4 outlines about how different AI technologies can be used in healthcare domain. Section 3.5 elaborates the need of technological analysis, Section 3.6 focus on future aspects of AI in Healthcare and Medical Engineering, finally section 3.7 concludes this chapter.

3.2   Background Work

With the use of artificial intelligence, numerous researchers have developed and presented numerous clinical assistance systems since the middle of the 20th century. Rule-based artificial intelligence systems have many success stories in the 1970s, such as interpreting ECGs and diagnosing various diseases and providing and choosing between the relevant treatments and also, they are used to assist the physicians in generating clinical reports in complex patient cases [2]. Anyhow, the rule based Artificial Intelligence systems are very expensive and brittle to use as they require a lot of human-authored updates. Also, in rule-based AI, it is also difficult to encrypt different pieces of knowledge given by different experts. These types of AI are dependent on the data given to them while, recent or latest Artificial Intelligence leverages various learning methods, which can help us by identifying the patterns from the data.

There are two types of fundamental machine learning algorithms: supervised and unsupervised. In supervised learning, the process of gathering a sizable sample of test cases with input and output for accurate labels and then analyzing the data to produce the accurate output label for new data. Unsupervised learning deduces the patterns in unlabeled data to find sub clusters of original data.

The Machine Learning Algorithms enables the enhancement of the Artificial Intelligence applications which can easily facilitate discovery of unrecognized patterns in the data which was previously not known hence the Machine Learning becomes the preferred framework for creating the Artificial Intelligent utilities.

Since 2012, Deep Learning has also shown improvement in image classification which involves training in Artificial Neural Networks with many layers on very big data.

3.2.1   Recent Technologies in Healthcare and Medical Engineering

Most of the technologies are pertinent to the medical and healthcare field but specific processes vary widely. Some of the Technologies of high importance to medical and healthcare are listed below.

3.2.1.1   The Internet of Medical Things

The usage of connected devices and sensors in the healthcare sector is referred to as the "Internet of Medical Things" (IoMT). These tools and sensors can be used to gather and communicate information on the health and conditions of patients, which can subsequently be used to improve patient outcomes and guide medical decisions [3].

Wearable fitness trackers, smart watches, and smart pills are examples of IoMT devices that can gather data on patients' heart rates, activity levels, and other vital signs. The internet can also be connected to medical devices like insulin pumps, inhalers, and glucose monitors, allowing for real-time monitoring of patients' health data as shown in Figure 3.1.

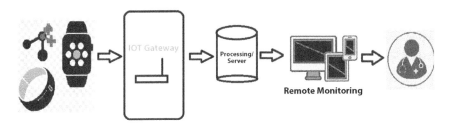

Figure 3.1 Internet of medical things in medical engineering.

One of the main advantages of IoMT is that it makes it possible to monitor patients from a distance. This is especially helpful for people who have chronic conditions or who live in remote areas. Patients will not have to travel so far to get to their appointments as a result of this, which can help ease access to care.

By allowing healthcare providers to share patient data, IoMT has the potential to also boost the effectiveness and efficiency of the healthcare system. For instance, healthcare providers can access patients' medical histories, test results, and other data in real time with the assistance of electronic health records (EHRs) and other data-sharing systems. This can help to improve continuity of care and reduce the likelihood of errors.

However, data security and privacy concerns are also raised by the Internet of Medical Things. It is critical that security measures are in place to safeguard sensitive personal data from unauthorized access, breaches, and hacking given that these devices collect and transmit personal data.

3.2.1.2   Blockchain

Blockchain technology is a decentralized system that uses cryptography to secure and validate transactions. In the healthcare industry, blockchain technology can be used to create secure, tamper-proof digital records of patients' health information. This may contribute to enhanced patient data security and privacy as well as improved interprofessional communication [4].

One of the main advantages of blockchain technology in healthcare is that it can contribute to the development of a more secure and effective

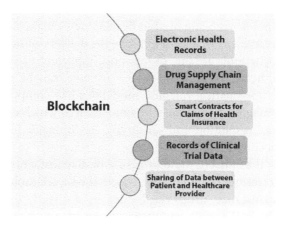

Figure 3.2 Application of blockchain in healthcare.

method for storing and exchanging patient data. With the use of blockchain, patient medical records may be safely maintained and distributed among different healthcare providers, improving continuity of treatment and reducing the possibility of mistakes. Additionally, blockchain can be used to create secure, tamper-resistant records of clinical trial data, thereby lowering the risk of fraud, and enhancing research integrity as shown in Figure 3.2.

Supply chain management is another area where blockchain could be used in the healthcare industry. With the use of blockchain, it is possible to build a tamper-proof record of the flow of medications and other medical items through the supply chain, which can help reduce the risk of fake medications and improve medical product traceability.

Additionally, medical data exchange between patients, healthcare professionals, and researchers can be made safe via blockchain technology. Smart contracts are software programmes that self-execute complex instructions and lower the costs of contracting, monitoring, and enforcing contracts and making payments [5].

However, as with any new technology, blockchain in healthcare also presents challenges. It requires regulations and guidelines to safeguard patient privacy and secure data sharing, as well as a level of standardization and interoperability between various systems, which is one of the main obstacles. The healthcare system must also be able to adapt to new technologies and the infrastructure necessary to support them.

3.2.1.3   Nanotechnology

Nanotechnology is the manipulation and engineering of materials on a very small scale, typically at the level of atoms and molecules [6]. In healthcare, nanotechnology is being used to develop new diagnostic tools, treatments, and therapies, as well as to improve the delivery of existing drugs.

New diagnostic tools are one of the most important uses of nanotechnology in healthcare. Nanoparticles, for instance, can be used to make contrast agents for medical imaging modalities like computed tomography (CT) and magnetic resonance imaging (MRI), which can help boost these modalities' resolution and sensitivity. Additionally, biosensors that can identify specific chemicals or diseases can be created using nanoparticles, improving the efficiency and precision of diagnostic operations. New therapies and treatments are another way that nanotechnology is used in healthcare. For instance, drugs can be delivered directly to specific cells or tissues in the body using nanoparticles, which can help reduce drug side effects and increase their effectiveness. Nanoparticles can also be used to create new materials that can be used in prosthetics and implants to improve their biocompatibility and mechanical properties.

Additionally, nanotechnology is being utilized to enhance drug delivery. For instance, nanoparticles can be used to target drugs to specific cells or tissues in the body, which can help to reduce side effects and increase efficacy. They can also be used to encapsulate drugs, which can help to protect them from degradation and increase their solubility [7].

However, nanotechnology in healthcare faces the same difficulties as any new technology. The safety and toxicity of nanoparticles, which may have unintended effects on living things and possess properties distinct from those of bulk materials, are one of the main obstacles. In addition, the regulatory framework for the development and application of nanotechnology in healthcare is still in the process of developing, and additional research is needed to comprehend the potential merits and demerits of these technologies.

3.2.1.4   Cloud Computing

Cloud computing in healthcare refers to the use of remote servers and storage systems to store, manage, and process healthcare data. Cloud computing can be especially beneficial in healthcare, as it allows for the sharing and analysis of large amounts of data, which can help to improve patient health status and minimize costs [8].

The ability to share and analyze vast volumes of data is one of the key advantages of cloud computing in the healthcare industry. With the help of cloud-based platforms, healthcare providers can access and share patient data, such as electronic health records (EHRs), imaging studies, and lab results, which can help to improve continuity of care and reduce the risk of errors.

Additionally, large amounts of data, such as genomics data and medical literature, can be analyzed using cloud-based platforms, which can aid in the creation of new therapies and treatments.

The remote delivery of healthcare services is another advantage of cloud computing in the healthcare industry. Healthcare providers are able to provide telemedicine services, such as virtual consultations and remote monitoring, with the assistance of cloud-based platforms, which can assist in enhancing access to care and lowering costs.

Machine learning and other advanced analytics tools can also be used with cloud computing to find patterns and trends in patient data, which can help improve disease diagnosis and treatment.

Cloud computing also has its challenges. One of the main challenges is the security and privacy of patient data, as it is important that the data are protected from unauthorized access, breaches, or hacking. Additionally, there is a need for regulatory compliance, particularly with regard to the storage, sharing and access of sensitive patient data.

3.2.1.5   Big Data and E-Health

The term "Big Data" refers to information assets with a large volume, velocity, and/or diversity that necessitate cutting-edge, economical methods of processing the data in order to enhance insight, decision making, and process automation, according to the Gartner Glossary. The vast, varied collections of data that are expanding at an ever-increasing rate are referred to as "big data." Big data has been utilized more frequently in recent years to enhance and optimize healthcare management, analysis, and forecasting. For instance, the switch to electronic health records (EHR) can aid in the organization, storage, and acceleration of patient data processing. Big data also encompasses the diversity or scope of the data points being shielded. The utilization of big data systems is also additionally involved in the management of medical practices has the power to decrease the number of medical errors, decrease the expenditure of care, and enhance service quality and efficiency. In point of fact, the rapid expansion of big data in the healthcare industry is due to the widespread use of EHRs in recent years. Data on healthcare providers which can be pharmaceuticals, logistics, genetics, or other information are also included in big data applications in healthcare [9].

3.2.1.6   Virtual Clinical Trials

Virtual clinical trials are another recent and promising area of medical research [10]. These include wearable sensors, tablets, smartphone apps, and other technology for remote person health related data retrieval. These systems are frequently referred to as virtual interventional studies, remote trials, patient-specific trials, or hybrid trials [11]. The procedure entails finding patients, getting their permission, and gathering information. When physical venues and in-person patient contact are no longer necessary, a virtual interventional study is a system [12].

3.2.1.7   3D Printing for Healthcare and Medical Engineering

Healthcare has increasingly adopted 3D printing technology over the past ten years. The technology for creating organ models and permanent implants has advanced to this stage in medical 3D printing, and it is now more dependable [15]. The study by Cheng et al. showed that biodegradable materials employed in 3D printing may exhibit improved behaviour [16]. Researchers in the United States and elsewhere have started to look at the prospect of 3D printing organs and blood arteries utilizing printed tissues and organs, even if direct printing of tissues and organs is still in its early stages [17].

In reality, the surgeon can provide a physical 3D model of the desired patient's anatomy spot thanks to 3D printing technology. This model can be used to precisely plan access and cross-sectional 3D imaging. Additionally, prior to implantation, the prosthesis components' sizes can be selected with high precision using 3D printing. Additionally, unique implants and surgical tools can be created via 3D printing, allowing for the personalization of devices and prosthetics without raising expenses [18].

In healthcare, 3D printing is being used in a variety of ways to improve patient outcomes and streamline processes. Some examples of how 3D printing is being used in healthcare include:

Medical models: 3D printing can be used to create detailed models of bones, organs, and other parts of the body. These models can be used for patient education, surgical planning, and medical student training.

Prosthetics and orthotics: 3D printing can be used to create custom-fit prosthetic limbs, orthotic devices, and other assistive devices for patients. This can improve the comfort, functionality, and appearance of these devices.

Tissue engineering: 3D printing can be used to create living tissues, such as blood vessels and heart valves, which can be used for transplants and other medical procedures.

Medical equipment: 3D printing can be used to create medical equipment, such as surgical instruments, which can be tailored to the specific needs of patients.

Drugs: 3D printing can be used to create customized dosages of drugs, which can be tailored to the specific needs of patients.

However, 3D printing also has some limitations, such as the cost, the need for specialized software and hardware, and the need for specific skills to operate the machines, as well as the possibility of errors or inconsistencies in the printed product.

3.2.1.8   Telemedicine

Using telecommunications technologies, telemedicine enables medical professionals to assess, identify, and treat patients in distant locations [12]. Telemedicine has benefits, such as the capacity to gather, store, and exchange medical data [13]. Additionally, telemedicine enables patient movement tracking, distance learning, better healthcare administration and management, integration of health data systems, and remote patient monitoring [14].

Telemedicine can be used for a variety of healthcare services, including consultations, follow-up appointments, and the management of chronic conditions. It can also be used for mental health services, such as therapy and counselling.

One of the most popular forms of telemedicine is telehealth, which uses videoconferencing technology to connect patients with healthcare providers. This can be done through a computer, smartphone, or tablet, and it allows patients to receive medical care from the comfort of their own homes.

However, telemedicine also has some limitations, such as technical difficulties, lack of trust from patients and providers, and legal and regulatory challenges. Additionally, telemedicine can't replace the physical examination entirely, and in some cases, the provider might need to refer the patient for an in-person visit.

Telemedicine is a powerful tool that can help to improve access to healthcare, reduce costs, and improve patient outcomes. As technology

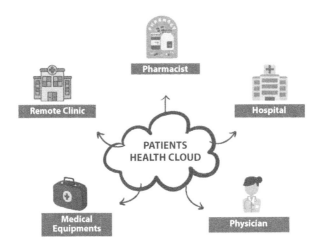

Figure 3.3 Telemedicine applications.

continues to advance, it is likely that telemedicine will play an increasingly important role in healthcare in the future as depicted in Figure 3.3.

3.2.2   Advancement in Healthcare and Medical Engineering

The advancement in healthcare and medical engineering has led to significant improvements in the diagnosis and treatment of diseases, as well as an overall increase in the quality of life for patients. One of the most significant developments in healthcare in recent years has been the incorporation of technology and engineering principles into the practice of medicine.

One of the main areas where technology has had a major impact is in the field of imaging. With the advent of new technologies such as magnetic resonance imaging (MRI) and computed tomography (CT) scans, doctors are now able to obtain detailed images of the human body, which has greatly improved their ability to diagnose and treat a wide range of diseases. Additionally, advancements in ultrasound technology have made it possible for doctors to obtain real-time images of internal organs and blood vessels, which have greatly improved the accuracy of diagnostic procedures.

Another area where technology has had a major impact is in the field of robotics and automation. Robotics and automation have been used to develop new surgical instruments and procedures that are more precise, less invasive, and have shorter recovery times. Robotics has also been used in the field of telemedicine, allowing doctors to remotely operate on patients in remote or hard-to-reach areas [19].

The field of biotechnology has also seen significant advancements in recent years. Biotechnology has been used to develop new drugs, therapies, and treatments that are more effective and have fewer side effects. Additionally, biotechnology has been used to develop new diagnostic tools and techniques that are more accurate and can detect diseases at an earlier stage.

In the field of medical devices, the advancements in the miniaturization of electronics and the advent of new materials have led to the development of smaller and more sophisticated devices, such as implantable pacemakers, artificial joints, and artificial organs. This has led to an increase in the quality of life for patients, as well as an overall increase in the longevity of the population.

In addition to the advancements mentioned above, there have also been significant developments in the field of genetic engineering and personalized medicine. Genetic engineering has allowed for the identification of specific genetic markers associated with certain diseases, which has led to the development of targeted therapies and treatments. Personalized medicine, which is a form of medicine that takes into account an individual's genetic makeup, lifestyle, and environment, has also been made possible by advances in genetic engineering.

Another area of healthcare where technology has had a significant impact is in the field of medical informatics. Electronic health records (EHRs), CPOE systems, and other clinical decision support systems were all developed as a result of medical informatics, which is the use of information technology to store and organize healthcare data. These technologies have greatly improved the efficiency and accuracy of healthcare delivery and have also led to better patient outcomes.

One of the most promising areas of healthcare technology is artificial intelligence (AI). AI has been used in a variety of applications, such as image analysis, natural language processing, and machine learning. In healthcare, AI has been used to develop systems that can assist doctors in diagnosing diseases, predicting patient outcomes, and identifying potential health risks.

Finally, the field of nanotechnology has also been making significant contributions to healthcare. The use of nanotechnology has led to the development of new materials, sensors, and devices that are smaller, more sensitive, and more biocompatible. This has led to the development of new diagnostic tools, such as lab-on-a-chip devices, as well as new therapies, such as targeted drug delivery systems.

3.3   Current Scenario of Public Healthcare System and Medical Engineering

The medical care situation in any nation is quickly changing, equally in terms of the public health challenges as well as medical healthcare systems and difficult to face and how to respond. As India grows and gains access to more resources, our responses to health issues must reflect our shifting health and socioeconomic status. Many developing country like India experiencing significant challenges when it comes to the health of children and women. India is one of the few countries where maternal mortality has decreased significantly. India still has a long way to go before it achieves the Millennium Development Goals. Despite the government's adoption of a number of policies geared toward growth, the health sector is having trouble due to growing economic, regional, and gender disparities. Public health must prioritize the socioeconomic determinants of health, illness prevention and control, and health promotion in order to lessen the burden of disease. Through coordinated societal action, the objective of public Mediclaim or healthcare is to effect change at the policy level for both disease prevention and health promotion.

In point of fact, our current healthcare system places a greater emphasis on disease prevention than on health improvement. When one's health improves, everything about life changes. In terms of health and other aspects, we must accept the responsibility of making the world a "Better Place." India, the largest nation in the globe, faces a plethora of public health issues, including communicable and no communicable diseases. Maternal, infant, and child mortality rates are among the highest in the world in India. India's public health has undergone significant transformations, despite significant progress in some areas. Several immediate concerns regarding public health persist.30 percent of Indian deaths, according to estimates, continue to occur without medical attention. Universal access to essential services must be guaranteed. The promotion and prevention of disease will be pursued in an effort to cut costs associated with curative treatment. This puts an emphasis on making healthcare more accessible to the poor, marginalized, and underserved [20].

In the majority of Indian states, there is a severe shortage of healthcare workers. To fill the gap, management, support employees, and health service providers are needed. Some states of India are unable to consistently offer essential healthcare systems that can save lives. For instance, they typically not up to the mark in vaccination coverage for measles and other likely diseases that can be prevented by vaccination.

The people who deliver healthcare to those in need are the backbone of health systems and professions in medicine. Health professionals are still in limited availability across the country. Government have not any solution to this difficult issue, but there are steps that must be taken right now. To see results in the coming years, immediate action is required. As a result of an increase in the prevalence of long-term health issues among India's aging population and their own workforce, there has been an even greater demand for health workers. Now more than ever, a national strategy for managing the workforce is required. It is crucial to prioritize the workforce. However, the government must invest in healthcare worker education. The objective ought to be to make primary healthcare available to everyone, including those living in urban slums. The healthcare system must be strengthened, public-private partnerships must be improved, and the workforce in public health must be expanded with a dedicated public health cadre.

The challenges facing the healthcare industry today are significantly more complicated. Because of the complexities of culture and customs, economic circumstances, geography, ethnicity, and political circumstances, the challenges posed by public health are unique to each state. The issues that Indians face, such as the high prevalence of communicable diseases, low performance of maternal and child health indicators, and nutritional issues, particularly those affecting women and children, persist in almost all parts of the country even today. This is in addition to the burden of chronic no communicable diseases as well as other economic and social factors.

3.4   Role of AI in Healthcare

Figure 3.4 shows the various role of AI in healthcare and Medical science. A comprehensive survey of AI technology in healthcare would cover a wide range of topics, including but not limited to:

It is worth noting that AI technology in healthcare is an emerging and rapidly evolving field, and new applications and developments are being made all the time.

The increasing of chronic and normal patients and the advancing age of the population make disease prevention an essential component of healthcare. As a means of maintaining a healthier environment and preventing serious conditions from getting worse, prevention encompasses regular exercise, healthy eating, and periodic preventive measures. To meet the needs of patients, the future upcoming medical treatment places must

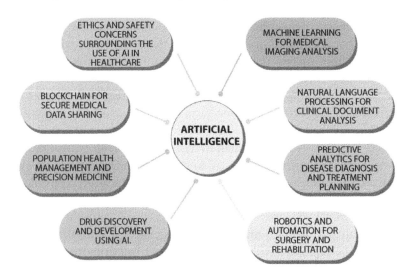

Figure 3.4 Various AI technologies in healthcare.

address an increasing number of chronic conditions and a lack of facilities. Recently, COVID-19 has emphasized the significance of e-healthcare that is quick, complete, and accurate as well as intelligent healthcare that uses a variety of medical equipment and functional data to diagnose the virus.

Developing enhanced technology-based caring policies and behavioural study systems can aid in the early identification of probable medical issues and the scheduling of the necessary actions, such as concurrently monitoring treatments and creating new assessments. Between 2020 and 2027, the global market for smart health is anticipated to expand at an annual pace of 16.2%, reaching USD 143.6 billion in 2019 [21]. Diverse actors play a role in intelligent medical treatment, including staff, hospitals, doctors, and research organizations. The management of healthcare, patient decision-making, sickness prevention and identification, calculation and estimation, and medical research are just a few of its many facets. Automated networks like the Internet of Things (IoT), mobile Internet, cloud networking, big data, 5G, artificial intelligence (AI), and evolving biotechnology are all components of intelligent healthcare.

Intelligent technology, computerization, and robotic signal processing have gradually integrated sensors into a variety of our daily systems. Sensor-generated data can help doctors and patients better understand their symptoms and potential treatments by allowing them to recognize critical situations more quickly and consistently. Patients and the healthcare industry benefit from personal and multimedia information and assistance provided by intrusive and non-intrusive tools, such as temperature-reading devices and dialysis control systems.

Electrocardiograms (ECGs), electroencephalograms (EEGs), electroglottography (EGGs), electrooculogram (EOGs), electromyograms (EMGs), body temperature, blood pressure (BP), and heart rate are examples of 1D and 2D medical signals. These medical signals could be used by a healthcare monitoring system to keep an eye on a patient.

Through healthcare, the Internet of Things is slowly beginning to connect consumers and doctors. Patients' health is still being monitored using a variety of methods, including ultrasounds, blood pressure readings, glucose receptors, electroencephalograms, and electrocardiograms. Important conditions include doctor's visits for follow-up. Smart beds, which are capable of automatically adjusting to the appropriate angle and location in response to a patient's movement; have begun to be used in a number of healthcare facilities. The presently used term Internet of Medical Things (IoMT) is referred for the utilization of IoT in the field of medical and healthcare. The IoMT has the potential to play a significant role in the creation of a fully integrated health environment.

Occasionally, depending just on one form of medical signal may not be sufficient to make a thorough diagnosis of a disease. In these circumstances, a more accurate diagnosis can be made using multimodal medical signals. This process is carried out at the data level, feature level, and classification level. While blending signals, many challenges could appear. Among these challenges include data buffering, feature normalization, classification fusion, and synchronization when gathering inputs from numerous sensors.

The development of machine learning and artificial intelligence algorithms within the context of deep learning (DL) and local area wireless network (WLAN) technologies has altered intelligent healthcare in order to assure the happiness of patients and stakeholders. The medical industry has been able to manage multiple medical signals from the same user, simultaneously increasing disease detection and prediction precision, thanks to these technologies' high computing performance, high data volume, and support for numerous terminal units, and the introduction of 5G and beyond 5G wireless technology [22].

3.5 Technological Analysis for Healthcare System and Medical Engineering

Technological analysis plays a critical role in the healthcare system and medical engineering. It is used to evaluate the effectiveness, efficiency, and safety of various technologies and techniques used in the healthcare system. This includes analysing the effectiveness of new drugs, medical devices, and surgical procedures, as well as the costs and benefits associated with these technologies.

One specific example of a technological analysis in healthcare is the use of cost-effectiveness analysis (CEA) to evaluate the cost-effectiveness of new drugs or medical devices. CEA is a method used to compare the costs and benefits of different healthcare interventions, considering factors such as the effectiveness of the intervention, the number of patients treated, and the cost of the intervention. This analysis can help policymakers and healthcare providers to make informed decisions about which technologies and treatments to adopt and fund [23].

Another example is the use of system dynamics modelling to analyze the impact of new technologies on the healthcare system as a whole. This method is used to simulate the interactions between different components of the healthcare system, such as patients, healthcare providers, and healthcare facilities, in order to predict how new technologies will impact the system over time [24].

Technology analysis is used to design and evaluate medical devices like prosthetics and implants in medical engineering. Computer-aided design (CAD) and finite element analysis (FEA) are common methods for predicting these devices' bodily functions and mechanical properties. Medical devices' performance can also be evaluated using simulation and modelling under a variety of conditions, including extreme temperatures and loads.

3.5.1   Need of Advancement in Public Healthcare System

There is a growing need for advancements in public healthcare systems due to several factors, including:

1. **An aging population**: As the population ages, there is an increased demand for healthcare services, particularly for chronic conditions such as heart disease, diabetes, and cancer.
2. **Rising healthcare costs**: The cost of healthcare is rising, making it increasingly difficult for individuals and governments to afford adequate healthcare coverage.
3. **Limited access to healthcare**: Despite advances in technology and medicine, many individuals, particularly those living in rural or underserved areas, still lack access to basic healthcare services.
4. **Shortage of healthcare professionals**: There is a shortage of healthcare professionals, particularly in rural and underserved areas, making it difficult to provide adequate healthcare services.
5. **Increasing burden of chronic diseases**: The burden of chronic diseases such as diabetes, heart disease, and cancer is increasing, putting a strain on healthcare systems and increasing healthcare costs.
6. **Growing demand for mental health services**: Mental health issues are becoming more prevalent, and there is an increase in the need for mental health services.
7. **Advancements in medical technology**: The rapid pace of technological advancements has led to the development of new medical treatments and technologies, which need to be integrated into healthcare systems.

8. **Data explosion**: The amount of data generated by electronic health records, wearables, and other sources is growing exponentially, and healthcare systems need to be able to manage, analyze and use this data to improve care.

9. **The need for more efficient and effective healthcare delivery**: With the increasing demands on healthcare systems, there is a need to find more efficient and effective ways of delivering healthcare services.

10. **The need for better healthcare data management**: With the growing amount of data generated by electronic health records, wearable's, and other sources, healthcare systems need to find ways to manage, analyse, and use this data to improve care.

11. **The need for better healthcare coordination**: With an aging population and a growing number of individuals with chronic conditions, there is a need to coordinate care across different healthcare providers and settings.

12. **The need for better healthcare accessibility**: Advances in telemedicine and virtual consultations can improve access to healthcare for individuals in remote or underserved areas.

13. **The need for better healthcare security**: The security of healthcare data must be ensured in order to protect patient privacy with the growing usage of electronic health records and other digital technologies.

14. **The need for better healthcare affordability**: Rising healthcare costs are making it increasingly difficult for individuals and governments to afford adequate healthcare coverage. Advancements in healthcare delivery and technology have the potential to reduce costs and make healthcare more affordable.

15. **The need for more patient-centered healthcare**: Advances in machine learning and other technologies have the potential to provide more personalized and patient-centered healthcare.

16. **The need for more efficient healthcare management**: With the growing demand for healthcare services, there is a need for more efficient healthcare management to ensure that resources are used effectively.

17. **The need for more effective disease prevention**: Advances in predictive analytics and machine learning can be used to

identify individuals at risk of developing chronic conditions and provide targeted interventions to prevent or delay onset.

18. **The need for more effective emergency response**: With the increasing threat of natural disasters and other emergencies, healthcare systems need to be able to respond effectively to ensure the safety and well-being of individuals.

19. **The need for more effective care for marginalized communities**: Advances in technology and healthcare delivery can help to ensure that marginalized communities have access to the same level of healthcare as the general population.

20. **The need for more effective healthcare for non-communicable diseases**: Healthcare systems must develop strategies to enhance care for non-communicable diseases like diabetes, heart disease, and cancer given their growing burden. Overall, advancements in public healthcare systems are needed to meet the growing demand for healthcare services and to ensure that all individuals have access to high-quality, affordable healthcare. These advancements can be achieved by investing in technology, training healthcare professionals, and improving healthcare infrastructure, and by involving the community in the design and implementation of healthcare policies.

3.5.2   Advance Technology Role in Healthcare System

The healthcare system has been significantly improved by technological advancements. Accessing and sharing patient data has become easier for medical professionals thanks to electronic health records (EHRs). Access to medical care has increased, particularly in rural and remote areas, thanks to telemedicine. The diagnostic capabilities of medical imaging technologies like MRI and CT scans have also greatly improved. In addition, the application of robotics and artificial intelligence (AI) to surgical and other medical procedures has reduced recovery times and improved precision. In summary, technology has made healthcare more efficient and effective as well as improved patient outcomes.

Technology is also playing a big role in disease management and prevention, in addition to the examples I gave earlier. Patients can track their health and fitness data using wearable devices and mobile apps, as well as monitor chronic conditions like diabetes. Additionally, these devices have the ability to notify patients and healthcare providers of potential health issues, assisting them in better managing their conditions.

New therapies and treatments are also being developed with the help of technology. For instance, genomics and precision medicine are assisting in the identification of specific genetic markers for diseases, which may serve as a basis for the creation of treatments that are more specific and efficient. Big data and machine learning are also being used to analyze a lot of health data to find patterns and trends that can help make new medicines and treatments.

Telehealth and telemedicine, which are becoming more common, are another way technology is affecting healthcare. Patients who live in remote or underserved areas, have mobility issues, or are unable to take time off from their jobs can now have virtual consultations with their healthcare providers thanks to technology. Patients won't have to travel so far for appointments as a result of this, which can help make medical care more accessible to more people.

Medical research methods are also being improved through the use of technology. For instance, a lot of medical data is being analyzed with the help of AI and machine learning, which can help find patterns and trends that can help develop new therapies and treatments. Organ models and prosthetics are also being made with the help of 3D printing technology, which can help with surgical planning and training [25].

Drug development and personalized medicine are two additional areas where technology is having a significant impact. Researchers are now able to identify specific genetic markers for diseases with the help of genomics, which can help develop treatments that are more specific and effective. New drugs like CAR-T therapy, a cancer treatment that uses genetically modified cells from a patient's own immune system to fight cancer, are also being developed using technology. The field of medical imaging is another important area where technology is having a significant impact. Doctors and radiologists can now create detailed, high-resolution images of the internal structures of the body with the assistance of advanced imaging techniques like MRI and CT scans. This makes it possible to diagnose diseases and injuries with greater precision and can also assist in directing surgical procedures. For instance, using robots and other forms of automation in surgery can both reduce recovery times and improve precision. Surgeons can, for instance, perform procedures with greater precision and control thanks to robotic-assisted surgery, which can also lower the likelihood of complications.

The study of an individual's genetic makeup, or genomics, is another area where technology is having a significant impact. Researchers are now able to analyze an individual's entire genome with the assistance of next-generation sequencing, which can assist in the identification of genetic markers for various diseases [26–33]. Both personalized medicine and the creation of more specific and efficient treatments can benefit from this information.

Additionally, technology is being utilized to enhance the management and dissemination of medical data. For instance, medical records of patients can be securely stored and shared among various healthcare providers with the assistance of blockchain technology, thereby enhancing continuity of care and decreasing the likelihood of errors.

3.6   Future Aspects of AI in Healthcare and Medical Engineering

The future of AI in healthcare systems is expected to bring many advancements and improvements to the way healthcare is delivered and received. Some potential future aspects of AI in healthcare include:

1. Increased personalization of medicine: AI-driven predictive analytics will be used to tailor treatments to the unique characteristics and needs of individual patients, leading to better health outcomes.
2. Remote patient monitoring: AI-powered sensors and devices will enable continuous monitoring of patients' vital signs and health status, allowing for early detection of potential health issues.
3. Improved clinical decision making: AI-powered systems will assist doctors and nurses in making more accurate and efficient diagnoses, leading to better patient outcomes.
4. Automation of routine tasks: AI will be used to automate routine tasks, such as data entry and scheduling, freeing up healthcare professionals to focus on more critical tasks.
5. Advancement in healthcare research: AI will be used to analyze large data sets and identify new patterns and insights, leading to the discovery of new drugs and treatments.
6. AI-powered Chabot's, virtual assistants, and other interactive tools will be used to improve the patient experience, providing quick and easy access to health information, and enabling patients to communicate with their providers more easily.
7. Real-time language translation in virtual consultations and telemedicine to break language barriers.

8. AI-powered drug development and clinical trial process optimization, leading to faster and more cost-effective drug development.

9. AI-driven medical imaging and diagnostic tools for early detection and diagnosis of diseases such as cancer, heart disease, and other chronic conditions.

10. Robotic and automation of surgical procedures and rehabilitation, leading to improved precision and reduced recovery time.

11. AI-powered virtual assistants and Chabot's for mental health support and assistance, providing 24/7 access to mental health resources and reducing the stigma around mental health.

12. AI-powered medical robots for home-based care, aiding and support for older adults and people with chronic conditions who require long-term care.

13. Predictive analytics and machine learning for population, health management, identifying individuals at risk of developing chronic conditions and providing targeted interventions to prevent or delay onset.

14. Advancement in AI-powered wearable devices and sensors, providing continuous monitoring of vital signs and enabling proactive care management.

15. AI-powered virtual medical consultations and triage, providing remote access to healthcare for individuals in rural or underserved areas.

16. AI-powered patient engagement and education, providing personalized health information and educational resources to patients.

17. AI-powered hospital operations and management, optimizing patient flow, reducing wait times, and improving overall efficiency in healthcare facilities.

18. AI-powered medical equipment and device maintenance, reducing downtime and improving equipment availability.

19. AI-powered clinical trial recruitment, identifying and recruiting eligible participants more efficiently.

20. AI-powered medical device security, preventing cyber-attacks and ensuring patient safety.

21. AI-powered genomics, using genetic data to better understand the underlying causes of diseases and develop more effective treatments.

22. AI-powered clinical trial design, using machine learning algorithms to optimize study design and increase the chances of success.

23. AI-powered patient-generated data, using data from wearable's, mobile apps, and other sources to gain a more complete understanding of patients' health and well-being.

24. AI-powered drug pricing and reimbursement, using data analysis to optimize drug pricing and reimbursement strategies.

25. AI-powered patient safety, using machine learning algorithms to identify and mitigate safety risks in healthcare settings.

26. AI-powered medical education, using virtual reality, simulations, and other technologies to improve the training of medical professionals.

27. AI-powered medical research, using machine learning algorithms to identify new research opportunities and accelerate the discovery of new treatments and cures.

28. AI-powered public health surveillance, using data from various sources to identify and track disease outbreaks and other public health threats.

29. AI-powered patient-provider communication, using natural language processing and other techniques to improve the quality and effectiveness of communication between patients and healthcare providers.

30. AI-powered healthcare fraud detection and prevention, using machine learning algorithms to identify and prevent fraudulent activity in the healthcare system.

31. AI-powered drug development and discovery, using computational biology and bioinformatics techniques to identify new drug targets, design new drugs, and optimize drug development.

32. AI-powered electronic health records, using natural language processing and other techniques to extract relevant data from electronic health records and improve healthcare decision-making.

33. AI-powered medical imaging and diagnostic tools, using machine learning algorithms to improve the accuracy and speed of medical imaging and diagnostic processes.

34. AI-powered medical device security and regulatory compliance, using machine learning algorithms to ensure that

medical devices are secure and compliant with regulatory requirements.

35. AI-powered patient-centric healthcare, using machine learning algorithms to provide personalized patient-centric care and improve patient satisfaction.

36. AI-powered clinical trial data management, using machine learning algorithms to automate data management tasks such as data cleaning, data integration, and data analysis.

37. AI-powered medical device testing, using machine learning algorithms to automate the testing and validation of medical devices to improve efficiency and reduce costs.

38. AI-powered virtual reality-based surgery and therapy, using virtual reality technologies to simulate surgeries and therapies and improve training and education for medical professionals.

39. AI-powered personalized nutrition, using machine learning algorithms to recommend personalized diets based on genetic, environmental, and lifestyle data.

While AI in healthcare has the potential to significantly improve the healthcare system, it is essential to implement it ethically and responsibly, taking into consideration issues like data privacy, bias, and interpretability. The integration and interoperability of AI systems with existing healthcare systems, as well as the implications for the workforce and the healthcare system as a whole must also be taken into consideration.

3.7   Conclusion

The nation's public healthcare system must keep up with technological changes and how they affect people's health. AI has many potential benefits for the practice of medicine, like accelerating research or assisting clinicians in making wiser judgements. It is clear that the moment has come for healthcare technology businesses to bring about real, long-lasting change that will benefit patients and clinicians across the country. The continued acceptance of cutting-edge technology and the emergence of a digital workplace will enable this transition. The research gap for developing effective decision support systems for medical applications is filled in part by this study. It is essential that public health practices have a scientific foundation. Research is essential to public health globally because it produces insights and technologies that address health issues. In this study, emerging technology developments in health services applications and systems are looked at, and suggestions are given. This chapter highlights current developments in healthcare and medical engineering, including applications of artificial intelligence (AI) in clinical settings, as well as other applications.

3.8   Future Aspect

Like any other system, it has strengths and weaknesses. IoT, AI, and machine learning has significant drawbacks, and managing billion of an active network with many sensors and devices, that stand gathering trillions of gigabytes of data is one of the largest difficulties. Security is followed by privacy. It is unethical and unlawful to provide patient information to unauthorized parties. In order to strengthen advance technical systems without risking people's security and privacy, several nations have formed policies, statutes, and regulations, and several more are in the process of doing so. Enabling low-cost, community-based healthcare while both enhancing medical results and creating a knowledge economy. Additionally, technology will help and update patients to receive precise information and also provide clear data monitoring along with individualized care, which results to save time of frequent visit of hospitals. The global market had a value of $22.5 billion in 2016 and is expected to increase at a composite annual growth rate of 26.2% to reach $72.02 billion by 2021, according to Frost & Sullivan's estimate. This chapter quickly categorizes and summarizes the various concepts and applications that are updated as a result of the integration of IoT, AI, machine learning, and cloud computing in healthcare and medical sciences.

References

1. Tumen, V., SpiCoNET: A hybrid deep learning model to diagnose COVID-19 and pneumonia using chest X-ray images. *Trait. du Signal*, 39, 4, 1169–1180, 2022.
2. Yu, K.H., Beam, A.L., Kohane, I.S., Artificial intelligence in healthcare. *Nat. Biomed. Eng.*, 2, 10, 719–731, 2018.
3. Vishnu, S., Ramson, S.J., Jegan, R., Internet of medical things (IoMT) - an overview, in: *2020 5th International Conference on Devices, Circuits, and Systems (ICDCS)*, IEEE, pp. 101–104, 2020, March.

4. Rai, A., Karatangi, S.V., Agarwal, R., Prakash, O., Smart sensors transform healthcare system, in: *Deep Learning and IoT in Healthcare Systems*, pp. 191–214, Apple Academic Press, New York, 2021.

5. Zheng, Z., Xie, S., Dai, H.N., Chen, W., Chen, X., Weng, J., Imran, M., An overview on smart contracts: Challenges, advances, and platforms. *Future Gener. Comput. Syst.*, 105, 475–491, 2020.

6. Morrison, D.W., Dokmeci, M.R., Demirci, U. T. K. A. N., Khademhosseini, A., Clinical applications of micro-and nanoscale biosensors, in: *Biomedical Nanostructures*, vol. 1, pp. 433–458, 2008.

7. Anjum, S., Ishaque, S., Fatima, H., Farooq, W., Hano, C., Abbasi, B.H., Anjum, I., Emerging applications of nanotechnology in healthcare systems: Grand challenges and perspectives. *Pharmaceuticals*, 14, 8, 707, 2021.

8. Sultan, N., Making use of cloud computing for healthcare provision: Opportunities and challenges. *Int. J. Inf. Manag.*, 34, 2, 177–184, 2014.

9. Dash, S., Shakyawar, S.K., Sharma, M., Kaushik, S., Big data in healthcare: Management, analysis and future prospects. *J. Big Data*, 6, 1, 1–25, 2019.

10. Rai, A., Sharma, D., Rai, S., Singh, A., Singh, K.K., IoT-aided robotics development and applications with AI, in: *Emergence of Cyber Physical System and IoT in Smart Automation and Robotics: Computer Engineering in Automation*, pp. 1–14, Springer International Publishing, Cham, 2021.

11. Senbekov, M., Saliev, T., Bukeyeva, Z., Almabayeva, A., Zhanaliyeva, M., Aitenova, N., Fakhradiyev, I., The recent progress and applications of digital technologies in healthcare: A review. *Int. J. Telemed. Appl.*, 2020, 1–18, 2020.

12. Nayak, S., Mantri, S., Nayak, M., Rai, A., Introduction to e-monitoring for healthcare, in: *Book Machine Learning, Deep Learning, Big Data, and Internet of Things for Healthcare*, pp. 1–11, Chapman and Hall/CRC, New York, 2022.

13. Acharibasam, J.W. and Wynn, R., Telemental health in low- and middle-income countries: A systematic review. *Int. J. Telemed. Appl.*, 10 pages, 2018.

14. Molfenter, T., Brown, R., O'Neill, A., Kopetsky, E., Toy, A., Use of telemedicine in addiction treatment: Current practices and organizational implementation characteristics. *Int. J. Telemed. Appl.*, 8 pages, 2018.

15. Cheng, Y., Shi, X., Jiang, X., Wang, X., Qin, H., Printability of a cellulose derivative for extrusion-based 3D printing: The application on a biodegradable support material. *Front. Mater.*, 7, 86, 2020.

16. Yan, Q., Dong, H., Su, J., Han, J., Song, B., Wei, Q., Shi, Y., A review of 3D printing technology for medical applications. *Engineering*, 4, 5, 729–742, 2018.

17. Aimar, A., Palermo, A., Innocenti, B., The role of 3D printing in medical applications: A state of the art. *J. Healthc Eng.*, 11 pages, 2019.

18. Pugliese, L., Marconi, S., Negrello, E., Mauri, V., Peri, A., Gallo, V., Pietrabissa, A., The clinical use of 3D printing in surgery. *Updates Surg.*, 70, 3, 381–388, 2018.

19. National Academies of Sciences, Engineering, and Medicine., *Leveraging artificial intelligence and machine learning to advance environmental health*

research and decisions: Proceedings of a workshop—In brief, National Academies Press, Washington, DC, 2019.

20. Kumar, J.R., Role of public health systems in the present health scenario: Key challenges. *Indian J. Public Health*, 57, 3, 133. 41, 2013.

21. Ahmed, Q.W., Garg, S., Rai, A., Ramachandran, M., Jhanjhi, N.Z., Masud, M., Baz, M., AI-based resource allocation techniques in wireless sensor internet of things networks in energy efficiency with data optimization. *Electronics*, 11, 13, 2071, 2022.

22. Muhammad, G., Alshehri, F., Karray, F., El Saddik, A., Alsulaiman, M., Falk, T.H., A comprehensive survey on multimodal medical signals fusion for smart healthcare systems. *Inf. Fusion*, 76, 355–375, 2021.

23. Detsky, A.S. and Naglie, I.G., A clinician's guide to cost-effectiveness analysis. *Ann. Intern. Med.*, 113, 2, 147–154, 1990.

24. Galea, S., Hall, C., Kaplan, G.A., Social epidemiology and complex system dynamic modelling as applied to health behaviour and drug use research. *Int. J. Drug Policy*, 20, 3, 209–216, 2009.

25. Ventola, C.L., Medical applications for 3D printing: Current and projected uses. *Pharm. Ther.*, 39, 10, 704, 2014.

26. Mishra, A.R., Pippal, S.K., Asif, Kumar, A., Singh, D., Singh, A., Clear vision - Obstacle detection using bat algorithm optimization technique. *2021 9th International Conference on Reliability, Infocom Technologies and Optimization (Trends and Future Directions) (ICRITO)*, pp. 1–5, 2021.

27. De Magalhães, J.P., Finch, C.E., Janssens, G., Next-generation sequencing in aging research: Emerging applications, problems, pitfalls and possible solutions. *Ageing Res. Rev.*, 9, 3, 315–323, 2010.

29. Sharma, N. and Shambharkar, P.G., Applicability of ML-IoT in smart healthcare systems: Challenges, solutions & future direction, in: *2022 International Conference on Computer Communication and Informatics (ICCCI)*, IEEE, pp. 1–7, 2022, January.

30. Rai, A., Singh, R.P., Jain, N., Role of IoT in sustainable healthcare systems, in: *Ambient Intelligence and Interneto of Things: Convergent Technologies*, John Wiley & Sons Publications, United States, 2022.

31. Nittari, G., Khuman, R., Baldoni, S., Pallotta, G., Battineni, G., Sirignano, A., Ricci, G., Telemedicine practice: Review of the current ethical and legal challenges. *Telemed. E-Health*, 26, 12, 1427–1437. 7, 2020.

32. Prokofieva, M. and Miah, S.J., Blockchain in healthcare. *Australas. J. Inf. Syst.*, 23, 1–20, 2019.

33. Miseta, E., What exactly is a virtual clinical trial?, in: *National Academies of Sciences, Engineering, and Medicine; Health and Medicine Division; Board on Health Sciences Policy; Forum on Drug Discovery, Development, and Translation.* Shore, C., Khandekar, E., Alper, J. (eds.), National Academies Press (US, Washington (DC), 2019 Jul 23.

4

Role of Genomics in Smart Era and Its Application in COVID-19

Sunil Kumar and Biswajit R. Bhowmik*

BRICS Laboratory, Department of Computer Science and Engineering, National Institute of Technology Karnataka, India

Abstract

Genomics is a rapidly developing field that aims to understand the whole inherited traits of an organism, including its structure, function, and evolution. The purpose of genomics is to gain a detailed understanding of the biological basis for human disease, to explore the genetic variation of several species and humans, and also to enhance rural livelihoods and farming practices. The motivation to completely comprehend the complex biological processes that regulate life on earth and to put this knowledge to enhance people's lives, improve food security, and safeguard the environment has driven the growth of genomics technologies. The discovery of the genetic roots of human diseases and other complex traits is one of the main goals of genomics, which may lead to the development of treatments and medications. Researchers can find similar genetic pathways and mechanisms to develop drugs and medicines for a broad range of diseases by comparing the genomes of many species. With the introduction of new technologies and advancements in deoxyribonucleic acid sequencing, genomics has evolved into a powerful tool for solving life's riddles and transforming the lives of people from all over the world. By comparing the genomes of DNA sequencing disorders, researchers can uncover the genes responsible for desirable characteristics such as improved genetics, disease resistance, and better efficiency. This information is essential to develop populations of organisms better adaptable to evolving biological conditions. This chapter provides an overview of genomics, including its background, key attributes, and various types and application areas. The numerous challenges in genomics are also addressed in this chapter, including dealing with large genomes, sequencing and retrieving genetic data, comprehending the features of potential pathogens, and analyzing pathogen sequence trends. The chapter also addresses recent advances

---

Corresponding author: brb@nitk.edu.in

Amit Kumar Tyagi (ed.) Privacy Preservation of Genomic and Medical Data, (73–112) © 2024 Scrivener Publishing LLC

in genomics, such as its involvement in the COVID-19 pandemic and the most sophisticated techniques used in the discipline. The development of artificial intelligence in genomics and its usage in COVID-19 research are also discussed in this chapter. Moreover, this chapter provides a comprehensive insight into the evolution, present condition, and future potential of genomics research. Overall, the purpose of the chapter is to understand the problems and accomplishments in genomics and how it may assist healthcare systems.

Keywords: DNA and RNA, genomics and genetics, DNA computing, genome sequencing, COVID-19, SARS variants, convolutional neural networks, AI in genomics.

4.1   Introduction

Before the genomics era, the main focus of genetic and heredity research was the analysis of specific genes and their function. This was known as the "era of gene genetics [1]." Since that time, scientists have used traditional genetic concepts like mating trials, linkage analysis, and DNA profiling to identify and explore the role of specific genes. These initiatives led to the discovery of several inherited human notions, including dominant and recessive genotypes, gene mutation, and genetic linkage, as well as a deep understanding of the genetic basis of various traits and diseases. However, the restrictions of these approaches, such as the difficulties of identifying genes that contribute to complicated features, prompted a transition to a more comprehensive, genome-wide system introduced in the genomics era.

The genomics era in Bharat (India) may be found in ancient to the late 1990s and early 2000s when Bharat's first genome sequencing programs were initiated. Since then, Bharat has achieved a remarkable breakthrough, focusing on integrating genomic technology for disease detection and tailored treatment. The Human Genome Project in Bharat (HGP-Bharat) was launched in 2001 to sequence the genomes of Bharat and develop a complete database of the genetic diversity in the country. The Department of Biotechnology (DBT), the Council of Scientific and Industrial Research (CSIR), and other prominent academic and research institutes in Bharat collaborated on this project [2].

Another notable event in 2019 was the launching of the National Health Stack (NHS), which aimed to provide the country with a uniform health information platform. The NHS aims to enhance healthcare delivery by integrating and providing access to health data from various sources, including genetic data, to healthcare researchers and practitioners.

With a focus on improving health outcomes and addressing the unique health concerns encountered by the Bharat people, the genomics era in Bharat has witnessed a rapid expansion of genomics research and infrastructure in the country [3].

The genomics era commenced in the late 20th century when the attention of genetics and heredity research evolved to the sequencing, assembly, and analysis of entire genomes of various organisms. The Human Genome Project was completed in 2003, laying the groundwork for substantial genome sequencing efforts for multiple species, from microorganisms through crops to mammals [4]. The availability of this genetic information has contributed to several breakthroughs in fields such as health, agriculture, and evolutionary biology. It has provided us with a wealth of new information and insights into the biology and development of life on Earth. The genomics era is still ongoing, shaping our perspective of the natural world.

Genomics studies an organism's whole collection of genetic information called its genome. The field of genomics explores the structure, function, and evolution of genomes, which encompass all of the genetic data inherent in living organisms. It is a rapidly developing field that combines the characteristics of genetics, biochemistry, molecular biology, bioinformatics, and computing to analyze and grasp the data contained in genomes [5]. It entails the mapping, sequencing, and analyzing of DNA and its properties. The purpose of studying genomics is to understand how gene mutation influences an organism's traits and behaviors and to identify genetic susceptibility to diseases and other characteristics. The emergence of high-throughput sequencing technologies has resulted in substantial developments in the field, allowing for large-scale, rapid, and cost-effective genetic sequencing. Moreover, genomics can assist in developing personalized medicine, farming, and biotechnology.

Genetics is the study of inheritance and variation within species. It requires knowledge about how the genetic code, DNA, transfers characteristics from parents to children. The DNA in all living things contains the instructions for their growth and maintenance; variations in DNA result in different traits. There are numerous uses for genetic research in biotechnology, agriculture, and medicine. DNA computing is a field that uses DNA molecules to analyze and store data. It uses self-replication and highly information-dense DNA molecules to perform computation. In DNA computing, cognitive functions are carried out by altering DNA sequences encoded into programs. Although the field is still in inception, it has the potential to revolutionize computers by offering fresh thoughts for data processing, assessment, and preservation.

Bharat has contributed to genetic research in the last 20 years. The enthusiasm for human genome research has assisted plant and microbial sequencing endeavors. Many corporate organizations, mainly as outsourcing hubs, have started working in the field of genomics in addition to government institutions.

Organization of the Chapter

The rest of the chapter is organized as follows: Section 4.2 discusses the basics of genomics. Section 4.3 explores the development of genomics. Section 4.4 discusses the characteristics of genomics and DNA computing. Section 4.5 explores the many types of genomics. Section 4.6 discusses the application area of genomics and DNA computing. Section 4.7 discusses the application area of DNA computing. Section 4.8 discusses the role of genomics and DNA computing in COVID-19. Section 4.9 explores the issue of genomics and DNA computing. Section 4.10 discusses the tools and technology utilized in genomics systems. Section 4.11 explores the role of artificial intelligence (AI) technologies in genomics. Section 4.12 discusses the related works. Section 4.13 discusses the future research dimension. Section 4.14 concludes the chapter.

4.2 Basics of Genomics

The study of an organism's entire genome, or collection of genetic data, is known as genomics. The exact meaning of "genome" is challenging. It often refers to the DNA or ribonucleic acid (RNA) molecules that contain genetic information in an organism. However, determining which nucleotide to incorporate into the concept can take time—for instance, bacteria store the required transgene in one or two enormous DNA strand pairs of chromosomes [6]. Moreover, they also have smaller molecules called extra-chromosomal plasmids that carry essential genetic information. The term "genome" in scientific literature refers to the large chromosomal DNA molecules found in bacteria.

The concept of heredity and genetics in ancient Bharat was limited and primarily based on observations of how physical traits were handed down from one generation to the next. A deeper understanding of genetics was required, as well as a thorough investigation of the fundamental mechanisms of inheritance. The Charaka Samhita and the Sushruta Samhita, which were penned between the second century BCE and the second century CE, explain how some physical traits, like eye and skin color, are transmitted from parents to children. Ayurveda and Siddha medicine, which have been used for thousands of years, are far ancient Bharat medical cannabis systems that included components of what can be called early genetic knowledge. Practitioners of Ayurveda, for example, are aware of the significance of gene history and the hereditary transmission of disease. Overall, early genetic knowledge was incorporated into ancient Bharat's medical institutions and practices even if the concept of genomics as we know it today did not exist then.

Hans Winkler, a botany professor at the University of Hamburg in Germany, coined the term "genome" in 1920 [7]. Figure 4.1 is a graphical representation of humane genomes. The study of an organism's total or a part of its epigenetic or genetic sequence data is referred to as genomics, and it intends to comprehend the structure and function among these sequences as well as the subsequent biochemical. The research of genomics in a wide variety of health includes the molecular mechanisms that underlie disease as well as the relationships between molecular data, medical therapies, and environmental factors. Figure 4.2 illustrates a key component of genomic-based healthcare which is using an individual's genomic data in clinical decision-making (i.e., for making a diagnosis or selecting a course of treatment) while considering the potential consequences.

Another emerging area of genomics is genetics. The study of genes, genetic diversity, and inheritance in species is known as genetics. It is a significant branch of biology since heredity is essential to the evolution of

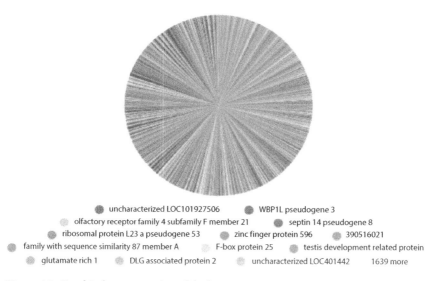

Figure 4.1 Graphical representation of the human genome.

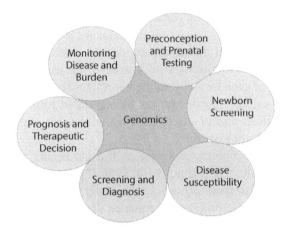

Figure 4.2 A conceptual overview of the usages of genomics in healthcare.

organisms. Genetics was initially studied scientifically by Gregor Mendel, a Moravian Augustinian priest who worked in Brno in the 19th century [8]. Mendel studied trait inheritance, the process by which features are passed down from parents to children over time. He found that organisms (pea plants) inherit characteristics in distinct units of heredity. This word, which is still used nowadays, is a slightly unclear definition of what is often alluded to as a gene. Festetics claimed that apparent transformations in domesticated animals, crops, and humans are the consequences of scientific principles. Festetics arrived at the empirical conclusion that traits are inherited rather than acquired by organisms. To distinguish genetic traits and inherent variation, he proposed that features from previous generations may emerge subsequently and even that species could produce offspring with a variety of attributes. These findings, providing a necessary theoretical basis for genetics in the 20th century, act as an essential precursor to Mendel's theory of particle inheritance as it includes a transformation of heredity from myth to scientific discipline.

DNA computing was initially discussed by USC professor Leonard Adleman in the Science article Molecular Computations of Solutions to Combinatorial Problems from November 1994 [9]. Adleman showed how DNA might be utilized for massively parallel computing, data storage, and even computation. It is a branch of natural analysis that accomplishes logical and mathematical operations by using molecular mechanisms of DNA by swapping typical carbon/silicon circuits with synthetic biology. That allows a massively parallel computation and takes less time to solve complicated mathematical equations or problems. The information or data is now preserved in bases adenine, thymine, guanine, and cytosine instead of binary digits. The ability to synthesize DNA sequences permits these sequences to be applied as input for systems.

James Watson and Francis Crick's initial proposal for the structure of DNA [10] was followed by a concept for a replication process depicted in Figure 4.3. The significant distinction between genetics and genomics is that genetics focuses on the structure and operation of a single gene. In contrast, genomics examines all genes and their interactions to determine how they collectively affect the growth and development of an organism. The human genomes of approximately three billion base pairs have been sequenced, and about 25,000 genes have been discovered, but just 1% of the complete genome has been related to protein coding. It will probably take decades of more research to determine the functional significance of noncoding DNA and the causes and effects of sequence variations across individuals. The human genome serves as the epicenter. No other databases stimulate our imagination and curiosity in the same way, but none offer the same possibility of improving human health. Genes, which are stored on 23 pairs of chromosomes crammed into the nucleus of a biological system, control protein synthesis with the help of enzymes and messenger peptides. A messenger ribonucleic acid (mRNA) molecule is created when an enzyme transfers data from a gene's DNA (mRNA). The ribosome integrates the amino acids essential to the mRNA to form the protein molecule. With the help of data, the ribosome links amino acids together

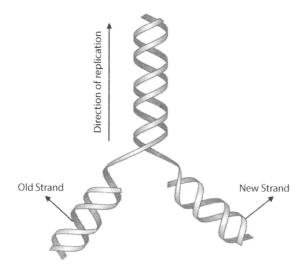

Figure 4.3 A conceptual overview of the replication process.

in the proper sequence to create a particular protein. Proteins coordinate chemical changes, transmit messages within organisms, and produce bio-molecules like cells and tissues. The DNA in a mutant cell may have an abnormal gene, which can impair healthy organ systems and cause malig-nancies like cancer.

4.3   Evolution of Genomics

The history of genomics in Bharat has been marked by several vital break-throughs and turning milestones that have shaped the field and made Bharat a significant player in the international genomics community. Rapid expansion, innovation, and collaboration in DNA sequencing and genetic research have characterized the emergence of genomics in Bharat. Participation in the Human Genome Project, the establishment of new facilities and institutions to support the needs of the genomics community, the development of newer technologies for DNA sequencing and genome analysis, the formation of the Bharat Genome Variation Consortium, and the launch of the Genome Bharat Project are all significant developments and milestones. These initiatives have aided in establishing Bharat as a sig-nificant player in the global genomics community as well as in our under-standing of the genetic basis of many diseases and the creation of new diagnostic tools and treatments [11].

Watson and Crick's major scientific paper [12] specifying how DNA's double-helix structure works was published in 1953. In their research, they made the observations that "as far as is known, the sequence of bases along the chain is irregular" and "the sequence of bases on a single chain does not appear restricted in any way,"—two characteristics that imply that DNA plays a role in the collection of genetic data and emphasize the significance of figuring out the precise base sequence along the system. The first biolog-ical molecule was sequenced in 1953. Using an enhanced partition chro-matographic technique, Sanger was able to sequence the two chains of the insulin protein. His process comprises randomly degenerating proteins, analyzing each fragment separately, and overlapping the sequences from each piece to produce an entire consensus sequence. Before nucleic acids, proteins were sequenced, but many of the same principles applied, opening the door for contemporary DNA sequencing. Regarding nucleic acids in 1965, the 76-base-long alanine tRNA from *Saccharomyces cerevisiae* took the lead since it has been used successfully to cleave RNA fragments since the 1940s.

RNA was first broken up into smaller pieces using RNA A and T1 to determine the insulin sequence. The fragments were then separated using chromatography, and the results were employed. DNA sequencing lagged behind RNA sequencing at the four ends of the 1960s. The complementary endpoints of the bacteriophage k cos-site, which were 12 bases long, became the first DNA molecules to be sequenced. A group led by Sanger used 32P-labeled RNA and a technique based on paper fractionation to identify the 120-base-pair (bp)-long 5s rRNA that same year. The first gene to be sequenced was the 510-bp coat protein gene from the RNA virus phage MS2, and it was done in 1972 by Fiers [13]. By converting its DNA into RNA, the 24 bases of the lactose-repressor binding site for *Escherichia coli* were first identified by Gilbert and Maxam in 1973. In 1976, the 3,569-bp RNA genome of the phage MS2 became the first organism to be sequenced entirely.

Consequently, estimations of respective variables using genome and phenotype data are less precise within one or two decades than for three generations. This results in less accurate heritability calculations using genomes from selected humans and animals. As a result, combining all genetic and phenotypic data in the analysis can improve the prediction accuracy. Figure 4.4 illustrates a brief overview of the development of

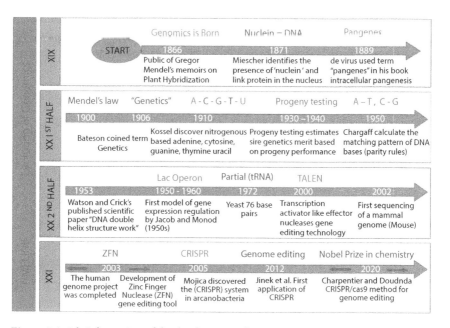

Figure 4.4 A brief overview of the development of genomics.

genomics. Classic genetic knowledge has unquestionably grown out of Mendel's observations about the inheritance of traits in plants in the 19th century. Concepts of genes and chromosomal theory were solidified in the early 20th century. Later, developments in the chemical basis of inheritance, the deciphering of the genetic code, and discoveries related to gene control highlighted the growth of genomics and the creation of genomic tools in animal research over the 20th century. The decoding of the entire human genome at the beginning of the 21st century significantly impacted genomics, as did the eventual use of this knowledge in the creation of gene-editing tools. As a result, two female researchers, Charpentier and Doudna, were given the Nobel Prize in 2020.

The third-generation sequencing (TGS) era of innovative new technologies emerged in the 2010s. Even though other TGS techniques often refer to machinery that can sequence a single DNA molecule without replicating it, these frameworks enable reads that are hundreds of Mbps longer than NGS. The use of long reads is a significant aspect of genome assembly because the difficulty of detecting overlaps between NGS short reads reduces the ability to create long, sustained consensus sequences [14], affecting the overall assembly quality. Population genomics, genetic disorder, diagnosis, specific treatment programs, cancer care, and prenatal care have indeed contributed to genome sequencing and assembly developments during the last decade. Using these approaches to better comprehend biological and evolutionary processes is becoming more common in non-model species. The dedication to comparative genome sequencing and assembly has increased from single-species initiatives to multi-species

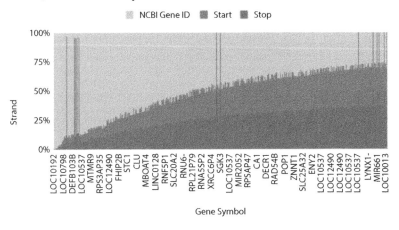

Figure 4.5 Graphical representation of gene data using *Homo sapiens* genome.

collaborative efforts. For most organisms, steps are in progress to make high genomes using a mix of NGS and TGS methods. Figure 4.5 illustrates a graphical representation of gene data using the *Homo sapiens* genome to validate Chr8 (chromosome 8) gene for protein feature coding.

4.4   Characteristics of Genomics and DNA Computing

As stated, the study of genomes' structure, function, evolution, and mapping, which are the complete sets of genetic information present in an organism, is known as genomics. On the other hand, DNA computing is a field that studies the use of DNA molecules for computation and information storage—both present multiple features. The following are the fundamentals of genomics and DNA computing.

4.4.1   Genomics

The basic features of genomics include the following:

- This generic and all-encompassing concept refers to any genomic area with some annotated function. An example of this might include a gene, protein coding sequence (CDS), messenger RNA (mRNA), transfer ribonucleic acid (tRNA), ribosomal ribonucleic acid (rRNA), repeat sequence, inverted repeat, microRNAs (miRNA), small interfering RNA (siRNA), or origin of replication.
- A particular genomic feature may comprise several different genomic sites that collectively make up the genomic feature [15].
- For instance, a gene with several exons that codes for proteins is called a protein-coding gene (CDS). Create a mature mRNA, and each exon is spliced together. As a result, the actual CDS feature is made up of numerous nearby genomic sites.
- It aims to uncover DNA changes such as single-nucleotide polymorphisms, insertions and deletions, and more enormous structural differences in organisms.
- Analysis of enormous volumes of genomic data using bioinformatics tools.

- It is crucial in personalized medicine because it provides information on an individual's genetic structure, which may be used to predict their risk for specific diseases and guide the development of precision medicine.

4.4.2 DNA Computing

The basic characteristics of DNA computing include:

- Instead of the binary alphabet 1 and 0, DNA computing encodes information using a four-letter genetic alphabet A [adenine], G [guanine], C [cytosine], and T [thymine].
- Small DNA molecules with arbitrary sequences are feasibly synthesized into order.
- In the quickest and easiest scenario, DNA molecules with specific DNA sequences are applied as the input to an algorithm.
- Laboratory procedures are employed to execute the instructions, such as sorting the molecules by length or chopping strands containing specific sequences.
- The outcome is defined as some attribute of the final group of molecules, including the presence or absence of a particular sequence.
- DNA functions like a computer hard disc in that it stores gene information indelibly.

Both genomics and DNA computing include the modification and investigation of DNA molecules; however, genomics is focused on comprehending the genetic makeup of organisms, whereas DNA computing is concerned with exploiting DNA molecules for computational and data storage [16].

4.5 Types of Genomics

Genomics is a multidisciplinary field that can be divided into several areas of study, such as structure genomics, function genomics, metagenomics, and epigenomics, depicted as Figure 4.6. Each of the sub-fields is discussed here.

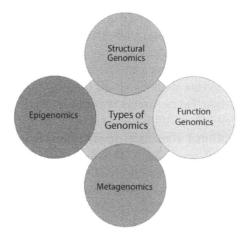

Figure 4.6 A conceptual overview of the types of genomics.

4.5.1   Structural Genomics

Structural genomics deals with the physical nature of genomes, including the sequencing and mapping of genomes. Figure 4.7 gives an overview of structural genomics and illustrates a genetic modification's role in

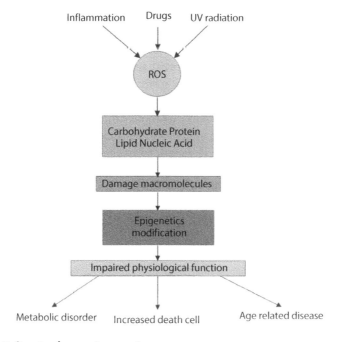

Figure 4.7 Structural genomics overview.

the development of impaired metabolic processes. In structural genomics, every protein encoded by an individual genome is explained in terms of its three-dimensional structure. With a combination of experimental and modeling techniques, this genome-based methodology enables a high-throughput structure determination method instead of concentrating on only one protein. Every protein encoded by the DNA will be identified by structural genomics. This is the main distinction between structural genomics and traditional structural prediction. Determining a protein molecule by structural genomics is often but sometimes only done after something about its protein function is selected. The significant issues in structural bio-informatics include determining cellular processes from the three-dimensional structure. When whole genome sequences are accessible, structure prediction can be completed more quickly by combining experimental and modeling methods [17]. That is certainly relevant now that there is a massive proportion of sequenced genomes and completed protein molecules accessible, allowing scientists to base their protein structure models on homology structures solved earlier. It incorporates a variety of techniques to structure identification.

4.5.2   Function Genomics

It is another subfield of molecular genetics that aims to define the connections and roles of genes and proteins by using the enormous amount of information generated by genomic projects, such as genome sequencing programs. Figure 4.8, a conceptual overview of function genomics, illustrates a diagrammatic representation of genome analysis to explore the combination of the transcriptome, proteome, and metabolome data and how these connections affect metabolic functions. Further genomics addresses dynamic factors like gene transcription, translation, and binding proteins instead of the static elements of genetic information like DNA sequence or structures. It aims to provide information on how DNA functions at the level of genes, RNA transcripts, and protein products. The genome-wide approach that functional genomics research takes to these issues rather than the more conventional "gene-by-gene" approach is one of their primary distinguishing features [18].

4.5.3   Metagenomics

Metagenomics studies genomes, or genetic material, extracted directly from sediment samples. As shown in Figure 4.9, a conceptual overview of

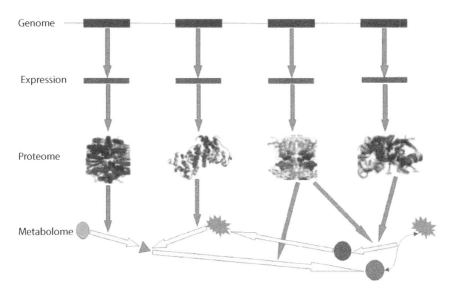

Figure 4.8 A conceptual overview of function genomics.

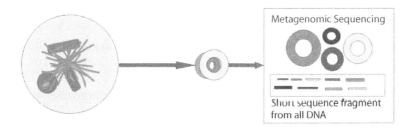

Figure 4.9 A conceptual overview of metagenomics.

metagenomics, while exposure to environmental, genetic sequencing replicated specific genes to provide a profile of variety in a clinical specimen, conventional microbiology and bacterial genome sequencing depend on growing clonal organisms. Such analysis revealed that cultivation-based methods have mostly disregarded microorganism diversity [19]. Recent findings obtain an essentially impartial sampling of every gene from the surveyed community using shotgun sequencing. Metagenomics is commonly used to examine a particular demographic of microbes, for instance, those found in soil, water, and even human organs.

4.5.4   Epigenomics

Epigenomics studies the physical changes, connections, and conformational changes of inherited nucleotide sequences to link them to genetic

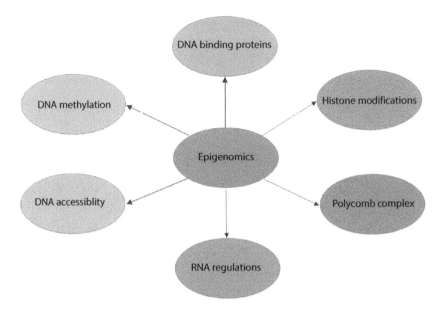

Figure 4.10 A conceptual overview of epigenomics.

memory, biological identities, and stem cell functions. A growing curiosity about epigenetic mechanisms inside complicated and heterogeneous tissues fuels the development of single-cell epigenomics. In contrast, current techniques characterize average epigenomics features across enormous cell ensembles [20]. Detecting DNA methylation, chromatin permeability, chromatin remodeling, genome shape, and replicating dynamics are a few of the new single-cell techniques depicted in Figure 4.10. Combining these approaches has proven increasingly crucial for evaluating biological variety and adaptation, as demonstrated by progenitor cells and cancer.

4.6   Application Area of Genomics

Genomics research can be used in various fields, including biotechnology, social sciences, and medicine. Although many industries already use genomics, science has the potential to change all those who deal with humans and other forms of life on Earth. Figure 4.11 depicts the diverse genomics applications currently in use or development.

- **Biotechnology Application:** The synthetic biology and bio-engineering field has several uses for genomic research.

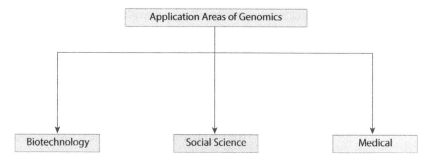

Figure 4.11 Primary application areas of genomics.

Scientific research has shown that it is possible to create partially synthetic bacteria species [21]. Researchers from the J. Craig Venter Institute developed the synthetic bacterium *Mycoplasma laboratorium* in 2010 using the genome of *Mycoplasma genitalium,* which differs from the original organism in several ways. Figure 4.12 illustrates the primary usage of biotechnology applications in respective fields.

- **Social Science Applications:** In the growing field of population genomics, genomic sequencing techniques are being used to comprehensively compare DNA sequences among populations, going beyond the capabilities of conventional population genetic markers like short-range PCR products or micro-satellites. Population genomics investigates gene

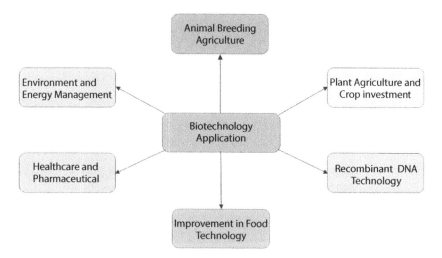

Figure 4.12 Essential usage of biotechnology.

expression effects to comprehend micro-evolution better and gain knowledge of a population's phylogenetic history and demography. Numerous disciplines use population genomic techniques, including biological evolution, ecology, biodiversity, environmental science, and fishery. Environmental genomics, which uses genomic approaches to find connections between environmental and genetic variation patterns, has similarly evolved from landscape genetics [22]. Figure 4.13 illustrates various disciplines used in social science genomic fields.

- Medical Applications: Medical researchers and professionals now have multiple features due to recent advancements in the technology used to collect genomic data, but since data has been collected more efficiently than previously, and this enhanced the understanding of genetics and genes' role in either causing or preventing disease. Figure 4.14 illustrates a cycle for such vital aspects of incorporating genomic information into medical care.

  ❖ Healthcare professionals from all specialties can diagnose patients with severe genetic diseases using genomic technologies. Due to the use of these approaches by scientists, who are discovering new genes that trigger genetic disease at an incredible rate [23], approximately 4,000 disorders now have a specific biological factor, compared with approximately 50 in 1990.

  ❖ To better comprehend how prevalent and uncommon gene mutations lead to the formation of common diseases

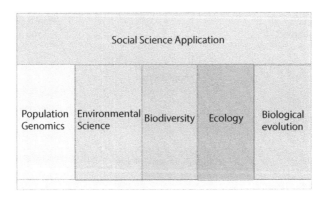

Figure 4.13 Using genomics for social science application.

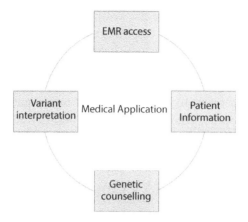

Figure 4.14 A conceptual overview of incorporating genomic information into Medical care.

like diabetes, cancer, and hypertension, genomic technologies are becoming more widely used.

❖ It is used to identify the extent to which people will react to a specific drug, how quickly they will adapt to such a drug, and whether or not they will experience any adverse effects from using that drug. That allows their treating team to formulate personalized recommendations regarding the most appropriate treatment for them. In other cases, such as cancer, researchers can highlight the genetic causes of the disease and then deliver drugs that target that specific system.

❖ In children, genetic disorders are usually severe, causing significant impairment or death. Early treatment of genetic disorders provides people with the option of continuing their pregnancy or enabling early detection and treatment in the womb or at birth. While early prenatal screening methods could threaten the pregnancy, modern genomic technology-based techniques can look directly at the fetus's DNA from a maternal blood test without increasing the risk of miscarriage; this is non-invasive prenatal testing. Next-generation sequencing (NGS) and array technology are also used in prenatal samples to increase diagnostic yields during pregnancy.

❖ The genomes of the microorganisms that trigger respiratory diseases can be sequenced to determine the precise organism producing the symptoms, track the source of the incidence of the respiratory disease, and assess which drugs are most likely to be helpful in treatments.

❖ The infusion of DNA or RNA to mend a genetic defect or alter gene expression is called gene therapy. Genome editing refers to using molecular techniques to change the genome; genome editing can add, subtract, or replace segments of the DNA sequence.

4.7 Application of DNA Computing

DNA computing has evolved as an enticing fusion of computer science and molecular genetics. The field is an exciting information processing technology catalyst for sharing knowledge between cognitive processing, nanotechnology, and biological molecules. Figure 4.15 illustrates an essential application for DNA computing fields. This research area has the chance to change the perception of computer principles and applications significantly. Below are a few of the vital and valuable applications of DNA bases that are currently in use or development:

- Leonard Adleman introduced the first DNA computer prototype in 1994. A test tube called the TT-100 contained

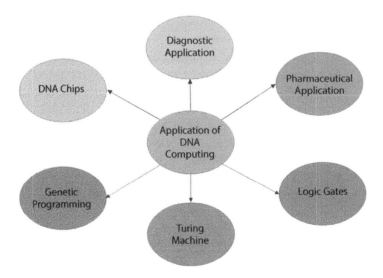

Figure 4.15 Application areas of DNA computing.

100 µL of a DNA solution. The directed Hamiltonian path problem was one of the challenges he could address [24]. The Hamiltonian Path Problem, sometimes known as the "traveling salesman problem," was used in Adleman's experiment. Several DNA segments representing a city that needed to be visited were generated to do this. Each of these nodes can be connected to the other nodes produced. In a test tube, these DNA fragments were created and combined. The little fragments, representing the many travel routes, combine to produce larger ones in seconds. The DNA segments representing the lengthier routes were removed using a chemical process.

- Recent studies have suggested using DNA computing to address the problem of matching types in DSP approaches and the adaptability of the DNA computing algorithm to computer vision in automated visual biomechanics and control systems. DNA computing is also proposed for message encryption, data encryption, and image security assessment in information technology and security, increasing the efficacy of privacy, safety, and ample data storage.

- DNA computing has also benefited big data in clinical situations, especially in detecting and treating diseases, developing small-scale computers to track patients' states, and simultaneously analyzing various gene expressions. To accurately modify the medication concentration and release of pharmaceuticals, self-explanatory DNA identification chips and bio-sensors are also produced. The development of DNA computing is expected to transform computers, particularly in the area of medicine.

4.8   Genomics and DNA Computing in COVID-19 Epidemic

Coronavirus disease 2019 (COVID-19) is a highly contagious respiratory disease characterized by SARS-CoV-2, a novel (new) coronavirus. The epidemic, initially detected in Wuhan, China, in December 2019, has expanded globally and was proclaimed a global epidemic on March 11, 2020 by the World Health Organization (WHO) [25, 26]. The virus is transmitted mainly through droplets in the air, and symptoms vary from mild to severe, comprising fever, cough, and breathing difficulties. The impact of COVID-19 on global health and economy has been enormous. The world is still attempting to prevent its spread through immunization, social distancing, mask use, and regular washing of hands. The COVID-19 epidemic has significantly impacted Bharat's economy and health. The country has reported many diseases and fatalities, and the medical system is overwhelmed. The epidemic has also caused enormous job losses and financial distress, with several industries struggling to remain afloat. The government has implemented precautions such as lockdowns and vaccination drives to prevent the virus from spreading and to mitigate its consequences [27, 28].

The peer-reviewed study of severe diseases like heart disease, asthma, diabetes, and cancer is incorporated into genomics since these disorders are frequently triggered by a combination of genetic and environmental factors instead of single genes—for example, Global Initiative on Sharing Avian Influenza Data (GISAID), Nextstrain, and Pango's identified etymology mechanisms for labeling and monitoring SARS-CoV-2 biological variants are present. They will continue to be applied by researchers and in scientific investigations. Genomic sequencing enables researchers to classify a virus as a specific variant and identify its lineage, extending beyond screening for SARS-CoV-2. Throughout the COVID-19 epidemic, genomic surveillance has been a significant aspect of public healthcare [25, 26]. The WHO formed a team of scientists from the WHO Virus Evolution Working Group, the WHO COVID-19 benchmark research lab channel, the committee from GISAID, Nextstrain, and Pango, and also other specialists in virological and microbiological classification and information exchange from several countries and organizations to consider convenient and non-convenient labels for variants of interest and varietals of concern. The Pango nomenclature is used by researchers and organizations that focus on public health to keep track of the spread and transmission of SARS-CoV-2 and other versions of the virus. Using genetic information about pathogens for the study's purposes and enhancing public health is the goal of the open-source research study Nextstrain.

The GISAID established a nomenclature structure resulting in diverse forms based on marker mutants in eight high-level phylogenetic clusters, from the initial split of S and L to the continued evolution of L into V and G, and afterwards of G into GH, GR, and GV, and even more recently of GR into GRY. The significant progress established currently in preventing the spread of this pathogen is at risk of becoming reversed by the emergence of new severe acute respiratory variant strains. The genetic analysis of the genomes of virus strains is an effective method for identifying any new genetic mutations of SARS-CoV-2 that are migrating into countries, especially in the context of a worldwide disease outbreak [29]. Numerous variants have been discovered. However, only a few of these versions are considered to be variants of concern due to their impact on the healthcare system. This scientific report aims to describe these updated versions of the concerns and the most recent treatment for COVID-19 in humans. The WHO and the Centers for Disease Control and Prevention have developed different classification methods in response to numerous variations. This system categorizes the evolving SARS-CoV-2 into the variants of concern and interest shown in Figure 4.16 and Figure 4.17. Integrating genomics and other omics technologies was crucial in developing new diagnostics, treatments, and vaccines. Overall, by revealing an advice about the genetic structure of the virus, tracking its progress, and identifying drug therapies and vaccines, genomics and DNA computing have played an essential role in the COVID-19 epidemic [30].

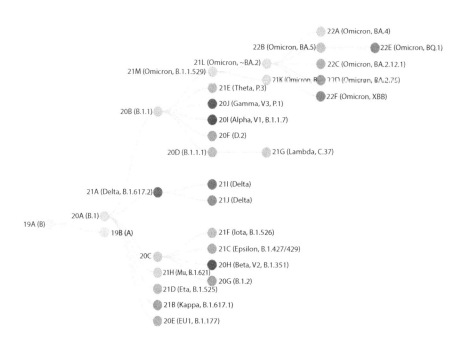

Figure 4.16 Nextstrain SARS-CoV-2 biological connections.

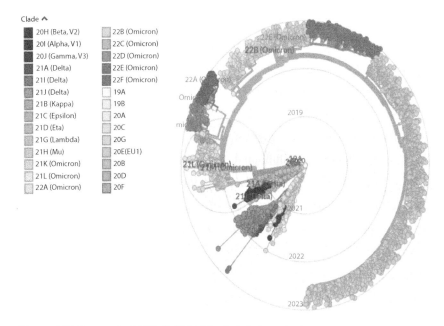

Figure 4.17 Nextstrain SARS-CoV-2 biological clade variants.

4.9   Issues in Genomics and DNA Computing

Gene mutations present in every cell in the body produce many hereditary diseases. These disorders consequently often affect many body systems, and the overwhelming fraction cannot be healed. DNA is the next generation of data processing due to its many benefits. The short storage life of DNA, which has a maximum shelf life of 6 months, and the slow metabolomics activities utilized in the calculation algorithms imply that the development of DNA computing still needs to be revamped. On the other hand, implementing DNA computing has significant restrictions and issues [31].

- In large genomes, extraction and sequencing are the most challenging tasks.
- cDNA libraries only depict exons; alternative splicing is not considered.
- The process of whole genome sequencing (WGS) produces a large amount of data, which is its main drawback.
- The enormous amount of data generated needs much more storage space and analysis time.

- The cost and the amount of time needed for analysis will increase as a result.
- One major problem is its accuracy because there is a chance for errors like mismatched pairs and because it is highly dependent on the precision of the enzymes used.
- DNA computing uses enormous amounts of data, exponentially increasing the probability of inaccuracy.
- The concurrent processes' time-consuming nature necessitates an extensive human and mechanical interaction between steps to hours or days.
- Unlike other cryptographic methods, DNA cryptography lacks a developed theoretical base.
- It also has an implementation issue due to the high cost of the laboratory and biological experiments required to create a reliable DNA cryptography system.
- The primary ethical concerns when planning and reviewing genetic information studies are privacy, confidentiality, informed consent, and data return.

4.10   Tools and Technology Used in Genomics Systems

There are many different types of tools and technology used in genomic research. Some of the essential tools are included here.

- **DNA Sequencing Technologies:** These include Sanger sequencing, NGS technologies such as single-molecule real-time sequencing, and technologies like Illumina, PacBio, Nanopore, etc. [32].
- **Annotation Tools:** These are used to classify and label the different components of a genome, including genes, introns, exons, and regulatory regions. Examples include MAKER, AUGUSTUS, and BRAKER [33].
- **Genome Assembly Software:** These tools are used to put together DNA sequencing sequences into a whole genome. SPAdes, ABySS, and SOAPdenovo are a few examples [34].
- **Bioinformatics Tools:** These are used to analyze and comprehend the vast amounts of information generated by

genomics research. Some examples are BLAST, SAMtools, and BEDtools [35].

- **Cloud Computing:** The increasing volume of genomic data makes processing and storing difficult. Google Cloud Platform and Amazon Web Services are increasingly used for data storage and processing [36].
- **CRISPR-Based Technologies:** Clustered Regularly Interspaced Short Palindromic Repeats (CRISPR) allows for the precise editing of specific genomic areas. New medicines are being developed using CRISPR-based technologies to comprehend gene function and disease processes better [37].
- **Machine Learning:** Machine learning algorithms analyze genomic data to predict gene function, therapeutic response, and disease risk.

4.11   Role of AI Technology Used in Genomics Systems

Artificial Intelligence and related technologies, such as deep learning, machine learning, and data analysis, can accelerate the process of generating valuable intelligence while leading to a more effective global response. The need for computational methods that make it possible to analyze massive, complex, and high-dimensional genomic data sets is growing. Despite specifying precise rules and interests at various stages of the genomic data pipeline, artificial intelligence might encourage discoveries in these data sets. Artificial intelligence analysis and perception stages with genomic data sets have experienced the most development. The genomics field of study is increasing the use of computational methods such as artificial intelligence and machine learning to help find the hidden patterns in large and complex genomes data sets from crucial medical research efforts. Figure 4.18 illustrates the relationship between artificial intelligence with genomics and genetics. Artificial intelligence has contributed to significant incremental advances in clinical genome analysis, such as phenotyping in unusual syndromes, cancer, its variants research, and explanation. However, most artificially intelligent genetic studies are still in its development [38]. Machine and deep learning approaches are in high demand for functional genomics analysis. These techniques have traced almost every

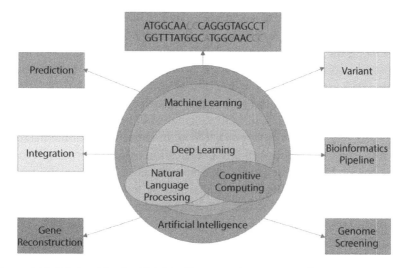

Figure 4.18 Relationship of artificial intelligence with genomics and genetics.

element of genome analysis, from genome sequencing to phenotyping and variation detection to downstream analysis. Nowadays, advancements in the computing system, artificial intelligence, and the expansion of biological data allow for improvements in existing service domains.

4.12   Related Works and Challenges

Since December 2019, the coronavirus infection 2019 has started spreading globally from Wuhan, China, and has significantly impacted public health. A study of the research on the DNA characteristics of SARS-CoV-2, the virus involved in the COVID-19 epidemic, may also include research on the genetic profile and phylogeny of the disease. One of the earliest databases, OriDB, incorporates statistics for DNA synthesis similar to all those discussed with all publicly accessible data on the origin of DNA replication for eukaryotic genomes. It comes after GenBank, which contains more than 300,000 wholly accepted organisms' DNA molecules.

The researchers concluded that the small dataset needed for this study works best with such a novel feature extraction approach using random DNA sequences. The researcher investigated and compared three deep-learning methodologies for diagnosing COVID-19, SARS-CoV-2,

MERS, and Ebola genomic sequences using machine learning to classify the DNA sequences. They reached 97% for sensitivity and 99.19% for specificity using the MLP classifier and 30% for mismatch using RT-PCR and our pseudo-convolutional method. In summary, a study of the literature on the DNA characteristics of SARS-CoV-2 would spotlight the genetic makeup and mutation of the virus, and it may implement strategic efforts to develop effective treatments and vaccinations [39].

Conard et al. [40] introduced OriDB as an entirely functional database, one of the first to combine all DNA replication origin information that is public for budding yeast. Those who are actively engaged in the field of DNA replication may find this database to be a beneficial resource. His goal is to build OriDB to include simultaneous datasets for different organisms with statistics on DNA replication similar to those discussed.

Benson et al. [41] refers to the GenBank, a centralized repository that includes the DNA molecules of more than 300,000 fully recognized species. These genomes are accessible to everyone. Submissions primarily obtain these sequences from single labs and batch contributions from substantial sequencing efforts, such as DNA sequencing and ecological monitoring approaches. Several large-scale sequencing projects also contributed lines. GenBank experts assign accession numbers as soon as the data are obtained, and the bulk of contributions are produced using the web-based BankIt tool or the separate Sequin tool.

Solis-Reyes et al. [42] points to KAMERIS, an open-source, supervised sequencing genotyping technique, using k-mers frequencies in HIV-1 genotypes as features. The paper compares this approach to four different cutting-edge methodologies. The researchers revealed an overall accuracy of 97% and a processing throughput with over 1,500 sequences by KAMERIS during testing with 2,784 humanly chosen actual HIV-1 sequences. It excelled in other approaches to ensuring security and privacy, rendering data transparent, and enabling it to replicate. It seems advantageous for individuals who need to transfer HIV-1 sequence data via the Internet to remote servers. These approaches were employed to identify the viral genotypes of influenza A, hepatitis B, and hepatitis C.

DLAMINI et al. [43] investigated innate dinucleotide genetic patterns for SARS-CoV-2 and seven other pathogens. Whole genomes were decoded to dinucleotide frequency, identified using XGBoost, and discriminated among these eight species and various SARS-CoV-2 genomes. Our approach achieved 100% in all eight species assessment metrics and tests. The study demonstrated 67% overall accuracy when classifying

SARS-CoV-2 sequences into six regions and 86% overall accuracy in iden-tifying SARS-CoV-2 samples as Asian or not.

Mousavizadeh *et al.* [44] suggested the beta-coronavirus premised on its phylogeny and genomes. SARS-CoV2, SARS-CoV, and MERS-CoV have various features, although their genomic and phenotypic characteristics can impact their pathogenesis. COVID-19 has single-stranded positive-sense RNA together in the matrix–protein capsid. A typical COVID has six ORFs. In pathogenesis, COVID-19's both genetic and phenotypic struc-tures are crucial. This paper highlights the most relevant beta-coronavirus characteristics.

Zhang *et al.* [45] compared DNA sequence classifying algorithms and five distinguished approaches across four large databases. A total of 14 sig-nificant contributions include using random DNA sequences to determine length-based attributes. They examined whether it could replace primers. Latest-state approaches from computer vision and natural processing, like CNN's or N-gram probabilistic models, can reach above 99% accuracy on DNA sequence classifiers, given enough sample data. The 3-g approach is simple and effective with different datasets. The novel feature extraction approach based on random DNA sequences performed the best on the small SARS-Cov-2 dataset and is thus promising for DNA classification issues with little data.

Deorowicz *et al.* [46] considered FQSqueezer as an innovative data compression technique for sequencing data capable of dealing with sin-gle paired end reads of different lengths. Dynamic Markov coder meth-ods and partial matching to get a precise prediction, both from the field of overall compressors techniques, were used as models for this system's development. Most of the time, the compression ratios are superior by 10% compared with those offered in the most sophisticated technology.

Rincon *et al.* [47] pointed out that artificial intelligence and deep learn-ing were coupled to identify SARS-CoV-2 with 98.73% accuracy. The National Genomics Data Center's 553 genomes have been used to train a convolutional neural network that reliably distinguishes between corona-virus genotypes. Then, a single sequence is selected to form a test against the primer's set and other recent specific primers. Subsequently, the primer is produced and tested on $n = 6$ positive patient samples. The suggested technique has a significant advantage over the existing methods because it can autonomously identify potential primer sets for a pathogen from limited datasets and generate efficient outcomes rapidly.

Hu *et al.* [48] discussed the fundamentals of SARS virology, CoV-2, espe-cially gene characteristics and receptor usage, intending to emphasize the virus's primary distinction from other viral pathogens that have recently been discovered. They also summarize what is presently known on the clinical, epidemiologic, and pathogen features of COVID-19, in addition to the most recent developments in animal studies and antiviral therapeutic modalities for SARS-CoV-2 infection.

Using CNN, CNN-LSTM, and CNN-bidirectional LSTM models, Label, and K-mer encoding to classify DNA sequences, Gunasekaran et al. [49] evaluated and compared three deep learning methodologies. Several various classification measures are employed in the assessment of the models. Based on the outcomes of the tests, both CNN and the CNN-bidirectional LSTM with K-mer encoding provide high accuracy on testing data, with respective parameters of 93.16% and 93.13%.

Gomes et al. [50] noted a novel approach to represent DNA sequences using co-occurrence matrices and pseudo-convolution. The alignment of multiple sequences is eliminated. Through the suggested technique, virus DNA patterns from 24 viral families, including SARS-CoV-2, can be determined. They attained 97% for SARS-CoV-2 sensitivity and 99.19% for specificity with MLP classifier and 30% mismatch. They used MLP and 50% overlaps to achieve 99% for SARS-CoV-2 sensitivity and 99.86% for specificity for healthy DNA sequences. Using RT-PCR and our pseudo-convolutional technique to identify SARS-CoV-2 DNA sequences can assist in the diagnosis of COVID-19.

Ahmed et al. [51] showed an AI-based approach to analyze COVID-19, SARS, and Ebola genomic sequences. They compare COVID-19 and other genome sequences by retrieving nucleotide composition, frequency, tri-nucleotide composition, amino acid count, alignment, and DNA similarity information. They evaluated virus genome sequences using different layering approaches and identified these using support vector machines based on machine learning. The model identifies COVID-19, SARS, MERS, and Ebola genome sequences with 97%, 96%, and 95% accuracy, respectively.

Adetiba et al. [52] suggest a genomic sequence classification system based on GSP, deep learning, and genetic datasets from SARS-CoV-2, SARS-CoV, and MERS-CoV. After a validation accuracy of 98.33%, Z-Curve images for MERS-CoV, SARS-CoV, and SARS-CoV-2 exhibit unique features. Higher layers of CNN enhance the significant discriminating characteristics of input images, supporting the relevance of deep learning and GSP in virus detection. Table 4.1 summarizes the relative performance and challenges by the different methods discussed in the state of the art.

Table 4.1 Characteristics and relative performance by a previous method on COVID-19 DNA sequences.

Author	Objective	Datasets	Techniques used	Accuracy	Pros	Limitation
Conrad A et al. [40]	It aims to provide a comprehensive and up-to-date resource for the identification and labelling of DNA replication origins in various species.	OriDB	DNA sequence	-	A useful tool for researchers studying DNAreplication and working in a related field.	It does not hold data on protein components that bind to origins or replication inhibition.
Benson et al. [41]	It aims to provide an accessible repository of top-notch genomic sequencing in-formation.	National Center for Biotechnology Information	DNA sequence	-	More than 300,000 genomes species are stored	It does not contain information about the species that inherit the genes' anatomyor physiology.
Solis-Reyes et al. [42]	It aims to develop a machine-learning tool that can classify HIV-1 genomes quickly and precisely.	Los Alamos sequence (LANL)	KAMERIS (k-mer frequencies)	Overall accuracy of 97%, with 1,500 sequences per second.	It is quite effective in identifying HIV-1 strains quickly and accurately.	Replication and quick sequence variance problem during training time.

(Continued)

Table 4.1 Characteristics and relative performance by a previous method on COVID-19 DNA sequences. (*Continued*)

Author	Objective	Datasets	Techniques used	Accuracy	Pros	Limitation
DLAMINI *et al.* [43]	It uses machine learning and base pair frequency to distinguish COVID-19 and other pathogenic genes.	WGS data in FASTA format for eight pathogenic species.	Extreme gradient boosting (XGBoost) model	67 for six regions and 86% for either emerging from Asia or others.	Easily demonstrate the usages of base pair relative frequencies for discriminating and identifying similar species.	The statistics could not only be addressed with sequencing and characterization methods from the source.
Mousavizadeh *et al.* [44]	A review of SARS-CoV-2 is a pathogenesis of COVID-19 is not.	-	Role of pathogenesis	-	It is useful to identify the precise molecular information of the virus.	-
Zhang *et al.* [45]	It performs a DNA classification approach using machine learning methods combined with and without feature extraction.	Hepatitis C virus (World Gene bank), influenza virus, and SARS-Cov-2 dataset (NCBI)	Feature extraction method	99% for DNA classifier	Random DNA sequence method are promising methods could be deployed is the diagnosis of diseases.	Better performances on larger datasets.

(*Continued*)

Table 4.1 Characteristics and relative performance by a previous method on COVID-19 DNA sequences. (*Continued*)

Author	Objective	Datasets	Techniques used	Accuracy	Pros	Limitation
Deorowicz et al. [46]	It used an FQsqueezer tool for compressing sequencing data.	DNA sequence compression	FQSqueezer	10% better for sophisticated technology for com pressing.	For most data, achieve a compression ratio of up to 95%.	Large memory and time requirements.
Rincon et al. [47]	Designed a specific primer for detecting SARS-CoV-2 using a deep-learning algorithm.	National Genomics Data Center repository, NCBI dataset (A& B), GISAID and Primer 3plus FastPCR	DCNN with cDNA	98.73%	Deliver effective results in a min imal amount of time.	Not consider degenerate primer sets.
Hu et al. [48]	A review of SARS-CoV-2 and COVID-19 characteristics	-	Approaches for SARS- CoV-2 infection.	-	Addressing the gene mutation and receptor used.	Cross-species infectious trans mission is still unknown.

(Continued)

Table 4.1 Characteristics and relative performance by a previous method on COVID-19 DNA sequences. (*Continued*)

Author	Objective	Datasets	Techniques used	Accuracy	Pros	Limitation
Gunasekaran et al. [49]	Uses CNN and hybrid model analysis for classifying DNA sequences.	Nucleotide sequence database: NCBI	With label encoding and K-mer encoding, CNN, CNN-LSTM, and CNN bidirectional LSTM	93.16% and 93.13%	The best approach for achieving high testing and validation accuracy is using K-mers.	While CNN with label encoding exceeds the other model, test ing accuracy is surprisingly low.
Gomes et al. [50]	Enhance the possible RT-PCR results for COVID-19 diagnostic testing.	National Institute of Allergy and Infectious Diseases (NIAID)	Pseudo-convolutional feature ex traction	97% for SARS-CoV-2 sensitivity and 99.19% for multi- layer perceptron classifier and 30% mismatch	RT-PCR and pseudo-convolutional approaches can improve the specificity and sensitivity of COVID-19 molecular diagnostics.	The overlap was tested for 30%, 50%, and 70%.

(*Continued*)

Table 4.1 Characteristics and relative performance by a previous method on COVID-19 DNA sequences. (*Continued*)

Author	Objective	Datasets	Techniques used	Accuracy	Pros	Limitation
Ahmed *et al.* [51]	It aims to make feasible artificial intelligence-based genomic sequence characterization of COVID-19 and related viruses.	NCBI	ML-based classifier	95% for MERS and Ebola, 95% for SARS, and % for COVID-19.	Achieves good classification results compared with others.	-
Adetiba *et al.* [52]	Develop a deep COVID-19 model for the classification of COVID-19 pathogen sequences using deep learning and genomic signal processing.	National Center for Biotechnology Information (NCBI)	Transfer learning-based approach	98.33% validation	Despite their substantial similarity, DeepCOVID-19 can effectively separate the genomes of the three coronavirus variants.	Memory for storing multi-genome sequences and the computation requirements.

4.13   Future Research Dimension

Genomic sequence tools have the potential to enhance global health equality. The genetic health disparity must be contained and, eventually, bridged by equitable economic investment, clinical research, and the worldwide provision and use of genomic services. The exchange of old information, expertise, and technology between high- and low-income nations helps accelerate this process. As genomics is an overgrowing field, several research areas will likely be necessary. DNA computing will be more efficient and faster than electronic computing. DNA computers will address complex issues. DNA computers will be able to solve medical, biological, engineering, encryption, artificial intelligence, and data analysis challenges in the coming few years. Some of the critical areas of future genomics research involve the following:

- Genomic medicine will be utilized to diagnose and forecast medical illnesses in the future. Liquid biopsy for early disease diagnosis will be a significant advancement in healthcare and will be achievable.
- The use of synthetic biology techniques to develop and construct new biochemical pathways will increase genomics research directions. That could entail developing novel gene editing tools and new species with desired traits.
- Genome-wide association studies will become increasingly frequent in identifying genetic variations connected to complex diseases such as cancer, diabetes, and heart disease.
- The use of computational techniques to predict the behavior of genome sequences will increase in importance. That could result in a better understanding of gene interactions and aid in discovering new drug targets.
- With the development of genomics, the use of artificial intelligence will become ever more critical. Identifying new therapies and detecting illness risk will help analyze large amounts of genomic data and identify patterns.

4.14   Conclusion

This chapter provides a comprehensive overview of genomics and DNA computing with respect to the healthcare sector. Particular interest has been given to COVID-19 treatment using these fields. Genomics and DNA computing have been essential in comprehending the virus's inherited traits and assisting in developing effective therapies and vaccines. Furthermore, AI in genomics and DNA computing has contributed immensely to assessing vast volumes of genetic data, ramping up new drugs, and enhancing forecast and diagnostic reliability. Because data security and privacy are important factors for ethical implications and due to the necessity for rapid and cost-effective secured remedies, the literature review demonstrated a surge in research and advancement in the area, underlining the importance of this interdisciplinary scope. Genomics is continually evolving, and it has a wide range of applications. The possibilities are limitless with the emergence of new technologies like genome sequencing and bioinformatics. One can anticipate a future in which people's health becomes more reliable and sustainable as genetics advances. Further studies are required to overcome privacy and ethical issues concerning using genomic data in healthcare.

References

1. Durmaz, Karaca, E., Demkow, U., Toruner, G., Schoumans, J., Cogulu, O., Evolution of genetic techniques: Past, present, and beyond. *BioMed. Res. Int.*, 2015, 1–7, 2015.
2. Dharmapalan, Two decades of human genome project. *Science Reporter*, 58, 1–4, 2021.
3. Bajpai, N. and Wadhwa, M., India's national digital health mission. ICT India Working Paper, Tech. Rep., 2020.
4. Collins, F.S., Morgan, M., Patrinos, A., The human genome project: Lessons from large-scale biology. *Science*, 300, 5617, 286–290, 2003.
5. Tefferi, Genomics basics: DNA structure, gene expression, cloning, genetic mapping, and molecular tests. *Semin. Cardiothorac. Vasc. Anesth.*, 10, 4, 282–290, 2006, Sage Publications Sage CA: Thousand Oaks, CA.
6. Satzinger, H., Theodor and Marcella Boveri: Chromosomes and cytoplasm in heredity and development. *Nat. Rev. Genet.*, 9, 3, 231–238, 2008.
7. Winkler, H. and Winkler, H.K.A., *Verbreitung und ursache der parthenogenesis im pflanzen-und tierreiche*, G. FIscher, Germany, 1920.
8. Griffiths, Miller, J., Suzuki, D., Lewontin, R., Gelbart, W., Genetics and the organism, in: *An Introduction to Genetic Analysis*, 7th edition, Freeman WH, New York, 2000.
9. Church, G.M., Gao, Y., Kosuri, S., Next-generation digital information storage in DNA. *Science*, 337, 6102, 1628–1628, 2012.

10. Watson, J. and Crick, F., Cold spring harbor laboratory press, in: *Cold Spring Harbor Symposia on Quantitative Biology*, pp. 123–131, 1953.
11. Brahmachari, S.K., Majumder, P., Mukerji, M., Habib, S., Dash, D., Ray, K., Bahl, S., Batra, J., Consortium, I.G.V. *et al.*, Genetic landscape of the people of India: A canvas for disease gene exploration. *J. Genet.*, 87, 1, 3–20, 2008.
12. Watson, J., *The double helix*, Hachette UK, London, 2012.
13. Jou, W.M., Haegeman, G., Ysebaert, M., Fiers, W., Nucleotide sequence of the gene coding for the bacteriophage MS2 coat protein. *Nature*, 237, 5350, 82–88, 1972.
14. Alkan, Sajjadian, S., Eichler, E.E., Limitations of next-generation genome sequence assembly. *Nat. Methods*, 8, 1, 61–65, 2011.
15. Klasberg, S., Bitard-Feildel, T., Mallet, L., Computational identification of novel genes: Current and future perspectives. *Bioinf. Biol. Insights*, 10, BBI–S39 950, 2016.
16. Erlich, Y. and Zielinski, D., DNA fountain enables a robust and efficient storage architecture. *Science*, 355, 6328, 950–954, 2017.
17. Brenner, S.E., A tour of structural genomics. *Nat. Rev. Genet.*, 2, 10, 801–809, 2001.
18. Przybyla, L. and Gilbert, L.A., A new era in functional genomics screens. *Nat. Rev. Genet.*, 23, 2, 89–103, 2022.
19. Hugenholtz, P., Goebel, B.M., Pace, N.R., Impact of culture-independent studies on the emerging phylogenetic view of bacterial diversity. *J. Bacteriol.*, 180, 18, 4765–4774, 1998.
20. Laird, P.W., Principles and challenges of genome-wide DNA methylation analysis. *Nat. Rev. Genet.*, 11, 3, 191–203, 2010.
21. Lu, Y.-F., Goldstein, D.B., Angrist, M., Cavalleri, G., Personalized medicine and human genetic diversity. *Cold Spring Harb. Perspect. Med.*, 4, 9, a008581, 2014.
22. Baker, M., The next step for the synthetic genome. *Nature*, 473, 7347, 403–408, 2011.
23. Horton, R.H. and Lucassen, A.M., Recent developments in genetic/genomic medicine. *Clin. Sci.*, 133, 5, 697–708, 2019.
24. Braich, R.S., Johnson, C., Rothemund, P.W., Hwang, D., Chelyapov, N., Adleman, L.M., Solution of a satisfiability problem on a gel-based DNA computer, in: *DNA Computing: 6th International Workshop on DNA-Based Computers, DNA 2000 Leiden, The Netherlands, June 13–17, 2000 Revised Papers 6*, Springer, pp. 27–42, 2001.
25. Bhowmik, B.R., Varna, S.A., Kumar, A., Kumar, R., Reducing false prediction on COVID-19 detection using deep learning, in: *2021 IEEE International Midwest Symposium on Circuits and Systems (MWSCAS)*, IEEE, pp. 404–407, 2021.
26. Bhowmik, B.R., Varna, S.A., Kumar, A., Kumar, R., Deep neural networks in healthcare systems, in: *Machine Learning and Deep Learning in Efficacy Improvement of Healthcare Systems*, pp. 195–226, CRC Press, Taylor and Francis, USA, 2021.

27. Hindu, A. and Bhowmik, B.R., An IoT-enabled stress detection scheme using facial expression, in: *2022 IEEE 19th India Council International Conference (INDICON) (INDICON-2022)*, pp. 1–6, CUSAT, Bharat, Nov. 2022.

28. G. @ of India, *Ministry of Health anf Family Welfare (MoHFW)*, 2023, https://www.mohfw.gov. in/, [Accessed 16-Feb-2023].

29. Aleem, Samad, A.B.A., Slenker, A.K., Emerging variants of SARS-CoV-2 and novel therapeutics against coronavirus (COVID-19), in: *StatPearls [Internet]*, StatPearls Publishing, Florida, 2022.

30. Hadfieldl, Nextstrain: Real time tracking of pathogen evolution. *Bioinformatics*, 34, 4121–4123, 2018.

31. El-Seoud, S.A., Mohamed, R., Ghoneimy, S., DNA computing: Challenges and application. *Int. J. Interact. Mob. Technol.*, 11, 2, 74–87, 2017.

32. Slatko, B.E., Gardner, A.F., Ausubel, F.M., Overview of next-generation sequencing technologies. *Curr. Protoc. Mol. Biol.*, 122, 1, e59, 2018.

33. Dong, Y., Li, C., Kim, K., Cui, L., Liu, X., Genome annotation of disease-causing microorganisms. *Briefings Bioinf.*, 22, 2, 845–854, 2021.

34. Bankevich, Nurk, S., Antipov, D., Gurevich, A.A., Dvorkin, M., Kulikov, A.S., Lesin, V.M., Nikolenko, S.I., Pham, S., Prjibelski, A.D. *et al.*, Spades: A new genome assembly algorithm and its applications to single-cell sequencing. *J. Comput. Biol.*, 19, 5, 455–477, 2012.

35. Roumpeka, D., Wallace, R.J., Escalettes, F., Fotheringham, I., Watson, M., A review of bioinformatics tools for bio-prospecting from metagenomic sequence data. *Front. Genet.*, 8, 1–10, 2017.

36. Langmead, and Nellore, A., Cloud computing for genomic data analysis and collaboration. *Nat. Rev. Genet.*, 19, 4, 208–219, 2018.

37. Li, H., Yang, Y., Hong, W., Huang, M., Wu, M., Zhao, X., Applications of genome editing technology in the targeted therapy of human diseases: Mechanisms, advances and prospects. *Signal Transduction Targeted Ther.*, 5, 1, 1, 2020.

38. Dias, R. and Torkamani, A., Artificial intelligence in clinical and genomic diagnostics. *Genome Med.*, 11, 1, 1–12, 2019.

39. Wang, H., Li, X., Li, T., Zhang, S., Wang, L., Wu, X., Liu, J., The genetic sequence, origin, and diagnosis of SARS-CoV-2. *Eur. J. Clin. Microbiol. Infect. Dis.*, 39, 1629–1635, 2020.

40. Nieduszynski, C.A., Hiraga, S.-I., Ak, P., Benham, C.J., Donaldson, A.D., OriDB: A DNA replication origin database. *Nucleic Acids Res.*, 35, suppl_1, D40–D46, 2007.

41. Benson, Clark, K., Karsch-Mizrachi, I., Lipman, D.J., Ostell, J., Sayers, E.W., Genbank. *Nucleic Acids Res.*, 43, Database issue, D30, 2015.

42. Solis-Reyes, S., Avino, M., Poon, A., Kari, L., An open-source k-mer based machine learning tool for fast and accurate subtyping of HIV-1 genomes. *PLoS One*, 13, 11, e0206409, 2018.

43. Dlamini, S., Müller, S.J., Meraba, R.L., Young, R.A., Mashiyane, J., Chiwewe, T., Mapiye, D.S., Classification of COVID-19 and other pathogenic sequences:

A dinucleotide frequency and machine learning approach. *IEEE Access*, 8, 195 263–195 273, 2020.

44. Mousavizadeh, L. and Ghasemi, S., Genotype and phenotype of COVID-19: Their roles in pathogenesis. *J. Microbiol. Immunol. Infect.*, 54, 2, 159–163, 2021.

45. Zhang, X., Beinke, B., Kindhi, B.A., Wiering, M., Comparing machine learning algorithms with or without feature extraction for DNA classification, *arXiv preprint arXiv:2011.00485*, 1–17, 2020.

46. Deorowicz, S., Fqsqueezer: K-mer-based compression of sequencing data. *Sci. Rep.*, 10, 1, 1–9, 2020.

47. Lopez-Rincon, A., Tonda, A., Lucero Mendoza-Maldonado, D., Mulders, G., Molenkamp, R., Claassen, E., Garssen, J., Kraneveld, A.D., Specific primer design for accurate detection of SARS-CoV-2 using deep learning. Preprint. *Bull. World Health Organ. E-pub*, 27, 1–17, 2020.

48. Hu, B., Guo, H., Zhou, P., Shi, Z.-L., Characteristics of SARS-CoV-2 and COVID-19. *Nat. Rev. Microbiol.*, 19, 3, 141–154, 2021.

49. Gunasekaran, Ramalakshmi, K., Rex Macedo Arokiaraj, A., Deepa Kanmani, S., Venkatesan, C., Suresh Gnana Dhas, C., Analysis of DNA sequence classification using CNN and hybrid models. *Comput. Math. Methods Med.*, 2021, 1–12, 2021.

50. Gomes, J.C., Masood, A.I., d. S. Silva, L.H., da Cruz Ferreira, J.R.B., Freire Junior, A.A., d. S. Rocha, A.L., de Oliveira, L.C.P., da Silva, N.R.C., Fernandes, B.J.T., Dos Santos, W.P., COVID-19 diagnosis by combining RT-PCR and pseudo-convolutional machines to characterize virus sequences. *Sci. Rep.*, 11, 1, 1–28, 2021.

51. Ahmed, and Jeon, G., Enabling artificial intelligence for genome sequence analysis of COVID-19 and alike viruses. *Interdiscip. Sci.: Comput. Life Sci.*, 14, 2, 504–519, 2022.

52. Adetiba, E., Abolarinwa, J.A., Adegoke, A.A., Taiwo, T.B., Ajayi, O.T., Abayomi, A., Adetiba, J.N., Badejo, J.A., DeepCOVID-19: A model for identification of COVID-19 virus sequences with genomic signal processing and deep learning. *Cogent Eng.*, 9, 1, 2017580, 2022.

Part 2
METHODS AND APPLICATIONS

5

Novel Cutting-Edge Security Tools for Medical and Genomic Data With Privacy Preservation Techniques

A. Rehash Rushmi Pavitra[1]*, I. Daniel Lawrence[2], J. Sarojini Premalatha[3], P. Kalaiselvi[1], D. Jena Catherine Bel[3], C. Esther[3], G.B. Zionna Sen[3] and G. Gomathy[3]

[1]Department of Artificial Intelligence and Data Science, Sri Sairam Engineering College, Chennai, India
[2]Department of Mechanical Engineering, Agni College of Technology, Chennai, India
[3]Sathyabama Institute of Science and Technology, Chennai, India

Abstract

A variety of field applications in contemporary healthcare are being made possible by the amazing technological advancements in genetic analysis and the substantial decrease in the cost of genome sequencing. The possibility of advancements in improved preventive and individualized medicine is particularly highlighted by the growing understanding of the human genome and its relationship to illnesses, health, and treatment responses. Unfortunately, the effect on security and privacy is exceptional. The genome serves as the most definitive form of identification and, in the event of a data breach, can reveal sensitive and private information about us, including our genetic susceptibility to certain diseases such as leukaemia or Parkinson's and other family's health complications. In this study, we examine the problem of developing cutting-edge security tools to protect genomic and medical data. In order to overcome the privacy and security issues that prohibit specialized medicine from attaining its complete capacity, the objective is to expedite the use of cutting-edge security tools in the medical industry.

Keywords: Genomic, medical, security, shared data, data protection

Corresponding author: Pavitra.ai@sairam.edu.in

Amit Kumar Tyagi (ed.) Privacy Preservation of Genomic and Medical Data, (115–130) © 2024 Scrivener Publishing LLC

5.1 Introduction

The history of privacy issues is quite extensive. The first cutting-edge observation and identification device that endangered user privacy was indeed the photography system, which was launched at the end of the 19th century. Since then, a number of additional gadgets have grown ubiquitous, including cameras, credit cards, web browsers, and cell phones [1]. These instruments can all expose a lot of personal information about us, such as the patterns and availability in various aspects of life, or even communication and physical movement. This issue could become significantly worse due to the recent exponential growth in DNA sequencing usage. The fundamental physical identity is represented by the DNA, which also holds a great deal of private data about family relatives and our health. If used inappropriately, it can provide access to a multitude of concerns and exploits that are currently not properly known [2].

When the Human Genome Project was considered finished in April 2003, the genomic era officially started. Consequently, a significant genomic revolution has taken place in medicine as a result of the remarkable decline in genome-sequencing expenses and the quick development of next-generation sequencing technology. At the moment of writing, a growing number of individuals are possessing their genomes sequenced, and it is not inconceivable to imagine that in the not too away future, the large number of us will be regularly inspected in order to benefit from new preventive diagnoses and treatments accommodated to with us genetic make-up [3]. While the complicated connection between the genome, illness, health, and phenotype remains only partially understood, genomic data can already be collected, stored, processed, and disseminated in ways that were inconceivable just a decade ago. Better preventive and customized treatment are greatly improved by the increased availability, usage, and sharing of such genetic information as well as their increasing integration with electronic health record (EHR) systems. However, it also raises previously unprecedented privacy and ethical issues.

The following significant privacy issues are generally brought on by access to genetic data, (a) Re-identification of people using the genome is possible. (b) It can provide details about their susceptibility to serious illnesses like Parkinson's, leukemia, or depression as well as genetic diseases like cystic fibrosis. (c) It contains details on relatives, children, and siblings, and publishing it might (potentially against the family's interests) provide interesting facts about the health problems that affect the entire family.

Additionally, it is challenging to determine or quantify the volume of personal data that may one day be obtained from the genome [4]. Thousands of individuals have seen their hospitals and doctors during the recent years, and cyberattacks on data housed in hospitals, insurers, and clinical laboratories have compromised the medical information of millions of people in the past few years.

5.2   Background of Genomic

Double-stranded DNA molecules, which are made up of two complementary polymer chains, contain the data for the human genome. Each chain is made up of little nucleotide units which are represented by the letters A, C, G and T in the alphabet respectively.

Medical Care
It has been established that changes in a person's genetic make-up can affect how well they are doing. Particularly, changes in the reaction to medication and changes in the susceptibility to a particular disease can be attributed to genetic abnormalities. The latter is especially employed in oncology [5]. As a result, an individual's genetic makeup can be considered for early diagnosis and therapy.

Research in Genomic
All throughout the world, research studies are being carried out to investigate how the genome works. Nearly every week, researchers learn something new about the relationship between the genome and various diseases and treatment outcomes [6]. Finding and validating associations with effect sizes, sensitivity, and specificity that enable advising about risk beyond what is anticipated by conventional clinical criteria is a challenge.

Competitive Genomics
In the past few years, direct-to-consumer (DTC) services for medical data in general and genetic data in particular have grown significantly. With the help of these services, people may now directly participate in the gathering, processing, and even the analysis of their own medical and genomic data at a price they can pay. Some well-known examples include www.ancestry.com, which offer their customers information based on their genotype about their ethnic make-up, their potential kinship, and their susceptibility to disease [7].

Legitimate and Forensic Genomics
Genomic data is also employed for investigation purposes because it has a characteristic and reliably recognizes a person [8].

Variation in Genetic
Approximately 99.9% of the entire human genome is identical between any two people that were already noted. Variation in genetic is used to describe the remainder (around 0.1% of the total). Here, single nucleotide polymorphisms are the most prevalent source of this genetic diversity (SNPs). For example, a single unique nucleotide is present at a specific genetic location in two sequenced DNA fragments from two individuals. However, there are a variety of less common genetic variations that also include multiple nucleotides, such as insertions, deletions, duplications, copy number variations and more intricate structural variations [9]. Figure 5.1 depicts the architecture for single nucleotide polymorphism.

A particular genetic locus can have numerous alternative versions (or alleles) with various genetic variants in the human population. A human genome consists of two sets of chromosomes, one inherited from each parent, due to the fact that somatic human cells are diploid. As a result, every individual either possesses two copies of the same gene or variation (homozygous) or two copies of two distinct alleles or variants (heterozygous). By comparing a genome with the reference human genome, a digital sequence of nucleotides thought to be indicative of the human genetic

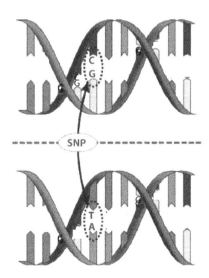

Figure 5.1 Single nucleotide polymorphism.

make-up, genetic variations in a specific individual genome are detected [10]. A genetic variation is often biallelic, meaning it can have two distinct alleles: a reference allele, which is the form found on the reference human genome, and an alternate allele, which is the alternative version found in the human population. The alternative allele frequency measures how frequent the latter is [10]. It is vital to remember that a variation may only be considered such if it has at least one alternative allele. Therefore, at a particular locus, an individual can be homozygous reference (i.e., take two reference alleles) and not have a variation, be heterozygous (i.e., having one alternate allele and one reference allele), or be homozygous alternate (two alternate alleles). Assume, for instance, that "X" represents the alternative allele and "T" represents the reference allele for a hypothetical SNP site (both "A" and "R" are from the set "X, Y, Z, R").

Combination of Genotype-Phenotype
Diseases and more generalised features known as phenotypes can be linked to genetic variations. For instance, the existence of some genetic variations might either enhance a person's propensity to eventually acquire a disease or act as a protective factor against it. GWAS (genome-wide association studies) and phenome-wide association studies (PNAS) are the typical methods used to investigate these connections (PheWAS). The effect size, which is expressed as $= \log (ro)$, where ro is the value of odd ratio which is typically used to measure the strength of the genome-phenome link [11]. The odds are the ratio of the likelihood that a disease will spread inside a certain group to the likelihood that it will not spread within that same group. The odds ratio is the probability in the population of people who carry a genetic variation divided by the probability in the population of people who do not, then the ro is $(Npg/Nqg)/(Npn/Nqn)$.

Correlations of Genetic Data
Physically adjacent variations are frequently associated because genetic segments (or haplotypes) are inherited in blocks. Linkage disequilibrium is the term used to describe this association. It may be used to deduce the value (or genome) of a particular variation from the genotype of other polymorphisms and is often assessed by the correlation coefficient.

Cryptography Background
The study of methods for protecting digital data, interactions, and distributed operations is known as cryptographic algorithms in the scientific community. Here, the two types of encryption are typically distinguished as symmetric and asymmetric [12]. The same key is used to encrypt and

decode the message in symmetric encryption, which is shared by the sender and the recipient. Hashing operations, message encryption, and authentication codes for messages are the principal applications for symmetric encryption.

As opposed to this, with asymmetric encryption, the communication is encrypted and decrypted using distinct keys. A set of keys, including a public key and a secret key, is given to the recipient. In order to encrypt the plaintext, the sender needs the recipient's public key, and in order to decode the ciphertext, the recipient uses his secret key.

Key exchange and digital signatures both frequently employ asymmetric encryption. Generally speaking, cryptographic approaches limit the algorithms' efficiency while adding storage and computing overhead, prohibiting users from accessing the data, and attackers without access to the secret key from reading or manipulating the data. However, there are particular forms of encryption that permit access to the encrypted data at the cost of lowered security or efficiency [13]. We give a high-level description of elliptic curve and property-preserving cryptography in the subsequent sections.

Encryption Technique
Instead of making ciphertext incomprehensible and useless like typical probabilistic encryption does, property-preserving encryption (PPE) maintains some of the qualities of the plaintexts.

Homomorphic Encryption
A unique kind of asymmetric encryption known as homomorphic encryption (HE) allows computation to be done on encrypted data. It is probable to use homomorphic encryption [14]. It offers semantic security, which prevents anyone who does not have the secret key from computing any function of the plaintext from the ciphertext.

5.3   Literature Review

Genomic data privacy protection is getting more attention, but integrity protection for this persistent and extremely sensitive data is getting far less. They investigate a related industries situation where the genetic data of a patient is preserved over an extended period of time and frequently accessed by authorised parties like doctors and clinicians. In such case, a protective system is provided that maintains the integrity of the genetic data over a 100-year time frame. Because cryptographic systems may mal-function over such a protracted period, our system enables updating the integrity protection. Furthermore, it is possible to confirm the accuracy of some genetic data while keeping the confidentiality of the collected infor-mation [15].

There has been several timestamping-based long-term integrity pro-tection systems proposed in the literature [16] for a variety of use cases. These methods do not, however, maintain the shielded data's long-term secrecy since they reveal information to the relevant timestamp services. Long-term integrity and long-term secrecy protection are combined using pledges that are unconditionally hidden. They do not take into account the security of genomic databases' many relatively little data pieces, which are far more numerous than the one huge data item they take into account. Since every data item needs to be secured by a unique signature-timestamp pair, which is expensive to make and maintain, their scheme's computation and storage costs scale poorly for large databases [17].

Regarding new research on integrity protection based on blockchains, the same thing may be argued [18]. While decentralised blockchain tech-nology is a unique and optimistic method of timestamped data integrity, it has the same long-term security vulnerabilities as any other system that does not incorporate routine hash function updates. Consequently, these efforts do not address the issue of long-term security [19].

Important and determining factors in the creation of such governance systems include public expectations about the gathering and use of genetic data. Previous survey research has typically concentrated on the constrained environment of research biobanks maintained by academic organisations and has highlighted the idea that the people donating their genetic data are behaving as altruistic biospecimen donors. Respondents were questioned about their attitudes on sharing their data with researchers, whether or not their data should be stored for speculative future research purposes, and how their privacy should be maintained [23].

The background of earlier studies, however, only provides a partial pic-ture of what the public anticipates from the regulation of genetic databases. We observe that two rising social phenomena growing public knowledge of the economic worth of genomic data and the escalating privacy dan-gers for those giving data will influence future governance expectations for genetic databases [24]. The importance of genetic data for business has recently been made more widely known by recent media coverage of agree-ments like Glasko Smith Kline's relationship with 23andme and Roche's acquisition of Flatiron Health.

5.4   Highlights of the Proposed Methodologies

In general, to create a system that protects privacy for the processing, retrieval and storing the files. A framework called privacy was created in the field of cryptography to secure personal data, and it is presently being heavily studied for the release of genetic data. Additionally, it is widely employed in the fields of deep learning and medicine [20]. The notion behind differential privacy is that it is very hard to discriminate between two nearby datasets that vary by only one factor. This component is chosen depending on the data that has to be secured, which, in the case of genetic data, frequently represents a single person or one family. The parameter > 0 in differential privacy evaluates the degree of privacy, and the definition of -differential privacy is as follows.

In high-throughput analysis of genomic datasets, such as GWAS, the top K significant SNP based on 2-statistics have to be made public while maintaining differential privacy. We thus assume that in the following methods, the statistics vector g is made up of 2-statistics. We start by thinking about applying a basic compressive technique on the genetic data. This approach concentrates on counting the number of nonzero items in the sparse vector [21]. In addition, we integrate the laplace, compressive mechanism, wavelet transform and the ability to release important SNP with high precision. Therefore it provides theoretical support for this method's compliance with differential privacy.

When visiting a doctor or hospital on a frequent basis, typical personalised medicine workflows need access to a few genetic variants. For elderly patients who frequently require medical attention, this random access to genetic variation data is typically necessary once every month at most. Likewise, ancestry and paternity tests, which largely access tandem repeat variants, are accurate.

Here, we take into account a customised medicine application scenario including a patient, a sequencing facility, a verified genome database, the patient's physicians, and hospitals. Doctors frequently request portions of the patient's genome, which is kept in a trusted database which identify the best medication and dosage, or to detect possible genomic predispositions. The patient could also wish to demonstrate the validity of their genetic data to a third party validate. Hence, an application situation in broad strokes while the following subsections into deeper.

Generation of Data

The information is subsequently sent to the genome database. Since our method functions on any type of data blocks, the data may be kept in plain-text blocks, encrypted using a symmetric block-cipher, or exchanged in secret. To conceal the accessible places, a pseudo-random permutation might be added to each block's 32-bit index. To concentrate on the long-term integrity of data blocks instead of performing a thorough examination of the various types of block storage.

Data Accessing

Assume about a physician that needs to determine the optimal prescription and dosages for their patient or find any potential genetic predispositions that could affect therapy in the future. If the partitions are kept classified, the patient, a named healthcare doctor, or a facility would be responsible for keeping track of the secret keys that would be used to aid in the decryption of the recovered data blocks.

Standard of Genomic Data

Genetic data provides a lot of private information about the person who owns it, including his or her forebears, physical characteristics, and the genomic information of their relations (leading to interdependent privacy risks). People share a tonne of data online, and some of this data may be used huge infer things about their genome. As a result, it is crucial to comprehend the privacy dangers associated with individual's genetic data while taking into account publically accessible information online. In order to use genetic data for research and healthcare, it is essential to safeguard individual users' genomic privacy.

This proposed work contain two primary goals are to (i) create a new, all-encompassing framework for quantifying an individual's genomic privacy and (ii) create a comprehensive framework for using, sharing, and verifying genomic data while protecting privacy under threat scenarios that are relevant to real-world situations. The new quantification framework will be built upon the applicant's prior graph-based, iterative algorithms, which were created to quickly evaluate and draw conclusions from huge data. Use of cryptography technologies, information theory methods, and statistics (differential privacy) will be made in order to meet the overall genomic privacy target.

The information contained in a genome is extremely private and delicate. Numerous individuals begin to generalise their digital genomes as the price of whole genome sequencing decreases and the interpretation of genomic data improves in significance and use. It becomes crucial to prioritise protection of personal genetic data. In this paper, we discuss about genetic data's uniqueness, the privacy risk associated with genomic data leaking, and potential reasons why it could be insecure and vulnerable.

Then additionally focus about what everyone is doing to better preserve genetic data.

When compared to other sensitive data, genomic data is uniquely sensitive and has its own unique features. With a few exceptions brought on by sequencing errors or the shortening of DNA strands caused by age, the profile of a germ line genome initially remains nearly unchanging over the course of a person's lifetime. The problem of a lost credit card can be resolved by replacing the credit card number, but it is impossible to change the information on your DNA. This irreversible future's security issue is that genetic data leaking might result in a person being defrauded for their whole existence.

In addition, because to the high degree of genetic similarity across individuals' genomes, genomic data include not just the individual's own genetic information but also that of their siblings, offspring and ancestors [22]. As a result, even those whose genomes have never been sequenced may still be vulnerable to attack by blood relations. The enormous range of uses for one's digital genome in health and behaviour, including paternity testing, predicting hazardous medication responses, identifying one's genealogy, and diagnosing diseases, makes genomic data extremely valuable.

The interpretation of one's genetic data may also be improved in the future due to the rapid expansion of scientific knowledge brought about by extensive studies involving genome research. You might never know what will be feasible with your DNA in ten or twenty years. Therefore, given all the unique qualities, the topic of genetic data security and privacy is one that is both urgent and crucial.

Security Risk of Genomic Data

Personal information, such as a person's name and contact information are removed in order to protect privacy and aggregate genomic data, which is then combined with that of other people. However, research has demonstrated that conventional anonymization methods are inadequate for use with genetic data, and as a result, disguised genomes may be used to re-identify individuals.

The greatest privacy risk associated with human genetic data is re-identification. summarised genetic privacy violations, and show the methods they employed to re-identify a person utilising the anonymous genomic data and certain fundamental demographic variables. The province and number of this individual were discovered using the information, and Ysearch, a free genetic genealogy database, was then used to discover the person's identity.

Additionally, a database of probable candidates was created using public record search sites like PeopleFinders.com. The individual can also be triangulated via pedigree analysis or social engineering. The significance of safeguarding data originators' genetic privacy is highlighted by this groundbreaking study.

Genomic data leaks might result in catastrophic consequences like genetic discrimination or extortion. The laws and policies safeguarding the privacy of genetic information about individuals are far from ideal. Since anonymized data are not covered by the Health Insurance Portability and Accountability Act, the United States passed the Genetic Information Nondiscrimination Act in 2009, which outlaws specific forms of discrimination in hiring and receiving health insurance. A long-term care insurance firm may punish a person for a genetic predisposition to a particular condition, such as cancer or Alzheimer's disease, because GINA does not apply to life insurance or the military.

Vulnerability in Bioinformatics Techniques
The development of bioinformatics tools and pipelines used for sequencing analysis has accelerated due to the fast advancement of next-generation sequencing technology. These Bioinformatics pipelines for next-generation sequencing are often created by small research teams and made available as open source. However, security is not always considered when creating these technologies. One group examined the software security in a large number of DNA processing applications, and they discovered that biological analysis programmes now in use that were built in C frequently used unsafe calls to runtime library functions like strcpy, sprintf, or strcat. These function calls may result in buffer overflows and software crashes, which may then be turned into vulnerabilities.

In a supply chain that consists of bioBanks, laboratories, hospitals, research organisations, genetic testing services, and individuals, NGS data are often examined and shared. The high flexibility, strong scalability, and low cost of NoSQL application databases, notably MongoDB, are luring research groups and businesses because biomedical data always have a broad range of data types and high dimensionality, and particularly genomic data are huge and fast expanding. Genomics England, a firm owned by the UK government, is adopting MongoDB, according to a recent MongoDB article. 1000 complete genomes from patients with uncommon disorders and their families, as well as individuals with common malignancies, are being sequenced as part of Genomics England's flagship project.

The poor security of this type of NoSQL database will, however, lead to significant problems without robust security backing and cautious configuration. Password credentials are not immediately necessary because MongoDB has Authentication Weakness by default. Second, it is automatically connected to the internet. Additionally, due to the fact that all data is delivered in clear text, it is possible to intercept it via a man-in-the-middle or ARP Poison attack. The Least Privilege principle, which states that each user should only have access to the minimal set of rights required to perform their assigned duties, is also violated by the fact that each newly formed user has default access to the whole database in read-only mode. Numerous databases are being attacked without proper settings.

5.5　Results and Discussion

Actions throughout data collection, storage, transmission, analysis, and sharing are necessary to safeguard genetic data and reduce possible dangers. Biobanks, data centres, researchers, decision-makers, and individual users all work together to accomplish all of these.

Sensitive genetic data should not initially be shared over the internet using clear text protocols like FTP or HTTP. The first and most crucial step in guaranteeing data security is the encryption of data during storage and transmission. When developing a data analysis pipeline for an organisation or data centre, vulnerability scanning is a crucial step in identifying possible risks. A tight least-privileged authorization approach and restricted data access based on personal role will lessen the danger of sensitive data leaking.

Additionally, the danger of reidentification of anonymous genomic data will be reduced by physically separating metadata and genetic data. It is crucial for researchers to prioritise data security and be aware of typical risks while creating new bioinformatic tools or constructing. To bridge the gap between the rapid progress of next-generation sequencing and the protection of sensitive data's privacy, policymakers must work diligently. New laws and regulations have been enacted so far to secure genetic data. As an illustration, the EU General Data Protection Regulation (GDPR), which took effect on May 25, 2018, has made it impossible to use the public genetic genealogy database Ysearch.org, which was utilised in the process of re-identification. A robust privacy protection law known as the California Consumer Privacy Act (CCPA) was signed this year by the governor of California and will go into effect in 2020.

Further, researchers are suggested to refer articles [25–30] to know about current progress towards privacy issues and its preservation mechanisms for their future research work.

5.6   Conclusion

We should be informed of the advantages and disadvantages of sequencing our genome. We may have our genome sequenced at some point in our lives as more and more individuals, particularly those with life-threatening diseases like cancer, benefit from genomic and other "omic" investigations. Therefore, it is crucial for people to understand their rights, the organization's data policy, and how their data will be utilised. Next-generation sequencing technologies are developing quickly, offering previously unheard-of prospects to transform healthcare delivery. Finding out our genomic information becomes crucial for evaluating our health in precision medicine. In the near future, it is also possible that you will be able to sequence and retrieve your genetic data via your smartphone. The security and privacy dilemma of such unique and highly sensitive genetic data calls for much more thought and effort.

References

1. Ayday, E., De Cristofaro, E., Hubaux, J.P., Tsudik, G., The chills and thrills of whole genome sequencing. *Computer*, 2013.
2. Raisaro, J.L., Ayday, E., Hubaux, J.P., Patient privacy in the genomic era. *Praxis*, 103, 10, 579–86, 2014.
3. Adam, N R and Worthmann, J.C., Security control methods for statistical databases: A comparative study. *ACM Comput. Surv. (CSUR)*, 21, 4, 515–556, 1989.
4. Aguilar-Melchor, C., Barrier, J., Guelton, S., Guinet, A., Killijian, M.O., Tancrede Lepoint, NFLlib: NTT-based fast lattice library, in: *Cryptographers' Track at the RSA Conference*, pp. 341–356, 2016.
5. Arthur, R., Schulz-Trieglaff, O., Cox, A.J., O'Connell, J., AKT: Ancestry and kinship toolkit. *Bioinformatics*, 33, 1, 142–144, 2016.
6. Botstein, D. and Risch, N., Discovering genotypes underlying human phenotypes: Past successes for mendelian disease, future approaches for complex disease. *Nat. Genet.*, 33, 3s, 228–238, 2003.
7. Bresson, E., Catalano, D., Pointcheval, D., A simple public-key cryptosystem with a double trapdoor decryption mechanism and its applications. *Proc. Asiacrypt*, 3, 37–54, 2003.
8. Browning, B.L. and Browning, S.R., Genotype imputation with millions of reference samples. *Am. J. Hum. Genet.*, 98, 1, 116–126, 2016.
9. Yu, F. and Ji, Z., Scalable privacy-preserving data sharing methodology for genome-wide association studies: An application to iDASH healthcare privacy protection challenge. *BMC Med. Inform. Decis. Mak.*, 14, S3, 2014.

10. Yuan, X. and Haimi-Cohen, R., *Image compression based on compressive sensing: End-to-end comparison with jpeg*, vol. 22, pp. 2889–2904, IEEE Transactions on Multimedia, 2020.
11. Rehash Rushmi Pavitra, A., Parkavi, G., Uma Maheswari, P., Karthikeyan, K., Daniel Lawrence, I., An illustrative review on machine learning techniques along with software tools and its evaluation. *Neuroquantology*, 20, 16, 233–236, 2022, doi: 10.14704/NQ.2022.20.16.NQ88026.
12. Zhang, Y., Blanton, M., Almashaqbeh, Secure distributed genome analysis for GWAS and sequence comparison computation. *BMC Med. Inform. Decis. Mak*, 15 Suppl 5, 2015.
13. Rehash Rushmi Pavitra, A., Daniel Lawrence, I., Uma Maheswari, P., To identify the accessibility and performance of smart healthcare systems in IoT-based environments, in: *Using Multimedia Systems, Tools, and Technologies for Smart Healthcare Services*, pp. 229–243, 2022, doi: 10.4018/978-1-6684-5741-2.ch014.
14. Lionnie, R. and Alaydrus, M., An analysis of haar wavelet transformation for androgenic hair pattern recognition. *International Conference on Informatics and Computing (ICIC)*, pp. 22–26, 2016.
15. Yamamoto, A. and Shibuya, T., Differentially private linkage analysis with TDT — The case of two affected children per family. *IEEE International Conference on Bioinformatics and Biomedicine (BIBM)*, pp. 765–770, 2021.
16. Vigil, M., Buchmann, J., Cabarcas, D., Weinert, C., Wiesmaier, A., Integrity, authenticity, non-repudiation, and proof of existence for long-term archiving: A survey. *Comput. Secur.*, 50, 16–32, 2015.
17. Weinert, C., Demirel, D., Vigil, M., Geihs, M., Buchmann, J., Mops: A modular protection scheme for long-term storage, in: *Proceedings of the ACM on Asia Conference on Computer and Communications Security. ASIA CCS '17*, pp. 436–448, 2017.
18. Jalko, J., Lagerspetz, E., Haukka, J., Tarkoma, S., Honkela, A., Kaski, S., Privacy-preserving data sharing via probabilistic modeling. *Patterns (N Y)*, 2, 7, 100271, 2021.
19. Cortes, J., Dullerud, G.E., Han, S., Le Ny, J., Mitra, S., Pappas, G.J., Differential privacy in control and network systems. *IEEE 55th Conference on Decision and Control (CDC)*, pp. 4252–4272, 2016.
20. Alnemari, A., Raj, R.K., Romanowski, C.J., Mishra, S., Interactive range queries for healthcare data under differential privacy. *IEEE 9th International Conference on Healthcare Informatics (ICHI)*, pp. 228–237, 2021.
21. Rehash Rushmi Pavitra, A., Parkavi, G., Uma Maheswari, P., Karthikeyan, K., Daniel Lawrence, I., An illustrative review on machine learning techniques along with software tools and its evaluation. *Neuroquantology*, 20, 16, 233–236, 2022, doi: 10.14704/nq.2022.20.16.nq88026.
22. Rehash Rushmi Pavitra, A., Daniel Lawrence, I., Uma Maheswari, P., To identify the accessibility and performance of smart healthcare systems in IoT-based environments, in: *Using Multimedia Systems, Tools, and Technologies*

for Smart Healthcare Services, pp. 229–243, 2022, doi: 10.4018/978-1-6684-5741-2.ch014.

23. Kaufman, D., Murphy, J., Scott, J., Hudson, K., Subjects matter: A survey of public opinions about a large genetic cohort study. *Genet. Med.*, 10, 831–839, 2008. pmid:19011407.

24. Selk, A., *The ingenious and 'dystopian' DNA technique police used to hunt the 'Golden State Killer' suspect*, Washington Post, USA, 2018.

25. Sai, G.H., Tyagi, A.K., Sreenath, N., Biometric security in Internet of Things based system against identity theft attacks. *2023 International Conference on Computer Communication and Informatics (ICCCI)*, Coimbatore, India, pp. 1–7, 2023.

26. Tyagi, A.K., Nair, M.M., Sreenath, N., Abraham, A., Security, privacy research issues in various computing platforms: A survey and the road ahead. *J. Inf. Assur. Secur.*, 15, 1, 1–16, 2020.

27. Nair, M.M. and Tyagi, A.K., Privacy: History, statistics, policy, laws, preservation and threat analysis. *J. Inf. Assur. Secur.*, 16, 1, 24–34, 2021.

28. Tyagi, A.K., Rekha, G., Sreenath, N., Beyond the hype: Internet of Things concepts, security and privacy concerns. In: S. Satapathy, K. Raju, K. Shyamala, D. Krishna, M. Favorskaya (eds), *Advances in Decision Sciences, Image Processing, Security and Computer Vision. ICETE 2019. Learning and Analytics in Intelligent Systems*, vol. 3, Springer, Cham, 2020. https://doi.org/10.1007/978-3-030-24322-7_50

29. Tyagi, A.K., Agarwal, K., Goyal, D., Sreenath, N., A review on security and privacy issues in Internet of Things. In: H. Sharma, K. Govindan, R. Poonia, S. Kumar, W. El-Medany (eds), *Advances in Computing and Intelligent Systems. Algorithms for Intelligent Systems*. Springer, Singapore, 2020. https://doi.org/10.1007/978-981-15-0222-4_46.

30. Tyagi A.K. and Goyal, D., A survey of privacy leakage and security vulnerabilities in the Internet of Things. *2020 5th International Conference on Communication and Electronics Systems (ICCES)*, pp. 386–394, 2020.

6

Genomic Data Analysis With Optimized Convolutional Neural Network (CNN) for Edge Applications

Sneha Venkateshalu*, Santosh Deshpande and Bharathi Pannyagol

Department of Computer Science Engineering, Visvesvaraya Technological University, Belagavi, India

Abstract

Deep learning shows potential for empowering devices to help individuals in the examination of extensive, massive data sets through developing specific algorithms that get effective with its use. Extensions of learning algorithms towards the processing of samples from genetic analysis, such as the identification of nucleotide sequences and statistics from epigenetic, proteomic, or metabolomics origins. The protein that contains the genetic code data necessary for an individual to develop and function is known genetic material acid, or DNA. Fascinating molecule DNA is really what defines each of us unique. The massive expansion of Nucleotide sequences due to advances in genomic technologies these have driven the analysis of gene sequences through into big data era. Artificial learning is an effective method for examining data because it gathers up information by itself. The machine learning CNN solves analyzing DNA data for identifying the genome with network model features that extract the depth of DNA, RNA attributes. The under fitting issue generated when the model is too simpler for our genomic data, so to solve this the CNN provided to build the model complex, less regularization, larger quantity of features with number of layers. A protein sequences is an approach used in genetics to assemble DNA, RNA, or protein sequences in order to determine patterns of commonality which may derive from practical, molecular, or genetic correlations between the strands.

Corresponding author: snehavenkateshalu@gmail.com

Amit Kumar Tyagi (ed.) Privacy Preservation of Genomic and Medical Data, (131–150) © 2024 Scrivener Publishing LLC

Keywords: Convolutional neural network, pattern matching, pair sequencing, probabilistic decision tree, activation function, hyper-parameter tuning, regularization

6.1   Introduction

The design and use of complex algorithms that get improved of is the target of the discipline of deep learning. Diverse sectors of bioinformatics have been confined to the application of mathematical approaches. Deep learning is being used to identify a broad range of gene sequence elements, but it may be most helpful for the interpretation of large genomic large data sets [21, 27–29, 32]. Deep learning approaches, for instance, is used to intended learning to find the location of transcribing. Algorithms can similarly be trained to identify and collect genetic information from DNA molecule. Deep neural networks (CNNs) are a class of neural network that are specifically designed for processing input with a matrix design, such as an image. A digital image is a numeric representation of sensory input. Each of the pixels, which are arrayed in a matrix pattern, seems to have a pixel count to define how intense as well as what tone it ought to be.

The individual brain starts analyzing a huge volume of data as soon as we receive a picture. Every neuron has a unique perceptron, and since they are connected to each other, they aggregate encompass the entire central vision. Identical to how well the neuron in the genetic targeting system responses to sensory input only in the restricted portion of the peripheral vision identified as the region of interest, so every neuron in a Network analyses the data in its region of interest. The layers first collect on edges, curves, and other simpler patterns before proceeding on to more complex patterns like faces and items. By using a Network, one can allow perception to systems.

Convolution Layer

The fundamental component of the CNN is the convolution layer. It performs the majority of the computational complexity on the network. In this stage, two weight vectors—the core, which is a scale parameter that can be learned, and the restricted area of the region of interest paired continuously [15–17]. The kernel is denser but tiny in length than an image. This signifies if the image has three (RGB) channels, the kernel length and width will be relatively tiny, but the intensity will improve to include all different channels.

In this stage, two weight vectors—the core, which is a scale parameter that can be learned, and the restricted area of the region of interest paired continuously. The kernel is denser but tiny in length than an image. This signifies if the image has three (RGB) channels, the kernel length and width will be relatively tiny, but the intensity will improve to include all different channels.

During the forward throw, the core traverses the image's minimum and maximum values, yielding an image of this same focused region. As a consequence, an activation pattern multiplex rendering of the image is designed, exposing the processor's response through each pixel of the image [6, 7, 13].

The CNN filters applied to go through the genomic features to extract the DNA four properties. A double helix, which is split into two linked strands that wrap around one another to mimic a coiled spiral, is the form of DNA. The basic structure of every helix is mainly composed of deoxyribose and phosphate groups that rotate. Every molecule is linked to one of the nucleotide elements: adenine (A), cytosine (C), guanine (G), or thymine (T). To combine two strands, cytosine makes a chemical bond with guanine, while adenine forms a chemical bond with thymine. The gene product along the DNA double helix can carry genetic material such as the instructions for building a protein or an RNA molecule.

Although each layer is layered together to build the full network and has exactly one input and output, a CNN may be implemented as a Sequential model refer Figure 6.1. Especially when the data sets are vast and complicated, the bioinformatics applications required techniques and software tools for analyzing biological data. CNN employed with sequential procedure applicable for analyzing genomic data. The genomic data with a sequence alignment is a data input given to the CNN system model. When DNA, RNA, or protein sequences are arranged in order to discover correlations with both each other that could be the result of systematic, operational, or genetic correlations, the whole process is known as DNA sequencing. Segments in arrays are commonly used to display genetic or amino acid sequence alignments. Gaps are inserted in between sequences to coordinate connected or unique sequences in successive columns.

If diverse set in a sequence share a predecessor, errors and spaces could be construed as genetic alterations and addition or removal genetic changes, accordingly, established with one or even both lines since individuals parted from each other. Indicators of how conserved a particular region or nucleotide feature is across groups can be determined using the measure of correlation among amino acid residues at a precise area in a molecule's code. When there are no alterations even if very conservative transpositions in a limited subset of the genome, that part of the succession

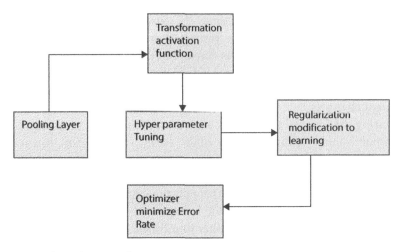

Figure 6.1 Flow of CNN analytics.

could have functional or structural importance. (i.e., limited subset of amino acids whose side chains have similar biochemical characteristics).

An approach for organizing DNA, RNA, or gene products to identify regions of similarity is called a sequence alignment. The two primary algorithmic methods for aligning sequences are multilateral similarities and nearby connections. When a global similarity is calculated, the pattern is "forced" to span the total length of all query strings. From the other hand, nearby similarities highlight areas of similarity within extended distances, and that are typically much diversified generally. Nearby patterns are typically the great decision, so they might be harder to calculate because it can be harder to find the locations of similarity.

A number of algorithmic techniques are often used to confront the problem of sanger sequencing. Which include time-consuming but technically accurate methods like nonlinear optimization. Many such include the efficient statistical or predictive methods [22, 34–38, 41, 42] designed for extensive selected databases, even without any assurance that they will uncover the right solution. Sequence analysis is a technique used to assemble protein (or DNA) strands in terms of determining of commonality this might be the product of genetic connections between strands.

Organization of Chapter
The rest of the chapter is outlined as follow. Section 6.2 shows about related work, section 6.3 outlines about proposed methodology, finally section 6.4 concludes this chapter.

6.2   Related Work

Comparing CNN to other neural networks that deal with single, two-dimensional feature extraction, CNN has the finest compatibility features. On the basis of extracting spatial data, CNN's architectural model was constructed with significant categories. With the capacity to extract numerous features, it can increase the channel and mapping features of a neural network model and extract depth, height, width, and multipath features using filters. This allows it to quickly and effectively learn from data representations. The neural network's architecture was improved with its model employing activation functions and error functions, enabling how effectively the model working. Using hyper-parameter adjustment of the learning weights and parameter optimizers of regularization approaches, CNN performance can be improved [23–26]. The characteristics of the activation function cover differentiable, zero-centered, computationally expensive, and vanishing gradient problems. Gradient algorithms are used by neural networks to train the network and add the required parameters to the model. This algorithm's goal is to use the back propagation approach to reduce mistakes in every epoch. Because of the depth features in the network, gradients frequently disappear, moving value to zero. In order to solve this issue, activation functions were utilized to move the gradient in the direction of zero. Calculating functions repeatedly at completely linked layers or at each layer reduces the cost of computation. Layers in a neural network's gradient descent process must be least differentiable or differentiable among the network's components [1, 30–33]. Neural networks do feature extraction and other image processing tasks, as well as video analyzing in time series. This feature, which returns the model with accuracy analysis in time process of the video frames in a network, is offered by the ReLU activation function. Mathematical examination of this activation function does not involve a lot of computing because it is easy to calculate. The function's sparseness, which also causes the matrix to be sparse, is a benefit. Sparsity gives the model swift, accurate prediction power with reduced overfitting because neurons only process the necessary data features. ReLU avoids the vanishing gradient issue and improves model convergence for bigger inputs [2, 3].

The assignment of functional annotations to genes has also been widely used in machine learning applications. Gene Ontology term assignments are the most used format for such annotations. Any one or more of a wide range of data types, such as the genomic sequence, gene expression profiles across diverse experimental conditions, or phenotype, can be used as input to predictive algorithms. Through the training of a network model, more advanced techniques aim to jointly model the expression of all the genes in a cell [4]. A biological macromolecule is DNA, also known as deoxyribonucleic acid. Information storage is its primary purpose. Since advances in generation sequencing, Genomic DNA input is presently growing at an accelerated rate, ushering the field of Nucleotide sequence analysis through into big data era. Furthermore, deep learning, which learns by itself is a powerful technique for analyzing enormous quantities of data. It has received many scientific accomplishments and has been widely employed in DNA sequence data analysis. The review begins by introducing the sequencing technology development process and explaining the concepts of DNA sequence data structure and sequence similarity [5].

A number of algorithmic techniques are often used to confront the problem of sanger sequencing. Which include time-consuming but technically accurate methods like nonlinear optimization. Many such include the efficient statistical or predictive methods designed for extensive selected databases, even without any assurance that they will uncover the right solution. Sequence analysis is a technique used to assemble protein (or DNA) strands in terms of determining of commonality this might be the product of genetic connections between strands. The fully connected layer, subsampling/pooling layer, and convolutional layer are the three different types of functional layers in the CPNN. Before the convolutional layer, the input patterns are subjected to the polynomial expansion, which results in a single piece of data that is formatted as a polynomial term. The polynomial term is then convolved with several filters in the subsequent convolutional layer, and then the dimensionality is decreased by subsampling and pooling. The fully linked layer receives these sub-features for classification. In other words, the polynomial expansion-based filters break the original input patterns into their component parts, and the resulting nonlinear features are then classified using nonlinear bounds [7].

A DNA sequence could be statistically examined to understand more about the sequence's features, genetic basis, composition, and development. This process is known as sequence analysis. Finding the nucleotide base order of DNA molecules is known as DNA sequencing. Genomic sequencing is the method employed when the nucleotide sequence of an individual is employed as the targeted DNA. Consequently, a variety of purposes together with basic biological investigation make extensive utilization of this technique. The basic Genetic code is an essential piece of information used in numerous different types of research, including forensic science, biotechnology, genetic manipulation, medicine research, farming, and biological studies [8]. To identify where specific DNA sequence fragments are located on each segment of a standard genomic sequences, studies utilized software applications called binders. The regions where unique human genetic information varies from those other genomic data variants are then called out by "mutation responders." The gene variants offer a variety of lengths. Single-nucleotide variants, often referred to as systematic variations, that included incisions and omissions, can range from minor with one Genetic letter, several more letters long, or considerably bigger genetic syndromes. The gene mutations might have no negative health consequences or they could immediately harm the body, genetic uncommon syndromes, or various other more prevalent diseases [9].

The supervised and unsupervised learning are typically feasible for systems. Discrete learning and testing dataset streams being supplied to systems during deep classification. By simulating ways neurons throughout the human brain communicate between one another, a deep neural network algorithm analyses a sample to discover patterns and sensitive data. Artificial neural networks (ANNs) are the techniques; ANN models are a type of software platform that imitate the brain's capacity to assess the perceived importance of various types of information and manage with bias. The variety and sophistication of certain sets of data will continue expanding as a consequence of Genetic analysis and some other biological methods. ML-based statistical methods that really are designed for handling, identifying, and understanding the vital information hidden within this massive data stream [10]. In the area of genetic predictive model, convolution techniques have been taken into consideration. The learning techniques are stochastic algorithms that offer adaptability to dynamic relations among input and output as well as the capacity to adapt to extremely complex patterns. Prediction models, that are subcategories of empirical "moderately evaluation modeling techniques," assemble multiple computational convolution layers, which are all composed of a significant number of neurons, in order to summarize artificial neural networks. Once more, the activation affects the product transmitted to the layer below that accepts the data as input. The neurons throughout the stack beneath use the product of the neurons within level preceding it as an input [11].

Substantial data can be mined for meaningful ideas specifically for data science. However, compared to other fields, bioinformatics is enduring a faster rate of data development. Genetic code has 2 aspects. The organized arrays of sequences that make up the uniform sequence alignment data seem to be on one side. Both are frequently aligned to the gene in individual genetics and utilized to yield protection or variable statistical data. The engineering processes in biological sciences, significantly linked with genetics, in terms of Quantitative, Substantial Deep learning is often made of as three steps: extraction, analyzing the collected samples, and modifying or evaluating the model to guarantee its precision. Well-known methods called hidden Markov models (HMMs) are utilized to model the flow or consecutive relationships among signals or occurrences. Classifiers have been employed in the discipline of bioinformatics to characterize genes, estimate epigenetic conditions, and investigate birthrate genetic code. Similar to orientation input weights, CNN's convolution kernels can analyze genetic patterns and identify patterns [12].

Scientists have given minimization a lot of focus because it is a crucial component of deep learning. Optimization algorithms in deep learning experience expanding unique challenges to the incredibly rapid expansion of data volume and the rise in computational cost. In Probabilistic deep learning, variable estimation is a beneficial prediction method that seeks to predict the procedure yields. It is conceivably an efficiency problem. Seeking the perfect transformation matrix to optimize the gradient descent of the base classifiers is really the aim of deep classification. A sequential first-order improved algorithm for limited optimization algorithms is the Frank-Wolfe technique. Neural network have battled with quasi optimum, that further creates the enhancement to frequently generate a relatively rather than an optimal solution resolution [13].

Enhanced predictive performance in computational weather forecast (NWP) and climate analysis utilizing splitting, inclusive greater cognitive flow models are primarily hampered by model error. Major innovations in the framework of inadequate 4D-Var have demonstrated that it is possible to predict and adjust for a significant portion of systematic model error that occurs in the atmosphere placed above a white limited prediction intervals within a new analytical paradigm. The outstanding result of deep learning and machine learning strategies in a variety of application categories has involving the ability an increase in involvement in all these developments. The application of the insufficient approach for prototype debugging to the complete weather stack may be increased by integrating ANN models into the four-dimensional insufficient architecture. Consequently, designers go over the benefits and drawbacks of the deep learning techniques in NWP threads [14].

Convolutional layers (CNNs) were used as foundation for a paradigm for extracting features in video sequences. This extracted features is dependent on Graphics processor parallelization of video streams to generate brightness and alter objects each moment. CNN need to be more precise and demonstrate how well it depicts image features like scaling, categorizing image information, etc. After that, CNN has been used in the second stage, where SBD has been local binary patterns, to extract the features.

CNN can be beneficial because it can accurately depict the content while filtering out ambient noise [15].

The principle behind the internet of things is to rapidly interconnect almost anything to the online, effectively enhancing our interactions and life satisfaction. Algorithms that analyze media streaming dataset seem to be content and processing and computationally demanding, so machine learning inside the framework of computing for the IoT devices, neural model methods seem to be essential for the practical implementation among these programs. Video sequence correction factor is employed to generate slow motion video, enhance video clock speed, and then use deep neural networks to evaluate and improve the quality of interlaced images in order to achieve real-time picture quality in streaming content. An input data of a stack with in cnn architecture is transformed into an activation signal using the batch normalization node nonlinear activation [16].

Data analysis on end devices became problematic due to real-time machine learning on streaming content. Deep learning models are the subject of extensive study because they effectively address complex mathematical problems and have increased processing capacity. Gradient boosting is the current internet algorithm being used reconfigure the deep convolution network's weighting factors. The training series is handed a confined constraint implemented to an endless dataset. Approximation analysis was used to measure the data variance factors through its constraining actions. The maximum parameters ensure that these strategies will resolve everywhere throughout the nonlinear structure. The primary determinant is indeed the fact that a penalizing condition is not necessary to acquire a succession of weight training with limits. Using transfer learning and the formulation of kernel function, aggregate computational resources were directed at reducing the amount of energy that memory was consuming. Similar to the stream forward carry process, array scaling is employed as an optimal solution [17].

With the astronomical increase in the volume of genetic information, there is indeed a huge bang in the discipline of genomics. Processes are used in genetics to assemble and examine genetic information. The two techniques being used carry out genomics processes are coordination and sequencing. Big data, however, provides a myriad of issues for such strategies. The management of big data throughout system operation is among the difficulties. Numerous transformed coordination and sequencing methodologies have been implied to manage big data since the inception of big data [18]. The several notable genomic errors, nevertheless, including the quick development of founder and transcription factors and the identifiers of notable modules. The instant analysis of vast nucleotide sequences, Genetic material, and nutrient sequences, and the quick query processing on sequential and diverse big data relative paucity conventional big data frameworks and methods [19]. Distribution area prediction delays is crucial for programs powered by ai (AI). Computing is a distributed processing strategy which distributes application software traffic to different databases like nearby edge devices or Wireless sensor networks (IoT) devices. When data are close to its origin, stand to gain from rapid findings, quick and efficient latencies, and more broadband being made accessible. There will be connectivity and lag limitations as a description of the findings gathered by end devices being sent to a data storage center or the cloud. Data processing permits a rapid and more detailed input analytical method [20].

6.3   Proposed Methodology

Stages of machine learning for genomic dataset
A model for discovering genes. It is demonstrated a simplified gene-finding model that encapsulates the fundamental characteristics of a protein-coding gene. The model outputs comprehensive gene annotations after receiving the entire or a portion of a chromosome's DNA sequence as input. The streamlined model is unable to distinguish between overlapping genes or different isoforms of the same gene.

> ➢ As insight to a learning approach, Nucleotide sequences and Boolean labels showing the extent to which every nucleotide is focused on a transcription begin site (TSS) are given.
> ➢ A model is created by the learning process and can then be used, in conjunction with to label unlabeled test sequences with predicted labels (such "TSS" or "not TSS") using a prediction algorithm.

The predictive model can either find different genes that are similar towards the gene mutations in the training session using these learning new features.The genomic data processing is large enough for computations given to the model is simple then the under fitting occurs. The under fitting occurs when CNN model is too simple for the processing data. The underfitting issue occur in machine learning degrade the performance of model. Each machine learning model's primary objective is to generalize effectively. The ability of an ML model to adjust the provided set of unknown input to produce an acceptable output is defined here as generalization. It indicates that it can generate trustworthy and accurate output after receiving training on the dataset. As a result, underfitting and overfitting are the key terms that need to be analyzed in order to determine how effectively the model performs and generalizes.

Underfitting happens while our algorithm for machine learning is incapable of recognize the underlying pattern in the data. To prevent overfitting in the model, the loading of dataset could be halted ahead of schedule, but this could prohibit the framework from obtaining adequately from the learning algorithm. Because of this, it could be unable to recognise the dominant pattern in the best fit of the data.

When an algorithm could indeed understand adequately from the training data, underfitting happens, which lessens efficacy and produces inaccurate estimates. An underfitted framework is characterized by high bias and low variation.

Combative methods for underfitting:

➢ Create an intricate model.
➢ Minimal regularization
➢ Wider variety of features.

Measures to create an intricate model:

- Consider applying a more effective model with more parameters that is ensemble learned with more layers or neurons per layer.
- Ensemble technique in CNN, Combining CNN models is one method, known as ensemble, for improving detection performance in the case of a two-stage detector.
- The region proposals produced by each CNN model are merged, analyzed, and then selected upon in the ensemble approach.
- The single-stage detector that does not produce region suggestions but instead recognises and categorises DNA properties. Combining CNN models is one method, known as ensemble, for improving detection accuracy in the case of a two-stage detector.
- The region proposals produced by each CNN model are merged, categorised, and then voted upon in the ensemble approach.

- To increase complementary strength, different aspects of the CNN models taken into account choosing to use in the ensemble technique.
- Ensemble deep learning comprises random forests, enhancing, and bagging. They all share the ability to create ensembles of base classifiers and guarantee their diversity by exposing them to various collections of training samples as shown in Figure 6.2.

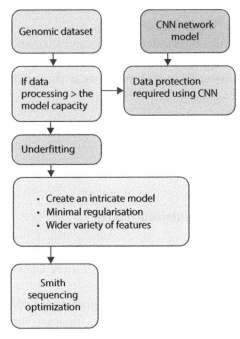

Figure 6.2 Genomic data analysis with CNN.

Consequence:
The approximate $\dot{\hat{\theta}}_v$ of $\theta(F)$.
for i=1,..... V_s do
    Create a new sample $A_{v,i}^*$ choosing v components from A_v and repeating them;
    Calculate $\dot{\hat{\theta}}_{v,i} = \theta(A_{v,i}^*)$;
end
Approximate $\dot{\hat{\theta}}_v = \sum_{i=1}^{V_s} \hat{\theta}_{v,i} / V_s$;
Approximate $\sigma^2(\dot{\hat{\theta}}_v) = \sum_{i=1}^{V_s} (\hat{\theta}_{v,i} - \dot{\hat{\theta}}_v)^2 / V_s$;

Minimal learning algorithm:

- **Regularization technique: The gradient regression**
  It is also referred to as reduced regression and modifies under-fitted models by applying a penalty equal to the sum of the squares of the coefficient magnitude. The gradient regression method solve the underfitting problem when the CNN learning model is small with large enough genomic data input. The network prototype with high bias of incapability model size created this problem solved by gradient factor.

  As a result, coefficients are produced and the mathematical function that represents CNN machine learning model that is minimised. The coefficients' magnitudes are squared and summed. Ridge Regression applies regularisation by reducing the number of coefficients. The cost function of ridge regression is shown in the function below.

Cost factor:

$$\text{Cost variable} = \text{Reduction} + \lambda * \sum \|v\|^2$$

Here,
Reduction – Total of the residuals squared
λ = Consequences for the faults
v = The curve's incline
The penalized factor is represented by Lambda in the gradient descent. To regulate the penalty term, required by adjusting the variables of the correction factor. The value of the variables reduces as the penalty increases. The parameters are trimmed. As a result, it serves to prevent autocorrelation problem and, through factor reduction, reduce the model's complexity.

Quantity of functionalities:

- A wider number of functions. Take advantage of extra characteristics, feature engineering, polynomial features, etc.
- Polynomial features with introducing non-linearity can improve the quantity of functions.

- Non-linearity can be achieved using the exponential expansion principle.
- Optimization with Forward pass and Back propagation can improve the non-linearity introducing PReLU activation function.

$$f(v_i) = \{\ v_i,\ if\ v_i > 0\ else\ s_i v_i,\ if\ v_i <= 0$$

Updating required for activation function to prevent model not to enter into the saturation mode of the learning genomic task.

$$\partial \varepsilon / \partial s_i = \sum_{v_i} \frac{\partial \varepsilon}{\partial f(v_i)} \frac{f(v_i)}{\partial(s_i)}$$

Applying back propagation along with gradient the activation function specified by:

$$\partial f(v_i) / \partial s_i = \{\ 0,\ if\ v_i > 0\ else\ s_i,\ if\ v_i <= 0$$

Summing up the channels sharing of the gradient s and finally Σi is applied all over the layers in neural network.

$$\partial \varepsilon / \partial s_i = \sum_{i} \sum_{v_i} \frac{\partial \varepsilon}{\partial f(v_i)} \frac{f(v_i)}{\partial(s_i)}$$

Optimization of CNN for analyzing DNA sequencing:

➤ Target.1: Adapting global alignment to determine whether a given two-kind data sets of gene DNA is similar or different. [Global alignment, using the Needleman-Wunsch approach, is preferred since it is appropriate for highly related sequences]
- Initialization -> Filling of the matrix -> Traceback
- Manually align two sequences using Needleman's approach

➤ Target.2: Determining which illness-causing gene is detected by the two-paring sequencing method.

Target.1: Adapting global alignment:
In global matching, the entire sequence is considered to be aligned (end-to-end alignment). Every letter from both the query and target sequences is present in a global alignment. Two series are acceptable with global matching if they are relatively similar and around the same length. Appropriate for matching two sequences that are closely linked. Global matching implied for going through the genes comparison with the same functionality or comparing two functionalities to know the DNA of gene. The best algorithm suggested with Needleman-Wunsch Global Align Nucleotide Sequences (Specialized BLAST) for further sequence match processing.

Target.2: Determining which illness-causing gene is detected by the two-paring sequencing method.

DNA sequencing
Adenine, thymine, cytosine, and guanine are the four genetic units that make up the Genetic material and carry considerable genetic data. The method of determining the order of these bases is known as DNA sequencing. The four elements in the double helix of DNA generate nucleotide sequences when they form a particular bond with one another. The bases adenine (A) and thymine (T) and cytosine (C) and guanine (G) couple (G). The 3 billion base combinations which compose the human genome contain the required to create and maintain an organism. Genetic code is well adapted for the storing of a considerable amount of genetic data owing to its base-paired architecture.

The technique through which DNA strands are replicated, processed, and transformed is dependent on this template strand, which further serves as the foundation for the majority of DNA sequencing techniques. Entire genetic analysis is now feasible and cost effective as a result of the significant advancements in Genome sequencing methods and technologies.

It is possible to check the Genetic code for distinctive traits in genes. For the purpose of comparing identical Genetic code from various organisms to analyze genetic variation among species. Genetic variations which may lead to disease can be identified using DNA sequencing.

DNA Progression Procedures
The two essential Specific DNA bases make up a base combination that together constitutes a "rung of the DNA ladder." The structure of DNA is a double helix, which is made up of two connected strands that loop around one another to form a convoluted helix. On the contrasting strands of the double helix of DNA are molecules called nucleotides that

interact chemically. The two strands of DNA are held together by these chemical bonds, which function similar hierarchical levels on a ladder. DNA contains the nucleotides adenine (A), cytosine (C), guanine (G), and thymine (T). These bases come in particular pairs (A with T, and G with C).

Mathematical functionalities implied for DNA sequences
The approaches to effectively evaluate DNA sequences and identify similarities and variances among them by attributing statistical classifiers to the strands. It is essential to look into the many diverse techniques in use to identify which, if any, optimally fulfills the requirements essential to categorize Nucleotide sequence.

Decision trees implied for the evaluation of pair sequences of DNA strands with small count of levels in decision making tree. Employing gini-index and entropy attribute facilitate a best precision of evaluating the node quality incense of its level of identifying between the pair sequences of provided gene DNA strands. Identification of gene sample taken with feature extraction of genetic dataset and further undergo diagnosing gene in detail.

Two pair-coding with binary procedure is Genomic DNA translation to binary:
Pairing order for two DNA strands: A with T: Adenine pairs with thymine and C with G: Cytosine pairs with guanine as followed in Figure 6.3.

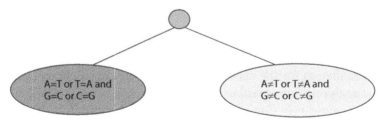

Left node specifying Normal gene factor

Right node specifies Risk in gene factor

Figure 6.3 Multivariate splits of DNA pair sequencing.

Flow 1: Process DNA strand:
N=TACGCCATCGTTCGAA (Binary sequence)
Flow 2: Translate the TACG into pointer:
¨, s = is member(N, 'TACG');
Flow 3: Numerical strands to translate the pointer:
V = {'00', '01', '10', '11'};

Flow 4: Translate the pointer into numerical strands:
Product = cell2mat(V(s));

Base pair sample:
The following DNA sequences illustrate pair double-stranded patterns. By convention, the top strand is written from the 5′-end to the 3′-end; thus, the bottom strand is written 3′ to 5′.

A base-paired DNA sequence:
Given pair sequence: TGAGCTCTAATCGATGCG
Target pair sequence: ACTCGAGATTAGCTACGC

6.4   Conclusion

The use of machine learning has increased. It is not a common use case in the field of computational biology and bioinformatics. Technologies based on machine learning are incredibly rare. Most tools are developed with deterministic techniques and algorithms. The CNN With the help of network model features that extract the depth of DNA and RNA properties, CNN resolves the problem of evaluating DNA data for genome identification. The underfitting problem arises when the model is too simple for our genomic data, thus CNN offered to create the model complex, less regularised, with a greater number of layers and features with best matching and sequencing using smith algorithm. The precision of proposed system evaluated using Decision trees with multivariate splits. Overall resolving the underfitting issue and deploying parameterised CNN on the edge nodes for saving the power constraint directly with improved space and time.

References

1. Sanjar, K., Bekhzod, O., Kim, J., Kim, J., Paul, A., Kim, J., Improved U-net: Fully convolutional network model for skin-lesion segmentation. *Appl. Sci. (Switzerland)*, 10, 2020. https://doi.org/10.3390/app10103658.
2. Mathai, V., Baby, A., Sabu, A., Jose, J., Kuriakose, B., *Video frame interpolation using deep convolutional neural network*, Springer International Publishing, 2019, https://doi.org/10.1007/978-3-030-00665-5_82.
3. Goel, S., *PReLU activation. This paper introduced both the PReLU*, Medium, 2019, https://medium.com/@shoray.goel/prelu-activation-e294bb21fefa, last accessed 2021/04/07.
4. Libbrecht, M.W. and Noble, W.S., Machine learning applications in genetics and genomics. *Nat. Rev. Gen.*, 16, 6, 321–332, 2015. https://doi.org/10.1038/nrg3920.

5. Yang, A., Zhang, W., Wang, J., Yang, K., Han, Y., Zhang, L., Review on the application of machine learning algorithms in the sequence data mining of DNA. *Front. Bioeng. Biotechnol.*, 8, September, 1–13, 2020. https://doi.org/10.3389/fbioe.2020.01032.

6. Wickramarachchi, A., *Machine learning for genomics*, 2020.

7. Cui, C., *Convolutional polynomial neural network for improved face recognition*, 2017. https://ecommons.udayton.edu/graduate_theses/1276/.

8. Ananthanarayanan, G., Bahl, P., Bodik, P., Chintalapudi, K., Philipose, M., Ravindranath, L., Sinha, S., Real-time video analytics: The killer app for edge computing. *Computer, 50*, 10, 58–67, 2017, https://doi.org/10.1109/MC.2017.3641638

9. Prjibelski, A.D., Korobeynikov, A.I, Lapidus, A.L., Sequence analysis, in: *Encyclopedia of Bioinformatics and Computational Biology: ABC of Bioinformatics*, vol. 1–3, 2018, https://doi.org/10.1016/B978-0-12-809633-8.20106-4.

10. Marco, S., Machine learning and artificial intelligence, in: *Volatile Biomarkers for Human Health: From Nature to Artificial Senses*, pp. 454–471, 2022, https://doi.org/10.4324/9780429318795-15.

11. National Human Genome Research Institute., Genomic data science, in: *Fact Sheet*, 2022, https://www.genome.gov/about-genomics/fact-sheets/Genomic-Data-Science.

12. Kristiani, E., Yang, C.T., Phuong Nguyen, K.L., Optimization of deep learning inference on edge devices. *Proceedings - 2020 International Conference on Pervasive Artificial Intelligence, ICPAI 2020*, pp. 264–267, 2020, https://doi.org/10.1109/ICPAI51961.2020.00056.

13. Kashyap, H., Ahmed, H.A., Hoque, N., Roy, S., Bhattacharyya, D.K., *Big data analytics in bioinformatics: A machine learning perspective*, vol. *13*, 9, pp. 1–20, 2015, http://arxiv.org/abs/1506.05101.

14. Nunes, R.T.P. and Deshpande, S.L., Big-data approaches for bioinformatics workflows: A comparative assessment, in: *Communications in Computer and Information Science, 628 CCIS*, pp. 647–654, 2016, https://doi.org/10.1007/978-981-10-3433-6_78.

15. Deshpande, S. and Venkateshalu, S., Asymptotic analysis of convolutional neural network with minimization of computational resources for real time short video applications. *The IUP Journal of Computer Sciences,* 15, 3, pp. 44–51, July 2021.

16. Venkateshalu, S. and Deshpande, S., *Performance optimization of short video using convolutional neural network for IOT applications*, pp. 743–754, 2022, https://doi.org/10.1007/978-981-16-5747-4_64.

17. Venkatesh, S., Goudar, R.H., Deshpande, S., A fast robust approach for video shot boundary detection based on CNN feature. *Int. J. Pure Appl. Math., 120*, 6, 12065–12075, 2018.

18. Bonavita, M. and Laloyaux, P., Machine learning for model error inference and correction. *J. Adv. Model. Earth Syst.*, 12, 12, 1–22, 2020. https://doi.org/10.1029/2020MS002232.

19. Sun, S., Cao, Z., Zhu, H., Zhao, J., A survey of optimization methods from a machine learning perspective, *IEEE Trans. Cybern.*, *50*, 8, 3668–3681, 2020, https://doi.org/10.1109/TCYB.2019.2950779.

20. Navarro, F.C.P., Mohsen, H., Yan, C., Li, S., Gu, M., Meyerson, W., Gerstein, M., Genomics and data science: An application within an umbrella. *Genome Biol.*, *20*, 1, 1–11, 2019. https://doi.org/10.1186/s13059-019-1724-1.

21. Libbrecht, M.W. and Noble, W.S., Machine learning applications in genetics and genomics. *Nat. Rev. Genet.*, *16*, 6, 321–332, 2015. https://doi.org/10.1038/nrg3920

22. Ananthanarayanan, G., Bahl, P., Bodik, P., Chintalapudi, K., Philipose, M., Ravindranath, L., Sinha, S., Real-time video analytics: The killer app for edge computing. *Computer*, *50*, 10, 58–67, 2017. https://doi.org/10.1109/MC.2017.3641638.

23. Niklaus, S., Mai, L., Liu, F., Video frame interpolation via adaptive convolution. *Proceedings - 30th IEEE Conference on Computer Vision and Pattern Recognition, CVPR 2017*, 2017-January, pp. 2270–2279, 2017.

24. Parihar, A.S., Varshney, D., Pandya, K., Aggarwal, A., *A comprehensive survey on video frame interpolation techniques*, 2021, https://doi.org/10.1007/s00371-020-02016-y.

25. Ahn, H.E., Jeong, J., Kim, J.W., Kwon, S., Yoo, J., A fast 4K video frame interpolation using a multi-scale optical flow reconstruction network. *Symmetry*, 11, 1–12, 2019. https://doi.org/10.3390/sym11101251.

26. Niklaus, S., Mai, L., Liu, F., *Video frame interpolation via adaptive separable convolution*, 2017.

27. Nabi, J., *Hyper-parameter tuning techniques in deep learning*, Towards Data Science, 2019, https://towardsdatascience.com/hyper-parameter-tuning-techniques-in-deep-learning-4dad592c63c8, last accessed 2021/04/05.

28. Patel, A., *Chapter-7 Under-fitting, over-fitting and its solution*, ML Research Lab Medium, 2018, https://medium.com/ml-research-lab/under-fitting-over-fitting-and-its-solution-dc6191e34250, last accessed 2021/04/05.

29. *Online courses & education programs for professionals*, 2020, upGrad, https://www.upgrad.com/, last accessed 2021/04/05.

30. Jiang, H., Sun, D., Jampani, V., Yang, M.H., Learned-Miller, E., Kautz, J., Super SloMo: High quality estimation of multiple intermediate frames for video interpolation. *Proceedings of the IEEE Computer Society Conference on Computer Vision and Pattern Recognition*, pp. 9000–9008, 2018, https://doi.org/10.1109/CVPR.2018.00938.

31. Meyer, S., Djelouah, A., McWilliams, B., Sorkine-Hornung, A., Gross, M., Schroers, C., PhaseNet for video frame interpolation. *Proceedings of the IEEE Computer Society Conference on Computer Vision and Pattern Recognition*, pp. 498–507, 2018, https://doi.org/10.1109/CVPR.2018.00059.

32. Sanjar, K., Bekhzod, O., Kim, J., Kim, J., Paul, A., Kim, J., Improved U-net: Fully convolutional network model for skin-lesion segmentation. *Appl. Sci. (Switzerland)*, 10, 2020. https://doi.org/10.3390/app10103658.

33. Mathai, V., Baby, A., Sabu, A., Jose, J., Kuriakose, B., *Video frame interpolation using deep convolutional neural network*, Springer International Publishing, 2019, https://doi.org/10.1007/978-3-030-00665-5_82.
34. Kang, D., Romero, F., Bailis, P., Kozyrakis, C., VIVA : An end-to-end system for interactive video analytics, in: *Proceedings of 12th Conference on Innovative Data Systems Research (CIDR'22)*, vol. 1, 1, Association for Computing Machinery.
35. Lee, R., Venieris, S.I., Lane, N.D., Deep neural network based enhancement for image and video streaming systems: A survey and future directions. *ACM Comput. Surveys*, 54, 8, 2022. https://doi.org/10.1145/3469094
36. Khallaf, R. and Khallaf, M., Automation in construction classification and analysis of deep learning applications in construction: A systematic literature review. *Autom. Constr.*, 129, June, 103760, 2021. https://doi.org/10.1016/j.autcon.2021.103760.
37. Baek, S., Jung, W., Han, S.H., Automation in construction A critical review of text-based research in construction: Data source, analysis method, and implications. *Autom. Constr.*, 132, September, 103915, 2021, https://doi.org/10.1016/j.autcon.2021.103915.
38. Benito-picazo, J., Domínguez, E., Palomo, E.J., López-rubio, E., Deep learning-based video surveillance system managed by low cost hardware and panoramic cameras uncorrect proof version uncorrected. *IIntegr. Comput. Aided Eng.*, 1, 1–15, 2020. https://doi.org/10.3233/ICA-200632.
39. Zhang, C., Cao, Q., Member, S., Jiang, H., A fast filtering mechanism to improve efficiency of large-scale video analytics. *IEEE Transactions on Computers*, 69, 6, 914–928, 2020.
40. Q. Zhang, H. Sun, X. Wu and H. Zhong, Edge video analytics for public safety: A review, in: *Proceedings of the IEEE*, 107, 8, 1675–1696, Aug. 2019.
41. Liu, P., Qi, B., Banerjee, S., EdgeEye - An edge service framework for real-time intelligent video analytics. *EdgeSys 2018 - Proceedings of the 1st ACM International Workshop on Edge Systems, Analytics and Networking, Part of MobiSys*, pp. 1–6, 2018, https://doi.org/10.1145/3213344.3213345.
42. Ran, X., Chen, H., Zhu, X., Liu, Z., Chen, J., DeepDecision: A mobile deep learning framework for edge video analytics. *Proceedings - IEEE INFOCOM*, 2018- April, pp. 1421–1429, 2018, https://doi.org/10.1109/INFOCOM.2018.8485905.
43. Zhang, C., Cao, Q., Jiang, H., Zhang, W., Li, J., Yao, J., FFS-VA: A fast filtering system for large-scale video analytics. *ACM International Conference Proceeding Series*, 2018, https://doi.org/10.1145/3225058.3225103.

7

Real-World Estimation of Malaria Prevalence From Genome of Vectors and Climate Analysis

Ashvath Narayanan C., Pavitra Vasudevan, Maheswari R.*, Parvathi R.
and Pattabiraman V.

*School of Computer Science and Engineering, Vellore Institute of Technology,
Chennai, India*

Abstract

Malaria has always been one of the world's most common vector-borne diseases. Remarkably, over the past decades, this disease has been eradicated in a number of nations. However, there are still several obstacles to overcome in order to achieve a greater level of control and to continue the eradication process in the direction of a world free of this illness. India is extremely vulnerable to the effects of vector-borne diseases due to its large population and good geo-ecological environment. Vector-borne diseases (VBDs) are illnesses brought on by parasites, viruses, and micro-organisms. These VBDs include lymphatic filariasis, Kyasanur Forest disease, Japanese Encephalitis (JE), Dengue, Chikungunya, and Malaria (KFD). In India, malaria remains a major public health concern [1]. In Tamil Nadu, Chengalpet being our place of residence, piqued our interest. Since malaria is endemic in south Indian cities like Chennai, the prevalence of the disease in a nearby coastal region like Chengalpet was investigated. The problem statement was viewed from two different perspectives, one was used to determine the mosquito type and species using classification models and the other way of tackling this was by regression resulting in the gender and age of the people who got affected by malaria to determine the best possible results. Twelve years worth of monthly climate and malaria data with the information of which mosquito genomes and species has caused the spread, from public sources in Chengalpet were collected as part of the dataset. Both classification and regression were performed, and it was observed that nonlinear regression gave the best result with 85% accuracy.

Corresponding author: maheswari.r@vit.ac.in

Amit Kumar Tyagi (ed.) *Privacy Preservation of Genomic and Medical Data*, (151–170) © 2024
Scrivener Publishing LLC

Keywords: Vector-borne diseases (VBDs), climate, species

7.1 Introduction

Vector-borne diseases (VBDs) are illnesses that are transmitted to humans and animals by blood-feeding arthropods, such as mosquitoes, ticks, and fleas. VBDs thrive given our population's lifestyles, hygiene standards, and rate of disease transmission. Mosquito-borne illnesses can have significant impacts on human health and well-being, and their spread is closely tied to climatic conditions. The climate of a region directly affects the spread of vector-borne diseases. Temperature plays a major role in the spread of vector-borne diseases. Warmer temperatures can lead to an increased population of vectors, as well as a shorter incubation period for the pathogens they transmit. For example, the warmer temperatures found in tropical regions are conducive to the development and proliferation of mosquitoes, which are responsible for transmitting diseases, such as malaria and dengue fever.

Precipitation also plays a role in the spread of vector-borne diseases. Adequate precipitation is essential for the development of mosquito larvae, and heavy rainfall can lead to an increase in the mosquito population. Conversely, drought conditions can lead to a reduction in the mosquito population. Relative humidity also affects the transmission of vector-borne diseases. High humidity can lead to an increased survival rate of vectors, while low humidity can lead to a decrease in vector survival. In addition, high humidity can increase the rate of evaporation, which can lead to an increase in the number of mosquitoes found near water sources. Climate change is also affecting the spread of vector-borne diseases. Rising temperatures and changes in precipitation patterns are leading to an expansion of the geographic range of vectors and the emergence of new disease vectors. For example, as temperatures have risen, mosquitoes that can transmit West Nile virus have expanded their range from the southern US to the northern US.

To combat the spread of vector-borne diseases, it is important to consider the ways in which climatic conditions affect the populations of vectors. This can include measures such as reducing mosquito breeding sites, using mosquito nets and repellents, and controlling tick and flea populations. In addition, it is important to be aware of the ways in which climate change is affecting the spread of vector-borne diseases and to take steps to adapt to these changes. It can be observed that the climatic conditions have a significant impact on the spread of vector-borne diseases.

Temperature, precipitation, and relative humidity all play a role in the population dynamics of vectors and the transmission of pathogens. Climate change is also making the problem worse, leading to an expansion of the geographic range of vectors and the emergence of new disease vectors. To combat the spread of vector-borne diseases, it is important to consider and understand the ways in which climatic conditions affect the populations of vectors and take steps to adapt to these changes.

Mosquitoes with different genome sequencing proliferate under different climatic conditions. The temperature of an area impacts the seasonal pattern or temporal distribution of illnesses that are carried and transmitted by vectors since the vector animals typically flourish in certain climate conditions. When it comes to Malaria, the primary vectors are mosquitoes. Genome sequencing of mosquitoes has boosted our knowledge of basic molecular level biological processes. It thereby has the potential to be used to control mosquito populations and curb the transmission of diseases carried by them [2]. Warm and wet environments make suitable breeding grounds for mosquitoes. If the mosquitoes happen to be the type of species, which can transmit the disease, then the spread of that disease is more likely in an infected region. Based on the climatic cycle, different regions suffer the spread of vector-borne diseases at different times of the year on a wider scale. Malaria, which is the disease focused largely in this study, can occur if a mosquito infected with the Plasmodium parasite bites a person. There are four types of Plasmodium parasites, which are *Plasmodium falciparum* (or *P. falciparum*), *Plasmodium malariae* (or *P. malariae*), *Plasmodium vivax* (or *P. vivax*), and *Plasmodium ovale* (or *P. ovale*).

The outcome of this study is to predict and classify mosquito genome type and species that have infected a patient who has Malaria. The parasites are carried by the Anopheles mosquitoes. Anopheles mosquitoes thrive in regions with heavy rainfall, high humidity, and warm temperatures. Therefore, tropical and subtropical areas are excellent. Additionally, warm temperatures are necessary for malaria parasites to finish their life cycle in mosquitoes. It is well established that the climate can have an impact on the transmission dynamics, geographic distribution, and re-emergence of certain transmittable diseases. The diseases caused by vectors have shown to spread more readily in tropical areas. When compared to rich countries, developing nations are more prone to these diseases since they are economically underdeveloped and have subpar healthcare. India is extremely vulnerable to the effects of VBDs due to its large population and suitable geo-ecological environment. Plasmodium falciparum, a parasite, cannot complete its life cycle in mosquitoes at temperatures below 20°C or 68°F; hence, it cannot be transmitted at those temperatures. *Plasmodium vivax,* a different type of the malaria parasite, can complete its life cycle in colder environments. With the changing climate, the proliferation of the mosquitoes and parasite change thus being a contributing factor in the transmission of malaria. Along with these types, the study also takes into account the mosquitoes that are indigenous and imported. Identifying people who are contagious and treating them effectively and continuously as soon as possible in government primary/public health centers in our country's rural areas are some of the numerous ways to prevent this communicable disease. As machine learning, deep learning, and Internet of things (IoT) technologies advance rapidly, they can be used to analyze, detect, forecast, predict, and even advise modifications that would aid in preventing the spread of these diseases.

The dataset used has the climate data of each month for the past 12 years. The dataset was taken from a public healthcare center in Chengelpet, with the monthly climate data from the meteorological department available on the Internet. The attributes taken into consideration include average temperature, humidity, rainfall, number of rainy days, precipitation, maximum and minimum temperature. This month-wise data are combined with the Malaria data which consists of the age category, gender (male or female), ward number of the Chengalpet district and other attributes like the type of mosquito and species of mosquito that has infected the patient. Analysis of the dataset was done in order to extract those attributes that contributed to our objective. Machine learning learners and classifiers were utilized to predict the number of people affected and categorize the mosquito type and species.

7.2   Significance of Estimation of Malaria Prevalence From Genome of Vectors and Climate Analysis

Prediction and estimation of spread of a vector-borne disease of any region using the climatic conditions and its variations.

7.2.1   Related Work

The study aims to understand the relationship between climate change and vector-borne illnesses on a regional level [3]. The authors of the study conducted a comprehensive review of existing literature and data to assess the evidence for how the epidemiology of vector-borne diseases is directly impacted by interannual and interdecadal climate variability at the continental level. Interannual climate variability refers to the natural variation in climate that occurs from year to year, such as changes in temperature and precipitation. Interdecadal variability, on the other hand, refers to longer-term climate patterns that can span several decades. By examining both types of variability, the study was able to gain a more complete understanding of how climate change is affecting the spread of vector-borne illnesses. The study also helped to forecast and identify the potential consequences of climate change on vector-borne illnesses in the future. By analyzing the existing evidence and identifying patterns, the authors were able to make predictions about how changes in temperature, precipitation, and other climatic factors may affect the spread of diseases transmitted by vectors in the coming years and decades.

The study focused on understanding the potential impacts of climate change on vector-borne diseases [4]. The authors examined various climate change scenarios and how they may affect the circumstances and patterns under which vector-borne diseases are expected to vary. They outlined the requirements that must be satisfied in order to draw the conclusion that vector-borne diseases are being impacted by climate change. These requirements include, for example, identifying a clear relationship between changes in climate and changes in the incidence or distribution of vector-borne diseases, and demonstrating that this relationship cannot be explained by other factors. The study also looked at the quality of the data and methods used in previous studies, as well as the strength of the evidence presented. Using a number of examples from the literature, the authors demonstrated how some studies satisfy these requirements while others do not. They analyzed previous research on the relationship between climate change and vector-borne diseases, and evaluated the quality of the evidence presented and the methods used. By doing so, they were able to identify which studies provided strong evidence for a relationship between climate change and vector-borne diseases, and which studies did not.

The main objective of the paper in question was to use machine learning techniques to provide a reliable prediction of the outbreak of three vector-borne diseases: malaria, dengue, and Chikungunya across the Indian subcontinent [5]. The authors of the paper gathered data from 2013 to 2017 across India, which they then used to analyze and improve their model. Specifically, they used a technique called multiclass classification to classify the data into one of the three diseases. This technique is used when there are multiple classes or categories to classify an input data into, in this case, malaria, dengue, and Chikungunya. The authors then applied an outbreak risk prediction algorithm implemented using a specific type of neural network called convolutional neural network (CNN) to analyze the data.

CNNs are neural networks that are particularly well suited for image and video data, but they can also be used for other types of data such as time series data. The authors used the CNN to analyze the data from the Indian subcontinent and developed a model that could predict the outbreak of vector-borne diseases with a high degree of accuracy. The proposed CNN algorithm was able to achieve an accuracy of 88% in predicting the outbreak of malaria, dengue, and Chikungunya.

This paper aimed to explore the potential of deep learning and machine learning techniques for predicting and preventing outbreaks of lethal diseases [6]. In order to achieve this goal, the authors conducted a comprehensive review of previous research in this area. They examined the current state of the field, the difficulties and challenges faced when using these techniques for predicting disease outbreaks, and the possible applications of deep learning and machine learning in this context. They looked at various aspects of previous research, such as the methodology used, the datasets employed, the factors that influence the performance of these techniques, and the indicators used to evaluate their performance. The authors also considered the different types of diseases that have been studied using these techniques and the specific methods and models used for each disease. They analyzed the advantages and limitations of different approaches and identified opportunities for future research in this field.

This study aims to improve the prediction of dengue epidemics in Pakistan using a combination of satellite imagery and machine learning techniques [7]. The authors used a specific type of neural network called a Convolutional Neural Network (CNN) to analyze satellite images of the landscape in London. The CNN was trained using a large dataset called Imagenet, which contains a wide variety of images of different objects and scenes. The authors used the trained CNN to label the terrain attributes in satellite images from London, such as the presence of water bodies, vegetation, and built-up areas. This information was then merged with data on dengue cases in Pakistan from 2012 to 2016. This merged data were then fed into a mathematical model called the susceptible-infectious-recovered (SIR) epidemic model. The SIR model is a framework for understanding the spread of infectious diseases in a population, and it describes the dynamics of how a disease spreads and how it affects different groups of people. By combining the satellite-collected landscape data with information on dengue cases, the authors were able to improve the predictions of the SIR model. The results of the study showed that combining satellite-collected landscape data with information on dengue cases could improve the key component of proactive and tactical surveillance and control programs.

This approach can provide valuable information for public health officials to take actions to prevent the spread of dengue in a specific area.

This research study explores the use of transfer learning models to improve the detection and forecasting of vector-borne diseases for which significant data are currently unavailable [8]. Transfer learning is a machine learning technique where a model that has been trained on one task is used to improve the performance of another related task. In this case, the authors propose using models that have been trained on dengue time series data to detect and forecast the spread of Chikungunya and Zika, which are both related diseases that are also transmitted by mosquitoes. The authors of the study used two families of models for forecasting Chikungunya and Zika in two Brazilian cities, Rio de Janeiro, and Fortaleza. The first family of models is forecasting models, which are statistical models used to predict future values based on historical data. The second family of models is LSTM, which stands for Long Short-Term Memory, a type of recurrent neural network (RNN) that is capable of learning long-term dependencies. The LSTM models are designed to handle time series data, which makes them well suited for predicting the spread of diseases over time. The authors used data from dengue time series to train the models and then applied them to the task of detecting and forecasting Chikungunya and Zika. The results showed that the transfer learning models performed well in both cities, and were able to detect and forecast the spread of the diseases with a high level of accuracy.

This study developed a multiclass mosquito identification system using InceptionV3, a transfer learning model implemented using Tensorflow [9]. The objective of this system is to accurately identify different species of mosquitoes based on the sound they make. The study used spectrogram images of six different mosquito species produced from recordings made using a smartphone. Spectrogram images are visual representations of sound that show how the frequency and amplitude of a sound change over time. InceptionV3 is a pre-trained model that was trained on a large dataset of images, and it has been shown to be effective at image classification tasks. TensorFlow is an open-source machine learning library that was used to implement the transfer learning model. The authors used the pre-trained weights of the InceptionV3 model and fine-tuned it on the spectrogram images of the six different mosquito species. The results showed that the multiclass mosquito identification system was able to detect 85% of the species that were previously available in the reference library. However, the system was not able to correctly identify new invasive species that were not present in the reference library. This is an important limitation of the system as invasive species can cause significant damage to the ecosystem and public health.

This paper states that quantitative projections of future climate-sensitive health effects are difficult [10] due to several reasons. One of the reasons is that many infections are sensitive to weather conditions and the interactions between climatic and nonclimatic parameters are complex. Additionally, adaptation to changes in climate can also impact the spread of vector-borne diseases. The authors of this paper have confirmed that monitoring weather forecasts can assist in identifying early signs of outbreaks of diseases that are transmitted by vectors. This can act as a risk reduction early warning system. By keeping track of weather patterns and identifying areas where the conditions are favorable for the spread of vector-borne diseases, public health officials can take proactive measures to prevent or control outbreaks. For example, if the weather forecast predicts that an area is going to experience a prolonged period of high temperatures and high humidity, which are favorable conditions for the spread of malaria, public health officials can take steps to control the mosquito population in that area and distribute bed nets to protect people from being bitten by mosquitoes.

This study aimed to identify areas in Chennai with a high incidence of malaria, using the ArcGIS tool for hot spot analysis [11]. The study used data on monthly cases of malaria reported by the Chennai Corporation's Vector Control Office between 2005 and 2011, and also obtained monthly data on various climate variables from the Indian Meteorological Department in Chennai. The analysis revealed that malaria cases were most prevalent during the months of August, September, and October. It was also found that the highest number of cases were recorded in the Basin bridge zone, followed by the Adyar zone. The study also found that rainfall and mean temperature were strongly correlated with the number of malaria cases in a given area. This information can be used to target malaria control efforts in specific areas and months, and to better understand the relationship between climate conditions and the spread of malaria.

This study [12] focused on the impact of climate change on the spread of malaria in six countries in the Sub-Saharan Africa region, specifically Burkina Faso, Mali, Niger Republic, Nigeria, Cameroon, and DRC. The study aimed to identify patterns and trends in the incidence of malaria in relation to climate variables. The researchers used data from the World Health Organization's data repository on confirmed malaria occurrences per 1000 population and climate data from the National Centre for Atmospheric Research's repository. They implemented a malaria incidence classification model, which incorporates k-means clustering to detect outliers and the XGBoost algorithm for classification. The results of the study showed that the accuracy of the model significantly improved after feature engineering, achieving 90+% for all six countries, and is significantly better than the machine learning models used for comparison.

The study [13] aims to investigate the relationship between the Indian National Malaria Control Program's malaria prevention efforts and meteorological conditions, and their impact on malaria outbreaks between January 2009 and December 2015. The study used data from the frequency of implementation of preventative approaches following each epidemic to evaluate the effectiveness of the measures taken by the Indian National Malaria Control Program. The results of the study showed that fever surveys and anti-larval activities were the most beneficial measures in controlling malaria outbreaks. The study also found that winter had a detrimental effect on the overall rate of malaria, while summer and fall were the seasons when epidemics were most likely to occur. These findings are important in understanding the role of climate variability in malaria outbreaks and the measures that are being taken in India to control it.

The study [14] focuses on the Sundargarh district of Odisha, an Indian state that is particularly susceptible to malaria due to its climate. The study found that maximum surface temperatures in the district range between 27°C and 40°C during the summer and monsoon seasons, and relative humidity values are between 60% and 85%. These conditions are conducive for the transmission of malaria, and it was observed that the number of malaria cases was on the rise during the monsoon and post-monsoon seasons. To analyze the data and predict the incidence of malaria, the study used two machine learning classifiers: WEKA's J48 and MLP (Multi-layer Perceptron). The performance of these classifiers was evaluated using 10-fold cross-validation, which is a technique used to measure the performance of a machine learning model on unseen data. The results of the study showed that the J48 model outperformed the MLP model in all performance metrics. It was concluded that the J48 model was more accurate and efficient in predicting the incidence of malaria in the Sundargarh district of Odisha. These findings are important in understanding the factors that contribute to the transmission of malaria in this region and can be used to develop more effective malaria control strategies.

7.3   Proposed Methodology

Monthly climate data from January 2010 to September 2022 were obtained from [15], and includes information such as the month, week one to four, minimum temperature, maximum temperature, and average temperature in Fahrenheit for that month, the dew point in Fahrenheit, wind speed in mph, humidity in percentage, precipitation, and the number of days it rained in that month. According to research, the two primary malaria vectors [16] are Plasmodium falciparum, Pf, and Plasmodium vivax, Pv. Imported and indigenous Pf and Pv species have been encoded to generate four distinct mosquito genome types. Male and female gender categories along with five different age categories are included in the Malaria data obtained. The data also contains the total number of cases in male, female and the death count.

The 12 years worth of malaria data and monthly climate data were combined to create a dataset with a total of 613 records, with mosquito types 1 and 4 each accounting for 24% of the data and types 2 and 3, each making up for 27%. There are six age groups: 0–10, 11–20, 21–40, 41–50, and 51–80. The majority of malaria cases were seen in people aged 51 to 80, with an annual average of around 200 cases.

The dataset has undergone a lot of modifications to make it ready for training the prepared models. Columns like maximum temperature and minimum temperature were condensed to average temperature and additional values, like ward number, that are trivial to training the model are truncated. The names of the months are encoded into numbers for training purposes. The mentioned processes were carried out in Google colab's ipython notebook with the libraries pandas for manipulating the dataset as a dataframe and numpy for encoding attributes and transforming data.

The dataset is split into training and testing sets with 70% and 30% of the original dataset respectively. The dataset is transformed to be training compatible with 11 inputs and 3 outputs for number of cases prediction.

Tropical weather prevails in the areas in and around Chennai, with the rainy season lasting from July to December and the dry weather lasting from January to May. Due to the north-east monsoon or receding monsoon, the most rainfall occurs from mid-October to mid-December. A similar trend is seen in Chengalpet, the area of study. To prove that temperature has less weightage, and attributes like precipitation, humidity and number of rainy days have more weightage in the occurrence of the number of malaria cases, the trend in the dataset was observed. In Figure 7.1, it can be seen that the number of rainy days increases starting from June and drops after peaking in October.

The trend followed by precipitation in the span of a year (Figure 7.2) also starts increasing around June and peaks in October and November before going downhill. In Chengalpet, Tamil Nadu, September to November experience the most rainfall in a year, explaining the precipitation increase

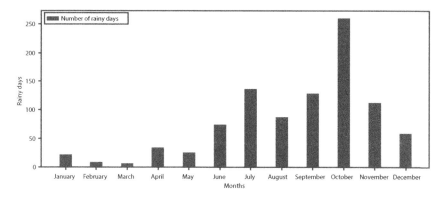

Figure 7.1 Number of rainy days in each month.

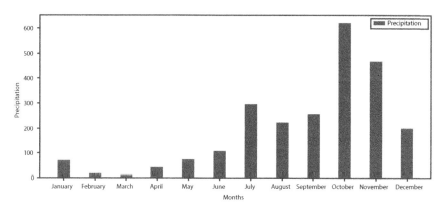

Figure 7.2 Amount of precipitation in a month.

in these months. Mid February till Mid June is considered as Summer, so the precipitation goes down.

Average temperature peaks after every two months as observed from Figure 7.3. However, the overall shape of the graph looks like August through December have less average temperatures compared to March, May and June, the summer months in the place of study. Though the rising temperature is a cause of increased vector survival, reproduction and pathogen growth and survival, the dataset did not show the expected positive trend for the same.

Coastal areas, such as Tamil Nadu, are perpetually humid. The monsoon season in the rest of India begins in July, while Tamil Nadu has rainy weather from September through December. As a result, summers last

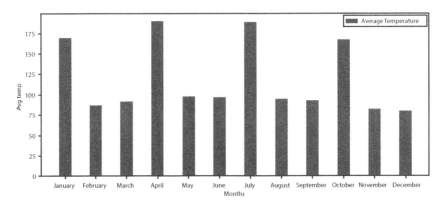

Figure 7.3 Average temperature in a month.

longer and are more humid. However, as shown in Figure 7.4, the rainy months are humid, particularly October, which has the most rainfall in a year.

The trend in the average temperature, precipitation, humidity, and number of rainy days p.a can be seen in Figures 7.2 to 7.5. It has been noted that from July through December, the values of precipitation, rainy days, and, to some extent, humidity, are more substantial than the rest of the year. A similar pattern emerges when the number of malaria cases in a year is considered (Figure 7.5). We therefore come to the conclusion that some attributes, as described, have a greater influence on the outcomes than others.

The problem statement was viewed from two different perspectives to determine the best possible results. Both classification and regression were performed with the combined dataset.

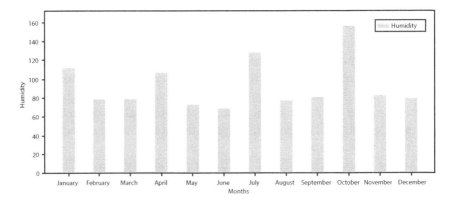

Figure 7.4 Percentage of humidity per month.

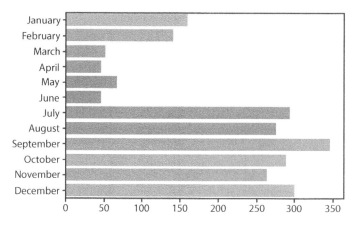

Figure 7.5 Number of malaria occurrences per month.

7.3.1   Classification Approach

The following models were built using Python's Sklearn package. The aim was to take all the climate variables, age category, gender and the number of Malaria cases to predict the mosquito type and species. Given the data, this model can output what kind of mosquito has caused the disease and with this information appropriate medication can be prescribed. The results yielded by the models can be seen in Table 7.1. Species of mosquito was considered as the class for one set of training and testing while the type of mosquito was taken as the category for classification in the next set of training and testing of the same model. The course of handling the problem was changed, results of which are tabulated in the following section. It was observed that among all the models, KNN performed the best with an accuracy of 65%.

The decision tree model is considered one of the most interpretable models, as it is visualized as a tree, making it easy to understand the factors and rules that lead to a certain prediction. The model is easily updated with new data as it becomes available, making it a useful tool for ongoing disease surveillance and prediction. The model creates a tree-like structure of decisions and their possible consequences, where each internal node represents a decision based on an input feature, and each leaf node represents the outcome or prediction.

The KNN algorithm is based on the principle that similar instances are more likely to have similar outcomes. It is used to make predictions about the incidence of malaria in a new region based on the similarity of the weather conditions and other environmental factors in that region to the conditions in the training dataset. One of the advantages of KNN is that

Table 7.1 Classifiers for the given problem statement.

Model	Class	Accuracy	Class	Accuracy
Decision tree	Species	57.7%	Mosquito	41.1%
K-nearest neighbors	Species	65%	Mosquito	47.9%
Random forest	Species	56.9%	Mosquito	45.5%
XGBoost	Species	56.9%	Mosquito	45.5%
Support vector machine	Species	56.9%	Mosquito	49.5%
Multilayer perceptron	Species	53.6%	Mosquito	48.7%
Logistic regression	Species	55.2%	Mosquito	53.6%
AdaBoost	Species	50.4%	Mosquito	45.5%

it is simple to implement and understand. It also has the ability to handle nonlinearly separable data and can work well with small datasets. However, its performance is highly dependent on the quality and size of the training dataset, and it is computationally expensive for large datasets.

The Random Forest algorithm is an extension of the decision tree algorithm, which builds multiple decision trees and combines them to make a prediction. The Random Forest algorithm works by creating a large number of decision trees, each of which is trained on a random subset of the data. The final prediction is made by averaging the predictions of all the decision trees. This approach improves the accuracy and stability of the model by reducing the variance and bias of a single decision tree. It has the ability to indicate the relative importance of each feature in the dataset, which is useful in identifying the most important factors that influence the incidence of vector-borne diseases. Additionally, Random Forest algorithms handle missing data and outliers and can work well with both small and large datasets.

XGBoost (eXtreme Gradient Boosting) is a machine learning algorithm that is commonly used for classification and regression problems. In the context of vector-borne disease prediction, it is used to analyze and classify a large dataset of historical vector-borne disease cases and related environmental factors. By identifying patterns and relationships in this data, the XGBoost model is trained to predict the likelihood of future disease outbreaks in a specific region. The algorithm is particularly useful in this context because it is able to handle large datasets with high dimensionality and has the ability to handle missing values.

Support Vector Machine uses a boundary, known as the decision boundary, to separate the data into different classes. The SVM algorithm finds the optimal decision boundary by maximizing the margin between the different classes. SVM is applied to classify the different types of vectors by using the morphological characteristics, which are obtained from images, as input features. The output of the model will be the vector species, which helps in understanding the vector-borne disease transmission.

The MLP model is trained by adjusting the weights of the connections between the neurons in the network. The input layer of the network receives data on environmental factors such as temperature, humidity, and rainfall. The output layer produces a prediction of the likelihood of a disease outbreak. The model is fine-tuned by adjusting the number of layers and neurons in the network, and by adjusting the learning rate and other parameters. The model is also used to identify areas that are at high risk of a disease outbreak, and to provide early warning of potential outbreaks. This helps public health officials to take preventative measures to reduce the spread of the disease.

Logistic regression is a statistical method used for binary classification problems, where the goal is to predict the probability of an outcome belonging to one of two classes. It is used to predict the likelihood of a specific disease outbreak based on certain input features, such as temperature, humidity, and mosquito population density. The model is used to make predictions on new data, such as current weather conditions and mosquito population density, to estimate the likelihood of an outbreak occurring. Logistic regression is extended to multi-class classification problems where the goal is to predict the probability of the disease outbreak from multiple classes.

The AdaBoost process begins by training a simple classifier on the dataset and then identifying instances that are misclassified. The algorithm then focuses on those instances and trains a new classifier, giving more weight to the misclassified instances. This process is repeated multiple times, each time adjusting the weights of the instances and training new classifiers. The final classifier is a combination of all the trained classifiers, and their weights are determined by their individual accuracy.

7.3.2   Nonlinear Regression Approach

This model was built using Python's tensorflow package. It is a sequential model with two dense layers, having 11 input attributes and 3 output attributes. The aim was to take all the climate variables and the mosquito type as input to produce a three-dimensional output. The outputs include the gender—male or female—and what age group they belong to. This model works to show how many people of each gender are affected in a particular age group, given the climatic conditions. Refer to Table 7.2 for the results obtained. This approach to the problem has given better results, with Tanh+Orthogonal giving the highest result of 85% accuracy.

The tanh (hyperbolic tangent) activation function is a mathematical function that is commonly used in artificial neural networks to introduce nonlinearity and enable the model to learn more complex relationships in the data. In vector-borne disease prediction, a neural network model with a tanh activation function in its hidden layers is used to analyze a variety of factors related to the spread of diseases, such as weather conditions, population density, and travel patterns. The model then uses this information to make predictions about the likelihood of outbreaks in different regions. The tanh function is particularly useful in this context because it maps input values to outputs between −1 and 1, which is useful for predicting probabilities.

The sigmoid activation function maps input values to output values within a specific range, typically between 0 and 1. The output of the sigmoid function is interpreted as a probability or likelihood that a given input belongs to a certain class or category. In the context of vector-borne disease prediction, the sigmoid function is used to predict the probability of a disease outbreak based on certain input variables, such as temperature, humidity, and mosquito population density. The sigmoid function is used in a logistic regression model, which is a simple and widely used statistical method for predicting the probability of an event occurring based on certain input variables.

Table 7.2 Nonlinear regression for the given problem statement.

Activation function	Kernel initialiser	Input dim	Output dim	Accuracy
Tanh	Orthogonal	11	3	85%
sigmoid	Orthogonal	11	3	82%
Tanh	GlorotUniform	11	3	78%
sigmoid	GlorotUniform	11	3	78%
softmax	Orthogonal	11	3	70%

The softmax activation function maps the output of the last layer of neurons to a probability distribution over the classes. It is particularly useful when the task is to predict the probability of multiple classes, such as in multiclass classification problems. The softmax activation function allows the model to output a probability distribution of the likelihood of each disease occurring in a certain area, providing a more nuanced prediction than a simple binary classification of "outbreak" or "no outbreak."

The GlorotUniform method, also known as Xavier Uniform, is a weight initialization technique for deep neural networks. It is used to initialize the weights of the layers in the network so that the values are randomly sampled from a uniform distribution, with the scale of the distribution determined by the number of input and output units in the layer. The purpose of this initialization method is to ensure that the variance of the activations and gradients in the network remains the same across all layers.

Orthogonal kernel initializers, on the other hand, are used to initialize the weight matrices of the convolutional layers in a neural network. The weights are initialized such that the rows of the weight matrix are orthogonal to each other. This initialization method is used to prevent the gradients from exploding or vanishing during training, as it ensures that the weight matrices have a unit norm.

Both GlorotUniform and orthogonal kernel initializers used to improve the performance of the model and prevent overfitting. The GlorotUniform method is used to initialize the weights of the layers in the neural network while the orthogonal kernel initializers is used to initialize the weight matrices of the convolutional layers.

7.4   Conclusion

More than 17% of all infectious diseases are vector-borne, and they account for more than 700,000 annual fatalities. They may be brought on by viruses, bacteria, or parasites. Malaria has caused an estimated 219 million cases globally, and results in more than 400,000 deaths every year. There is an increasing need to prevent and treat if affected by these diseases. The primary objective of this system was to minimize the people's dependency on hospitals, especially in rural areas where the availability of medical professionals is relatively low compared to cities. The dataset used contains data going back 12 years in Chengalpet and comprises monthly climate and malaria data together with mosquito genomic information from public sources. The data were examined to assess the relationship between climate and disease spread in the region. According to research, factors, including precipitation, humidity, and the number of rainy days, are more significant in determining the frequency of malaria cases. Warmer conditions will affect the mosquito parasite's growth cycle, allowing it to mature faster and increase transmission, affecting the disease burden in lower altitudes where malaria is already a concern [17]. After performing classification using the species of mosquitoes as classes and regression to determine the occurrence of malaria based on climate, the best accuracy of 85% was attained using a two-layer sequential model for nonlinear regression with activation function Tanh and Orthogonal Kernel Initializer. It was observed that classification did not perform well for this data.

References

1. https://www.severemalaria.org/countries/india-0
2. Severson, D.W. and Behura, S.K., Mosquito genomics: Progress and challenges. *Annu. Rev. Entomol.*, 57, 143–66, 2012.
3. Githeko, A.K., Lindsay, S.W., Confalonieri, U.E., Patz, J.A., Climate change and vector-borne diseases: A regional analysis. *Bull. World Health Organ.*, 78, 9, 1136–1147, 2000.
4. Rogers, D.J. and Randolph, S.E., Climate change and vector-borne diseases. *Adv. Parasitol.*, 62, 345–381, 2006.
5. Raizada, S., Mala, S., Shankar, A., Vector borne disease outbreak prediction by machine learning, in: *2020 International Conference on Smart Technologies in Computing, Electrical and Electronics (ICSTCEE)*, pp. 213–218, IEEE, 2020, October.
6. Kaur, I., Sandhu, A.K., Kumar, Y., Analyzing and minimizing the effects of vector-borne diseases using machine and deep learning techniques: A systematic review, in: *2021 Sixth International Conference on Image Information Processing (ICIIP)*, vol. 6, pp. 69–74, IEEE, 2021, November.
7. Abdur Rehman, N., Saif, U., Chunara, R., Deep landscape features for improving vector-borne disease prediction, in: *Proceedings of the IEEE/CVF Conference on Computer Vision and Pattern Recognition Workshops*, pp. 44–51, 2019.
8. Coelho, F.C., De Holanda, N.L., Coimbra, B., *Transfer learning applied to the forecast of mosquito-borne diseases*, MedRxiv, 2020.
9. Khalighifar, A., Jiménez-García, D., Campbell, L.P., Ahadji-Dabla, K.M., Aboagye-Antwi, F., Ibarra-Juárez, L.A., Peterson, A.T., Application of deep learning to community-science-based mosquito monitoring and detection of novel species. *J. Med. Entomol.*, 59, 1, 355–362, 2022.
10. Semenza, J.C. and Suk, J.E., Vector-borne diseases and climate change: A european perspective. *FEMS Microbiol. Lett.*, 365, 2, fnx244, 2018.

11. Kumar, D.S., Andimuthu, R., Rajan, R. *et al.*, Spatial trend, environmental and socioeconomic factors associated with malaria prevalence in Chennai. *Malar J.*, 13, 14, 2014. https://doi.org/10.1186/1475-2875-13-14.

12. Nkiruka, O., Prasad, R., Clement, O., Prediction of malaria incidence using climate variability and machine learning. *Inf. Med. Unlocked*, 22, 100508, 2021.

13. Baghbanzadeh, M., Kumar, D., Yavasoglu, S.I., Manning, S., Hanafi-Bojd, A.A., Ghasemzadeh, H., Sikder, I., Kumar, D., Murmu, N., Haque, U., Malaria epidemics in India: Role of climatic condition and control measures. *Sci. Total Environ.*, 712, 136368, 2020.

14. Mohapatra, P., Tripathi, N.K., Pal, I., Shrestha, S., Determining suitable machine learning classifier technique for prediction of malaria incidents attributed to climate of Odisha. *Int. J. Environ. Health Res.*, 32, 8, 1716–1732, 2022.

15. https://www.wunderground.com

16. https://www.cdc.gov/malaria/about/biology/index.html

17. Sutherst, R.W., Implications of global change and climate variability for vector-borne diseases: Generic approaches to impact assessments. *Int. J. Parasitol.*, 28, 935–945, 1998.

8

Revolutionizing Internet of Medical Things for Blockchain-Based 5G Healthcare Security and Privacy for Genomic Data

Shyam Mohan J. S.[1]*, Guddeti Theekshana[2] and Guddeti Likhit Kumar Reddy[3]

[1]Department of Computer Science Engineering, GITAM University, Bangalore, India
[2]Dept. of Computer Science and Engineering, SCSVMV, Enathur, Kanchipuram, Tamil Nadu, India
[3]Wichita State University, Wichita, Kansas, USA

Abstract

Recent developments in the Internet of things (IoT), Internet of medical things (IoMT), and blockchain technology (BCT) have created disruptions in health-care. This chapter explores and provides insights to the application of IoT, IoMT for BC-based 5G healthcare security and privacy. Leveraging IoMT and BCT to healthcare applications are beneficial due to decentralization, privacy, and security as they ensure secure access to medical data for patients and various stakeholders. Adopting IoT and BCT for 5G healthcare provides clinicians and healthcare professionals to diagnosis the patient on time. In this chapter, we have used genomics data for building individual strategies, for diagnosis and decision making by utilizing patient's genomic information. We have also explored about genomics data and its privacy and security issues in 5G healthcare using IoT and BCT and possible ways to implement them. In the last, we have provided the details of core and enabling technologies that can be used to build a strong 5G security model.

Keywords: Genomic data, healthcare, security, privacy

Corresponding author: sjayaram@gitam.edu

Amit Kumar Tyagi (ed.) Privacy Preservation of Genomic and Medical Data, (171–188) © 2024
Scrivener Publishing LLC

8.1   Introduction

The healthcare management models that rely on blockchain technology are designed to protect the sensitive data of the patients and provide better efficiency. Blockchain's decentralized architecture is capable of processing massive amounts of data and storing it in a secure manner. Blockchain is an example of a distributed ledger technology that enables healthcare organizations to improve the transparency, privacy, and traceability of their patient records [1]. It can also be used for security administration in healthcare applications. Instead of relying on third-party agencies for securing the data, BCT provides an efficient and tamper-proof handling of healthcare data. Blockchain can reduce the barriers in data sharing across healthcare providers and organizations without disrupting the communication process and avoids unauthorized access. Trust, privacy, and authenticity are the three most critical factors that healthcare organizations have to consider when sharing patient data. Blockchain-based solutions help minimize these issues by implementing trust-based security and authentication protocols. Biometric systems rely on robust security schemes to prevent unauthorized access and minimize the risk of data loss and theft. These systems are used to handle various types of attacks [2]. This paper aims to introduce blockchain technology to improve the security of medical data. A blockchain is a distributed ledger system that enables people to store and record transactions. Unlike cryptocurrencies, blockchains are not backed by any physical commodities. Through precision medicine, scientists can predict which preventive and therapeutic approaches will most effectively work for certain patients. This is possible through the use of electronic health records (EHRs). Figure 8.1 shows the typical applications of BCT.

8.1.1   Genomics Data

Genomic data is the data collected and processed by scientists related to organisms. This type of data is usually stored in large databases and needs specialized software to analyze its [3]. A comprehensive analysis of a large volume of genomic data is conducted through various steps. These include data sequencing, data analysis, and variation analysis. The goal of these processes is to find out the functions of specific genes.

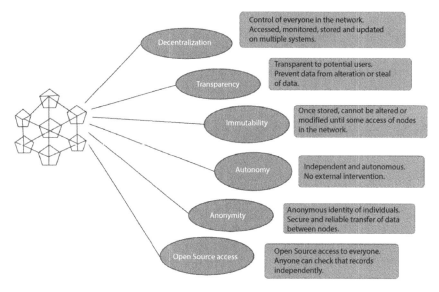

Figure 8.1 Applications of blockchain technology.

8.2   Internet of Things in Healthcare and Medical Applications (IoMT)

The Internet of Things is a broad term that refers to the various devices that can be linked to each other through wireless networks. These gadgets can communicate autonomously without requiring a human to do so. The term "Internet of things" was first used by John Ashton in a presentation about RFID. It was not main stream until 2010, when Google's Street View became widely used. Due to the emergence of distributed networks, it has become possible to create networks that are responsible for the maintenance and monitoring of smart environments. The Internet of Things is an interconnected network of various devices and systems that are used for gathering, processing, and analyzing the data. Its various components are typically linked remotely. The security of the data is a major concern for the various industries that use it [4]. Wearable devices can collect data about an individual's health status, such as their electrical consumption. This information can help track their lifestyle and provide insight into their medical condition. Kevin Ashton first introduced the concept of the Internet of Things in 1999 by incorporating sensors that can identify the presence of an embedded Internet [5]. As of 2020, around 127 million new devices are expected to be deployed with the web-based platform. The number of connected devices globally has increased significantly during the past couple of years. The evolution of the Internet of Things has greatly changed the way people communicate with each other. Its massive size and complexity have raised various concerns related to the security and privacy of the data collected by the networks.

The Internet of Things is made up of various components, such as wireless networking technology, advanced data analytics, and cloud computing. A physical device is typically linked to a central area or a remote region. The data collected by these devices is then stored in various locations. It is then processed by artificial intelligence and machine learning. A smart thermostat, for instance, uses this data to perform various actions, such as regulating the temperature. The data collected by a smart thermostat is then analyzed by a third-party app to improve its efficiency. It sends the temperature readings to an energy provider's database. The Internet of Things is a broad term that refers to the connectivity of various devices and systems that collect data. Some of its terms are: edge computing, big data analytics, machine learning, and digital twin [6].

Data is the core of IoT, and it is used to collect information about the physical world. The Internet of Things has numerous ways to collect this data. The industrial Internet of Things is often used to describe the various applications of this technology. Some of these include industrial robots, wearable devices, and medical equipment.

The proposed work aims to improve the remote monitoring of patients through the use of the Internet of medical things (IoMT). This technology can help improve the efficiency and safety of healthcare and medical applications. The increasing popularity of IoMT has led to the development of healthcare frameworks that can help lower healthcare expenses and enhance the performance of the system [7]. The next-generation 5G network will allow the frameworks to work seamlessly and provide faster connectivity. Due to the privacy and security concerns associated with 5G technology, its implementation has become a major challenge. To address these issues, we focused on the various security considerations that are necessary to ensure the immutability and privacy of the data being exchanged over the network. The goal of this study is to provide a layered model that describes the various aspects of the data storage and its transparency. The concept of recognizing the cluster head (CH) and the various steps involved in keeping the ledger updated are also discussed.

8.2.1 Benefits of IoMT

The Internet of things (IoMT) is a powerful tool that healthcare sectors can use to improve their processes and overall operations. It can also collect and store vast amounts of data that can be used to improve their offerings and services. It is also easier to IoMT than any other traditional methods.

1. As its popularity grows, more social and environmental benefits will also be realized.
2. For instance, smart cities will allow citizens to make informed decisions regarding their environment.
3. The immense amount of data that can be collected by smart cities and the Internet of Things will allow people to gain new insights into previously limited areas.

8.2.2 Adopting Blockchain Technology in Healthcare and Medical Applications—A General Scenario

Blockchain is a distributed ledger technology that enables people to transact securely in a new generation of transactions. Its creator, Satoshi Nakamoto, created it based on cryptographic algorithms. The only way to modify a block is to modify it at the same time. This method makes the data on the network immutable. Blockchain is becoming more prevalent in various industries such as healthcare, banking, and retailers. Its decentralized nature enables businesses to transact seamlessly. The healthcare industry is one of the industries that are looking to implement blockchain technology. Due to its decentralized nature, it is often considered as the most popular platform for adoption. Ethereum and Ripple have established themselves in the global finance markets. Most blockchain deployments involve public ledgers that allow anyone to participate. Despite the hype surrounding Bitcoin, blockchain still has plenty of potential. Its immutability and security are key factors that are driving the adoption of this technology in banking and insurance. American Express has been working with various blockchain-related companies such as Ripple. They also launched a blockchain for member rewards.

8.2.3 The Cryptography Behind Blockchain

The blockchain is a distributed ledger system that enables people to store and record transactions on it. Its goal is to create a trusted record of all transactions on the system. Bitcoin is the most popular example of this.

8.2.4 Hash Functions

A hash function is a type of math function that takes any number as an input. It produces a fixed output in a range of numbers. In order to be considered secure, the function has to be collision-resistant. To implement this, a hash function must meet certain security requirements. These requirements are usually met if the function has no weaknesses and outputs a large number of possible outputs [8].

8.2.5 Public Key Cryptography

Another type of cryptography used in blockchain is public key cryptography. This algorithm can be used to protect a message from its intended recipient. It can also generate a digital signature. In public key cryptography, both of the encryption keys are public. The private key is used to secure messages and generate digital signatures, while the public key is used to distribute them. The public key is usually obtained from public sources.

8.3 Limitations of Existing Technologies in Healthcare Applications

The importance of human factors in the design of healthcare apps was highlighted by the FDA in the US. In the UK, the MHRA has also started regulating some apps that are tied to medical devices. University of Nottingham researchers have been developing a wide range of apps for years, mostly for clinical studies. Some of these are designed to help people with special needs monitor their physiological signals while they're undergoing treatment. Researchers are interested in the kinds of assessments that can be performed using smartphones. These tools allow patients to collect data from various medical devices and monitor their condition more easily than using paper-based methods. Following the initial experiences of co-design, it has been revealed that there are a number of issues that need to be considered when it comes to collecting and storing personal data. One of these is the security of the data that is collected [9, 10]. The ethical considerations involved when it comes to data collection are numerous. How often should patients be asked to provide data collection? If they are suffering from an illness, how often should they be expected to self-monitor? Aside from having the necessary skills and credentials, the cognitive abilities of the users also need to be taken into account when it comes to designing an app.

This is because the people who use it often have different habits and attitudes when it comes to using technology. Since most healthcare app users do not keep their devices charged up, it could result in data loss or inconvenient. This is one of the main considerations that the authors are working on in developing a protocol for the app design.

8.4   Solving Healthcare Problems Using BCT

While the usage of blockchain in finance is still relatively new, its applications in healthcare are gaining momentum. There are various industries that are now providing blockchain-focused solutions.

8.4.1   Problems in Drug Discovery

Counterfeiting is a major issue in the pharmaceutical industry. According to the WHO, around 16% of the drugs sold globally are fake. It costs the industry around $200 billion annually. Most of the time, fake drugs are not as effective as the original versions. Also, they can be very different in terms of their chemical composition. This could be dangerous for patients.

8.4.2   Blockchain Application to Solve Problems in Drug Discovery

Security is the main characteristic that makes blockchain technology useful in drug traceability. Each transaction is time stamped and is easily verifiable. Only blockchains that are controlled by a central entity can be used to prevent fake drugs from entering the market. A company that has access to the drug blockchain would be able to prove that the drugs it produces are authentic. Each time a new batch of drugs is introduced into the market, its data is stored on the blockchain, which makes it easy to trace [11]. This eliminates the need for companies to find out about any issues regarding the batch. The use of blockchain technology in drug traceability has two main advantages. First, it allows companies to keep track of their products throughout the supply chain, which is an important component of keeping the drugs market safe.

8.4.3   Patient Data Management

One of the main issues that the healthcare industry has is the management of patient data. Due to the unique characteristics of each patient, it is very important that their records are kept up-to-date. Also, it is necessary that the right treatment is adapted to the individual. Despite the prevalence of social media platforms, doctors still use these tools to share patient data. Unfortunately, the lack of secure structure in these networks can prevent researchers from accessing the data and making legitimate discoveries.

8.4.4   Blockchain Application to Solve Patient Data Management

Healthcare organizations collect patient data from various sources, such as hospitals, laboratories, and doctors. The collected data are stored in their existing databases and can be shared with the blockchain. Smart contracts help healthcare organizations obtain and manage patient data. They can query the blockchain to find the location of the data and allow the patient to share his full medical record. For instance, a patient could share his data with a healthcare organization and a pharmaceutical company [12, 13]. The patient would then have the ability to control who he wants to see his data and how it is used. This technology also allows people to control who can access it. Through an API, the patient can set the conditions under which he or she would like to see his data. After the data is secured, the providers can access it if the patient is conscious. Regardless of how it is used, the patient still has full control over his medical records. As the Internet of things continues to develop, wearable devices will become more useful sources of information for patients. They can help track their activities and provide helpful suggestions on how to improve their health.

8.5   Proposed Model for 5G Healthcare

BCT has many advantages for the healthcare industry. One of them is its ability to reduce the cost of monitoring and managing sensitive medical data, while at the same time, providing a secure and reliable method of storing and accessing patient records [14]. Health information exchange (HIE) is a process that enables people to collect and share medical data. This method is powered by blockchain technology and can solve various problems such as keeping track of all the details of a patient [15, 16].

Electronic health records are the digital versions of data that contain a patient's medical history, lab results, and treatment plans. They are secure and available at any time. In this Paper, we will implement security using Python code. Python is an excellent language for developing blockchain projects. Python has plenty of free packages for building blockchains. Even though C++ is the main language used for building blockchains, many developers prefer to work with other languages instead.

The trust model is introduced as a means of introducing an additional level of authentication which is based on the blockchain paradigm. The concentric authentication is based on the concept of trust models in which an individual is authenticated by a central authority and the additional level of authentication introduced by the trust model is based on the concept of concentric authentication in which a user is authenticated by a central authority and then authorized for a specific task by a specific person or system. Both of the authentication models are introduced using the blockchain paradigm. This is achieved by creating a smart contract which is based on the conditional logic.

Since Python is supported by a large community of developers, it has undergone significant evolution and is now at an advanced stage. This language is more stable and secure than ever before. It allows developers to get started quickly and easily. Python is a language that is very simple to use, and it has a philosophy of being minimalistic. Its code transparency and simplicity make it an excellent choice for developing blockchain. It makes the work of building blocks with the relevant information and linking them together a much easier one to do.

8.5.1   Access Security and Data Privacy

Blockchain technology is well-equipped to address the issue of how to secure the data. Its decentralized nature and cross-verifying system make it secure and resilient. Its robust security measures prevent hackers from

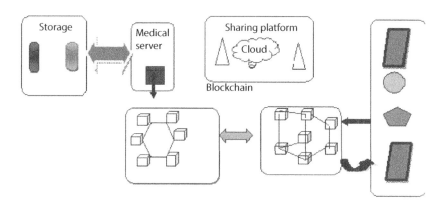

Figure 8.2 Architecture of blockchain technology.

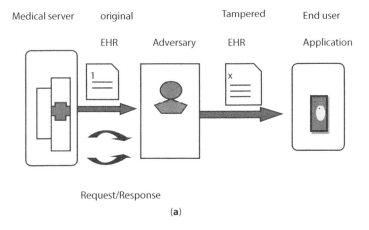

(a)

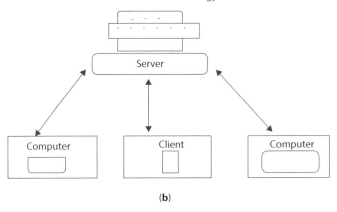

(b)

Figure 8.3 (a) Data tampering attack. (b) Server and client-based blockchain technology.

accessing the data without requiring multiple registrations. Blockchain is an encrypted technology that enables proper validation. Its unique features such as trust factor and multi-authority permissions help users gain control over their data [17, 18]. With flexible access control permissions, users would be able to set their own terms and conditions for accessing their data. This feature would allow users to modify the permissions at any given time. Its transparency provides an environment where the user can make their own decisions. After a user is granted access to their health data, a healthcare provider can make queries on the blockchain to authenticate the data refer Figures 8.2 and 8.3 for the same.

8.5.2   Algorithm

Step-1: Import these packages tkinter.
Step-2: import numpy as np.
Step-3: import matplotlib.pyplot as plt
Step-4: import pandas as Pd
Step-5: import os
Step-6: from datetime import-datetime
Step-7: import socket
Step-8: from threading import thread
Step-9: from socketserver import ThreadingMixIn
Step-10: import json
Step-11: By importing these packages we can successfully run the program and we can execute it.

8.6   Experimental Setup and Discussion

This work has been carried out in Windows 7 Operating system and Python 3.7 version. We have designed two applications namely, Privacy 5G Server and healthcare users, the first application is used to upload Genomic dataset and then encrypt and encode data to provide security and privacy and then store data in Blockchain server. After that 5G server is started that will receive genes data from healthcare application that identifies gene family and sends result back to healthcare application. The later one sends the gene data to 5G server and gets the family name from the genes.

Human genome dataset has two data columns; the first one is the sequence column that shows the DNA sequences. Blockchain is a distributed server technology that enables users to run applications on multiple servers. If a server gets attacked, then the users can access the data from other servers without getting interrupted. Data security is ensured by blockchain by using hash code for each block. Whenever a block is changed, its hash code will be changed. Each block is verified before it is stored. If a change is made in the hash code of a block, it will prevent the data from being stored correctly.

Example of test data as it appears is given below:
ATGTGTGGCATTTGGGCGCTGTTTGGCAGTGATGATTGCCTT
TCTGTTCAGTGTCTGAGTGCTATGAAGATTGCACACAGAGGTC
ATGAAGCTTGTCAACATCTGGCTGCTTCTGCTCGTGGTTTTG
CTCTGTG

ATGCTCCAGTTCCCTCACATCAGCCAGTGCGAAGAGCTG
CGGCTCAGCCTCG
ATGATTATAAGCACACCACAGAGACTAACCAGTTCAGGAAG
TGTTCTGATTGGGAGTCCATATACCCCTGCACCAGCAATGG
Example of human genome test data as it appears is given below:
Sequence class
ATGCCCCAACTAAATACTACCGTATGGCCCACCA
TAATTACCCCCATACTCCTTACACTATTCCTCATCACCCAACT
AAAAATATTAAACACAAACTACCACCTACCTCCCTCACCAAAGC
CCATAAAAATAAAAAATTATAACAAACCCTGAGAACCAAAATGA
ACGAAAATCTGTTCGCTTCATTCATTGCCCCCACAATCCTAG4

For implementation, we used Python API to store secured and encrypted Genomic data in blocks that are finally stored in a blockchain network.

8.7　Results

The results obtained are shown in Figure 8.4 - . The user clicks on *Upload DNA Genomics Dataset* button to upload dataset. Dataset *human.txt genomics file* is then uploaded.

Figure 8.5 shows setting up of path for the dataset, the dataset is loaded with a click on 'Preprocess Dataset' button to read all the dataset and then separate dataset into different families of genes.

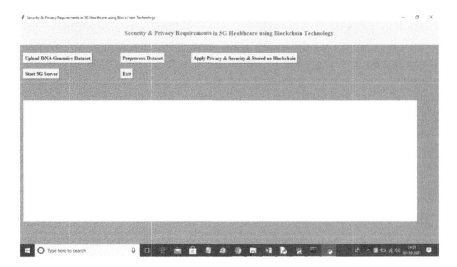

Figure 8.4　Initial screen of the proposed model.

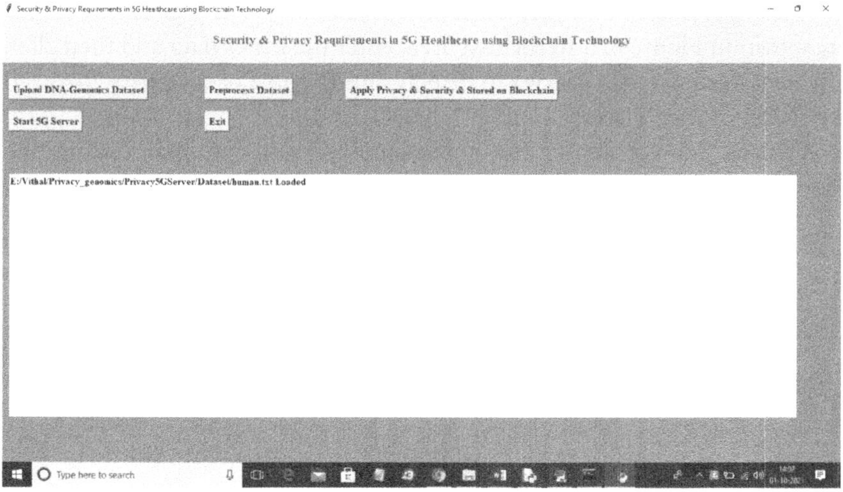

Figure 8.5 Setting up path.

Figure 8.6 shows the text highlighted text is the encrypted genomic data for first record that is block 1 in Blockchain and with each block we can see previous and current hash code.

By scrolling down the text, we can view all the records and with each record we can see the previous hash code of current record that is validated along with the current hash code of last record. This step is called Proof-of-work. Human genome data is stored on Blockchain server. The

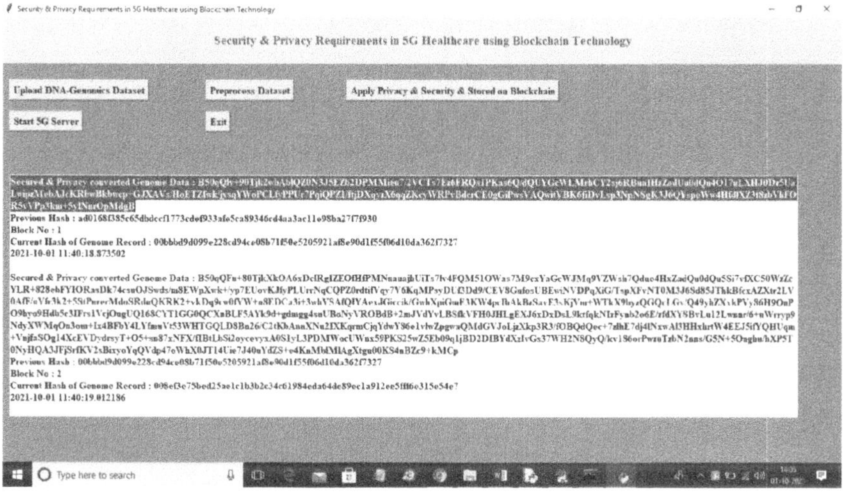

Figure 8.6 Hash code generated for human genome data.

5G Server is started and then click on 'run.bat' file from 'Healthcare Users' as shown in Figure 8.7. In the text area, enter the genes data and then click on *Send Requests to 5G Server* to display family name of the genes. This can be found in *testData.txt*.

Figures 8.8–8.9 shows the subsequent results obtained during the implementation.

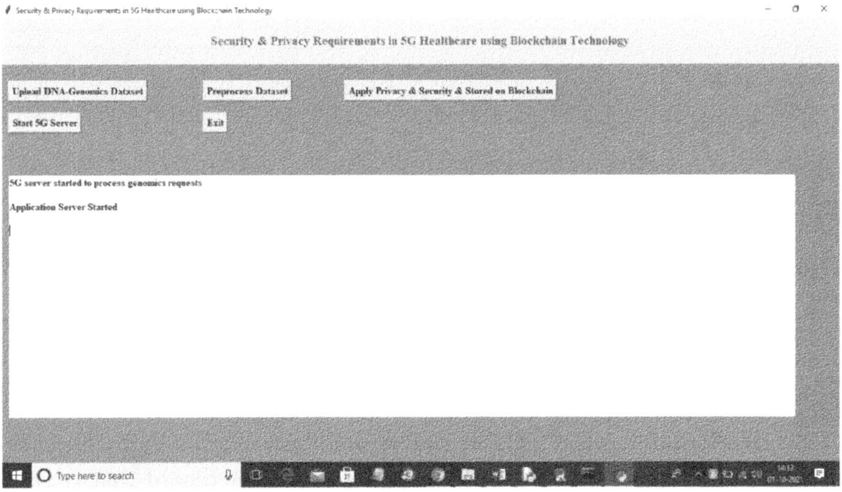

Figure 8.7 Initializing 5G server.

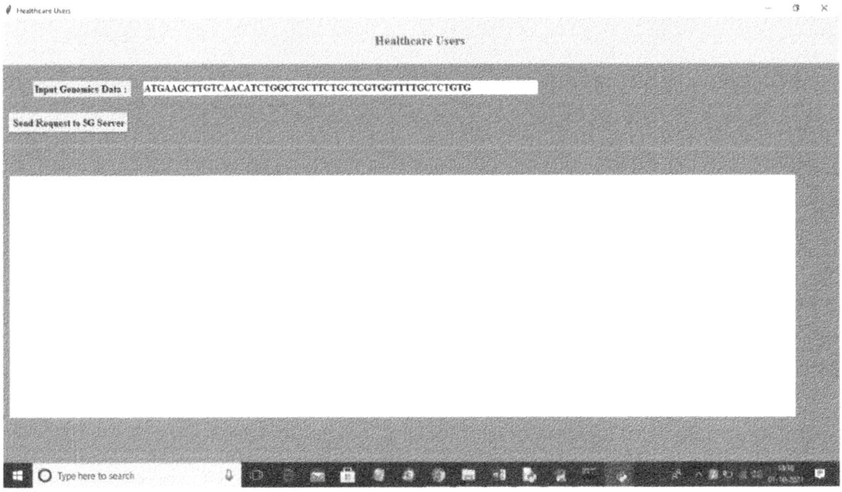

Figure 8.8 Setting up of input data.

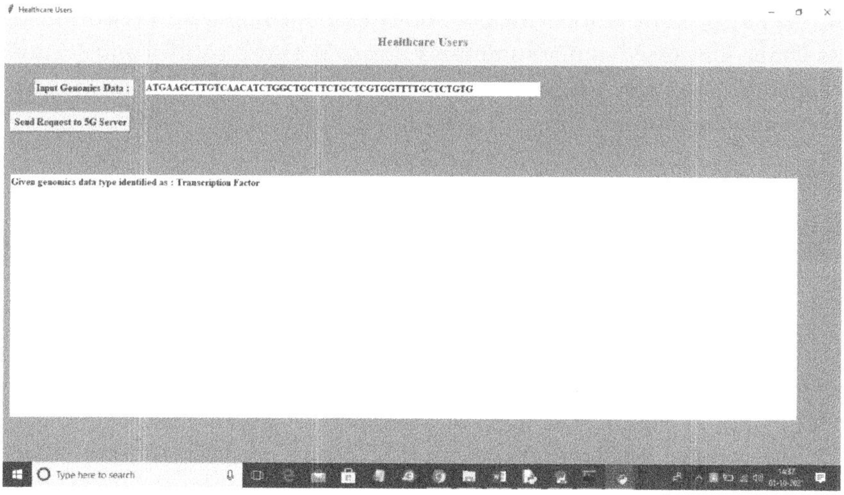

Figure 8.9 Final results.

8.8   Conclusion

The goal of this chapter is to provide a secure and encrypted way to store and protect sensitive data in healthcare facilities. It uses the blockchain paradigm to provide trust validation through an API. The goal is to provide a secure and private sharing environment for biomedical systems. The decentralized nature of the blockchain technology combined with its ability to classify sharing instances helps minimize the complexity of the authentication process The global annual health spending reached $7 trillion in 2015. By 2020, it is expected to reach over $8.734 trillion. Through blockchain technology, the healthcare industry can save a huge sum of money annually by reducing data breaches, frauds, and other expenses. According to a report by Technavio, the use of blockchain in the healthcare industry is expected to grow at a robust rate of 63.85% during the next five years, to reach a value of over $5.61 billion. The report also mentioned that the use of blockchain for data exchange will account for the largest share of the market during the forecast period. Blockchain has gone past crypto-monetary legislation and is now revolutionizing numerous sectors. The excitement extends beyond the speculation as many companies are embarking on a technology focused Blockchain to boost business requirements. Similarly, this applies to the 5G network and beyond the 5G network, since numerous experiments have been carried out to promote

Blockchain's 5G networks. The possibility that upcoming 5G networks will be widely dispersed and autonomous means network control and section challenges are more prominent and challenging than highly centralized previous generation.

References

1. Haddad, Z., Founda, M.M., Mahmoud, M., Abdallah, M., Blockchain-based authentication for 5G networks, *in: IEEE International Conference on Informatics, IoT, and Enabling Technologies (ICIoT)*, pp. 189–194, Doha, Qatar, 2020.
2. Su, Q., Zhang, R., Xue, R.,Revocable attribute-based signature for block-chain-based healthcare system, in: *IEEE Access*, vol. 8, 99. 127884–127896, 2020.
3. Chukwu, E. and Garg, L., A systemic review of blockchain in healthcare frameworks, prototypes, and implementations, in: *IEEE Access*, vol. 8, pp. 21196–21214, 2020.
4. Bhatti, A., Siyal, A.A., Mehdi, A., Shah, H., Kumar, H., Bohyo, M.A., Development of cost-effective tele-monitoring system for remote area patients, in: *IEEE Conference on Engineering and Emerging Technologies (ICEET)*, pp. 1–7, Lahore, Pakistan, 2018.
5. Hang, L., Kim, B., Kim, K., Kim, D., A permissioned blockchain-based clinical trial service platform to improve trial data transparency. *Biomed. Res. Int.*, 2021, 5554487, 2021.
6. Kubyshkin, A. and Ponomareva, D., Blockchain and genomic research legal regulation: Element in mechanism for interest's balancing, in: *SHS Web Conf.* 134, 00073, 2022.
7. *SecuringIndustry.com - applying blockchain technology to medicine traceability*, https://www.securingindustry.com/pharmaceuticals/applying-blockchain-technology-to-medicinetraceability/s40/a2766/ (accessed Dec. 29, 2021.
8. Abinaya, B. and Santhi, S., A survey on genomic data by privacy-preserving techniques perspective. *Comput. Biology Chem.*, 93, 107538, 2021. https://doi.org/10.1016/j.compbiolchem.2021.107538.
9. Piras, E.M., Cabitza, F., Lewkowicz, M., Bannon, L., Personal health records and patiet-oriented infrastructures: Building technology, shaping (new) patients and healthcare practitioners. *Comput. Support. Cooper. Work CSCW*, 28, 1001–1009, 2019.
10. Tsai, M.F., Hung, S.Y., Yu, W.J., Chen, C.C., Yen, D.C., Understanding physicians adoption of electronic medical records: Healthcare technology self-efficacy, service level and risk perspectives. *Comput. Stand. Interfaces*, 66, 103342, 2019.

11. Muthu, B.A., Sivaparthipan, C.B., Manogaran, G., Sundarasekar, R., Kadry, S., Shanthini, A., Dasel, A., IOT based wearable sensor for diseases prediction and symptom analysis in healthcare sector. *Peer Peer Netw. Appl.*, 1–12, 2020, doi: 10.1007/s12083-019-00823-2.

12. Baskar, S., Shakeel, P.M., Kumar, R., Burhanuddin, M.A., Sampath, R., A dynamic and interoperable communication framework for controlling the operations of wearable sensors in smart healthcare applications. *Comput. Commun.*, 149, 17–26, 2020.

13. Gu, D., Li, T., Wang, X., Yang, X., Yu, Z., Visualizing the intellectual structure and evolution of electronic health and telemedicine research. *Int. J. Med. Inform.*, 130, 103947, 2019.

14. Manogaran, G. and Lopez, D., A survey of big data architectures and machine learning algorithms in healthcare. *Int. J. Biomed. Eng. Technol.*, 25, 182–211, 2017.

15. Enaizan, O., Zaidan, A.A., Alwi, N.H.M., Zaidan, B.B., Alsalem, M.A., Albahri, O.S., Albahri, A.S., Electronic medical record systems: Decision support examination framework for individual, security and privacy concerns using multi-perspective analysis. *Health Technol.*, 10, 795–822, 2018.

16. Yakubu, A.M. and Chen, Y.P.P., Ensuring privacy and security of genomic data and functionalities. *Brief. Bioinform.*, 21, 2, 511–526, March 2020.

17. Bonomi, L., Huang, Y., Ohno-Machado, L., Privacy challenges and research opportunities for genomic data sharing. *Nat. Genet.*, 52, 7, 646–654, 2020. 29 June 2020.

9

Preserve Privacy-HD: A Privacy-Preserving Distributed Framework for Health Data

Aswathy Ravikumar and Harini Sriraman*

School of Computer Science and Engineering, Vellore Institute of Technology, Chennai, India

Abstract

A distributed software framework called Preserve Privacy-HD trains deep neural network models in numerous decentralized edge systems. Every edge system will have a data-parallel model and provide the model with incoming input. In each edge device, the model is run concurrently. They will send an asynchronous message to the multi-parameter server including the local weights computed by each edge device. The model is updated by the multi-parameter server, which determines the global weights based on the local weights. The edge device then downloads the model for additional processing. Healthcare data are not shared with other devices, thanks to Preserve Privacy-HD. Instead, only the weights are shared to adjust the model. The suggested framework's metrics for accuracy, training duration, and privacy have all been confirmed. Maintaining the original client data on local systems protects their privacy while leveraging the server in subsequent layers and using all information from each system during training increases learning performance.

Keywords: Privacy, distributed deep learning, digital health, edge computing, federated learning

9.1 Introduction

In several real-world applications, such as medical image analysis [1, 2], active identification [3], face recognition [4–6], it has been proved that

---

Corresponding author: harini.s@vit.ac.in

Amit Kumar Tyagi (ed.) Privacy Preservation of Genomic and Medical Data, (189–212) © 2024 Scrivener Publishing LLC

machine learning produces astounding outcomes. Typically, a single person runs DL algorithms using training data. DL models trained with more data are usually more reliable. In smart healthcare, one hospital collects minimal data, but multiple corporations gather enormous and diversified data. Thus, data users want to create DL models utilizing dispersed data from multiple data owners, forcing academics to run DL distribution, whereas if data user protocols do not effectively address data owners' security concerns, data providers will be unwilling to engage in distributed deep learning.

As the world becomes more digital, there is a rise in electronic data. It is essential to study the socioeconomic developments of society's members. Privacy issues are significant when data sharing is considered. For example, medical data may include sensitive information, since it may contain details about individuals' ailments. Before making these data accessible for data mining, it is necessary to ensure its privacy. In medical contexts, it is crucial to protect the mining model with adequate privacy; otherwise, erroneous and inappropriate predictions would result. Personal information that may otherwise be deemed unethical must not be exposed. Whenever data mining is conducted on aggregate findings, privacy may be defined as the protection of unintended publication of information. Privacy must be considered at all levels throughout mining operations.

Distributed evaluation of services is a key challenge in distributed computing, and monitoring inquiries make up a substantial fraction of the operations carried out across distributed networks. streams. In certain instances, these inquiries might be as simple as comparing the total of a dispersed collection of variables to a preset threshold or detecting frequently occurring elements in a collection of dispersed streams. In other instances, the inquiries demand non-linear systems that need more complex calculations to score functions monitoring the sum of square errors in feature selection or relative to a baseline to detect unusual activity. While monitoring algorithms allows or enhances applications, such as fraud detection, early illness identification is made possible by monitoring algorithms. They respond rapidly to epidemics and security-related situations need access to vast volumes of information, which is often personal. As the collection of such data becomes more convenient and cheaper, there is an increasing understanding of the privacy implications and risks. For instance, an examination of the privacy implications of collaborative recommender systems revealed that even aggregative algorithms that analyze vast quantities of data might compromise privacy, leaking confidential information on specific people. Such paintings highlight the significance of formal and verifiable privacy protections in algorithm design. Differential privacy demands that the probability distribution have a certain shape only slightly impacted by the results of the calculation of each incoming record. In differential privacy, each piece of information is shielded. The sharing of information about persons incurs an expense in terms of privacy. Any new information exchange incurs expenses and accumulates. To prevent privacy breaches, information flow is restricted and should be terminated once the expense accumulates beyond a certain limit (a privacy budget). Theoretical infeasibility findings indicate that these limitations are inherent in information processing safeguarding privacy. Nonetheless, the lifespan of a stream monitoring system may be significantly increased without breaching privacy restrictions. Moreover, even systems where usefulness overcomes privacy (when the system is utilitarian) should continue running regardless of any violations of privacy), privacy issues and possible damage might be mitigated using monitoring algorithms that include privacy protection procedures economically.

Lack of trust, data sharing restrictions, such as HIPAA [7], and restricted patient permission significantly hamper health collaboration. Cooperative training of distributed deep learning models without sharing data is preferred in situations where different organizations hold different modalities of patient information in the form of electronic health records, picture annotating and communication systems for diagnostic imaging as well as other imaging information, pathology lab tests, or other sensitive information, such as genetic markers for disease. Deep learning approaches have found widespread applications in biology, clinical medicine, genetics, and public health. To avoid unwanted inspection by other entities, it is necessary to train distributed deep learning models to avoid exchanging model topologies and parameters, as well as raw data. Take the use case of building a deep learning model for diagnostic testing via cooperation between two entities storing pathology testing results or radiological data, respectively, as a specific example in the field of medicine. Due to these considerations, these organizations cannot exchange their original data with one another. However, the diagnostic accuracy of the distributed deep learning model is strongly dependent on its ability to use training data from both institutions.

Emerging technologies in fields, such as medicine, healthcare, and economics, might benefit from distributed deep-learning techniques that enable several organizations to build a deeper neural network without the need for data exchange or resource consolidation in a single location. Specifically, we are focused on distributed deep learning algorithms that bridge the gap between dispersed medical sources and a strong central computing capacity, with the restriction that local sources of data of clients cannot be shared with the server or even other clients.

In this research, we investigate how distributed machine deep learning from federated medical data sources that protect privacy might aid in healthcare governance.

9.1.1   Motivation

By proposing data-sharing protocols and guidelines that aim to harmonize regulatory regimes and research oversight, certain studies have attempted to enhance and safeguard data-sharing procedures to motivate linked researchers, as well as institutions to share their data openly and embrace transparency. Despite efforts to make data sharing universal, societal issues over data sharing remain pertinent. Due to restricted data storage facilities and manpower, large clinical investigations are equally hampered in their capacity to collect data. To conduct new studies retrospectively, it is required to contact all cooperating institutions once again, which is time-consuming and impedes scientific progress. In addition, medical institutions prefer not to trade patient information to protect patient confidentiality. Obtaining the confidence and trust of patients with different degrees of sensitivity regarding the use of their private information is essential.

Privacy problems, implemented modifications, and model outputs are covered by distributed learning network confidentiality. Data confidentiality is accomplished via anonymization and prohibiting information from leaving medical facilities. Cryptography, differential security, and weight leaking prevention may secure the distributed learning model. Multiparty calculations and communications are protected by these cryptographic approaches. To preserve the model's outputs, online users must be able to utilize it locally or in a secure environment to learn from personal data. Not all deep learning technique creators are users. Thus, documentation and automated information eligibility requirements are beneficial: eligibility checks verify that the correct input data are provided before starting the model.

9.1.2   Medical Data and Interoperatability

Data are an asset, especially now when cloud technology, big data, and ML are combined. This unprecedented period of technology convergence presents formidable obstacles to data privacy and protection. Even more, the danger exists for Electronic Medical data, following a recent analysis, the number of medical records disclosed each year has been on the rise. More than one data breach in the healthcare industry occurs every day. Privacy legislation, like the HIPAA in the USA or the GDPR in Europe, necessitates information to be kept and shared in a safe and confidential manner and may impose serious punishments for healthcare data breaches to enhance medical data leadership.

Privacy is closely connected to security but has its focus, including ensuring that private details are lawfully obtained, utilized, and safeguarded. The confidentiality and security of health data must be safeguarded not just from potential hackers but also from unwanted access inside the network or the system. Consequently, new approaches, structures, or computer paradigms may be required to solve security and privacy issues in the field of medical data exchange.

Privacy is closely related to security, but has distinct objectives, such as ensuring that private information is legitimately collected, employed, and protected.

The privacy and safety of health information must be protected not just from prospective hackers but also from unauthorized network or system access. Therefore, new methodologies, structures, or computing paradigms may be necessary to handle security and privacy challenges in the area of medical data exchange, such as non-repudiation, anonymity, and unlikability. Each of the abovementioned needs is discussed briefly in the context of digital health systems below.

(a) Integrity—ensuring that health data acquired by a system or transmitted to an organization is an accurate representation of the regarding appropriate and has not been altered

(b) Confidentiality—ensuring that the health information of patients is never divulged to unauthorized parties.

(c) Authentication—verifies that the entity seeking access is legitimate. In healthcare systems, it is necessary to verify both the information supplied by healthcare professionals and the identity of the organizations utilizing such information.

(d) Accountability—the duty to be accountable considering the agreed-upon standards. Patients or organizations designated by patients should oversee the use of personal patient data at hospitals, pharmacies, insurance companies, etc.

(e) Audit—ensuring that all healthcare data are protected and that all data access operations in the e-Health clouds are tracked.

(f) Non-Repudiation—repudiate threats include users who reject after taking an action with the data. Inside the healthcare context, neither patients nor physicians can refute misappropriation of health information.

(g) Anonymity—refers to the condition in which a person cannot be recognized. When patients save their health information in the cloud, for instance, their identities may be anonymized so that cloud servers cannot determine their identities.

(h) Unlinkability—refers to the various uses of resources or objects of interest by a user without ability of other users or subjects to interlink these uses. Furthermore, the information received from diverse flows of health data should not be sufficient for unauthorized actors to establish likability.

9.2 Organization of Chapter

The rest of the chapter is outlined as follow. Section 9.3 shows about related work, section 9.4 shows about proposed methodology, section 9.5 shows complexity analysis, finally section 9.6 concludes this chapter.

9.3 Related Work

Achieving effective, economical, and privately distributed deep learning is difficult. There are few privacy-preserving distributed deep learning approaches [7–9]. Papernot *et al.* [10] proposed PATE, a model of confidentiality machine learning, where each user is given access to a trainer model using its own (local) personal set of data, in addition to the user aims to fully understand a student technique that employs the unlabeled publicly available data to imitate this same result of an ensemble of a teacher model, i.e., the students learn to create forecasts that are the same as the most accurate teacher model. PATE needs a trustworthy aggregator to offer a privacy-preserving query interface, through which a data user may query the ensembles of a teacher model using unlabeled publicly accessible data to collect the tags for the learning of the student model. However, in most of all distributed deep learning cases in the real world, a perfectly trustworthy aggregator is relatively unusual. Some works mix MPC, DP, and secret sharing. Because the MPC approach is implemented through a corrupted circuit whose size is dependent upon the number of parameters of the neural network, it tends to be more effective & non-scalable when training bigger neural network models. Secret sharing requires two honest, non-colluding data consumers, which may not be achievable. Differentially Private Stochastic Gradient Descent [11, 12] develops centralized deep neural networks with differential privacy. It utilizes the Gaussian process for a random selection of data to create a noisy slope for model optimization. This method's source code is not accessible to the public.

Differentially Private Federated Learning [11] discreetly optimizes federations. In place of merely averaging the scattered client model updates, an alternate technique incorporating random sampling as well as a Gaussian mechanism on the sum of client updates is offered. The curator accumulates disruptive modifications to optimize the model of the central server. Since the original study attempts to ensure client-level privacy but not sample-level privacy, DP-FL is examined using the author's published code with simple changes to offer sample-level privacy protection. Local Differential Privacy [13] eliminates the centralized differential privacy's authorized administrator. LDP offers the information owner greater actual control over the information others have. LDP for statistical data collection and estimation has been studied for decades [14–16]. Bayesian inference [17], frequent item mining [17], and probability density estimates [18] employ DP and LDP. Few recent studies use LDP for deep learning. Centralized scenario, Abadi *et al.* [19] suggest training a deep network using stochastic gradient descent and differential privacy. The detailed summary of related works is given in Table 9.1.

9.4   Proposed Methodology

This research aims to provide a platform for distributed deep learning that protects user privacy in the medical data processing. The de facto benchmark for deep learning that protects privacy is [25], which operates as follows. Initially, distributed platforms get the training model from a centralized server and then train it using their data locally. The revised model parameters/weights are then aggregated towards the server. Each device continues to download the model from the server. While this method aids in preventing privacy leaks by preventing the exchange of raw and original information, it requires a vast bandwidth utilization to communicate models and attributes and execute computation on every platform.

Table 9.1 Existing works.

Data	Target disease	Methods	Tools	Result	Reference
5 locations with 287CT and RT lung cancer data	dyspnea	Bayesian network + Distributed learning The master node communicates only the weights	Varian learning	Area under the curve 0.61	[20]
5 locations with 268 patients	dyspnea grade ≥ 2.	Direction Method of Multipliers + SVM	Varian learning	Area under the curve 0.62	[21]
258 patients with schizophrenia and 222 patients without schizophrenia data from 4 locations	schizophrenia	SVM + Multi-sample models	VBM8 toolbox MATLAB ML tools	NA	[22]
698 patients with lung cancer, from two locations	NSCLC 2-year survival after radiation therapy	Distributed learning + Bayesian network	Varian learning portal	Area under the curve 0.662	[23]
Heart data from 10 locations in for 5 years	Cardiac arrest	SVM + cPDS algorithm	NA	Area under the curve 0.56	[24]
227 data from 6 locations	thyroid cancer	Inferential regression analysis + Learning Analyzer Proxy	COBRA	NA	[25]

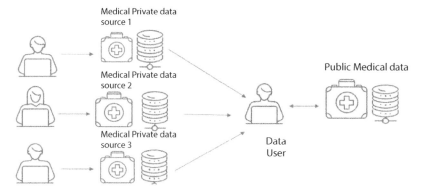

Figure 9.1 Problem in medical data sharing.

Furthermore, this issue gets more pronounced as the model goes deeper and bigger, which is inevitable in medical applications of deep learning for highly accurate patient diagnosis. Figure 9.1 shows the problems faced in medical data sharing for which we need a distributed framework.

Privacy-preserving: The problem is one of achieving a balance between the privacy of digital medical records and research data access. This problem is projected to grow more acute because of future changes in healthcare, including increasing costs, an older population, personalized medicine, global healthcare, and the rise of noncommunicable illnesses. However, new advancements in legislation, such as the General Data Protection Regulation (GDPR) of the European Union, tend to retain the old approach that appears to prioritize individuality over cooperation. In the new law, individualism is reinforced. In respect to the ongoing uncertainty of the legal environment for research including the use and reuse of huge data sets and the linkage of data sets, the GDPR lacks clarity in re-identification of persons. Part of the difficulty is evident for the GDPR: when data, when combined with other data, can identify an individual, then those data are personal information and are regulated. The dilemma is whether this is unconditional (any option, irrespective matter how distant) or if there is a criterion for reasonableness. It is evident from this review of legal issues that their impediments to data acquisition in big data, deep learning, contexts, and approaches. The Privacy preserving issue addressed in the medical data is shown in Figure 9.1.

Distributed federated learning: Brendan McMahan introduced federated learning in 2016 [26]. Local data are used to acquire and integrate the present paradigm. Integrating the locally trained model creates a single federated and updated global model for devices [27]. FL lets ML access many data sets. This method lets many organizations work on a model without sharing sensitive information. Shared models were trained on a broad range of data across numerous rounds. FL favors ML without data centralization. The model was trained in many domains. FL trains algorithms on linked devices or systems using non-shared local training data sets. The server handles the following training steps: Applying the training algorithm, Combining device-related learning outcomes. Modelling framework modification, notifying devices of global model-based augmentation and preparing for training.

FL is a new learning system that improves agent learning without revealing sensitive data, patterns, or learning objectives. To construct a new ML application, the FL model is being built together with system components and on-site examination. It hides activities and saves sensitive data in electronic gadgets. Local machine intelligence training minimizes data transmission. Learned and shared models aggregate and transmit user data on a distant database. Before analyzing, this research compares ML deployment topologies. FL allows agents to use and learn from each other without a global model, unlike FL, which normally needs an intermediary controller to coordinate practice and learning sessions. FL delivers data security and privacy. Importing, viewing, and sharing location data was impossible. The position-split database is hard to retrieve [28]. FL shares just ML variables. Key cryptography may boost security. Encoding these concerns before exchanging them across learning cycles allows correct computations without disclosing encrypted data. In addition to these considerations, these variables may give information about tiny data samples by querying databases. Decoupling privacy and robust integration may address the spatial performance assumption [29]. Successful assessment as a privacy risk in federated learning limits DL model implementation [30, 31].

FL prioritizes privacy. Privacy splitting and K-Order confidentially are different [32]. Federated learning protects user privacy by communicating protected restrictions [33]. FL assurance and GDPR issues would not affect data privacy during hardware. FL might be horizontal, basic, or approach-based for data dissemination [34]. The authors may use the switch to solve data or ID gaps when the two databases' user and device attributes coincide. FL research multi-device distribution and distributed systems [35]. Distributed publishing models, information, and ML affect distributed ML.

Proposed solution: For data-parallel computing of neural networks, the proposed framework is designed with two primary purposes in mind: scalability and a framework for privacy preservation. Deep learning experts often face two scaling issues while training models: scaling network size and expanding training data. Even though model size and complexity might enhance precision, there is a limitation to the amount that a single system can accept. Increasing model size may also increase computations and training times. Since training requires loading all training data into memory, not all algorithms scale training data equally effectively. They only scale vertically and to ever bigger instance types. Scaling training data typically results in longer training durations. Smaller models can be trained with a limited amount of data, but as larger models have been built, the need for information processing has outpaced the equipment's computational capabilities. Later, it became more rational to distribute the work of deep learning over several computers rather than a centralized system. The volume of data has reached a point where it cannot be transferred or centralized. Even in large businesses where data processing is so extensive that the necessary data are stored in a separate location, centralized solutions are unsuitable. Utilizing a cluster, distributed deep learning speeds the training of neural networks. Parallel training accelerates the fine-tuning of hyper-parameters in a network by examining many configurations concurrently. Mini-batch stochastic gradient descent is the most used training method for neural networks. Mini-batch SGD [35] has several advantages. In the first place, its iterative design minimizes training time according to the quantity of data. Second, in a specific mini-batch, the model processes each record's cross-communication independently beyond the final gradients' mean. Mini-batch processing lends itself nicely to parallelization and distribution. The most prevalent deep learning distribution method is data parallel distributed learning, which parallelizes SGD by distributing mini-data batches over many processing units. Data parallel training is an efficient distribution strategy for increasing the mini-batch size and accelerating the processing of each mini-batch. Nonetheless, data-parallel training adds the complexity of calculating the mini-batch gradients average with gradient emanating from all workers and interacting with all employees. The secure means of weight sharing among the nodes during parallel SGD is shown in Figure 9.2. Message Passing Interface may be used for efficient communication between nodes and represents a growing overhead as the training cluster is enlarged, which may also drastically decrease training time if not improperly built or operated on unsuitable hardware. Another key aim is to provide a user-friendly evaluation of things for distributed data-parallel deep learning that is readily deployable on AWS Sage maker in Python and MPI that can speed training.

The Message Passing Interface is a modular and standardized message-passing platform intended for both distributed and parallel computation. MPI offers parallel hardware providers with a well-defined, easily implementable basic set of functions. Therefore, hardware providers may use

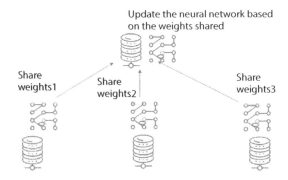

Figure 9.2 Secure weight sharing.

this set of standard low-level procedures to develop higher-level strategies for the distributed-memory communications provided with their parallel computers. Accessibility and efficiency are the benefits of MPI above other message-passing frameworks. It was built for almost any distributed memory design, and each implementation is optimized for the hardware it operates on. A crucial element in the MPI programming paradigm is the communicators, which identify processes that may interact with one another. As a unique identifier, each process inside a communicator is ranked. MPI Send and MPI Recv are the fundamental point-to-point interfaces of MPI. A send operator allows a process to transmit data to another unit (specified by its rank).

Similarly, a process may receive data from a particular process using the recv operator. In addition to conventional point-to-point operators, several MPI implementations include a variety of collective operators enabling distributed communication. Collective operators require interaction amongst all processes within a group of communicators. MPI Bcast, MPI Allreduce, MPI Reduce, etc., are standard collective operators. OpenMPI collaborates academia, research, and industrial partners for open-source MPI implementations. Open MPI integrates technology and assets from several different projects. mpi4py offers MPI standard bindings for the Python language, enabling any Python application to use multiple processors.

MPI is a major independent library used for congruence between explicit distributed framework methods. The basic version of MPI was presented in 1994. Later, a lot of adjustments were made. Alterations were made to give new functionality in various versions. In the recent past, several obstacles, including environmental The MPI 3.0 version addressed architecture, message passing in heterogeneous cluster systems, blocking/nonblocking data distribution and reception. Although the initial development of MPI did not take Exascale into account, its steady improvement has made it a viable option for growing HPC systems. Exascale computing systems need several issues, including low power-consuming mechanisms for message forwarding across heterogeneous cores, synchronized handling in non-blocking schemes, and memory management techniques.

Most enterprises want an "ideal" machine learning platform that can assist them in navigating all phases of the ML lifecycle, including creating, training, and deploying. Due to its adaptability and scalability, AWS SageMaker comes close to becoming the ideal platform, despite our belief that there is no such thing. SageMaker provides various compute instances with varying quantities of CPU Processors and GPU processors with different RAMs. Depending on the application's requirements, one may choose a computing instance. There is no need to manage security groups or IP addresses for these instances. SageMaker includes Amazon's repositories, including high-performing techniques, which may be used to train the model utilizing Amazon's pre-trained models. Both of the algorithms and models are substantially tuned for AWS service execution. SageMaker allows the model to be hosted on an endpoint and afterward called from any standard programming language. AWS also provides access to a network of data analysts, software engineers, ML researchers, and industry professionals with extensive expertise in machine learning. SageMaker provides sophisticated hyperparameter tuning options for several models. One may schedule a tuning task anytime you would like, and SageMaker will display the optimal hyperparameter depending on this. AWS SageMaker's price structure is one of the most significant benefits. Due to the necessity to install, execute the code, and afterward shut down the machine, the cost of utilizing such platforms is often remarkably high.

In contrast, SageMaker allows you to utilize a computer instance for much less than a minute, invoiced at a few dollars an hour, and you will still be paid for the seconds used. You may use this dynamic pricing by employing a low-cost instance to host your laptop and a powerful GPU to train it. SageMaker provides a diversity of computing instances you can pick depending on your needs and budget. In addition, you are not required to pay for unused resources using SageMaker. For data scientists, AWS SageMaker offers Jupyter notebooks. The data analyst community widely values this benefit since they can utilize Jupyter notebooks for the complete machine learning (ML) lifecycle, including creating, training, and deploying. Utilizing Pandas & Mllib, R & ggplot2, etc., data scientists may analyze, clean, and convert data into any desired format using these notebooks. The detailed scheme of the proposed model with the experimental setup in the AWS node with the neural network structure is shown in Figure 9.3.

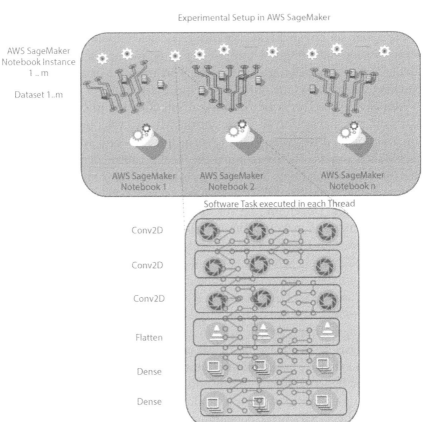

Figure 9.3 Proposed model.

Algorithm 1:

Input: Data Set, Model (CNN Model)
Output: Synchronised model output with the updated parameters and prediction made
D2N2 ACCEL ()
{
If master node:
{
Exec()
}
Else if worker node:
    {
Data split()

```
Exec()
}
      Exex():
{
Weight initialization
Model building
Model compile
Modelfit()
}

Model fit()
      {
      Gather weights layer-wise for each epoch
      Reduce weights
      Broadcast weights to nodes
}
}
```

In distributed training, there is a group of employees, and each performs training. But we could give each employee a distinct function so that some serve as parameter servers and the remainder as training workers. The server that saves model parameters centrally is known as a Parameter Server. It is often implemented as a key-value store, but various implementations are possible. When there are hundreds and thousands of parameters or many workers within the cluster, a single PS node may not be enough due to network bandwidth constraints between the workers and the PS. Parameter server model structure is shown in Figure 9.4. For a substantial

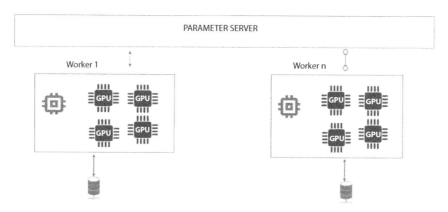

Figure 9.4 Parameter server logic.

number of parameters, parameters may be load balanced among numerous server nodes, with each parameter server storing a subset of parameters. The term for this is sharded key-value store. Server nodes interact with one another to duplicate and transfer scaling and reliability characteristics. A server manager controls the consistency of all server nodes. The parameter servers oversee storing the model's parameters and maintaining the model's global state. Whereas the training workers execute the real training cycle and generate gradients and loss from the data provided, the training workers conduct the training loop. The procedure may be summed up as follows: replicate the model across all our employees, with each worker using a portion of data for training purposes. Each worker in training retrieves parameters from parameter servers. Each training worker executes a training cycle and transmits the gradients to all parameter servers, which subsequently updates the model's parameters.

The PS model consists of the four phases outlined below and is shown in Figure 9.5:

1. All workers get the model weights from the centralized parameter server.
2. Every worker node trains its local model using its local training data partition and produces local gradients. Then, each slaver uploads its local gradient to the centralized PS.
3. Aggregate Gradients: Following collecting all gradients supplied by the worker node, the PS will total all gradients

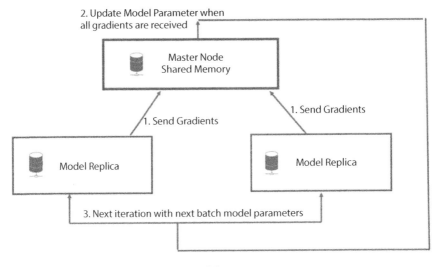

Figure 9.5 Synchronous data parallel model.

4. And once aggregated gradient has been computed, the parameter server utilizes them to update the model's parameters on this centralized server.

A distributed training technique in which a data set is partitioned among several processing nodes, and each processing node holds a copy of the network. Each node gets a unique batch of the data set, does a forward and backward pass, and exchanges weight adjustments with other nodes for synchronization before moving on to the following collection and, eventually, the next epoch. Data parallelism occurs when the same model is used for each thread but is fed distinct data portions. In neural nets, this implies that data parallelism employs the same weights but separate mini-batches on each line; gradients must be synchronized or averaged after each run through a mini-batch. There is no communication during the forward pass, and gradients are synchronized throughout the reverse pass. The most problematic aspect of this method is that, during the backward pass, the entire gradient must be sent to all other nodes. There are two data parallelism configurations: parameter server and All reduce.

Data parallel model mathematical explanation using the stochastic gradient descent (SGD):

$$
\frac{\partial Loss}{\partial w} = \frac{\partial[\frac{1}{n}\sum_{i=1}^{n} f(xi, yi)]}{\partial w}
$$

$$
= \frac{1}{n}\sum_{i=1}^{n}\frac{\partial f(xi, yi)}{\partial w}
$$

$$
= \frac{p1}{n}\frac{\partial\left[\frac{1}{p1}\sum_{i=1}^{p1} f(xi, yi)\right]}{\partial w} + \frac{p2}{n}\frac{\partial\left[\frac{1}{p2}\sum_{i=1}^{p2} f(xi, yi)\right]}{\partial w}
$$

$$
+ \ldots + \frac{pk}{n}\frac{\partial\left[\frac{1}{pk}\sum_{i=1}^{pk} f(xi, yi)\right]}{\partial w}
$$

$$
= \frac{p1}{n}\frac{\partial l1}{\partial w} + \frac{p2}{n}\frac{\partial l2}{\partial w} + \ldots + \frac{pk}{n}\frac{\partial lk}{\partial w} \tag{9.1}
$$

w is the model parameters, x and y the features of a particular data point, f(xi,yi) represents the loss calculated at a particular data point i in the forward pass of the network, n represents the total data points in the data set, k represents the number of nodes, pk represents the number of data points assigned to node k,

$$\frac{\partial Loss}{\partial w} = \frac{1}{k}\left[\frac{\partial l1}{\partial w} + \frac{\partial l2}{\partial w} + \ldots + \frac{\partial lk}{\partial w}\right] \qquad (9.2)$$

Using the same settings for each node's forward propagation, transmit a small sample of distinct data to every node, calculate the gradient conventionally, and return the gradients to a root node. This stage is asynchronous since the speeds of the individual nodes vary somewhat. Once we get all of the gradients perform synchronization, compute the mean of the gradients and utilize that value to update the parameters. Then, repeat the same steps for the subsequent iteration.

9.5   Complexity Analysis

To develop a neural net model to identify input photos, five key stages are required: (1) modify and reformat the photos to suit a multidimensional matrix. the artificial neural algorithm necessity; (2) completely at the random sample and dividing the picture information into two uneven portion parts, the schooling and the verifying data sets; (3) design a sequence of procedures to extract the crucial aspects from the image data sets; (4) ascertain an optimizing automated system and set the parameters correspondingly; and (5) applying this same model on the validation data set to determine if the accuracy and loss meet the objective. In addition to the volume and dimensions of the pictures, the neural network model structure in terms of layer design and their related parameters significantly adds to the exhaustion of computational resources, hence significantly extending the entire processing time.

The neural network classification of images is an experimental and iterative process in which the model architecture is continuously improved, and the parameters are fine-tuned to approximate the predicted outcome. Undoubtedly, the quality (major feature extraction) of the pictures will impact the classification accuracy; thus, identifying and excluding low-quality photos from the classification process will minimize training time and improve the model's accuracy. Time complexity is an assessment of the result versus the time required to apply a certain model configuration.

In general, remember that matrices are used to accomplish back-propagation while training an MLP. The complexity of mathematical operations in terms of

The temporal complexity of **Mij Mjk** multiplications is only **O(*ij*)**

Note that we are using the simplest multiplying method here; alternative techniques with slightly great experience complexity exist.

Feedforward pass method: Following is indeed the feedforward propagation method.

Firstly, to move from layer i to j, perform equation 9.3.

$$Sj = Wji * Zi \tag{9.3}$$

After this proceed with activation as given in equation 9.4

$$Zj = f(Sj) \tag{9.4}$$

If there are N layers, such as the input and output layers, it will be executed N-1 times.

For the analysis let us consider an instance and calculate the time complexity of the forward move method for just an MLP with four layers, where i represent the number of input nodes, j is the number of nodes inside the second layer, k represents the number of nodes inside the third layer, and l represents the number of nodes inside the output layer.

Because there are four levels, three matrices are required to express the weights between such layers. Let us refer to them as Wji, Wkj, and Wlk, where Wji is a matrix consisting of j rows and I columns.

Suppose you have instances of t training. We must first propagate from layer I to layer j using equation 9.5

$$Sjt = Wji * Zit \tag{9.5}$$

matrix multiplication has the temporal complexity of O(jit). Therefore, the activating function is applied as shown in equation 9.6.

$$Zjt = f(Sjt) \tag{9.6}$$

This has temporal complexity of O(jt) since it is an element-by-element operation.

Perform equation 9.7

$$O(j * i * t + j * t) = O(j * t * (i + 1)) = O(j * i * t) \qquad (9.7)$$

In the same way, derive is derived for jk and is derived for kl.

The overall temporal complexity of feedforward propagation calculated using equation 9.8

$$O(j * i * t + k * j * t + l * k * t) = O(t * (ij + jk + kl)) \qquad (9.8)$$

Back-propagation Pass

The algorithm for back-propagation operates as follows. We calculate the error signal, Elt, a matrix comprising the error signals of all nodes at the hidden layer, beginning with the output layer lk using equation 9.9.

$$Elt = f(Slt) \odot (Zlt - Olt) \qquad (9.9)$$

for element-wise multiplication

Now consider that Elt contains l rows and t columns, which indicates that each column in Elt represents the error signal for learning example t.

Proceed for delta weight calculation using equation 9.10.

$$Dlk = Elt * Ztk \qquad (9.10)$$

Ztk is the transposition of Zkt.

After that adjust weights using equation 9.11

$$Wlk = Wlk - Dlk \qquad (9.11)$$

Thus, the temporal complexity of lk is given by equation 9.12

$$O(lt + lt + ltk + lk) = O(ltk) \qquad (9.12)$$

Now returning from kj. Proceed using equations 9.13, 9.14, and 9.15

$$Ekt = f'(Skt) \odot (Wkl * Elt) \qquad (9.13)$$

$$Dkj = Ekt * Ztj \qquad (9.14)$$

$$Wkj = Wkj - Dkj \qquad (9.15)$$

Wkl is the transposition of **Wlk**. For k→j, we get the temporal complexity $O\,(kt + klt + ktj + kj) = O\,(k * t(l + j))$

The final expression for ji is $O(jt(k + i))$. Overall, we have

$$O\,(ltk + tk(l + j) + tj(k + i)) = O(t * (lk + kj + ji)) \qquad (9.16)$$

according to the feedforward pass technique. Given that they are identical, the overall time complexity for a single epoch is $O(t(ij + jk + kl))$.

The number of iterations increases this temporal complexity (epochs). Thus, the complexity is $O(nt(ij + jk + kl))$, where n is the number of iterations. Notice that such matrix operations are very parallelizable on cloud and HPC. We chose the most straightforward type of matrix multiplication, which has a cubic time complexity. The stochastic gradient descent approach was used.

For the distributed framework with M nodes, the complexity is $O(nt(ij + jk + kl))/M$

9.6   Conclusion

In this chapter, we provide a framework for distributed machine learning and privacy-preserving computation. Simple setups of distributed deep learning are insufficient for a variety of actual cooperation arrangements. throughout health organizations. We suggest unique configurations for a previously proposed distribution system. The proposed method is a distributed deep learning methodology that is much more resource-efficient than existing methods- federated learning and huge batch synchronous learning are ways of distributed deep learning that are already accessible. In health and beyond, the generation of such unique combinations is a promising area for future research. Currently, a combination of laws and morals makes it impossible to do so. Sharing data is difficult even for scientific research. Included in the inquiries are the legal justifications for preprocessing and privacy protection. There has been pushback to informed consent as the legal basis for processing inside the manner of processing in the interest of the public, there are concerns about the reidentification of individuals when aggregated and anonymized data are available. Environments. A feasible alternative would be to allow researchers to train their models for machine learning without ever getting access to the information leaving the clinics, which we address in this paper characterized by scattered learning. This secure method permits the examination of health records and may be applied to several medical specialities. A constraint on its application, however, is that medical facilities be regulators be convinced to partake in such conduct, and it must be recognized that suitable precautions have been installed.

References

1. John, J., Ravikumar, A., Abraham, B., Prostate cancer prediction from multiple pretrained computer vision model. *Health Technol.*, 11, 5, 1003–1011, Sep. 2021.

2. Perez, F., Avila, S., Valle, E., *Solo or ensemble? Choosing a CNN architecture for melanoma classification*, arXiv, Apr. 29, 2019, Accessed: Dec. 18, 2022. [Online].Available: http://arxiv.org/abs/1904.12724.

3. Calisto, F.M., Nunes, N.J., Nascimento, J.C., BreastScreening: On the use of multi-modality in medical imaging diagnosis, in: *Proceedings of the International Conference on Advanced Visual Interfaces*, pp. 1–5, Sep. 2020.

4. Ravikumar, A., Sriraman, H., Saketh, P.M.S., Lokesh, S., Karanam, A., Effect of neural network structure in accelerating performance and accuracy of a convolutional neural network with GPU/TPU for image analytics. *PeerJ Comput. Sci.*, 8, e909, Mar. 2022.

5. Zhuang, D. and Chang, J.M., PeerHunter: Detecting peer-to-peer botnets through community behavior analysis, in: *2017 IEEE Conference on Dependable and Secure Computing*, pp. 493–500, 2017.

6. Ravikumar, A. and Sriraman, H., Staleness and stagglers in distibuted deep image analytics, in: *International Conference on Artificial Intelligence and Smart Systems (ICAIS), Coimbatore, India*, pp. 848–852, 2021.

7. Mercuri, R.T., The HIPAA-potamus in healthcare data security. *Commun. ACM*, 47, 7, 25–28, Jul. 2004.

8. Nasr, M., Shokri, R., Houmansadr, A., Comprehensive privacy analysis of deep learning: Passive and active white-box inference attacks against centralized and federated learning. *Presented at the 2019 IEEE Symposium on Security and Privacy (SP)*, pp. 739–753, May 2019.

9. Shokri, R., Stronati, M., Song, C., Shmatikov, V., Membership inference attacks against machine learning models, in: *2017 IEEE Symposium on Security and Privacy (SP)*, San Jose, CA, USA, pp. 3–18, May 2017.

10. Papernot, N., Abadi, M., Erlingsson, Ú., Goodfellow, I., Talwar, K., *Semisupervised knowledge transfer for deep learning from private training data*, arXiv, Mar. 03, 2017, Accessed: Jan. 08, 2023, [Online], Available: http://arxiv.org/abs/1610.05755.

11. Geyer, R.C., Klein, T., Nabi, M., *Differentially private federated learning: A client level perspective*, arXiv, Mar. 01, 2018, Accessed: Jan. 08, 2023, [Online], Available: http://arxiv.org/abs/1712.07557.

12. Abadi, M. *et al.*, Deep learning with differential privacy, in: *Proceedings of the 2016 ACM SIGSAC Conference on Computer and Communications Security*, New York, NY, USA, pp. 308–318, 2016.

13. Wang, T., Li, N., Jha, S., Locally differentially private frequent itemset mining, in: *2018 IEEE Symposium on Security and Privacy (SP)*, pp. 127–143, 2018.

14. Bittau, A. *et al.*, Prochlo: Strong privacy for analytics in the crowd, in: *Proceedings of the 26th Symposium on Operating Systems Principles*, Shanghai China, pp. 441–459, Oct. 2017.

15. Ding, B., Kulkarni, J., Yekhanin, S., *Collecting telemetry data privately*, arXiv, Dec. 05, 2017, Accessed: Jan. 08, 2023, [Online], Available: http://arxiv.org/abs/1712.01524.

16. Cormode, G., Jha, S., Kulkarni, T., Li, N., Srivastava, D., Wang, T., Privacy at scale: Local differential privacy in practice, in: *Proceedings of the 2018 International Conference on Management of Data*, Houston TX USA, pp. 1655–1658, May 2018.

17. Yilmaz, E., Al-Rubaie, M., Chang, J.M., *Locally differentially private naive bayes classification*, arXiv, May 03, 2019, Accessed: Jan. 08, 2023, [Online], Available: http://arxiv.org/abs/1905.01039.

18. Murakami, T., Hino, H., Sakuma, J., Toward distribution estimation under local differential privacy with small samples. *Proc. Priv. Enh. Technol.*, 2018, 3, 84–104, Jun. 2018.

19. Abadi, M. *et al.*, Deep learning with differential privacy, in: *Proceedings of the 2016 ACM SIGSAC Conference on Computer and Communications Security*, New York, NY, USA, pp. 308–318, 2016.

20. Chowdhury, M., Zaharia, M., Ma, J., Jordan, M.I., Stoica, I., Managing data transfers in computer clusters with orchestra, in: *Proceedings of the ACM SIGCOMM 2011 Conference (SIGCOMM '11)*. Association for Computing Machinery, p. 12. New York, NY, USA, 98–109.

21. Deist, T.M. *et al.*, Infrastructure and distributed learning methodology for privacy-preserving multi-centric rapid learning healthcare: EuroCAT. *Clin. Transl. Radiat. Oncol.*, 4, 24–31, Jun. 2017.

22. Dluhoš, P. *et al.*, Multi-center machine learning in imaging psychiatry: A meta-model approach. *NeuroImage*, 155, 10–24, Jul. 2017.

23. Jochems, A. *et al.*, Developing and validating a survival prediction model for NSCLC patients through distributed learning across 3 countries. *Int. J. Radiat. Oncol. Biol. Phys.*, 99, 2, 344–352, Oct. 2017.

24. Brisimi, T.S., Chen, R., Mela, T., Olshevsky, A., Paschalidis, I.C.H., Shi, W., Federated learning of predictive models from federated electronic health records. *Int. J. Med. Inf.*, 112, 59–67, Apr. 2018.

25. Tagliaferri, L. *et al.*, A new standardized data collection system for interdisciplinary thyroid cancer management: Thyroid COBRA. *Eur. J. Intern. Med.*, 53, 73–78, Jul. 2018.

26. McMahan, H.B., Moore, E., Ramage, D., Hampson, S., Arcas, B.A.Y., *Communication-efficient learning of deep networks from decentralized data*, arXiv, Feb. 28, 2017, Accessed: Jan. 08, 2023, [Online], Available: http://arxiv.org/abs/1602.05629.

27. Qi, Y., Hossain, M.S., Nie, J., Li, X., Privacy-preserving blockchain-based federated learning for traffic flow prediction. *Future Gener. Comput. Syst.*, 117, 328–337, Apr. 2021, doi: 10.1016/j.future.2020.12.003.

28. Junxu, L. and Xiaofeng, M., Survey on privacy-preserving machine learning. *J. Comput. Res. Dev.*, 57, 2, 346, Feb. 2020.

29. Truex, S. *et al.*, *A hybrid approach to privacy-preserving federated learning*, arXiv, Aug. 14, 2019, Accessed: Jan. 08, 2023, [Online], Available: http://arxiv.org/abs/1812.03224.

29. Yang, Z., Chen, M., Wong, K.-K., Poor, H.V., Cui, S., *Federated learning for 6G: Applications, challenges, and opportunities*, arXiv, Jan. 04, 2021, Accessed: Jan. 08, 2023, [Online], Available: http://arxiv.org/abs/2101.01338.

30. Mammen, P.M., *Federated learning: Opportunities and challenges*, arXiv, Jan. 13, 2021, Accessed: Jan. 08, 2023, [Online], Available: http://arxiv.org/abs/2101.05428.

31. Huang, Y. *et al.*, *Personalized cross-silo federated learning on non-IID data*, arXiv, Dec. 13, 2021, Accessed: Jan. 08, 2023, [Online], Available: http://arxiv.org/abs/2007.03797.

32. Bui, D. *et al.*, *Federated user representation learning*, arXiv, Sep. 27, 2019, Accessed: Jan. 08, 2023, [Online], Available: http://arxiv.org/abs/1909.12535.

33. Peterson, D., Kanani, P., Marathe, V.J., *Private federated learning with domain adaptation*, arXiv, Dec. 13, 2019, Accessed: Jan. 08, 2023, [Online], Available: http://arxiv.org/abs/1912.06733.

34. Guler, B. and Yener, A., *Sustainable federated learning*, arXiv, Feb. 22, 2021, Accessed: Jan. 08, 2023, [Online], Available: http://arxiv.org/abs/2102.11274.

35. Das, D. *et al.*, *Distributed deep learning using synchronous stochastic gradient descent*, arXiv, Feb. 22, 2016, Accessed: Jun. 26, 2022, [Online], Available: http://arxiv.org/abs/1602.06709.

Part 3

FUTURE-BASED APPLICATIONS

10

Decision and Recommendation System Services for Patients Using Artificial Intelligence

Arjun Tandon[1], Raghav Dangey[1], Anand Kumar Mishra[2], G. Balamurugan[3] and Amit Kumar Tyagi[4*]

[1]*School of Computer Science and Engineering, Vellore Institute of Technology, Chennai, Tamilnadu, India*
[2]*NIIT University, Neemrana, Rajasthan, India*
[3]*Department of Computing Technologies, SRM Institute of Science and Technology, Kattankulathur Campus, Chengalpattu, Tamilnadu, India*
[4]*Department of Fashion Technology, National Institute of Fashion Technology, New Delhi, Delhi, India*

Abstract

Recent advancements in the Internet of Things (IoT) have made it possible to create intelligent surroundings. With any technology, the IoT idea is thought to carry considerable security and privacy threats. The various potential incursions that may be made pose privacy and security issues. The creation of an intrusion detection system is necessary to identify attacks and anomalies in the IoT system. This study presents a Deep Belief Network (DBN) algorithm model for the intrusion detection system. The CICIDS 2017 dataset is used in the performance analysis of the current IDS model for assaults and anomaly detection. All of the metrics, including accuracy, recall, precision, F1-score, detection rate, and others, were improved by the recommended technique. The way that people get health-care has been transformed by IoT technology. Due to the integration of network-enabled IoT devices with healthcare network organizations, medical institutions are extremely worried about IoT security. This research presents a machine learning-based detection mechanism for dangerous behaviors in such IoT network contexts. The suggested two-phase LSTM detection technique establishes the network's traffic protocol to detect IoT abnormalities. The study illustrates the

Corresponding author: amitkrtyagi025@gmail.com

Amit Kumar Tyagi (ed.) Privacy Preservation of Genomic and Medical Data, (215–242) © 2024 Scrivener Publishing LLC

consequences of unbalanced data on model training and provides a workable solution because the bulk of the data is unbalanced and there is just a small quantity of malicious traffic. The experimental results show that the proposed two-phase LSTM classification model outperforms other classification models, as well as one-phase one.

Keywords: IoT, deep learning, anomaly detection, intrusion detection, DBN, Internet of Things, machine learning

10.1 Introduction

The Internet of Things (IoT) is a network that links everything to the Internet using sensing data devices and a specified protocol. It enables data sharing and exchanges as well as intelligent identification, tracking, placement, administration, and monitoring. A network of physical objects is the standard definition of the Internet of Things. However, the Internet has developed into a network of objects of various sizes and forms, including furniture, vehicles, toys, cameras, medical equipment, household appliances, cellphones, and modern buildings, as well as humans, animals, and other living things. These interconnected gadgets all share and exchange data by predefined protocols [1]. The IoT is an Internet comprising three different types of relationships.

- Man to machine or thing,
- Man to man,
- Internet-based communication between machines and objects [2].

The goal of the IoT is to enable connections between things at anytime, anywhere, with anything, and with anyone, ideally using any pathways, networks, and supports [1]. There are numerous uses for the IoT. IoT is a technology that utilizes networks to connect and communicate with the physical environment. Smart homes, smart transportation, and intelligent healthcare are just a few of the many applications that the Internet of Things can be used for [3]. The market for IoT in healthcare has grown in recent years. Cyber-physical systems (CPS), which connect IoT medical devices like blood glucose machines, inhalers for asthma, pulse oximeters, and other wearables, have been widely used by healthcare institutions. IoT healthcare apps may track patients, samples, and supplies, as well as enhance service quality and job efficiency, by leveraging biometric data and measurements gathered by sensors. Due to the healthcare industry's stringent security regulations and HIPAA compliance, security concerns must be taken into account along with the ease and benefits of emerging technology. Through IoT medical equipment, patient data have been unlawfully acquired and transmitted.

10.1.1   Effect of Internet of Medical Things Attacks

An IoT-focused attack often does greater harm to the healthcare sector than it does to other industries as a whole. IoT security incidents have escalated since 2019 as a result of the expanding number of IoTs installed in healthcare companies and the vulnerabilities of these smart devices [4]. Adversaries have a financial advantage in the business of cybercrime. Attacks against IoMT devices have the potential to injure patients gravely and perhaps endanger their lives. In light of their significance for safety and security, IoMT devices and healthcare infrastructure have therefore emerged as prime targets for attacks. Ransomware is one of the deadliest risks from cyberattacks for all industries. Healthcare businesses were, regrettably, the most often targeted by ransomware attacks [5]. They are the most in need and willing to pay when it comes to the COVID problem.

The frequency and complexity of the assaults are predicted to rise. Because any malfunction might compromise patient safety and privacy, security concerns with IoTs should be a major alarm for administrators in the health industry. To ensure that the advantages of IoT can be realized in the healthcare industry, a solid defensive plan is essential.

10.1.2   Basic Structure of Defensive Plan

Several formal IoT cybersecurity guidelines and recommendations [6] have been made by the National Institute of Standards and Technology (NIST) for consumers and manufacturers. Such publications also help to address the challenges raised in the recently approved IoT Cybersecurity Improvement Act of 2020 and begin to provide the guidelines the law needs. Since attackers have discovered vulnerable IoT, the healthcare sector needs to be more proactive. Healthcare organizations rely heavily on connected devices to provide efficient patient care, but many of these devices operate on outdated platforms, rendering them vulnerable to endpoint attacks [7]. In modern healthcare network settings, a lot of IoT device data is collected. Layered networking is a good way to describe network architecture [8]. The lowest data collection layer collects biological data and monitoring data from IoT devices and saves it in healthcare database systems, while the data management layer analyses and processes the gathered data for usage by the highest, application service layer. Models are perceived as being challenging, which puts the security benefit that the solution provides in jeopardy. Due to the lack of thorough technical information on the solution and the timetable for its adoption by final cloud customers, it is highly challenging to make the concluding remark.

10.1.3   Security/Defense Mechanism

The internal network is connected to by the IoT devices without any security measures. They collaborate with others and play a big part in the infrastructure that makes sure each essential component is safe. Although the majority of IoT devices lack security features, they have evolved into IP-capable endpoints of the hospital network architecture. Despite their many advantages, these devices expose the healthcare industry to further security and privacy risks by creating new attack surfaces. Due to the unique characteristics of IoT devices, typical security solutions are insufficient for effectively detecting IoT assaults [9]. As a consequence, developing a strategic plan for IoT devices is quite challenging. The majority of current research has been focused on establishing authentication and encryption solutions for wearable medical devices [10]. Additionally, many IoT devices could use various communication protocols, such as TCP/IP, Ethernet, EtherCAT, Modbus, and EtherNet/IP, which complicates attack detection. To effectively defend against cyberattacks in the healthcare industry, it is essential to recognize abnormal activities in the aforementioned diverse network environments. An intrusion detection system is one such defense mechanism. According to our examination of the literature, previous research tended to concentrate on a particular technique and very seldom addressed cyberattacks in diverse network situations. On the contrary side, most information that is currently available was acquired from real-world scenarios in which the vast majority of traffic is benign and just a small percentage is malicious. Studies from the past hardly ever examined the implications of unbalanced data and data labeling. The following research issues will be addressed to close the aforementioned gaps:

- Create a reliable detection model for detecting aberrant traffic in IoT network settings with a variety of topologies?
- How may an uneven collection be used to prepare a detection algorithm?
- How does database identification affect detection efficiency?

Just when training an ML model demands a neutral dataset, the study proposes an up-sampling method to mitigate the impacts of an imbalanced dataset. This research proposes a two-phase classification technique for detecting abnormalities in various network contexts. A more sophisticated artificial neural network architecture known as long short-term memory (LSTM) incorporates feedback connections and can assess single data points as well as data sequences such as time series traffic and flows. In the first step, it determines the network protocol of the traffic, and in the second, it detects anomalies.

10.2 Literature Review

10.2.1 Healthcare Safety

The Health Insurance Portability and Accountability Act of 1996 (HIPAA) [11] was enacted as federal legislation and a nationwide standard to prevent sensitive patient health info from being disclosed without the patient's consent. To maintain information security, healthcare providers, healthcare clearinghouses, health plans, and business partners must follow the HIPAA Security Rule. Its five basic components are administrative safeties, technological safeguards, physical safeguards, policy, organizational requirements, procedure, and documentation requirements. The following steps must be taken by all covered entities to comply can with the HIPAA Security Rule:

- Ensure the privacy, security, and accessibility of all healthcare data;
- Identify and guard against risks to information security;
- Protect against expected prohibited usage or exposures; and
- Validate that all workers have been educated in these processes.

One of a nation's most important infrastructures is its medical organizations. Due to their greater susceptibility to intrusions than other businesses, hackers have lately targeted hospitals and clinics. Cyberattacks on medical institutions have had a significant impact on their everyday operations and put patients' safety in danger. Worldwide cyberattacks on hospitals resulted in severe data breaches [12], and ransomware operations also affected numerous hospitals in Germany [13].

10.2.2 Intrusion Detection

Intrusion detection is a crucial security tool for controlling network assaults and spotting malicious activity in computer network traffic. It plays a crucial part in data security and aids in finding, choosing, identifying unauthorized access, copying, altering, and destruction of data and data frameworks [14]. The network security framework and the host security framework are two common security frameworks that guard against unauthorized access, malfunction, damage, and change for the basic network and systems. These two frameworks might include a variety of coordinated security approaches, including firewalls, antivirus software, and intrusion detection systems (IDS), that permit a network to be watched and to get alert whenever malicious activity occurs [15].

10.2.2.1 Types of Techniques in Intrusion Detection Systems

The IDSs may be broadly categorized into three types of techniques:

A. Misuse Identification: To find infiltration, misuse identification techniques employ predetermined signatures of malicious behavior. As a result, they are used to recognize known assaults.

B. Anomaly Detection: Anomaly detection techniques describe usual patterns and identify harmful behavior based on how those patterns depart from the norm. This is how anomaly-based identification methods may recognize zero-day assaults [16].

C. Hybrid Technique: Hybrid approaches aim to increase the detection rates of known incursions while reducing the false positives of unknown assaults [17]. Both anomaly and anomaly detection approaches are used in hybrid methods. Intruder detection was a significant advancement in safeguarding the safety of IoT networks. As a result, intrusion detection is merely one of the numerous techniques for dealing with security flaws within any of the four architectural levels of IoT depicted in Figure 10.1. IDS techniques can take several forms, including those based on statistical analytics, ANNs, cluster analytics, or deep learning. Deep learning intrusion detection surpasses other systems in this group due to its strong ability for self-adaption, generalization, self-learning, and the identification of unknown attack actions [18].

10.2.3   Anomaly Detection

Anomalies are a crucial component of any framework due to the extensive IoT, creating a massive amount of information. These abnormalities could be a sign of resource depletion in an industrial setting.

An important situation at recognizing anomalous performance of medical devices, etc. Therefore, the ability to spot abnormalities might have a significant impact on the overall performance of any model being watched. In those models, identifying the precise boundaries between abnormal and normal activities is the major challenge in anomaly perception.

10.2.3.1   Process of Identifying Anomalies

The first step in the framework for identifying anomalies is to comprehend the relationship architecture as well as the nature of obtained data movement, which is frequently binary, discrete, or continuous. This connection framework illustrates whether the information is graphical, spatial, or time series information. Anomalies, examinations, or expectancies can be detected using the appropriate procedure with the help of relationship type identification. Finding the type of anomaly from the preset list comes next (for example, point, collective, or contextual anomaly). The after step is to comprehend the existence of training data to create a framework for anomaly identification. We may classify the information as supervised, semi-supervised, or unsupervised depending on its presence and the explanation provided. In supervised learning, the availability of information with a class label and its core learning style is used to detect the framework's anomalous behavior. Unsupervised learning yields data but no trustworthy findings. Furthermore, we have restricted models with a class label and unlabeled data elsewhere in semi-supervised learning.

10.2.3.2   Researches on Anomaly Detection

One of the most popular protection strategies against cyberattacks is the use of intrusion detection systems (IDS). Two typical methods for detecting intrusions are:

- Knowledge-based detection, or SD, cannot identify novel assaults since it is dependent on information from existing attacks or weaknesses. Anomaly detection, also known as outlier identification, locates inappropriate actions by setting them out from the vast majority of typical users.

In a research by Chacko and Hayajneh [19], the security hazards of IoMT were examined. By showcasing several attacks, it highlighted the significance of security and privacy problems in the healthcare industry. A defense-in-depth approach is advised to comply with HIPAA, where many levels of protection are set up to guard against certain dangers. IoMT problems with the high moral standards of the medical occupation, including safety, dependability, and security, were noted in another research study [20]. A system that uses an open-source IoT data generator tool to produce both benign and malicious IoT traffic for research purposes was reported in a paper [21], and it may contribute to the development of context-aware IoT security solutions for IoT healthcare settings.

Because most detection algorithms rely on supervised learning, researchers [9] used a semi-supervised fuzzy algorithm to identify unusual IoT traffic. According to one research [22], deep learning (DL) algorithms may be vulnerable to adversary assaults if protective models against adversarial perturbations are not taken into account. The bulk of studies employed deep learning algorithms to recognize COVID-19 events in data gathered from IoMT devices. In a research by Hussain *et al.* [23], network traffic data were transformed into images and a CNN model was trained to recognize IoT DDoS assaults. The internet traffic statistics, rather than IoT-specific data, were used to train and test the techniques for IoT threat detection. A similar technique was employed in different research [24], this one concentrating more on telecommunication networks, to identify DDoS assaults for CPS. To circumvent man-in-the-middle attacks, Taylor and Sharif [25] advocate using an out-of-band communication channel to incorporate these IoT devices into a CPS network.

IoMT also generates a high dimensional and visible dynamicity of the traffic data used in such systems, making it possible to properly diagnose patients and remotely monitor their health conditions [26]. According to the study, which is based on the aforementioned research, a system for healthcare attack detection that uses both network and biometric data as characteristics outperforms one that uses only one of the two types of features. The study made the assumption that the alerts had already been divided into the physical and virtual worlds given its understanding of the device protocols. The evaluation's findings indicate that dynamically modifying the alert windows' size improves alert correlation performance.

10.2.3.3   Types of Anomalies

The idea of the necessary anomaly is a key component of an anomaly identification approach. The three categories below can be used to classify anomalies:

- Point anomalies: A data model contains point anomalies if it may be said to be aberrant about the remaining information. Since they are the most fundamental kind of anomaly, they have primarily been the focus of studies on anomaly detection. Let us use the identification of credit card scams as a real-world example and compare the dataset to a person's credit trades. A point anomaly is a monetary transaction that is larger than what the person would typically spend.
- Contextual anomalies: Contextual anomalies are data models that behave abnormally in one setting but not another (likewise stated as conditional anomalies). Contextual characteristics are used to determine the context for that model; in geographical datasets, they include an area's latitude and longitude. Time is the contextual feature in time-series data that determines a model's condition on the overall order.
- Behavioral attributes: These describe a model's noncontextually properties; for example, the measure of rainfall in every location is the behavioral property in a geographical dataset that defines the average for rainfall. The characteristics of the behavioral attribute within the specific environment are used to resolve the anomalous behavior. While the contextual anomalies in the given context may be represented using a data model.
- Collective anomalies: The term "having collective anomalies" refers to an accumulation of relevant data models that are anomalous about the entire dataset. This anomaly's data models might not be unusual on their own, but the aggregate of such events makes the anomaly. Investigations into

collective anomalies are done for the organization, graph, and geographical data.

- The fact that point anomalies can appear in any dataset, unlike collective anomalies, which can only happen in datasets with connected data models, should be emphasized. The distinction is that a contextual anomaly's existence depends on the data's capacity to access context-specific attributes. A collective anomaly or a point anomaly might become a contextual anomaly when the context is considered. In this way, issues with identifying point or collective anomalies might become problems with identifying contextual anomalies by merging the context information [27].

10.2.4   Machine Learning

Deep learning has been used to construct several machine learning (ML) algorithms that have impressive classification and grouping skills. One of them is the use of supervised ML algorithms for anomaly identification. When performing a classification job, data are divided into groups based on knowledge gained from the training data, where each instance in the training dataset has a single "target value" (i.e., class label) and several "attributes" (i.e., features or observed variables). The goal of a supervised learning method is to create a model that classifies or predicts the test data's target values using just the test data's attributes. Zidi *et al.* [28] employed an SVM classification model to discover defects in wireless sensor networks concluded that fault detection has to be precise to avoid false alarms and speedy to avoid loss. Their analysis revealed that SVM is superior to other approaches in terms of effectiveness.

Neural network (NN) modeling is one of the most used ML techniques for anomaly detection, and academics have utilized their improved models to get better results. In a research by Radford *et al.* [29], LSTM was used to identify anomalous network traffic and to understand how two IP addresses communicate. Another study [30] used a natural language model and LSTM to extract information from domain names and identify HTTPS irregularities. According to the experimental findings, the LSTM classification model performs better than the RF model. Kim and Ho [31] suggested a NN model for identifying abnormalities in online traffic and used CNN to extract spatial information and LSTM temporal features.

10.3 Proposed Methodology

The literature review found that network access was a component of the vast majority of cyberattacks. Previous research has shown that LSTM is appropriate for time-series data and that ML approaches provide accurate classification results. An LSTM classification model is used in this work to find abnormalities. This paper suggests a two-phase detection method to increase detection efficiency. The first phase identifies the protocol type, and the second phase uses an LSTM classification model to identify bogus data. The preprocess module gathers the network's unprocessed traffic, corrects any errors, concatenates the packet-based data into flows, and transforms the unprocessed data into a readable format. The trained detection model detects malicious activities, the Protocol Categorization module gathers and encodes attributes for recognizing anomalous behaviors, and the Protocol Categorization module categorizes the protocol type for each flow of data (refer to Figure 10.1).

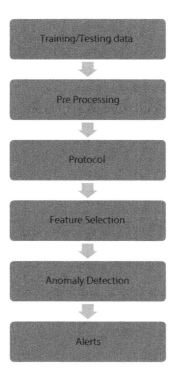

Figure 10.1 Proposal methodology for our work.

10.3.1 Pre-Processing

The network's raw data are gathered in pcap format and converted to human-readable CSV format. Our preliminary study suggests that a flow rather than a single packet may contain aberrant network behavior because a single packet may not be harmful, such as a packet carrying a TCP session beginning or closing. For this research to take into account anomalies in the flow basis, the module preprocess combines the packet-based traffic data into flow form.

10.3.1.1 *Categorization of Protocols*

In earlier publications [32–34], ML models were used to categorize network protocols. Two ML models must be used—one for identifying network protocols and the other for detecting anomalies—to uncover abnormalities in heterogeneous networks. Processing is demanding, and models must be trained. Even if each device in a heterogeneous network communicates with the others using a distinct protocol, it is fair to assume that each protocol is understood to create network monitoring security measures. This study classifies the communication protocol used in a certain packet based on the header information to save time. The Modbus communication protocol coexists with the TCP/IP protocol stack, which is the one of the most frequently used in IoT networks. The module Protocol Categorization can recognize the protocol by looking at the header using knowledge of the protocol formats and the range of each field in the headers. For example, since the Modbus header is 7 bytes long, the first 7 bytes are checked to verify if they fall within the field's acceptable ranges. By gathering and

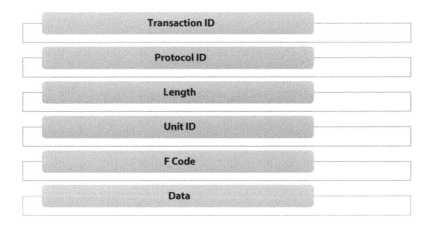

Figure 10.2 Description of Modbus format.

examining the TCP payload, it is possible to determine the kind of proto-col used when a connection uses TCP/IP, such as Ethernet over TCP/IP or Modbus over TCP/IP. The Modbus format is shown in the illustration in Figure 10.2.

The data fields of all the network's communication protocol, as well as payload length, payload, and payload entropy, make up the feature set that was chosen. The following TCP/IP-related data is retrieved for protocols via TCP/IP: destination IP, source IP, destination port, and packet count. The following header information for Modbus is extracted: Transaction ID, Protocol ID, payload length, Unit ID, and Function Code. It includes both categorical and numerical data, with payload length and packet count being under the numerical category and protocol type being categorical data. Before applying an ML model to categorical characteristics, a trans-formation must be applied as ML models only operate with numerical val-ues. Additionally, this study uses data normalization for numerical data to assess the importance of the feature values. The approaches used for feature encoding are described below.

- One-hot encoding, which removes the order of a categorical variable, is a popular method for encoding categorical char-acteristics. Therefore, categorical data are converted into binary form in this study using one-hot encoding. A one-hot encoding transform is shown in Table 10.1 where each value in the field translates to a column of the encoding.

The MinMax Scaler standardization method was used in this study to scale the data to a preset range while maintaining the shape of the original

Table 10.1 Description of one-hot encoding transform.

Categorical feature	Description
Source IP	The source of the flow
Destination IP	The destination of the flow
Ports	The communication port
Unit ID	The destination ID of the Modbus packet
Function Code	The operation ID of the Modbus packet
Transaction ID	The transaction ID of the Modbus packet
Modbus Protocol ID	The protocol ID of the Modbus packet

distribution. The minimum value that is removed from each element's X value determines the range, which is the difference between the element's original maximum and lowest value. The formula for MinMaxScaler:

The formula for MinMaxScaler standardization is as follows, where max and min represent the maximum and lowest values of feature X, respectively, and Xstd is the standardized value of feature X with a range of 0 to 1.

$$X^{std} = \frac{X - min}{max - min}$$

10.3.1.2   Detection Model

IoT devices often carry out a specific set of duties, some of which may be periodic, like ECG or patient monitoring systems in intensive care units. As a result, the communication's contents include regular and steady data. According to the literature review, the LSTM is capable of learning time series and periodic patterns.

The suggested LSTM detection model is shown in Figure 10.3.

A flow from Kc is shown, which further divides into three flows of k1, k2, and k3, leading toward the output. Also, the flow's destination and its source can be observed. The flows that are sent to a specific destination indicated as K1, K2, and K3; are ordered chronologically to determine whether an attack has occurred at that destination. The proposed LSTM model uses present and previous flows as inputs to categorize the flow. The

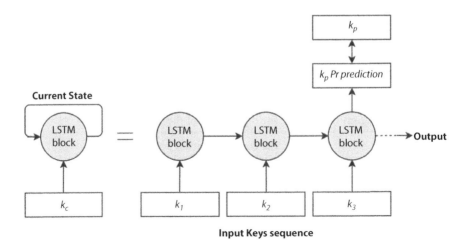

Figure 10.3 LSTM detection model.

output is the flow Kc's detection result, where Kp Pr Prediction and Kp are based on our preliminary experiment. The suggested model uses binary cross-entropy as the loss function as a binary classifier. To create a strong detection model, cross-entropy loss increases since the anticipated probability differ from the actual label. The stochastic gradient descent method is the foundation of the majority of model learning optimizers. RMSprop [35] is appropriate for knowing a model from a large or out-of-work dataset since it employs an adjustable learning rate as opposed to considering the learning rate as a hyperparameter. RMSprop is used in this study's model optimization because the training data, which includes recurring traffic patterns, fulfills the aforementioned definition.

Performance Evaluation

To answer the suggested research questions, this study develops the subsequent evaluation.

- Experiment 1 assesses the effects of various data balancing techniques on accuracy.
- Experiment 2 assesses the efficiency of the suggested 2-phase categorization paradigm.
- Experiment 3 assesses the efficiency of the suggested Machine Learning detection model.

Performance indicators in this study include accuracy, precision, recall, and F1 score. The proportion of actual cases among the projected instances is known as precision, sometimes known as a positive predictive value. The ratio of the total number of accurately detected occurrences to the total of instances that were projected to be positive is called recall, also known as sensitivity. The percentage of accurate predictions out of all the instances that were analyzed is known as accuracy. The F1 score, which includes precision and recall, was employed in this study as the harmonic mean of accuracy to compare the 2 models. Biomedical data make up the majority of healthcare datasets [36, 37], which lack network traffic information for IoMT intrusions. Previous research evaluated their IoMT attack detection approaches using internet network traffic, which might not have the features of IoT data. As a result, the datasets used in this investigation are taken from several sources [38–40] and divided into training and testing in an 8:2 ratio. Multiple datasets that include ordinary traffic, data injection, system failure, reconnaissance, command injection, and DoS assaults are contained in the dataset source [38]. The dataset CSET [41] includes regular communication, C&C traffic, and fictitious orders to IoT devices.

Table 10.2 Examined datasets.

Dataset	Size (MB)	Ratio M: B	Protocols	Attacks
Morris	288	3:7	Modbus, TCP/IP	Various types of commands injection and data injection attacks, line maintenance, DoS, reconnaissance, and system faults.
CSET	238	3:7	Modbus	Fake commands, C&C, uploading, and characterization tracking.
4SICS	350	1:9	Modbus, TCP, TCP/IP	Port scanning HTTP scan, SSH connection.

Different sorts of reconnaissance attacks, such as HTTP scans, port scans, and password guessing for SSH connection attempts, are included in the 4SICS Geek Lounge [40]. The examined datasets are listed in Table 10.2.

Experiment 1: Data Labeling and Unbalanced Data

A balanced class distribution—or one that is more balanced—is necessary for effective model training. However, in actual network settings, the majority of traffic is benign; as a result, the datasets gathered from actual environments are unbalanced, with benign traffic being a majority class and malicious traffic a minority class. Sampling is the process of resampling data, where *upsampling* is the process of raising a minority class's sampling rate and *downsampling* is the process of lowering a majority class's sample rate. On the other hand, resampling depends on the fundamental data labeling unit. Most studies used packet-based traffic statistics. Our early research shows that a flow, not a single packet, may be used to detect an unusual network activity since some packets from a malicious network flow may be identical to those from a benign flow. For instance, there is no prepared payload in the first packet of a TCP connection that is being established. To enhance the detection performance, this study takes flow-based abnormalities into account. Experiment 1 verifies the aforementioned claims by comparing the effectiveness of two resampling techniques for addressing the problem of unbalanced data: up-sampling employs the

Synthetic Minority Oversampling Technique (SMOTE) technique, while down-sampling uses the Fourier approach. Up-sampling is preferable to down-sampling because Machine Learning model training needs a lot of data, whereas shrinking decreases the size of the training data and might have an impact on training effectiveness. Since packet resampling could damage a flow's integrity, resampling by flows performs better than resampling by packets. In summary, upsampling by flows produces the best outcomes.

Experiment 2: The Two-Phase Classification Method's Efficacy
Our first studies show that the protocol type is a key element of the proposed detection model that locates attacks in a heterogeneous network environment. The data format of any communication protocol is made up of a collection of header data fields and a distinct payload field. It's crucial to extract the correct feature values from a given protocol to prevent inaccurate detection. Experiment 2 looks at how well the proposed classification model performs with and occasionally without protocol categorization. The two-phase classification model performs better because the chosen features are better able to capture the characteristics of each protocol's inappropriate actions.

Experiment 3: Evaluation of the Detection Model's Performance
The previous study [42] used SVM to detect anomalies in the Morris dataset, treating anomalies as outliers, and obtained 98.13% accuracy, 96% recall, 98% precision, and an F1 score of 0.9707. Another experiment on anomaly detection [38] used the CNN model and attained accuracy, recall, and precision rates of 99.13%, 98.12%, and 99.03%. The ML models mentioned above from previous research had excellent performance; however, they were only tested with one set of data. Experiment 3 uses several datasets to assess the performance of the proposed system under various network circumstances before comparing it to the two models

Table 10.3 Comparison of LSTM over SVM and CNN.

	LSTM	SVM	CNN
Accuracy	**97.06%**	92.45%	91.59%
Precision	**94.85%**	89.60%	93.84%
Recall	**97.42%**	90.43%	92.74%
F1	**0.961211631**	0.900146829	0.89775075

mentioned above. The training approach for the two models mentioned above involves upsampling the datasets using flow data labeling. The comparative findings are summarized in Table 10.3, which shows that the suggested LSTM model performs better than the other two detection models.

10.4   Implementation and Results Analysis

A. Dataset Description

The CICIDS2017 dataset served as the research's guide. In general, many DDoS attack datasets are inconsistent due to several obstacles including redundant data or irrelevant information. Recent network similar data may be found in the CICIDS2017 dataset. This dataset was acquired over five days, including both normal data and different attacks. This dataset comes close to representing actual network data since it includes both network information with and without assaults. Since the dataset's unevenness had a significant influence on the deep learning approach's training, we employed a duplicating strategy to make sure the testing was balanced [43]. This study was carried out using Keras on a 64-bit Intel Core-i7 CPU with 16 GB of RAM running Windows 7 and the Tensorflow deep learning package. In MATLAB, the machine learning method was put to use.

- **Heartbleed Attack:** The OpenSSL protocol is used by attackers to incorporate malicious data, which grants the attacker unauthorized access to sensitive data.
- **Web Attack–SQL Injection:** Data-driven programs and malicious SQL queries that are entered in section regions for implementation are the focus of the code injection method known as SQL injection.
- **Infiltration:** Attackers use infiltration techniques and software to get full access to networked system information and perform unauthorized logins.
- **Web Attack – XSS:** Attackers inject innocent web apps and widely trusted websites with malicious material to spread them.
- **Web Attack – Brute Force:** Using trial and error, the attackers try to get privileged information, such as PINs and passwords.
- **Bot:** Trojans are used by the attackers to bypass the security on several victim machines, taking ownership of every

device in the Bot network so that it may be utilized and controlled by the attackers.

- **DoSSlowhttptest:** Attackers prevent other users from accessing and provide themselves the opportunity to allow many HTTP connections with a comparable server by manipulating the number of HTTP connections allowed on the server using the HTTP Get request.
- **DoSslowloris:** The attackers carry out a DoS attack using Slow Loris tools.
- **SSH-Patator:** SSH Patator is used by attackers to attempt brute force assaults to discover the SSH login credentials.
- **FTP-Patator:**The attackers try to carry out brute force assaults using FTP Patator to discover the FTP login credentials.
- **DoSGoldenEye:** The GoldenEye tool is used by the attackers to carry out a DoS attack.
- **DDoS:** To attack one target machine, the attackers need several devices that cooperate.
- **PortScan:** Through the forwarding of packets with various destination points, the attackers try to obtain information associated with the target system, such as the type of OS and services currently in use
- **DoS Hulk:** DoS assaults on web servers are carried out by the attackers using the HULK program, which generates large amounts of inconsistent and chaotic traffic. Furthermore, the generated traffic could avoid cache systems and target the server's immediate resource pool.
- **Benign:** Regular traffic patterns [12].

10.5   Results and Discussion

The performance of the model's subset was used to assess the model's correctness. One of the metrics used to evaluate the categorization models was accuracy.

The equation representing the accuracy estimation:

$$Accuracy = \frac{TP + TN}{TP + TN + FP + FN}$$

Precision denotes a high degree of accuracy. It is a percentage of all genuine positives that the model claims are connected with all positives that the model demands.

The rate of precision is presented in this equation:

$$Precision = \frac{TP}{TP + FP}$$

The recall is sometimes referred to as the TP value, which compares the precise total of positives in the information with the total positives in the system states. The rate of recall is presented in this equation:

$$Recall = \frac{TP}{(TP + FN)}$$

Model performance might also be estimated using the F1 score. It is the model's recall and accuracy weighted average. The value of the F1 Score is presented in the following equation:

$$F1Score = \frac{2*TP}{2*TP + FP + FN}$$

The level of intrusion incidents is represented by the detection rate (DR). The value of the detection rate is presented in this equation:

$$Detection\ Rate\ (DR) = \frac{TP}{TP + FN}$$

whereas TP, true positive; FP, false positive; FN, false negative; TN, true negative

The minority attack classes were grouped in this study because they exhibit comparable traits and behaviors. Comparable classes have been integrated, and it appears that this has improved the class of the majority of distinct attack labels. The predominance of the major class (benign) was 83.34% in the table, while the minority class was 0.00039% (heart bleed). Given the stark disparity in the prevalence numbers, prospective detectors could lean toward benign. The benign label was described as a normal label, and the given DBN's performance analysis was assessed and compared to other detection methods. A new label for the bot was introduced: Botnet ARES. This label had a frequency of 0.06% and had 1966 occurrences. The suggested method outperformed other conventional and current strategies in terms of performance for all parameters. About this Botnet ARES label, an accuracy of 97.93% and a detection rate of 98.51% were attained. Due to their comparable traits and behaviors, the FTP-Patator and SSH-Patator labels were merged to form the Brute Force labels. These labels were combined to create a new label with 13,835 instances and a prevalence of 0.48%.

DoS/DDoS was a brand-new term for the mashup of DDoS, DoSGoldenEye, DoSHulk, DoSSlowhttptest, DoSslowloris, and Heartbleed. The proposed approach was used to execute 294,506 cases with a 10.4% prevalence using all of these labels, and the outcomes were improved concerning all of the suggested criteria. the performance evaluation for detecting DoS/DDoS attacks. The 36 occurrences of the infiltration attack had a prevalence ratio of 0.001%, the lowest of all the instances. There were 158,930 cases of the PortScan label, with a prevalence ratio of 5.61% in all instances. The suggested strategy for both assaults performed better in all the parameters, with an accuracy of 96.37 for the infiltration assault and 97.71% for the PortScan attack. For every one of the suggested settings, the enhanced performance was clear. With 2,180 cases and a 0.07% prevalence ratio, the Web Attack category contained Web Attack-SQL Injection, Web Attack-Brute Force, and Web Attack-XSS. The proposed technique delivered high-performance results for each of the above parameters when compared to the alternative attack labels. The current approach for the normal attack labels, which was 99.37% accurate, and the model for the Web attack labels, which was 98.37% accurate, achieved the greatest performance values found in this study (refer Table 10.4 and Figure 10.4).

Table 10.4 Comparisons of all metrics.

Sl no.	Attack detection method	Accuracy	Precision	Recall	F1-score	Detection rate
1	DBNIDS[@]	98.37%	97.21%	98.34%	0.97	98.31%
2	SVMIDS[†]	97.45%	96.32%	97.15%	0.96	97.12%
3	RNNIDS[*]	96.00%	94.93%	95.59%	0.97	95.50%
4	SNNIDS[$]	91.00%	90.05%	90.25%	0.93	90.11%
5	FNNIDS[$$]	90.35%	89.04%	89.13%	0.90	89.01%

Web Attack Detection (which includes the attack label "Web Attack - Brute Force, Web Attack - SQL Injection & Web Attack - XSS").

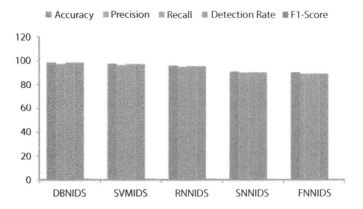

Figure 10.4 Performance analysis of web attack detection.

Further, several useful works related to cloud computing, blockchain technology, internet of things which can help to increase trust in location-based services (LBS) can be found in articles [46–60].

10.6   Conclusion

Healthcare network infrastructure has become susceptible and complex as a result of IoT implementation. As a result, the majority of healthcare businesses have experienced IoT-focused hacks. Cyberattacks on the health industry can be devastating, and if essential infrastructure were to be hacked, patient safety may even be in jeopardy. To detect harmful network activities in diverse IoT network contexts, this study suggests a two-phase ML-based anomaly detection methodology. The suggested technique classifies traffic flow protocol types first, then finds the abnormalities of each protocol type to increase detection performance. A two-phase strategy like this decreases model training time and boosts detection effectiveness in diverse network settings. The majority of prior research has been on enhancing performance by testing several ML models. This study emphasizes how most ML models are affected by unbalanced training data and the fundamental unit of data labeling. In addition, this study shows that up-sampling enhances model learning effectiveness and lessens the effects of unbalanced data.

Based on an IoT intrusion detection system, this study provided and investigated several assaults and anomaly types. We evaluated the performance of the proposed deep learning model DBN-IDS system using the

CICIDS dataset for attack detection. This dataset had several attacks with numerous labels and a large number of assaults. We went to great lengths in this study on the dataset used to assess performance. In this dataset, numerous factors, including DoS/DDoS, botnets, brute force attacks, web attacks, infiltration, and port scans, cause IoT system failure. The analyses' assessment criteria were detection rate, F1 score, precision, recall, and precision. The suggested model outperformed existing approaches generally. Future upgrades to the proposed IDS will enable it to recognize other systemic IoT threats and a wider range of intrusion detection datasets. Along with intrusion detection, this suggested method may also be utilized for classification and identification.

Previous research has used per-packet analysis to identify malicious network traffic, but this study finds that per-flow analysis produces superior detection results and that the fundamental data resampling unit may have an impact on detection performance. The attack surface is expanded by the multilayered convergence of a modern healthcare network environment. Defense in depth might improve security at several levels. The subject of further research may be how to combine current safety measures with those against IoT threats.

References

1. Kcyur, K.P. and Sunil, M.P., Internet of things-IoT: Definition, characteristics, architecture, enabling technologies, application & future challenges. *Int. J. Eng. Sci. Comput.*, 6, 5, 6122–6131, 2016.

2. HaddadPajouh, H., Dehghantanha, A., Khayami, R., Choo, K.-K.-R., A deep recurrent neural network-based approach for internet of things malware threat hunting. *Future Gener. Comput. Syst.*, 85, 88–96, Aug. 2018.

3. Al-Garadi, M.A., Mohamed, A., Al-Ali, A.K., Du, X., Ali, I., Guizani, M., A survey of machine and deep learning methods for Internet of Things (IoT) security, in: *IEEE Communications Surveys & Tutorials*, vol. 22, no. 3, pp. 1646–1685, thirdquarter 2020.

4. Pascu, L., *Medical IoT security incidents on the rise in 2019*, Survey says. https://www.bitdefender.com/box/blog/iot-news/medical-iot-security-incidents-rise-2019-survey-says/ (accessed: Jun. 12, 2021).

5. Graham, J., Hospitals hit hardest by ransomware attacks, study says. https://techxplore.com/news/2020-10-hospitals-hardest-ransomware.html (accessed: Jun. 12, 2021).

6. Boutin, C., NIST releases draft guidance on internet of things device cybersecurity. https://www.nist.gov/news-events/news/2020/12/nist-releases-draft-guidance-internet-things-device-cybersecurity (accessed: Jun. 12, 2021).

7. Davis, J., Cybersecurity in 2020: IoT medical devices, ransomware, legacy OS. https://healthitsecurity.com/news/cybersecurity-in-2020-iot-medical-devices-ransomware-legacy-os (accessed: Jun. 12, 2021).

8. Zhang, Y., Qiu, M., Tsai, C.-W., Hassan, M., Alamri, A., Health-CPS: Healthcare cyber-physical system assisted by cloud and big data. *IEEE Syst. J.*, 11, 1–8, 08/24 2015.

9. Rathore, S. and Park, J., Semi-supervised learning based distributed attack detection framework for IoT. *Appl. Soft Comput.*, 72, 79–89, 07/01 2018.

10. Thamilarasu, G., Odesile, A., Hoang, A., An intrusion detection system for internet of medical things. *IEEE Access*, 8, 181560–181576, 2020.

11. Center of Disease Control and Prevention. Health Insurance Portability and Accountability Act of 1996 (HIPAA). https://www.cdc.gov/phlp/publications/topic/hipaa.html (accessed: Jun. 12, 2021).

12. Emsisoft Malware Lab. State of Ransomware in the U.S.: 2019 Report for Q1 to Q3. https://blog.emsisoft.com/en/34193/state-of-ransomware-in-the-u-s-2019-report-for-q1-to-q3/ (accessed: Apr. 25, 2021).

13. Steffen, S., Hackers hold German hospital data hostage. https://www.dw.com/en/hackers-hold-german-hospital-data-hostage/a-19076030?maca=en-rss-en-all-1573-rdf (accessed: Apr. 22, 2021)..

14. Hassija, V., Chamola, V., Saxena, V., Jain, D., Goyal, P., Sikdar, B., A survey on IoT security: Application areas, security threats, and solution architectures. *IEEE Access*, 7, 82721–82743, 2019.

15. Fahim, M. and Sillitti, A., Anomaly detection, analysis and prediction techniques in IoT environment: A systematic literature review. *IEEE Access*, 7, 81664–81681, 2019.

16. Gurina, A. and Eliseev, V., Anomaly-based method for detecting multiple classes of network attacks. *Information*, 10, 3, 84, Feb. 2019.

17. Mahdavifar, S. and Ghorbani, A.A., Application of deep learning to cybersecurity: A survey. *Neurocomputing*, 347, 149–176, Jun. 2019.

18. Zhang, Y., Li, P., Wang, X., Intrusion detection for IoT based on improved genetic algorithm and deep belief network. *IEEE Access*, 7, 31711–31722, 2019.

19. Chacko, A. and Hayajneh, T., Security and privacy issues with IoT in healthcare. *EAI Endorsed Trans. Pervasive Health Technol.*, 4, 14, 2018.

20. Kagita, M.K., Thilakarathne, N., Gadekallu, T.R., Maddikunta, P.K.R., *A review on security and privacy of internet of medical things*, 2020, arXiv preprint arXiv:2009.05394.

21. Hussain, F. *et al.*, A framework for malicious traffic detection in IoT healthcare environment. *Sensors*, 21, 9, 3025, 2021.

22. Rahman, A., Hossain, M.S., Alrajeh, N.A., Alsolami, F., Adversarial examples–security threats to COVID-19 deep learning systems in medical IoT devices. *IEEE Internet Things J.*, 8, 12, 9603–9610, 2020.

23. Hussain, F., Abbas, S.G., Husnain, M., Fayyaz, U.U., Shahzad, F., Shah, G.A., *IoTDoS and DDoS attack detection using ResNet*, 2020, arXiv preprint arXiv:2012.01971.
24. Hussain, B., Du, Q., Sun, B., Han, Z., Deep learning based DDoS-attack detection for cyber–physical system over 5G network. *IEEE Trans. Industr. Inform.*, 17, 2, 860–870, 2020.
25. Taylor, J.M. and Sharif, H.R., "Enhancing integrity of modbus TCP through covert channels, in: *2017 11th International Conference on Signal Processing and Communication Systems (ICSPCS)*, IEEE, pp. 1–6, 2017.
26. Hady, A.A., Ghubaish, A., Salman, T., Unal, D., Jain, R., Intrusion detection system for healthcare systems using medical and network data: A comparison study. *IEEE Access*, 8, 106576–106584, 2020.
27. Roopak, M., Yun Tian, G., Chambers, J., Deep learning models for cyber security in IoT networks, in: *Proc. IEEE 9th Annu. Comput. Commun. Workshop Conf. (CCWC)*, pp. 0452–0457, Jan. 2019.
28. Zidi, S., Moulahi, T., Alaya, B.J.I.S.J., Fault detection in wireless sensor networks through SVM classifier. in *IEEE Senors J.*, 18, 1, 340–347, 2017.
29. Radford, B.J., Apolonio, L.M., Trias, A.J., Simpson, J.A., *Network traffic anomaly detection using recurrent neural networks*, 2018, arXiv preprint arXiv:1803.10769.
30. Prasse, P., Machlica, L., Pevný, T., Havelka, J., Scheffer, T., Malware detection by analysing network traffic with neural networks, in: *2017 IEEE Security and Privacy Workshops (SPW)*, IEEE, pp. 205–210, 2017.
31. Kim, T.-Y. and Cho, S.-B., Web traffic anomaly detection using C-LSTM neural networks. *Expert Systems with Applications,* 106, 66–76, 15 September 2018.
32. Jeong, C., Ahn, M., Lee, H., Jung, Y., Automatic classification of transformed protocols using deep learning, in: *International Conference on Parallel and Distributed Computing: Applications and Technologies*, Springer, pp. 153–158, 2018.
33. Xue, J., Chen, Y., Li, O., Li, F., Classification and identification of unknown network protocols based on CNN and T-SNE, in: *Journal of Physics: Conference Series*, vol. 1617, IOP Publishing, p. 012071, 2020.
34. Lin, R., Li, O., Li, Q., Liu, Y., Unknown network protocol classification method based on semi-supervised learning, in: *2015 IEEE International Conference on Computer and Communications (ICCC)*, IEEE, pp. 300–308, 2015.
35. Tyagi, A.K., Using multimedia systems, tools, and technologies for smart healthcare services, IGI Global, 2022.
36. ODSC., *15 Open datasets for healthcare*, (Accessed: Aug. 12, 2022).
37. Kaggle, *Healthcare datasets*, (Accessed: 12 Aug., 2022).
38. Adhikari, U., Pan, S., Morris, T., *Industrial control system (ICS) cyber attack datasets*, (Accessed: 12 Aug., 2022).
39. Lemay, A., *A SCADA Dataset*, (accessed: 12 Aug., 2022).

40. Gomathi, L., Mishra, A.K., Tyagi, A.K., Industry 5.0 for healthcare 5.0: Opportunities, challenges and future research possibilities, in: *2023 7th International Conference on Trends in Electronics and Informatics (ICOEI)*, pp. 204–213, Tirunelveli, India, 2023.

41. Lemay, A. and Fernandez, J.M., Providing SCADA network datasets for intrusion detection research, in: *9th Workshop on Cyber Security Experimentation and Test*, 2016.

42. Li, Y., Zhang, T., Ma, Y.Y., Zhou, C., Anomaly detection of user behavior for database security audit based on ocsvm, in: *2016 3rd International Conference on Information Science and Control Engineering (ICISCE)*, IEEE, pp. 214–219, 2016.

43. Sharafaldin, I., Habibi Lashkari, A., Ghorbani, A.A., Toward generating a new intrusion detection dataset and intrusion traffic characterization, in: *Proc. 4th Int. Conf. Inf. Syst. Secur. Privacy*, pp. 108–116, 2018.

44. Manimurugan, S. *et al.*, Effective attack detection in internet of medical things smart environment using a deep belief neural network. *IEEE Access*, 8, 77396–77404, 2020. 10.1109/access.2020.2986013, Accessed 12 Aug 2022.

45. Li, C. *et al.*, Machine learning-based detection of internet of thing attacks in healthcare environments. *IT Industry*, 9, 2, 2021, 2021, Accessed 12 Aug. 2022.

46. Shreyas Madhav, A.V., Ilavarasi, A.K., Tyagi, A.K., The Heroes and Villains of the Mix Zone: The Preservation and Leaking of USer's Privacy in Future Vehicles, in: *Microelectronic Devices, Circuits and Systems. ICMDCS 2022. Communications in Computer and Information Science*, Springer, Cham, vol. 1743, 2022, https://doi.org/10.1007/978-3-031-23973-1_12.

47. Sharma, D. and Tyagi, A.K., Preserving privacy in Internet of Things (IoT)-based devices, in: *Proceedings of Third International Conference on Computing, Communications, and Cyber-Security. Lecture Notes in Networks and Systems*, Springer, Singapore, p. 421, 2023, https://doi.org/10.1007/978-981-19-1142-2_63.

48. Tyagi, A.K., Rekha, G., Sreenath, N., Is your privacy safe with aadhaar? An open discussion, in: *2018 Fifth International Conference on Parallel, Distributed and Grid Computing (PDGC)*, pp. 318–323, 2018.

49. Nair, Manoj, M., Tyagi, Kumar, A., Privacy: History, statistics, policy, laws, preservation and threat analysis. *J. Inf. Assur. Secur.*, 16, 1, 24–34, 11p, 2021.

50. Tyagi, A.K., Fernandez, T.F., Mishra, S., Kumari, S., Intelligent automation systems at the core of industry 4.0, in: *Intelligent Systems Design and Applications. ISDA 2020*, Advances in Intelligent Systems and Computing, vol. 1351, A. Abraham, V. Piuri, N. Gandhi, P. Siarry, A. Kaklauskas, A. Madureira (Eds.), Springer, Cham, 2021, https://doi.org/10.1007/978-3-030-71187-0_1.

51. Tyagi, A.K., Nair, M.M., Niladhuri, S., Abraham, A., Security, privacy research issues in various computing platforms: A survey and the road ahead. *J. Inf. Assur. Secur.*, 15, 1, 1–16, 16p, 2020.

52. Tyagi, A.K., Kumari, S., Fernandez, T.F., Aravindan, C., P3 block: Privacy preserved, trusted smart parking allotment for future vehicles of tomorrow, in: *Computational Science and Its Applications – ICCSA 2020. ICCSA 2020,* Lecture Notes in Computer Science, vol. 12254, O. Gervasi, *et al.* (Eds.), Springer, Cham, 2020, https://doi.org/10.1007/978-3-030-58817-5_56.

53. A., Mohan Krishna, Tyagi, A.K., Prasad, S.V.A.V., Preserving privacy in future vehicles of tomorrow. *JCR,* 7, 19, 6675–6684, 2020.

54. Tyagi, A.K. and Sreenath, N., Preserving location privacy in location based services against sybil attacks. *Int. J. Secur. its Appl.,* 9, 12, 189–210, December 2015.

55. Tyagi, A.K. and Sreenath, N., A comparative study on privacy preserving techniques for location based services. *Br. J. Math. Comput. Sci.,* 10, 4, 1–25, July 2015.

56. Tyagi, A.K. and Sreenath, N., Providing safe, secure and trusted communication among vehicular ad-hoc networks' users: A vision paper. *Int. J. Inf. Technol. Electric. Eng.,* 5, 1, 35–44, February 2016.

57. Tyagi, A., Niladhuri, S., Priya, R., Never trust anyone: Trust-privacy trade-offs in vehicular Ad-Hoc networks. *J. Adv. Math. Comput. Sci.,* 19, 6, 1–23, 2016. https://doi.org/10.9734/BJMCS/2016/27737.

58. Tyagi, A.K. and Sreenath, N., Providing trust enabled services in vehicular cloud computing, in: *Proceedings of the International Conference on Informatics and Analytics (ICIA-16),* Association for Computing Machinery, New York, NY, USA, pp. Article 3, 1–10, 2016, https://doi.org/10.1145/2980258.2980263.

59. Tyagi, A.K. and Sreenath, N., Providing trust enabled services in vehicular cloud computing. *2016 International Conference on Research Advances in Integrated Navigation Systems (RAINS),* pp. 1–7, 2016.

60. Tyagi, A.K., Krishna, A.M., Malik, S., Nair, M.M., Niladhuri, S., Trust and reputation mechanisms in vehicular ad-hoc networks: A systematic review. *Adv. Sci. Technol. Eng. Syst. J.,* 5, 1, 387–402, 2020.

11

MPHDRDNN: Meticulous Presaging of Heart Disease by Regularized DNN Through GUI

Ritu Aggarwal* and Suneet Kumar

Department of Computer Science Engineering, Maharishi Markendeshwar Engineering College, Mullana, India

Abstract

Various intelligent and automated diagnosis models have been by the other researchers by using the various machine learning model and techniques. To control the death rate and increase the chance of survival rate of patient's early detection of disease is necessary. Heart disease prediction at early stages is very challenging task that poses a serious threat of life shortening. In this proposed model an intelligent and automated is designed with the help of GUI features used by the Python Jupyter notebook. The analysis is based on real time database using the machine learning models which are to be trained and tested on the same dataset. The various parameters of machine learning with dataset computed results and predict heart disease. This regularized deep leaning network (L1 & L2) with some intelligent detecting easily predict the disease at early stages and the proposed model could help the doctors for prescribing medications in timely manner. This current study develops a GUI application by which the prediction of heart disease could be easily identified by their clinical parameters.

Keywords: Graphical user interface, heart disease, L1 & L2 regularization

Corresponding author: errituaggarwal@gmail.com

Amit Kumar Tyagi (ed.) Privacy Preservation of Genomic and Medical Data, (243–262) © 2024
Scrivener Publishing LLC

11.1　Introduction

In the previous research the deep learning-based prediction system developed. To develop the intelligent automated detection system the basic idea is based on the develop the deep learning based intelligent system through which relevant features have to be selected. The DNN regularized the data by providing to structured form. Intelligent system automatically detect the disease by the patients clinical parameters.DNN provides the intelligent through the regularization methods, such as L1-regularization, L2-regularization, drop our hold validation method. The regularization methods are developed to remove the problem of under fitting and overfitting the data. It automatically used the feature engineering and deep learning selects the brain neurons by which it forms the complex patterns from the data.

Regularization is a set of techniques that can prevent overfitting in neural networks which improve the accuracy of intelligent system. New data when entered to the system at the of training and testing the data various problems occurred, at that time regularization is needed. Prediction of disease could be done by deep learning and machine learning techniques according the entered the patient data. Regularization has achieved by the different techniques as previous mentioned. On the basis of results to overcomes all the problems by the designing and developed the graphical user interface. This interface automatically detects the patient disease by their clinical parameters. This study is projected section as follows: 11.1 introduction about the domain about of work, in section 11.2 literature study by which how the other researcher works on the DNN, section 11.3 proposed work methods and in section 11.4 performance evaluation, in section 11.5 results and discussions, finally section 11.6 concludes this chapter

11.2　Literature Study

Subhadra and Boddu [1] used a multilayer perceptron neural network, the suggested system of heart disease prediction and suitable diagnosis has been developed. Back propagation algorithm was used to train the data and compare the parameters iteratively for accurate prediction. Up until a minimal error rate was noticed, the propagation method was repeated. The findings shown in the previous section make it abundantly clear that the accuracy rate is maximized. Results show that, when compared to other methods, the suggested strategy accurately predicts heart disease using the

14 features. By taking into account more factors, this work can be expanded to forecast and examine the severity of the condition.

Chen et al. [2] proposed model in which Data in cyberspace is growing as a result of the advancement of new technology that is used for network communication. Massive amounts of redundant data pose serious issues for network connectivity and security. Therefore, the foundation for solving this challenge understands how to accurately detect the same information for the neural network. Main issue for every training data is overfitting and under fitting in DNN. Researchers resolve this issue with the assigning and adding the weights to the given nodes

Xiao et al. [3] projected a heart disease by the clinical parameters of patient. It develops a DNN model for the prediction of heart disease. In this study, the DNN is replaced with DRNN and obtained a 95% accuracy as compared to CNN using ML techniques as accuracy for logistic regression is 87%; Random Forest, 83%; Native Bayes, 80%; Decision Tree, 68%.

Mukherjee et al. [4] projected an idea for in healthcare. In the current era of growing health issues and chronic diseases, various statistical analyses are conducted to make health solutions more accurate and faultless as we discuss affordability and quality assurance in the healthcare business. It is amazing how data-driven intelligent technologies have advanced in terms of disease diagnosis, detection, treatment, and research. The area where the most sought-after minds are working is medical image analysis and symptom-based disease prediction. With the help of ECG analysis and symptom-based detection, we want to provide our proposed model for the prediction of diagnosis of cardio vascular illness in this study. The model seeks to be investigated and developed further.

Li et al. [5] projected that one of the more difficult ailments is heart disease, which affected a large number of people worldwide. Heart illness must be promptly and accurately diagnosed in order to be treated, especially in the field of cardiology. In this work, we suggested a machine learning-based approach for diagnosing cardiac disease that is both effective and accurate. The system was created using classification algorithms, where standard feature selection algorithms like relief, minimal redundancy maximal relevance, least absolute shrinkage selection operator, and local learning have been used to omit unnecessary and redundant features. Other feature selection algorithms include support vector machine, logistic regression, artificial neural network, K-nearest neighbour, Nave bays, and Decision tree. To address this issue, we have provided a brand-new, quick conditional mutual information feature selection approach.

Zhou et al. [6] developed a cloud video surveillance (CVS) has gained a lot of attention in recent years due to the rapid growth of IoT, AI, and cloud computing technologies. This is especially true when real-time analysis is needed for smart application development. Generally, object detection is crucial to surveillance system sensor systems and activity tracking. We now have the chance to manage the continuously created massive volume of surveillance data locally across IoT systems thanks to the growing edge-cloud computing architecture. However, because of the complicated surveillance environment, the predictive accuracy is still far from satisfactory. The multi- target detection for real-time monitoring in intelligent IoT systems is the main topic of this study. A-YONet is a recently developed deep neural network model that is created by fusing the benefits.

Due to its noteworthy expressiveness, flexibility, and scalability, attribute-based access control (ABAC) has gained increasing interest as network research has advanced quickly [7]. Unfortunately, gathering user characteristics is required to finish the typical ABAC decision-making process, which raises the danger of privacy leakage. This issue inhibits the spread of ABAC and raises public scepticism about it. This work introduces a unique hash-based binary search tree to introduce a privacy-protected and efficient attribute-based access control (EPABAC) system to avoid the privacy leakage of access subject in the decision-making process of ABAC. The results of the analysis and experimental assessments demonstrate that the EPABAC protects user privacy during the decision-making process with a tolerable increase in computational cost.

11.3   Proposed Methodology

This proposed work is to predict the heart disease in an individual in view of responding to a couple of inquiries utilizing DNN models in a start to finish process. The examination is carried on a framework with the accompanying framework configurations and programming: Python 3. Proposed diagram of the current work showed the how the DNN and GUI work for disease prediction as shown in Figure 11.1. In this regularization method to profound the neurons of brain organized to predict the heart disease. For indemnifying the disease and the practical examinations carried out on using the Cleveland dataset that have 303 instances and selected pre-processed 14 attributes. Some of attributes in given instance have missing values. DNN has following layers by their working is based such as (key) input/output and secret layer as shown in Figure 11.1.

This the basic structure of DNN neurons by which shows the working of this model. The basic idea for this as three different kinds of nodes and accordingly the weight assigned to each nodes.

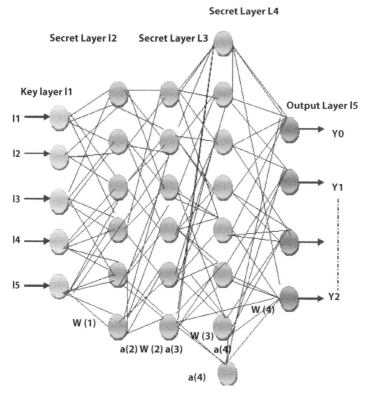

Figure 11.1 DNN neuron architecture.

11.3.1   Proposed Flowchart of Work

The current study develops a GUI based application by which easily predicts the heart disease. As shown in Figure 11.2.

Overfitting means that when samples are collected to predict the disease, it could be easily trained and predicted [3] but at the time of validation and testing the data due to generalization and poor performance on dataset, it occurs. Any of the strategies could be following to overcome this problem [4]. In the proposed work the DNN used we could reduce the complexity through reducing the numbers of hidden layers present in neural network. The current proposed work designed for the Cleveland dataset but to increase the number of samples or for multimodal datasets we could overcome the overfitting problem [6]. The main method is L1 or L2 regularization method that applying to penalty factor to the loss function.

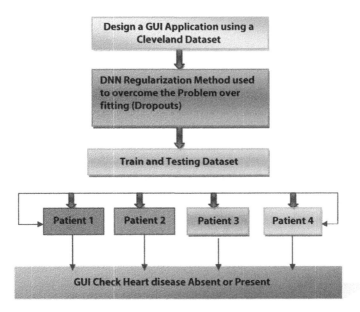

Figure 11.2 Proposed workflow.

DNN

It is an analytic method that we planned utilizes standard completely associated with neural networks. For DNN, the heart disease analysis which accessible by including TensorFlow, Keras, Paddle, Caffe, MagmaDNN, and so forth [1]. The main building block for the DNN is the network framework augmentation, which is accessible to use through exceptionally improved numerical libraries like CUBLAS, CUDNN, MKL, MAGMA [13], and others. A parameterized DNN in Python, involving NumPy as a backend for the straight variable based math schedules required. The code is vectorized for execution, communicated with regards to grid lattice augmentations, and in this manner can be handily ported to C/C++ code, calling profoundly advanced BLAS/GEMM executions, which gives useful and execution transportability across different registering structures. The structure plan, documentations, and principal computational advances that we research are il- lustrated on the brain network is coordinated into L completely associated "layers" (I = 1, .. L) with ni vectors (or artificial neurons) per layer that capability together to make a pre-phrasing. The associations between layers I − 1 and I are addressed by mathematical loads, put away in network Wi by size ni and other vectors by length represented as by ni-, defines the resultant layer I the given vector as the following formula is used as flows:

$$Zi = WiAi - 1 + bi, \tag{11.1}$$

where "+" add the segments of nb of the subsequent network. The Forward design process, given by stages 0, …, L, addresses a non-straight hypothe-sister/expectation capability HW,b(X) ≡ AL for given inputs X and fixed loads W, b. The loads should be altered with the goal that the expectations HW,b(X) become near given/realized results put away in Y. This is known as a characterization issue and is an instance of supposed regulated learning [8]. The change of the loads is characterized as a minimization issue on a raised expense capability J, e.g.,

$$\min (W, b) = -\Sigma \, y \log (\,) + (1 -) \log(1 - H(x \,)) \tag{11.2}$$

where it is used to compute the entropy and mutual information for regularization.

This is tackled by a clump stochastic inclination plummet technique - an iterative calculation utilizing a group of nb preparing models all at once. The subordinates of J regarding the loads (W and b) are Inferred over the layers utilizing the chain rule for separating syntheses of capabilities. They are registered then by the regressive proliferation steps L+1, , 2L, and used to alter their particular loads Wi, bi during the iterative preparation process for each layer I as:

$$Wi = Wi - \lambda dWi, \, bi = bi - \lambda dbi, \tag{11.3}$$

Where λ is a hyper parameter alluded to as learning rate. The σ1, σL capabilities are the initiation capabilities (perhaps unique) for the various layers of the organization, and σJ are their subsidiaries. We have coded initiation capability decisions for ReLU, sigmoid, tanh, and broken ReLU. The ".*" documentation is for point-wise duplication is a standard strategy that forestalls overfitting by punishing huge weight values. DNNs will quite often dole out higher weight values for specific preparation pieces of information, which relates to a high fluctuation. Regularization assists address the issue of high fluctuation on preparing information, which with canning further develop exactness on test information for regularization is as α ||W, b||2 to the expense capability J, where ||W, b|| is some standard of the loads, e.g., L1 or L2. The regularization boundary α forces a punishment on enormous loads, in this way guaranteeing that we do not overfit preparing information. One more benefit of regularization is that it can keep a calculation from gaining from information exceptions, which is fundamental for a more modest dataset like the coronary illness patient set utilized in this examination [2]. Regularization makes the anomalies stay in the dataset, yet decreases the calculation's probability of gaining from these qualities [9].

Hyper Parametric Optimization

The numbers of layers in CNN have a huge network with 16-19 weighting layers to develop a VGG network. The computation.

$$\text{hparams} = [L, n1 \dots nL, \sigma1, \dots, \sigma L, \lambda, \alpha, nb, \text{epochs}] \qquad (11.4)$$

Data about dataset 1

Dataset taken from the University of California Irvine AI archive. Information has been preprocessed. The missing value finds in dataset. It has 303 instances and 14 attributes. The different clinical attributes such as age, sex, chest type, resting blood sugar. During ECG the ST fragment is a comparative approach to outwardly surveying the hearts capability when it should course more blood, on account of activity [14]. pulse, 5) cholesterol, 6) fasting glucose, 7) resting electrocardiographic outcomes, 8) greatest pulse accomplished, 9) work out prompted angina, 10) ST gloom, and 11) incline of the pinnacle practice ST fragment. These characteristics have been chosen as ideal highlights by different scientists utilizing this dataset [1] in light of the fact that they are viewed as generally firmly connected to heart disease. This dataset is utilized in light of the fact that it is openly available and thusly works on the reproducibility of results. Hparams utilizes these eleven highlights to analyze coronary illness on account of their variety, accessibility, and capacity to recognize coronary illness at various progressive phases. The blend of these highlights can make a model that precisely assesses connections between different patient circumstances and coronary illness conclusion [18].

Impact of Regularization

While the unregularized DNN shows an inconsistency between preparing exactness and test (close to 100% on preparing, 93% on test), regularization expanded the precision on test information to close to 100%. The regularization worked on the precision on test information by decreasing the effect of exceptions (as well as missing information) on preparing information. On a somewhat little dataset, exceptions can hinder the calculation's capacity to gain from predictable connections in preparing information, and do not add logical worth. Consequently, by controlling the impact of anomalies on learning, regularization further develops the calculations capacity to sum up while keeping up with a similar logical norm. Since

Table 11.1 Nodes presents in DNN.

Parameter	Setting
Total types or Number of layers	3
Input layer nodes	14
Output layer nodes	1
Secret layer nodes	14
Dropout	0.5
Batch Size	32
Epochs	150

regularization diminishes overfitting on preparing information, the calculations precision is supposed to diminish on preparing information as shown by Tables 11.1 and 11.2 [16].

Some of the activation used by DNN
Sigmoid Function
The sigmoid function is plotted as in shape of "S" graph. The following formula is used to evaluate the sigmoid function, such as [20]

$$B = 1/(1 + e{-}x) \qquad (11.5)$$

It is also known as no linear function by which the X values of -2 to 2. These values are steep values means that if any slightly change in the value of x, it could be possible it changed at large extent. The value lies between the ranges 0 to 1. The prediction result could easily get by if lies 1or greater than 0.5 [17].

Activation Function
This function decides which neuron is selected and activated. According to each neurons assigns the weight and then add it .it checks the non linearity of each assigned nodes with their and sum that produces.

Tanh function
This function is also a non linear function in which one or more real values entered as input number −1, 1. The output is a zero centered for the inputs given that has a range as neutral, strongly negative and positive [19].

ReLU Function: (Rectified Linear Unit)
This function provides features or work benefit same as sigmoid function. It gives better performance when compared both functions [21]. The basic idea is used implement the ReLu function is that to solve the vanishing gradients problems. The range lies between from max to 0,y.

11.4   Performance Evaluation Metrics

The current model implements and evaluated for the various metrics such as accuracy, LOSS and ROC etc.

LOSS
In the DNN the loss is the key element for any training data computation. With the help of training the correct behavior of target could be easily predicted by the loss function. GUI application performed the function using the loss function because it gives the optimal results at the time of training the application specific model. For computed the binary classification problems is used as binary cross-entropy loss function. Loss can be computed by the following formula. Such as

$$\textbf{Loss} = \textbf{y\_1} - \textbf{hat y\_i})^\textbf{2} \, \textbf{L} = (\textbf{yi} - \textbf{y\textasciicircum i)2} \qquad (11.6)$$

The performance of the framework was tried on the Cleveland coronary illness dataset. The proficiency of Reg-DNN was assessed by utilizing the hold-out approval method.70% information was utilized for preparing the model and 30% information was utilized for testing the model. Two sorts of models of DNN were made: traditional DNN and regularized DNN. Tests were performed with the two sorts of models to dissect the impact of regularization on model exactness. Regularized DNN was created by applying dropout and L2 regularization. Model precision and misfortune with ordinary and regularized DNN are displayed. In the advancement of DNN, it is important to guarantee that overfitting does not happen. Improper organization setup prompts overfitting of the model. When overfitting happens network is exceptionally fitted with preparing information and gives great exactness with preparing information however gives a horrible showing with testing information. In Reg-DNN, the issue of overfitting was overwhelmed by regularization. Precision and loss of customary DNN and regularized DNN over the quantity of epochs.

11.4.1   L1 Regularization

It is also called lasoo regression and denoted as Ω. It is computed by the formula in that the absolute values in weight matrix as in weight parameters. It is the most common weight decay or ride regression in all type of regularizations used in DNN. With the help of regularization reduces the overfitting problem.

Dropout
Dropout AI Regularization is one of the most normally involved strategies for Profound Learning Frameworks. Profound Brain Nets are strong AI Frameworks. What is more, overfitting could be a difficult issue to counter in these enormous Brain Nets. Dropout is an AI Regularization strategy that approximates preparing countless brain networks with various structures in equal. It is accomplished by obstructing or Dropping haphazardly chosen neurons during preparing. Dropout can be effectively executed in input as well as covered up information. In this regularization procedure, the neurons are haphazardly discarded, and the current neurons on various levels lead to make up for decreased limit with respect to the expectation. This powers the organization to learn complex inner portrayal. The organization becomes heartless toward specific neurons and improves speculations for the general preparation information. The primary benefit of the Dropout strategy is that it forestalls every one of the neurons in the organization from merging toward a similar objective and working simul taneously. With the Dropout method, you can de-connect the loads and make the Profound Learning Model perform better speculation undertakings and Expectations.

11.4.2   Implementation With L1 and L2 Reg-DNN

Dropout regularization is a method for regularizing L2 and L1. During training, this is a pretty straightforward process. It is founded on probability [9]. The pooled area's unit value sorting is utilized to develop the unit (neuron) discarding technique, and wireless communications and mobile computing are used to design the maximum pooling dropout. The second step is to create the weight attenuation by including a penalty term into the backpropagation. The implementation process: theoretical analysis and experimental comparison show that the strategy used in this study may successfully prevent overfitting and improve the network's generalization capabilities [5]. However, the technique proposed in this study has the following flaws. The top convolutional layer's semilinear activation function (ReLU) may result in non-maximal output.

11.4.2.1 How to Implement in This Proposed Work L2 and L1 Regularization

L2 and L1 are the most well-known sorts of regularization. Regularization deals with the reason that more modest loads lead to easier models which in results helps in staying away from overfitting. So to get a more modest weight network, these methods add a "regularization term" alongside the misfortune to get the expense capability.

Cost capability = Misfortune + Regularization term

Where to Utilize Regularization

In the above segment, we have perceived how we can regularize the loads of the brain organizations yet we as a whole realize there are such circumstances where we might have to apply the regularization methods. A portion of the circumstances are recorded beneath. We can utilize them with any brain network since it is a conventional methodology for making the model exhibition higher. However, it is proposed to utilize particularly with the LSTM models. It very well may be generally utilized with successive info and such associations which are repetitive.

Assuming in any circumstance the size of information values are not comparable we can utilize the regularization as a result of its extraordinary capacity to refresh the information variable to have a similar scale, the enormous organizations for the most part become overfitted to the preparation information we can use for regularization with the huge organizations.

Pre-prepared brain networks are better with those information just on which they are prepared and to use with fresher information or various data sources we can utilize the regularization. It assists the organization with playing out different information that are insignificant to one another.

As we have found in the article that L1 and L2 both of the regularization approach is helpful and furthermore we can apply the two of them as opposed to picking between them. In the relapse technique, we have seen the outcome of the versatile net where both of the punishments are utilized [10, 11]. We can likewise attempt this methodology in brain organizations. Additionally, we utilize the little upsides of the hyper parameter in the regularization that aides in controlling the commitment of each weight to the punishment. Physically doling out worth to the hyper parameter we can

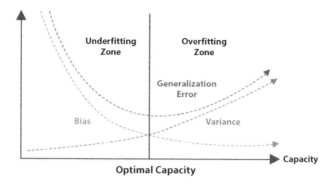

Figure 11.3 Regularized capacity. https://medium.com/analytics-vidhya/regularization-understanding-l1-and-l2-regularization-for-deep-learning-a7b9e4a409bf.

utilize the network scan strategy for picking the right hyper parameter for better execution as shown in Figure 11.3.

11.4.2.2 Lasso Relapse

The coefficients are punished to where they arrive at zero at all outright shrinkage and choice administrator (or rope) relapse [12, 13]. It disposes of the immaterial free factors. The L1 standard is utilized for regularization in this method.

> L1-standard is added as a punishment.
> The beta coefficients' outright worth is L1.
> The L1 regularization is one more name for it.
> L1 regularization produces inadequate outcomes.

At the point when there is a great deal of factors, this system proves to be useful on the grounds that it could be used as an element determination strategy all alone.

11.4.2.3 Edge Relapse

At the point when the factors in a model are multicollinear, the Edge relapse approach is utilized to dissect it. It limits the quantity of unimportant free factors yet does not thoroughly dispose of them. The L2 standard is utilized for regularization in this kind of regularization. As a discipline, it utilizes the L2-standard as shown in Table 11.2.

Table 11.2 Accuracy results.

DNN model	Accuracy	Loss	Drop out
L1+L2 Regn_DNN	96.5%	1.52%	34%
L1-Norm	90.5%	1.40%	67%
Dropout	78.8%	1.36%	70%
K_n+ Sparsity	90%	1.38%	80%
Dropout +Maxnorm	91.5%	1.25%	87.6%

The L2 punishment is equivalent to the square of the extents of the beta coefficients.

It is likewise alluded to as L2-regularization as shown by Figure 11.4.

L2 lessens the coefficients yet never carries them to nothing.

L2 regularization produces non-inadequate outcomes.

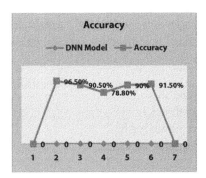
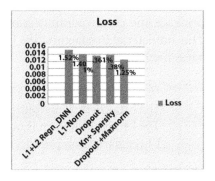

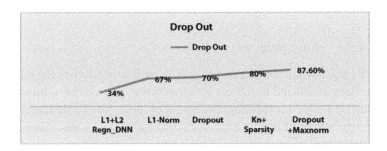

Figure 11.4 Implementation results for loss, dropout, loss.

11.4.3   Graphical User System Model

In this section, a graphical user interface is developed for making intelligent system for meticulous presaging of heart disease. The GUI is easy to use. The output and data input given to the system is shown in Figure 11.1. This GUI consists of clinical parameters of different patients and developed the model which easy to handle. It gives results according to the selected data from the patient history. The basic idea to develop this model is to predicts whether a patient have heart disease or not. The results conclude the input and output data given to the system with their clinical parameters that finally informed the person should consult a cardiologist and start their treatments with some prescription mentioned by doctor. Intelligent system developed by using an regularized deep neural network for heart disease predition. L1 and L2 regularization, dropout methods and max norm methods are used to prevent the overfitting problem in DNN. The performance of system model is based on computed the performance evaluation metrics, such as accuracy, loss, AUC with their ROC characteristics. It obtained accuracy for L1+L2 Regn_DNN 96.5% and loss 1.52% and dropout is 34. The graphical user interface could be helpful for the doctors for detect the disease. The automated intelligent heart disease prediction system model reduce the error rate because the prediction and detection, diagnosis most accurately found out with GUI as shown by Figure 11.5.

11.5   Results and Implementation Process for Building a GUI

To build a GUI-based application for heart disease, tkinter is used .input the clinical attributes of patient as per Cleveland dataset used for creating the GUI. In this framework, four types of patient data are input according their results obtained when treated it as for heart disease. Every patient's input gives results according to data input by the physicians. The prediction is checked with the help of prediction button. This button is used to check the patient is suffering from heart disease or not. The results obtained by GUI are as follows.

=============== RESTART: C:\Users\lenovo\OneDrive\Desktop\ GUI.py ===============

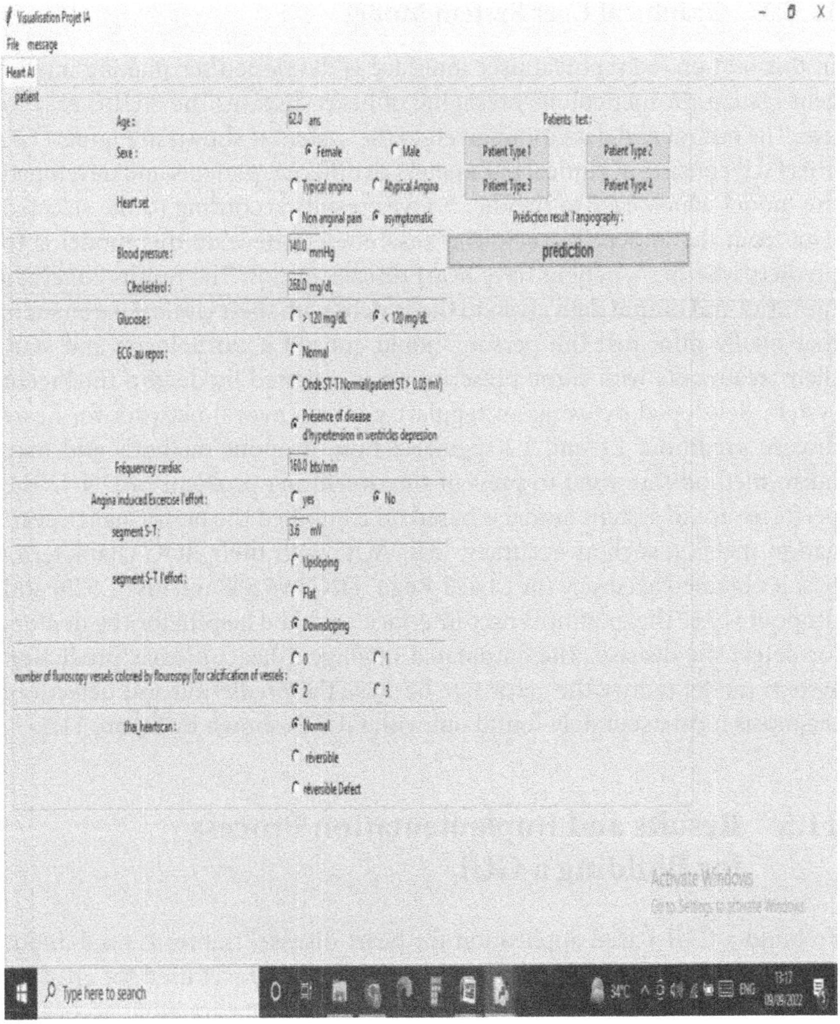

Figure 11.5 GUI interface for heart disease prediction.

Patient 1:3.0

62.0 0.0 4.0 140.0 268.0 0.0 2.0 160.0 0.0 3.6 3.0 2.0 3.0

62.0 0.0 4.0 140.0 268.0 0.0 2.0 160.0 0.0 3.6 3.0 2.0 3.0

Patient 2 7.0

44.0 1.0 2.0 120.0 263.0 0.0 0.0 173.0 0.0 0.0 1.0 0.0 7.0

44.0 1.0 2.0 120.0 263.0 0.0 0.0 173.0 0.0 0.0 1.0 0.0 7.0

Patient 3 7.0

67.0 1.0 4.0 120.0 229.0 0.0 2.0 129.0 1.0 2.6 2.0 2.0 7.0

67.0 1.0 4.0 120.0 229.0 0.0 2.0 129.0 1.0 2.6 2.0 2.0 7.0

Patient 4:7.0

60.0 1.0 4.0 117.0 230.0 1.0 0.0 160.0 1.0 1.4 1.0 2.0 7.0

60.0 1.0 4.0 117.0 230.0 1.0 0.0 160.0 1.0 1.4 1.0 2.0 7.0

The GUI shows prediction results for different patients input given to the system. It is an intelligent automated detection GUI system. That shows prediction of disease.

11.6   Conclusion and Future Scope

In this application various activation function and regularization methods are studying that is used to build the intelligent system. Deep neural network is used to detect the heart disease by developing GUI and computed the number the dropouts and Epchos according to evaluation metrics. The results obtained and computed according to DNN model for L1+L2 Regn_ DNN is 96.5% and dropout is 34 % and loss is 1.52%.in future another DNN model is implemented for the same for heart disease prediction. GUI using Jpython will be developed for multimodal dataset by which any of dataset could give prediction rate of heart.

11.6.1   Comparative Performance Reg-DNN
With Other Existing Work

In the literature review, many systems already existing for predicting and diagnosing the heart disease, when compared with other system model

Table 11.3 Comparison of the Reg-DNN with existing systems.

Reference	Year	Method	Accuracy
A. Ashiquzzaman, A. K. Tushar, M. R. Islam *et al.* [18]	2017	DNN	88.41
Mukherjee, Soumonos & Sharma [4]	2019	DNN and ECG signal	Not defined
K. H. Cha, N. Petrick, A. Pezeshk, C. G. Graff, and B. Sahiner [15]	2019	Faster R-CNN	Image refinement by DNN
Subhadra, K. & Boddu [1]	2019	MLP	Achieved accuracy higher (not defined)
X. Chen *et al.* [2]	2020	DNN	70
Xiao *et al.* [3]	2020	DRNN	95
Li *et al.* [5]	2020	FCMIM_SVM	92.37
Zhou *et al.* [6]	2020	Control (EPABAC	Not defined
Xu and Zeng [7]	2020	IOT systemwith DNN	Not defined
Our Work	2022	DNN modelfor L1+L2 Regn	Reg_DNN L1+L2 is 96.5% and dropout is 34 % andloss is 1.52%

Reg-DNN performance is good because it reduces the problem of over-fitting. The compared performance is shown in Table 11.3 and also the accuracy comparison.

Acknowledgment

This research work aims to design the GUI-based application and L1 and L2 used for regularization and reduce the problems of overfitting.

References

1. Subhadra, K. and Vikas, B., Neural network based intelligent system for predicting heart disease. *IJITEE.*, 8, 484–487, 2019.
2. Chen, X., Li, C., Wang, D. *et al.*, Android HIV: A study of repackaging malware for evading machine-learning detection. *IEEE Trans. Inf. Forensics Secur.*, 15, 1, 987–1001, 2020. [2].
3. Xiao, N., Zou, Y., Yin, Y., Liu, P., Tang, R., DRNN: Deep residual neural network for heart disease prediction, in: *Journal of Physics: Conference Series*, vol. 1682, 1, IOP Publishing, p. 012065, 2020, November.
4. Mukherjee, S. and Sharma, A., Intelligent heart disease prediction using neural network. *Int. J. Recent Technol. Eng.*, 7, 402–405, 2019.
5. Li, J.P., Haq, A.U., Din, S.U., Khan, J., Khan, A., Saboor, A., Heart disease identification method using machine learning classification in E-healthcare. *IEEE Access*, vol, 107562–107582, 2020.
6. Lin, G., Wen, S., Han, Q., Zhang, J., Xiang, Y., Software vulnerability detection using deep neural networks: A survey. *Proc. IEEE*, 108, 10, 1825–1848, 2020.
7. Xu, Y., Zhang, C., Wang, G., Qin, Z., Zeng, Q., A blockchain-enabled deduplicatable data auditing mechanism for network storage services. *IEEE Trans. Emerg. Top. Comput.*, 9, 3, 1421–32, 2020.
8. Zhou X, Xu X, Liang W, Zeng Z, Yan Z. Deep-learning-enhanced multitarget detection for end–edge–cloud surveillance in smart IoT. *IEEE Internet of Things Journal.*, 4, 8, 16, 12588–96, 2021 May.
9. Xu, Y., Ren, J., Zhang, Y., Zhang, C., Shen, B., Zhang, Y., Blockchain empowered arbitrable data auditing scheme for network storage as a service. *IEEE Trans. Serv. Comput.*, 13, 2, 289–300, 2020.
10. Qi, L., Hu, C., Zhang, X. *et al.*, Privacy-aware data fusion and prediction with spatial-temporal context for smart city industrial environment. *IEEE Trans. Industr. Inform.*, 17, 6, 4159–4167, 2021.
11. Xu, Y., Zeng, Q., Wang, G., Zhang, C., Ren, J., Zhang, Y., An efficient privacy-enhanced attribute-based access control mechanism. *Concurr. Comput. Pract. Exp.*, 32, 5, 1–10, 2020.
12. Zhou, X., Liang, W., Shimizu, S., Ma, J., Jin, Q., Siamese neural network based few-shot learning for anomaly detection in industrial cyber-physical systems. *IEEE Trans. Indstr. Inform.*, 17, 8, 5790–5798, 2021.

13. Xu, Y., Yan, X., Wu, Y., Hu, Y., Liang, W., Zhang, J., Hierarchical bidirectional RNN for safety-enhanced B5G heterogeneous networks. *IEEE Trans. Netw. Sci. Eng.*, 8, 4, 2946–57, 2021.

14. Yang, X., Li, X., Guan, Y., Song, J., Wang, R., Overfitting reduction of pose estimation for deep learning visual odometry. *China Commun.*, 17, 6, 196–210, 2020.

15. Cha, K.H., Petrick, N., Pezeshk, A., Graff, C.G., Sahiner, B., Reducing overfitting of a deep learning breast mass detection algorithm in mammography using synthetic images, in: *Progress in Biomedical Optics and Imaging-Proceedings of SPIE*, pp. 188–194, San Diego, CA, USA, March 2019.

16. González, G., Ash, S.Y., San José Estépar, R., Washko, G.R., Reply to Mummadi *et al.*: Overfitting and use of mismatched cohorts in deep learning models: Preventable design limitations. *Am. J. Respir. Crit. Care Med.*, 198, 4, 545–555, 2018.

17. Ashiquzzaman, A., Tushar, A.K., Islam, M.R. *et al.*, Reduction of overfitting in diabetes prediction using deep learning neural network, in: *IT Convergence and Security 2017*, Lecture Notes in Electrical Engineering, vol. 449, pp. 35–43, Springer, Singapore, 2018.

18. Zhang, S., Gong, Y., Wang, J., The development of deep convolutional neural networks and their applications in the field of computer vision. *Chin. J. Comput.*, 42, 3, 453–482, 2019.

19. Xu, Y., Zhang, C., Zeng, Q., Wang, G., Ren, J., Zhang, Y., Blockchain-enabled accountability mechanism against information leakage in vertical industry services. *IEEE Trans. Netw. Sci. Eng.*, 8, 2, 1202–1213, 2021.

20. Gong, T., Fan, T., Guo, J., Cai, Z., GPU-based parallel optimization of immune convolutional neural network and embedded system. *Eng. Appl. Artif. Intell.*, 62, 25, 384–395, 2017.

21. Liu, D. and Liu, J., Neural network model for deep learning overfitting problem. *J. Nat. Sci. Xiangtan Univ.*, 40, 2, 96–99, 2018.

12

Techniques for Removing Hair From Dermoscopic Images: A Survey of Current Approaches

Ranjita Rout[1], Priyadarsan Parida[1]*, Sonali Dash[2] and Sandipan Mallik[3]

[1]*Department of Electronics and Communication Engineering, GIET University, Gunupur, Odisha, India*
[2]*Department of Computer Science Engineering, Chandigarh University, Chandigarh, Punjab, India*
[3]*Department of Electronics and Communication Engineering, NIST, Berhampur, Odisha, India*

Abstract

One of the prevalent and severe forms of skin cancer is melanoma. If not caught in time, it poses a threat to human life. The survival rate may be increased with early identification. For the purpose of effectively diagnosing melanoma, computer-aided diagnostic (CAD) systems are crucial. However, the work presents a challenge for the CAD system because of the existence of artefacts like hairs, gels, ruler lines, etc. It has been discovered that the majority of dermoscopic pictures include hairs, which have an immediate impact on the CAD system. For the improvement of the accuracy of the diagnosis, it is crucial to eliminate hairs and other artefacts from the dermoscopic pictures. This research analyzes several hair removal methods, including unsupervised and supervised algorithms, using dermoscopic pictures. The result demonstrates the superiority of supervised methods over unsupervised methods for the identification of hairs from dermoscopic pictures.

Keywords: Computer-aided diagnostic (CAD), melanoma, hair removal

*Corresponding author: priyadarsanparida@giet.edu

Amit Kumar Tyagi (ed.) Privacy Preservation of Genomic and Medical Data, (263–282) © 2024 Scrivener Publishing LLC

12.1 Introduction

Skin cancer is one of the most common malignancies in the world. The three different kinds of skin cancer include melanoma, basal cell carcinoma, and squamous cell carcinoma. Malignant melanoma, another name for melanoma, is one of the three kinds of skin cancer that may be lethal. Melanoma is brought on by the melanocytes' aberrant cell proliferation. If not caught in time, it is less prevalent and more dangerous to human life. In the United States, 197,700 new instances of melanoma are anticipated in 2022, according to the Skin Cancer Foundation. Out of that, 7650 fatalities attributed to melanoma are anticipated. Early diagnosis and identification are thus crucial for improving survival rates and saving human lives. Basically, the dermatologist does the physical examination according to the asymmetry, border, color, diameter, evolving (ABCDE) [1] guidelines. However, owing to the complexity of melanoma, it is also exceedingly difficult for doctors to find it through physical examination. Therefore, proper melanoma detection is crucial since it aids in diagnosis and lowers the likelihood that melanoma would be the cause of mortality. As a result, the CAD [2] system is highly advised since it improves the accuracy of melanoma early detection and aids in melanoma diagnosis. Pre-processing is regarded as the first and most important stage in a CAD system since it aids in removing undesirable artefacts from the dermoscopic pictures, such as hairs, ruler markings, gels, and bubbles. Dermoscopic pictures with unwanted artefacts provide accurate results for the CAD system. The researchers have created a variety of pre-processing methods to get rid of unwanted artefacts, including light and thick hair removal, texture area enhancement, lesion border identification, etc. Hairs are one of the most prevalent artefacts in dermoscopic pictures from various datasets, and this may directly impact how correctly melanoma may be detected using a CAD system. Therefore, it is crucial to remove artefacts including hairs, from dermoscopic pictures. In order to remove hairs from dermoscopic pictures, many hair removal techniques are explored in this work.

12.1.1 Organization of Chapter

The remaining sections of the study are organized as follows: Sections 12.2 and 12.3 discuss various inpainting and hair removal techniques applied to dermoscopic pictures. The findings and discussion of the various methods to remove hair are presented in Section 12.4, and the study is then completed in Section 12.5.

12.2   Inpainting Techniques Used for Hair Removal From Dermoscopic Images

Due to its outstanding achievements in precisely removing the lesion zone from dermoscopic pictures in recent years, CAD systems have become more important. This is made possible by efficient pre-processing approaches. The dermoscopic pictures' unwanted artefacts may be found and removed using pre-processing procedures. Repairing or repainting the missing section or region in the original picture is very necessary after eliminating the undesirable artefacts. Based on the background data, inpainting aids in restoring the missing or damaged portions in a picture. By eliminating the chosen item and replacing it with its surrounding areas, it enhances the picture quality for future processing. It aids in completing the information that is lacking from a picture. That is why it is also known as image completion. It may be used for a variety of purposes, including picture de-noising, image editing, image restoration, and multimedia editing. The main principles of how the image inpainting process works are structure and texture. Geometric methods are used in structural inpainting to fill in the empty space. However, texture inpainting utilizes texture synthesis to fill in the blanks or missing information by gathering pixel values from nearby pixels. Therefore, it is crucial to choose the right approach based on the situation. In the literature, there are several approaches for picture inpainting that are diffusion-based, texture synthesis-based, exemplar and search-based, wavelet transform-based, fast marching method (FMM), and deep learning-based.

12.2.1   Diffusion-Based Inpainting

The partial differential equation (PDE) and the variation approach are the basic building blocks of the diffusion-based inpainting process. Utilizing what are known as isophotes and the diffusion process, they fill in any gaps or flaws in the pictures. PDE-based methods were created by Bertalmio *et al.* [3] and come in a variety of shapes, such as linear, non-linear, isotropic (where diffusion happens in all directions at the same rate), and anisotropic (where diffusion varies with regard to direction). The primary drawback of the PDE-based technique is that while filling in hair patches, it produces a blurring effect in the photos that is obvious upon visual examination.

12.2.2　Texture Synthesis-Based Inpainting

The texture synthesis-based inpainting [4] method performs admirably for straightforward images but fails miserably for complex dermoscopic images. It primarily relies on stealing or copying pixels from nearby pixels to fill in the gaps left by missing pictures. It works effectively to fill up little missing areas in photos of simple structures. The texture synthesis-based inpainting approach has certain downsides, one of which is that it is sluggish since the filling of empty areas is carried out in a pixel-by-pixel way.

12.2.3　Exemplar and Search-Based Inpainting

One of the most often used picture inpainting techniques is exemplar-based inpainting [4], which combines the two techniques of texture synthesis and non-linear-PDE diffusion. Priority setting for each of the nearby patches and choosing the top candidate patch are the two processes that make up this process. The adjacent pixels in the same patch's gap are filled using the inpainting method. It produces superior results when compared to diffusion-based techniques, however one of the drawbacks of this approach is deciding which patches should be filled in what order. Filling in the texture and structure in the gaps at the same time is a difficult job.

12.2.4　Wavelet Transform-Based Inpainting

Wavelet decomposition [5] picture inpainting fixes the damaged images by utilizing both the textural and structural approaches. Using both the textural and structural methods, wavelet-based image inpainting [5] inpaints or fixes the damaged image. Since it employs both techniques, wavelet processing is used to separate the defect image's texture and structural components. The total vibrational (TV) model [6], which essentially operates on the Euler-Lagrange equation, is utilized to reconstruct the structure images. The texture synthesis technique is used to fix the texture images. The interaction between the structure and texture wavelet reconstruction or restored images, results in the final restored image. As it makes use of both the texture and the structure of images, the inpainting technique enhances the quality of the image.

12.2.5　Fast Marching Method Inpainting

The inpainting methodology and the fast-marching method (FMM) put out by Telea *et al.* [7] both rely on the weighted average, which determines an image's smoothness based on the pixel's known pixel neighbourhood.

The FMM inpainting technique's disadvantage is that it blurs when an area needs to be painted that is thicker than ten pixels.

12.2.6   Deep Learning Image Inpainting

Due to its incredible performance in comparison to conventional methods, convolution neural networks (CNNs), a sort of deep learning approach, are increasingly frequently employed in image processing as well as inpainting. The CNNs must be trained using a collection of training images in order to paint in the regions or sections that are missing. The actual image, known as the Ground Truth image (GT), and the masked image, known as the image with the gap area, make up the usual input pair for training CNNs. The network needs to first be trained before it can fill in the missing region.

12.3   Hair Removal Approaches From Dermoscopic Images

After hair removal and detection, inpainting techniques are employed to fill in or fill in the hair gaps in the dermoscopic images. Researchers have created a number of algorithms that can be divided into two categories to detect and remove hairs from dermoscopic images. Those are supervised and unsupervised approaches. In CAD systems, both unsupervised and supervised approaches are frequently employed to remove hair from dermoscopic pictures because they produce better results and enable automatic melanoma identification.

12.3.1   Unsupervised Approaches

For the purpose of removing hairs from dermoscopic images, several unsupervised techniques, including filtering, morphological, and edge-based techniques, have been developed by various researchers. Lee *et al.* [8] widely used unsupervised method, which is capable of precisely locating and removing the dark and dense hairs from dermoscopic pictures. Below are some details about unattended hair removal techniques. Table 12.1 shows the different hair removal approaches by various researchers using inpainting approaches.

12.3.1.1   Filtering-Based Hair Removal Approaches

The easiest method for identifying hair in dermoscopic images is image filtering. It increases the accuracy of lesion detection. Therefore, several

Table 12.1 Comparison of filtering-based techniques for hair removal in dermoscopy.

Method	Hair detector	Inpainting by
Alfed *et al.* [9]	64 Directional Gabor filters	—
Choudhary *et al.* [10]	Frangi vesselness filtering	Fast marching method
Huang *et al.* [11]	Multiscale matched filters	Linear discriminant analysis (LDA)
Omar *et al.* [13]	84 directional filters	Partial differential equation (PDE) based
Barata *et al.* [14]	64 directional filters	Partial differential equation (PDE) based
Abbas *et al.* [12]	Matched filter and first-order derivative of Gaussian (MF-FDOG)	Fast marching method
Zhou *et al.* [15]	Line detection Curve fitting	Feature guided exemplar-based
Blandón *et al.* [16]	Derivative of Gaussian (DOG)	Multiscale morphological reconstruction
Jaishakti *et al.* [17]	Frangi vesselness filtering	Fast marching method
Vasconcelos *et al.* [18]	Gaussian and median filters	—
Nguyena *et al.* [19]	Universal matched filter	—
Du *et al.* [20]	Top-Hat transform Multi-scale curvilinear Matched filtering	

researchers have created a variety of filtering-based hair removal techniques to address this. Alfed *et al.* [9] utilize 64 directional Gabor filters to detect hairs in images and apply an inpainting process to remove artefacts to boost the segmentation result's accuracy. In addition to hairs, dermoscopic images also contain various artefacts like skin lines, blood vessels, ruler markings, etc., which makes segmentation and feature extraction more difficult. Choudhary *et al.* [10] effective method for removing hairs and other artefacts from dermoscopic pictures uses Frangi vesselness filtering. The contrast limited adaptive histogram equalization (CLAHE) algorithm is used in this method to enhance the images. Additionally, hairs and other artefacts are found and removed from the enhanced photos using the Frangi vesselness approach. Finally, the deleted hair pixels are repaired using FMM inpainting.

The software DullRazor [8] cannot remove thin or light hairs because it is only effective on thick hairs. If the hairs are set to a specific tint, it also does not work very well. In order to solve the aforementioned difficulties, Huang *et al.* [11] used multiscale matched filters, and it was found that this increased the identification of fine hairs as well as hairs found in the shadows. The approach restores the gap hair intersections using linear discriminant analysis (LDA). LDA uses two metrics to divide data sample classes, namely the class-specific scatter matrix and the matrix of the between-class scatter measure. The objective of class separation is to increase the between-class measure and decrease the within-class measure. By utilizing the local LDA results based on pixel color information and region growth techniques, it is feasible to accurately reconstruct hair intersections.

Abbas *et al.* [12] devised a revolutionary technique to find and get rid of the hairs. The two components of the suggested approach are inpainting and hair detection. To begin with, the rough hairs are discovered using a combination of the matching filter and first-order derivative of the Gaussian (DOG) filter. Only curved forms, such as hair, can be detected using the first DOG filter in combination with the matching filter. Additionally, a few little particles identified as the pigmented network are seen in the dermoscopic pictures. In order to correctly substitute those recognized pixels, those must be strengthened, made smoother, and cleared of any unwelcome non-hair like objects. At this refinement stage, the algorithm also employs morphological edge-based approaches. Finally, using the quick marching procedure, the excised hairs are restored or repainted without harming the area around the lesion.

Dermoscopic images reveal that there is a significant range in the thickness and intensity of the hairs. The dermoscopic images show both dark and thick hairs and pale and thin hairs. Numerous academics have created an algorithm to distinguish between light hairs, dark hairs, and both light and dark hairs. Using curvilinear structure analysis, Zhou *et al.* [15] created an algorithm that exclusively picks up ruler markings and dark hairs. The approach employs a feature guided exemplar-based inpainting method to replace the hair pixels. The algorithm is put to the test on 460 dermoscopic images, and the results show that it accurately recognizes and removes hairs from images.

Using a derivative of the Gaussian filter (DOG), Blandón *et al.* [16] was created to recognize hairs in dermoscopic images. The multiscale morphological reproduction inpainting calculation is utilized to fix the pixels of the hair in the pictures after the hairs have been identified and eliminated from the images. The result of the repairing or refining step is the ability to keep the texture and the numerous attributes present in the chosen area.

12.3.1.2   *Morphological-Based Hair Removal Approaches*

Many researchers have created a variety of hair removal methods that are morphologically based. Accurately identifying both bright and dark hairs in dermoscopic images is crucial. The scientists are capable to precisely identify the hairs (light and dark) by utilizing morphological operators, according to the methods currently in use. The morphological closing-based top-hat operator is used in an unsupervised hair removal algorithm created by Ying *et al.* [21] to enhance both thick and thin hairs. The suggested approach employs an elongate feature function to precisely excerpt hairs from dermoscopic images, and then pixels of hair are replaced with non-hair pixels to complete the restoration. The segmentation outcomes are improved because the suggested method can extract hairs, including thick and thin hairs. One of the most popular hair removal methods, DullRazor, uses the morphological closure operator to identify dense, black hairs. The image's binary hair mask is created by using a thresholding technique. Bilinear interpolation is then used to switch out the hair pixels for the two non-hair pixel values. Only thick and black hairs perform better when using the DullRazor algorithm, and processing is laborious due to the interpolation technique.

Zaqout *et al.* [22] developed a block-based hair removal algorithm that uses the morphological bottom-hat operator on the Y-channel picture of the YIQ color model to identify hairs. The algorithm operates on 256 non-overlapping blocks, and the removal step is determined based on the operations performed on each block's histogram. Following this, a morphological closure action is carried out. Sultana *et al.* [23] proposed a method that combines the Top-Hat transform with other morphological opening and closing procedures to identify thin and thick hairs and generate the corresponding hair mask. This method involves post-processing the image. The method utilized for hair removal employs the patch-based inpainting class, which is evaluated for its ability to account for both light and thin, as well as dark and dense hairs. The outcomes indicate that the algorithm can effectively remove hairs, regardless of their thickness or color, without disrupting the surrounding area. Additionally, a technique developed by Fiorese *et al.* [24], which combines the Top Hat operator with a PDE-based hair inpainting methodology, has been successful in identifying and eliminating black hairs from photographs.

In their study, Xie *et al.* [25] proposed a technique that combines the top-hat operator, based on morphologic closure, with the elongate feature function and an inpainting algorithm that uses partial differential equations (PDEs). The morphologic closure-based top-hat operator enhances both strong and weak hairs simultaneously. The elongate function, introduced in their study, accurately captures the elongation of band-like connected regions, making for precise hair measurement. Finally, the researchers employed an inpainting method based on PDEs to replace the hair pixels.

Koehoorn *et al.* [26] have developed an algorithm that combines morphological gap detection with a fast marching inpainting approach to achieve remarkable results in identifying and removing hairs from dermoscopic images. The algorithm's performance is tested against previous approaches using over 300 photos. Meanwhile, Saugeona *et al.* [2] have found that the morphological closure operator with a spherical structuring element in the L* u* v* color space is more effective than linear color space transformations at isolating hairs. The morphological closing operator is used to detect the hairs, while a hard threshold is applied to obtain the hair masks. Finally, an interpolation method is used to replace the hair pixels with non-hair pixels, without damaging the lesion area. Table 12.2 provides a summary of morphologically-based unsupervised hair removal techniques.

12.3.1.3   Edge-Based Hair Removal Approaches

There are many different images in the dermoscopic images, including images with light and dark hairs, thick and thin hairs, etc. It is one of the crucial elements in precisely detecting the edge of the hairs. Researchers use a variety of edge detection techniques to identify thick and thin hairs in dermoscopic pictures. Toossi *et al.* [29] employ an adaptive canny edge detector to pinpoint the borders of the hairs. The morphological dilation operator is used to segment the hairs after the edges have been detected. The multi-resolution coherence transport approach, which combines the wavelet decomposition/reconstruction method with the fundamental coherence transport inpainting methodology, is used to repair or inpaint the hair pixels. The algorithm was evaluated on 50 dermoscopic images, and the assessment results show that it is capable of both accurately identifying and removing hairs.

A hair removal method was created by Borys *et al.* [30] employing a clever edge detector. The suggested approach first locates the margins of

Table 12.2 Comparison of morphological techniques for hair removal in dermoscopy.

Method	Hair detector	Inpainting by
Ying *et al.* [21]	Morphological closing-based top-hat operator	Elongate feature function
DullRazor [8]	Morphological closing	Bilinear interpolation
Zaqout *et al.* [22]	Morphological bottom-hat operator	Block-based histogram function & morphological close
Sultana *et al.* [23]	Top Hat operator	Patch – based class
Fiorese *et al.* [24]	Top Hat operator	Partial differential equation (PDE) based
Xie *et al.* [25]	Morphologic closing-based top-hat operator and elongate feature function	Partial differential equation (PDE) based
Koehoorn *et al.* [26]	Multiscale skeletons/ morphological operators	Fast marching method
Bibiloni *et al.* [27]	Color top-hat	Morphological inpainting
Maglogiannis *et al.* [28]	Bottom-Hat transform, Laplacian of Gaussian, Logsobel	Interpolation
Saugeon *et al.* [2]	Morphological closing operator	Interpolation

the hair, then employs morphological operation to filter out inappropriate objects before removing the hairs from dermoscopic images deprived of disturbing the lesion area. The Prewitt edge detector can precisely identify the hairs just like the clever edge detector. Radon transform and Prewitt edge filters are both used in an algorithm created by Kiani *et al.* [31].

Use the Radon transform to determine an image's linear characteristics. Both bright and dark colored hair may be recognized by the application. A few pixels with skin-like grey levels fill the space left by the hairs once they have been located and removed. The suggested algorithm is put to

Table 12.3 An overview of edge-based approaches for hair removal in dermoscopy.

Method	Hair detector	Inpainting by
Toossi *et al.* [29]	Adaptive canny edge detector	Multi-resolution coherence transport
Borys *et al.* [30]	Canny edge detector	Morphological operation
Kiani *et al.* [31]	Radon Transform + Prewitt edge detector	Averaging method
Saugeon *et al.* [22]	Morphological-edge detection	Linear interpolation

the test by being compared to the well-known DullRazor [8] hair removal method, and it is found to be faster and more effective in removing hairs. Table 12.3 displays the researchers' inpainting techniques as well as edge-based strategies for hair recognition.

12.3.2 Supervised Approaches

Numerous academics have created a variety of unsupervised hair recognition and removal algorithms, which were covered in detail in the previous section. The hair algorithms are discovered to essentially consist of two stages: (i) hair recognition and removal and (ii) hair inpainting. The researchers have employed a variety of techniques for locating and painting hairs in dermoscopic images. However, the investigation noted a number of limitations to unsupervised hair removal techniques, including;

(i) Thickness of the hairs (thick or thin).
(ii) Variation of intensity of hairs (light or dark hairs).
(iii) To precisely eliminate the hairs and other artefacts from the dermoscopic pictures without affecting the lesion, such as gel, ruler markings, air bubbles, etc.
(iv) Hair length, such as short or long.
(v) Overlapping hairs and the hairs that match the color of underlying skin.

Light and thin hairs cannot be removed from photos using DullRazor, one of the most popular unsupervised hair removal algorithms. It accurately removes from photographs the thick, black hairs by detecting them.

As a result, Kiani *et al.* [31] developed a modified DullRazor dubbed the E-shaver, which is excellent for identifying and removing both light and dark hairs. The method of Huang et al can only identify short hairs; it is not appropriate for long hairs. After hair removal, it has been noticed that some unsupervised procedures also produce blurry images, which could result in erroneous lesion region and feature extraction.

Supervised approaches may be used to overcome the aforementioned issues, and deep convolutional neural networks (CNNs) have recently gained significant significance in the field of biological image analysis and classification. Through a series of trainable filters, deep CNN can automatically learn the features from the dataset. To train, massive datasets of images are used, allowing for the extraction of additional features. Because hair removal in CAD systems is crucial, it is crucial to locate and remove hairs and other artefacts from dermoscopic pictures without disrupting the lesion site. As a result, numerous deep CNN algorithms have been created by researchers in order to solve the issues with classic approaches and also to improve segmentation and classification performance.

Table 12.4 presents the deep convolutional neural network (CNN) techniques developed by researchers for hair removal from dermoscopic images. The U-Net architecture is a popular CNN model used for both segmentation and classification in medical image analysis. Li *et al.* [32] utilized a U-Net model for hair detection in dermoscopic images, followed by a transfer learning method based on SN-Patch GAN and gated convolution for filling in the hair gaps. Attia *et al.* [33] proposed a hybrid network with convolutional and recurrent layers for hair segmentation, which used deep encoded information to remove hair and fill in the gaps. The model was evaluated using the ISBI 2017 dataset and outperformed other methods. Lidia *et al.* [35] developed a CNN-based encoder-decoder architecture that incorporated a loss function in the network's training phase for hair detection and removal. Bardou *et al.* [34] proposed a hair removal algorithm using a variational auto-encoder (VAE) encoder, which generated hairless images at the cost of losing image quality. To overcome this, three loss functions, including the structural similarity index (SSIM), L1-norm, and L2-norm, were integrated into the method to enhance image quality.

12.4   Results and Discussion

This section goes into great detail about both the supervised and unsupervised processes' results. Numerous unsupervised techniques have been developed by researchers to identify and remove hairs from dermoscopic

Table 12.4 Comparison of supervised techniques for hair removal in dermoscopy.

Method	Hair detector	Inpainting by	Dataset
Li *et al.* [32]	U-Net	A combination of Gated convolution and SN-PatchGAN	ISIC 2018
Attia *et al.* [33]	Hybrid convolutional + Recurrent neural network (RNN)	Using information from the neighbouring pixels.	ISBI 2017
Bardou *et al.* [34]	Variational auto-encoder (VAE)	Applying several metrics to a combined loss function	HAM10000
Lidia *et al.* [35]	Convolutional encoder-decoder	—	618 images from different datasets
Xiaowei *et al.* [36]	Maximum variance fuzzy clustering algorithm	Improved Criminisi priorities, matching criteria and matching paths	ISIC 2019

images in order to improve the precision of the CAD system's segmentation and categorization of lesions. To test and confirm the hair removal technique, the researchers used open-source dermoscopic datasets as ISIC, PH2, HAM 10000, EDRA2002, etc. Figure 12.1 shows the results of the various unattended hair eradication techniques. The original photographs that the researchers gathered from various datasets are shown in Figure 12.1(a), and they demonstrate the great variety of hair types that may be found, including thin, thick, light, dark, short, and long hairs, among others. To reduce complexity, the original RGB photographs are converted into the corresponding grey level image, which is shown in Figure 12.1. For further image processing, it is imperative to remove hairs from dermoscopic images. Hair removal algorithms proposed by different researchers are tabulated in Section 12.2 along with the outcomes of those algorithms, which are displayed in Figure 12.1 (c). For the removal of the hairs from the photos, it is necessary to use the hair detection and inpainting algorithm.

The process of recognizing and removing hair regions from images while preserving lesion regions can be achieved with the hair recognition method. After hair removal, hair mending or inpainting algorithms can be used to produce the desired results. The researchers' unsupervised hair recognition and inpainting techniques are summarized in Tables 12.1, 12.2, and 12.3. The unsupervised methods examined produced images that showed certain algorithms could only remove light or dark hairs or both, but not other artifacts.

It has been observed that the use of certain hair removal algorithms can lead to blurriness and loss of lesion patches in images, which can negatively impact subsequent image processing. To address this issue, researchers have developed a variety of supervised algorithms. Figure 12.2 illustrates the results obtained from these supervised approaches.

The original photos that the researchers from the various datasets took into consideration are shown in Figure 12.2(a). Figure 12.2 displays the final images produced using supervised hair removal algorithms (b). Different

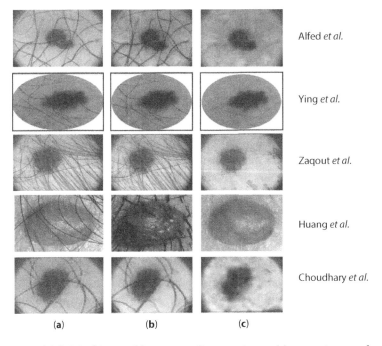

| (a) | (b) | (c) |

Figure 12.1 (a) Original image, (b) corresponding grey image, (c) output images after hair removal techniques.

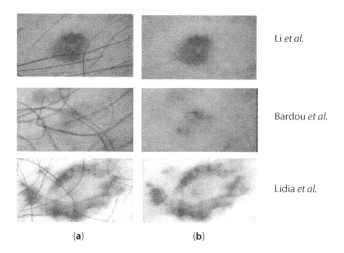

Li *et al.*

Bardou *et al.*

Lidia *et al.*

(a)   (b)

Figure 12.2 (a) Original image, (b) output images after hair removal techniques.

Table 12.5 An overview of various hair removal techniques in dermoscopy.

Method	DA	Sensitivity	Specificity
DullRazor [8]	68.03	88.65	—
Xie *et al.* [25]	72.5	87.03	—
Toossi *et al.* [29]	88.3	93.2	—
Zaqout *et al.* [22]	95.75	97.36	95.78
Okuboyejo *et al.* [41]	96.10	98.27	93.75
Saugeon *et al.* [2]	71.00	7864	—
Abbas *et al.* [37]	81.20	86.27	—
Vasconcelos [18]	79.46	91.72	—
Pennisi *et al.* [38]	79.38	80.24	—
Choudhary *et al.* [10]	81.49	93.88	—
Al-masni *et al.* [39]	80.82	93.72	—
Patino *et al.* [40]	78.34	91.04	—
Li *et al.* [32]	99.08	95.74	99.85

performance indicators, to demonstrate the efficacy of the supervised hair removal techniques in comparison to the unsupervised approaches, the researchers gathered data, such as diagnostic accuracy (DA) [10], sensitivity [10], and specificity [22]. The summary been demonstrated in Table 12.5.

12.5　Conclusion

The accuracy of the CAD system used to identify melanoma is improved by removing the hairs from dermoscopic pictures. So, in this study, we spoke about many hair removal methods, including supervised and unsupervised methods. Although some are limited to hair intensity, thickness, and length, among other factors, unsupervised techniques are capable of successfully identifying hairs from dermoscopic pictures. So, supervised techniques are strongly advised to both minimize complexity and get over the afore-mentioned restrictions. Due to its superior performance in pre-processing as well as segmentation and classification, supervised techniques utilizing deep CNN are commonly employed in biomedical imaging.

Acknowledgment

The authors would like to express their deepest gratitude to GIET University for their invaluable support and contributions to this chapter. Their expertise and guidance have been instrumental in shaping and refining my ideas. We are also grateful to all the coauthors for their helpful feedback and encouragement.

References

1. Senan, E.M. and Jadhav, M.E., Analysis of dermoscopy images by using ABCD rule for early detection of skin cancer. *Global Transition Proc.*, 2, 1, 1–7, Jun. 2021.
2. Schmid-Saugeona, P., Guillodb, J., Thirana, J.-P., Towards a computer-aided diagnosis system for pigmented skin lesions. *Comput. Med. Imaging Graph.*, 27, 1, 65–78, Jan. 2003.
3. Bertalmio, M., Bertozzi, A.L., Sapiro, G., Navier-stokes, fluid dynamics, and image and video inpainting, in: *Proceedings of the 2001 IEEE Computer Society Conference on Computer Vision and Pattern Recognition. CVPR 2001*, vol. 1, pp. I-355-I–362, 2001.

4. Shivaranjani, S. and Priyadharsini, R., A survey on inpainting techniques, in: *2016 International Conference on Electrical, Electronics, and Optimization Techniques (ICEEOT)*, pp. 2934–2937, Mar. 2016.

5. Xu, Y. and Wang, S., Image inpainting based on wavelet transformation, in: *2014 IEEE 5th International Conference on Software Engineering and Service Science*, pp. 541–544, Jun. 2014.

6. Zhang, H. and Dai, S., Image inpainting based on wavelet decomposition. *Procedia Eng.*, 29, 3674–3678, 2012.

7. Telea, A., An image inpainting technique based on the fast marching method. *J. Graphics Tools*, 9, 1, 23–34, Jan. 2004.

8. Lee, T., Ng, V., Gallagher, R., Coldman, A., McLean, D., Dullrazor®: A software approach to hair removal from images. *Comput. Biol. Med.*, 27, 6, 533–543, Nov. 1997.

9. Alfed, N. and Khelifi, F., Bagged textural and color features for melanoma skin cancer detection in dermoscopic and standard images. *Expert Syst. Appl.*, 90, 101–110, 2017.

10. Choudhary, P., Singhai, J., Yadav, J.S., Curvelet and fast marching method-based technique for efficient artifact detection and removal in dermoscopic images. *Int. J. Imaging Syst. Technol.*, 31, 4, 2334–2345, Dec. 2021.

11. Huang, A., Kwan, S.Y., Chang, W.Y., Liu, M.Y., Chi, M.H., Chen, G.S., A robust hair segmentation and removal approach for clinical images of skin lesions, in: *2013 35th Annual International Conference of the IEEE Engineering in Medicine and Biology Society (EMBC)*, pp. 3315–3318, Jul. 2013.

12. Abbas, Q., Garcia, I.F., Emre Celebi, M., Ahmad, W., A feature-preserving hair removal algorithm for dermoscopy images. *Skin Res. Technol.*, 19, 1, e27–e36, Feb. 2013.

13. Abuzaghleh, O., Barkana, B.D., Faezipour, M., Noninvasive real-time automated skin lesion analysis system for melanoma early detection and prevention. *IEEE J. Transl. Eng. Health Med.*, 3, 1–12, 2015.

14. Barata, C., Marques, J.S., Rozeira, J., A system for the detection of pigment network in dermoscopy images using directional filters. *IEEE Trans. Biomed. Eng.*, 59, 10, 2744–2754, Oct. 2012.

15. Zhou, H. *et al.*, Feature-preserving artifact removal from dermoscopy images. *Proc. SPIE 6914, Medical Imaging 2008: Image Processing*, 69141B, Mar. 2008.

16. Ocampo-Blandón, C.F., Restrepo-Parra, E., Riaño-Rojas, J.C., Jaramillo, F., Multiscale morphological reconstruction for hair removal in dermoscopy images. *Modern Appl. Sci.*, 12, 12, 90, Nov. 2018.

17. Jaisakthi, S.M., Mirunalini, P., Aravindan, C., Automated skin lesion segmentation of dermoscopic images using GrabCut and kmeans algorithms. *IET Comput. Vis.*, 12, 8, 1088–1095, 2018.

18. Ximenes Vasconcelos, F.F., Medeiros, A.G., Peixoto, S.A., Rebouças Filho, P.P., Automatic skin lesions segmentation based on a new morphological approach via geodesic active contour. *Cogn. Syst. Res.*, 55, 44–59, 2019.

19. Nguyen, N.H., Lee, T.K., Atkins, M.S., Segmentation of light and dark hair in dermoscopic images: A hybrid approach using a universal kernel. *Proc. SPIE 7623, Medical Imaging 2010: Image Processing*, 76234N, Mar. 2010.

20. Lee, I., Du, X., Anthony, B., Hair segmentation using adaptive threshold from edge and branch length measures. *Comput. Biol. Med.*, 89, 314–324, Oct. 2017.

21. Xie, F.-Y., Qin, S.-Y., Jiang, Z.-G., Meng, R.-S., Xu, B., *An approach to unsupervised hair removal from skin melanoma image*, p. 712729, SPIE, Beijing, China, Oct. 2008.

22. Zaqout, I.S., An efficient block-based algorithm for hair removal in dermoscopic images. *Comput. Opt.*, 41, 4, 521–527, Jan. 2017.

23. Sultana, A., Dumitrache, I., Vocurek, M., Ciuc, M., Removal of artifacts from dermatoscopic images, in: *2014 10th International Conference on Communications (COMM)*, pp. 1–4, May 2014.

24. Fiorese, M., Peserico, E., Silletti, A., VirtualShave: Automated hair removal from digital dermatoscopic images, in: *2011 Annual International Conference of the IEEE Engineering in Medicine and Biology Society*, pp. 5145–5148, Aug. 2011.

25. Xie, F.-Y., Qin, S.-Y., Jiang, Z.-G., Meng, R.-S., PDE-based unsupervised repair of hair-occluded information in dermoscopy images of melanoma. *Comput. Med. Imaging Graph.*, 33, 4, 275–282, Jun. 2009.

26. Koehoorn, J. *et al.*, *Automated digital hair removal by threshold decomposition and morphological analysis*, pp. 15–26, Springer International Publishing Switzerland, Reykjavik, Iceland, 2015.

27. Bibiloni, P., González-Hidalgo, M., Massanet, S., *Skin hair removal in dermoscopic images using soft color morphology*, pp. 322–326, Springer International Publishing Switzerland, Vienna, Austria, 2017.

28. Maglogiannis, I. and Delibasis, K., Hair removal on dermoscopy images, in: *2015 37th Annual International Conference of the IEEE Engineering in Medicine and Biology Society (EMBC)*, pp. 2960–2963, Aug. 2015.

29. Toossi, M.T.B., Pourreza, H.R., Zare, H., Sigari, M.-H., Layegh, P., Azimi, A., An effective hair removal algorithm for dermoscopy images. *Skin Res. Technol.*, 19, 3, 230–235, Aug. 2013.

30. Borys, D., Kowalska, P., Frackiewicz, M., Ostrowski, Z., *A simple hair removal algorithm from dermoscopic images*, pp. 262–273, Springer International Publishing Switzerland, Granada, Spain, 2015.

31. Kiani, K. and Sharafat, A.R., E-shaver: An improved DullRazor® for digitally removing dark and light-colored hairs in dermoscopic images. *Comput. Biol. Med.*, 41, 3, 139–145, Mar. 2011.

32. Li, W., Joseph Raj, A.N., Tjahjadi, T., Zhuang, Z., Digital hair removal by deep learning for skin lesion segmentation. *Pattern Recogn.*, 117, 107994, Sep. 2021.

33. Attia, M., Hossny, M., Zhou, H., Nahavandi, S., Asadi, H., Yazdabadi, A., Digital hair segmentation using hybrid convolutional and recurrent neural

networks architecture. *Comput. Methods Programs Biomed.*, 177, 17–30, Aug. 2019.

34. Bardou, D., Bouaziz, H., Lv, L., Zhang, T., Hair removal in dermoscopy images using variational autoencoders. *Skin Res. Technol.*, 28, 3, 445–454, May 2022.

35. Talavera-Martinez, L., Bibiloni, P., Gonzalez-Hidalgo, M., Hair segmentation and removal in dermoscopic images using deep learning. *IEEE Access*, 9, 2694–2704, 2021.

36. Song, X. *et al.*, Research on hair removal algorithm of dermatoscopic images based on maximum variance fuzzy clustering and optimization criminisi algorithm. *Biomed. Signal Process. Control*, 78, 103967, Sep. 2022.

37. Abbas, Q., Fondón, I., Rashid, M., Unsupervised skin lesions border detection via two-dimensional image analysis. *Comput. Methods Programs Biomed.*, 104, 3, e1–e15, Dec. 2011.

38. Pennisi, A., Bloisi, D.D., Nardi, D., Giampetruzzi, A.R., Mondino, C., Facchiano, A., Skin lesion image segmentation using delaunay triangulation for melanoma detection. *Comput. Med. Imaging Graph.*, 52, 89–103, Sep. 2016.

39. Al-masni, M.A., Al-antari, M.A., Choi, M.T., Han, S.M., Kim, T.S., Skin lesion segmentation in dermoscopy images via deep full resolution convolutional networks. *Comput. Methods Programs Biomed.*, 162, 221–231, 2018.

40. Patiño, D., Avendaño, J., Branch, J.W., *Automatic skin lesion segmentation on dermoscopic images by the means of superpixel merging*, pp. 728–736, Springer International Publishing Switzerland, Granada, Spain, 2018.

41. Okuboyejo, D. *et al.*, Unsupervised restoration of hair-occluded lesion in dermoscopic images. *Annual Conference on Medical Image Understanding and Analysis*, 2014.

13

The Emergence of Blockchain Technology in Industrial Revolution 5.0

Meenu Gupta[1], Chetanya Ved[2*], Saransh Khetarpaul[2], Anmol Dhingra[2] and Sanjana Deswal[2]

[1]*Department of Computer Science and Engineering, Chandigarh University, Punjab, India*
[2]*Department of Information Technology, Bharati Vidyapeeth's College of Engineering, New Delhi, India*

Abstract

As we move toward a business-driven value generation approach in Industrial Revolution 5.0, it becomes imperative to look at some of the key chauffeurs of the generation which bring a sense of security, transparency, and trust. One such technology is blockchain, which essentially means a chain or network of interconnected blocks. Its mechanization is crucial to study due to its decentralized and secure essence. The impact of blockchain can be estimated with the record-high increase of global spendings, which is estimated at $19 Billion by end of the year 2024. This transition owes to the wide range of features that this decentralized ledger offers to industries. This book chapter is divided into eight sections followed by a concluding note. Throughout the chapter, we will be focusing on key factors driving the blockchain trends and what this technology holds for us in upcoming years. We will then look at the basic terms governing the lifecycle of a blockchain network. The next discourse will uncover the applications of blockchain in industries. The next section covers the decentralized model and how it brings about a generation without intermediate parties followed by the positive impacts of blockchain in different domains. We finally summarize this work by discussing the economic overview and the impact analysis of the blockchain ledger and briefly unveiling the upcoming opportunities in various industries.

Corresponding author: chetanyaved@gmail.com

Amit Kumar Tyagi (ed.) Privacy Preservation of Genomic and Medical Data, (283–326) © 2024
Scrivener Publishing LLC

Keywords: Blockchain, energy, healthcare, cryptocurrency, consensus mechanisms, protocols, Industrial Revolution 5.0

13.1   Introduction

As the world is immersed in technological evolutions, the main cause of this change will be brought up by the fifth generation of the Industrial Revolution, which is slowly and steadily changing the way of living, working and other life utility processes. Industrial Revolution 5.0 (or Industry 5.0) has been predicted to bring the enormous change in way of interactions among the machines, computers and humans as connectivity is enhanced in an incremental way, which ultimately leads to humongous productions and methodical dividends, improvements in the quality of life and hence the capability to develop a sustainable environment [1]. The correct estimation of the Fifth industrial revolution is that it will be based on trusted networks that are capable enough to remove middlemen from processes. Fifth-generation of the Industrial revolution is capable enough to blur the line between the physical and digital worlds [2], blockchain technology is a currently emerging and empowering computing resource in both private and public sectors [3]. Blockchain as an emerging technology allows digital product memories to follow physical objects and guide them through the supply chain [4, 5]. Blockchain is capable enough to introduce a "trustless" [6] based network that can drive the entirely new type of business models [7–9]. Blockchain's importance could be wit by the fact that the Global Blockchain Market is expected to progress at a compound rate of annual growth (CAGR) by almost 29% in the upcoming period of 2020 to 2024. This technology is developing with the aim of providing services, the product with a completely secured and traceable network so that it can protect one's right over its product or services [10].

In this notable chapter, we will initially focus on the comparison of various latest articles and research papers in section 13.2. In the next section, we will unfold the evolution of web technology starting from Web 1.0 to Web 3.0 associated with blockchain. Explanation of some of the basic terms used in the blockchain industries is provided in section 13.4. Some of the key terms described, such as distributed ledger technology (DLT), mining, consensus mechanisms, and their protocols. Industrial components, such as cryptocurrencies, DApps, and smart contracts associated with blockchain, are thoroughly explained in section 13.5. Further, the next section comprises the contribution of blockchain for revolutionizing industrial aspects. Section 13.7 focuses on the transformation of industrial sectors after using blockchain technology. The next section analyzes the economical impact of blockchain over each industry followed up by the conclusion.

This chapter initially reveals some ongoing research work surveys conducted by Blockchain experts in the age of Industrial Revolution 4.0 and 5.0. Section 13.2 provides a literature survey of some research papers followed by a table summarizing them. Section 13.3 gives a detailed understanding of how Web Technology has evolved over the past three decades and how it is helping various industry sectors. This is followed by section 13.4, which introduces all key terminologies used with Blockchain. Next, we explore the industrial components associated with the Blockchain in Section 13.5 and Section 13.6 discusses how Blockchain is revolutionizing the Industries. Further, Section 13.7 studies a wide range of industries that are impacted with the inception of Blockchain including Pharmaceutical sectors, Internet and security services, banking and finance sectors, token economy sectors and Real Estate agencies. Towards the end of the chapter, Section 13.8 discusses some of the key applications of Blockchain in various economic sectors and respective use-cases followed by a conclusion.

13.2   Literature Survey

We have surveyed the latest research articles and papers which are discussed below: In the study by Giliazov [11], the author discusses one of the unique features of blockchain that provides a framework for creating distributed consensus in the digital world and that it can encourage the development of a democratic, open and scalable digital economy.

The article focuses on analyzing the advantages of using a blockchain. It also examines the types and implementation of blockchain pools, attacks on them, and investigates the possibility of using existing software tools to study the stability of blockchain-type protocols. At last, it concludes with an analysis of the two most popular cryptocurrencies and smart contracts, as well as the safety problems associated with them.

Al Omar *et al.* [12] gave an overview related to issues regarding the data security of electronic health record (EHR) and the privacy of patients in the healthcare industry. It explains about the blockchain's characteristics of decentralization through a P-2-P network where different parties can store and power the network while keeping the sensitive health data records secure and private. Development further in the field of encryption technology will disrupt the blockchain-based systems to resolve the data preserving vulnerabilities. Next, the accountability, integrity, pseudonymity, security, and privacy have been briefly discussed in the context of the management system presented.

Further, Lee [13] discusses the evolution of blockchain technology with amalgamation of cryptocurrency, their connection, and contribution in developing a token economy through introducing various business models. It has the potential to introduce us with a new economic system by revolutionizing the way communication occurs over the Internet. It can enhance information security, transparency, and reliability by sharing encrypted data among P-2-P networks.

Farouk *et al.* [14] discusses the impact of integration of blockchain and IoT with the healthcare system. The amalgamation of the two technologies enables the security and unhamparable transmission of medical data. It will allow delivery of medical supplies to be traced throughout the supply chain. Further, the article discusses blockchain technology and its architecture, and introduces various healthcare–related applications.

Cho [15] explains about important protocols being the core mechanism of a blockchain network. Proof-of-Work (PoW) being a commonly used consensus protocol which requires significant computation resources to mine a new valid block. Further, it gives a brief overview related to application-specific integrated circuits (ASICs), which are specifically designed for hampering the mining process of PoW. It is capable enough to expose vulnerabilities in blockchain systems. The article proposes PoW mechanisms to disincentivize the use of ASICs in the consensus operation. Employing multiple hash functions in the PoW computation is one of the commonly adopted approaches to achieve such ASIC resistance. The authors evaluate the level of ASIC-resistance of the multi-hash PoW mechanisms based on the performance gap between ASICs and general purpose computing platforms through experiments. The results reveal that ASIC resistance of these PoW mechanisms is not strong enough to prevent ASIC-based mining.

Tapscott *et al.* [16] bring the reader's attention to the need of revolutionizing finance industries. This work has tried to stress over the inefficient procedures of finance industries and how blockchain can help transform towards the betterment of the business and further reducing friction caused by burdensome and inconvenient paperwork. It is worth noting that more than 45% of the banking and finance negotiations be it through stock exchanges, remittances or even through payment mediators suffer from economic crimes every year. Stress is also laid on how principles of blockchain like peer-to-peer networking, the immutability of records, computationally expensive mining procedures, and distributed ledger technology can help reduce the friction and overdue costs.

Mikaand Goudz [17] draw the reader's attention toward the sustainability of blockchain in the sector of power generation. Taking the reference from the recent developments made in Germany, it talks on how blockchain can help transfigure the energy sector in the current era of industrialization. Further, as renewable resources have added fuel to the power generation revolution it becomes imperative to discuss the potential obstacles being faced in the deployment of blockchain-based systems in the short term. The author has also focused on how a prosumer-based system can help improve the energy economy by an equity profit development and how factors like low participation are affecting their economic growth. It measures the ability of blockchain to establish digitalization of the energy revolution and finally examine if it is a driver of innovations in the energy sector. It focuses on how the inherent capabilities of blockchain can lead to economic and social growth in the coming years and what could be challenging to achieve the goal.

Kumar et al. [18] discussed the ill effects of counterfeiting drugs on the health of patients and the general public. They stressed the root causes of the manufacturing of these products,which generally lack traceability of the right and active ingredient to manufacture drugs, and how this lack of traceability can lead to safety concerns.

These facilities are affecting the pharmaceutical supply chain. The proposed ideology also aims to secure the network by different attacks like replay and man-in-middle attacks. The proposed framework ensures the drug security and authenticity of the manufacturer. The framework takes advantage of the inherent properties of blockchain like immutability of records and cryptographic security features. Additional advantages of drug supply chain management tools include end-to-end tracking of the medical equipment, establishing their identity ensuring social and economical benefits.

In the study by Kalla et al. [19], the challenges people are facing due to the novel Coronavirus pandemic are discussed. It terms blockchain as a key growth chauffeur to drive the economic and social development post-pandemic. Potential use cases are discussed to wit the power of this revolutionary technology in the industrial revolution 5.0. A few applications of blockchain discussed in the research are contact tracing, disaster relief and insurance to worst affected people, information sharing among healthcare collaborators and stakeholders. Advanced study of the paperwork presents an application of blockchain in immigration and emigration procedures taking the benefit of the immutability of the blockchain ledger records and inherent security offered by Smart Contracts. Finally, some challenges are discussed which pose a problem to the deployment of the blockchain-based models like privacy requirements, latency, and scalability.

In the study by Andoni *et al.* [20], the author presents an all-inclusive overview of fundamental principles of blockchain that govern its work. It also identifies the business application related to the power generation sector. This paper is one of the first systematic reviews of blockchain in the energy sector and unpins the potential scope and models that can disrupt the energy market. The review stresses how energy systems are developing to accommodate energy generated by renewable energy sources (RES) like solar PV and wind. Since the availability of energy through RES is primarily dependent on weather and atmospheric conditions, more stable and flexible operations need to be configured to sustain the ever-increasing demand for energy through renewable resources. The paper also uncovers the challenges and the market barriers hampering the sustainability of blockchain in energy markets and how we can overcome these challenges to adopt this revolutionary technology in the mainstream.

Money is an integral asset that is used for organized utilization and managing the allocation of finite resources. However, presently established monetary frameworks are run by sophisticated centralized Institutions. Takemiya [21] introduced a token-based financial framework that is automatic, can change the amount of tokens to give liquidity on a case-by-case basis. A version named Sora DAE has been executed on a blockchain framework. It is a dual token framework (the XOR token and the XST token), that permits the production of tokens for monetary development and stability of transactions.

Based on the study done above, we have categorized these literature works in two broad brackets. Table 13.1 below summarizes the genre on which the respective works have been done.

Table 13.1 Summarizing literature work.

Ref. no.	Scope	Contextual factors	Findings
[1]	Blockchain- A Distributed Consensus	Consensus Protocols, Cryptocurrencies and scalability of Blockchain protocols	The authors present a view of how Blockchain can encourage sustained development paired with a scalable economy.

(Continued)

Table 13.1 Summarizing literature work. (*Continued*)

Ref. no.	Scope	Contextual factors	Findings
[2]	Healthcare Applications of Blockchain	Safeguarding patient's health records, the role of Blockchain in data storage and privacy concerns.	In this paper, the authors present an approach using Blockchain designed to protect patients' integrity and privacy.
[3]	Evolution of Cryptocurrency	Creation of token economy, Role of Blockchain in ensuring transparency	The authors briefly describe the advancement of Blockchain paired with cryptocurrency in the creation of digital assets.
[4]	Blockchain and IoT	An amalgamation of two technologies, impact on healthcare industries and their applications.	The authors present various applications of Blockchain paired with IoT in the healthcare sector and their quantified impacts.
[5]	Consensus Protocols in Blockchain	Proof-of-Work protocol, use of ASIC in operations and potential network threats.	The authors have experimentally evaluated levels of ASIC resistance of PoW mechanisms.
[6]	Blockchain in Finance Sector	Inefficient banking procedures and principles of Blockchain as a rescue.	In this paper, authors lay stress on the inefficient Banking procedures leading to more than 45% of negotiations ending in economic crisis.
[7]	Blockchain in Energy Sector	Blockchain in energy sector, renewable resources, prosumer-based system.	The author emphasizes on a prosumer-based system that can incentivize the energy economy by equitable profitable approach.

(*Continued*)

Table 13.1 Summarizing literature work. (*Continued*)

Ref. no.	Scope	Contextual factors	Findings
[8]	Supply chain Management	Counterfeiting drugs, trust and traceability issues and network security using Blockchain.	The author proposes a supply chain management theory as potential solution for counterfeiting aiming at secure network transmission
[9]	Blockchain as a futuristic technology	Blockchain, post-pandemic development and sustainability..	In this paper, author discusses about the post-COVID use cases of blockchain in healthcare sector.
[10]	Blockchain and renewable resources	Energy Sector, use cases of Blockchain, solar PV and wind energy.	In this paper, the author has proposed numerous applications of Blockchain utilizing green energy to minimize carbon footprints.
[11]	Token economics of Blockchain	Decentralized economy, token-based system and advantages.	The author discusses a token-based economic system that can support regulation and liquidity.

13.3 Evolution of Web Technology in Association With Blockchain

Web in itself is an abstract concept encapsulating the entire Internet and its facilities. With its inception in 1989 with Web 1.0, this wave stirred up the entire globe with the idea of decentralization. It came up with the ideology of a decentralized network of devices through which anyone can access the information using a set of protocols. It could be understood by a typical operation of accessibility to blogs and websites.

The semantic web came into existence to make data on the Internet machine-readable so it can be processed to generate meaningful results. This opened opportunities for establishing multiple peers to peer networks regarding the wide cross-application interpolation offered through Web 2.0. This empowered the users to share and control their data freely without any involvement of external authority. Social media platforms served as the basis for this technology.

Finally, as we progressed toward the end of the decade, technology leapt employing Web 3.0. As the term says, this concept is further a notch up of previous versions of the Web and Internet. Data present on the Internet can now be very well "understood" and interpreted by machines. Web 3.0 technology has pioneered the Internet by:

13.3.1   Superior Security and Privacy

With its very decentralized nature, Web 3.0 commits to deliver secure and superior connectivity. Unlike traditional systems which store data at a single location that is controlled by security systems, a blockchain network copies these data to many places creating a distributed ledger.

Accuracy is maintained when all these nodes communicate to validate this data. Further, challenges like decrypting the hash value and modifying a node in the existing chain of data make blockchain tamper-proof.

All these features, namely consensus, cryptography, and data duplication at the different network endpoints together make blockchain immune to frauds.

13.3.2   Gravitation Toward Cryptocurrency

Being the future of currency, Web 3.0 enables its customers to interact with crypto coins. According to a report in reference [22], Ethereum coins were processed more than 1.1 million times per day. The digital ecosystem has given this new and promising addition to digital payments. Cryptocurrency transactions being fraud-proof has gained a lot of attraction from the public eyeball. Since every transaction is stored over a public ledger and identities are verified and encrypted, it becomes record tamper-less. Further, due to the fact of this currency form not being centrally owned, it becomes a safe option to invest in. Instant settlement and accessibility are among the other reasons that keep fraud-proofs the investors hitched.

13.3.3   Participant Providence in Industries by Web 3.0

Blockchain owing to its decentralized nature, intangibility across peer networks and integrity maintenance properties has opened the doors for an altogether new paradigm of trustless network and Decentralized Applications, which are popularly known as DApps.

With the help of pioneering approaches like Crowdfunding and Initial Coin Offering (ICO), blockchain has given novel definition to the Internet and better scope of economic growth forecasts. It has expanded itself into many industries and has made itself an indispensable part of human lives.

13.3.3.1   Currency Exchange Procedures

As the Internet has been intelligent enough to process human natural queries into machine-readable knowledge, it has also given the opportunity to new ways of exchanging digital currency. Web 3.0 has stirred up ways for generating and storing digital currencies be it in terms of digital gold or cryptocurrency coins. It offers a bouquet of benefits to both participating agencies. A few of them are listed below:

- Digital currency mechanisms are highly immune to hacking processes.
- Helps to establish end-user control over the currency.
- Overhead transaction cost has been drastically reduced
- The transfer time of a currency between sender and receiver is drastically reduced.

13.3.3.2   Social Media and Messaging Platforms

This is one of the most crucial aspect of our generation. Today, people cannot imagine their lives without networking, and social media helps to interact with an individual from the comfort of one's home. The control has moved out of the hands of makers to end-users. It offers the following benefits to consumers:

- It takes your privacy as priority
- Web 3.0 has enhanced the way information is retrieved, managed, and delivered.
- There is no centralized authority to control data access.

13.3.3.3   Browsers

Late in the Web 2.0 revolution, a need was felt to make web browsing safer and less prone to the security loopholes present today with web surfing. A service provided by Web 3.0 should be capable of safeguarding end user's data from security breaches and protecting the user Internet usage patterns externally for monetary benefits. Browsers and extensions like Brave and Metamask are bridging the gaps between browsers today and the distributed web of tomorrow's generation by:

- End-users have a choice to sell their Internet usage patterns and data.
- Privacy is duly maintained by these browsers.
- Encrypting data ensures the least security setbacks.

13.3.3.4   *Banking and Finance Industries*

With the advent of Web 3.0, Banking firms have started using the extensive features of futuristic technologies like blockchain and the Internet of Things. This has led to the development of a transparent economy that can be sustained with the help of identifying user's identities. It further reduces the need for centralization and hence can drastically reduce fraud. In further sections, we have discussed how blockchain approaches aim to improve transparency in this sector with its salient features.

Distributed Ledger technology serves as a backbone of Web 3.0, making this approach a success. The main protocols that route the blockchain toward a sustainable future are:

- **Consensus Algorithms:** These algorithms are the set of protocols that guide through the process of attaching a block of a transaction into an intangible chain of previous transactions. For instance Proof of Stake and Proof of Work algorithms.
- **Block Validation:** This is done by a set of peer networks that are called miners who are involved in the block validation to provide a secure system of transactions to maintain the integrity of the network transactions.

The next section uncovers a detailed overview of all the basic terminologies involved in a successful blockchain transaction including consensus algorithms and validation by peers in a network.

13.4   Understanding of Basic Key Terminologies

In this section, we will be having the expository view of basic terminologies used over the blockchain industry since it is important to have some familiarity with the key terms used to further understand the implementation of blockchain in real world application.

13.4.1 Distributed Ledger Technology

It refers to the technological instrument, which consists of protocols to govern simultaneous validation and updation in immutable way across the distributed network without any concern of geographical locations. The objective of developing this tool is to develop the decentralized network of peer-to-peer nodes, which can overpower the mechanism of centralization. It is develop with a motive to haute the trust over the third party involvement. Decentralized database can be enabled through this technology. It eliminates the requirement of central authority to monitor the manipulation in transactions.

DLT uses the technique of cryptography to store all type of information, and it is immutable in nature (i.e., cannot be modified once entered) [11]. Cryptography signatures and keys are majorly used to access these ledgers and it is governed by the protocols of the network. They are introduced to provide immunity against the attackers and malicious hackers. Its tamper-proof, if one node gets maliciously attack then other copies of ledger, which are distributed over the network will not be tampered, and they will be secured by making the blockchain invalid over the attack node. It is a computational effective and economically viable solution to the organizations since it makes the process faster and effective due to its data distributive capability. In further upcoming sections, we will be unveiling its wide range of diverse industrial application.

13.4.2 Mining

Blockchain mining is a P-2-P computational process, utilized for security and verification of digital currency (bitcoin) transactions. Mining includes blockchain excavators also known as miners who are responsible for adding bitcoin-related exchange information to Bitcoin's worldwide public ledger. In the records, blockchain miners are responsible for the security of blocks and are associated with one another establishing a chain.

As compared to conventional financial services frameworks, Bitcoins don't have a financial organization as an authority. Bitcoin exchanges are by and large confirmed in decentralized clearing frameworks wherein individuals contribute computing assets to check the validity of records, which produces a unique record (ledger). Here no single person is in charge of checking the legitimacy and uniqueness of records on blockchain.

This soperation of confirming exchanges is called mining. In this whole interaction, it is significant that there is no single person who is in charge of checking the legitimacy and uniqueness of records on blockchain.

13.4.3   Consensus Mechanisms and Protocols

A process of agreement among the distributed computational system or processes in the branch of computer science, it is known as consensus algorithm. These algorithms are developed for the purpose of rectifying two major current issues of blockchain that is double spending and Byzantine general problem. These problems are below more elaborated.

13.4.3.1   Double Spending Problem

An error in scheme of virtual cash and that is not spending virtual token twice or more. This problem occurs, since virtual currencies are associated with digital file which cannot be further identicated. The prevention of this problem further categorized into two parts centralized and decentralized. Centralized solution is implemented via third-party application, which can authenticate whether the token was used or not. It basically represents a single point of failure and view.

13.4.3.2   Byzantine General Problem

This problem is related with one short story, group of generals belong to Byzantine army camped with their troops which are surrounded with city of rival. The generals have to agree upon a common battle plan since they are able to communicate through the messages only. So there can be a possibility of one or more generals can be traitor who will manipulate the message. Same problem occurs in computer nodes who are connected with a blockchain, major problem statement is how all nodes can agree with state of data transaction. It is difficult to authorize every nodes data state should be correct or not. That is where consensus mechanism come into an action to resolve such type of problems.

Table 13.2 gives brief overview on different type of consensus protocol. Also, this table draws the comparison between how protocols are different in terms of mining and functionality. Below mentioned are some of the consensus mechanism, which comes into an action to avoid above discussed problems:

- **Proof of Work:** This algorithm works by making every node to solve cryptographic puzzle. In this, all miners participate to solve the complex puzzle which is binded with cryptographical manner. And the first one who solves it will win the reward in terms of cryptocurrency. It rewards on the basis of computational sources utilized for mining. To make it more efficient group of miners can create a mining pole, which ultimately combines their hashing power and distribute their incentives accordingly who are connected with a pole. The major disadvantage of this algorithm is it utilizes electricity in massive amount. People who can afford large resources for computational have main advantage in this power of economics at massive scale.

- **Proof of Stake:** This mechanism does not have set of miners it has set of validators and valid condition for being validator is to have their stake in cryptocurrency network. Mining is not allowed in this mechanism instead mining, forge or minting of blocks are allowed. The point of measure in forging the next block is the amount of stakes it holds, more the stakes higher will be probability to forge or mint the next block. The major responsibility of validator is to check whether transactions are correctly made or not, then node signs off the block and add into the blockchain. After that, validator receives an incentive based on the fees associated inside the block. Also, if node is not actively participating in validation process, his stakes, as well as his transaction fee, which he got will be released after certain period of time. POS is more efficient in comparison to PoW since it does not base on power utilization.

- **Delegated Proof of Stake (DPoS):** In this protocol, users have to conduct a real-time voting to create a panel of trusted parties, who are called as witnesses. They are having the right and create a block and add it to the chain. In this, witnesses are made to those who hold sufficient amount of tokens. It means the influence over the network will be of those who hold more tokens in comparison to who hold few tokens. The voting process is continuous process, therefore, the witnesses must carry out their functions for the higher standard or they will lose their position. This model is based on decentralized consensus model. It has to main advantage higher transaction rates and low energy consumption.

- **Practical Byzantine Fault Tolerance (PBFT):** This mechanism created a breakthrough in environment of distributed computing which comes out in 1999. It was a replication

Table 13.2 Comparison of functionality and mining processes in different consensus mechanism.

Consensus protocol	Functionality	Mining
Proof of Work (PoW)	• It works by making every node to solve cryptographic puzzles. • It rewards on the basis of computational sources utilized for mining.	All miners participate to solve the complex puzzle
Proof of Stake (PoS)	• Instead of mining, forging or minting of blocks are allowed. • The point of measure in forging the next block is amount of stakes it holds, more the stakes higher will be probability to forge or mint the next block	It does not have set of miners; It has set of validators Validators should have stake in cryptocurrency network
Delegated Proof of Stake (DPoS)	• Users have to conduct a real-time voting to create a panel of trusted parties, who are called as witnesses. • Witnesses have the right to create a block and add it to the chain.	No miners are there; Set of witnesses casts vote The influence over the network will be of those who hold more tokens in comparison to who hold few tokens.
Practical Byzantine Fault Tolerance (PBFT)	• It possesses a multiple verification process for authentication purpose, where at initial phase verification is done by selected nodes only, as process increments it requires more confirmations. • It achieves a consensus of variability in distributed computing environment	Participants are responsible to create a block and coordinate together in decentralized network

algorithm which was developed to overcome the faults of Byzantine. It achieves a consensus of variability in distributed computing environment. It is currently used by many distributed computing networks and frameworks, such as Ripple, Stellar, and Hyper Ledger. It possess a multiple verification process for authentication purpose, where at initial phase verification is done by selected nodes only, as process increments it requires more confirmations. The "PeerCoin" was the initial virtual currency which used PoS mechanism. Scalability issues in blockchain were resolved by the DPoS method. It also helped in speeding up the transaction and creation of blocks. PBFT addresses the issues related to Byzantine General failures. The most difficult class of failure modes in

Byzantine failure due to generation of garbage value by node during transaction which can be difficult to handle.

13.5   Industrial Components Associated With Blockchain

In the following section, we will be discussing the different industrial components which are presently associated with blockchain. To have a deep insight about the working principles of blockchain technology in the real world. This section will give deep insight about the application of different blockchain-based components in coalescence with industry.

13.5.1   Cryptocurrency

In Figure 13.1, validating a transaction in a blockchain network goes through a series of steps. Once initiated, it passes through a consensus mechanism. This ensures that the transaction is validated by other participating nodes resulting in fewer frauds. Post verification, a transaction is added into a chain of blocks and it becomes immutable to any further modifications.

A cryptocurrency is a form of money stored in a digital format of significant worth which is mainly used for the purchase and sale of products, services, or other assets [26]. Examples of cryptocurrency include bitcoin, litecoin and many others. Bitcoin, the first publicly presented blockchain,

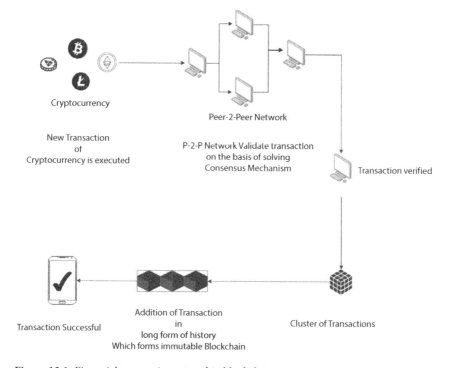

Figure 13.1 Financial transactions stored in blockchain.

is an electronic cash framework, which can replace mediator organizations such as financial institutions and save costs. Presently there are more than 1500 types of cryptocurrencies in blockchain-based networks with aggregate market capitalization of around $500 billion, which is presently dominated by Bitcoin having a market capitalization of around 37% of the total, and the ETH and Ripple holding the second and third places respectively.

The blockchain is the innovation that can protect cryptocurrencies cryptographically from forgery and fraud. It acts as a distributed ledger and permits an organization to maintain consensus. Distributed consensus allows the framework to follow exchanges, and empowers the exchange of significant worth and data. In the framework, cryptocurrencies also referred to as tokens are recognized as modes of payment for services during transactions or to give rewards [30].

Cryptocurrencies commonly have four principle benefits over normal monetary standards. First, money transactions involving a cryptocurrency, either locally or globally are not required to go through monetary cryptocurrency intermediaries or money transfer operators (MTOs), which offer services, for example, cash trade or exchange repayment. The second is the processing and settlement of transactions involving cryptocurrencies is quicker than those involving other payment techniques. The third benefit is that the transaction charges imposed on digital monetary transfers are much lower when compared to traditional methods, or sometimes no charges at all. These faster, less expensive, and more proficient exchanges can be accomplished by being handled in a framework utilizing blockchain innovation. At long last, quite possibly the most important advantage of digital money is that they have inherent inflation protection. Any fiat monetary standards can be printed at the discretion of the national bank, making them inflationary in nature. On account of digital forms of money, they have a controlled creation that is restricted by a cap, and, thus, no monetary organization can control the amount issued.

13.5.2 Decentralized Applications (DApps)

In centralized architecture there is one source and multiple receivers, on the other hand, in decentralized architecture, there are multiple nodes, which can both transmit and receive information. It is a decentralized application that needs a smart contract-based API to get the information from the blockchain framework. Here, the API gets replaced by a smart contract interface, and the smart contract will fetch the data from the blockchain framework, which acts as the backend. In Figure 13.2, contrast between centralized and decentralized applications has been shown.

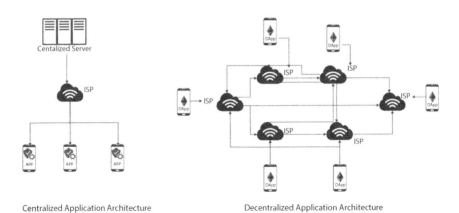

Centralized Application Architecture   Decentralized Application Architecture

Figure 13.2 Difference between centralized and decentralized application.

The blockchain framework is certifiably not a centralized authority for putting away data, it's a decentralized system where the individual members (the miners) support and corroborate every transaction that is happening to utilize the smart contract on the blockchain framework [29].

A Dapp comprises a support code that is deployed on a distributed peer to peer framework. It is a final product expected to be used in service in the Ethereum framework without being obliged by a centralized system, and that is the primary difference that it gives direct association between the end-customers and the decentralized application benefactors. Dapp allows the backend code and data to be decentralized, and that is the fundamental plan of any Dapp. A representative token is used as fuel for the decentralized application to run.

13.5.3   Smart Contracts

A smart contract is a simple computer program that permits the exchange of any critical asset between two groups. It very well may be cash, shares, property, or whatever other advanced assets that organizations might want to exchange. Anyone on the Ethereum system can make these arrangements. The agreement involves primarily the conditions and arrangements ordinarily discussed and agreed to between the groups [29]. The significant component of a smart contract is that whenever it is executed, it cannot be altered, and any exchange that happens on top of the smart contract is enrolled forever. So whether or not you decide to change the smart contract, later on, the conditions and transactions relating to the principal conditions will not get changed, you can't modify them.

The smart contracts comprise a verification procedure that is finished by unknown members of the network without the prerequisite for a central authority, and that is what makes the execution of a smart contract on Ethereum a decentralized execution. The trading of any asset or monetary resource is done in a reliable and transparent manner, and the data of the two organizations is securely stored on the Ethereum framework. After the completion of the exchange, the records of the sender and recipient are refreshed likewise, and this process winds up increasing trust between the organizations.

The most wanted and admired utilization of a smart contract is a financial derivative. The hurdle in the development of monetary agreements is that the vast majority of them require that a reference should an external price calculator or indicator, for instance, an application that is a smart

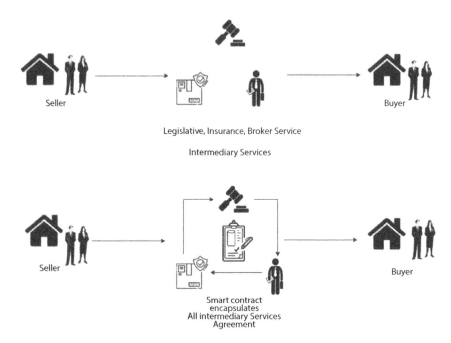

Figure 13.3 Application of smart contract in real estate dealing.

contract that secures against the instability of ether (or any other digital currency) regarding the US dollar, for doing this the consent to comprehend what the value of ETH/USD is necessary [28].

In Figure 13.3, two scenarios are depicted. In the first one the transaction goes through intermediary services and in the second, the transaction goes through a smart contract which encapsulates all intermediary services. After the completion of the transaction the information gets stored in the distributed ledger.

13.6   Contribution of Blockchain for Revolutionizing Industrial Aspects

It is time to explore the contribution of blockchain in bringing the Industrial Revolution 5.0. In the following section, we will be analyzing the implementation and its implications of blockchain over the existing industry, which are able to generate economical benefits and develop a sustainable environment for the upcoming generation.

13.6.1   Introducing the Ethereum Network

Ethereum is a blockchain-based registering system which enables the developers to build and assemble decentralized applications—which implies not represented by a centralized system. For a decentralized application, the members of that specific application would be the intended final decision-making authority [29]. In 2018, market capitalization for Ethereum, crested at $134 billion, and many decentralized applications going from informal organizations to monetary networks have been created over Ethereum. Also, the smart contract market is assessed to develop at a compound annual growth rate of 32% during the period 2017 to 2023 [47].

The goal of Ethereum is to unite and refine the perceptions about scripting, altcoins, and on-chain meta-shows, and permit specialists to make self-assertive agreement-based applications that improve the adaptability, normalization, feature-completeness, simplicity of development, and interoperability offered by these various ideal models all simultaneously. Ethereum performs the function by developing the definitive unique foundation: a blockchain-based network with an inherent Turing-complete programming language, permitting the public to compose smart contracts and decentralized applications (DApps) where they can define their own set of rules for ownership and transaction configurations [28].

In Ethereum, the state consists of articles called "accounts," with each record having a 20-byte address and state advances being immediate transactions of utility and data between accounts. The following four fields make up an ethereum account.

- The nonce, a counter used to ensure every exchange must be handled once
- The record's present ether balance
- The record's agreement code, if present
- The record's storage

"Messages" in Ethereum are fairly like "exchanges" in Bitcoin, however with three significant contrasts. First, an Ethereum message can be made either by an outside establishment of an agreement, while a Bitcoin exchange has to be made remotely. Second, there is an unequivocal option for Ethereum messages to contain information. At last, the beneficiary of an Ethereum message, in the event that it is a contract account, has the alternative to return a reaction; this implies that Ethereum messages additionally incorporate the idea of functions.

Generally, Ethereum has three kinds of applications. The first class consists of monetary applications, giving clients all the more remarkable methods for management and commencing contracts utilizing their cash. The second class is semi-monetary applications, where money is included; however, there is additionally a non-financial side to what exactly is being done. At last, there are applications such as online voting and decentralized governance that are not monetary by any stretch.

A significant quantity of ICOs depends on Ethereum blockchain for the conveyance and the regulation of their tokens. Initial Coin Offerings (ICO) are public proposals of new digital agreement of funds in return of existing ones, expected to fund projects, majorly for the advancement in blockchain-based or crowdfunded projects. The ease of transacting assets through blockchain-based exchanges, and their desire to get exceptional yields even before the business drive arrives at the market—on the grounds that ICO tokens are exchanged promptly on cryptographic platforms—grow exponentially. In the second half of 2017, the aggregate sum raised by ICOs surpassed 4 billion US$ and defeated the investment piped toward cutting edge drives at the same time [49]. Recently, a large number of ICOs running on Ethereum blockchain are overseen through Smart Contracts, and specifically through ERC-20 Token Standard Contract.

Implementation of Ethereum Smart contracts comes with risks and challenges such as smart contracts should essentially contain three properties: they should be deterministic, isolated and terminable. Here deterministic, the first property means the requirement to process the same output every time it runs. The second property is isolation that states the smart contracts may not contain viruses and bugs as they can be uploaded by anyone, therefore it needs to be isolated in a sandbox. Basically isolation provides the immunity to smart contracts from bug and viruses which makes these technologies trustless. A broadly revealed bug in the DAO contract in June 2016 misused callbacks to take $150M, however there are numerous different bugs identified with callbacks that did not get as much consideration [48].

13.6.1.1   Ethereum Virtual Machine

EVM is built to develop and support as a runtime environment for compilation and deployment of Ethereum-based contracts [29]. EVM is the framework that can understand and process the meaning and conditions of smart contracts, which are developed in the Solidity language for Ethereum. EVM is utilized in a sandbox environment where you can build up your independent environment, that can further be used as a testing and developmental environment, and you can run and test your smart contract any number of times, verify it, and a while later whenever you are satisfied with the results and the operability of the contract, you can send it on the Ethereum primary framework.

13.6.1.2   Cloud Computing

The Ethereum Virtual Machine innovation referenced above can be used to build up a supporting computing environment, allowing customers to demand that others do computations and every now and then request verifications that computations at certain discretionarily chosen points were done precisely. This considers the arrangement of a distributed computing framework permitting anybody to participate with their own specific workstations, and spot-checking alongside security stores can be used to ensure that the system is reliable.

13.6.2   Implementation of Blockchain for Enhancing Security and Privacy

With the rapid pace of advancement, the number of IoT devices has increased. Generally, the quantity of IoT gadgets presented in the market is moving toward the mark of 25 billion and which is normal according to the current scenario of rapid development, this number is estimated to reach 50 billion before the end of 2025. IoT Devices consist of various sensors to set up a framework and to empower gathered data transmission to a distant hub. By empowering cooperation with a wide scope of devices such as smart watches, mobile devices, cameras, screen display units, which is capable enough to produce, operate, and trade enormous data that is safety-critical as well as privacy-sensitive [27]. Traditional methodologies for enforcement of safety and privacy cannot be applied straightforwardly because of scalability issues [34]. Most of the security systems utilized as of recently are extremely centralized and accordingly are not appropriate for structures of IoT because of the single position of collapse, nature of the traffic that is many-to-one, and position of scale [33].

To secure client protection, Traditional techniques ensure client security by disclosing fragmented or noisy information, which may cause harm to information and impact offering customized services. Therefore, Internet-connected devices require a shield that is scalable, distributed, and lightweight. Because of its private, secure and decentralized nature, the blockchain has an extraordinary potential to overcome these previously mentioned difficulties [31].

Public key infrastructure (PKI) could be used to provide security and transparency of data. Rather than depending upon an outsider, we can depend on encryption-based strategies for keeping up with security and protection [32]. It can be coordinated to the IoT-based devices and information of these devices for giving secure access control with tampered-less transmission. It produces a history of trades that are time-stamped and therefore can't be altered and can be associated with each other giving explicit services. For lightweight security reasons, symmetric encryption can be used for gadgets to achieve accessibility and protection. In this manner, key security assaults like Distributed Denial of Service (DDOS) and associating assaults can be deterred and the overheads activated could be relatively little [31].

13.6.3 Development of Token Economy Based on Cryptocurrency

Token Economy can be explained by an arrangement of incentives based on digital currencies that support and construct attractive practices in the blockchain ecosystem. It requires miners to validate the approved services for exchanges to form a consensus. This form of economy in time can become apprehensive in terms of incentives to miners for offering better assistance on the framework [24].

For example: Token Economics, which boosts the assistance gave on the blockchain framework

In the blockchain framework, tokens are needed in place of money for ease of transactions. The token economy is planned considering the blockchain frameworks that permit it to outline frameworks from service executions to customer incentives through a program-based monetary plan in online systems.

An appropriately designed token economy would keep the check on measure of token issuance, pay for members, rearrangement of assets, and clients' continuous commitment. However, assuming the token economy is executed perfectly, the members can prioritize their preferences to seek after their own advantages, resulting in quality improvement, in all aspects. In such a manner, possibly the main feature for the effective implementation of a blockchain-based business model is the strong foundation of the compensation framework for participants [25].

However, based on blockchain and digital currencies, another token economy model that compensates for the quality of service has come into view [25]. This model uses blockchain innovation and gives incentives to a client for its services and commitments. This commitment can be voting, giving suggestions, posting, or creating content in the case of a social streaming service. These crypto token-based models have created a new method that rewards the content creators by paying them directly. This starts a moral cycle wherein content makers are more likely to bound themselves in on improving the quality of their services as their reward progressively increases with better services.

13.6.4   Developing the Market for Smart Real Estate

Real estate entities generally prefer managing transactions face to face with different organizations. However, the introduction of blockchain can change this way of conducting business. The concept of smart contracts in blockchain frameworks will authorize organizations to tokenize assets such as real estate and recognize their transactions like cryptocurrencies such as bitcoin and ether [23].

In Figure 13.4, the transaction regarding real estate settlement is managed by the smart contract. On successful completion of the transaction, the information regarding the entities with digital signature gets stored in the distributed ledger.

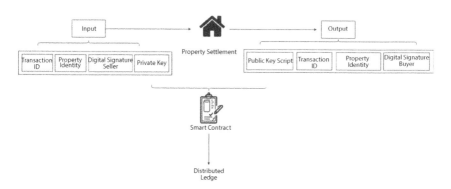

Figure 13.4 Application of DLT and smart contract in real estate.

13.6.4.1 Platforms and Marketplaces

For decades the development in real estate technology has been focused on connecting buyers and sellers and listings. But blockchain technology has enabled better ways for trading real estate and allows modified trading frameworks and online platforms to enhance real estate transactions. Blockchain also allows for the tokenization of assets like real estate and then traded online just like stocks on any exchange platforms. After tokenization real property assets can be operated like a stock sale and similar assets can be dissolved using online frameworks through the token sale. At last, the assembled tokens can be transacted for paper money allowing buyers to own a stake of the property.

13.6.4.2 No Intermediaries

The real estate market has for long been dependent on dealers, attorneys, and banks. In any case, blockchain may make a significant change in their jobs and cooperation in asset transactions. The latest evolved frameworks can soon start with features like payments, listings, and legitimate documentation process. Eliminating the middle men will bring about purchasers and merchants getting more out of their cash as they save money on commissions and expenses. Hence it makes the transaction channelised in a faster way due to elimination of intermediaries.

13.6.4.3 Illiquid Characteristics of Real Estate

Real estate for quite some time has been thought of as an illiquid resource since it requires some investment and time for deals to close. That isn't the situation with digital currencies and tokens as they can, in principle, be promptly exchanged for fiat currency. But on the other hand, tokenized real estate assets can be promptly exchanged. A seller won't need to hang tight for a purchaser who can bear the cost of the entire property to get some worth out of their property.

13.6.4.4 Fractional Ownership of Real Estate

By permitting fractional possession, blockchain likewise brings down the traditionally built walls for investing in real estate. Normally, ventures would require critical cash beforehand to obtain property. On the other hand, financial backers could likewise pool their cash to procure greater real estate assets. Using blockchain, financial backers would just need to get to an exchanging application to purchase and sell even parts of tokens as they see fit. Furthermore, while having fractional possession token owners wouldn't need to take care of the entire asset themselves.

13.6.4.5   Decentralization

As a decentralized technology, blockchain empowers trust and security. Data stored in the decentralized ledger is available to anyone having access to the framework, making information transparent and immutable. Since data are verified by all members, purchasers and sellers can have more trust in managing exchanges. Forgery and fraud would be easy to recognize and simultaneously its attempts would decrease. With time, smart contracts would progressively turn out to be permissible records.

13.6.4.6   Costs

The transparency related to a decentralized framework can likewise manage down costs related to real property asset exchanges. After the money saved by removing intermediaries' professional expenses and commissions, there are different expenses, for example, assessments charges, enlistment charges, credit expenses, and tax duties related to the assets. These charges vary as the territory of the asset changes. Similar to intermediaries, these intermediate costs can be decreased or even dispensed when the concerned platforms automate these procedures and make them part of the framework.

13.6.5   Development of Supply Chain Management Systems Based on Distributed Ledgers

In Figure 13.5, the shipment of goods from the manufacturer to the customer occurs. The information about the transaction regarding transportation between one step to another gets stored over the blockchain until it reaches the customer. At each and every incremental step, the smart contract implicitly updates the information of the shipment on the distributed ledger.

The traditional supply chain system can be digitized by using blockchain innovation going about as the organization's central framework. The structure can be empowered and engaged by the Internet of Things (IoT) which gives an enlarged framework, refined information gathering, and high-performance analytical abilities. GPS instruments and intelligent

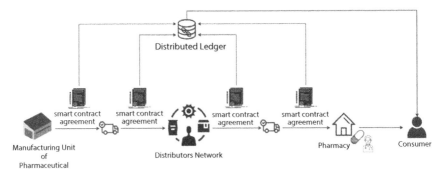

Supply chain Management system based on smart contract and Distributed Ledger Technology

Figure 13.5 Application of distributed ledger and smart contract in supply chain management.

sensors are delivered by the supporting IoT environment that can connect appliances or objects with data, engaging more effective assembling procedures, and new business frameworks. At the core of the supply chain structure, blockchain empowers security and transparency in exchanges through smart contracts automating information transmissions across the entire framework. The consistent physical-to-digital and back-to-physical procedures give considerable improvement in contrast with conventional supply chains.

Data collected from the IoT appliances connected to a supply chain can be used in the review system. A review framework plays a significant part in the E-Commerce platform. It has been observed that online item reviews fundamentally influence the purchase patterns of items. Sixty percent of consumers consider appraisals and audits significant while exploring an item. A survey framework is a significant segment in Ecommerce applications. Existing incorporated review frameworks are controlled and are inclined to frauds. A new blockchain-based framework, which is decentralized, immutable, and auditable in nature, is fit to forestall fake and controlled surveys based on smart contracts. IBM and Maersk, the biggest container transport administrator on earth, have employed a complete digitized supply chain framework utilizing decentralized ledger technology. IBM plans to shift out of 70 million compartments; 10 million compartments are transported every year on the blockchain deployed using Hyperledger Fabric by the end-year. Container transportation approaches 50% of all sea exchange that is an enormous lump of worldwide GDP.

13.7   Transformation of Industrial Sectors by Blockchain

In the following section, we will be unveiling the transformation made by blockchain in the Healthcare, Energy and O&G sectors. To understand the implications of implementing this technology on the recent grounds of real world application. Also discovering the socio and economic aspects of this technology in these sectors.

13.7.1   Healthcare Sector

The emergence of decentralized technology played a major role in the healthcare sector economically. It was estimated $34.47 million approximately revenue was valued, also it is predicted by 2024 revenue will be close to $1415.59 million. And expected Compound Annual Growth Rate (CAGR) will be around 70.45% between 2018 and 2024 [41]. The blockchain has the capability to build decentralized system which makes it tamper proof and uncompromisable with data, which enhances the security and privacy of each data point. Majorly medical industry is approaching to integrate this technology with their hardware commodity, which provides the security from man-made or natural disasters. Healthcare and medical professionals are seeking it as opportunity for their research purpose, also since decentralized systems are power efficient which can be utilized by researchers to make convoluted calculations for the purpose of finding cures, drugs, and treatments of various disease and disorder.

The transaction get stored over the chain only after it gets verified by the majority of other nodes. It maintains the integrity as well as authentication of genuine data. It is beneficial for researchers to use this property to study massive amount of confidential information of specific group of people, it will be helpful in assisting the longitudinal studies which can be used for developing precision medicine for effective treatment.

13.7.1.1   Patient Monitoring

It can be used to record the patient's vitals such as blood pressure and sugar level in real-time via wdevice. The doctors can be assist with certain system of monitoring 24×7 who are more prone to risk, which is integrated with alert system, it immediately alarms the doctor or medical professional as soon as vitals overshoots or get undervalued. Saveonmedical introduces a new method that allows patients to track down the cheapest MRI, radiology, drug store in their area.

13.7.1.2 Medical Supply Chain Management

It has been observed current supply-chain (SC) is insecured as well as tampered. Since in the SC, the drugs are manufactured in their centers. Then they are transferred to their local distributors. And from there, it goes to retail companies which finally sell out to customers. This wholesome process of drugs distribution holds lots of leaks and make it more prone to frauderies and counterfeiting of drugs. Immutability feature of blockchain comes into role play to resolve such below mentioned issues:

- **Drug Verification:** It assists the manufacturers to keep a check and track of all ingredients used for drug manufacturing. which ensures the composition of drug should be upto medical standards.
- **Traceability:** The drug counterfeiting can be prevented using blockchain technology, healthcare organizations can trace the source through this feature of blockchain since each and every step of a drug gets recorded as a transaction in a distributed ledger which gets updated at each and every step of SC which enhances the tracking and traceability feature of the system and safeguard it from drug counterfeiting.

13.7.1.3 Medical Record Storage

Presently of all analytical information in the sector clinical images account for about 70%, which is a significant reason for diagnosis of diseases. Also, information leaks related to medical records have happened in over 90% clinical establishments therefore it becomes necessary to utilize this technology to ensure the integrity of all medical records on a higher level [50]. The medical records can be produced and stored over the electronic medical record (EMR) system. These are decentralized record softwares which are shared with medical and health organization. It stores patients' medical history, treatment records, and other important vitals. It is distributed among several organization but each organization is having the access restrictions. Since the blockchain is holding the capability of immutability, it maintains the integrity of patients medical records, which is critical from both side medical, as well as legal point of view.

13.7.1.4 Stakeholders Benefits

Pharma companies can collect real-time data of patients which allows them to offer a variety of medical products and treatment which specifically designed according to patients medical requirements. For pharmacies, it will be an effective approach, on the basis of data recorded in ledgers the can effectively guide the patients how they must take the drug. All medical professionals whether the doctor or nurses can easily access the patients data related to their condition. All the wearable technology can contribute sufficiently by alerting them in case of emergency.

In upcoming years we may observe blockchain will be disrupting this industry with the boom of healthcare app development using blockchain technology. Since this industry involves highly confidential data and privacy, it is more suitable for the blockchain industry to step over in this sector to bring new data revolution.

13.7.2   Energy Sector

The energy sector is currently undergoing the process of digital transformation. The major role is backed by blockchain technology to bring emerging trends in this sector. It has been observed recently that the energy industry is continuously catalyzed with innovative solutions to develop a sustainable environment. According reference [42], it has been predicted by the experts that the investment in blockchain technology in the market of energy will appreciate from 200 million USD to 18 billion USD by 2025. Population of many countries are moving towards the culture of energy parity which ultimately leads to cost reduction in retailing of traditional energy supply. This technology is turning the individual customers to become producers also and hence they are called prosumers. They are capable of producing, trading, and exchanging the energy units in a Peer-to-Peer (P-2-P) network. The trade and exchange will be possible through microgrids (MG). These are clusters of loads and distributed energy resources (DERs), which are interconnected with each other. Currently, Power Ledger, an Australian-based company is working on the implementation of this idea. Turning the group of P-2-P nodes into communities of microgrids. Majorly this technology aims to provide efficiency and control over the energy generation sources for the purpose of reduction in energy waste. Development and Investment in the energy sector will fuel advancement for electric vehicles.

This technology will going to impact below mentioned data

- Traditional Market Prices
- Marginal Costs
- Energy fuel prices

This technology will also cater to make the records of prices and transactions public, which directly leads to increase in transparency. Since it has been observed data gets manipulated or omitted which leads to detrimental errors to government and businesses. Several market analysis firms are working and identifying the several aspects of blockchain which can benefit providers and it via distributed ledger technology. This aspect of blockchain can be beneficial to develop the system of transparent transactions of energy and currency distribution.

13.7.2.1   Impact Analysis of Blockchain Over Oil Exploration and Refining Industry

Several companies, startups and organizations who belong to this sector are working over the blockchain to find optimal solutions for maintaining the trading system. Till now, it has been explored the potential use case of blockchain, such as cost reduction in data management, visibility, and transaction settlement delays and inter system communications. A pilot project of BTL group, a blockchain-related enterprise which was associated with ENI, BP, and Wein Energie has been completed which showcased the cost reduction by 30% to 40% approximately in tracking of gas trades [44]. In Figure 13.6, it has been depicted that oil and gas industry categorized into three segments:

- Upstream
- Midstream
- Downstream

The organizations who are dedicated to upstream of industry are majorly responsible for resource exploration and extraction processes. This stream is considered as one of the most technologically complex parts of the industry. It consists of high risk because exploring vast natural resources is a very tedious task to perform. It offers the opportunity of drilling wells,

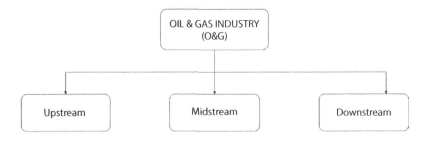

Figure 13.6 Major division of O&G Industry.

which are hundreds of miles below the surface, which also includes geopolitical legislative issues and highly unregulated jurisdiction. Due to which, hundreds of stakeholders are being part of this process which ultimately leads to issues in financial transactions. Organization faces several challenges related to cooperation, reconciliation of payments and attestation of performance across several stakeholders, and it also leads to some friction for some organizations to coordinate.

13.7.2.2   Use Cases of Blockchain in O&G Upstream Industry

Figure 13.7 shows the major application focus over over the blockchain in Upstream segment of O&G Industry. Explore each applications in-depth in the below following sections:

- **Financial Reconciliation:** It has been known while making entries in the system related to financial transactions or organization details, naturally, there is almost 25% to 30% probability will be always there of causing typo errors by humans, which can take days to rectify those errors. Due to this, huge loss will be bear by the organizations and other stakeholders who were part of that transaction. To make the process of reconciliation seamless developers introduced the blockchain technology through distributed ledgers. Basically, every stakeholder holds the information of every employer in the form of unique identities and certifications over the blockchain. Those will be distributed and shared

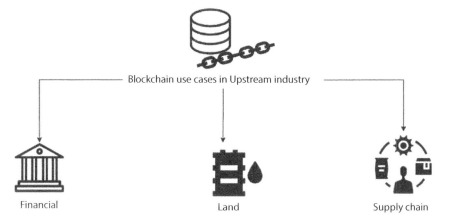

Figure 13.7 Use case of blockchain in O&G Upstream Industry.

with other stakeholders for the purpose of maintaining transparency. A second major role will be if any errors are caused due to typo or misinformation, it can be easily rectified through distributed network. Since the information will be stored over the distributed ledgers and every stakeholder holds the authentic copy of ledger which can make this task of problem identification and rectification financially be solved within minimum time and cost. Due to major diversification among the different organization, the reconciliation process gets delayed and backlogs of transactions starts getting piled up. So distributed ledger technology comes into an action to prevent such cases every transaction will be recorded over the ledger which gets implicitly updated to all the stakeholders about the transaction performed in a network. Hence, no staggering and pending backlogs of transactions will be caused, and no extra cost will be added in payment reconciliation process.

- **Obtaining rights for lands:** The process of tracking the ownership of land before any drilling or excavating, Is one of the most laborious and tedious tasks to perform. where organizations have to make sure they have correct authorization and rights transfer to authorities before performing any activity. Blockchain technology is highly suitable for such cases, since every lands ownership is recorded over government blockchain records. And these records have great feature of immutability and distribution which leads to fast updation of ownership rights transferring from one organization to another since they are recorded over the government ledger it gets implicit updated internally without involvement of government authorities. Also this process will be handled and monitored by the smart contracts. Smart contracts will create an agreement among the parties with an aim of providing a highly secure ownership rights transaction.

- **Maintaining Transparency in Supply Chain:** It has been observed in reference [43] the problem faced by supply chain is majorly over the data faults and failures among the different stages of supply chain. Where distributed and shareable system comes into major role play to develop a transparent environment among different stakeholders, it will provide the capability to companies have transparency over the entire system from extraction of over single drop of oil to its consumer. Research over the data can be easily segmented and studied for the purpose of improving the organization's efficiency in standard operating procedures.

13.7.2.3   Use Cases of Blockchain in O&G Midstream Industry

Midstream segment deals with the transportation and storage of O&G-related products is a low-risk taking sector of the industry [45]. This sector act as a bridge between drop of oil from reservoir to consumers. After the extraction process is done then comes to an transportation and storage parts which fall into this stream. This segment requires the feature of data transparency of blockchain technology. Below, exploring more key uses of blockchain technology in the midstream segment:

- **Heavy Asset Tracking:** The transportation task is very much laborious and manual task to perform. When crude oil is transported from reservoir to refineries it has to be handle with care, since the pipeline of transportation is pretty diverse and it's the utmost importance for oil and gas stakeholders. In recent times, crude oil spilling over the oceans and water bodies have been experienced by the world which leads to hampering ecosystem and biodiversity. Organization requires the full proof view of the crude oil transportation over the various network. The blockchain can provide optimal solution for tracking those heavy assets by capturing each move into the distributed ledger which several stakeholders can monitor the movement of the asset. Also, it has been observed that while transportation, the health of petroleum products gets tampered due to the mixture of other compounds present in the compound. For this, technology of blockchain came up with the solution of providing quality certificate after blending process, and it can be updated to distributed ledger which can be monitored by the stakeholders. And in the pre-blending process, the gasoline and ethanol have been also certified so that each and every mixture is in good health till its last production usage. These certifications will help in increasing the visibility and location of their assets to the major stakeholders who are involved in transporting the asset from one place to another with safety measures. This will have great significance in O&G distributor network.

- **Maintenance of O&G Infrastructure:** The task of maintenance of pipelines, industry equipment, tankers, containers, and transportation pipelines from one state to another or one country to another is a pretty tedious task to manage. Since several organizations are involved in maintenance of infrastructure which requires to build trust an integrity among them blockchain has major role to play in this problem. It has been analyzed for maintaining the records by each and every stakeholder over the papers is quite laborious and manual task. To eliminate this problem, distributed ledger technology can provide the facility of establish a peer-to-peer network among the several stakeholders related to maintenance and update their progress over the distributed ledger. Also if any problem occurs in the refinery plant or any failure in equipment will occur, it can be reported to the ledger where other stakeholders can immediately act upon the damage. So this technology can also facilitate in damage control also [45].

13.7.2.4 Use Cases of Blockchain in O&G Downstream Industry

This segment is dedicated to final stage of processing of crude oil into a finished products, which can be used for consumption purpose by the consumer. Crude oil consists of hundreds of hydrocarbon components, which have different boiling and weight points. Various heat and steaming techniques are used to separate complex compound from crude oil to obtain a simplified petroleum and gasoline products. These products are used across various industries, such as lubricants, are used in metal and transportation industry, fuels are used for heavy transportation and aviation industry, synthetic rubbers, and plastics are made by manufacturing industries and many more [46].

The products belong to downstream O&G faces major globalization impact since this segment is based over economical driven business model. The prices get fluctuate on the basis of geopolitical trend. Therefore, emerging technology of blockchain offers massive opportunity for from economic point of view to the downstream stakeholders. Some benefits are mentioned below of blockchain implementation over this industry:

- **Reconciliation Process:** It has been noted there are larger number of participants with hundreds of different petroleum and gasoline-based products, which makes the supply chain more complex. It leads to several complex issues, such as related to regulatory or legislative perspective. Generally, these issues arise due to data management and visibility problems. Since a complex network of supply chain would lead to create issues, which are based over trust, data integrity and ownership of assets. Yet, no stable solution is developed to eradicate this problem over a scalable platform. Blockchain can turn out to be revolutionizing solution for this problem, since it has capability to develop the private consortium networks for performing among the stakeholders, it will facilitate the organization with transparency and visibility. Hence, trust will be established and restored. The integration of smart contract will further facilitate data is shared with authentic stakeholders only and restricts the accessibility, i.e., only permitted and authorized stake holder can access the particular data with certain rights and privileges is provided. From this, organization will gain confidence over the data handling and management, which would further lead to automate the processes with greater security.

- **Compromise with Safety and Environmental Regulations:** In downstream segment of O&G many stakeholders get indulge in malpractices and compromise with social regulations. The load of expenses will be over to the stakeholders and system of supply chain. It can cause lot of environmental and financial damages. The regulations gets hampered intentionally or purposefully due to mishandling of tonnes of data generated at regular interval of time or churn of high employees. Also, these malicious acts create a unnoticeable loopholes in the system and causes corruption [14]. According to models of distributed blockchain systems, it creates a trustless network where regulations can be programmed over the smart contracts and keeps the check over the entire standard operating procedure of the supply chain. According to our propose model of blockchain, it will keep the check over the organization transaction ledger, any unrecorded entry in one block of transaction but present over the other connected nodes transaction. It will be detected as malpractice according to our system, that is how blockchain solutions can drive this industry effectively and economically [46].

According to above models and analyzing above facts and figures, it can be noted that emerging technology of blockchain in industry will lead to profitable future with no compromise in safety standards and regulation. From this, it can be observed, autonomously, tonnes of data can be handled by the distributed ledger technology and smart contracts without compromising data security and privacy. The blockchain-enabled solution leads the way to prosperous future in energy sector.

13.8   Economical Impact Analysis of Blockchain Over Each Industry

Figure 13.8 shows a comparative study of average Blockchain spending in different industrial sectors in years 2017 and 2021. It could be seen that the finance and supply chain (distribution and service) industry contribute to the majority of spending.

When we acclaim blockchain as a futuristic technology, it becomes of imperative importance to discuss the impacts of blockchain on Industries in all ways. We all are well aware of the fact that shortly, as we move towards

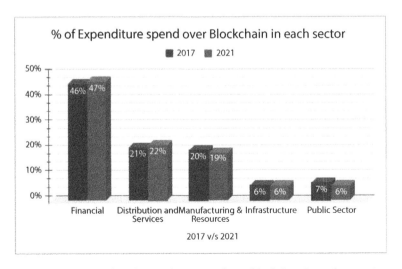

Figure 13.8 Percentage of total expenditure spend over blockchain by each sector in world [35].

rapid development in terms of industrialization and switching to secure servers it would be correct to say that data is the most valuable asset to us nowadays. As this resource flows around us, maybe when we get personalized recommendations on products or develop insights on these data, we will need a carrier that can circulate these data in a secure, transparent, and intangible way from one source to another. Blockchain is an efficient approach that tends to solve this problem. It not only keeps your data chain secure and error-free but will also prevent any kind of malicious attack from corrupting your data.

Blockchain being decentralized in nature has no central authority to control data. Moreover, it provides an efficient way to provide an extra layer of security to the data containers. As per blockchain market reports, blockchain will be able to contribute more than 120 million dollars to the industry by the end of the 6 years in 2024. The Distributed Ledger technology is aiming to bring drastic changes in the conventional way industries work.

13.8.1   Banking and Financial Institutions

Simplifying the banking procedures, it has become a lot easier for Banks to have identity verification and asset management ledgers.

Blockchain facilitates quicker and secure ways of transactions between parties with the help of Decentralized ledger technologies like Bitcoin and Ethereum with lower costs. This has further led to an increase in the popularity of Bitcoin by a 600% increase in daily transactions from 2014 to 2021. On average, more than 400,000 transactions took place through Bitcoins daily in January 2021 [22]. Blockchain makes it easier to share financial information between institutions by storing patron's information into decentralized blocks helping customer KYC and fewer frauds. Blockchain can generate enormous security features in any transaction market. Hence, it can maintain more efficient markets throughout the world.

13.8.2   Healthcare Sector

The Drug Supply chain [36] is evolving as the most innovative solution by Healthcare industries. This utilizes the advantages of Blockchain to enable streamlined visibility of associates and drugs in the supply chain across any geographical region.

It is worth noting that infringement and feigned pharmaceutical products pose particular risks both socially and economically. According to a report on counterfeit pharmaceutical products, every year almost 250,000 children die due to the consumption of counterfeit drugs [37]. Blockchain and distributed Ledger can tap on the journey of a drug from producer to patients decreasing the risk of counterfeiting in pharmaceutical drugs and medicines. Cryptocurrencies, like Ethereum and Bitcoin, have enabled medical shareholders to make payments using these currencies. This tends to develop a trustable environment.

13.8.3   Retail Market

Blockchain due to its inherent property of being transparent and decentralized has bridged the gaps between producer and consumers in the Market. With blockchain solutions, we need not require third party interference to buy or sell a commodity. With the introduction of concepts like prosumers which means any consumer can be a producer, blockchain is creating an environment where equity distribution of profits can exist. Blockchain helps companies to manage their inventories efficiently and with ease. Automating the product shortage and surplus scenarios, blockchain has helped retail enterprises to save a lot more money. The distribution market of blockchain is predicted to achieve USD 1936.26 million by 2026 according to Adhikari *et al.* [38].

13.8.4   Energy Market

The inception of Blockchain has brought a drastic transformation within the energy market. The introduction of concepts like smart contracts and energy Internet has shifted the focus to the environmental benefits of using renewable resources of energy. Smart grids with the help of Blockchain aim to bring transition to methods of fetching costly energy from conventional grids. Currently, gain has been observed by 13% of the world population living in a shortage of energy [39]. Smart grids utilize present day information and communication technology (ICT) architecture in a smart way aimed for constructing a sustainable metropolitan climate and enhancing the quality of life. Further integration with blockchain will empower two appliances to impart and trade information and assets in a decentralized P-2-P–based framework. With technologies like energy Internet, it is possible to create an ever-expanding network of energy transmission between multiple peer mesh. Furthermore, it enables the establishment of the introduction of an equitable distribution of energy in the world at much lower prices than conventional grid offerings.

13.9   Conclusion

The inception of Blockchain has opened a door to many potential solutions and has proposed new ways to deal with problems like insecurity in transactions, lack of transparency, and trust in centralized authority. As per the above discussion, blockchain can help in establishing a trustless environment where all transactions happen in a decentralized fashion and maintaining the integrity of the participating authorities by establishing immutable blocks of transactions. Blockchain is no longer limited to a few cryptocurrencies and the Banking industry. It has the power to disrupt the industries with its essence. Its market size is expected to grow at a rate of 67.3% in the period 2020 to 2025 with a monetary value of USD 39.7 billion [40]. Hence, it would be wise to say that blockchain stores an ocean of opportunities to explore in the Industrial Revolution 5.0 and can contribute as a backbone for a trustless generation.

References

1. Chinnasamy, P. *et al.*, Blockchain technology: A step towards sustainable development. *International Journal of Innovative Technology and Exploring Engineering (IJITEE)*, 9, 2S2, 1034–1040, 2019.
2. Yano, M. *et al.*, *Blockchain and crypto currency: Building a high quality marketplace for crypt data*, Springer Nature, Singapore, 2020.
3. Treleaven, P., Gendal Brown, R., Yang, D., Blockchain technology in finance, in: *Computer*, vol. 50, pp. 14–17, 2017.
4. Dabbagh, M., Sookhak, M., Safa, N.S., The evolution of blockchain: A bibliometric study. *IEEE Access*, 7, 19212–19221, 2019.
5. Li, Z. *et al.*, A hybrid blockchain ledger for supply chain visibility. *2018 17th International Symposium on Parallel and Distributed Computing (ISPDC)*, IEEE, 2018.
6. Klems, M. *et al.*, Trustless intermediation in blockchain-based decentralized service marketplaces. *International Conference on Service-Oriented Computing*, Springer, Cham, 2017.
7. Weking, J. *et al.*, The impact of blockchain technology on business models–A taxonomy and archetypal patterns. *Electron. Markets*, 19, 3, 285–305, 2019.
8. Nowiński, W. and Kozma, M., How can blockchain technology disrupt the existing business models? *Entrep. Bus. Econ. Rev.*, 5, 3, 173–188, 2017.
9. Mendling, J. *et al.*, Blockchains for business process management-challenges and opportunities. *ACM Transactions on Management Information Systems (TMIS)*, 9, 1, 1–16, 2018.

10. Zyskind, G. and Oz, N., Decentralizing privacy: Using blockchain to protect personal data. *2015 IEEE Security and Privacy Workshops*, IEEE, 2015.

11. Giliazov, R.R., Blockchain protocol study, in: *Sovremennye Informacionnye Tehnologii i IT-obrazovanie = Modern Information Technologies and It-Education*, vol. 15, pp. 190–199, 2019.

12. Al Omar, A., Rahman, M.S., Basu, A., Kiyomoto, S., *MediBchain: A blockchain based privacy preserving platform for healthcare data*, Lecture notes in computer science, pp. 534–543, Springer Link, Germany, 2017.

13. Lee, J.Y., A decentralized token economy: How blockchain and cryptocurrency can revolutionize business. *Bus. Horiz.*, 2019.

14. Farouk, A. *et al.*, Blockchain platform for industrial healthcare: Vision and future opportunities. *Comput. Commun.*, 154, 223–2355, 2020.

15. Cho, H., ASIC-resistance of multi-hash proof-of-work mechanisms for blockchain consensus protocols. *IEEE Access*, 6, 66210–66222, 1–1, 2018.

16. Tapscott, A. and Tapscott, D., *How blockchain is changing finance*, vol. 1, pp. 2–5, Harvard Business Review, USA, 2017.

17. Mika, B. and Goudz, A., Blockchain-technology in the energy industry: Blockchain as a driver of the energy revolution? With focus on the situation in Germany. *Energy Syst.*, 12, 285–355, 2021.

18. Kumar, R. and Tripathi, R., Traceability of counterfeit medicine supply chain through blockchain. *2019 11th International Conference on Communication Systems & Networks (COMSNETS)*, IEEE, 2019.

19. Kalla, A. *et al.*, The role of blockchain to fight against COVID-19. *IEEE Eng. Manag. Rev.*, 48, 3, 85–96, 2020.

20. Andoni, M. *et al.*, Blockchain technology in the energy sector: A systematic review of challenges and opportunities. *Renew. Sustain. Energy Rev.*, 100, 143–174, 2019.

21. Takemiya, M., Sora: A decentralized autonomous economy. *2019 IEEE International Conference on Blockchain and Cryptocurrency (ICBC)*, 2019.

22. *Daily cryptocurrency transactions 2017-2021*, Statista, German, 28 May 2021.

23. *How blockchain technology is changing real estate*, Accessed Date 10 May 2021.

24. *Token economics #2: Comparison review of token economy*, Hacker Noon, Accessed Date 7 May 2021, 2019.

25. Lee, J.Y., A decentralized token economy: How blockchain and cryptocurrency can revolutionize business. *Bus. Horiz.*, 2019.

26. *Blockchain vs cryptocurrency*, Weteachblockchain.Org, Accessed Date 6 May 2021.

27. Mushtaq, A. and Haq, I.U., Implications of blockchain in industry 4.O. *2019 International Conference on Engineering and Emerging Technologies (ICEET)*, 2019.

28. Buterin, V., *A next-generation smart contract and decentralized application platform*, vol. 3, 37, white paper, 2014.

29. *What is ethereum: Understanding its features and applications*, Accessed Date 12 May 2021.
30. *Blockchain definition: What you need to know*, Accessed Date 6 May 2021.
31. Dorri, A., Kanhere, S.S., Jurdak, R., Gauravaram, P., Blockchain for IoT security and privacy: The case study of a smart home, in: *Pervasive Computing and Communications Workshops (PerCom Workshops), 2017 IEEE International Conference on*, IEEE, pp. 618–623, 2017.
32. Aitzhan, N.Z. and Svetinovic, D., Security and privacy in decentralized energy trading through multi-signatures, blockchain and anonymous messaging streams. *IEEE Trans. Dependable Secure Comput.*, 15, 5, 840–852, 2018.
33. Roman, R., Zhou, J., Lopez, J., On the features and challenges of security and privacy in distributed internet of things. *Comput. Netw.*, 57, 10, 2266–2279, 2013.
34. Sicari, S., Rizzardi, A., Grieco, L.A., Coen-Porisini, A., Security, privacy and trust in internet of things: The road ahead. *Comput. Netw.*, 76, 146–164, 2015.
35. *A comprehensive list of blockchain platforms*, ValueCoders, Accessed (2021, June 10).
36. Agbo, C.C., Mahmoud, Q.H., Eklund, J.M., Blockchain technology in healthcare: A systematic review. *Healthcare*, 7, 2, 56, 2019. Multidisciplinary Digital Publishing Institute.
37. Fake drugs kill more than 250,000 children a year, doctors warn, in: *Science*, The Guardian, UK, 5 June 2021.
38. Blockchain in retail market, in: *Growth, Trends, and Forecast (2021-2026)*, 10 June 2021.
39. *Access to energy - Our world in data*, Our World in Data, University of Oxford, 10 June 2021.
40. *Blockchain market size, growth, trends and forecast to 2025*, Markets sand Markets, India, 3 June 2021.
41. *Impact of blockchain technology on healthcare sector*, Peerbits, India, 19 May 2021.
42. *Blockchain technology in energy market to hit $3bn by 2025*, Global Market Insights, Inc, USA, 5 June 2021.
43. Ondiflo, *Blockchain use cases and benefits for upstream oil & gas*, ConsenSys Media, USA, 7 June 2021.
44. *Blockchain in the energy sector: Uses and applications*, ConsenSys, USA, 7 May 2021.
45. Ondiflo, *Blockchain use cases for midstream oil and gas*, ConsenSys Media, USA, September 26, 2018, https://media.consensys.net/blockchain-use-cases-for-midstream-oil-gas-609033457e33
46. Ondiflo, *Blockchain use cases for downstream oil and gas*, ConsenSys Media, USA, September 18, 2018, Accessed from https://media.consensys.net/blockchain-use-cases-and-benefits-for-downstream-oil-gas-ac8de9da6dca

47. Li, C. and Palanisamy, B., Decentralized privacy-preserving timed execution in blockchain-based smart contract platforms. *2018 IEEE 25th International Conference on High Performance Computing (HiPC)*, 2018.

48. Harris, C.G., The risks and challenges of implementing ethereum smart contracts. *2019 IEEE International Conference on Blockchain and Cryptocurrency (ICBC)*, 2019.

49. Fenu, G., Marchesi, L., Marchesi, M., Tonelli, R., The ICO phenomenon and its relationships with ethereum smart contract environment. *2018 International Workshop on Blockchain Oriented Software Engineering (IWBOSE)*, 2018.

50. Tang, H., Tong, N., Ouyang, J., Medical images sharing system based on blockchain and smart contract of credit scores. *2018 1st IEEE International Conference on Hot Information-Centric Networking (HotICN)*, 2018.

14

Cervical Cancer Detection Using Big Data Analytics and Their Comparative Analysis

V. Lakshmi Narasimhan and W. Tumisang Zaphaniah*

Southern Georgia University, Statesboro, USA

Abstract

The detection of cervix-based cancer cells relies heavily on artificial neural networks (ANNs). It is a huge challenge to detect cervical cancer because this cancer occurs with little or no observable symptoms. In order to quickly and precisely identify cervical cells, ANNs employ various architectures and strategies. This paper presents a systematic performance analysis of three deep learning algorithms, namely, backpropagation neural network (BPN), multilayer perceptron (MLP), and recurrent neural network (RNN) for predicting cervical cancer. It is concluded that the most appropriate technique to use for cervical cancer analysis is the multilayer perceptron (MLP) because it gives a higher accuracy of 90% when compared with BPN (60%) and RNN algorithms (88%). MLP is also faster in performance (70%) when compared with the RNN algorithm (0%).

Keywords: Artificial neural networks (ANN), multilayer perceptron (MLP), recurrent neural networks (RNN), backpropagation neural networks (BPN)

14.1 Introduction

A woman's reproductive system has, the cervix, uterus, vagina, and ovaries. The cervix, which we will be focusing on in this paper is the opening to the uterus from the vagina where cervical cancer occurs [1] see Figure 14.1 to view the female reproductive system. The highest cause of cervical cancer is Sexually transmitted human papillomavirus (HPV) [2, 3].

Corresponding author: wapelozaphaniaha@gmail.com

Amit Kumar Tyagi (ed.) Privacy Preservation of Genomic and Medical Data, (327–360) © 2024
Scrivener Publishing LLC

Its occurrence is high in low- and middle-economic countries [4]. Screening for cervical cancer is crucial. An ideal screening test is the least invasive, the easiest to perform, the most agreeable to the subjects, the cheapest, and most effective at identifying disease in its early stages when treatment is straightforward. Cervical cytology, also known as the Pap smear test, biopsy, Schiller, and Hinselmann are the four screening methods. Because there is a significant barrier to effective access to cervical screening methods, cervical cancer continues to be a significant cause of death worldwide. Due to a lack of screening programs, Botswana has a high rate of cervical cancer. About 60% of cervical cancer patients are HIV positive also [2], in addition to the fact that most women when detected were at an advanced stage of cervical cancer. Within Botswana, cervical cancer is the leading cause of cancer death [3]. In most cases, people are falsely diagnosed with cervical cancer scaring them unnecessarily; others are given false hope and later die of the disease. Advances have been made in the treatment of pre-invasive and invasive cancers thanks to several initiatives launched by the Botswana Ministry of Health and several strategic partnerships. The national See and Treat program for cervical cancer is also expanding. Beginning in 2015, school-aged girls will receive HPV vaccinations. A multidisciplinary clinic has been established at the main oncology hospital to streamline care for invasive cancer treatment [5]. An approach to medicine known as personalized healthcare (PHC) emphasizes prediction, prevention, intense patient engagement, shared healthcare decision-making, and care coordination in reducing the number of deaths caused by cervical cancer and save money [6].

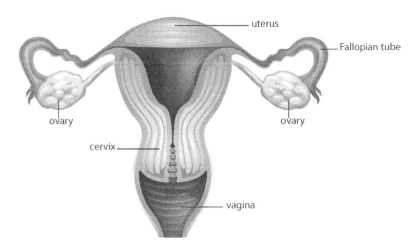

Figure 14.1 Female reproductive system.

Predictive analysis is carried out in biomedical research using data mining methods like decision tree algorithms. The dataset used in this study was obtained from the archive belonging to the University of California, Irvine [7]. The dataset was balanced using the Synthetic Minority Oversampling Technique (SMOTE) [17]. The number of deaths caused by cervical cancer has increased over time due to a lack of effective access to cervical screening methods [8]. Age, number of pregnancies, contraceptive use, smoking habits, and chronological records of sexually transmitted diseases (STDs) are included in the dataset. Using data mining techniques like artificial neural networks (ANNs) [15], this paper primarily focuses on cervical cancer prediction through various screening methods.

The system presented in this paper provides doctors with information on the detection of cervical cancer at an early stage. This can be done by observing various samples, which will then be used to generate data to easily identify cervical cancer at an earlier stage. This helps in reducing false negatives and false positives of the disease in the patients. The remaining parts of the paper are laid out as follows: The literature review is covered in section 14.2, and the machine learning algorithms used are covered in section 14.3. Section 14.4 explains about data used in this research work. Section 14.5 specifies required parameter used for ANNS. Further, section 14.6 contains the results of the work, while the conclusion (in section 14.7) summarizes the paper and offers pointers for further research work in this arena.

14.2 Related Literature

In low-income nations, cervical cancer remains a significant cause of death. However, if it is discovered in its early stages, it can frequently be treated by removing the affected tissues [8]. Women between the ages of 35 and 44 years receive the diagnosis the most frequently, with the average age at diagnosis being 40 years. It rarely occurs in women younger than 20 years. There are a lot of older women who are unaware that they are still at risk for developing cervical cancer. Women over the age of 65 years accounts for more than 20% of cases of cervical cancer. However, women who had regular screenings for cervical cancer before the age of 65 years are less likely to develop these cancers [9]. As a result, it is important to make cervical screening programs, specifically digital colposcopy, a low-cost method with a high potential for scalability, accessible to everyone in a timely manner. In the past ten years, the computer vision and machine learning communities have paid close attention to the development of computer-aided diagnosis systems for the automated processing of digital colposcopies. As a result, a wide range of computational tasks and solutions have been born.

However, there is a dearth of a unified framework for discussing and evaluating the primary responsibilities [9]. The accuracy, dependability, and productivity of electronic devices are all being improved by the Internet of Medical Things (IoMT) in the healthcare sector [10].

Methods for data mining, particularly tree-based algorithms, make accurate predictions regarding cervical cancer possible. The SMOTE method was used to solve the dataset problem [11], which was that there were too few patients with cancer compared to those without cancer. The boosted decision tree outperforms the decision forest and decision jungle approaches in terms of predictive ability, as indicated by the value of the AUROC curve [12]. One will be able to determine the most effective cervical cancer screening method with the rapidly developing methods for analyzing the data and the expanding collection of data from cervical cancer patients [1]. Even though advances in screening and early detection with the Pap test have reduced the number of cases of cervical cancer in recent years, 300,000 women worldwide die annually from the disease [9]. However, depending on the size of the tumor and its stage, cervical cancer can be treated in a variety of ways. A biopsy, Citology, Schiller, or Hinselmann procedure is one option for treatment [8]. There are two types of biopsies: a cone or Sentinel lymph node biopsy [12].

In the early stages, a Sentinel lymph node biopsy is done to see if the Sentinel lymph node has cancer. A cone-shaped piece of tissue is removed from the cervix and the endocervical canal during the procedure known as the cone biopsy [13]. Women with Stage 1A1 cervical cancer or women who are still trying to conceive are the primary recipients of this surgery [9]. Some cases of cervical cancer require a trachelectomy, hysterectomy, pelvic exenteration, or ovarian transposition if cancer has progressed further [14]. There is not much information available online about using machine learning to detect cervical cancer. The goal of this paper is to make sure that there are more false positives than false negatives because false negatives could kill someone. As soon as cancer cells are discovered in a patient's body, this method enables accurate diagnosis, thereby saving their lives.

14.3 Machine Learning Algorithms Used

Three machine learning algorithms are used for the analysis, namely, Multi-Layer Perceptron (MLP), Backpropagation Neural Network (BPN), and Recurrent Neural Network (RNN). A brief explanation of the three algorithms is given below:

14.3.1   Multi-Layer Perceptron

Networks that contain more than one layer of artificial neurons, which allow unidirectional forward connections of inputs and outputs, are called Multi-Layered Perceptron's (MLP) or Multi-layered Feed-forward Neural Networks. An MLP consists of a set of input layers, an output neural layer, and several layers of hidden nodes between the input terminals and the output layer.

1. Send the first pattern's inputs to the input layer.
2. Sum the weighted inputs to the next layer and calculate their activation using the following equation:

$$\Delta W_{ij} \propto \left(\frac{\partial E}{\partial W_{ij}} \right) = -\left(\frac{\partial E}{\partial a_i} \right)\left(\frac{\partial a_i}{\partial W_{ij}} \right) = 2(t_i - a_i)a_i(1 - a_i)a_j$$

3. Repeating (2) until the output layer's activations are known, send activations to the next layer.
4. Compare output activations to the target values for the pattern and calculate deltas for the output layer where n is the iteration number, using the equation below:

$$\delta_i = (t_i - a_i)a_i(1 - u_i).$$

5. Propagate error backward by using the output layer deltas to calculate the deltas for the previous layer using the following equation:

$$\delta_i = (\sum_k \delta_k W_{ki})a_i(1 - a_i)$$

6. Use these deltas to calculate those of the previous layer, repeating until the first layer is reached
7. Calculate the weight changes for all weights and biases (treat biases as weights from a unit having an activation of 1)

$$\Delta W_{ij}(n+1) = \epsilon \delta_i a_j + \alpha \Delta W_{ij}(n),$$

8. If training by pattern, update all the weights and biases, else repeat the cycle for all patterns, summing the changes and applying at the end of the epoch
9. Repeat the entire procedure until the total sum of squared errors is less than a specified criterion

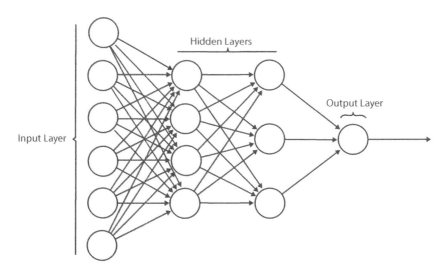

Figure 14.2 Architectural structure of the MLP.

```
Start with a random initial weight
Set epoch={50,100,200,250,500,1000}
While no error{
    For each set epoch{
        For each set(){
            For all output node j{
                Calculate activation(j)
                Error_j= Target value_j_for_set epoch= Activation_j
                For all input Nodes I to output node j{
                    Delta_weight = learning constant= Error_j*Activation_i
                    Weight=weight*Delta_weight
        }
      }
     }
    }
   }
```

Figure 14.3 Pseudocode for MLP implementation.

Figure 14.2 shows the architectural structure of the MLP showing the input layer, hidden layers, and output layer.

Figure 14.3 shows the pseudocode for the implementation of the MLP algorithm.

14.3.2   Backpropagation Neural Network

The following steps present the operation of Backpropagation Neural Network (BPN):

1. Inputs X, arrives through the preconnected path
2. Input is modeled using real weights W. The weights are usually randomly selected.
3. Calculate the output for every neuron from the input layer to the hidden layers, to the output layer.
4. Calculate the error in the outputs **Error= Actual Output – Desired Output**
5. Travel back from the output layer to the hidden layer to adjust the weights such that the error is decreased.
6. Keep repeating the process until the desired output is achieved.

Figure 14.4 shows the architectural structure of BPN showing the input layer, hidden layers, and output layer.

Figure 14.5 presents the pseudocode for BPN implementation.

14.3.3   Recurrent Neural Network

The following steps present the operation of recurrent neural network (RNN):

1. A single-time step of the input is provided to the network.
2. Then calculate its current state using a set of current input and the previous state.
3. The current state becomes the previous state for the next time step.
4. One can go as many time steps according to the problem and join the information from all the previous states.

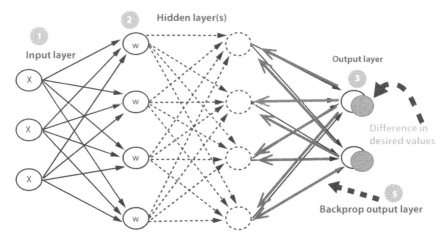

Figure 14.4 Architectural structure of the backpropagation.

```
Start with random initial weight w;
Set  epoch={50,100,200,250,500,1000};
While no_error{
          For each set epoch{
                    Calculate e^p(w) for each epoch;
                    E1:=  Σ p=1 e^p( w ) ^T e^p( w ) ;
                    Calculate J^p(w)for each pattern;
                    repeat
                              Calculate Δw;
                              E2:= Σ p=1 e^p( w  +  Δw) ^T e^p( w  +  Δw) ;
                              If (E1<= E2) Then μ=μ*β;
          Until  (E2<E1);
          μ:=μ/ β;
          w=w + Δw;
            }
          }
```

Figure 14.5 Pseudocode for Backpropagation algorithm implementation.

5. Once all the time steps are completed the final current state is used to calculate the output.
6. The output is then compared to the actual output, i.e., the target output and the error is generated.
7. The error is then backpropagated to the network to update the weights and hence the network (RNN) is trained.

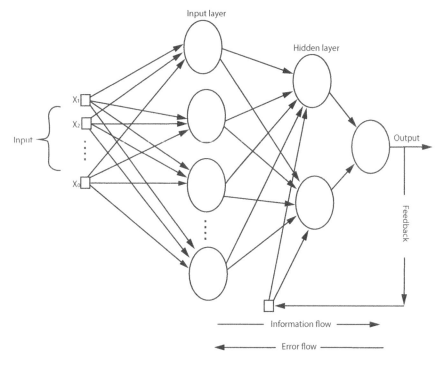

Figure 14.6 Architectural structure of RNN.

Figure 14.6 represents the architectural structure of RNN showing the input layer, hidden layer, and output layer.

Figure 14.7 below presents the pseudocode for RNN implementation.

14.4   Description of the Dataset

The dataset, "Cervical Cancer Risk Factors" was obtained from the UCI Repository [7], which was collected by Fernandes, Cardoso, and Fernandes in 2017 at the "Hospital Universitario de Caracas" in Caracas, Venezuela. The dataset contains habits, demographic information, and the medical history of 858 patients from the hospital. There are many missing values in this dataset, due to many patients not answering questions because of privacy concerns. The dataset consists of 858 instances, with 36 attributes, consisting of 32 risk factors, and 4 target variables (the last four attributes) as shown in Table 14.1.

Algorithm 1 RNN-LF algorithm.

1: **Input:** $DB = \{DB_1, DB_2...DB_r\}$: The long-term traffic flows database.

σ: Activation function.

L: The number of layers excluding the input and the output layers.

2: **Output:**

$\Omega = \{\omega_{l-1}^{mj} | l \in [1...L], m \in [1..|l|], j \in [1..|l-1|]\}$.

3: **for** l=1 to L **do**

4:     **for** j=1 to $|l-1|$ **do**

5:         **for** m=1 to $|l|$ **do**

6:             $\omega_{l-1}^{mj} \leftarrow GenerateRandomValue(0, 1)$.

7:         **end for**

8:     **end for**

9: **end for**

10: **for** i=1 to r **do**

11:     **for** m=1 to p **do**

12:         $s_1^m \leftarrow W_{im}$.

13:     **end for**

14:     **for** l=2 to L **do**

15:         **for** j=1 to $|l-1|$ **do**

16:             **for** m=1 to $|l|$ **do**

17:                 $Computing(s_l^m, \sigma)$. {Eq. 3}

18:             **end for**

19:         **end for**

20:     **end for**

21:     $UpdatingWeight(\Omega)$. {Eq. 4}

22: **end for**

23: **return** Ω

Figure 14.7 Pseudocode for RNN implementation.

This dataset has the target variables as the Hinselmann, Schiller, Cytology, and Biopsy, their values have more 0s than 1s. This means that it contains more people who have tested negative for cancer than those who tested positive for it. The Pie chart in Figure 14.8 illustrates the percentage of the 0s and 1s in the dataset.

Table 14.1 Dataset attributes.

(int) Age
(int) Number of sexual partners
(int) First sexual intercourse (age)
(int) Num of pregnancies
(bool) Smokes
(bool) Smokes (years)
(bool) Smokes (packs/year)
(bool) Hormonal Contraceptives
(int) Hormonal Contraceptives (years)
(bool) IUD
(int) IUD (years)
(bool) STDs
(int) STDs (number)
(bool) STDs:condylomatosis
(bool) STDs: cervical condylomatosis
(bool) STDs: vaginal condylomatosis
(bool) STDs:vulvo-perineal condylomatosis
(bool) STDs: syphilis
(bool) STDs: pelvic inflammatory disease
(bool) STDs: genital herpes
(bool) STDs:molluscum contagiosum
(bool) STDs: AIDS
(bool) STDs: HIV
(bool) STDs: Hepatitis B
(bool) STDs: HPV
(int) STDs: Number of diagnosis
(int) STDs: Time since first diagnosis
(int) STDs: Time since last diagnosis
(bool) Dx: Cancer
(bool) Dx: CIN
(bool) Dx: HPV
(bool) Dx
(bool) Hinselmann: target variable
(bool) Schiller: target variable
(bool) Cytology: target variable
(bool) Biopsy: target variable

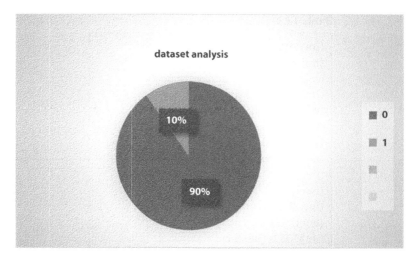

Figure 14.8 Target values analysis pie chart.

14.4.1   Bias in the Dataset

There are some biases in the dataset due to the data collection process and missing values. Since the data was only collected from one hospital in Venezuela, the results could be very different than if the data had been collected from a hospital in Botswana, or multiple locations around the world. Although there are some attributes in the dataset corresponding to lifestyle choices, which could result in a higher risk of cervical cancer (e.g., smoking, hormonal contraceptives, etc.), there are still some major differences between Venezuelan women and Botswana women, which are not accounted for in the dataset and, which could have some effect on the results (such as living conditions, access to healthcare, access to contraceptives, etc.) Additionally, since some of the missing data contain sensitive issues, there is no right way to replace/remove those values

14.4.2   Sorting the Dataset

The cervical cancer dataset has several negative results than positive results; therefore prediction of positive cases was not captured properly. In the dataset, the 1s on the four targets meant that the person did have cervical cancer, and, the 0s represents that the person does not have cervical cancer. The training data was therefore split in two, one where we collected only the 1s (representing the positive test of cervical cancer). Then selected a few entries from the original training set randomly to make a complete training set. In the second half, we kept it the way it was for easy comparison between the two.

14.4.3   Visualization of the Dataset

The **scatter matrix** of the dataset is shown in Figure 14.9, which reveals strong correlations between specific attributes. The "Target" columns (the furthest right) in the scatterplot show attributes with no or little correlations, thereby implying that these attributes are redundant or irrelevant and could be removed from the training set. The **area plot** graph (Figure 14.9) shows each attribute on a different curve and then stacks all the curves on top of each other. It is interesting to see that the two dominating features on this graph are "age" and "biopsy." As a result of these two findings, a histogram showing the relation between "age" and "biopsy," to which there is a strong correlation is shown in Figure 14.10. The graph shows a biopsy occurred when the women were between the ages of 20 and 30 years. This preliminary result supports the fact given earlier that biopsies are often performed on women who still want to have children since most women still wanting to have children would be between the ages of 20 and 30 years.

14.4.4   Pre-Processing

An advantage of this dataset is that it contains all numerical values, meaning that no transformations need to take place to convert categorical values to numerical values.

14.4.5   Standardization and Normalization

Since some of the attributes in the dataset are binary values and some are not, standardizing and normalizing the dataset is advantageous in evening out the values and helping to solve imbalance problems. Standardizing

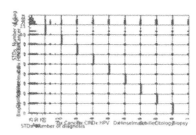 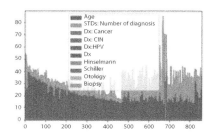

Figure 14.9 Scatter matrix and area plot of the targets.

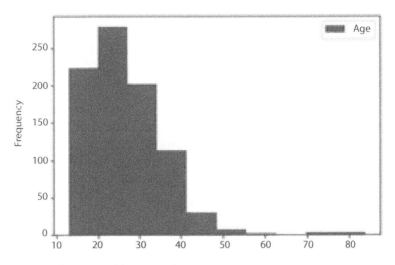

Figure 14.10 Histogram of the age attribute.

makes the entire dataset have a specific value, and in this case, we standardized the mean and normalized the variance. It is important to do this kind of standardization so that larger values do not dominate when developing models based on them. Additionally, many classification methods perform better when the dataset is standardized and/or normalized, and some even require the data to be standardized. Using a built-in function for standardizing/normalizing data in *Scikit*-learn [16], the dataset now has a mean value of -1.4389896095932891e-17 and a variance value of 0.9561828874675149.

14.4.6 Missing Values Management

Due to the large number of missing values in this dataset, it was decided to replace the missing values, instead of eliminating, them so that one does not lose any important data and further, make a better estimate of the missing data. The missing values are replaced with the most frequent, mean, and median values of the row or column in which the missing value was located. Therefore, one can test which approach gives better results.

14.4.7 Splitting of Dataset Into Training and Testing

The dataset needs to be split into two parts, namely, the training part and the testing part. To study the perturbation, the split ratio on the dataset has been set as 50–50, 60–40, 70–30, 80–20, and 90–10 for training to testing respectively.

14.5   Parameter Specification on the ANNs

This section will discuss few parameters which are required for ANNs as:

a. **Backpropagation Neural Network (BPN)**
The model contains one input layer, 5 hidden layers, and only 1 output layer. The input layer contains 55 nodes, the first hidden layer contains 50 nodes, the second hidden layer contains 35 nodes, the third hidden layer contains 20 nodes, the fourth hidden layer contains 14 nodes and the fifth hidden layer contains 8 nodes. There is only one node on the output layer. The initial weights are set to small random numbers and a stochastic gradient descent algorithm is used for optimization. The sigmoid function is used as an activation function, which maps any value to a value between 0 and 1. To get the learning rate to reduce the losses, the *Adam* optimizer is used. The Mean Square Error (MSE) was used to calculate the loss.

b. **Multilayer Perceptron**
The multilayer perceptron (MLP) contains one input layer, two hidden layers, and only one output. The input layer and hidden layer have 100 nodes each along with one output with only one node. Kernel regularizer is used to reduce the weights W (excluding bias). The Relu activation function is used, which greatly accelerates the convergence of stochastic gradient descent compared to the Sigmoid function.

The learning rate was set at 0.001, because if the learning rate is low, then training is more reliable, but optimization will take time because steps toward the minimum of the loss function are small. Binary cross entropy I used to calculate loss because it minimizes the distance between two probability distributions—predicted and actual; it also makes sure that the difference between the two probabilities is minimized. The Stochastic Gradient Descent (SGD) optimizer is used because it performs redundant computations for large data sets, and recomputes gradients for similar examples before each parameter update. SGD does away with this redundancy by performing one update at a time and hence is usually fast.

c. **Recurrent Neural Networks**

The RNN has three layers, an input layer, a hidden layer, and an output layer. The number of nodes in the first input layer is 512 and in the second layer, it is 256. The number of nodes in the output layer is only one. The sigmoid function is used as the activation function because it can map any value to a value between 0 and 1. It is especially used for models where one needs to predict the probability as an output. Since the probability of anything exists only between the range of 0 and 1, Sigmoid is the right choice. To get the learning rate to reduce the losses, the *Adam* optimizer is used, because it uses the squared gradients to scale the learning rate (e.g., *RMSprop*) and it takes advantage of momentum by using the moving average of the gradient, instead of the gradient itself (similar to stochastic gradient descent with momentum). The mean square error (MSE) was used to calculate the loss. Keras layers were used to uniformly set the initial random weights, initially to small random numbers; this is an expectation of the stochastic gradient descent algorithm.

Further, interesting research/facts related to healthcare can be found in articles [18–21].

14.6   Analysis of Results

14.6.1   Backpropagation Neural Network

The data were trained on epochs 50, 100, 500, and 1000; median values of respective parameters were chosen to clean the dataset, however, the results remained the same whether mean or mode was used. For the training-to-testing ratio of 80:20, the stopping criteria are 1000 epochs because the accuracy graph goes into convergence with no change in the data accuracies. Similarly, for the training-to-testing ratio of 70:30, the stopping criteria is 1000 epochs; for the training-to-testing ratio of 60:40, the stopping criteria is 50 epochs; for the training-to-testing ratio of 50:50, the stopping criteria is 50 epoch; for the training to the testing ratio of 90:10, the stopping criteria is 500 epochs. It can be noted from Table 14.2

Table 14.2 Mean/mode/median values for various data with data splitting of 80:20 and 1000 epochs.

Target	Mean	Mode	Median
Hinselman	52.17	52.17	52.17
Citology	60.87	60.87	60.87
Biopsy	60.80	60.80	60.80
Schiller	78.26	78.26	78.26

that a training-to-testing ratio of 80:20 yielded the highest accuracy compared to the rest. The corresponding confusion matrix is shown in Figures 14.11, 14.13, 14.15, and 14.17.

Figure 14.11 shows the TP= 6, TN=6, FP=0, and FN=7. This means that 12 were correctly predicted and 7 were falsely predicted.

Figure 14.12 shows the model accuracy for biopsy using BPN of up to 1000 epochs.

Figure 14.13 shows the TP= 9, TN=4, FP=2, and FN=8. This means that 13 were correctly predicted and 10 were falsely predicted.

Figure 14.14 above shows the model accuracy for Hinselmann using BPN with an epoch up to 1000.

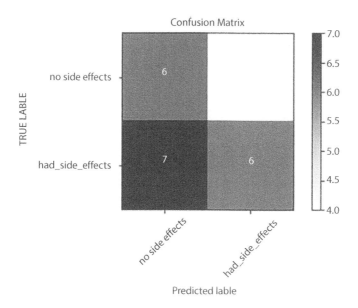

Figure 14.11 Confusion matrix.

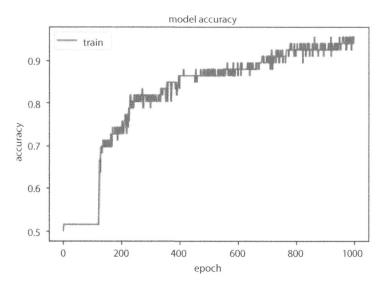

Figure 14.12 Model accuracy for biopsy BPN.

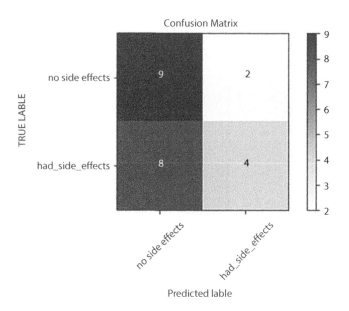

Figure 14.13 Confusion matrix for Hinselmann BPN.

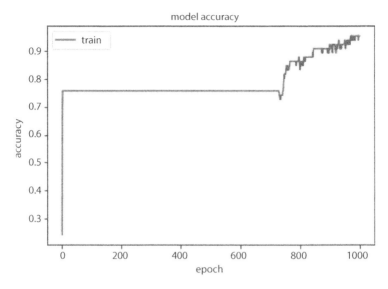

Figure 14.14 Model accuracy for Hinselmann BPN.

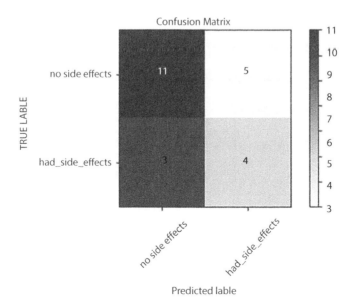

Figure 14.15 Confusion matrix for citology BPN.

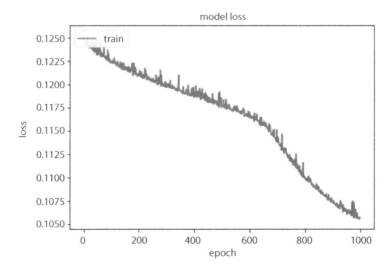

Figure 14.16 Model loss for citology BPN.

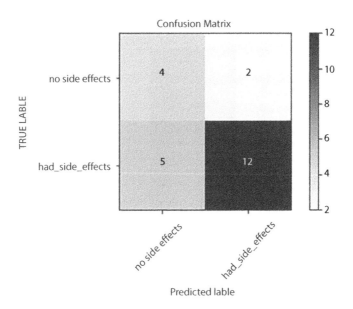

Figure 14.17 Confusion matrix for Schiller BPN.

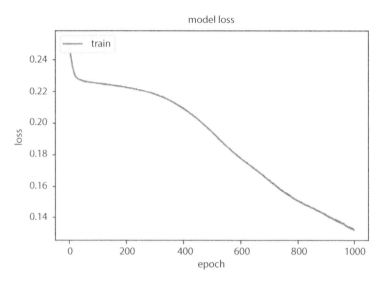

Figure 14.18 Model loss for Schiller BPN.

Figure 14.15 shows the TP= 11, TN=4, FP=5, and FN=3; this implies that 15 were correctly predicted and 8 were falsely predicted.

Figure 14.16 shows the model loss for Citology using BPN with an epoch of up to 1000.

Figure 14.17 shows the TP= 4, TN=12, FP=2, and FN=5. This implies that 16 were correctly predicted and 7 were falsely predicted.

Figure 14.18 shows the model loss for Schiller using BPN.

14.6.2   Multilayer Perceptron

Data were trained on epochs 50, 100, 500, 1000, and 2000. The most frequent (i.e., mode value) was used for cleaning the dataset. With the training-to-testing ratio set as 80:20 and the stopping criteria set at 50 epochs, there is no change in the accuracies. With the ratio set as 70:30 and the stopping criteria set as 1000 epochs, there is no change in the accuracies. With the ratio set as 60:40 and the stopping criteria set as 50 epochs, there is no change in the accuracies. With the ratio set at 50:50 and the stopping criteria set at 50 epochs, there are no changes or inaccuracies. When the said ratio is 90:10 and the stopping criteria of 500 epochs, there is no change in the data accuracies. The ratio training to the testing set as

70:30 gave a higher accuracy when compared to the rest. This can be noted in Table 14.3. The corresponding confusion matrix is shown in Figures 14.19, 14.21, 14.23, and 14.25.

Figure 14.19 shows the model accuracy for Hinselmann using MLP.

Figure 14.20 shows the TP=72, TN=0, FP=0, and FN=13, implying that 72 were correctly predicted and 13 were falsely predicted.

Figure 14.21 presents the accuracy graph for citology using MLP.

Figure 14.22 shows TP=121, TN=0, FP=0, FN=20. This matrix shows that 121 were correctly classified and only 20 were incorrect.

Figure 14.23 shows the model accuracy for Biopsy using MLP.

Table 14.3 Mean/mode/median values for various data with data splitting of 70:30 and 1000 epochs.

Target	Mean	Mode	Median
Hinselman	90.5	90.1	90.2
Citology	87.3	81.5	86.9
Biopsy	83.4	82.3	83.1
Schiller	86.3	85.8	86.2

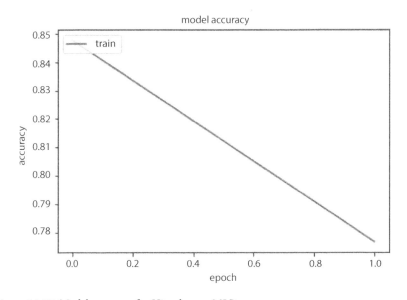

Figure 14.19 Model accuracy for Hinselmann MLP.

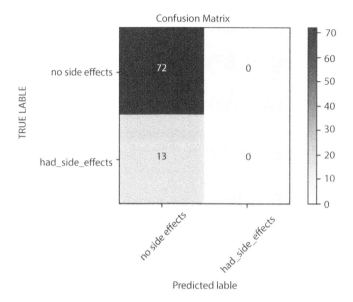

Figure 14.20 Confusion matrix for Hinselmann MLP.

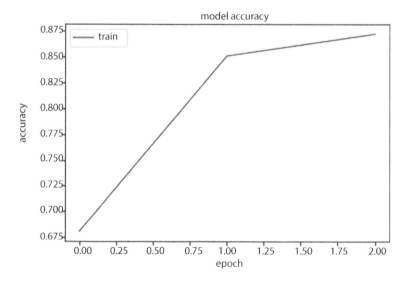

Figure 14.21 Accuracy graph for citology MLP.

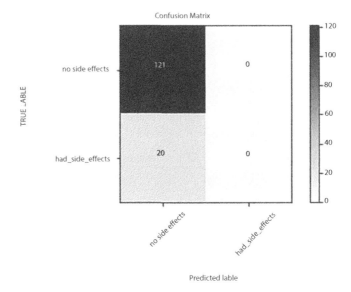

Figure 14.22 Confusion matrix for citology results MLP.

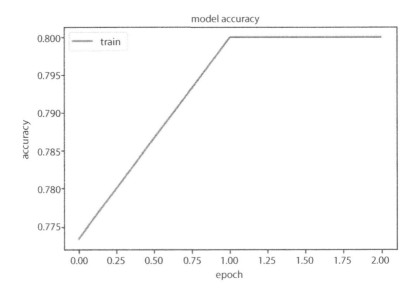

Figure 14.23 Model accuracy for biopsy MLP.

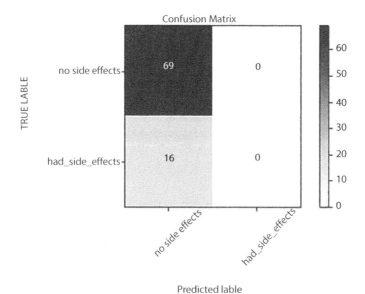

Figure 14.24 Confusion matrix for biopsy results MLP.

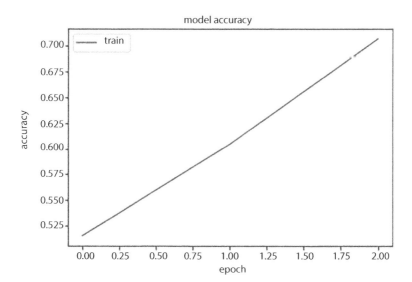

Figure 14.25 Model accuracy for Schiller MLP.

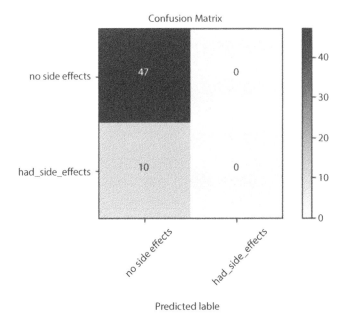

Figure 14.26 Confusion matrix for Schiller results MLP.

Figure 14.24 shows the confusion matrix whereby the TP=69 TN=0, FP=0, and FN=16. It shows that 69 were correctly predicted and 16 were incorrectly predicted.

Figure 14.25 shows the model accuracy for Schiller using MLP.

Figure 14.26 shows the confusion matrix for the model. TP=47, TN=0, FP=0, and FN=10. It shows that 47 were correctly predicted and only 10 were falsely predicted.

14.6.3 Recurrent Neural Network

The dataset was trained on epochs 50, 100, 200, 500, and 1000. The mean value appeared to be the best method to use for handling missing data. With the training-to-testing ratio set as 80:20 and the stopping criteria set as 200 epochs, there is a change in the accuracies. With the ratio set as 70:30 and the stopping criteria as 50 epochs, there is no change in the accuracies. With the ratio of 60:40 and the stopping criteria as 200 epochs, there is no change in the accuracies. With the ratio set as 50:50 and the stopping criteria as 100 epochs, there is no change in the data accuracies. With the ratio set as 90:10 and the stopping criteria as 100 epochs, there is no change in the accuracies. The ratio of 50:50 gave the highest accuracy when compared to the rest. This can be noted in Table 14.4. The corresponding confusion matrix is shown in Figures 14.27, 14.29, 14.31, and 14.33.

Figure 14.27 shows the model accuracy for Hinselmann using RNN.

Figure 14.28 shows the confusion matrix. where TP=26,TN=8, FP=12 and FN=10. 34 were correctly predicted and 22 were incorrectly predicted.

Table 14.4 Mean/mode/median values for various data with data splitting of 50:50 and 100 epochs.

Targets	Mean	Mode	Median
Hinselmann	89.0	88.1	80.5
Citology	82.1	83.2	80.7
Biopsy	91.3	80.1	89.8
Schiller	80.7	87.3	81.2

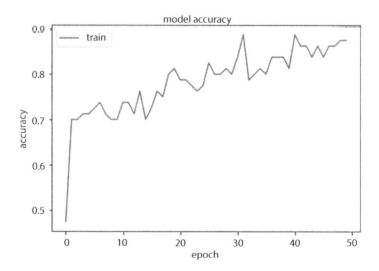

Figure 14.27 Model accuracy for Hinselmann RNN.

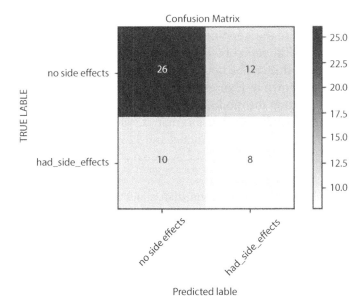

Figure 14.28 Confusion matrix for Hinselmann RNN results.

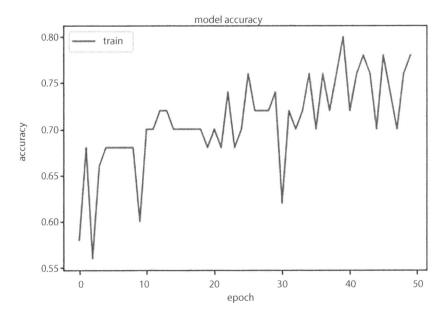

Figure 14.29 Model accuracy for citology RNN.

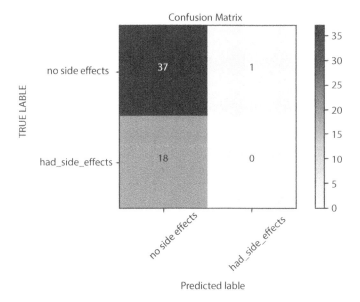

Figure 14.30 Confusion matrix for citology RNN results.

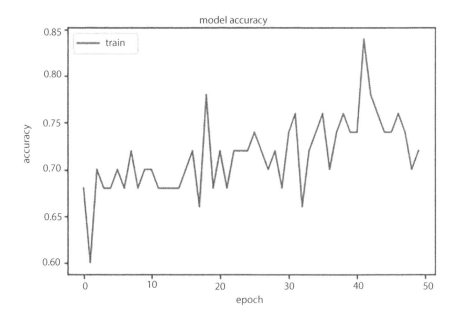

Figure 14.31 Model accuracy for biopsy RNN.

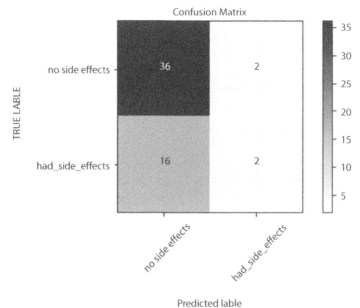

Figure 14.32 Confusion matrix for biopsy RNN results.

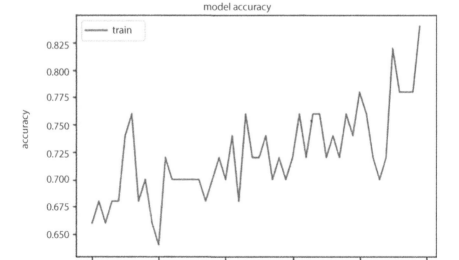

Figure 14.33 Model accuracy for Schiller RNN.

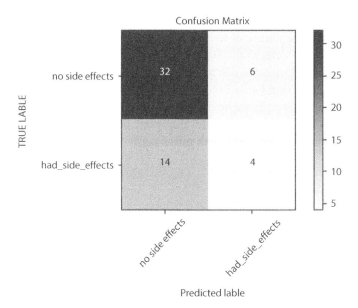

Figure 14.34 Confusion matrix for the RNN Schiller results.

Figure 14.29 shows the model accuracy for citology using RNN.

Figure 14.30 shows the confusion matrix. where TP=37, TN=0, FP=1 and FN=18. 37 were correctly predicted and 19 were incorrectly predicted.

Figure 14.31 shows the model accuracy for Biopsy using RNN.

Figure 14.32 shows the confusion matrix, where TP=36, TN=2, FP=2, and FN=16. 38 were correctly predicted and 18 were incorrectly predicted.

Figure 14.33 shows the model accuracy for Schiller using RNN.

Figure 14.34 shows the confusion matrix, where TP=32, TN=6, FP=14, and FN=4. 36 were correctly predicted and 20 were incorrectly predicted.

14.7 Conclusions

This chapter presented a systematic performance analysis of three deep learning algorithms, namely, backpropagation (BPN), multilayer percep-tron (MLP), and recurrent neural network (RNN) for predicting Cervical cancer. It is concluded that the most appropriate technique to use for cer-vical cancer analysis is the Multilayer perceptron (MLP) because it gives a higher accuracy of 90% when compared with backpropagation (60%) and RNN algorithms (88%). MLP is also faster in performance (70%) when compared with the RNN algorithm (0%). However, it is pointed out that the method to employ for cleaning the dataset is determined by the kind of algorithm and the nature of the dataset. In this paper, the different methods used for the detection of cervical cancer based on neural networks and their architecture are discussed. Further work in this arena includes the development of a Gene Feedforward Neural Network (GFNN) with a combination genetic algorithm for detecting many forms of cancer types, including cervical cancer. The development of a comprehensive Cancer APP will also be something worth pursuing.

References

1. Mahboob, T. *et al.*, Cervical cancer prediction through different screening methods using data mining. *International Journal of Advanced Computer Science and Applications (IJACSA)*, 10, 2, p 388, March 2019.

2. Oncol, F., 2015, November 3. https://www.ncbi.nlm.nih.gov/. Retrieved from https://www.ncbi.nlm.nih.gov/pmc/articles/PMC4630577/ (28th December 2020).

3. Winter, S.C., 2019, March 18. https://bmcpublichealth.biomedcentral.com/. Retrieved from https://bmcpublichealth.biomedcentral.com/articles/10.1186/s12889-019-6638-z (28th December 2020).

4. Enrique Alba, F.C., *Training neural networks with GA hybrid algorithms*, Research gate, USA, 2004, january, Retrieved from Training Neural Networks with GA Hybrid Algorithms: https://www.researchgate.net/publication/220743543_Training_Neural_Networks_with_GA_Hybrid_Algorithms (28th December 2020).

5. Ramogola-Masire, *et al.*, Cervical cancer prevention in HIV-infected women using the "see and treat" approach in Botswana. *J. Acquir Immune Defic. Syndr.*, 59, 3, 2012 Mar 1.

6. Lakshmi Narasimhan, V., *Proactive personalized primary care information system – P3CIS*, Lecture Notes in Electrical Engineering (LNEE) Series, Springer Series, USA, 2021.

7. Dua, D. and Graff, C., *UCI machine learning repository*, the University of California, School of Information and Computer Science, Irvine, CA, 2019, [https://archive.ics.uci.edu/ml/datasets/Cervical+cancer+%28Risk+Factors%29].

8. Fernandes, K., Cardoso, J.S., Fernández, J., Automated methods for the decision support of cervical cancer screening using digital colposcopies. *IEEE Access*, 4, 99, May 2018.

9. The American Cancer Society medical and editorial content team, 2020. https://www.cancer.org/cancer/acs-medical-content-and-news-staff.html (28th July 2021).

10. Lakshmi Narasimhan, V., *Internet of medical things (IoMT)*, Proc. of AICTE-ATAL Academy (International), University Grants Commission (UGC), India, 21-25 Sept. 2020.

11. Alam, T.M. *et al.*, Cervical cancer prediction through different screening methods using data mining. *Int. J. Adv. Comput. Sci. Appl.*, 10, 2, 388–396, 2019.

12. Noviyanti, T. and Sagala, M., A comparative study of data mining methods to diagnose cervical cancer. *J. Phys.: Conf. Ser.* 1255, 012022, 2019.

13. Andikyan, V., Khoury-Collado, F., Denesopolis, J., Park, K.J., Hussein, Y.R., Brown, C.L., Sonoda, Y., Chi, D.S., Barakat, R.R., Abu-Rustum, N.R., Cervical conization and sentinel lymph node mapping in the treatment of stage I cervical cancer: Is less enough? *Int. J. Gynecol Cancer*, 24, 1, 113–7, 2014 Jan.

14. de Juan, A. *et al.*, SEOM clinical guidelines for cervical cancer (2019). *Clin. Guides Oncol.*, 22, 271, 24 January 2020.

15. Sampath Kumar, V. and Lakshmi Narasimhan, V., Using deep learning for assessing cybersecurity economic risks in virtual power plants. *IEEE Intl. Conf. on Electrical Energy Systems (ICEES – 2021)*, IEEE Xplore, Feb.11-13, 2021.

16. Brownlee, J., *How to normalize and standardize time series data in python*, San Francisco, 2019, https://machinelearningmastery.com/normalize-standardize-time-series-data-python/, (28th July 2021).

17. Brownlee, J., *How to scale data for long short-term memory networks in python*, 5th August 2019, https://machinelearningmastery.com/how-to-scale-data-for-long-short-term-memory-networks-in-python/ (28th July 2021).

18. Gomathi, L., Mishra, A.K., Tyagi, A.K., Industry 5.0 for healthcare 5.0: Opportunities, challenges and future research possibilities. *2023 7th International Conference on Trends in Electronics and Informatics (ICOEI)*, Tirunelveli, India, pp. 204–213, 2023.

19. Adebiyi, M.O., Afolayan, J.O., Arowolo, M.O., Tyagi, A.K., Adebiyi, A.A., Breast cancer detection using a PSO-ANN machine learning technique. In: *Using Multimedia Systems, Tools, and Technologies for Smart Healthcare Services*, A. Tyagi (Ed.), IGI Global, pp. 96–116, 2023, https://doi.org/10.4018/978-1-6684-5741-2.ch007.

20. Sai, G.H., Tripathi, K., Tyagi, A.K., Internet of Things-based e-Healthcare: Key challenges and recommended solutions for future. In: *Proceedings of Third International Conference on Computing, Communications, and Cyber-Security*, Lecture Notes in Networks and Systems, vol. 421, P.K. Singh, S.T. Wierzchoń, S. Tanwar, J.J.P.C. Rodrigues, M. Ganzha (Eds.), Springer, Singapore, 2023, https://doi.org/10.1007/978-981-19-1142-2_37.

21. Jayaprakash, V. and Tyagi, A.K. Security optimization of resource-constrained internet of healthcare things (IoHT) devices using asymmetric cryptography for blockchain network. In: *Proceedings of International Conference on Network Security and Blockchain Technology. ICNSBT 2021.* Lecture Notes in Networks and Systems, vol. 481, D. Giri, J.K. Mandal, K. Sakurai, D. De (Eds.), Springer, Singapore, 2022, https://doi.org/10.1007/978-981-19-3182-6_18.

Smart Walking Stick for Visually Impaired People

Dhilip Karthik M.*, **Rizwan Mohamed Kareem, Nisha V. M. and Sajidha S. A.**

Department of Computer Science Engineering, Chennai, India

Abstract

We have all witnessed visually challenged persons stumbling over objects in front of them as they continually tap the ground to check for obstacles in their path. Visually challenged people rely on their sense of touch and sound to navigate their surroundings, but this can be challenging in unfamiliar environments or when obstacles are present. A smart walking stick equipped with sensors and navigation technology can enhance the safety and independence of blind individuals by providing real-time audio cues about the environment and alerting them to obstacles. The proposed intelligent walking stick takes away the need for them to be constantly on guard. It increases their level of safety and lowers their risk of tripping and falling.

Keywords: Visually challenged people, walking stick, security, IOT, smart assist devices

15.1 Introduction

Visually challenged people are individuals who are unable to see or have limited vision. Blindness can be caused by various factors, including genetic conditions, injuries, or diseases. People who are blind faces unique challenges in their daily lives and often need to use alternative methods to navigate and perform tasks. Visually challenged individuals often have limitations in areas such as mobility, access to information, and education.

Corresponding author: dhilipkarthik.m2019@vitstudent.ac.in

Amit Kumar Tyagi (ed.) *Privacy Preservation of Genomic and Medical Data*, (361–382) © 2024 Scrivener Publishing LLC

They may require the assistance of a guide or a service animal to navigate unfamiliar environments. The use of Braille, audio books, and other assistive technologies can help blind individuals access information and education, but these resources may not always be readily available. Additionally, blind individuals may also face discrimination in the workplace, which can limit their employment opportunities and impact their financial stability. Despite these limitations, blind individuals are often highly capable and resilient. With the help of assistive technologies and supportive communities, many visually challenged people are able to live normal and meaningful lives. It is important to recognize and address the challenges faced by blind individuals, and to create a society that is accessible and inclusive for all.

A. IoT and Future Generation Computing

The Internet of Things (IoT) is a rapidly growing field that is transforming the way we interact with technology and shaping the future of computing. IoT refers to a network of physical devices, vehicles, home appliances, and other items that are embedded with sensors, software, and network connectivity, enabling them to collect and exchange data. This data can then be used to improve and automate various aspects of our lives, from controlling the temperature in our homes to monitoring our health and fitness. In the future, IoT technology is expected to play a major role in shaping the way we live, work, and interact with each other [1]. With the increasing number of connected devices, IoT is creating new opportunities for businesses to collect and analyze data, and to create innovative products and services. For example, smart homes and cities are becoming more prevalent, and devices are being designed to work together in an interconnected way. As technology continues to evolve, it is likely to revolutionize the way we approach problem-solving and decision-making. In the near future, we can expect that IoT will play a crucial role in shaping the future of computing, with the development of cutting-edge technologies such as artificial intelligence, machine learning, and big data analytics. By enabling seamless communication between devices, IoT is creating new opportunities for data-driven decision-making and empowering organizations to make more informed decisions based on real-time data. IoT is also helping to transform industries such as healthcare, transportation, and manufacturing by improving efficiency and reducing costs. As the technology continues to evolve and the number of connected devices grows, the impact of IoT on our daily lives and the world as a whole is expected to be profound.

The future of computing is exciting, and IoT is playing a key role in shaping this future.

The Internet of Things (IoT) and Future Generation Computing have the potential to revolutionize the way society operates and provide new and innovative solutions to pressing social problems. These new technologies can serve the needs of marginalized and underserved populations by providing access to essential services such as healthcare, education, and communication. For example, IoT-enabled wearable devices can monitor the health of individuals living in remote and rural areas, providing real-time data to healthcare professionals for prompt diagnosis and treatment. The integration of AI and machine learning algorithms into these devices can also enhance their accuracy and improve their ability to predict and prevent health problems. In the field of education, the integration of IoT and Future Generation Computing can provide equal access to quality education for all, regardless of their geographic location. This can be achieved through the use of virtual classrooms, online learning platforms, and e-books that provide interactive and personalized learning experiences. Additionally, the use of IoT-enabled devices such as smart boards and smart classrooms can enhance the teaching and learning experience by providing real-time feedback, personalized assessments, and gamified learning activities.

The integration of IoT and Future Generation Computing can also help to address issues of poverty, hunger, and homelessness by providing better access to essential services such as food and shelter. For example, IoT-enabled smart homes can help manage energy consumption and reduce waste, making them more affordable for low-income families. The use of smart agriculture and IoT-enabled food supply chains can also help to increase food security and reduce food waste by optimizing crop production, reducing spoilage, and improving the distribution of food to those in need. In conclusion, the integration of IoT and Future Generation Computing has the potential to greatly benefit society, especially those in need. By providing access to essential services such as healthcare, education, and basic necessities, these technologies can help to address some of the most pressing social problems and improve the quality of life for people around the world.

B. Difference Between a Traditional Walking Stick and a Smart Walking Stick

A traditional walking stick, also known as a white cane, has been a standard tool used by individuals who are blind or have low vision for many years.

However, while a traditional walking stick provides basic support for mobility, it has several limitations when compared to a smart walking stick, which is a type of assistive technology cane. One of the main limitations of a traditional walking stick is its lack of advanced features for navigation and safety. A traditional walking stick does not have any sensors or other technologies that can detect and alert the user to the presence of obstacles. This means that the user must rely solely on their own ability to detect obstacles and navigate through their environment, which can be particularly challenging in unfamiliar or complex environments. Another limitation of a traditional walking stick is that it does not provide any feedback on the environment. A traditional walking stick does not give the user any information about the surroundings, such as the distance to an object or the height of an obstacle. This can make it difficult for the user to navigate with confidence and increase the risk of accidents. In contrast, a smart walking stick is equipped with advanced technologies that can provide real-time information about the environment to the user. For example, a smart walking stick may be equipped with sensors, cameras, and other technologies that can detect obstacles and alert the user to their presence. Some smart walking sticks can also provide audio or haptic feedback to guide the user in the right direction and provide information about the surroundings. Additionally, some smart walking sticks can connect to other devices, such as smartphones, providing even more information and connectivity options for the user.

One of the main benefits of a smart walking stick is improved safety. By providing real-time information about the environment and alerting the user to the presence of obstacles, a smart walking stick can help reduce the risk of accidents and improve the user's confidence when navigating. Additionally, the advanced features of a smart walking stick can help the user navigate with greater ease and independence, allowing them to live a more fulfilling life.

In conclusion, while a traditional walking stick has its place, a smart walking stick offers several advantages over a traditional walking stick, including improved safety, enhanced navigation, and additional features to support independent living. For individuals who are blind or have low vision, a smart walking stick can provide a more comprehensive solution that can greatly improve their quality of life.

C. Smart Walking Stick

Most of us take our vision for granted. We wake up each day and go about our lives without giving a second thought to the complex process that allows us to see. But for people with visual impairments, everyday activities like getting around can be a challenge. That is where our smart walking stick comes in.

It has an innovative design that helps visually impaired people move about like any other person. It makes use of various sensors to detect and inform the user about their surroundings.

The stick has the capacity to detect obstacles that are in the user's path; it has the ability to identify what kind of object is being detected and in which direction the obstacle is present. Because most people immediately avoid the path of a visually challenged person, the system is sophisticated enough to ignore individuals and solely detect obstacles in order to avoid false alarms. It also has the ability to alert other people and call for help if the user of the stick falls down. The stick will also be able to sense if there are any pits or water in the user's path. If the user has misplaced the stick anywhere, they can track their stick's location.

Our key strategy to reduce cost is by making use of the user's mobile phone to perform complex tasks rather than having a separate expensive computer. Since it is highly likely that users walk around with their mobile phones, we decided to harness its capabilities. We built our own Android application that can be integrated with the walking stick to perform the object detection task. We will also make use of the mobile phone's speaker rather than a separate speaker.

15.2   Related Work

There have been numerous attempts to create obstacle-avoidance tools for the blind with a constrained range of uses. This section will go over some of these attempts and their flaws.

For instance, Dada *et al.* [2] proposed a smart walking cane with only ultrasonic sensors and a buzzer.

In order to achieve this purpose, they fitted the cane with ultrasonic sensors at various locations, which activated the buzzer sound and informed the user about the surroundings. They suggested a low-cost, lightweight system with a microprocessor that processes signals and beeps to warn the visually challenged individual of any obstacles, water, or dark places. Obstacle and moisture detection sensors are used in the system to collect, process, and send signals to the alarm system, which then warns the user for quick action. The system was created, written in C language, tested for accuracy, and reviewed by a person who is blind. Within around 2 meters of the user, their device can identify obstructions. The only way the device responds to a scenario is through a buzzer. Although using ultrasonic sensors was a great idea, having a clear signal of what obstacle is being detected is important.

A brand-new design for a walking stick that enables blind and elderly persons to navigate new environments and keep an eye on their health was suggested by Singh and Singh [3]. In this technology, various sensors installed on a walking stick allow a person to conveniently traverse both indoors and outdoors while also keeping track of their health. They created a stick with various features integrated into a single stick, unlike prior electronic blind sticks that were useful in detecting obstacles and alerting users. This stick can detect obstacles, pits, and water up to a certain level on the ground as well as the user's location, pulse rate and body temperature. It can also send messages to notify others to a user's health problems or other emergencies. Although it is innovative to keep health monitoring in a walking stick, it is going to unnecessarily drive up the cost, preventing many people from getting access to the stick.

A nice way of accomplishing obstacle detection using the Raspberry Pi as the microcontroller was proposed by Mind *et al.* [4]. The Raspberry Pi microprocessor, obstacle-detection sensors, GPS module, speakers, and other connecting parts are included in the kit. After processing the data, the blind individual receives the necessary instructions. It gives a voice output, unlike a buzzer output in most literature. But despite that, it is not capable of identifying the type of object that was detected.

In order to identify obstacles in mobile robot applications, a novel way for building the transducer of a highly directed ultrasonic range sensor was proposed by Park *et al.* [5]. The wave generation, amplification, radiation, and counter mass sections make up the transducer. This design's working theory is based on the parametric array method, in which a low-frequency wave with a narrow aperture is produced by using the frequency difference between two ultrasonic waves. The objective of this study was to efficiently construct the best transducer for producing the two simultaneous longitudinal modes. The continuum model of a bar and counter mass and the compatibility requirement between a piezoelectric actuator and a linear horn were first combined to create an adequate mathematical model. Using a finite element approach, they next established the ideal lengths for the aluminum horn and piezoelectric actuator. The proposed sensor had a substantially greater directivity than the current standard ultrasonic range sensors, with a half-power bandwidth of less than ±1.3 degrees at 44.8 kHz.

A great design for an intelligent walking stick was proposed by García *et al.* [6]. Unlike other ideas, it does not provide a voice or a buzzer response to the user; it responds through haptic sensing. The cane vibrates when it wants to inform the user about an obstacle. A major drawback is that it detects obstacles only above the waistline. The long, conventional cane features an ergonomic design and an inbuilt electronic system that fits into the handle. Haptic sensing is used by the electronic system to find impediments higher than the waist. The cane vibrates or emits a sound when an obstruction is found. The interaction between blind and visually impaired people and the urban environment is investigated through experiments. In order to process experimental data, a J48 classifier is used. The output of the confusion matrix is good in terms of validation.

A sophisticated system that can distinguish between human and non-human targets in addition to alerting the user of potential difficulties as suggested by Cardillo *et al.* [7]. The technology allows the user to detect and recognize moving objects in the vicinity and obtain additional information about their size, distance, and speed. The system was designed and tested to work in different environments and lighting conditions, and the authors demonstrated its effectiveness in detecting and recognizing different types of moving objects, including pedestrians, cars, and bicycles. They also proposed an algorithm that uses machine learning to recognize human walking patterns and distinguish them from other moving objects.

The paper "An Astute Assistive Device for Mobility and Object Recognition for Visually Impaired People" proposes an assistive device that can help visually impaired individuals with both mobility and object recognition. The device is designed to be compact, lightweight, and easy to use. The proposed device consists of a wearable unit with an array of sensors, including an ultrasonic sensor for obstacle detection, a color sensor for object recognition, and an inertial measurement unit (IMU) [8] for motion tracking. The sensor data is processed by a microcontroller, which provides feedback to the user through a vibrating motor and an audio output. The device is also equipped with Bluetooth communication, allowing it to connect to a smartphone app that provides additional features such as GPS navigation and object recognition using machine learning algorithms. The paper describes the design and implementation of the device, as well as the results of a user study with visually impaired individuals. The study showed that the device was able to help users navigate unfamiliar environments and identify objects, and that the users found it easy to use and useful. Overall, the proposed assistive device shows promise in helping visually impaired individuals with mobility and object recognition, and could potentially improve their quality of life.

This paper proposes a Geographic Information System (GIS)-enabled model [9], which uses RFID to enable the user to move around in an unfamiliar environment through a user-friendly interface. Passive RFIDs may only detect objects within a short distance.

A basic system which uses an ultrasonic sensor to detect the distance of the obstacle and notifies the user with a buzzer alarm. The development of a smart cane with a distance measurement system [10] is the goal of this project. The system has an earphone as the output and an ultrasonic sensor as the input. The obstacle's distance is measured using an ultrasonic sensor. The National Instruments myRIO-1900 controller receives the data after which it processes it and outputs a beeping sound. LabVIEW was used to program the process graphically, using an FPGA as the desired target. Several verification tests have been used to determine the system's performance. Generally speaking, the gadget will use the audio output to warn blind individuals of the impediments. Since this is a basic system, it may not provide multiple features.

A cane equipped with ultrasonic sensors that can detect obstacles in front of the user and provide haptic feedback through a vibrating motor located on the handle of the cane was suggested by Zhou [11]. The sensors are connected to an Arduino microcontroller, which processes the sensor data and controls the vibration motor. The smart cane also features a GPS module that can provide location information to the user and a Bluetooth module that can connect to a smartphone or other device to provide additional features such as navigation or emergency notifications. The cane is powered by a rechargeable battery and can be charged through a USB port. The paper discusses the results of testing the smart cane with visually challenged participants and notes that the participants found the device helpful in detecting obstacles and providing haptic feedback. The paper also discusses future directions for improving the design and adding more features such as voice recognition and environmental sensing.

The stick integrates Internet of Things (IoT) and artificial intelligence (AI) technologies, allowing it to be an "AIoT-based" device. The smart stick is equipped with a range of sensors, including cameras, microphones, and ultrasonic sensors. These sensors collect information about the environment and transmit it to the AI algorithms [12] running on the device. The AI algorithms process the information and generate audio feedback to the user through the built-in speaker. For example, if there is an obstacle in front of the user, the AI algorithms would generate an audio warning, allowing the user to avoid the obstacle. In addition to the sensors and AI algorithms, the smart stick also includes a GPS module. This allows the device to provide directions to the user and alert them of any upcoming hazards. The stick also has a mobile application that can be used to manage and control the device. This application allows the user to set custom audio feedback, change the volume, and update the device software. The development of the smart stick required a deep understanding of the challenges faced by visually impaired individuals. The researchers conducted numerous studies and surveys to gather information about the needs and preferences of visually impaired people. This information was used to design and refine the smart stick to ensure it met the needs of the target audience. The researchers also noted that the device has the potential to be integrated with other assistive technologies, further increasing its potential to enhance the lives of visually impaired individuals.

The "Intelligent Assistance System for Visually Impaired/Blind People (ISVB)" is a research paper that focuses on developing an assistive technology for visually impaired or blind individuals. The system is designed to provide real-time information about the environment and enhance the safety and independence of visually impaired individuals. The ISVB is an AI-powered system that uses a combination of sensors and machine learning algorithms to provide audio feedback to the user. The ISVB system [13] is composed of several components, including an IoT device worn by the user, a smartphone application, and a cloud-based server. The IoT device is equipped with sensors, such as cameras, microphones, and ultrasonic sensors, that collect information about the environment. This information is transmitted to the cloud-based server, where it is processed by machine learning algorithms. The algorithms generate audio feedback, which is then transmitted to the user through the IoT device. The smartphone application is used to manage the ISVB system and provides additional functionality. For example, the user can set custom audio feedback, adjust the volume, and update the device software. The application also allows the user to access additional information, such as directions, maps, and point-of-interest information. The ISVB system was developed after conducting extensive research into the needs and preferences of visually impaired individuals. The researchers gathered information through surveys and studies, which was used to design and refine the ISVB system. The results of the research showed that the ISVB system significantly improved the safety and independence of visually impaired individuals, providing them with real-time information about their environment. The ISVB system also has the potential to be integrated with other assistive technologies, such as braille displays and screen readers, to further enhance the experience of visually impaired individuals. The researchers note that the ISVB system has the potential to be used in a wide range of environments, including indoors and outdoors, and for various activities, such as navigation, shopping, and education. In conclusion, the "Intelligent Assistance System for Visually Impaired/Blind People (ISVB)" is a significant contribution to the field of assistive technologies. The ISVB system provides visually impaired individuals with real-time information about their environment, enhancing their safety and independence. The research highlights the importance of incorporating the needs and preferences of the target audience when developing assistive technologies and serves as a model for future research in the field.

The "IoT-enabled Smart Blind Stick and Spectacles Mountable Eye-Piece equipped with Camera for Visually Challenged People" is a research paper that presents a novel assistive technology for visually challenged individuals. The technology consists of two devices—a smart blind stick and a spectacles mountable eye-piece equipped with a camera. The devices are IoT-enabled, allowing them to be connected to the internet and collect and transmit information about the environment. The smart blind stick [14] is equipped with sensors, including cameras, microphones, and ultrasonic sensors, which collect information about the environment and transmit it to the eye-piece. The eye-piece is equipped with a camera and a small screen that displays the information collected by the sensors in real-time. The eye-piece can be mounted on spectacles, allowing the user to see the information without having to take their eyes off the environment. The IoT-enabled devices are powered by AI algorithms, which process the information collected by the sensors to provide audio feedback to the user. For example, if there is an obstacle in front of the user, the AI algorithms would generate an audio warning, allowing the user to avoid the obstacle. The devices also have the ability to recognize and identify objects in the environment, such as doors, stairs, and signs, and provide relevant information to the user. The devices were developed after conducting extensive research into the needs and preferences of visually challenged individuals. The researchers gathered information through surveys and studies, which was used to design and refine the devices. The results of the research showed that the devices significantly improved the safety and independence of visually challenged individuals, providing them with real-time information about their environment. The devices are also equipped with a mobile application that can be used to manage and control the devices. The application allows the user to set custom audio feedback, change the volume, and update the device software. The devices have the potential to be integrated with other assistive technologies, such as braille displays and screen readers, to further enhance the experience of visually challenged individuals.

The research paper "Aerial Obstacle Detection With 3-D Mobile Devices" focuses on the development of an obstacle detection system for aerial vehicles, such as drones or unmanned aerial vehicles (UAVs). The system uses 3-D mobile devices, such as smartphones or tablets, to detect obstacles in real-time while the aerial vehicle is in flight. The obstacle detection system

[15] is based on computer vision algorithms and uses the camera of the 3-D mobile device to capture images of the environment. The algorithms process the images and generate a 3-D map of the environment, which is used to detect obstacles. The system is capable of detecting obstacles in real-time and providing feedback to the operator of the aerial vehicle. The researchers conducted experiments to evaluate the performance of the system and compare it to other obstacle detection systems. The results showed that the system was capable of accurately detecting obstacles, even in challenging environments. The system also had a low false positive rate, meaning that it was unlikely to generate false warnings about obstacles. The researchers also investigated the potential applications of the system, including its use for search and rescue missions, inspection of infrastructure, and aerial photography. The system has the potential to enhance the safety and efficiency of aerial vehicles, as it can help the operator avoid obstacles and maintain control of the vehicle in real-time. In conclusion, the "Aerial Obstacle Detection With 3-D Mobile Devices" research paper presents a promising solution for obstacle detection in aerial vehicles. The system uses 3-D mobile devices and computer vision algorithms to detect obstacles in real-time, providing the operator with valuable information about the environment. The research highlights the potential of mobile devices for obstacle detection in aerial vehicles and serves as a model for future research in the field.

The research paper "Design and Implementation of an Intelligent Assistive System for Visually Impaired People for Aerial Obstacle Avoidance and Fall Detection" presents a novel assistive technology [16] for visually impaired individuals. The system combines aerial obstacle avoidance and fall detection technologies to provide a comprehensive solution for the safety and independence of visually impaired individuals. The system consists of a wearable device that is equipped with sensors, including cameras, microphones, and accelerometers. The sensors collect information about the environment and transmit it to a central processing unit, where the information is processed and analyzed by AI algorithms. The algorithms generate audio feedback for the user, warning them of any obstacles or potential falls. The system also has the ability to detect falls in real-time and provide immediate assistance to the user. The system can notify a caregiver or emergency contact in the event of a fall, allowing them to provide support as quickly as possible. The researchers conducted extensive research into the needs and preferences of visually impaired individuals, gathering information through surveys and studies. The information was used to design and refine the system, ensuring that it meets the specific needs of the target audience. The results of the research showed that the system significantly improved the safety and independence of visually impaired individuals, providing them with real-time information about their environment and alerting them to potential falls.

The system is also equipped with a mobile application that can be used to manage and control the device. The application allows the user to set custom audio feedback, change the volume, and update the device software. The system has the potential to be integrated with other assistive technologies, such as braille displays and screen readers, to further enhance the experience of visually impaired individuals. In conclusion, the "Design and Implementation of an Intelligent Assistive System for Visually Impaired People for Aerial Obstacle Avoidance and Fall Detection" research paper presents a significant contribution to the field of assistive technologies. The system provides visually impaired individuals with a comprehensive solution for their safety and independence, combining aerial obstacle avoidance and fall detection technologies. The research highlights the importance of incorporating the needs and preferences of the target audience when developing assistive technologies and serves as a model for future research in the field.

15.3   System Architecture

The whole system can be viewed as a composition of hardware and software subsystems. The hardware sub-system comprises various sensors, Arduino module, batteries and mobile holder that all can be well embedded into the walking stick easily. Then coming to the software portion of the system, the only thing required is the user's mobile phone, which performs the task of object detection using the app installed on the user's phone, which is a major software component of the software sub-system. The integration and communication of these 2 major subsystems is carefully designed following the major connection protocols for the smooth working of the project. The complete architecture of the system is provided in the Figure 15.1 and Figure 15.2.

A. Architecture and Working of the Hardware Subsystem

The hardware architecture has various components to help the user to have hassle-free navigation. The various components present are gyroscopic sensor, buzzer, switch, Arduino, Bluetooth module, battery backup, RF-module (transmitter and receiver), Safe & Quick-release smart phone holder, Infrared sensor, ultrasonic sensor and water sensor. All these sensors will be accommodated in the walking stick itself in its most compact

Implementation Block Diagram

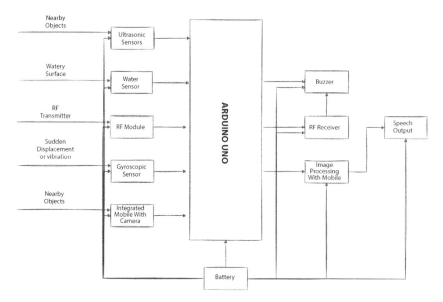

Figure 15.1 Implementation block diagram.

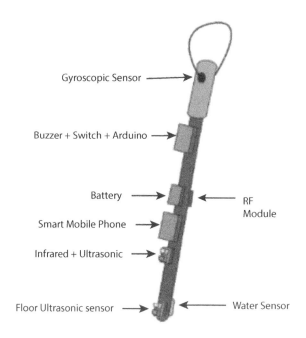

Figure 15.2 Model of the smart walking stick.

sense. The purpose, use and the working of each of these components will be explained clearly in the following section.

- Gyroscopic Sensor:
  These sensors are capable of detecting the angular velocity. Angular velocity can be understood as a change in rotation angle per second [17]. Let us assume a case where the user has slipped off the ground and has fallen down. In this case it would be really helpful if there is a kind of alarm that beeps out and alerts the nearby helpers. Gyroscopic sensor serves this purpose very well, when there is a fall, there will be an angular velocity, when this velocity is above any certain threshold value, the Arduino can send the signal to the software sub-system for further processing and also the buzzer alarm can produce sound in a different unique way as a gesture to alert nearby users.
- RF Module (Transmitter & Receiver):
  RF-Module has a transmitter and a receiver to send and receive signals. Assume a case where the user has misplaced the stick and also has forgotten the stick's location. In that situation, it would be really helpful if there is a device to know the location and position of the stick. There comes the RF-module whose receiver will be embedded into the stick and the transmitter is provided as a remote-control device to the user. The user can use the remote-control transmitter device to send a signal and the receiver in the stick will receive the signal and in turn, Arduino will detect this signal and produce sound through the buzzer to identify the stick's location.
- Passive Infrared Sensor:
  Passive Infrared Sensor (PIR) consists of two slots and when a human crosses these slots, it creates a positive and negative differential change between these two slots. This change is detected and a signal is produced. So, assume a case where the user is talking to a person nearby and at that time if the buzzer produces unwanted alert sounds continuously, it may irritate the users and his fellow beings. And other fellow humans are very well aware of the situation and thus alert is not necessary when there is any human in the path of the user. Thus, if any human is present as an obstacle, the PIR sensor detects [18] and produces a signal and the

Arduino can prevent the system from producing alerts by other ultrasonic sensors which may detect humans too as obstacles.

- Ultrasonic Sensor:
Ultrasonic sensor produces ultrasonic sound waves which get reflected back from the objects against them. Distance of the object can be detected with these reflected waves. When there is an obstacle within a specific range, the ultrasonic sensor produces a signal to the Arduino and activates the buzzer alarm and it also sends a signal to the mobile phone through the Bluetooth module to activate the software sub-system to detect and inform the user what the obstacle is. The ultrasonic sensors are placed in different directions to detect the direction in which the obstacle is present. There is also a floor ultrasonic sensor present at the bottom of the stick to detect any changes in the level of the ground.

- Water Sensor:
Water Sensor detects the water level. Therefore, if there is a slippery place, which contains water the water sensor, detects the water and informs the user about the water through Arduino and Bluetooth module, which sends signal to the mobile phone application, and the mobile application produces a speech alert about the water to the user.

- Arduino-UNO with Bluetooth module:
Arduino-UNO is the central unit for the system. It acts as a junction and helps in the interconnection of the hardware and software subsystem. It facilitates the communication of signals from various sensors to the mobile phone application through the Bluetooth module and also sends signals to the buzzer whenever needed [19]. It detects signals from various sensors and forwards the signal to the destination device to alert the user with an appropriate alert message.

- Buzzer:
A device that produces an alarming sound as a gesture to alert the user.

- Switch:
It helps in activating/deactivating the complete system.

- Battery Backup:
Provides the power necessary for various components in the system. Can be replaced with solar cells if needed.

- Safe & Quick-release Mobile Holder:
  Safe and easy-to-use mobile holding design to easily attach/detach the user's mobile phone into the stick.
- Mobile Phone:
  Mobile phones perform a crucial role in detecting and informing the user about what the object is. And it also provides various alerts received from various sensors to the user through earphones to keep the user alert of various conditions. The software sub-system (Mobile application) will be explained in great detail in the next section.

B. Architecture and Working of the Software Application

The purpose of the software is to identify and inform the user of the type of object that is located on the user's path. The system architecture of the software application is provided in Figure 15.3. We have used the following components to build the software:

1. Android—It is the operating system on top of which our application executes.
2. Phone Camera—It is used to capture an image of the user's path.
3. Phone Speaker—It is used to inform the user of the type of object
4. Google Cloud Vision API—Google Cloud Vision API is a machine learning service provided by Google Cloud Platform for image analysis. It allows developers to integrate image analysis into their applications, enabling them to identify objects, text, faces, explicit content and more in images [20]. The API provides pre-trained models that can be customized using user-defined data, and it can process images in real-time or batch mode. The API is accessible through REST and gRPC APIs and can be used to build a wide range of image-based applications, from automated image labeling to computer vision-based product search and more.
5. Android Text-to-Speech—Android text-to-speech (TTS) is a feature in Android that allows your device to "speak" text aloud. It can be used to read out loud the contents of a text or a prompt, or to convert text to speech for use in an app or other application. The Android TTS engine uses the TTS library built into the Android operating system to

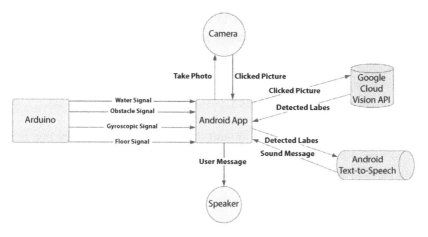

Figure 15.3 System architecture of the software application.

generate speech. This allows developers to easily integrate text-to-speech functionality into their apps, making it simple to add voice-based navigation, speech-to-text input, and other features.

The Arduino module sends four types of signals to the Android application via Bluetooth. After receiving the signal, the app first detects what type of signal was received. The first signal is the water signal. It informs the user that there is a puddle of water ahead of them. The next signal is the floor signal. It is used to inform the user about the change in floor height. The third is the gyroscopic signal. It sends a message along with the location to a pre-assigned contact saying that the user has fallen down. Finally, the fourth signal is the obstacle signal. It is used to trigger the object identification task. After the obstacle signal is received, the app triggers the phone camera to take a snap of the path ahead. After the picture is captured, it is sent back to the app by the camera application. Upon receiving the picture, it samples the image to a size of resolution 256x256. Then the app sends an API request to the Google Cloud Vision API, asking for label detection. After the image reaches the cloud, the obstacles in the image are detected, structured into a JSON format, and sent back to the user's phone as a reply. After receiving the response, the app sends the names as text to the Android Text-to-Speech application. That application converts the given text into an audio recording of a person reading the given text. Upon receiving the audio, the app plays it to the user via the phone speakers.

STEPS TO USE GOOGLE CLOUD VISION API

To use the Google Cloud Vision API, follow these steps:

1. Sign up for a Google Cloud account if you do not have one already.
2. Go to the Google Cloud Console and create a new project.
3. Enable the Cloud Vision API for the project.
4. Create a service account and download the private key file associated with the account.
5. Choose a programming language and install the necessary client library for making API calls (e.g. Google Cloud Client Library for Python).
6. In your code, use the private key file to authenticate and authorize your API requests.
7. Make API requests to the Cloud Vision API, passing in the image data and specifying the type of image analysis you want to perform (e.g. label detection).
8. Parse the JSON response from the API to extract the relevant information.

Implementation Details

The code first requests various permissions, including access to the device's camera and account information. Then it needs to ensure that the phone is connected with the Arduino bluetooth module. Then it then sets up a listener for a signal from the bluetooth module, and upon receiving the signal, it checks for the type of signal that was received. If the signal received is water signal, play an audio message of "Water Ahead." If the signal received is floor signal, play an audio message of "Uneven Floor Ahead." If the signal received is gyroscopic signal, send a message containing the user's location to all the pre-selected contacts. If the signal received is obstacle signal, then open the camera application and capture an image.

Once an image is taken or selected, the code converts it to a bitmap, converts the bitmap to a byte array, and then sends the image data to the Cloud Vision API to perform image labeling. The API returns a list of labels with their associated confidence scores, which the code then displays on the screen as text. Additionally, the code uses the Text-to-Speech API to speak out the labels.

15.4 Conclusion

The proposed system of a smart walking stick for visually impaired individuals has the potential to revolutionize the way they navigate and interact with their surroundings. The system is designed to be highly accurate, enabling visually impaired individuals to navigate from one location to another without the need for assistance from others, such as family members, friends, or guide dogs. This technology can be seen as a form of rudimentary artificial eyesight, helping visually impaired individuals regain some level of independence. The smart walking stick integrates multiple functional elements to create a real-time system that tracks the user's location and provides dual feedback. This enhances navigational security, and the stick alerts users to any obstacles or hazards in front of them via voice messages, rather than simply vibrating. The combination of these functional elements provides a comprehensive solution for navigation and safety, enabling visually impaired individuals to navigate their surroundings with greater confidence and ease. The proposed system has the potential to be further advanced with the incorporation of automation. This can be achieved by studying the user's daily activities and automatically performing actions based on that data. The development of wearable and handheld devices has made it easier for people with visual impairments to navigate their surroundings, and with advancements in technology, we can expect more projects and ideas to emerge in the future, helping visually impaired individuals even further. In conclusion, the proposed system of a smart walking stick for visually impaired individuals has the potential to make a significant impact on their lives by providing a comprehensive solution for navigation and safety. With the incorporation of automation and advancements in technology, we can expect this system to continually improve and help visually impaired individuals live more independently and confidently.

References

1. Shafique, K., Khawaja, B.A., Sabir, F., Qazi, S., Mustaqim, M., Internet of things (IoT) for next-generation smart systems: A review of current challenges, future trends and prospects for emerging 5G-IoT scenarios. *IEEE Access*, 8, 23022–23040, 2020.
2. Dada, E., Shani, A., Adekunle, A., Smart walking stick for visually impaired people using ultrasonic sensors and arduino. *Int. J. Eng. Technol.*, 9, 3435–3447, 2017.
3. Singh, S. and Singh, B., Intelligent walking stick for elderly and visually challenged people. *Int. J. Eng. Res. Technol. (IJERT)*, 09, 03, 19–22, March 2020.
4. Mind, P., Palkar, G., Mahamuni, A., Sahare, S., Smart stick for visually impaired. *Int. J. Eng. Res. Technol. (IJERT)*, 10, 06, 196–198, June 2021.

5. Park, J., Je, Y., Lee, H., Moon, W., Design of an ultrasonic sensor for measuring distance and detecting obstacles. *Ultrasonics*, 50, 3, 340–346, 2010, https://doi.org/10.1016/j.ultras.2009.10.013.

6. García, R., Fonseca, R., Durán, A., Electronic long cane for locomotion improving on visual impaired people. A case study. *2011 Pan American Healthcare Exchanges*, 2011, pp. 58–61, 2011.

7. Cardillo, E., Li, C., Caddemi, A., Millimeter-wave radar cane: A visually challenged people aid with moving human recognition capabilities. *IEEE J. Electromagn. RF Microw. Med. Biol.*, 6, 2, 204–211, June 2022.

8. Meshram, V.V., Patil, K., Meshram, V.A., Shu, F.C., An astute assistive device for mobility and object recognition for visually impaired people. *IEEE Trans. Hum. Mach. Syst.*, 49, 5, 449–460, Oct. 2019.

9. Faria, J., Lopes, S., Fernandes, H., Martins, P., Barroso, J., Electronic white cane for visually challenged people navigation assistance. *2010 World Automation Congress*, 2010, pp. 1–7, 2010.

10. Saaid, M.F., Mohammad, A.M., Megat Ali, M.S.A., Smart cane with range notification for visually challenged people. *2016 IEEE International Conference on Automatic Control and Intelligent Systems (I2CACIS)*, 2016, pp. 225–229, 2016.

11. Zhou, S., A smart cane to help the visually challenged people walk confidently. *2018 IOP Conf. Ser.: Mater. Sci. Eng*, vol. 439, p. 032121, 2018.

12. Jivrajani, K., *et al.*, A IoT-based smart stick for visually impaired person. *IEEE Trans. Instrum. Meas.*, 72, 1–11, Art no. 2501311, 2023.

13. Ghatwary, N., Abouzeina, A., Kantoush, A., Eltawil, B., Ramadan, M., Yasser, M., Intelligent assistance system for visually impaired/blind people (ISVB). *2022 5th International Conference on Communications, Signal Processing, and their Applications (ICCSPA)*, Cairo, Egypt, 2022, pp. 1–7, 2022.

14. Mude, R., Salunke, A., Patil, C., Kulkarni, A., IOT enabled smart blind stick and spectacles mountable eye-piece equipped with camera for visually challenged people. *2022 International Conference on Industry 4.0 Technology (I4Tech)*, Pune, India, 2022, pp. 1–5, 2022.

15. Sáez, J.M., Escolano, F., Lozano, M.A., Aerial obstacle detection with 3-D mobile devices. *IEEE J. Biomed. Health Inform.*, 19, 1, 74–80, Jan. 2015.

16. Chang, W.J., Chen, L.B., Chen, M.C., Su, J.P., Sie, C.Y., Yang, C.H., Design and implementation of an intelligent assistive system for visually impaired people for aerial obstacle avoidance and fall detection. *IEEE Sens. J.*, 20, 17, 10199–10210, 1 Sept.1, 2020.

17. Reyes Leiva, K.M., Jaén-Vargas, M., Codina, B., Serrano Olmedo, J.J., Inertial measurement unit sensors in assistive technologies for visually impaired people, a review. *Sensors*, 21, 14, 4767, 2021.

18. Shetty, A.D., Disha, B., S., K., S., Detection and tracking of a human using the infrared thermopile array sensor—"Grid-Eye". *2017 International Conference on Intelligent Computing, Instrumentation and Control Technologies (ICICICT)*, 2017, https://org/10.1109/icicict1.2017.8342790.

19. Malav, V., Bhagat, R.K., Saini, R., Mamodiya, U., Research paper on bluetooth based home automation using arduino. Poornima Institute of Engineering and Technology, Jaipur, India, 2018.

20. Mulfari, D., Celesti, A., Fazio, M., Villari, M., Puliafito, A., Using google cloud vision in assistive technology scenarios, in: *2016 IEEE Symposium on Computers and Communication (ISCC)*, pp. 214–219, IEEE, 2016, June.

Part 4
ISSUES AND CHALLENGES

16

Enhanced Security Measures in Genomic Data Management

Ambika N.

St. Francis College, Department of Computer Science & Applications, Bangalore, India

Abstract

Personal information like genetic information is protected by privacy laws. It is likely to use a well person's well-being position as indication for illness analysis and prediction of patient prognosis. Therefore, safety is essential. The previous work is A blockchain scheme with a decentralized request (DApp) and two distinct storage options—private and semi-private storage. The private storage contains encrypted gene data, while the semi-private repository contains noise-laden gene data. In addition, the DApp enables the owner of gene data to track usage and transmission information. Gene information with sound are kept in semi-isolated warehouse. They are not recovered from the previous facts by customer excluding moderately unreliable clients like insurance workers and researchers employed by external organizations. Lists of customers authorized to move encoded information and genetic factor facts with sound are also kept for access control purposes. The system verifies the blockchain system's availability whenever it receives a request to download gene data. The proposed system uses a better methodology to enhance security of stored data. increases security by 11.35% compared to previous contribution.

Keywords: Genetic data, DNA sequence, privacy, security, authorization, encryption, third-party access

Email: Ambika.nagaraj76@gmail.com; ORCID: 0000-0003-4452-5514

Amit Kumar Tyagi (ed.) Privacy Preservation of Genomic and Medical Data, (385–408) © 2024 Scrivener Publishing LLC

16.1 Introduction

Genomic succession [1] is the finished DNA construction of a living being. There are four nucleotides in the DNA sequence. Over the past few decades, studies in health science and related fields have been impacted by a significant advancement in genomic data. Since genomics uses data storage, health-related research on various medical datasets has become more realistic. Researchers interested in the relationship between genetic codes and health science have access to extensive and open genomic datasets. The expanding genomic dataset could support the creation of targeted therapies for specific diseases and enhance personalized medicine. As demonstrated by the effective use of DNA sequence in forensics, personal genomic data [2] can be effectively identified as an individual's identity because even a tiny subset of the DNA sequence [3] is sufficient to identify an individual or a relative. As a result, the genomic sequences pose a significant security threat. As a result, the cloud [4, 5] is used to store data. Because they guarantee a data owner's data security even in an untrusted environment, cryptographic techniques can address several genome data security issues.

It is a decentralized blockchain scheme and two distinct storage options—private and semi-private storage—are utilized in the previous method [7]. The genetic factor information is stowed in both stockpiles. It guarantees privacy and security. The facts are coded, or sound is summed to cover up segments including owner information. The private storage contains encoded gene knowledge, while the semi-private repository contains noise-laden gene data. In addition, the DApp enables the owner of gene data to track usage and transmission information. The original genetic factor details can be accessed and utilized by decrypting the encrypted sections in private storage, which is only accessible to internal staff members and highly trustworthy members. Hereditary information with sound are kept in semi-confidential warehouse. They will not be recovered from the original hereditary data by any other customers excluding comparatively unreliable clients like insurance workers and researchers employed by external organizations. It attaches the sound information to the sensitive discretion segment of the hereditary data using LDP. This model with two storage systems makes it less likely that private information might contain hereditary data. The file magnitude, formation/alteration period, hash price, secured sections of the knowledge, and other details on the hereditary data are all stored in each block. Lists of clients authorized to transfer encoded information and hereditary details with sound are also kept for access control purposes. The system verifies the blockchain system's availability whenever it receives a request to download hereditary data. The suggested scheme

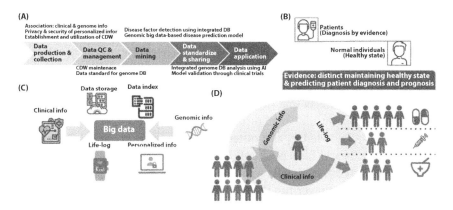

Figure 16.1 Summary of the genomic-data-based well-being administration [6].

sends the necessary data if the blockchain's smart contract returns "accept." External members does not access the sensitive portions of the hereditary data. It makes use of a private network and Ethereum. Figure 16.1 summarizes the genomic-data-based well-being administration.

The proposed work uses Merkle tree and Client ID to generate the hash key. For every session, a hash key is used to authenticate the system. The system authorizes the third-party only to view the documents. It increases security by 11.35% compared to previous contribution. The work is divided into seven divisions. Section two briefs various work. Segment three details the background of the study. Fourth section explains proposed work. The work is analysed in segment five. Sixth division briefs the future work. The suggestion is resolved in seventh unit.

16.2   Literature Survey

It [7] is a decentralized blockchain scheme [8, 9] with a decentralized application (DApp) and two distinct storage options—private and semi-private storage. The genetic factor information are stowed in both stockpiles. It guarantees privacy and security. The facts are coded, or sound is added to cover up sections that include owner information. The private storage contains encoded gene knowledge, while the semi-private repository contains noise-laden gene data. In addition, the DApp enables the owner of gene data to track usage and transmission information. The original genetic factor details can be accessed and utilized by decrypting the encrypted sections in private storage, which is only accessible to internal staff members and highly trustworthy members. Hereditary information with sound is kept in semi-confidential warehouse. They will not be recovered from the original hereditary data by any other customers excluding comparatively unreliable clients like insurance workers and researchers employed by external organizations. It attaches the sound information to the sensitive discretion segment of the hereditary data using LDP. This model with two storage systems makes it less likely that private information might contain hereditary data. The file magnitude, formation/alteration period, hash price, secured sections of the knowledge, and other details on the hereditary data are all stored in each block. Lists of clients authorized to transfer encoded information and hereditary details with sound are also kept for access control purposes. The system verifies the blockchain system's availability whenever it receives a request to download hereditary data. The suggested scheme sends the necessary data if the blockchain's smart contract returns "accept." External members will not be able to access the sensitive portions of the hereditary data. It makes use of a private network and Ethereum.

Policies and mechanisms that guarantee that threats and attacks are addressed at every stage of the big data [10] life cycle are included in the work [11]. Various data formats are collected from multiple sources during the information gathering stage. In the fact's transformation phase, the details are filtered and categorized according to their assembly, and any essential conversions are carried out for meaningful analysis. The information displaying stage is changed and put away ingot capacity arrangements, and the information handling examination is performed to create meaningful information. For feature selection and predictive modeling, supervised data mining methods like clustering and classification can use association in this phase. During the modeling phase, new information and valuable pieces of knowledge can be used by decision-makers. These made pieces of information are viewed as delicate information, particularly in a severe climate. Indeed, healthcare organizations are aware that sensitive data should not be made public.

Patient-centric personal data and an enhanced encryption scheme for access control have been considered in this framework [12]. To protect their identity, the user logs in with a client-name, key, and exclusive biometric data. Also, Solicitation for Administration is created by the confirmation office to get demand from the information base and outside outsiders. Thirdly, the well-being petitioner who requests admission to stowed private healthiness evidence is referred to as an information Entree Supplicant following the administrator's request for the service. Fourthly, a single point of contact verifies whether the client can admittance the facility following a request to access PHI. Administrators can easily access patients referred by a doctor or from a different hospital if the user is granted access to the service. Then, at that point, Individual Wellbeing Data is moved to Wellbeing Administration by utilizing another proposed system Mama ABE (Multi Authority Characteristic based encryption). The encryption method known as CP-ABE (cipher policy Attribute-based encryption) that was utilized to protected the e-health framework was average. A blended technique consolidates a subjective with a quantitative methodology. The suggestion was conducted using an online review that considered different statistics about respondents' satisfaction with security, privacy, and user experience. Twenty-five from the IT support group and 26 doctors responded.

A set of values for scheming a portable request that links pliability and confidentiality defence are presented in the system [13]. It is an organisation assessment of safety, privacy, and flexibility and their relationships. The app's purpose is to assist patients in scheduling appointments with their doctors based on their indications and local infirmary properties. The objective is to schedule an appointment at the patient-chosen hospital with the shortest possible patient wait time. A patient should first enter their healthcare information when registering for the app. After that, the data is sent over the radio linking and verified by a distant host that belongs to a healthcare database management authority. The patient must provide a brief symptom description once the intake data maps an entrance in the wellness warehouse. The application allows the patient to look over a few competitor emergency clinics. The application will access the wellness stockpile once more for verification and record the employment after receiving the decision. OS initiates a navigation option concurrently via the Google Maps steering provision. The application was created on a laptop running Windows 10 OS. Eclipse is the chief progress stage, integrating with the Java Development Kit (JDK) and Android Software Development Kit (SDK). The app is anticipated to function in a 2 G/4 G or WiFi wireless environment.

It is the Mobile Healthcare Network (MHN) [14]. Users, servers, wearable devices, and heterogeneous mobile networks make up MHNs. As the link between the mortal figure and the data biosphere, physiology detectors and low-energy calibration, message, and stowage components are integrated into wearable devices. These devices can detect a person's physiological limitations, wellbeing circumstances, signals, and place. Smartphones are used by patients, doctors, and their relatives to obtain perception info from wear instruments. They can transmit these fitness facts to hosts for added analysis and processing. The health data gathered from wearable devices or mobile users is stored, processed, and analyzed on the servers. Assorted portable systems, which include the cellular network, WiFi, and

D2D transmission, provide provision for MHNs for the transmission, sharing, and collection of health data from mobile users or wearable devices. During the transmission and sharing of health data, MHNs can seamlessly switch between numerous portable systems. Mobile users can access the Internet via WiFi or cellular networks, interact with others via Bluetooth or NFC, and browse local information via local servers with heterogeneous mobile networks.

A brand-new Modified Merkle Tree information framework with truthfulness organization capabilities is suggested [15]. The proposed system's architecture is made up of four functional parts: transactions, a three-phase amended Merkle tree, block components, and a sequence of blocks. The proposed system's available components each carry out four crucial tasks. The primary step in the data storage method is to use hashed transactions to create a Tree data structure. Input transactions underpin tree generation. A single marketing or many transactions can be in a block. It can use data in one or more transactions. The proposed system uses a brand-new Merkle Tree to validate the authenticity and integrity of stored data. The presented information authorization scheme checks to see if the transaction data has been altered or tampered with to ensure the integrity of stored data. By mining each block's hash and using the previous block's hash as on-chain growth, it validates the consistency of the blocks. There is an extreme number of dealings with either single or multiple input info in each block. It extracts original text from any of the P2P blockchain system nodes.

It is a home healthcare system [16] that is cloud-based and designed to give depressed patients more control over their treatment. Medication treatment organisation, nap, sunlit organisation, and bodily movement administration are the three main components of the services provided. Drug therapy management is intended to increase patient compliance with physician recommendations. The following stakeholders in the home healthcare scenario have healthcare professionals, druggists, fitness and well-being provision earners, patients and their families, and public authorities. Personal observing gadgets are utilized to screen and gather patients' active work information or rest data. In addition, the stockpile management provider provides structure as a service and podium as a provision for hosting applications for home healthcare. In some instances, delivery service providers also deliver medications to the patient's residence. The architecture of the TClouds home healthcare application is used. There are three types of processes: front-end, middle-tier, and back-end. A front end is an interface between an external entity and the middle tier. Commercial sense procedure that provides numerous facilities are middle-tiers.

The procedures that control information warehouse are known as backends. The home healthcare architecture of TClouds includes four kinds of back-end data stores. Subscriber monitoring data, such as information regarding physical activities and sleep monitoring, as well as private training advice given by well-being and fitness service providers, are the information that are stewed in the physical activity repository. The private wellness data of sick, which include information regarding treatments, physical activities, and sleep, an overview of personal medical and medication information, personal information, and a personal privacy policy, are the data kept in the PHR warehouse. The electronic health records of patients used for clinical purposes are the data held in the EHR repository. The information in the Treatment stockpile provides an summary of past drug purchases and prescriptions.

The electronic health system [17] is a new area with electronic processes and communications. A collecting of sick wellness info is an EHR or EMR. Facts, figures, sick therapeutic data, medications, infirmary or consulting room statistics, radiology images, billing data, and other delicate sick knowledge are all included in an electrical wellness information or electronic medical record (EMR). Stockpile calculation provides the price of efficiently stowage, dispensation, and apprising information with quality and efficacy. The advantage of cloud computing is accessing hosted services from multiple locations with various clients. E-health schemes promise quicker, more vigorous, and sought-after admittance to health facts, fewer therapeutic guidelines, and enhanced healthcare quality. However, they also echo sick confidential desecrations, inappropriate agreement, and the misappropriation of EHR information. Warehouse safety and confidential are essential necessities when distribution or retrieving enduring details. Figure 16.2 represents E-health framework in Stockpile.

Various transmission procedures are used to transmit the data of IoHT devices [18]. A cloud service, also known as a isolated host intended for rigorous calibration responsibilities, is where these medical data will end up. An IoHT employment has single detector instrument connected to a mobile device via Bluetooth, such as a heartbeat monitor. Information can be communicated to a doctor or Backup Reply Squad using portable transmission. After analyzing the data, it should install a specific application on the mobile device to generate alarms. Numerous detectors, midway gadgets, and central hosts connected to a centralized organization could complicate it. The therapeutic squad responds to emergencies by monitoring the patient's health. Using short-range procedures, midway gadgets like mobiles and PDAs talks with detectors, actuators, and healthcare servers via the Internet. In an emergency, hosts take the suitable action by

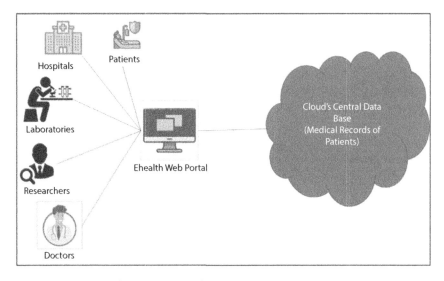

Figure 16.2 E-health framework in stockpile [17].

apprising the warehouse or communicating the proper doctors or immediate reply squad. IoT [19] application development makes use of this
straight forward figured architecture. There are limitations on each connected device, such as partial possession, memory, and battery warehouse,
and the applications are designed to use the limited resources at hand better. Sensors, such as electronic motors, drug pumps, and so on, produce
data that can be used to guide actuators, devices that can carry out specific actions. Implantable wellness instruments are inserted into the body.
The communication protocols and wireless standards that enable wireless
device communication make up the protocol layer. The devices in this layer
are responsible for sending information to powerful calibration warehouse
like stockpile owners. Information movement from the sensing elements
to warehouse for stowage, and additional examination is made possible by
these devices, which function as gateways. These devices support manifold
message procedures. The central component of the healthcare system is the
management and database servers. These servers receive and update the
sick information gathered by detectors. They can also assist physicians in
managing the patient's medication supply or prescribing a new one. In any
emergency, the surgeons and immediate reply squads give response and
contribute significantly to the healthcare system. Doctors and emergency
response teams at this layer reply to the scheme when it issues an alert.
Figure 16.3 represents the same.

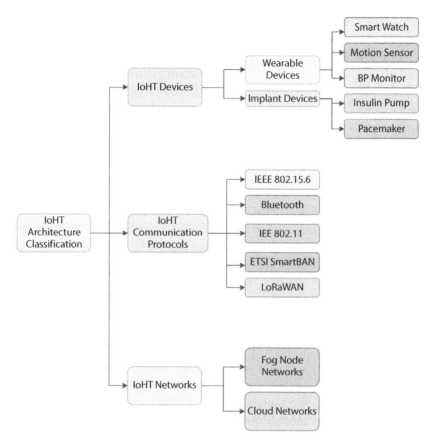

Figure 16.3 IoHT architecture classification [18].

The system [20] has five components: Overlay organization, Distributed storage, medical services suppliers, brilliant contracts, and sick outfitted with medical services wearable IoT gadgets [21]. Cloud storage organizes the client's information in matching blocks with a exclusive block number. The stockpile server transmits the hash of the info blocks to the overlay system when the details is stored in a block, and these warehouses are connected to overlay structure. Merkle Tree is used to calculate the single block's data hash. A distributed-architecture peer-to-peer network is known as an overlay. The hubs related with the group could be a PC, cell phone, tablet, or other IoT devices [22]. Each node in a network needs to show that they are certified by using a valid certificate. Patients or insurance companies appoint healthcare providers to perform medical procedures or tests. When they get an alert from the network, healthcare service providers take care of the treatment of patients. In addition, they are treated as a node in the network and have permission to download specific patient data from the cloud. Any Internet of Things device can use intelligent contracts to create agreements that are carried out when certain conditions are met. The IoT device [23, 24] will gather the Patient's entire health information. Sicks are the proprietors of their data and are in charge of yielding, rejecting, or cancelling information grant to any third gatherings, like wellness workers or insurance organizations. Figure 16.4 represents the same.

A patient query submodule [25] includes a smart contract, a database, and a private blockchain submodule. The patient sub-module helps users access patient privacy and copyright records and plays a crucial part in this procedure. It has functions for linking and querying different systems. A confidential blockchain for medics and fitness architecture with sick confidentiality is included in the blockchain subsystem. Employing a blockchain application programming interface (API), the user logs into the organisation and requests the respective patient health record. The smart contract triggers the privacy check. This savvy agreement will check for security and access control freedoms. Access to a particular PHR is granted to the applicant requesting if they are given authorized user rights; If not, access is restricted. The PHR is given to the user after the contract confirms that they have the appropriate privacy and access control rights. Each participant's authorization level is assessed following the access control policy. It is contingent on the access control rights of the users; A client can recite, inscribe, erase, add, and update. The intelligent contract tracks a patient's behavior, which also records the session and interactions. Figure 16.5 represents the same.

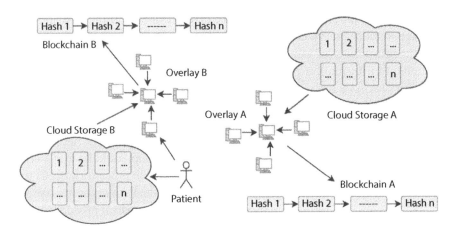

Figure 16.4 Overlay network [20].

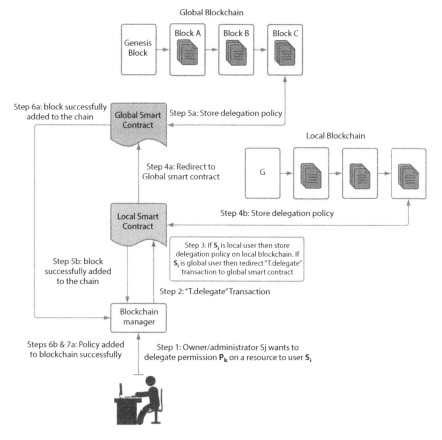

Figure 16.5 System architecture [25].

The electronic shareable health records' trust- and privacy-related specifications will be enhanced by the proposed BDL-IBS [26]. The system concentrated on minimizing adversary impact and maximizing the rate of sharing secured documents. The parts of the bio-clinical framework incorporate capacity and a clinical server. The digital wellness data of the end clients are stored in the storage. The therapeutic host is accountable for responding to user requests with the appropriate documents and processing them. A cloud-based common sharing platform and associated infrastructures share EHRs. The remedial host and end-consumer requests use the distributed ledger and blockchain. The belief and confidentiality aspects of the medical server blockchain are examined, whereas the end-user blockchain only evaluates the privacy aspects. Successful access and response to requests are among the trust factors, while convergence and complexity are necessary for privacy. Figure 16.6 represents the same.

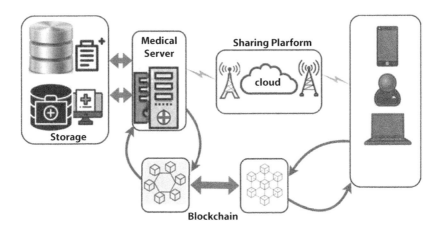

Figure 16.6 Biomedical security system with blockchain [26].

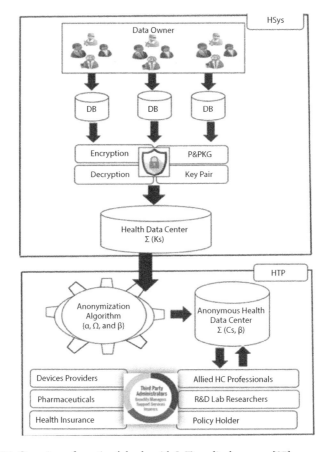

Figure 16.7 Overview of a patient's body with IoT medical sensors [27].

The two main components of the system model [27] are the HealthThird Party (HTP) and the Healthcare System (HYsy). The HSys incorporates the information proprietor, like patients and doctors, with their datasets (DB). The framework has a security motor to scramble the information with the characterized boundary. The parameters necessary to carry out the data anonymization process are stored on the HTP host. After all of the algorithm's steps have been carried out, it can access the anonymous data. The anonymized data can be returned to the system by the HTP. The client chooses the place and time to share it. When the client transmits data during the first session operation, the HSys key encrypts it. When the data are sent from the system to the HTP, cooperating infirmary, they are anonymized. Figure 16.7 represents the same.

A peer-to-peer network system is a foundation for the recommendation [28] using bitcoin's decentralized currency. Because of this, whenever a transaction takes place, the entire network is aware of it, and each miner who receives the business can confirm it using the signs included in the deal. Additionally, these miners have this actual business in their block.

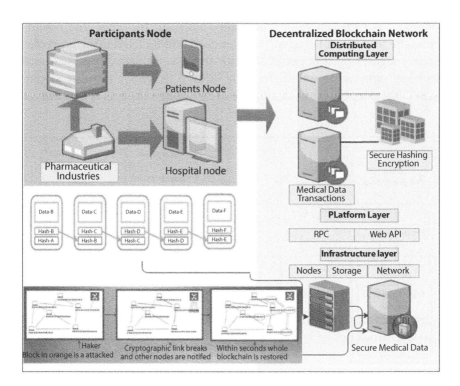

Figure 16.8 Framework of suggested system [28].

It demonstrates that multiple miners on the blockchain verify a single transaction's resolution. Figure 16.8 represents the same.

The data that the information gatherer [29] component collects data from a wide range of shrewd devices. Every device here provides details regarding an alternate part of the patient's vitals. These bits of information are combined into a single array in the data preparation module to show a patient's current state. The variety created by the data pre-processing module is sent to the anomaly detection module, which uses it to determine whether or not the SHS is being used maliciously. The action management module is used to notify the appropriate personnel of the SHS's harmful behavior. Figure 16.9 represents the same.

The recommendation [30] is a hybrid Context-Aware Reference management for E-Healthcare (HCARS-EHC). The sick can make entrance for succumbing the exploration demand. The medic will cause the encoded keyword for acquiescing the credentials. When the keywords used by the patient and the doctor are the same, the cloud-alike stage will begin. The evolutionary algorithm can be used with extremely enhanced resolves to compute all of these procedures. It can choose the generator at any given time. The elements are made by using the generator. It creates new group members, and the generator is computed alongside the other group members. The features of the group are designed and updated using an evolutionary algorithm. It is permissible for the new elements to persist until healthier options are found. They are utilized to resolve intricate system issues. The purpose of producing the cyclic group elements is to optimize

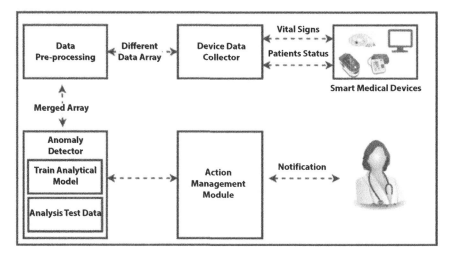

Figure 16.9 Smart healthcare system framework [29].

a solution to the ongoing difficulty in communicating with the patient and the doctor.

The proposal [31] is a blockchain that helped secure a framework for clinical IoT gadgets utilizing Lamport Merkle Computerized Mark (LMDS). The organization model incorporates a stockpile-IoT organization, IoT gadgets, clever agreements, distributed stowage, and CHC. The Cloud-IoT network is a shared organization that relies upon a disseminated climate. It incorporates IoT frameworks, distributed storage, CHC, and clinics. Every sick clinical information in IoT gadgets is stored in distributed storage. Then again, the CHC, with a few medical clinics, is attached to regulator the distributed packing. A clinical IoT framework incorporates a remote embedded sensor. In the instance of clothing detector or the affected role working with vesture medical services, IoT gadgets are put on the outer layer of the mortal, where they are gotten underway and makes fundamental signals fixed inside the person's tissue while execution various exercises. The IoT gadgets conveyed on the chest are battery-fueled. It gives two lead ECG estimations for ceaseless heart observing and checking for a different heartbeat on the ECG. Shrewd agreements empower executing gatherings to set conditions employing a cloud server so that the activity is performed consequently, which decreases the third party's effort. A brilliant deal likewise has its different location and account on the blockchain, and thus, each IoT gadget sees, furthermore, executes its directions, subsequently diminishing the correspondence above. The data sent by the IoT gadgets are put away in distributed storage. The data is stowed in the stockpile after getting a wariness message from the shrewd agreement. The gadgets, alongside the information, add a computerized sign before transfer clinical data over the cloud.

16.3   Background

A Merkle tree is made from a sequence of information blocks. The hash content of its children determines an interior device worth, and a leaf node's value is determined by the straight hash text of the info block to which it corresponds. The preimage-resistance belongings of the hash purpose means that it is computationally impossible to find the preimage of the given hash value during the tree construction process. Additionally, because this is a binary tree, the maximum depth from leaf to root for n data blocks is only "$\log 2n$." As a result, the Merkle tree serves as genuine data structure for adequate online content confirmation. Figure 16.10 represents the same.

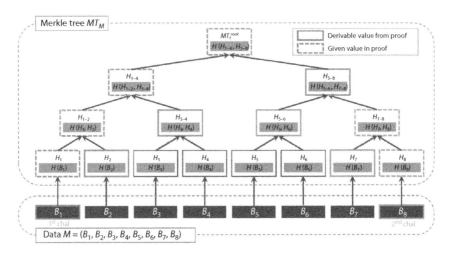

Figure 16.10 Merkle tree authentication for data [32].

The Merkle tree-based authentication method's side-channel attack vulnerabilities are the subject of this study [32]. To construct a Merkle tree, the magnitude of the information blocks and the guidelines for recognising precise information must be agreed upon by the prover and verifier. The prover first sends the verifier a data identifier to demonstrate complete possession of the data during the authentication process. An eavesdropper can estimate the underlying data size from a single verification resilient by watching how the prover and verifier communicate.

The work [33] advances the mesh system's safety against cyberattacks, and the system introduces a key distribution strategy that changes over time. The scheme has been used with concurrent verification of equals and effectual mesh safety connotation, two security protocols. All essential materials will be regularly updated as part of this strategy. To obtain a novel set of credentials before the termination of the existing vital materials, this is accomplished by initiating EAP or SAE authentication and 4-way handshaking.

16.4   Proposed Model

It [7] is a decentralized blockchain scheme [34] with a decentralized application (DApp) and two distinct storage options—private and semi-private storage. The genetic factor information is stowed in both stockpiles. It guarantees privacy and security. The facts are coded, or sound is added to cover up sections that include owner information. The private storage contains encoded gene knowledge, while the semi-private repository contains noise-laden gene data. In addition, the DApp enables the owner of gene data to track usage and transmission information. The original genetic factor details can be accessed and utilized by decrypting the encrypted sections in private storage, which is only accessible to internal staff members and highly trustworthy members. Hereditary information with sound is kept in semi-confidential warehouse. They will not be recovered from the original hereditary data by any other customers excluding comparatively unreliable clients like insurance workers and researchers employed by external organizations. It attaches the sound information to the sensitive discretion segment of the hereditary data using LDP. This model with two storage systems makes it less likely that private information might contain hereditary data. The file magnitude, formation/alteration period, hash price, secured sections of the knowledge, and other details on the hereditary data are all stored in each block. Lists of clients authorized to transfer encoded information and hereditary details with sound are also kept for access control purposes. The system verifies the blockchain system's availability whenever it receives a request to download hereditary data. The suggested scheme sends the necessary data if the blockchain's smart contract returns "accept." External members will not be able to access the sensitive portions of the hereditary data. It makes use of a private network and Ethereum. Figure 16.11 represents the same. Table 16.1 portrays symbolizations employed in the work.

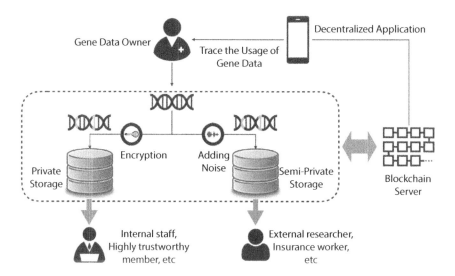

Figure 16.11 System model [7].

Table 16.1 Symbolisations employed in the work.

Representations utilized in the work	Explanation
C_i	Client
S	System
TP_i	Third party
ID_i	Client id
H_i	Generated hash key

Drawback

The gene data is shared with the third party like researchers and insurance workers. The client list authorized to transfer encoded and hereditary information with sound are also kept for access control purposes.

To overcome this problem, the third parties are given rights only to view the data. To keep it more secure, for every login different hash key is issued to the respective parties. It uses Merkle tree to derive the hash key. This hash key is used by the third parties to authenticate themselves and gain access to the system.

Let TP_i be the third party. The client C_i provides identification ID_i to the third party (insurance company). The same is represented in equation (16.1).

$$C_i \Rightarrow ID_i : TP_i \qquad (16.1)$$

The third party TP_i communicates the same to the system S, as shown in the equation (16.2).

$$TP_i \Rightarrow ID_i : S \qquad (16.2)$$

The system generates the hash key using the client ID stored in the system. For every session the hash key is different. This is communicated hash key H_i to the third party TP_i. Equation (16.3) represents the same.

$$S \Rightarrow H_i : TP_i \qquad (16.3)$$

This hash key is used as authentication key to view the data. Table 16.2 provides the procedure to make hash key.

Table 16.2 Procedure to make hash key.

Input – Client-ID (64 bits)
Phase 1—divide the input into two halves
Phase 2—XOR the bits from one with another forming Resultant bits (32 bits)
Phase 3—divide the bits into 3 parts (1 part—first 5 bits ; 2 part—22 bits ; 3 part—last 5 bits)
Phase 4—Xor 1 part with 3 part (resultant—5 bits + 22 bits)
Phase 5—divide the resultant bits into two halves
Phase 6—Insert the 1 parts in even position of the resultant and 2 part in odd position of the resultant
Phase 7—divide the resultant into two halves
Phase 8—apply right circular shift on the 1 part and left circular shift on 2 part (27 bits)

16.5   Analysis of the Work

It [7] is a decentralized blockchain scheme [34] with a decentralized application (DApp) and two distinct storage options—private and semi-private storage. The genetic factor information is stowed in both stockpiles. It guarantees privacy and security. The facts are coded, or sound is added to cover up sections that include owner information. The private storage contains encoded gene knowledge, while the semi-private repository contains noise-laden gene data. In addition, the DApp enables the owner of gene data to track usage and transmission information. The original genetic factor details can be accessed and utilized by decrypting the encrypted sections in private storage, which is only accessible to internal staff members and highly trustworthy members. Hereditary information with sound is kept in semi-confidential warehouse. They will not be recovered from the original hereditary data by any other customers excluding comparatively unreliable clients like insurance workers and researchers employed by external organizations. It attaches the sound information to the sensitive discretion segment of the hereditary data using LDP. This model with two storage systems makes it less likely that private information might contain hereditary data. The file magnitude, formation/alteration period, hash price, secured sections of the knowledge, and other details on the hereditary data are all stored in each block. Lists of clients authorized to transfer encoded information and hereditary details with sound are also kept for access control purposes. The system verifies the blockchain system's availability whenever it receives a request to download hereditary data. The suggested scheme sends the necessary data if the blockchain's smart contract returns "accept." External members will not be able to access the sensitive portions of the hereditary data. It makes use of a private network and Ethereum. Figure 16.11 represents the same.

Table 16.3 Parameters used in the work.

Parameters used in work	Description
Dimension of the network	200 m * 200m
Number of clients considered	3
Number of insurance companies	2
Length of the hash key	27 bits
Length of client-ID	64 bits
Maximum level of Merkle tree	16
Simulation time	60m

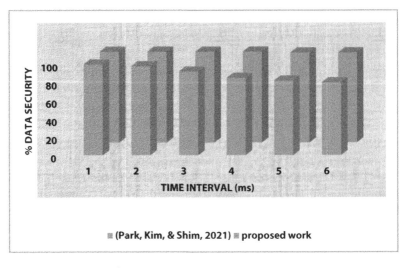

Figure 16.12 Security analysis.

To keep it more secure, for every login different hash key is issued to the respective parties. It uses Merkle tree to derive the hash key. This hash key is used by the third parties to authenticate themselves and gain access to the system.

The work is simulated using NS2. Table 16.3 lists the parameters used in the work

- **Security**
  - As the hash key is used to authenticate the system and as every time the hash key changes, security increases.
  - The system allows only to view the details of the patient.

The present work increases security by 11.35% compared to previous contribution [7]. Same is represented in Figure 16.12.

16.6   Future Work

The work uses Merkle tree and Client ID to generate the hash key. For every session, a hash key is used to authenticate the system. The system authorizes the third-party only to view the documents. The limitations of the system are:

- Client-id is used to generate Merkle tree. It limits to 16 reads.

16.7   Conclusion

There have been many shifts in the healthcare industry. To screen sick's medical data and give continuous facilities in real-time, wellness 4.0 stores the patient's records in a centralized EHR system. WDs and MDs that can be implanted can be used to monitor a patient's health. Patients' blood pressure, heart rate, temperature, and glucose level are all remotely measured by WDs utilizing a variety of healthcare sensors and stored in the tele health-care-branded centralized EHR. It provides the patient with better or more effective remote care. It is helpful to comprehend the patient's behavior.

The previous work is a decentralized blockchain scheme [34] with a decentralized application (DApp) and two distinct storage options—private and semi-private storage. The genetic factor information is stowed in both stockpiles. It guarantees privacy and security. The facts are coded, or sound is added to cover up sections that include owner information. The private storage contains encoded gene knowledge, while the semi-private repository contains noise-laden gene data. In addition, the DApp enables the owner of gene data to track usage and transmission information. The original genetic factor details can be accessed and utilized by decrypting the encrypted sections in private storage, which is only accessible to internal staff members and highly trustworthy members. Hereditary information with sound is kept in semi-confidential warehouse. They will not be recovered from the original hereditary data by any other customers excluding comparatively unreliable clients like insurance workers and researchers employed by external organizations. It attaches the sound information to the sensitive discretion segment of the hereditary data using LDP. This model with two storage systems makes it less likely that private information might contain hereditary data. The file magnitude, formation/alteration period, hash price, secured sections of the knowledge, and other details on the hereditary data are all stored in each block. Lists of clients authorized to transfer encoded information and hereditary details with sound are also kept for access control purposes. The system verifies the blockchain system's availability whenever it receives a request to download hereditary data. The suggested scheme sends the necessary data if the blockchain's smart contract returns "accept." External members will not be able to access the sensitive portions of the hereditary data. It makes use of a private network and Ethereum. Figure 16.11 represents the same.

The proposed system sends the necessary data if the blockchain's smart contract returns "accept." External members will not be able to access the sensitive portions of the gene data. It makes use of a private network and Ethereum.

The proposed work uses Merkle tree and Client ID to generate the hash key. For every session, a hash key is used to authenticate the system. The system authorizes the third-party only to view the documents. It increases security by 11.35% compared to previous contribution.

References

1. Kahn, S.D., On the future of genomic data. *Science*, 331, 6018, 728–729, 2011.
2. Durinck, S., Spellman, P.T., Birney, E., Huber, W., Mapping identifiers for the integration of genomic datasets with the R/bioconductor package biomaRt. *Nat. Protoc.*, 4, 8, 1184–1191, 2009.
3. Päun, G., Rozenberg, G., Salomaa, A., *DNA computing: New computing paradigms*, Springer, Berlin, 1998.
4. Devare, M.H., Convergence of manufacturing cloud and industrial IoT, in: *Applying Integration Techniques and Methods in Distributed Systems and Technologies*, pp. 49–78, IGI Global, US, 2019.

5. Devare, M.H., Challenges and opportunities in high performance cloud computing, in: *Handbook of Research on the IoT, Cloud Computing, and Wireless Network Optimization*, pp. 85–114, IGI Global, US, 2019.

6. Gim, J.-A., A genomic information management system for maintaining healthy genomic states and application of genomic big data in clinical research. *Int. J. Mol. Sci.*, 23, 11, 5963, 2022.

7. Park, Y.-H., Kim, Y., Shim, J., Blockchain-based privacy-preserving system for genomic data management using local differential privacy. *Electronics*, 10, 3019, 2021.

8. Ambika, N., A reliable blockchain-based image encryption scheme for IIoT networks, in: *Blockchain and AI Technology in the Industrial Internet of Things*, pp. 81–97, IGI Global, US, 2021.

9. Ambika, N., A reliable hybrid blockchain-based authentication system for iot network, in: *Revolutionary Applications of Blockchain-Enabled Privacy and Access Control*, pp. 219–233, IGI Global, US, 2021.

10. González García, C. and Álvarez-Fernández, E., What is (Not) big data based on its 7vs challenges: A survey. *Big Data Cogn. Comput.*, 6, 4, 158, 2022.

11. Abouelmehdi, K., Beni-Hessane, A., Khaloufi, H., Big healthcare data: Preserving security and privacy. *J. Big Data*, 5, 1, 1–18, 2018.

12. Shrestha, N.M., Alsadoon, A., Prasad, P.W.C., Hourany, L., Elchouemi, A., Enhanced e-health framework for security and privacy in healthcare system, in: *Sixth International Conference on Digital Information Processing and Communications (ICDIPC)*, Beirut, Lebanon, 2016.

13. Lin, W., Xu, M., He, J., Zhang, W., Privacy, security and resilience in mobile healthcare applications. *Enter. Inf. Syst.*, 17, 3, 1–15, 2021.

14. Zhang, K., Yang, K., Liang, X., Su, Z., Shen, X., Luo, H.H., Security and privacy for mobile healthcare networks: From a quality of protection perspective. *IEEE Wirel. Commun.*, 22, 4, 104–112, 2015.

15. Chelladurai, U. and Pandian, S., Hare: A new hash-based authenticated reliable and efficient modified merkle tree data structure to ensure integrity of data in the healthcare systems. *J. Ambient Intell. Humaniz. Comput.*, 2021, 1–15, 2021.

16. Deng, M., Petkovic, M., Nalin, M., Baroni, I., A home healthcare system in the cloud–Addressing security and privacy challenges, in: *IEEE 4th International Conference on Cloud Computing*, Washington, DC, USA, 2011.

17. Sivan, R., and Zukarnain, Z., Security and privacy in cloud-based e-health system. *Symmetry*, 13, 742, 2021.

18. Shahid, J., Ahmad, R., Kiani, A., Ahmad, T., Saeed, S., Almuhaideb, A., Data protection and privacy of the internet of healthcare things (IoHTs). *Appl. Sci.*, 12, 4, 1927, 2022.

19. Abdel-Basset, M., Manogaran, G., Mohamed, M., Internet of things (IoT) and its impact on supply chain: A framework for building smart, secure and efficient systems. *Future Gener. Comput. Syst.*, 86, 614–628, 2018.

20. Dwivedi, A., Srivastava, G., Dhar, S., Singh, R., A decentralized privacy-preserving healthcare blockchain for IoT. *Sensors*, 19, 326, 2019.

21. Nagaraj, A., *Introduction to sensors in IoT and cloud computing applications*, Bentham Science Publishers, UAE, 2021.
22. Abiodun, M., Awotunde, J., Ogundokun, R., Adeniyi, E., Arowolo, M., Security and information assurance for IoT-based big data, in: *Artificial Intelligence for Cyber Security: Methods, Issues and Possible Horizons or Opportunities*, vol. 972, Springer, Cham, 2021.
23. Abu-Tair, M., Djahel, S., Perry, P., Scotney, B., Zia, U., Carracedo, J., Sajjad, A., Towards secure and privacy-preserving IoT enabled smart home: Architecture and experimental study. *Sensors*, 20, 6131, 2020.
24. Ahmad, W., Rasool, A., Javed, A., Baker, T., Jalil, Z., Cyber security in IoT-based cloud computing: A comprehensive survey. *Electronics*, 11, 16, 2022.
25. Ali, A., Rahim, H., Pasha, M., Dowsley, R., Masud, M., Ali, J., Baz, M., Security, privacy, and reliability in digital healthcare systems using blockchain. *Electronics*, 10, 2034, 2021.
26. Liu, H., Crespo, R., Martínez, O., Enhancing privacy and data security across healthcare applications using blockchain and distributed ledger concepts. *Healthcare*, 8, 243, 2020.
27. Yin, X., Liu, Z., Ndibanje, B., Nkenyereye, L., Riazul Islam, S., An IoT-based anonymous function for security and privacy in healthcare sensor networks. *Sensors*, 19, 3146, 2019.
28. Kumar, A., Singh, A., Ahmad, I., Kumar Singh, P., Anushree, P., Alissa, K., Bajaj, M., Ur Rehman, A., Tag-Eldin, E., A novel decentralized blockchain architecture for the preservation of privacy and data security against cyber-attacks in healthcare. *Sensors*, 22, 5921, 2022.
29. Sundas, A., Badotra, S., Bharany, S., Almogren, A., Tag-ElDin, E., Rehman, A., HealthGuard: An intelligent healthcare system security framework based on machine learning. *Sustainability*, 14, 11934, 2022.
30. Deepa, N. and Pandiaraja, P., Hybrid context aware recommendation system for e-healthcare by merkle hash tree from cloud using evolutionary algorithm. *Soft Comput.*, 24, 7149–7161, 2020.
31. Alzubi, J.A., Blockchain-based lamport merkle digital signature: Authentication tool in IoT healthcare. *Comput. Commun.*, 170, 200–208, 2021.
32. Koo, D., Shin, Y., Yun, J., Hur, J., Improving security and reliability in merkle tree-based online data authentication with leakage resilience. *Appl. Sci.*, 8, 2532, 2018.
33. Hu, B. and Gharavi, H., Smart grid mesh network security using dynamic key distribution with merkle tree 4-way handshaking. *IEEE Trans. Smart Grid*, 5, 2, 550–558, 2013.
34. Nagaraj, A., Adapting blockchain for energy constrained IoT in healthcare environment, in: *Sustainable and Advanced Applications of Blockchain in Smart Computational Technologies*, p. 103, CRC Press, Boca Raton, Florida, 2022.

17

Industry 5.0: Potentials, Issues, Opportunities, and Challenges for Society 5.0

Amit Kumar Tyagi[1]*, R. Lakshmi Priya[2], Anand Kumar Mishra[3] and G. Balamurugan[4]

[1]Department of Fashion Technology, National Institute of Fashion Technology, New Delhi, Delhi, India
[2]GITAM University, Bangalore, India
[3]NIIT University, Neemrana, Rajasthan, India
[4]Department of Computing Technologies, SRM Institute of Science and Technology Kattankulathur Campus, Chengalpattu, India

Abstract

A new paradigm known as "Industry 5.0" envisions an industrial revolution that is "people-centric" and uses cutting-edge technology like Big Data and Artificial Intelligence (AI) to improve human creativity, problem-solving, and decision-making skills. In Industry 5.0, technology is not a replacement for humans, but a tool that can augment their capabilities and help them achieve better outcomes. On the other hand, the Society 5.0 movement, which has its roots in Japan, aspires to build a brand-new society that incorporates cutting-edge technologies like Big Data, Artificial Intelligence (AI), and the Internet of Things (IoT) into people's daily lives to enhance wellbeing and address social issues. Its foundation is the idea of "human-centric innovation," which puts people at the heart of technical advancement with the aim of fostering a better society for everybody. Industry 5.0 is the need of modern society. Hence, this chapter will discuss several interesting topics on Industry 5.0 and Society 5.0 in detail. We hope that our chapter will provide depth in information on these topics to future researchers and scientist.

Keywords: COBOTS (collaborative robots), industrial revolution, mass personalization, creativity, Internet of Things, big data, Artificial Intelligence

---

*Corresponding author: amitkrtyagi025@gmail.com
Amit Kumar Tyagi: ORCID: 0000-0003-2657-8700

Amit Kumar Tyagi (ed.) Privacy Preservation of Genomic and Medical Data, (409–432) © 2024 Scrivener Publishing LLC

17.1 Introduction

While Industry 4.0 continues to gain popularity and mature, Industry 5.0 is ready to take the stage. Industry 5.0 is viewed as the fifth industrial revolution, allowing customers to satisfy their unique needs based on preferences and expectations. In industry 4.0, which is at the customization stage, repetitive jobs are performed by robots [1], but industry 5.0 seeks to execute mass personalization with the aid of artificial intelligence. With increasing autonomy for collaborating robots, Industry 5.0 is predicted to change the manufacturing process. Industry 5.0 is a futuristic industrial revolution that will employ robots to carry out routine activities, which will promote creativity and innovation in the products. It is anticipated that it will make best use of human creativity and intelligence. Currently, the manufacturing industry is transitioning from mass production to custom manufacture, and this means that manufacturing systems digitization and intelligentization must advance quickly. Some important Industry 5.0 development models are shown in Figure 17.1.

17.1.1 Evolution of Industry 5.0

Following the beginning of the Industrial Revolution, manufacturing has undergone a series of advancements, from water and steam powered devices to electrical and digital electronic production, making manufacturing

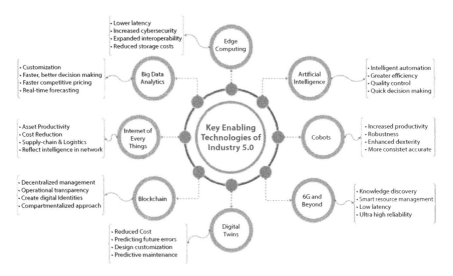

Figure 17.1 Key-enabling technologies of Industry 5.0.

Industry 5.0: Potential
Opportunities and Adoption
Challenges

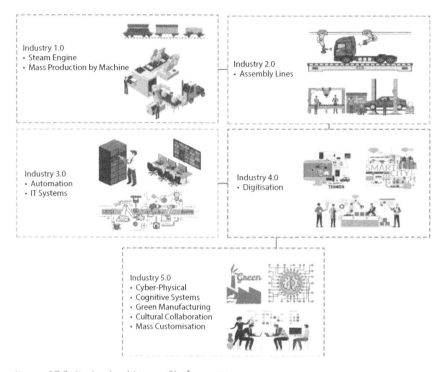

Figure 17.2 Evaluation history of Industry 5.0.

processes more complex, automatic, and sustainable so that machines can be operated simply, effectively, and persistently [1, 2, 7]. Today's consumers demand mass personalization with a human touch, and Industry 5.0 enables them to transition from mass manufacturing to mass personalization [4, 5]. Industry 5.0 is making mass customization a reality and, the fast advances in manufacturing techniques, production system digitization and intelligence are the needs of today's sector. Prior to Industry 4.0, mass customization was enabled, but this was insufficient. For instance, type 1 diabetes is difficult to manage because people have distinct levels of metabolism and distinct dimensions with distinct skin thicknesses, behaviors, lifestyles, etc. Shift to Industry 5.0 allows providing people with an application that follows their habits and routine, producing a diabetes control production method and eventually a lower, more discreet and reliable device tailored to the person. The capacity to produce an Industry 5.0 method would therefore be totally life-changing for diabetes sufferers.

Thus, after Industry 4.0, Industry 5.0 is the next stage of the industrial revolution (refer to Figure 17.2). It is defined by the incorporation of people and machines into the production process, with an emphasis on teamwork and the development of a more adaptable, sustainable, and effective manufacturing systems. While Industry 4.0 [14] was mainly concerned with automation and the application of digital technological advances like robotics, artificial intelligence, and the Internet of Things (IoT) [1, 2], Industry 5.0 seeks to restore the human touch and make it possible for humans and machines to coexist in a more productive and harmonious manner. In Industry 5.0, machines will take on the more repetitive and dangerous tasks, while humans will provide the creativity, problem-solving skills, and adaptability that machines currently lack. This collaborative approach will enable manufacturers to respond more quickly to changes in demand, introduce new products more quickly, and deliver higher-quality products to customers. Industry 5.0 will also place a greater emphasis on sustainability, with manufacturers using data analytics to optimize production processes and reduce waste, energy consumption, and emissions. In summary, Industry 5.0 has the potential to transform the manufacturing industry and create new opportunities for businesses to innovate, compete, and grow. In the last, the Society 5.0 vision [1, 8–12, 15] is based on five key pillars:

- Digital Transformation: Society 5.0 envisions a society that fully embraces digital technology, including AI, Big Data, and the IoT, to transform the way we live and work.
- Social Implementation: Creating a society where technologies is used to address social issues including bettering healthcare, education, and transportation is the goal of Society 5.0.
- Diversity: Society 5.0 recognizes the importance of diversity in society and aims to create an inclusive society that values diversity and promotes equal opportunities for everyone.
- Sustainability: Utilizing technologies to foster a circular economy and lessen waste, Society 5.0 seeks to build a sustainable society that strikes a balance between environmental conservation and economic progress.
- Ethics: Society 5.0 recognizes the importance of ethical considerations in the use of technology and aims to ensure that technology is developed and used in a responsible and ethical way that benefits society as a whole.

Ultimately, the goal of Society 5.0 is to establish a society that makes use of technological advances to enhance people's capacity for creativity, problem-solving, and decision-making while also fostering a better world for all. This was a vision that seeks to combine the benefits of technological advancement with the well-being of people and the planet.

17.2 Literature Review

According to the article [3], Industry 5.0 is a paradigm change from Industry 4.0 with a stronger focus on human-machine collaboration and a more flexible and adaptable manufacturing technology. It implies that Industry 5.0 has the ability to overcome many of Industry 4.0's shortcomings, including the lack of customization and personalization, and could result in new business models and economic prospects.

The article [4] gives a summary of the essential elements of Industry 5.0, such as the coexistence of people and robots, the application of cutting-edge digital technology, and the emphasis on sustainability and customer centricity. It suggests that Industry 5.0 could lead to significant improvements in efficiency, quality, and safety, while also addressing environmental concerns and meeting the needs of customers. Further, the article [5] provides a comprehensive overview of Industry 5.0, including its origins, key features, and potential benefits. With a stronger emphasis on collaboration, personalization, and sustainability, it implies that Industry 5.0 marks a significant change in production technologies. The adoption of Industry 5.0 presents both possibilities and challenges, and this article examines some of them. These include the need for new training and skills as well as the opportunity for new business models and revenue sources.

The article [6] examines artificial intelligence's (AI) function in Industry 5.0, stressing both the advantages and disadvantages of combining AI with human labor. It suggests that AI has the potential to enhance productivity, quality, and safety, while also enabling more flexible and adaptive manufacturing systems. However, it also highlights the need for ethical considerations and safeguards to prevent the displacement of human workers. Those studies collectively show that Industry 5.0 marks a dramatic transition in production technologies, placing a higher emphasis on sustainability, flexibility, and human-machine collaboration. While there are challenges associated with the adoption of Industry 5.0, such as the need for new skills and training, the potential benefits are significant, including improvements in productivity, quality, and customer satisfaction.

17.3   Role of Robots in Industry 5.0 and Society 5.0

Robots make an enormous contribution to works such as loading, unloading, painting, welding, etc. An autonomous robot is used to conduct a more accurate independent technique of manufacturing and to operate in locations where human employees are limited to operate. A cooperative robot, or so-called COBOT, which is meant to work alongside human employees to help them with a variety of tasks, is a significant trend. Industry 5.0 [10, 13, 19, 21] has devices interconnected to optimize productivity and human effectiveness.

17.3.1   Role of Big Data and Artificial Intelligence in Industry 5.0

Industry 5.0 can gain knowledge from big data, creating a network of digital knowledge, in order to produce symmetrical innovation. It uses cooperative robots to enhance performance and precision and is capable of carrying out human intentions. For instance, collaborative robots can be used on the operating table to perform distinctive surgery. Big Data comprises four aspects, according to Forrester's concept: information volume, information variety, information value, speed of creation of fresh information and interpretation. The Internet of Things (IoT), which automates numerous processes and collects vast volumes of new data kinds, is one of the enablers. IoT-equipped machines may transfer information to other connected machines and computer systems. Big data and IoT have already revolutionized industry 4.0, and they will have a stronger impact on industry 5.0. In order to make wise decisions, a large amount of data is created and analyzed utilizing big data analysis methods and AI algorithms. Also, industry 5.0, which is comprised of IoT, uses more sensors and intelligent devices to assure high quality, precision, and productivity with greater customization. New job opportunities are created by Industry 5.0, including those involving creative and imaginative thinking, utilizing technology, managing COBOTs, developing artificial algorithms, and many others. Furthermore, it is anticipated that robots will be a prominent part of both Industry 5.0 and Society 5.0. Here are some of the key roles that robots are expected to play in these contexts:

- Predictive maintenance: Big Data and AI may be employed to examine sensor and other information to forecast when machines and other equipment are likely to fail, allowing businesses to do maintenance before a breakdown happens.

This can reduce downtime, increase productivity, and lower maintenance costs.

- Quality control: Big Data and AI can be used to monitor the quality of products in real-time, identifying defects and other issues before they become more serious. This can help companies improve product quality and reduce waste.
- Supply chain optimization: Big Data and AI can be used to optimize supply chain operations by analyzing data from various sources such as suppliers, transportation, and inventory levels. This can help companies reduce costs, improve delivery times, and better manage inventory.
- Product design and development: Big Data and AI can be used to analyze customer feedback, market trends, and other data to inform product design and development. This can help companies create products that better meet customer needs and preferences.

Autonomous systems: Big Data and AI can be used to enable autonomous systems such as self-driving cars, drones, and robots. This can increase efficiency, reduce labor costs, and improve safety.

In conclusion, Big Data and AI are essential to the development of Industry 5.0 because they make it possible to implement autonomous systems, supply chain optimization, predictive maintenance, and quality control. As these technologies continue to evolve, they will likely have an even greater impact on industry, helping to create a more efficient, productive, and sustainable future.

17.3.2 Role of Big Data and Artificial Intelligence in Society 5.0

Society 5.0 is a concept that envisions a new society where technology is integrated seamlessly into everyday life, with a focus on human-centric values such as sustainability, inclusivity, and well-being. Big Data and Artificial Intelligence (AI) are two key technologies that are driving the transformation toward Society 5.0 [16–18, 20], and they play a critical role in shaping the future of our society. Here are some of the ways that Big Data and AI are impacting Society 5.0:

- Data-driven decision making: Big Data technologies are crucial for gathering, storing, and analyzing the huge amounts of information produced every day in order to get insights and make defensible judgments. Real-time data analysis by AI algorithms can produce insights that can be used by corporations, governments, and people to enhance their choices.

- Personalization: Big Data and AI can be used to personalize products and services to individual needs and preferences. For example, AI-powered recommendation engines can analyze a user's past behavior to suggest products or services that are relevant to them.

- Health and wellness: Big Data and AI are transforming the healthcare industry by enabling more accurate diagnoses, personalized treatment plans, and disease prevention. AI-powered medical devices can monitor patient health and alert medical professionals of any changes in real-time, helping to prevent health issues before they become serious.

- Smart cities: Big Data and AI can be used to manage urban infrastructure more efficiently, making cities more livable and sustainable. In hopes of optimizing the use of resources, AI algorithms can use data from sensors deployed in public areas to monitor things like air quality, traffic flow, and energy use.

- Education: Big Data and AI can be used to personalize education to individual students' needs, enabling more effective learning outcomes. AI-powered educational tools can analyze a student's learning patterns and adjust the curriculum to suit their individual learning style.

In summary, Big Data and AI are playing a critical role in shaping the future of our society, enabling data-driven decision making, personalization, improving health and wellness, creating smart cities, and transforming education. As these technologies continue to evolve, they will likely have an even greater impact on our society, helping to create a more inclusive, sustainable, and prosperous future. We will now talk more about the function that robots perform in industry 5.0 and society 5.0.

17.3.3   Role of Robots in Industry 5.0

Industry 5.0's use of robots can be analyzed as follows:

- Collaborative Manufacturing: In Industry 5.0 [21, 22, 24], robots are expected to collaborate with humans, working alongside them to achieve more efficient and effective production. This will enable humans to focus on more creative and complex tasks, while robots handle repetitive or hazardous work.

- Customization: Robots can play a key role in Industry 5.0 by enabling customized manufacturing. With the help of robots, manufacturers can quickly change production lines and reconfigure production processes to accommodate the demands of customers, resulting in a more customer-centric manufacturing system.

- Quality Control: Robots can be used to improve quality control in Industry 5.0. By using sensors and cameras, robots can detect defects or inconsistencies in products, leading to higher quality output.

- Sustainability: Robots can also help manufacturers to achieve more sustainable manufacturing practices. By automating and optimizing production processes, robots can reduce waste and energy consumption, leading to a more environmentally friendly manufacturing system.

17.3.4   Role of Robots in Society 5.0

The role of robots in Society 5.0 can be discussed as:

- Healthcare: In Society 5.0, robots can play a key role in healthcare, assisting doctors and nurses in patient care, monitoring patient vital signs, and delivering medications or other treatments.

- Elderly Care: Robots can also assist in elderly care, providing companionship and helping with activities of daily living, such as bathing, dressing, and eating.

- Education: Robots can also play a role in education, assisting teachers in the classroom, providing personalized learning experiences, and helping students with disabilities to access educational opportunities.

- Public Safety: Robots can also assist in public safety, providing surveillance and monitoring, assisting in disaster response, and performing hazardous tasks.

Consequently, robots are anticipated to play a big part in both Industry 5.0 and Society 5.0, facilitating more efficient, environmentally friendly, and customer-focused manufacturing, as well as enhancing quality of life in a variety of sectors like healthcare, education, and public safety.

17.4   Potentials of Industry 5.0 and Society 5.0

Industry 5.0 is the next development in the history of technologies or digitization, as was already mentioned. So, Industry 5.0 as a whole and Society 5.0 in particular have a wide range of potential. Such possibilities are covered in this section.

17.4.1   Potentials of Industry 5.0

In the next stage of the industrial revolution, known as industry 5.0, humans and machines will collaborate to develop more effective and efficient manufacturing processes. Here are a few of Industry 5.0's potentials:

- Improved Efficiency: Industry 5.0 will enable machines and humans to work collaboratively, leading to an increase in productivity and efficiency. This will result in faster turnaround times, reduced lead times, and fewer errors.
- Better Quality: Industry 5.0 will bring about improvements in quality control. With machines and humans working together, it will be possible to detect and address quality issues more quickly, resulting in better products.
- Increased Flexibility: Industry 5.0 will enable production systems to become more flexible and adaptable. This will speed up time-to-market by enabling producers to react swiftly to fluctuations in demand or the launch of new products.
- Enhanced Safety: Industry 5.0 will enable machines and humans to work together in a safer environment. By automating hazardous or repetitive tasks, the risk of accidents and injuries will be reduced.
- Sustainable Production: Industry 5.0 will help to reduce the environmental impact of manufacturing. By using data to optimize production processes, manufacturers can reduce waste, energy consumption, and emissions.
- Improved Customer Experience: Industry 5.0 will enable manufacturers to better understand and respond to customer needs. By using data analytics and customer

feedback, manufacturers can tailor products to meet customer demands, resulting in higher customer satisfaction.

In general, Industry 5.0 has the ability to transform the industrial sector and open up new avenues for enterprises to innovate, compete, and expand.

17.4.2   Potentials of Industry 5.0 in Society 5.0

Industry 5.0 and Society 5.0 are two related concepts that are expected to work together to create a better future for society. Here are some of the potential benefits of Industry 5.0 in the context of Society 5.0:

- Human-centered manufacturing: Industry 5.0 places a greater emphasis on human-machine collaboration and customization, which can lead to more customer-centric manufacturing. This strategy is consistent with Society 5.0's objectives, which are to build a society where human needs and welfare are at the core of technical innovation.
- Sustainable manufacturing: Industry 5.0 can also help to achieve more sustainable manufacturing practices, which is an important goal of Society 5.0. Industry 5.0 can help build a more ecologically friendly and sustainable society by streamlining manufacturing processes, as well as by consuming less energy and waste.
- Job creation: While there are concerns about the potential displacement of human workers with the increased adoption of Industry 5.0, it is also expected to create new job opportunities. As manufacturing becomes more flexible and adaptable, it is likely that new job roles will emerge, requiring new skills and training.
- Improved Quality of Life: The adoption of Industry 5.0 can lead to improved quality of life for individuals and communities. By enabling more customized and personalized manufacturing, Industry 5.0 can help to meet the diverse needs and preferences of people. Additionally, by improving the efficiency and safety of manufacturing processes, Industry 5.0 can help to reduce workplace injuries and improve the overall health and well-being of workers.
- Integration with other technologies: It is anticipated that Industry 5.0 would collaborate with other emerging

innovations, including blockchain, the Internet of Things (IoT), and artificial intelligence. These technologies can help to enable more efficient and effective production, as well as facilitate better communication and coordination between different stakeholders.

As a whole, the adoption of Industry 5.0 is anticipated to have a significant positive impact on Society 5.0, resulting in production that is more human-centered, environmentally friendly, and effective, as well as creating fresh employment possibilities and enhancing both individual and communal quality of life.

17.5   Open Issues Toward Industry 5.0 and Society 5.0

While Industry 5.0 and Society 5.0 hold great promise for a better future, there are also several challenges and issues that must be addressed. Here are some of the key issues facing Industry 5.0 and Society 5.0:

- Job Displacement: As machines improve in their ability to carry out duties that used to be carried out by humans, one of the main worries concerning Industry 5.0 is the possible displacement of human workers. This can lead to unemployment and inequality, particularly for those who lack the skills or training needed to transition to new roles.
- Privacy and Security: There are worries regarding privacy and security as Industry 5.0 and Society 5.0 rely more on digital technologies. Cyberattacks and data breaches can compromise sensitive information, while the collection and use of personal data can raise concerns about privacy and autonomy.
- Ethical and Social Issues: The adoption of Industry 5.0 and Society 5.0 raises significant ethical and social issues, such as the distribution of benefits and risks, the impact on human dignity, and the potential for bias and discrimination. There are also concerns about the impact of these technologies on social relations and cultural values.
- Infrastructure and Investment: The adoption of Industry 5.0 and Society 5.0 requires significant infrastructure and investment, which can be a barrier to entry for smaller businesses and less developed regions. This can also exacerbate existing inequalities and create new ones.

- Regulatory and Legal Frameworks: As new technologies are developed and adopted, there is a need for regulatory and legal frameworks to ensure safety, reliability, and accountability. However, the pace of technological change often outstrips the ability of regulators and policymakers to keep up.

17.6 Opportunities and Challenges Toward Industry 5.0 and Society 5.0

Industry 5.0 presents the opportunities and problems listed below (see Figure 17.3), which are described below as follows:

17.6.1 Opportunities of Industry 5.0

There are several opportunities toward industry 5.0, which can be summarized as (also refer Table 17.1):

- Increased automation will impact employment positively in many sectors through the deployment of next-generation technology.
- Customers have more customized options thanks to highly automated manufacturing techniques.
- Industry 5.0 increases the accessibility of employment opportunities for creatives, allowing for the improvement of labor productivity.
- Machines can be customized to fit worker needs to provide a high-level selection, and industry 5.0 will assist the client digitally in handling recurring follow-up assignments.
- Industry 5.0 creates higher-value employment than before because this gives back the liberty to people to be responsible for construction.
- In industry 5.0, the production cell operator is more involved in planning than in the more or less automated manufacturing approach.
- It enables greater customization and more individualized products while preserving creative freedom.
- It enables the automation of manufacturing methods better with Industry 5.0 by feeding the real-time information from the sector.

- Increased safety of the employees at the work floor because COBOTs can take up hazardous and dangerous works.
- More personalized products and services increase customer satisfaction, loyalty and attracts new customers, which results in increased profit and market share for the companies.
- It gives start-ups and entrepreneurs in creative and inventive fields fantastic opportunity to develop new goods and services related to industry 5.0, if enough money and infrastructure are available.
- With Industry 5.0, the field of human-machine interaction is given more weight and has access to a larger platform for research and development.
- With the aid of industry 5.0, quality services may be delivered in faraway locations, particularly in the healthcare sector where robots could be doing surgery.

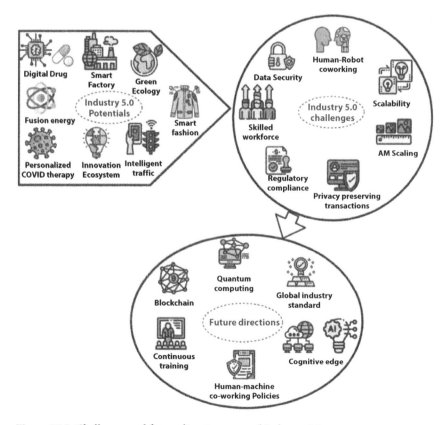

Figure 17.3 Challenges and future directions toward Industry 5.0.

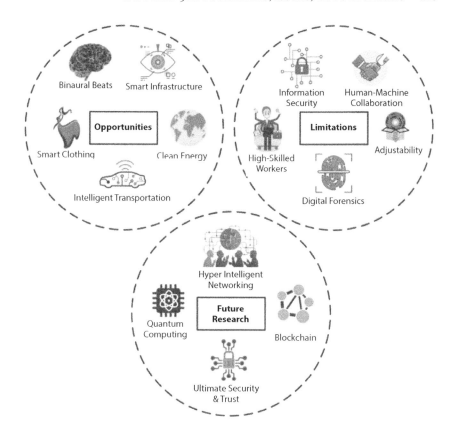

17.6.2   Challenges in Industry 5.0

There are various challenges exist in the era of Industry 5.0 which can be summarized as:

- This tendency exacerbates the polarization of the labor market, where middle-skill employment is declining and the workforce is divided into two groups: highly skilled and qualified workers who earn low wages, and unskilled workers who get low wages. The gap between the competent and unskilled in society might be narrowed as a result.
- Due mainly to highly automated production technologies, skill development is a massive task that includes preparing the workforce for the adoption of cutting-edge technology and causing behavior changes for interpersonal interactions.

Table 17.1 Industry 5.0 challenges and future directions.

Potentials Industry 5.0 applications	Industry 5.0 Challenges							Future Directions					
	Data security	Skilled workforce	Regulatory compliance	Privacy preserving transactions	AM scaling	Scalability	Human robot coworking	Blockchain	Continuous training	Human-machine CO-working policies	Cognitive edge	Global industry standard	Quantum computing
Digital Drug	✓	✓	✓	✓	✓	X	✓	✓	✓	✓	✓	✓	✓
Fusion Energy	✓	✓	✓	✓	✓	X	✓	✓	✓	✓	✓	✓	✓
Personalized Covid Therapy	✓	✓	✓✓	✓	✓	X	✓	✓	✓	✓		✓	✓
Innovation Ecosystem	✓	✓	✓	✓	X	✓	✓	✓	✓	✓	✓	✓	✓
Intelligent Traffic	✓	✓	✓	✓	✓	✓✓		✓	✓	✓	✓	✓	✓
Smart Fashion	✓	✓	✓	✓		✓	✓	✓	✓	✓	✓	✓	✓
Green Ecology	✓	✓	✓	✓	✓	✓	✓	✓	✓	✓	✓	✓	✓
Smart Factory	✓	✓	✓	✓	✓	✓	✓	✓	✓	✓	✓	✓	✓

- Collaborative robotics is the method of automation, which together with human co-workers also stays an important danger on the shop floor.
- More autonomy and sociality capacities are necessary for intelligent manufacturing platforms, which are essential components of self-organized processes. The absence of autonomy in the current systems, like as integrated decision making, makes the transition from the current setting to industry 5.0 challenging.
- From manufacturing technologies, it is challenging to obtain information of the highest quality and integrity, as well as to accommodate different information repositories.
- Because to its increased connection and utilization of common communications protocols, industry 5.0 poses a greater threat to cyber security in vital industrial operations and production lines.
- Industry 5.0 requires significant expenditure to properly execute all of its pillars, making it challenging for businesses, especially SMEs, to adopt. In the healthcare sector, for instance, industry 5.0 has enormous potential, but considerable accuracy and precision are required. The study on this front is still in its early stages and calls for substantial infrastructure and investments.
- It is challenging for startups and entrepreneurs since industry 5.0 demands high investments and infrastructure with cutting edge technology requirements.
- The presence of so much automation makes it difficult to develop regulatory frameworks for industry 5.0. For instance, who is responsible for failures and to what extent will they be held accountable.
- The industry 5.0 criteria must be met by modifying and customizing the current company strategy and business models due to increased levels of automation in the industries. Mass personalization will cause company strategy to place a greater emphasis on customer-centered procedures. It is challenging to often alter corporate strategies and business models since customer subjectivity evolves over time.
- Industry business models Due to varied customer preferences, version 5.0 calls for greater levels of dynamism to maintain competition.

In conclusion, industry 5.0 and society 5.0 are conceptions that are linked and present both opportunities and difficulties. Here, opportunities in industry 5.0:

- Greater Efficiency and Productivity: Industry 5.0 seeks to optimize production processes, increase efficiency, and enhance productivity. This can lead to lower costs, increased competitiveness, and greater profitability for businesses.
- Improved Customer Experience: Industry 5.0 emphasizes customization and personalization, which can lead to a more satisfying and engaging customer experience. This can increase customer loyalty and brand reputation.
- More Sustainable Manufacturing: Industry 5.0 can help to achieve more sustainable manufacturing practices, such as reducing waste and energy consumption. This is in line with Society 5.0's objectives, which are to build a society that is sustainable and environmentally friendly.
- Job Creation: While there are concerns about job displacement with the adoption of Industry 5.0, it is also expected to create new job opportunities, particularly in areas such as data analysis, robotics, and programming.
- Improved Quality of Life: Industry 5.0 can lead to improved quality of life for individuals and communities, by enabling more customized and personalized manufacturing, reducing workplace injuries, and improving overall health and well-being [28].

17.6.3   Challenges in Society 5.0

Although Society 5.0 presents numerous opportunities, it also faces numerous difficulties. The following are a few of the major issues facing Society 5.0:

- Ethical, Legal, and Social Implications: The integration of advanced technologies like AI, big data, and robotics raises ethical, legal, and social issues. For example, privacy, bias, and the potential for job displacement are significant concerns that need to be addressed.
- Inequality: There is a risk of creating a digital divide where some people are left behind due to lack of access to

technology and digital skills. There is also a concern that the benefits of technology will not be equally distributed.

- Security and Privacy: The use of connected devices and big data raises security and privacy concerns. Data breaches, cyber-attacks, and the misuse of personal data can undermine trust in the technology and society as a whole [29, 30].
- Education and Reskilling: High-skilled labor force capable of adjusting to the fast evolving technological environment is needed for Society 5.0. For the workforce to be ready for the latest technology developments, it is crucial to invest in education and reskilling initiatives.
- Environmental Sustainability: While Society 5.0 aims to promote sustainability, the production and disposal of technology can have a significant environmental impact. It is crucial to develop sustainable technology and ensure responsible disposal and recycling of electronic waste.

These are just a few of the challenges that need to be addressed while advancing toward Society 5.0. It is essential to ensure that the benefits of technology are accessible to all and do not come at the cost of social, ethical, or environmental harm.

17.6.4   Opportunities Toward Society 5.0

A future civilization called Society 5.0 has been envisioned, and it proposes a human-centered approach to technological development [23, 25–27]. It aims to integrate a number of cutting-edge innovations, including big data, robotics, the internet of things, artificial intelligence, and robotics, to build a society that is more sustainable, inclusive, and effective. There are numerous opportunities that Society 5.0 can offer. Some of the most promising opportunities are:

- Improved Healthcare: With advanced technologies like AI, big data, and telemedicine, healthcare can be made more accessible and affordable to all. The use of robotics can also help in providing better medical care.
- Sustainable Environment: Society 5.0 promotes sustainable development that can help in mitigating the effects of climate change. Energy usage and carbon emissions can be decreased by employing renewable energy, IoT, and smart grids.

- Enhanced Education: Education can be transformed with the use of personalized learning, augmented and virtual reality, and AI-powered adaptive learning systems. This can provide a more inclusive and equitable education system.
- Smart Cities: The use of IoT and big data can make cities more efficient, safe, and sustainable. Smart cities can enable better waste management, energy conservation, and traffic management, among other benefits.
- Digital Governance: Society 5.0 promotes digital governance that is more transparent, efficient, and responsive. With blockchain technology, secure and tamper-proof systems can be developed to ensure the accuracy and security of data.

These are just a few of the opportunities that Society 5.0 can offer. However, it is important to note that Society 5.0 also brings challenges, such as the need to address ethical, legal, and social implications of new technologies. It is crucial to consider both the opportunities and challenges while advancing toward Society 5.0

17.7 Conclusion

This industrial revolution relates to human-machine interaction to make jobs easier and quicker. The concept of personalization is advanced by Industry 5.0. Industry 5.0 is used with greater effectiveness to meet the extremely personalized demand and to build a virtual environment, advanced computers and information technologies. Industry 5.0 is the culmination of the best possible integration of big data, AI, the internet of things (IoT), cloud computing, COBOTS, innovation, and creativity. With greater latitude for creative thinking and innovation, Industry 5.0 is predicted to generate higher-value employment. It helps to improve the productivity of labor and greater opportunity for customization to customers. On the other hand, labor skill development is a huge task as a result of increasingly automated industrial systems. Due to industry 5.0's greater connectedness and adoption of common communications protocols, there is a heightened cyber security threat to crucial industrial facilities and production lines. Although industry 5.0 gives machines more autonomy, it is still up to humans to make crucial, morally sound decisions. In summary, industry 5.0 is anticipated to transform the manufacturing processes and systems by enabling increased human-robot interaction in the creation of specialized products for clients. With the help of programs like Make in India, Skill India, and Start-up India, India hopes to become a center for manufacturing. Industry 5.0 has great potential to integrate with these programs and initiatives in making India the forerunner in smart and collaborative manufacturing systems.

Hence on another side, With increased resilience and sustainability objectives, Industry 5.0 relates to robots and intelligent machines working alongside humans. Industry 4.0 concentrated on innovations such as the Internet of Things and big data, but Industry 5.0 aims to bring back human, environmental, and social factors. This is where Industry 5.0 can be considered as enhancing the developments of Industry 4.0 to support rather than replace humans. By incorporating critical reasoning and adaptation whereas still utilizing the accuracy and repeatability of machines, this allows people to step in when necessary and moves away from excessive automation.

A true revolution in society and humanity, the Era of 5.0 (industry and society) is centered on well-being on all fronts: quality of life, social, economic, and environmental. After the effects of the pandemic, climatic changes, war, societal divisions, and cyber dangers, amongst many others, these issues are at the top of the list and merit increased consideration from policymakers, corporations, and communities. As a result, the Industry 5.0 model is an advancement of the Industry 4.0 model, which centers the issue on the value of people by integrating the virtual and physical worlds using cutting-edge technology and applications. So, we are going to have a society (Society 5.0) with infrastructures and technology centered on people and addressing social and environmental issues, i.e., a society built on sustainability, human value, and resilience. Technology continues to advance industry, culture, and education, yet it is insufficient to bring about the anticipated advancements in humankind. There is a need for new learning and abilities in education in this situation of rapid evolution, transformation, and technological progress.

Hence, Education 5.0 arises, that should help students/trainees gain additional skills and competences in a holistic and human way, putting an emphasis on cooperation among peers and the community, relevant to the enhancement of individuals' lives and the social and human well-being. A higher standard of social order can be created by combining Industry 5.0 and Society 5.0, which can also enhance people's social lives. Future research could examine whether industry and education, in specific, are moving toward close cooperation in support of quality of life and economic, social, and environmental well-being in line with the SDGs. It could also examine how real contributions made by various actors in society to a future society focused on people, social responsibility, and sustainable development can be demonstrated through case studies.

References

1. Nair, M.M., Tyagi, A.K., Sreenath, N., The future with industry 4.0 at the core of society 5.0: Open issues, future opportunities and challenges, in: *2021 International Conference on Computer Communication and Informatics (ICCCI)*, pp. 1–7, 2021.

2. Tyagi, A.K., Fernandez, T.F., Mishra, S., Kumari, S., intelligent automation systems at the core of industry 4.0, in: *Intelligent Systems Design and Applications. ISDA 2020*, Advances in Intelligent Systems and Computing, vol. 1351, A. Abraham, V. Piuri, N. Gandhi, P. Siarry, A. Kaklauskas, A. Madureira (Eds.), Springer, Cham, 2021, https://doi.org/10.1007/978-3-030-71187-0_1.

3. Mihardjo, L.W.W., Sasmoko, S., Alamsjah, F., Djap, E., Boosting the firm transformation in industry 5.0: Experience-agility innovation model. *Int. J. Recent Technol. Eng.*, 8, 735–742, 2019.

4. Nahavandi, S., Industry 5.0—A human-centric solution. *Sustainability*, 11, 16, 4371, 2019. https://doi.org/10.3390/su11164371.

5. Adel, A., Future of industry 5.0 in society: Human-centric solutions, challenges and prospective research areas. *J. Cloud Comput. (Heidelb)*, 11, 1, 40, 2022.

6. Mishra, S. and Tyagi, A.K., The role of machine learning techniques in internet of things-based cloud applications, in: *Artificial Intelligence-Based Internet of Things Systems*, Internet of Things (Technology, Communications and Computing), S. Pal, D. De, R. Buyya (Eds.), Springer, Cham, 2022, https://doi.org/10.1007/978-3-030-87059-1_4.

7. Almada-Lobo, F., The industry 4.0 revolution and the future of manufacturing execution systems (MES). *J. Innov. Manag.*, 3, 16–21, 2015.

8. Savanevičienė, A., Statnickė, G., Vaitkevičiu, S., individual innovativeness of different generations in the context of the forthcoming society 5.0 in Lithuania. *Eng. Econ.*, 30, 211–222, 2019.

9. Ellitan, L. and Anatan, L., Achieving business continuity in industrial 4.0 and society 5.0. *Int. J. Trendin. Sci. Res. Dev.*, 4, 235–239, 2020.

10. Carayannis, E.G. and Morawska-Jancelewicz, J., The futures of Europe: Society 5.0 and industry 5.0 as driving forces of future universities. *J. Knowl. Econ.*, 13, 1–27, 2022.

11. Purnamasari, F., Nanda, H.I., Anugrahani, I.S., Muqorrobin, M.M., Juliardi, D., The late preparation of Ir 4.0 and society 5.0: Portrays on the accounting students' concerns. *South East Asia J. Contemp. Bus. Econ. Law*, 19, 212–217, 2019.

12. Önday, Ö., Society 5.0-its historical logic and its structural development. *J. Sci. Rep.*, 2, 32–42, 2020.
13. Saxena, A., Pant, D., Saxena, A., Patel, C., Emergence of educators for industry 5.0: An indological perspective. *Int. J. Innov. Technol. Explor. Eng. (IJITEE)*, 9, 359–363, 2020.
14. Raj, A., Dwivedi, G., Sharma, A., de Sousa Jabbour, A.B.L., Rajak, S., Barriers to the adoption of industry 4.0 technologies in the manufacturing sector: An inter-country comparative perspective. *Int. J. Prod. Econ.*, 224, 107546, 2020.
15. Pereira, A.G., Lima, T.M., Charrua-Santos, F., Industry 4.0 and society 5.0: Opportunities and threats. *Int. J. Recent Technol. Eng.*, 8, 3305–3308, 2020.
16. Zengin, Y., Naktiyok, S., Kaygın, E., Kavak, O., Topçuoğlu, E., An investigation upon industry 4.0 and society 5.0 within the context of sustainable development goals. *Sustainability*, 13, 2682, 2021.
17. Rojas, C.N.N., Peñafiel, G.A.A., Buitrago, D.F.L., Romero, C.A.T., Society 5.0: A japanese concept for a superintelligent society. *Sustainability*, 13, 6567, 2021.
18. Toprak, M., Bayraktar, Y., Özyilmazthe, A., Covid-19 pandemic and the digital transformation in turkish higher education: An evaluation from the perspective of industry 4.0 and society 5.0, in: *The COVID-19 Pandemic and its Economic, Social, and Political Impacts*, D. Demirbaş, V. Bozkurt, S. Yorğun (Eds.), pp. 148–198, Istanbul University Press, Istanbul, Turkey, 2020.
19. Saniuk, S., Grabowska, S., Straka, M., Identification of social and economic expectations: Contextual reasons for the transformation process of industry 4.0 into the industry 5.0 concept. *Sustainability*, 14, 1391, 2022.
20. Minchev, Z. and Boyanov, L., Future digital society 5.0: Adversaries & opportunities, in: *Proceedings of the 8th International Conference on Application of Information and Communication Technology and Statistics in Economy and Education (ICAICTSEE-2018)*, Sofia, Bulgaria, vol. 10, pp. 1–10, 18–20 October 2018.
21. Skobelev, P.O. and Borovik, S.Y., On the way from industry 4.0 to industry 5.0: From digital manufacturing to digital society. *Int. Sci. J. Ind.*, 2, 307–311, 4.02017.
22. Sharma, I., Garg, I., Kiran, D., Industry 5.0 and smart cities: A futuristic approach. *Eur. J. Mol. Clin. Med.*, 7, 2515–8260, 2020.
23. Darmaji, D., Mustiningsih, M., Arifin, I., Quality management education in the industrial revolution era 4.0 and society 5.0, in: *Proceedings of the 5th International Conference on Education and Technology (ICET 2019)*, Atlantis, Kota Batu, Indonesia, 3–5 October 2019.
24. Maddikunta, P.K.R., Pham, Q.-V., Prabadevi, B., Deepa, N., Dev, K., Gadekallu, T.R., Ruby, R., Liyanage, M., Industry 5.0: A survey on enabling technologies and potential applications. *J. Ind. Inf. Integr.*, 26, 100257, 2022.
25. Aoki, Y., Nakamura, K., Yuminaka, Y., Science education for society 5.0, in: *Proceedings of the International Conference on Technology and Social Science (ICTSS 2019)*, Kiryu, Japan, pp. 1–3, 8–10 May 2019.

26. Fukuyama, M., Society 5.0: Aiming for a new human-centered society. *Jpn. Spotlight*, 27, 47–50, 2018.

27. Falaq, Y., Education of citizenship in higher education as a fortress of nation characters in facing era society 5.0. *J. Educ. Sci.*, 4, 802–812, 2020.

28. Faruqi, U.A., Future service in industry 5.0. *J. Sist. Cerdas*, 2, 67–79, 2019.

29. Tyagi, A.K., Nair, M.M., Niladhuri, S., Abraham, A., Security, privacy research issues in various computing platforms: A survey and the road ahead. *J. Inf. Assur. Secur.*, 15, 1, 1–16, 16, 2020.

30. Nair, M.M. and Tyagi, A.K., Privacy: History, statistics, policy, laws, preservation and threat analysis. *J. Inf. Assur. Secur.*, 16, 1, 24–34, 11, 2021.

18

Artificial Intelligence—Blockchain Enabled Technology for Internet of Things: Research Statements, Open Issues, and Possible Applications in the Near Future

Shabnam Kumari* and P. Muthulakshmi

Department of Computer Science, SRM Institute of Science and Technology, Kattankulathur, Chennai, Tamil Nadu, India

Abstract

Today's world is surrounded by advanced technologies like Artificial Intelligence (AI), Blockchain, Internet of Things (IoT) and Cloud Computing. These technologies are improving the productivity of industries, enhancing communication levels, improving the results of many businesses, and many more. Today these technologies are being used almost in all applications/sectors like agriculture, businesses like retail, finance, healthcare, transportation, military to wearable devices. There are many benefits for these technologies individually and in the integration of each other. AI and cloud for the education sector, transportation, etc., Machine learning, IoT and Blockchain for weather forecasting or improving healthcare services, IoT and Cloud Computing for Logistics, etc. In this smart era, there are many important examples of these integration technologies. In summary, these technologies will be the king-maker for a business/industry and will change the smart era or style of living of human beings lining. These technologies will change the complete environment and will provide many benefits. But, on the other side, these technologies face a few serious issues and challenges. This article discusses all possible combinations of these technologies for many useful applications like agriculture, education, healthcare, etc. In last, we will discuss several critical challenges in the integration of these technologies in the near future and will conclude this work in brief by including several interesting remarks for future readers/researchers/scientists.

*Corresponding author: sk2581@srmist.edu.in

Amit Kumar Tyagi (ed.) Privacy Preservation of Genomic and Medical Data, (433–480) © 2024 Scrivener Publishing LLC

Keywords: Artificial intelligence, blockchain, Internet of things, internet of vehicles, industrial Internet of Things, machine learning

18.1   Introduction: Artificial Intelligence, Machine Learning, Internet of Things, and Blockchain Concepts

Artificial intelligence (AI) alludes to the imitation of human knowledge in PCs intended to think and emulate their conduct like people. The technique can likewise be applied to any framework that shows qualities connected to a human psyche, for example, learning and critical thinking. The Artificial Intelligence Era is coming. Using their minds and studying patterns of human actions, computers can solve what people do now, but at a quicker rate, reducing human involvement. In the current period, several experiments on the subject are going on, people are curious to get answers to questions such as how the computer can adapt a human behaviour just being them but in their way. These humans and AI are wired using a cross-disciplinary approach. The previous accomplishments in the field are obsolete as the world progresses and the canvas is set for the next major development. There is so much scope in this area, we have not even reached the start line, and so far, the end is [1]. Figure 18.1 depicts various frameworks of AI.

The method of inventing a humanoid is very difficult and brings a lot of effort and analysis into the process. AI is a man-made reasoning innovation or a type of digital intelligence that enables frameworks to take in and create for a fact consequently without being customized explicitly. AI focus on the pattern in which computer programs can learn themselves and process. There is a learning cycle for every model and each has different patterns of taking a decision, for example, models, direct insight, or direction. The main goal is that computers should work without the help of humans. Machine Learning is the subset of Artificial Intelligence, where people have come across the Machine Learning branch where they are still learning about AI. Some Machine Learning Methods [2, 3] exist:

- Supervised Learning
- Unsupervised Learning
- Semisupervised Learning
- Reinforcement Learning

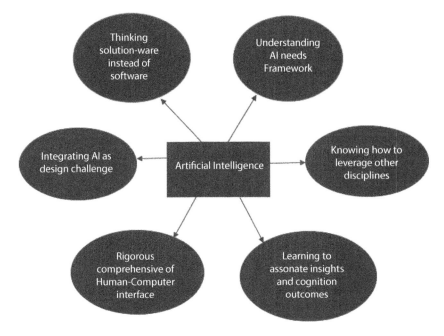

Figure 18.1 Artificial intelligence (AI) framework.

Machine Learning usually allows the analysis of major pieces of data, based on the principles of mathematics, to give accurate results in less time. In the processing of large volumes of knowledge, combining machine learning with AI and cognitive technology will make it even more efficient. A system program is said to profit by experience E according to some undertaking T and some yield measure P if its exhibition on T, as estimated by P, increments with experience E. In the accompanying circumstances, we need ML: Human information is missing (for instance, On Mars, exploring), People cannot depict their insight (for instance, Recognition for voice), changes in the solution with time (for example, Controlling Temperature). There is a sub-branch known as deep learning of Machine Learning. Machine learning, by its definition, is an area of computer science that emerged in artificial intelligence from studying pattern recognition (Human Patterns) and computational learning theory. It is the learning and creation of algorithms from which datasets can learn and make predictions. To settle on information-driven expectations or choices instead of following firm static program arranges, these strategies work by building a model from model data sources. Via algorithms, we build the future. Machine learning is based on the algorithm generated by

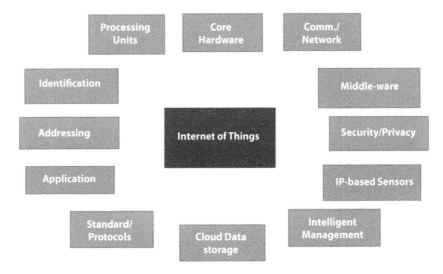

Figure 18.2 Internet of Things (IoT) components.

Maths for anything and all. Figure 18.2 depicts the various components of IoT and its related technical fields.

18.1.1   Scope of the Work

The scope is to bring out the various aspects of AI and Blockchain incorporation in IoT that gives so many opportunities for research specialists and many others who can develop and produce various angles of the system that can be potentially helpful for today's mankind.

18.2   Frameworks, Architectures, and Models for the Convergence of Machine Learning, IoTs, and Blockchain Technologies

Recently arising technology is Blockchain and that will be a better contender for IoT to produce better results. Without the requirement for a confided in an outsider to trade and validate data through exchanges, it is a decentralized, secure, and suitable arrangement. Hence, blockchain innovation has as of late been coordinated with modern Industrial Internet-of-Things (IIoT) to additionally accomplish the fourth mechanical upset. Even though blockchain-empowered IIoT organizations can possibly uphold the administrations and requests of cutting-edge organizations.

In taking care of a portion of the serious issues of blockchain-empowered IIoT organizations, Reinforcement Learning (RL) strategies are exceptionally valuable, for example, limiting square time and augmenting exchange throughput. Q-learning methodologies can likewise be utilized to bring down the recurrence of forking occasions by lessening the transmission delays for a miner. In spite of the fact that having a reasonable degree of unpredictability, the Q-learning approach could outflank the ravenous system. Blockchain development, the Internet of Things (IoT) and Artificial Intelligence (AI) areas of now seen as advances that can reinforce current business structures, develop new strategies and upset entire territories [4–10]. Blockchain will redesign the trust, transparency, security and assurance of any business cycle by offering a shared and decentralized appropriated record. Like a record, a blockchain may store a wide scope of properties. IoT atomizes the business cycles and usability of undertakings that are huge for every industry. Finally, by recognizing models and refining the effects of these cycles, AI updates the system. To this point, the association between these three developments is routinely ignored, and blockchain, IoT, and AI are customarily used freely. Nonetheless, these innovations can be applied together and may unite later on. The assortment and arrangement of information by IoT, the arrangement of the framework by blockchain and the foundation of commitment rules could be one potential connection between these advances, while AI advances cycles and rules. These three advances are reciprocal by plan and whenever consolidated, can amplify their maximum capacity. The principal advancements driving the following period of computerized change are blockchain, IoT, and AI. It very well may be contended that these advancements would combine and permit completely new models: self-sufficient specialists.

The formation of such independent plans of action and with it the computerized change of businesses could be driven by this union. Evidently, by combining blockchain advancement with IoT devices and AI, new strategies can be opened for the transformation of IoT contraptions. One such use case is light (e.g., a streetlight), which has its own blockchain-based character and limits with a blockchain-based edge. The light thusly gets the status of a self-administering substance running "without any other person." By using smart agreements, micropayments can be made clear to the light, allowing the light to turn on. At the point when an individual, an association, or even the public power pays for it, the light will shimmer. In this interesting circumstance, pay-per-use portion systems could be executed. Since the light cases a mechanized wallet, it can go probably like its own advantage network. Since all lights are related to a blockchain, they store, for example, experiences concerning their utilization, execution, and individual time.

This information can be utilized by ML and AI and can improve the network of executives. For instance, it may recommend more successive overhauling of much of the time utilized lights, just as dispatching the support group immediately in case of a breakdown. By improving the requesting cycle of networks or by serving to all the more precisely foresee the measure of new parts required, AI can likewise smooth the support cycle. Eventually, such help will bring about less space for the networks. Since lights can be tokenized as land, they can be made accessible to financial specialists. This program is a potential distinct advantage. The tokenization of such assets could move another surge of theories since monetary experts would be direct compensated with a bit of the appearance of the tokenized asset, for the present circumstance the light. The upsides of tokenization hold for lights just as all IoT items and thusly, a wide extent of current applications. For instance, these contraptions can be sensors, vehicles, PCs, cameras, trucks until they are related to the web and are related to a blockchain network. Blockchain, IoT, and AI are advancements that can be solidified into different estimations. Coordination of these headways will occur, as strategies, things and organizations will enable the mix of these turns of events. Such strategies may be for the most part applicable to each self-administering trained professional, for instance, sensors, vehicles, robots, trucks, cameras and other IoT things. These experts can send and get money self-administering and use AI and data assessment to make decisions as self-ruling financial trained professionals. Intermingling would fuel the development of such plans of action and the advanced change of mechanical firms.

18.3　Machine Learning Techniques for the Optimization of IoT-Based Services

We are emphatically getting smarter in various pieces of our consistently lives, with IoT and ML accepting a basic occupation in this. Outstanding appraisal pioneers, for instance, Bill Gates and Dr Judith Day Hoff (designer of "Neural Network Architectures: An Introduction") [12] ensure that our real inert world has been given a high-level tangible framework by the IoT. IoT has genuinely exploded throughout the late years, demonstrating its potential in applications going from wearables and self-administering vehicles to smart homes and sharp metropolitan networks, affecting everywhere. As demonstrated by progressing assessment by Gartner, there are around 16 billion contraptions associated with the IoT now, and this is needed to reach out to 25 billion by 2020. These associated gadgets make a surge of data that should be observed and broken down so they continually gain from the accessible arrangements of information and create themselves with no human mediation. That is how IoT gadgets are getting more intelligent. However, in what manner can quite a tremendous expanse of information be handled and checked? This is the place where the job of AI comes in [13]. There are different ML calculations and methods that are applied to quickly examine a lot of information in a limited capacity to focus time, expanding the proficiency of the IoT [11, 24–26]. Diverse ML draws near, for example, decision trees, clustering, neural, and Bayesian organizations, additionally assist gadgets with perceiving designs from various sources in various sorts of informational indexes and make proper choices based on their examination. Such issues are, specifically, looked at on account of inserted frameworks. Interestingly, there is no programming or coding help given to these gadgets now. ML improves the IoT yield by;

(a) Some information models fuse customary information analysis and are subsequently static and of no utilization when managing ceaselessly changing and unstructured information. In any case, the associations between a huge number of sensor inputs and different outer variables that produce a piece of great many information focus additionally should be shaped with regards to IoT. We realize that customary information examination requires a model dependent on past information and furthermore a well-qualified assessment to set up a connection between various factors. With regards to ML, it begins straightforwardly with the result factors and afterwards searches for various indicator factors and their connections right away. Hence, ML is useful when we choose what we need yet do not have a clue about the important information factors to go to that choice. Distinctive ML calculations gain from informational indexes that are fundamental to the accomplishment of this objective [14].

(b) ML is extremely useful for precisely foreseeing future occasions. All the diverse information models that are created utilizing conventional information examination are static; however, after some time, distinctive ML calculations are persistently changing as more information is gathered and absorbed. This suggests that the calculations utilized will conjecture, contrast, and their past expectations, see what really occurs, and afterwards adjust to turn out to be more precise.

(c) ML's prescient capacities are especially useful in assembling settings. By drawing the information from various sensors present in or on PCs, diverse ML calculations can really realize what is typical for the gadget and furthermore distinguish when something anomalous starts to happen [15].

(d) Machine learning assists with choosing whether a gadget connected to the IoT needs support; this is amazingly significant, converting into a great many dollars of saved expenses. Goldcorp, a mining firm, for instance, is presently utilizing ML to make expectations with more than 90% exactness on when upkeep is required, in this manner altogether lessening costs.

(e) We all realize that Amazon and Netflix use ML strategies to sort out our inclinations and give us better encounters, suggest various things we may like, and even have reasonable proposals for films and TV shows. On account of IoT, ML can be very helpful in forming our current circumstances to suit our preferences. For instance, the Nest Thermostat utilizes ML to figure out how hot or cold we need our homes to be, guaranteeing that the house is at the right temperature when we return home from work. In each IoT case, ML will truly help different organizations take the billions of information focuses they have and distil them down to something truly essential to them.

(f) All machines fit for delivering and afterwards amassing such Big Data will learn typical conduct utilizing ML and discover something outside the norm to dissect any IoT information assortment continuously (to precisely perceive the recently recognized and at no other time seen new examples).

Some ML implications that could potentially support IoT services [11];

- **Artificial Neural Networks:** This sort of learning procedure is likewise named neural networking. It is essentially a learning calculation that is motivated by the structure and useful parts of natural neural networks. Various calculations are organized as far as an interconnected classification comprising falsely modified neurons. This assists with preparing the information using the connection technique. They are essentially used to demonstrate the mind-boggling connections among sources of info and yields in the information, to discover designs.

- **K-means Algorithms:** This tackles a hub clustering issue that is generally utilized in light of the fact that it has straight intricacy and furthermore has a basic execution. The K-means truly steps in to fix diverse clustering issues. For the various groups to be beginning centroids, it arbitrarily chooses K nodes. It names every one of the nodes with its nearest centroid, with distance work. At that point, it re-figures the centroids by utilizing current nodes participation. It stops if the combination condition is found to be legitimate; else, it cycles back to the past point.

- **Inductive Logic Programming (ILP):** This is a technique used to screen the learning framework with the assistance of coherent programming as a portrayal of various information models, setting data and speculations. In the event that we have the encoding of any known setting information with explicit arrangements of models that speak to a consistent information base of reality, a conjectured rationale developer can be removed utilizing an ILP plot. This includes all sure and no negative cases and grasps any programming vocabulary to speak to the speculations.

- **Clustering:** This is a device used to allocate different perceptions to various clusters (sets) so that all the perceptions inside a similar bunch are comparable as indicated by certain pre-assigned rules. However, all the perceptions that are drawn from various bunches are extraordinary. Distinctive clustering approaches utilize different suppositions on the structure of information. This is regularly depicted by the utilization of certain likeness quantifies and is then determined. It is a sort of unsupervised learning.

- **Bayesian Networks:** This is a sort of graphical probabilistic model that utilizes a guided noncyclic diagram to speak to all its contingent autonomies in a bunch of arbitrary factors. It might, for example, clarify the probabilistic connections between different infections and their current side effects.

On the off chance that we know the side effects, at that point, this network can without much of a stretch decide the likelihood of the rate of different infections [16].

- **Decision tree learning:** Decision tree learning is a type of ML measure that uses a choice tree as its prescient model. This model guides the perceptions of an item to various suspicions about the thing's objective worth.

- **Learning the Association Rule:** This is a method utilized in expansive information bases to characterize distinctive fascinating relationships among all the factors present.

- **K-nearest Neighbors:** This is a directed learning calculation that characterizes an information test based on the names (likewise called yield estimations) of the close by information tests (additionally called a question point). Essentially, this calculation decides the K sorts of clusters to such an extent that the distance inside is little. For general arrangement, this is a kind of calculation.

- **Arduino MEGA:** In the energy area, it is utilized to diminish an espresso machine's energy costs. This is one of the easier usages of ML for IoT.

- **In Routing Traffic:** For directing traffic, the mix of different sensors and ML calculations is ordinarily executed. In a framework utilizing the LarKC stage, one such execution appeared in Figure 18.3, is. A few courses to a similar objective can be demonstrated by traffic and climate subtleties.

- **In the House:** For the house, IoT applications are exceptionally appropriate and are generally utilized in home robotization. They are utilized for light and stickiness control, just as for loft temperature sensors. IoT is currently being consolidated in pulse screens.

- **In Industry:** There are a few organizations and associations that utilization IoT and ML calculations for medical care, traffic light, and so forth In the car area, extensive HR can be saved with the assistance of an IoT framework that utilizes cameras and controls.

18.4   Machine Learning Techniques for Exchanging Data in a Blockchain

Machine learning's learning features can be extended to applications based on blockchains to make them smarter. Improvements can be made to the distributed ledger by using ML security [17]. By creating better data exchange paths, ML can also be used to increase the time taken to achieve consensus. In addition, taking advantage of BT's decentralized architecture [18] provides an opportunity to develop better models. In the BT-based smart application, we proposed Machine Learning adoption architecture, as shown in Figure 18.3. Here the smart application gathers data from various sources of data, such as sensors, smart devices, and IoT devices. As part of smart applications, data gathered from these devices is processed. As an integral part of these smart applications [19], the blockchain works.

At that point, ML [20] can be applied to the information for examination (Data investigation and ongoing analysis) and forecast of these applications. We could store the informational indexes utilized by ML models on a blockchain network. This dispenses with information blunders, for example, replication, missing estimation of information, mistakes, and clamour. Blockchains depend on the information, so it is conceivable to eliminate information-related issues in ML models [21]. Rather than the

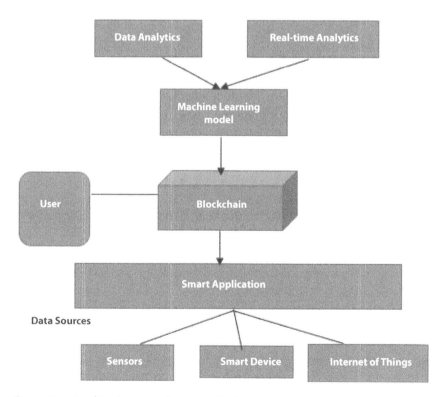

Figure 18.3 Machine learning adoption in blockchain.

whole dataset, ML models might be founded on specific portions of the chain. This could offer custom models, for example, misrepresentation location and data fraud discovery, for different applications. At the point when ML is applied, a couple of the advantages are portrayed underneath:

(a) User authentication is a valid user to request or to execute some blockchain network transaction.

(b) BT offers a high degree of security and confidence.

(c) To ensure that the conditions and terms previously negotiated are preserved, Blockchain incorporates public ML models into smart contracts.

(d) BT contributes to the reliable implementation of a framework based on rewards, thus enabling users/customers to contribute data. This enormous data will help boost the efficiency of the ML model [22].

(e) BT's on-chain environment can be modified on ML models at a small fee and off-chain, locally on a person A-Z computer at no cost.

(f) Users/customers should make good data contributions, regularly compute these data, and incentives can be offered to users [23].

(g) Different machines (with different hardware configurations) will test tamper-proof smart contracts; ML models will not diverge from their capacity and deliver results exactly as they do.

(h) Real-time payments with confidence in a blockchain world.

18.5 Machine Learning-Based Blockchain Transactions

Here, we have set the quantity of least expected transactions to 100, which has been resolved tentatively to be adequate to uncover basic transaction designs as of now. This is one of the standards that could be utilized in future work for the future centre, however is out of this current exploration's compass [27]. After the initial 100 transactions, a component extraction measure, portrayed in the past segment, starts, which changes over time arrangement information to plain information. The novelty recognition technique is then used to develop the irregularity identification model. This model is utilized to assess every transaction, to be either typical or bizarre, for the following j transaction. Once more, the j boundary can be additionally enhanced for the quantity of transaction assessed by the equivalent [28] oddity recognition model at the individual location, however, it is again outside the extent of this investigation that we have endeavoured to survey the handiness of the proposed cycle. Algorithm 1 shows the pseudocode of the framework [29]. Since our goal was to test the authenticity of the proposed procedure and not to find ideal conditions, we confined ourselves to using only one unmonitored inconsistency disclosure methodology: the Isolation Forest peculiarity area system [38], which disengages and parcels each trade into inliers (i.e., normal trades) and special cases (i.e., unusual trades) considering the number of decisions. All in all, there is no capacity to decide if the peculiarity identification component has effectively recognized the transaction as bizarre [30–32] or not. Some of the time, this is called curiosity distinguishing proof. Subsequently, we introduced the consequences of solo novelty transaction location in a period arrangement outline, where an abnormal transaction is identified.

Algorithm 1: Pseudocode of proposed method for identification of anomalous blockchain transactions.

Input:	*AD* unsupervised anomaly detection algorithm
	ad already built model for anomaly detection
	j update factor
	i number of transaction already used with this model
	W set of time frame windows
	F set of aggregation functions
	T transaction history of a blockchain address
	t transaction to be evaluated
Output:	*t_anomalous* anomaly detection results for transaction *t*
	i number of transactions evaluated with this model
	ad anomaly detection model

if $i == j$ **or** $ad.isnull()$ **then**

    $t\_features \leftarrow [t.valueUSD]$;

    for $w \in W$ **do**

        for $f \in F$ **do**

            $t\_features \leftarrow t\_features \cup f(T[w])$;

        end

    end

    $ad \leftarrow AD.fit\ Anomaly\ Detection\ (t\_features)$;

    $i \leftarrow 0$;

end

$t\_anomalous \leftarrow ad.predict\ (t\_features)$;

$i \leftarrow i + 1$;

return $t\_anomalous, i, ad$

The calculation is limited to a solitary unsupervised variation from the norm acknowledgement system, the Isolation Forest for Novelty Detection Method, which limits each trade and parcels them into standard trades and unpredictable trades, considering the number of decisions in the decision tree to separate the trade. The idea of abnormality location issues without marked occurrences is to such an extent that for the addresses there is no ground reality. At the end of the day, there is no capacity to decide if the novelty discovery instrument has appropriately distinguished the transaction as strange or not [33, 34].

The framework utilizes a progressive utilization of Machine Learning inside the blockchain advancements area, which is utilized to streamline the marking cycle while additionally securing the shopper against the systemized marking of an expected deceitful or broken blockchain transaction. The calculation is fused inside the program, which runs on top of blockchain innovation and with supposed blockchain-based advanced customer wallets. Furthermore, the structure for irregularity discovery runs and stores the information (for example the model for inconsistency recognition) on the client system, which is the centre of the automatic signature methods [35]. This calculation builds the availability and dependability of decentralized frameworks. Besides, in conditions requiring the nonstop execution of blockchain exchanges, for example, advanced cash trades, the utilization of the framework forestalls misrepresentation or other illegal exercises that may bring about the deficiency of assets kept in computerized wallets utilized in regular transactions [36]. The update factor j, which chooses how long the model is used until it is refitted, is one of the headway factors and is subsequently specially crafted to the instances of the individual area. Other independent peculiarities and peculiarity recognizable proof procedures have moreover been used in this strategy, from quantifiable to meta-heuristic, similarly, as a phoney neural network with typologies progressed for confined proportions of data. A correlation of results between the AI-based methodology and the first cycle reveals insight into the ease-of-use segment of the technique, clarifying its predominance in each other fields. It is stronger, more coordinated, and a lot speedier than a decentralized application than the first process [37].

18.6 IoT-Enabled Security Using Artificial Intelligence and Blockchain Technologies

Even though we have advancements in technology like AI, Blockchain, IoT and incorporating them in different combos to give useful products for society, there is always a pressing concern in the fields of security. How secure would these mechanisms be for public usage is an important question to be addressed.

This section will describe AI and Blockchain and how they give much more shielding effect to IoT in terms of security.

Securing the Internet of Things using Blockchain
Internet of Things frameworks store, make and cycle information and send this data over the Internet, making a lot of information to be utilized by different suppliers. Notwithstanding the central focuses, basic issues identified with security could emerge. The blockchain would expect an essential occupation in the course of action of decentralized applications that will run into billions of contraptions. Seeing how and when this headway can be utilized to give security and protection is a test, and a few scholars feature these issues [38, 39]. The creators examined, unequivocally as to the accompanying issues, the appropriateness of connecting Blockchain and IoT:

a) There are negligible abilities for commonplace IoT gadgets.
b) Transaction expenses can restrain connections.
c) Sleepy IoT endpoints are likewise accessible.

IoT-delivered data should be kept classified. It is hence important to examine whether everything developments can be applied appropriately. In such manner, the writing [40–49] tends to the accompanying: (i) A financially smart blockchain reasonable for low-limit gadgets (ii) Micropayments between information instalment sensors (iii) Computing and extricating data from delicate information (iv) Integration into brilliant homes, shrewd urban areas or shared economies.

The below points will give how much the IoT is secured using Blockchain and what changes can be made for IoT in several places to solves the privacy issues;
- **Providing Access Control and Anonymity:** To get an update, IoT contraptions ought to reliably be intended to use a substitute area, to make another area for and got to resource and not to use reevaluated networks. These measures are satisfactorily not to give complete anonymity, yet rather will give a degree of protection to character preservation. In data amassing and to give access control, the Blockchain can similarly be used. To save history data, using of the blockchain-based sensor can be used [50, 51]. All clients

approach exchanges and comprehend that the game plan of experiences made by the presence has the choice to be investigated by a specific client as the Blockchain is made public. Regardless, simply the people who have private keys can examine the step-by-step history that has been conveyed by the sensor. Ouaddah *et al.* [50] have proposed an Equal Access system that uses Blockchain to allow customers to follow their information. He reuses the Bitcoin code and presents two or three new sorts of exchanges used to give information access control, for example, "allowed" and "deny" access. In the model, there are sure people: the shared asset; the asset proprietor; and the clients. The transactions are utilized to give access control and the blockchain utilizes it to store and analyses the endorsements. The producers furnished evidence of thought with a Raspberry Pi and a camera ("the asset"). The proprietor controls asset access by systems for exchanges. To utilize the security given by Blockchain, Zyskind *et al.* [46] use the chain of blocks, data are being used. A Direct Hash Table (DHT) is utilized for limit, where there is a social link of focuses, picked to this point, committed for dealing with it. The information is imitated successfully to guarantee high accessibility. The middle person does not have the whole record to be viewed. The Blockchain is then used to screen where any information is and who approaches it. Thus, two new sorts of exchanges have been made, one for giving access control and one for controlling the designation of DHT information. Since Blockchain does not have an essential issue of thwarted expectation and is not worked by a solitary substance, it gives another class of businesses and decentralized assets, for example, the DNS root subject matter expert or the undertaking root affirmation authority. These inclinations have pushed Ali *et al.* [45] to utilize the blockchain to fabricate another decentralized PKI and perceiving affirmation system called Blockstack ID. The Blockstack withdraws the name record and the property from the openness, division of control and information of the related information. A name enlistment show is depicted by the control plane, setting up affiliations (name, hash). The control plane includes a block and a layer cleverly isolated from the control plane, which is liable for limit. The name of the proprietor key will be grasped on completely put aside information. The use of Blockchain for the handiness of IoT monetary exchanges was examined in an explicit proposition, incorporating the going with:

- **ADEPT [52]:** Automatic Decentralized P2P Telemetry is a decentralized IoT framework worked by an IBM-Samsung created effort that builds up a surrounded system network utilizing Bitcoin parts, permitting billions of contraptions to send exchanges to one another and perform self-upkeep, giving secure particular confirmation and endorsement. The ADEPT uses the blockchain to give the structure establishment, utilizing a blend of assertion of work and evidence of stake for stable exchanges.

- **Filament [55]:** A structure proposed to allow devices to have astounding characters and to have the choice to discover, give and interface with each other in a self-administering manner. They can, for example, offer information about biological conditions to a checking office. The fact is to make a file of devices that licenses IoT fibre devices to securely relate, send microtransactions, and execute smart agreements. The Filament uses five devices: block name; Tele-Hash; wise arrangements; Penny-bank; and BitTorrent. The Filament Devices can make an uncommon identifier that is taken care of and enlisted on a verifiable chip in the square. Tele-Hash, explicitly, gives encoded correspondence beginning to end-system, and BitTorrent awards record sharing. The Filament utilizes a show subject to Bitcoin for micro-transactions, named Penny-bank. On account of special constraints on IoT devices, Penny-bank offers an assurance organization between two IoT contraptions, enabling them to settle trades while they are on the web.

- **Watson IoT platform [53]:** This IBM stage permits information to be moved to a private blockchain by IoT gadgets. All neighbours who have this Blockchain can get to and give the gadget's information without focal control. Each trade can be checked, questions avoided and ensure that every accessory is liable for their employment in the overall trade.

- **IOTA [54]:** A cryptocurrency that was explicitly created for the offer of IoT gadget information. Rather than utilizing a worldwide Blockchain, the IOTA utilizes a DAG (Directed Acyclic Graph), the edges are transaction, and the loads have been checked by the occasions. The fundamental standard is that a hub should initially execute a progression of transaction checks to approve them and really at that time play out an exchange. There is no contrast between hubs. The obligation lies with the two of them for endorsing the exchanges. As indicated by the source, this guarantees more prominent versatility: the higher the quantity of exchanges, the more productive it becomes.

- **Ensuring safe smart home using blockchain:** Blockchain-based methodologies give decentralized wellbeing and security, yet require exorbitant utilization of energy and postponements for most asset compelled IoT applications that are not suitable. A lightweight IoT for Blockchain is given by Dorri *et al.* [55]. This work proposes a way to deal with joining Blockchain in boosting IoT, shedding the affirmation of work and the outlook of financial norms. The maker uses it to speak to the utilization of a smart house,

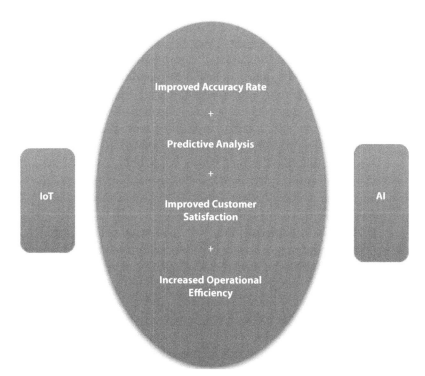

Figure 18.4 Internet of Things and Artificial Intelligence as together.

which involves three key structures: appropriated capacity, an overlay layer, and smart home. Each smart home is fitted with a system with more critical power that is reliably on the web. This system is such a "miner" and is responsible for dealing with all trades inside and outside the house. This system, which is used to manage and survey trades and to give access control between devices, keeps a hidden blockchain [56–58]. As appeared in Figure 18.4, IoT and AI will join to improve the examination of the framework, upgrade operational execution and improve the exactness rate.

In near future, we will see many developments based on the integration of AI, IoT and Blockchain.

18.7 Security, Privacy, and Trust Related Areas in Artificial Intelligence and Blockchain-Based IoT Applications

This section deals with the various application in which AI and Blockchain give a better improvement in IoT to produce eco-friendly products for the public and some of them are mentioned below:

Smart Healthcare: Smart medical care applications and administrations will be the greatest driving IoT applications and will have the option to screen and react to the medical services needs of patients and use cloud information analysis to improve the nature of medical services and patient experience while diminishing the expense of giving medical services administrations. Smart medical services security needs various highlights dependent on an emergency record's validity [62]. There are numerous advantages and downsides of information and choice combination in IoT for medical services. Information combination needs more transmission capacity to communicate crude tactile information, which can incorporate a few high-dimensionality highlights, for example, information from picture sensors utilized in endoscopy, while choice combination requires less transfer speed since the choice is sent over the organization with refined data. Since inborn adjusting mistakes in calculation dependent on the preparing precision of sensors will require crude tangible information handling, decision fusion brings about loss of exactness. On the other hand, information combination gives extra definite outcomes as the calculations are performed on sensor network doors that have more force. Choice combination devours the restricted intensity of the sensors to register and send information, while combination sensors utilize more capacity to communicate high-dimensional information. Since radio transmission utilizes more force than processor calculations [63].

Smart City built on Blockchain: To make the possibility of a shrewd city an authentic one, Bitcoin (BC) can be ideal. The idea for a smart city is centred on shrewd IoT gadgets [61]. In the conditions of smart urban communities, with IoT creating and prospering, a lot of information will be produced by various strategies. The smart city network is disengaged into two indisputable organizations, the centre affiliation and the edge affiliation, utilizing the BC strategy. High getting ready power and energy contraptions for mine centre points are associated with the centre structure, while the edge systems have low cut-off and power gadget managing. The miner hub is proposed to deliver the block and check the Proof of the Work (PoW). With the SDN regulator, every hub can offer unbelievable spryness and security, decline the expense of hardware association and comprehend the transparency of plan in the getting sorted out structure of the smart city [64].

Smart Home Built on Blockchain (BC): The BC-based savvy home has an arrangement standard that changes into an ACL that allows the owner to manage her structure's entire movement. The miner gives a split key between standing out systems concurring from the technique set by the proprietor in a contraption to gadget correspondence. The BC-based smart home structure gives trained acceptance to IoT information. It in addition ensures information validity, message transparency and course of action, close by flowed DDoS assault. The fundamental focuses of the BC-based savvy home are to choose BC issues through the as of late referred to the utilization of Proof of Work in Block Mining in 2019, for example, the second International Conference on Intelligent Computing, Instrumentation and Control Technology, Latency and Energy Use. Each block is mined with no other count to lessen computational power costs, including energy use. Moreover, the idleness of truncation approval, regardless of whether it is mined in a block, is diminished because of exchanges. For shrewd homes, the hypergraph-based blockchain worldview is pragmatic and can help save security and protection insurance necessities [65]. The exceptional disadvantage recognized in this plan, notwithstanding, is as depicted in:

- The decentralized structure is the indication of BC, however, in this arrangement the Home-Miner, Cluster Heads and distributed storage give the different layers a Single Point Failure (SPF).

- Most BC standards embrace exchanges and the determination of an arrangement from all hubs in the network. In this situation, the Cluster Heads have to choose if a block should be kept or dismissed.
- Only the Home Miner, without Proof of Work (PoW), mines a square, yet the level of obligation in PoW keeps the BC from twofold spending and taking data [66].

e-Business modes use IoT techniques based on blockchain to boost the company's income. The reason for these methodologies is to sell and purchase individual property utilizing Decentralized Autonomous Companies, for example, vehicles, bicycles and electronic gadgets. With no human intercession, the principle capacity of DAC is programmed and utilizes advanced truncations for decision making. This permits measurements to be shared quickly among complete proprietors, for example, machines, systems, individuals, clients, providers, and so forth moreover, since it goes about as a client support supplier, IoT gadgets utilized in the plan of action should be ensured. Fitness is improved by the nonattendance of the specialist in the e-plan of action by coordinating Blockchain innovation and IoT gadgets into the e-plan of action. The savvy gadget introduces the DAC model to buy and sell such offices, for example, power supply, updating of extra segments and applications, and so on the accompanying disadvantage to this procedure is 1. The board of IoT merchandise, for example, less handling space, little memory modules, and low force utilization, are essential for the unwieldy work. Incorporating BC with IoT prompts infringement of customer protection [67].

Supply Chain Management: In its entire supply network measure, the blockchain is a model system to support thing verification and transparency. Utilizing a computerized record to follow the beginning and moving items in a continuous climate can help. To discover the past item, current area and ecological status, for example, temperature, IoT gadgets utilized in the working environment, load trucks, stockpiling coolers associated with SCM computerized record decentralization [68]. In an activity associated with it, the streamlined Blockchain SCM is the following disadvantage.

- There is a fundamental issue of BC interfacing and diverse actual interface types, paying little mind to the blockchain's usable exhibition in SCM. Furthermore, the current position and condition of the item that sends one area to another area are physically changed in the current SCM.

Table 18.1 Blockchain-internet of thing: merits and security issues.

Applications	Merits	Security issues
Blockchain for IIoT	Solid, peer-peer and decentralized	Giving trust is perplexing between the individuals from the IoT and authority over the sharing of assets, for example, time, energy, administration.
Smart Healthcare in IoT with Blockchain	BC achieves on regularization of information design that is utilized to send information paying little mind to the skill of electronic wellbeing	The choice combination brings about the deficiency of rightness since crude tactile information will include explicit arranging blunders in the estimation of the exactness of sensors
Blockchain-based smart home	BC-based savvy home gadgets become unchanging and subsequently protected from digital assaults. It engages different people to get to exact zones and gadgets without giving total access rights	Proof of work is not utilized in these applications, so programmers hack the savvy home utilizing phoney assaults and twofold spending assault.
IoT eBusiness model using Blockchain	Exchange of resources and brilliant agreement esteem paid on the IoT with the assistance of P2P exchange dependent on the BC innovation	E-plan of action there will be the outsider to trade the cash, BC may not supplant it
Supply Chain Management	It will uphold in following and beginning item progressively climate utilizing the advanced record	Programmers bargain the whole SCM sensor hub and afterwards, they effectively hack and infuse bogus data in SCM. Overseeing trust is a testing issue.

- No other sensor hub decides the specific condition of this substance until it has arrived at the distribution centre in a decentralized situation. This sensor hub should subsequently be ensured to give a safe SCM to numerous sensor hubs utilized in the SCM to reveal the status of the item. At the point when hubs that are utilized in the SCM are trusted to incorporate with IoT gadgets, blockchain innovation is not fundamental.

Likewise, if the hubs utilized in the SCM do not look after trust, programmers bargain the whole SCM and afterwards, programmers infuse bogus data into the SCM without any problem. Table 18.1 shows the contrast between the Blockchain-based IoT stage and its security concerns.

The ability to automate IoT security monitoring, management and control would be the driver for protecting IoT devices and networks. AI intelligence procedures for upgrading stable IoT. To counter security hazards in IoT, AI procedures, for example, directed and solo AI, fortification learning and even deep learning are being proposed. The following demonstrates AI and machine learning [69];

(a) **Behavioural Modelling:** AI can be extended to all Network Traffic, Log & Audit Data, Net Nodes, Servers and all Smart IoT devices in real-time modelling.

(b) **Zero-Day Attacks:** AI modelling will mitigate new malware hazards that are unable to identify a "signature"

(c) **Advanced Persistent Threats (APTs):** The step-by-step penetration of APT malware can be identified by adaptive learning algorithms (Phishing, Trojans, Adware, Botnets, etc.).

18.8   Blockchain-Based Learning Automated Analytics Platforms

Limitation of Learning Analytics Platforms: Interoperability without some constraints is still difficult to achieve despite the existence of reference standards for maintaining LRS (Learning Registered Stores) learning data. These challenges involve:

(d) **Linking a learner's learning histories on various learning platforms on a single immutable path:** Even though students ordinarily move from the learning foundation of one supplier to another, separate LRSs independently and disconnectedly store their learning records. As a result, every framework needs to address the cost of developing student information without any preparation, aside from basic cases. Despite the fact that this may not be a rehashed endeavour for first-time learners, it is practically hard to tell whether they are genuinely newbies. This likewise causes a "cold start" issue in preparing suggestion frameworks because of the understudies' inaccessibility of earlier learning acts [70].

(e) **Maintaining privacy and ease of access control of student information:** When offering learning records to outsiders, this is another test experienced. Although learning examination assists with boosting student execution [71, 72], Alan and Kyle [72] contend that whatever the advantages of learning investigation are, in one wide and four restricted inquiries concerning student security conditions, they should be proportionate to ensuring the protection and related privileges of students [73, 74].

(f) **Integrating research and development processes for learning advancement:** The accessibility of information on learning encourages advancement. In situations where taking in information is received from cycles of improvement or potentially investigation, learning examination scientists are frequently gone up against with the heinous undertaking of anonymizing data that can be by and by recognized to ensure the protection of partners and accordingly negatively affect customized results [75]. Ground-breaking thoughts on the most proficient method to incorporate such consistent joining and interoperability of both examination and creation frameworks while keeping up the security of partners included are significant as ongoing learning information for learning investigation research turns out to be more appealing.

A blockchain is a distributed archive of all transactions or digital events conducted and shared between participants, or a public ledger database [77]. Below, we describe some of the features of blockchain technology that are central to the solution for the Blockchain-based Learning Analytics Application.

(a) **Distributed Consensus and Characteristics of Immutability:** Blockchain innovation depends on a dispersed agreement in which network hubs approach and screen all occasions that happen in the organization [76]. As lasting squares that are time stepped and tied, record passages are put away. All network hubs offer to add a new block to the record by contending with one another to settle a system serious riddle known as the Proof of Work to ensure the wellbeing and precision of record passages. These hubs are called miners and are compensated for being the first to propose the right response to the Proof of Work. The computational force important to tackle this riddle makes it harder to revise blocks since it would require the goal of related verification of work and the acknowledgement of such an answer by legitimate hubs. These blockchain innovation highlights incorporate answers with high information consistency to associate diverse taking in records from various learning suppliers.

(b) **Smart Protection, Security and Access Control dependent on contracts:** The blockchain innovation has a smart agreement work that makes it simpler to authorize the terms of understanding between two gatherings in an agreement; for this situation, among students and learning suppliers or between learning suppliers. To follow admittance to data and guarantee the security of students' information and the shared interests of learning suppliers [78], we propose approaches that can be executed on the blockchain.

(c) **Single Ledger, Multiple Participants:** To improve the interoperability of both exploration and creation measures, we influence the conveyed agreement and single record various members capacities of the blockchain innovation. We propose Learning Blockchain APIs and Datastore Wrappers for smooth and secure correspondence between the blockchain and LRSs of learning suppliers.

18.9   Blockchain- and Machine Learning-Based Solutions for Big Data Challenges

Information is viewed as an association's most significant asset in the present innovation and data-driven society. Information is ascending at an exceptional speed these days in view of the far-reaching appropriation of data innovation by most associations for the administration of their activities. 130 exabytes of information were produced and put away in 2005, as per the 2011 IDC Digital Universe Report. The total expanded to 1,227 exabytes in 2010 and is relied upon to ascend to 7,910 exabytes in 2015 at 45.2 per cent [79]. Because of significant value-based data, system data and social data, a considerable amount of this data impact starts and leads us into another field of data known as big data [80, 81]. Government offices have communicated their anxiety about the administration of Big Data [83–85]. In segments on the issues a lot of enormous information, driving logical diaries, for example, Science and nature additionally show their help for huge information [86, 87]. For a progression of informational indexes so huge and assorted, the term enormous information is utilized that it gets hard to handle them, as the data comes and keeps on growing from various, heterogeneous, self-sufficient sources with mind-boggling and evolving connections. The term "Big Data" is essentially used to portray colossal datasets with this huge expansion in tremendous worldwide information. Enormous information generally requires heaps of unstructured information as opposed to traditional information bases that require all the more constant investigation. Enormous data is tied in with developing issues looked at by networks when they manage expansive and quickly developing information or information sources, breaking down information blends. Information need not be restricted to numbers alone; they can be photos, recordings, outlines, words and expressions, and the rundown goes on. Client criticism on business sites, remarks on interpersonal interaction sites, photos and recordings shared on the web, electronic clinical records, and bank records are on the whole instances of enormous information. Enormous information is accessible in three sorts: structured, semiorganized, and unstructured [88]. The issues presented by big data are:

- **Decentralization:** Data storage and management decentralization help to improve protection by compartmentalizing the control flow. Decentralization means that there are copies of data that have not been compromised in a situation where a rogue data center employee attempts to delete or alter data. The attacker will need to access the majority of the network, which is very difficult to obtain, for a coordinated assault on the database. Decentralization also makes sure that such a model is inclusive in its governance. This is achieved by taking votes from all the interested parties who want to use the model to guarantee justice.

- **Data Immutability and Integrity:** Data immutability is of vital importance to big data businesses. The resulting study is bound to be of little benefit if the dataset that needs to be scrutinized is altered in some way. To save money, companies would naturally prefer to prevent such a situation. As blockchain provides a streamlined way to perform data integrity and audit trails, Blockchains can effectively ensure that. The two most critical issues facing broad datasets for businesses are: ensuring the knowledge has not been updated, ensuring the information originates from an authentic source.

Countermeasures/ Solutions for Big Data Challenges using Machine Learning:

In [2], Czarnowski. Jędrzejowicz recommends a way to deal with information decrease by joining stacking, revolution, and specialist populace taking in techniques for gaining from huge informational collections. This work shows that, by gaining from huge and complex datasets, the blend of the proposed strategies would build the exhibition of the classifier. The strategy depends on the classifier troupe model in which stacking sets have been made to guarantee their heterogeneity utilizing turn-based methods. To lessen the dimensionality of the information, information decrease in a model and capacity measurement was presented. Likewise examined in J's article was the diminishing in dimensionality.

Semichecked learning is a class of undertakings for ML in which both marked and unlabeled information produces a learning model. Some are tending to the subject of occasion choice and preparing set pre-processing. A few ways to deal with model choice dependent on testing are examined and differentiated. An exhaustive exploratory examination of the strategies considered is given in the paper Jedrzejowicz and P. Jedrzejowicz [100] proposing a way to deal with information stream mining. The issue has been conquered utilizing the steady Gene Expression Programming classifier with metagenes and information decrease. As found in the proposed depiction of metagenes, an expansion in the exactness of the characterization was guaranteed, while the decrease in information made it simpler to deal with computational time. The significance of the proposed arrangement likewise allows work to be finished with the information stream coming about because of the execution of basic float location components. Adaptability is additionally offered by the proposed approach by the capacity to change estimation times to the customer's requirements to the detriment of classification precision.

Z. H. Kilimci and Selim Akyokus [59] focus on the subject of text classification. To expand the adequacy of text classification, the creators propose ways to deal with ensemble learning and deep learning. In the classification of base classifiers proposed to take care of the thought about order issue, customary AI calculations, for example, innocent Bayes, uphold vector machine and irregular woods, and a deep learning-based Conventional Network classifier are incorporated. The distinctive archive portrayals and different troupe approaches were tried on eight separate datasets. At long last, it has been indicated that utilizing heterogeneous troupes expands the productivity of text classification, alongside deep learning approaches and word inserting. A. Nowak-Brzezińska [101] examines the subject of information on the board and proposes another way to deal with the structures of rule the executives for choice emotionally supportive networks. The methodology depends on the structure of a standard base that is progressively coordinated. Such a structure is delivered reliant on the clustering cycle. The proposed calculation, utilizing the procedure of comparability, intends to find new realities (new information) from existing guidelines and realities. A depiction of the effect of the proposed techniques on the viability of a choice help structure of progressive information portrayal is remembered for the computational trial.

The issue of complex control and assessment of intensity framework status is examined by Guo *et al.* [82]. As expressed, the paper presents a unique Big Data stage that is utilized as a logical instrument. Based on a contextual investigation, the creators tell the best way to improve the dynamic cycle in force frameworks.

18.10 Machine Learning Techniques for the Analysis of Sensor Records for Healthcare Applications

There is huge information about patient prosperity, as in the medical services area. So, it is hard to handle it for people. As a result, ML offers a strategy for recognizing patterns from huge information and utilizing calculations to estimate patients' expected results. ML in medical care permits individuals to comprehend the strength of current administrations and to discover the therapy that gives patients the best result contingent upon their condition. The information elements created by sensors, including time arrangement signals, which are an arranged grouping of sets, are sensor data. These information components are prepared by processing gadgets and can either be a basic mathematical or downright esteem or can be more mind-boggling information. The exploration is being completed on sensor information by the accompanying researchers. To distinguish Parkinson's disease (PD) utilizing information streams gathered from wearable sensors. The analysis was performed on 20 people and 6 individual development wearable sensors were recorded. Total 13 tasks were finished by people and the test was performed on a solitary day and rehashed fourteen days after the fact. For this, an aggregate of 41,802 information cuts was utilized. The information was prepared to utilize convolutional neural networks and an arbitrary woodland classifier for bradykinesia and quake location. The discoveries indicated that, with an AUROC estimation of 0.73 for bradykinesia recognition and 0.79 for quake identification, the arbitrary woods classifier performed better [86–98].

ML classifications were distinguished by David *et al.* [90] to recognize the threat of Array Development (AD) and Typical Development (TD) in newborn children. Utilizing Opal sensors appended to the baby's lower leg, long haul newborn child inertial movement was accounted for and the information was partitioned into two sets, 0 to a half year and 6 to a year, individually. A sum of 19 development highlights including development check, length, normal increasing speed and pinnacle quickening from two sets were separated utilizing univariate include determination techniques, which were Recursive Feature Elimination (RFE) and stepwise component choice. To help the vector machine, strategic regression and AdaBoost for expectation, the creators utilized three AI calculations, and the outcomes demonstrated that SVM performed best for 0 6 month babies with 90% exactness and AdaBoost for 6-year newborn children with 83 per cent precision.

The Bayesian organization hybrid approach and the neural network heuristic procedure were examined [92–99, 60] to recognize pressure utilizing the wireless detecting framework by estimating the estimation of Blood Pressure Monitor (BPM) and Heart Rate (HR). Information was gathered utilizing sensors mounted in cell phones and a half breed approach was utilized to arrange pressure utilizing estimations of BPM and HR. Accordingly, the hybrid approach performed well, with a precision of 92.86 per cent for BPM and 85.71 per cent for HR. A Deep-Belief Network (DBN) utilizing body sensor information to arrange human movement was recommended. To gather sensor information and concentrate significant highlights, Kernel Principal Component Analysis (KPCA) and Linear Discriminant Analysis were utilized (LDA). At that point, the model was prepared with 40 concealed layers utilizing a profound conviction network. It is obvious from the outcomes that the profound conviction network performed best for conduct discovery with 97.5 per cent accuracy.

An example of 40 female patients was taken from which 550,432 sensor information esteems were gotten, comprising of on-body information, natural information and self-report information on the passionate level gathered utilizing the cell phone application. Utilizing the hybrid CNN-LSTM model, the information was then pre-processed and prepared for feeling recognition. The consequence of the result indicated that with 95 per cent accuracy, the crossover approach proposed performed better. Four AI classifiers were examined utilizing a 3D-hub accelerometer fitted with a 6lowPAN wearable framework, including choice trees, troupe, calculated relapse and profound net for fall discovery in more established people. The accelerometer perusal was extracted and the capacity of utilizing the sliding window method was extricated. Fall was created utilizing AI classifiers and the result has indicated that the clustering algorithm performs best with 94 per cent exactness. Jessica *et al.* [96] presented a 90-second dread acceptance errand to gauge the movement of the member utilizing a wearable sensor to recognize small kids' nervousness and discouragement. Tests were taken from 64 youngsters and were exposed to a potential risk period of 20 seconds. The creators at that point exposed the information to the k-nearest neighbor model and demonstrated that the best outcome was given by the 75% exactness of the proposed model.

18.11   Blockchain-Enabled IoT Platforms for Automation in Intelligent Transportation Systems

Improvements in the Internet of vehicles (IoV) area are snappier than any time in recent memory, attributable to the advancements in Internet innovation and vehicle gear. Fundamentally, this energizing IoV area is proposed to improve the security of streams sooner rather than later, while upgrading vehicle offices, transportation in restructurings, and the way of life of residents. A tremendous proportion of information will be made and moved to the vehicles' cloud and edge reserves similarly to the vehicle benefits that will be improved for IoV. To give an expansive scope of utilization benefits, certain information and assets will be imparted to one another. Specifically, for AI applications, vehicles react to cloud and edge figuring hubs to release assignments and additionally measure undertakings locally by offering assets to one another to diminish inertness and data transfer capacity. There are numerous difficulties in coordinating the IoV worldview with current Internet innovations, including insurance, protection, trust, transparency, network and execution [97, 98]. The issues related to it will be presented with the headway of IoV availability. In such a manner, a significant number of the issues are interlinked with ITS. Truth be told, the IoV environment has various qualities and, all the more explicitly, a portion of these are exceptional contrasted with other IoT applications. Consequently, the IoV biological system could bear various novel difficulties;

(a)   Elevated mobility
(b)   Cellular Networks Difficulty
(c)   Critical Device Latency
(d)   Heterogeneity and Scalability
(e)   Artificial Intelligence (AI)

For most IoV applications, Blockchain can incorporate a tremendous scope of creative arrangements. Most IoV situations are ongoing and versatile, producing and sharing a lot of information. Specifically, numerous exemplary methods are probably not suitable and powerful in IoV circumstances. Additionally, expanding availability in such situations can give some attacking vectors to noxious elements [99]. Blockchain coordination into IoV improves security, insurance, and certainty, yet in addition upgrades the framework's proficiency and mechanization. To oblige adaptability and handle huge information, blockchain-like, solid innovations ought to along these lines be utilized. Coming up next are some major animating parts for the gathering of blockchain in IoV. Regardless of anything else, decentralization is one of the central excellencies of the blockchain. Blockchain enables decentralized IoV associations to be made and consolidates more dispersed components that can be RSUs, vehicles and individuals. These dispersed associations, simultaneously, can autonomously deal with their tasks. The working standards of the current IoV organization, which depend predominantly on focal dynamic, will be changed over into a decentralized model and smoothed out. Eventually, decentralization can upgrade the client experience of vehicle administrations. *Second,* blockchain diminishes the reliance on cloud-like frameworks on information stockpiling and upkeep.

Also, blockchain and smart contracts permit outsider elements, for example, the focal assistance director, control focus, heads, and confided in go-betweens to be taken out. All things being equal, clients of the blockchain organization will hold vehicle offices and exchanges all alone, adding to bring down running expenses. *Third,* the IoV blockchain appropriation would conceivably address security dangers, for example, disturbance, single-purpose of-failure, and attacks on ease of use. This is because of the synchronization and replication of the blockchain across all friend hubs associated with the network. In this way, despite the fact that at least one hub is included, the administrations are equipped for working easily. Then again, blockchain innovation depends on cutting edge cryptographic strategies to shield normal security and protection assets. Truth be told, cryptography for improved security and protection for IoV networks is accentuated by blockchain. *Fourthly*, blockchain gives high immutable IoV services and situations as the blocks keep a chain through the hash estimations of each square record to speak with one another in the blockchain. Hypothetically, this blockchain permanence highlight abstains from altering and information adjustment and furthermore assists with examining information proficiently. Besides, it empowers the sending and requirement with any predefined laws or contents with the assistance of a savvy contract. *Fifth*, distributed (p2p) [60] exchange, sharing, and coordinated effort between two elements are upheld by blockchain. Administration requesters and suppliers can grow direct interchanges through the p2p network between them. This p2p include is especially helpful for dividing information and assets among vehicles and RSUs safely for IoV situations. Since elements do not have to associate with any p2p network go-between, low idleness applications and administrations are viable. *Sixth*, heterogeneous elements that may not believe each other are connected by the IoV. Blockchain can make deep trust among even untrusted entertainers, driven by novel agreement systems. The shrewd agreement may likewise assume a significant job, notwithstanding agreement components, in managing trust issues and settling on choices with no confided in gathering. Likewise, the savvy contract additionally helps with accomplishing a coordinated and independent structure through its contents. At long last, the blockchain of people, in general, is un-approved and is by and largely open to all associations. At that point, the utilization of the public blockchain would make the way for full admittance to the blockchain's information. It can expand the receptiveness of the IoV environment, as well. In Table 18.2, we present different Blockchain-empowered IoV situations;

Military Applications: In today's advancement in technology, defence services have demonstrated incredible premium in blockchain innovation in nations, for example, the United States, Russia, China, and even NATO, and are beginning to analyse how to exploit the benefits of this innovation, to improve military strength. For armed forces, blockchain innovation may give focal points, for example, Cyber-assault counteraction by different countries or psychological militant gatherings, safeguard of delicate weapons frameworks, automatic frameworks, affirmation of requests and

Table 18.2 Blockchain-enabled IoV.

Application scenarios	Descriptions	How blockchain brings opportunities
Data Protection and Management	The vehicles share their created information in close by RSUs just as different vehicles. furthermore, use the put-away and shared information. The conditions of conveyed RSUs and vehicles for vehicular related administrations bring about the troubles to guarantee security and protection, for example, information respectability. information accessibility. furthermore, security of the vehicles while guaranteeing the trust among the RSUs without depending on any outsider.	Blockchain-helped IoV has demonstrated that blockchain offers decentralization of vehicle information of executives which dispose of the unified administration and control approaches through replication and agreement instruments. Blockchain has been used in vehicle information insurance because of its permanence and decentralization highlights to handle the information uprightness and accessibility issues. It has likewise offered significantly more productive vehicular information to the executives contrasted with customary dataset administration framework while guaranteeing security prerequisites through current cryptographic procedures.

(*Continued*)

Table 18.2 Blockchain-enabled IoV. (*Continued*)

Application scenarios	Descriptions	How blockchain brings opportunities
Data and Resource Trading	The IoV permits vehicles to exchange their produced information just as own figuring and correspondence assets through the Internet. Where the vehicles want immediate and free exchanging among others.	Blockchain has been used to set up shared (p2p) information just as asset exchanging among the vehicles were exchanging and instalment offices are conveyed in decentralized record network which is kept up by just the clients like vehicles This free exchanging has assisted with diminishing the exchange costs essentially.
Vehicle Management	Because of the heterogenicity and an enormous number of substances associated with IoV organization, for example, RSUs. vehicles and specialist organization units to give keen leaving like administrations, it is trying to safeguard the protection of clients just as actualize the entrance control while the framework is under unified control Moreover, the IoV network turns out to be more mind-boggling to oversee.	The utilization of blockchain has been possibly improved the vehicle administrations in savvy leaving and vehicle platooning frameworks by its decentralization include. The vehicle the executives over the decentralized organization has encouraged the check of the administration solicitations and commitments through the smart agreement.

(*Continued*)

Table 18.2 Blockchain-enabled IoV. (*Continued*)

Application scenarios	Descriptions	How blockchain brings opportunities
Ride Sharing	It is turning into a pattern to incorporate the vehicles and clients into ride-sharing administrations through the Internet which are normally founded on the cloud stage. Re-appropriating the data of clients to the cloud can bargain the weak security of clients.	Blockchain has offered better ride-sharing administrations contrasted with cloud-based administrations as far as lower correspondence delay and speedier information recovery. It has additionally offered vehicles and travellers looking and coordinating locally through RSUs as opposed to passing cloud stages.
Content Broadcasting	Content telecom is the ability of the IoV framework to spread both non–well-being and security substances through vehicles and RSUs, which might be semitrusted. nontrusted and assault inclined. Subsequently, the dependence of the vehicles and RSUs have put the danger of being adjusted the substance malignantly.	Blockchain has been received to guarantee the dependability of the substance. Keeping blockchain that contains the substance records in different hubs has encouraged quick distributing of substance. Also, the permanence include has made the substance solid obstruction against information trustworthiness attack.

(*Continued*)

Table 18.2 Blockchain-enabled IoV. (*Continued*)

Application scenarios	Descriptions	How blockchain brings opportunities
Traffic Control and Management	The vehicle traffic the board framework is reliant on information created by vehicles just as RSUs for capacity. This framework might be defenseless against security and protection.	Not the same as the conventional one which regularly uses incorporated control for traffic the board. blockchain use in rush hour gridlock framework has demonstrated that blockchain has furnished a decentralized administration and control with agreement systems The solid unchanging nature and multiple capacity highlights of blockchain have upgraded the openness yet at the same time guaranteed better security insurance against Denial of Service (DoS) assaults Moreover, the brilliant agreement executed in blockchain has been useful to deal with the board and control terms of confirmation and approval without depending on believed key age places and self-ruling recognition of malignant vehicle clients.

subtleties of combat zone or store network the executives, and coordinations. Numerous specialists accept that its utilization joined with artificial intelligence, will be more viable. A few assessments state that over 80% of organizations working in the protection business intend to coordinate this innovation into their various cycles in 2021. Solid and brisk contention: Every day, rivalry between countries is more noteworthy to fuse the capacities of the blockchain inside the military field, as it exhibits an upper hand over the contender and is viewed as an image of military predominance.

The United States is, at any rate formally, previously starting to investigate the conceivable outcomes of coordinating blockchain, similar to its NATO accomplices, into its military machines. The IoT (Internet of Things) advancement related to it is specifically noteworthy to them. In area 1646 of the 2018 National Security Doctrine Act, given by Congress, Blockchain has delegated an innovation that the military should give unique consideration to. In 2018, a coordinated effort with ITAMCO, an organization in Indiana, was declared by the United States Naval Aviation Command. They plan to strengthen the whole marine avionics industry by joining a blockchain into it. As indicated by them, this will permit the better aeroplane to save parts observing, prompting lower working expenses. The Defence Department of the United States has likewise caused to notice the blockchain. The whole production network through which $100 billion worth of hardware and supplies go through will be improved, as they would like to think. In 2015, a report was delivered that prominent all the constraints of the current coordination's arrangement of the US military. It was noticed that such weaknesses will be invalidated by the blockchain. It got known in 2016 that the Department of Advanced Research Projects (DARPA) began investigating blockchain under the Ministry of Defence to defend its information on various weapons, including codes for the dispatch of intercontinental ballistic rockets with atomic warheads. DARPA is not the lone military association that requirements to utilize blockchain innovation. The North Atlantic Treaty Organization (NATO), an intergovernmental military coalition covering 28 Member States, is likewise meaning to add blockchain-based answers for the military.

In April 2018, NATO declared that it was a time of problematic arrangements that are looking for new companies that can help assemble blockchain-based military applications pointed toward quickening ground-breaking, innovation answers for meet NATO C4ISR and digital prerequisites. NATO, nonetheless, is all the more comprehensively wanting to utilize the blockchain in military framework, preparing, and account. In Russia, the Russian Ministry of Defence declared in 2018 that it had set up a research centre for the investigation of digital danger insurance in the district. It tends to the abilities of the blockchain in distinguishing and fore-stalling gate crasher assaults on military foundation offices. As indicated by TASS, the Russian Defence Ministry is building up its encryption calculations based on decentralized advancements. They will be utilized for the sharing of data among armed force units. With respect to China, it began to fabricate a military coordination's framework dependent on blockchain innovation in 2016, and in 2019, the Global Times said the Chinese armed force had started an arrangement of impetuses and compensations for its staff and fighter's dependent on blockchain innovation.

In the most recent decade, with the rise of a few advances, AI and ML has gone through a restoration, including profound learning on monstrous marked coevolutionary neural network datasets (CNNs) and generous advancement towards the acknowledgement of self-driving vehicles, with certain appraisals foreseeing that 95%, all things considered, will act natu-rally driving vehicles by 2040. Be that as it may, in the assembling pipeline of AI and ML procedures, they have not discovered their way into military applications. There are valid justifications for this since these cutting-edge strategies presently endure certain inadequacies that make them inad-missible for use in the jumbled, contested, complex, and quickly moving conditions in which the US Army operates. The alleged "mist of war" will just increment as the war zone parts into different domains, going from traditional to metropolitan fighting, from actual space to virtual space, and from unmistakably delineated battle zones to an apparently incomprehen-sible social landscape. Army Research Laboratory (ARL) is attempting to tackle a portion of these issues with both modern and naturally created AI/ML strategies to determine the holes between best in class draws near and the military rules for operationalizing this innovation for the combat zone of things to come.

While assessing the idea of US Army task sets, obviously sent frame-works should be solid, rough, and adaptable. As usual, the Army should conform to an enormous scope of mission sets. The US Army, alongside a few experts, have anticipated in examinations such as] that the Army would work in "Thick Urban Environments," megacities clogged with individuals, complex framework, and overlaid with a digital social terri-tory that will require a multi-space approach and incorporate computer-ized reasoning that can react to consistently changing changes rapidly and powerfully. As a general rule, as per the United States Army Capabilities Integration Centre (ARCIC), problematic advances, for example, advanced robotized, self-sufficiency, AI, and digital fighting will be significant for megacities activities, and AI is portrayed as presumably the most trouble-some innovation of our time. ARL's modified essential examination has recognized three key exploration challenge regions for the AI and ML age that help centre examination endeavours around consider that will prompt the proper and extended capacities of the trooper:

(a) **Complex Data Environments Learning:** The US Army's operational climate is really overwhelming and frequently capricious. In conditions that contain a ton of "messiness" and "clog" past actual elements, however, even as far as the internet and social information, new AI and ML methods are expected to deal with datasets that have not many examples, uproarious information and capacity. Not exclusively is this information hard to access ahead of time and significantly harder to measure, however, it comprises a wide assortment of information types, including sound, video, text, network traffic, web-based media, news, remote and numerous other heterogeneous types of data. In this climate, a portion of the occasions and information streams (for example megacity) might be common and expected, while others might be tricky and antagonistic, purposefully created to upset the advancement of the Army. Challenged and tricky conditions will be particularly tested in managing complex and close companion adversaries, making the requirement for AI and ML techniques that are powerful and versatile, yet can likewise induce, evaluate and clarify the vulnerability of different situations.

(b) **Resource Limited Processing at the Point of Need:** Dissimilar to the business AI and ML application pipeline, which fundamentally depends on expansive and stable preparing information and generally static working conditions with admittance to critical figuring assets, the military's operational climate is one of learning in intricate, dynamic and to a great extent eccentric condition. Admittance to incredible distributed computing administrations will probably be restricted or inaccessible in military settings. Force on the combat zone is consistent including some built-in costs, and to guarantee that the mission can deal with the weight and size of parts, actual stacking should be improved. Later on, combat zone, this "war zone stuff" organization will require calculations comprising of many interconnected gadgets that run productively spread over a possibly enormous number of less incredible CPUs working with unreliable availability to take care of complex learning issues and give helpful, convenient examination and administrations to the war-fighter.

(c) **Generalizable and Predictable Artificial Intelligence:** Vulnerability measurement is essential for AI and ML strategies that, as referenced prior, will be utilized later in a combat zone. This infers that these techniques should be unsurprising so that mix-ups are not shocking and execution imperatives are known. The present business AI and ML strategies give off an impression of being exact and confined, and not general. The examination is expected to create strategies that sum up and that can move to gain starting with one model then onto the next, likewise in another space. This will incorporate methodologies that have implicit quantitative models that not just produce a progression of results dependent on an "ideal" choice or evaluation, but would incorporate some thought of the consistency of the judgment or appraisal and clarify the way toward thinking, furnishing the trooper with an avocation for the strategy. It might likewise be conceivable to remember arrangements for human-for the-circle preparing that will permit calculation programming to consent to the exhibition prerequisites

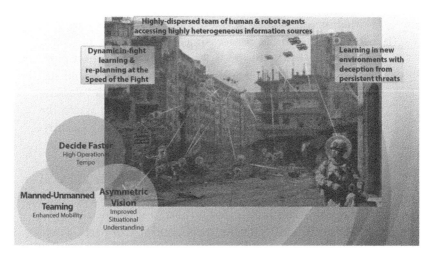

Figure 18.5 Future envision on battlefield using artificial intelligence and machine learning [3].

of explicit missions. Figure 18.5 depicts the future battlefield using AI and ML advancements.

Satellite Communications: Blockchain provides a new opportunity for ML algorithms used in communications and networking systems, thanks to the key features of blockchain, including decentralization, immutability, and transparency.

Further, readers are suggested to refer articles [102–110] to know recent trends with emerging technologies, i.e., as future work or for their research work.

18.12   Conclusion

Blockchain enhances the power of machine learning, a branch of artificial intelligence. Similar to how an IoT device's lifespan extends when it utilises cloud computing for the best possible storage. Hence, with the integration of AI, Blockchain, IoT, and Cloud Computing, we have witnessed significant evolutions in various industries and applications. This work offers numerous viewpoints on cutting-edge technology, including AI, IoT, Blockchain, and Cloud Computing, which may be useful in a variety of applications and industries. We also cover "how AI and Blockchain will benefit IoT in terms of architecture, system usage, and security" in this study. So, with the help of this trinity (AI, Blockchain and IoT), significant progress will be made in various areas, and it will be useful for many things in the near future. The main goal of this study is to briefly describe how AI and Blockchain may be used to support IoT and the difficulties that they may encounter when doing so. In conclusion, this work discusses a variety of topics, including AI and Blockchain incorporating IoT in industries like agriculture, healthcare, the military, education, CRM, and digital marketing, among others, as well as the difficulties that are encountered during the integration of these technologies. This chapter is also directed at other academics who may be able to use this work to develop new perspectives on AI and blockchain and create a more beneficial final result for society.

References

1. Nair, M.M. and Tyagi, A.K., Chapter 11 - AI, IoT, blockchain, and cloud computing: The necessity of the future, in: *Distributed Computing to Blockchain*, Pandey, R., Goundar, S., Fatima, S. (Eds.), pp. 189–206, Academic Press, 2023, https://doi.org/10.1016/B978-0-323-96146-2.00001-2.

2. Czarnowski, I., Jedrzejowicz, P., Chao, K.M., Yildirim, T., *Overcoming "Big Data"*, 2018.

3. Fossaceca, J.M. and Young, S.H., *Artificial intelligence and machine learning for future army applications*, 2018.

4. Tyagi, A.K., Bansal, R., Anshu, Dananjayan, S., A step-to-step guide to write a quality research article, in: *Intelligent Systems Design and Applications. ISDA 2022. Lecture Notes in Networks and Systems*, vol 717, Abraham, A., Pllana, S., Casalino, G., Ma, K., Bajaj, A. (Eds.). Springer, Cham, 2023. https://doi.org/10.1007/978-3-031-35510-3_36.

5. Website: https://www.geeksforgeeks.org/integration-of-blockchain-and ai

6. Holzinger, A., *Introduction in machine learning and knowledge extraction*, 2016.

7. Jordan, M.I. and Mitchell, T.M., Machine learning: Trends, perspectives, and prospects. *Science*, 349, 255–260, 2015.

8. Holzinger, A., Dehmer, M., Jurisica, I., Knowledge discovery and interactive data mining in bioinformatics - state-of-the-art, future challenges and research directions. *BMC Bioinformatics*, 15, Suppl 6, I1, 2014, https://doi.org/10.1186/1471-2105-15-S6-I1.

9. Ghahramani, Z., Probabilistic machine learning and artificial intelligence. *Nature*, 2015.

10. Domingos, P., The role of Occam's Razor in knowledge discovery. *Data Min. Knowl. Discov.*, 3, 409–425, 1999, https://doi.org/10.1023/A:1009868929893.

11. Shreyas Madhav, A.V., Mohan, A., Tyagi, A.K., IMPROVE: Intelligent machine learning based portable, reliable and optimal verification system for future vehicles. *2023 International Conference on Computer Communication and Informatics (ICCCI)*, pp. 1–6, Coimbatore, India, 2023.

12. Guo, B., Zhang, D., Yu, Z., Liang, Y., Wang, Z., Zhou, X., *From the internet of things to embedded intelligence*, Springer, 2012.

13. Preethi, N., Performance evaluation of IoT result for machine learning. *Transaction on Engineering Science.*, 2014.

14. Sindhura, V., Ramya, P., Yelisetti, S., Manne, S., A platform approach for unlocking the value of IoT (Internet of Things). *2017 Second International Conference on Electrical, Computer and Communication Technologies (ICECCT)*, pp. 1–7, Coimbatore, India, 2017.

15. Alsheikh, M.A., Lin, S., Niyato, D., Tan, H.P., Machine learning in wireless sensor networks: Algorithms, strategies, and applications. *IEEE Commun. Surv. Tutor.*, 16, 2014.

16. Bengio, Y., *Learning deep architectures for AI*, Foundations and Trends in Machine Learning, 2009. https://www.iro.umontreal.ca/~lisa/pointeurs/TR1312.pdf

17. Tanwar, S., Bhatia, Q., Patel, P., Kumari, A., Singh, P.K., Hong, W.C., Machine learning adoption in blockchain-based smart applications: The challenges, and a way forward, 2017.

18. Bodkhe, U., Bhattacharya, P., Tanwar, S., Tyagi, S., Kumar, N., Obaidat, M.S., Blohost: Blockchain enabled smart tourism and hospitality management.

International Conference on Computer, Information and Telecommunication Systems (CITS), Beijing, China, 2019.

19. Kuzmin, A. and Znak, E., Blockchain-base structures for a secure and operate network of semi-autonomous unmanned aerial vehicles. *IEEE International Conference on Service Operations and Logistics, and Informatics (SOLI)*, Singapore, 2018.

20. Zhao, Y., Yu, Y., Li, Y., Han, G., Du, X., Machine learning based privacy preserving fair data trading in big data market. *Inf. Sci.*, 478, 449–460, April 2019, https://doi.org/10.1016/j.ins.2018.11.028.

21. Salah, K., Rehman, M.H.U., Nizamuddin, N., Al-Fuqaha, A., Blockchain for ai: Review and open research challenges. *IEEE Access*, 7, 2019.

22. Ucci, D., Aniello, L., Baldoni, R., Survey of machine learning techniques for malware analysis. *Comput. Secur.*, 81, 123–147, March 2019, https://doi.org/10.1016/j.cose.2018.11.001.

23. Mitchell, T.M., *Machine learning*, 1997.

24. Zheng, Z., Xie, S., Dai, H., Chen, X., Wang, H., An overview of blockchain technology: Architecture, consensus, and future trends. *IEEE International Congress on Big Data (BigData Congress)*, Honolulu, HI, USA, 2017.

25. Mermer, G.B., Zeydan, E., Arslan, S.S., An overview of blockchain technologies: Principles, opportunities and challenges. *26th Signal Processing and Communications Applications Conference (SIU)*, Izmir, Turkey, 2018.

26. Tyagi, A.K., Chapter 2 - decentralized everything: Practical use of blockchain technology in future applications. In: *Distributed Computing to Blockchain*, Pandey, R., Goundar, S., Fatima, S. (Eds.), pp. 19–38, Academic Press, 2023, https://doi.org/10.1016/B978-0-323-96146-2.00010-3.

27. Jin, X., Sarkar, S., Mukherjee, K., Ray, A., Suboptimal partitioning of time-series data for anomaly detection. *Proceedings of the 48h IEEE Conference on Decision and Control (CDC) held jointly with 2009 28th Chinese Control Conference*, Shanghai, China, 2009.

28. Chan, P.K. and Mahoney, M.V., Modelling multiple time series for anomaly detection. *Fifth IEEE International Conference on Data Mining (ICDM'05)*, Houston, TX, USA, 2005.

29. Teng, M., Anomaly detection on time series. *IEEE International Conference on Progress in Informatics and Computing*, Shanghai, China, 2010.

30. Ma, J. and Perkins, S., Time-series novelty detection using one-class support vector machines. *Proceedings of the International Joint Conference on Neural Networks*, Portland, OR, USA, 2003.

31. Gupta, M., Gao, J., Aggarwal, C.C., Han, J., Outlier detection for temporal data: A survey. *IEEE Trans. Knowl. Data Eng.*, 2013.

32. Malhotra, P., Vig, L., Shroff, G., Agarwal, P., *Long short-term memory networks for anomaly detection in time series*, 2015.

33. Chandola, V., Banerjee, A., Kumar, V., *Outlier detection: A survey*, Citeseer, 2007.

34. Pimentel, M.A., Clifton, D.A., Clifton, L., Tarassenko, L., A review of novelty detection. *Signal Process.*, 99, 215–249, June 2014, https://doi.org/10.1016/j.sigpro.2013.12.026.

35. Mörchen, F., Time series feature extraction for data mining using DWT and DFT, 2003. Available at: https://www.mybytes.de/papers/moerchen03time.pdf

36. Deng, H., Runger, G., Tuv, E., Vladimir, M., A time series forest for classification and feature extraction. *Inf. Sci.*, 239, 142–153, 1 August 2013, https://doi.org/10.1016/j.ins.2013.02.030.

37. Li, L., Noorian, F., Moss, D.J., Leong, P.H., Rolling window time series prediction using MapReduce. *Proceedings of the 2014 IEEE 15th International Conference on Information Reuse and Integration (IEEE IRI 2014)*, Redwood City, CA, USA, 2014.

38. Zyskind, G., Nathan, O., Pentland, A., *Enigma: Decentralized computation platform with guaranteed privacy*, 2015, arXiv:1506.03471v1.

39. Conoscenti, M., Vetro, A., De Martin, J.C., Blockchain for the internet of things: A systematic literature review. *13th International Conference of Computer Systems and Applications (AICCSA)*, Agadir, Morocco, 2016.

40. Dorri, A., Kanhere, S.S., Jurdak, R., *Blockchain in internet of things: Challenges and solutions*, 2016, arXiv:1608.05187.

41. Dorri, A., Kanhere, S.S., Jurdak, R., Towards an optimized blockchain for IoT. *Second International Conference on Internet-of-Things Design and Implementation (IoTDI)*, Pittsburgh, PA, USA, 2017.

42. Dorri, A., Kanhere, S.S., Jurdak, R., Gauravaram, P., Blockchain for IoT security and privacy: The case study of a smart home. *IEEE International Conference on Pervasive Computing and Communications Workshops (PerCom Workshops)*, Kona, HI, USA, 2017.

43. Wörner, D. and Von Bomhard, T., When your sensor earns money: Exchanging data for cash with bitcoin. *Proceedings of the 2014 ACM International Joint Conference on Pervasive and Ubiquitous Computing*, Adjunct Publication, 2014.

44. Nguyen, K.T., Laurent, M., Oualha, N., Survey on secure communication protocols for the Internet of Things. *Ad Hoc Netw.*, 32, 17–31, September 2015, https://doi.org/10.1016/j.adhoc.2015.01.006.

45. Ali, M., Nelson, J.C., Shea, R., Freedman, M.J., *Blockstack: A global naming and storage system secured by blockchains*, USENIX Association, 2016.

46. Zyskind, G., Nathan, O., Pentland, A.S., Decentralizing privacy: Using blockchain to protect personal data. *IEEE Security and Privacy Workshops*, San Jose, CA, USA, 2015.

47. Gervais, A., Karame, G.O., Wüst, K., Glykantzis, V., Ritzdorf, H., Čapkun, S., On the security and performance of proof of work blockchains. *Proceedings of the 2016 ACM SIGSAC Conference on Computer and Communications Security*, 2015.

48. Tyagi, A.K. and Abraham, A. (Eds.), *Recent Trends in Blockchain for Information Systems Security and Privacy*, 1st ed, CRC Press, 2021, https://doi.org/10.1201/9781003139737.

49. Heilman, E., Kendler, A., Zohar, A., Goldberg, S., *Eclipse attacks on bitcoins peer-to-peer network*, Cryptology ePrint Archive, 2015.

50. Ouaddah, A., Abou Elkalam, A., Ait Ouahman, A., *FairAccess: A new block-chain-based access control framework for the internet of things*, 2017, https://onlinelibrary.wiley.com/doi/epdf/10.1002/sec.1748.

51. Sai, G.H., Tyagi, A.K., Sreenath, N., Biometric security in Internet of Things based system against identity theft attacks. *2023 International Conference on Computer Communication and Informatics (ICCCI)*, pp. 1–7, Coimbatore, India, 2023.

52. Kshetri, N., Can blockchain strengthen the internet of things? *IT Prof.*, 19, 2017.

53. Crosby, M., Pattanayak, P., Verma, S., Kalyanaraman, V., *Blockchain technology: Beyond bitcoin*, 2016.

54. Jesus, E.F., Chicarino, V.R.L., de Albuquerque, C.V.N., Rocha, A.A.D.A., A survey of how to use blockchain to secure internet of things and the stalker attack. *Secur. Commun. Netw.*, 2018.

55. Dorri, A., Kanhere, S.S., Jurdak, R., *Blockchain in internet of things: Challenges and solutions*, 2016, arXiv:1608.05187.

56. Sun, Y., Song, H., Jara, A.J., Bie, R., Internet of things and big data analytics for smart and connected communities. *IEEE Access*, 2016.

57. Zolotukhin, M. and Hämäläinen, T., On artificial intelligent malware tolerant networking for IoT. *IEEE Conference on Network Function Virtualization and Software Defined Networks (NFV-SDN)*, Verona, Italy, 2018.

58. Singh, S.K., Rathore, S., Park, J.H., BlockIoT intelligence: A blockchain enabled intelligent iot architecture with artificial intelligence. *Future Gener. Comput. Syst.*, 2018.

59. Kilimci, Z.H., Akyokus, S., Omurca, S.I., The evaluation of heterogeneous classifier ensembles for Turkish texts. *2017 IEEE International Conference on INnovations in Intelligent SysTems and Applications (INISTA)*, pp. 307–311, Gdynia, Poland, 2017.

60. Huang, J., Kong, L., Chen, G., Wu, M., Liu, X., Zeng, P., Towards secure industrial IoT: Blockchain system with credit-based consensus mechanism. *IEEE Trans. Industr. Inform.*, 15, 2019.

61. Salahuddin, M.A., Al-Fuqaha, A., Guizani, M., Shuaib, K., Sallabi, F., Softwarization of internet of things infrastructure for secure and smart healthcare. *Computer (Long. Beach. Calif)*, 2017.

62. Sharma, P.K. and Park, J.H., Blockchain based hybrid network architecture for the smart city. *Future Gener. Comput. Syst.*, 86, 650–655, September 2018, https://doi.org/10.1016/j.future.2018.04.060.

63. Qu, C., Tao, M., Yuan, R., A hypergraph-based blockchain model and application in internet of things-enabled smart homes. *Sensors*, 18, 9, 2784, 2018, https://doi.org/10.3390/s18092784

64. Nair, M.M. and Tyagi, A.K., Blockchain technology for next-generation society: Current trends and future opportunities for smart era. In: *Blockchain Technology for Secure Social Media Computing*, 2023.

65. Yu Zhang, J.W., The IoT electric business model: Using blockchain technology for the internet of things, 2018.

66. WIlliams, R., *How bitcoin's technology could make supply chains more transparent*, 2015.
67. Online-source: www.itu.int/en/ITUD/Conferences/GSR/Documents/GSR2018/documents/AISeriesSecurity AspectsModuleGSR18.pdf
68. Okubo, F., Yamashita, T., Shimada, A., Ogata, H., A neural network approach for students' performance prediction, in: *Proceedings of the Seventh International Learning Analytics & Knowledge Conference (LAK '17)*. Association for Computing Machinery, pp. 598–599, New York, NY, USA, 2017, https://doi.org/10.1145/3027385.3029479.
69. Sclater, N., Peasgood, A., Mullan, J., *Learning analytics in higher education*, 2016. https://www.jisc.ac.uk/sites/default/files/learning-analytics-in-he-v2_0.pdf
70. Rubel, A., and Jones, K.M.L., Student privacy in learning analytics: An information ethics perspective. *Info. Soc.*, 32, 2, 143–159, 2016.
71. Tene, O. and Polonetsky, J., Big data for all: Privacy and user control in the age of analytics. *Northwest J. Technol. Intellect. Prop.*, 2013.
72. Flanagan, B. and Ogata, H., *Integration of learning analytics research and production systems while protecting privacy*, 2017.
73. Srivastava, S., Anshu, Bansal, R., Soni, G., Tyagi, A.K., Blockchain enabled Internet of Things: Current scenario and open challenges for future. In: *Innovations in Bio-Inspired Computing and Applications. IBICA 2022. Lecture Notes in Networks and Systems*, Abraham, A., Bajaj, A., Gandhi, N., Madureira, A.M., Kahraman, C. (Eds.), vol. 649, Springer, Cham, 2023, https://doi.org/10.1007/978-3-031-27499-2_59.
74. Dahal, R.K., Bhatta, J., Dhamala, T.N., Performance analysis of sha-2 and sha-3 finalists. *International Journal on Cryptography and Information Security (IJCIS)*, 2013, https://pdfs.semanticscholar.org/8e14/93ae84dc-0c0bf89fc45dcc2ad1d936bbfcb1.pdf.
75. Barnes, T., and Stamper, J., Toward automatic hint generation for logic proof tutoring using historical student data. In: *Intelligent Tutoring Systems. ITS 2008. Lecture Notes in Computer Science*, Woolf, B.P., Aïmeur, E., Nkambou, R., Lajoie, S. (Eds.), vol 5091, Springer, Berlin, Heidelberg, 2008, https://doi.org/10.1007/978-3-540-69132-7_41.
76. IDC., *The digital universe study: Extracting value from chaos*, 2011.
77. Lohr, S., *The age of big data*, 2012.
78. *Drowning in numbers – digital data will flood the planet—And help us understand it better*, 2011. *Data, data everywhere*, 2010.
79. Noguchi, Y., *Following digital breadcrumbs to big data gold*, 2011.
80. Noguchi, Y., *The search for analysts to make sense of big data*, 2011.
81. Kalil, T., 2012, Online source: http://www.whitehouse.gov/blog/2012/03/29/big-data-big-deal.
82. Guo, Y., Yang, Z., Feng, S., Hu, J., Complex power system status monitoring and evaluation using big data platform and machine learning algorithms: A review and a case study. *Hindawi Complexity*, 2018.

83. Lonini, L., Dai, A., Shawen, N., Simuni, T., Poon, C., Shimanovich, L. *et al.*, Wearable sensors for Parkinson's disease: Which data are worth collecting for training symptom detection models, 2018.

84. Goodfellow, D., Zhi, R., Funke, R., Pulido, J.C., Mataric, M., Smith, B.A., *Predicting infant motor development status using day long movement data from wearable sensors*, 2018, arXiv:1807.02617.

85. Kitagawa, K., Uezono, T., Nagasaki, T., Nakano, S., Wada, C., Classification method of assistance motions for standing-up with different foot antero-posterior positions using wearable sensors. *International Conference on Information and Communication Technology Robotics (ICT-ROBOT)*, Busan, Korea (South), 2018.

86. Kaur, P. and Malhotra, S., *Improved SLreduct framework for stress detection using mobile phone-sensing mechanism in wireless sensor network*, Springer, 2019.

87. Hassan, M.M., Huda, S., Uddin, M.Z., Almogren, A., Alrubaian, M., *Human activity recognition from body sensor data using deep learning*, Springer, 2018.

88. Kanjo, E., Younis, E.M., Ang, C.S., Deep learning analysis of mobile physiological, environmental and location sensor data for emotion detection. *Inf. Fusion*, 49, 46–56, September 2019, https://doi.org/10.1016/j.inffus.2018.09.001.

89. Yacchirema, D., de Puga, J.S., Palau, C., Esteve, M., Fall detection system for elderly people using IoT and big data. *Procedia Comput. Sci.*, 130, 603–610, 2018, https://doi.org/10.1016/j.procs.2018.04.110.

90. McGinnis, R.S., McGinnis, E.W., Hruschak, J., Lopez-Duran, N.L., Fitzgerald, K., Rosenblum, K.L. *et al.*, Wearable sensors and machine learning diagnose anxiety and depression in young children. *EEE EMBS International Conference on Biomedical & Health Informatics (BHI)*, Las Vegas, NV, USA, 2018.

91. Chattopadhyay, A., Lam, K.-Y., Tavva, Y., Autonomous vehicle: Security by design. *IEEE Trans. Intell. Transp. Syst.*, 22, 11, 7015–7029, Nov. 2021.

92. Hahn, D.A., Munir, A., Behzadan, V., Security and privacy issues in intelligent transportation systems: Classification and challenges. *IEEE Intell. Transp. Syst. Mag.*, 2019.

93. Kang, J., Yu, R., Huang, X., Wu, M., Maharjan, S., Xie, S., Zhang, Y., Blockchain for secure and efficient data sharing in vehicular edge computing and networks. *EEE Internet Things J.*, 6, 2018.

94. Javaid, U., Aman, M.N., Sikdar, B., Drivman: Driving trust management and data sharing in VANET with blockchain and smart contracts. *IEEE 89th Vehicular Technology Conference (VTC2019-Spring)*, Kuala Lumpur, Malaysia, 2019.

95. Xu, L.D., He, W., Li, S., Internet of Things in industries: A survey. *IEEE Trans. Ind. Inform.*, 10, 4, 2233–2243, Nov. 2014.

96. Li, S., Zhao, S., Yang, P., Andriotis, P., Xu, L., Sun, Q., Distributed consensus algorithm for events detection in cyber physical systems. *IEEE Trans. Industr. Inform.*, 10, 2019.

97. Muller, J.M., Kiel, D., Voigt, K.-I., What drives the implementation of industry 4.0? The role of opportunities and challenges in the context of sustainability, 2018.

98. Kiel, D., Arnold, C., Voigt, K.-I., The influence of the industrial Internet of Things on business models of established manufacturing companies–A business level perspective. *Technovation*, 68, 4–19, December 2017, https://doi.org/10.1016/j.technovation.2017.09.003.

99. Perera, C., Talagala, D.S., Liu, C.H., Estrella, J.C., Energy efficient location and activity-aware on-demand mobile distributed sensing platform for sensing as a service in IoT Clouds. *IEEE Trans. Comput. Soc. Syst.*, 2, 2015.

100. Jedrzejowicz, P., *Ensemble classifier for mining data streams*, Elsevier, 2014.

101. Nowak-Brzezińska, A., Enhancing the efficiency of a decision support system through the clustering of complex rule-based knowledge bases and modification of the inference algorithm. *Hindawi Complex.*, 2018.

102. Tyagi, A.K. (Ed.), *Handbook of research on quantum computing for smart environments*, IGI Global, 2023, https://doi.org/10.4018/978-1-6684-6697-1.

103. V., S.A., Soni, G., Tyagi, A.K., A review on recent trends in quantum computation technology, in: *Handbook of Research on Quantum Computing for Smart Environments*, A. Tyagi (Ed.), pp. 48–64, IGI Global, 2023, https://doi.org/10.4018/978-1-6684-6697-1.ch003.

104. P., S., Soni, G., Tyagi, A.K., Kakulapati, V., J. S., S.M., Singh, R.K., Quantum computing and the qubit: The future of artificial intelligence, in: *Handbook of Research on Quantum Computing for Smart Environments*, A. Tyagi (Ed.), pp. 231–244, IGI Global, 2023, https://doi.org/10.4018/978-1-6684-6697-1.ch013.

105. Deshmukh, A., Patil, D.S., Soni, G., Tyagi, A.K., Cyber Security: New realities for industry 4.0 and society 5.0, in: *Handbook of Research on Quantum Computing for Smart Environments*, A. Tyagi (Ed.), pp. 299–325, IGI Global, 2023, https://doi.org/10.4018/978-1-6684-6697-1.ch017.

106. Tyagi, A., Kukreja, S., Nair, M.M., Tyagi, A.K., Machine learning: Past, present and future. *Neuroquantology*, 20, 8, 2022.

107. Goyal, D. and Tyagi, A., *A look at top 35 problems in the computer science field for the next decade*, 2020, 10.1201/9781003052098-40.

108. Mishra, S. and Tyagi, A.K., The role of machine learning techniques in internet of things-based cloud applications, in: *Artificial Intelligence-based Internet of Things Systems. Internet of Things (Technology, Communications and Computing)*, S. Pal, D. De, R. Buyya (Eds.), Springer, Cham, 2022, https://doi.org/10.1007/978-3-030-87059-1_4.

109. Nair, M.M., Tyagi, A.K., Sreenath, N., The future with industry 4.0 at the core of society 5.0: Open issues, future opportunities and challenges. *2021 International Conference on Computer Communication and Informatics (ICCCI)*, pp. 1–7, 2021.

110. Tyagi, A.K., Fernandez, T.F., Mishra, S., Kumari, S., Intelligent automation systems at the core of industry 4.0, in: *Intelligent Systems Design and Applications. ISDA 2020*, Advances in Intelligent Systems and Computing, vol. 1351, A. Abraham, V. Piuri, N. Gandhi, P. Siarry, A. Kaklauskas, A. Madureira (Eds.), Springer, Cham, 2021, https://doi.org/10.1007/978-3-030-71187-0_1.

Blockchain-Empowered Decentralized Applications: Current Trends and Challenges

Atharva Deshmukh[1], Anand Kumar Mishra[2], G. Balamurugan[3] and Amit Kumar Tyagi[4*]

[1]Department of Computer Science, Terna Engineering College, Navi Mumbai, Maharashtra, India
[2]Computer Science and Engineering, NIIT University, Neemrana, Rajasthan, India
[3]Department of Computing Technologies, SRM Institute of Science and Technology Kattankulathur Campus, Chengalpattu, Chennai, India
[4]Department of Fashion Technology, National Institute of Fashion Technology, New Delhi, Delhi, India

Abstract

Today, each application shifting itself toward decentralized and distributed technology to build trust and improve reliability among consumers/customers. Smart contract (blockchain 2.0) is one of the best applications of blockchain, which is being used today in land reforms, supply chain management, etc. A smart contract is an automated computerized protocol which is used to digitally facilitate, verify, or apply the agreement for the performance of a legal contract. Also, with this, many other uses of smart contracts and blockchain technology are increasing day by day, i.e., in agriculture, government welfare schemes, government records, healthcare, military uses, etc. Together, during the implementation of blockchain, many other serious issues, like scalability, standardization, lack of skilled people, security of data in blocks, etc., were raised in many applications. This work includes several blockchain-enabled several applications and discusses how blockchain has changed such applications' importance to a certain level for industry 4.0 and Society 5.0. Also, some other useful points/insights regarding blockchain for the smart era have been included in this work.

[*]Corresponding author: amitkrtyagi025@gmail.com

Amit Kumar Tyagi (ed.) Privacy Preservation of Genomic and Medical Data, (481–502) © 2024 Scrivener Publishing LLC

Keywords: Blockchain technology, decentralized technology, smart contract, smart era, privacy, security

19.1 Introduction

Blockchain is a revolutionary technology that is beginning to change the world today. It has gained a lot of popularity over recent years both in industry and academia. The blockchain was first implemented in 2009. Since then, it has been referred to and mentioned along with famous terms, such as cryptocurrency. However, they are not the same. The blockchain is the mechanism that makes it possible for cryptocurrencies to exist the way they do. Centralized systems of the global financial markets, made possible by sizable intermediaries like banks and investment companies, faltered and started to fall apart in the latter half of 2008 and early 2009. When the financial markets collapsed, confidence in these systems began to weaken, and fear spread throughout the whole world. A workable prototype of a peer-to-peer, decentralized digital currency system named bitcoin was to be introduced to the public at this point.

When neither verification nor audit methods are present, the issue of credibility and trust in information systems becomes incredibly difficult, especially when they deal with sensitive data like financial transactions involving digital currencies. In this framework, Satoshi Nakamoto introduced two revolutionary ideas in 2008 that have had a significant impact. The first of them is bitcoin, a digital money whose value is unaffected by any centralized authority or financial organization. Instead, a decentralized peer-to-peer network of actors that makes up a network that is auditable and verifiable holds the coin collectively and safely. The second idea is blockchain, whose acceptance has grown even more than that of cryptocurrencies. This system has no central authority or administration. This system's trust intermediation was made possible by blockchain-related software. Blockchain gave money transfers the software-based verification, validity, record keeping, and integrity they needed. Since its inception, bitcoin has remained operational without interruption. More than 200,000 transactions are delivered per day, according to blockchain charts [1].

People started to wonder, "If you can exchange digital currency, why not any other digital assets?" once it initially became successful. With the introduction of a code runtime environment on another well-known blockchain, Ethereum (https://ethereum.org), this topic was finally solved around 2013. The extension of the validation, verification and recording to more digital assets, associated transactions, and systems was an innovation. Therefore, by offering intermediaries and non-currency peer-to-peer transaction, blockchain can play a vital role in the implementation of decentralized systems. The key features of the blockchain technology include decentralization, persistence, anonymity, and audibility. Incorporating techniques like encrypted hash, digital signs based on asymmetric cryptography, and distributed consensus strategy would ensure that blockchain is likely to operate in a decentralized way. Using blockchain technology, a transaction can be carried out in a decentralized manner. Blockchain can therefore significantly reduce costs and increase efficiency.

Organization of this work
Section 19.2 discusses about literature survey. Further, section 19.3 discusses about key characteristics of blockchain and then in section 19.4, we have discussed some of the challenges faced by blockchain then in next few sections, we have discussed about smart contracts and then in section 19.8, we have discussed the application of blockchain. Then we talked about future data storage issues and solutions.

19.2   Literature Survey

Decentralized applications (DApps) are digital apps or programs that function on a peer to peer (P2P) network of computers rather than a single computer. DApps, or "Dapps," exist independently of a single authority's jurisdiction and control. The Ethereum platform is commonly used to develop DApps, which may be used for a variety of purposes like as gaming, banking, and social networking. Truffle [2], an Ethereum development framework for smart contracts, enables the production of formal test cases for JavaScript or Solidity-based smart contracts based on predefined mathematical principles and logic. These test cases may be written in JavaScript and executed on a test network to validate different smart contract attributes [3]. According to the methodology used for data collection in this research, Web of Science has been indexing about 7,000 scientific papers on its own recently. Comprehensive research investigations are required to investigate an overview of the present body of related information due to the rise of publications in the blockchain area. Through a few review papers, practitioners and researchers have been informed about recent advancements and difficulties in the field of the blockchain [4].

Blockchain has enabled consumers and producers to verify and validate the information they share about themselves [5]. In the case of a

10-block blockchain, block number 10 contains the hash of the previous block, and the data from the current block is used to construct a new block. As a result, every block in the current chain is linked to every other block in the chain. Even the prior transaction is linked to the present one. A simple change to any transaction will now significantly modify the hash of the block. When any information is changed, the hash data for all preceding blocks must be changed, which is a difficult and time-consuming procedure. Furthermore, when a miner generates a block, the network's other users validate it. As a consequence, any probable data change or fabrication will be detected by the network. As a result, blockchain is analogous to an immutable distributed ledger that is almost tamper-proof.

There are several ways in which quantum computing could potentially be used to enhance or improve upon existing blockchain technology. For example:

- Quantum computers could be used to help secure blockchain networks through the use of quantum-resistant cryptographic techniques.
- Quantum computers could be used to perform complex calculations that are necessary for certain blockchain-based applications, such as modeling financial markets or optimizing supply chain networks.
- Quantum computers could be used to help verify the integrity of data stored on a blockchain, by providing a means to perform checks that are beyond the capabilities of classical computers.

19.3 Key Characteristics of Blockchain

There are several unique characteristics of blockchain are, which can be discussed as:

Decentralized: Conventional centralized transaction frameworks require every single transaction to be verified by a human interpreter at their respective trusted agency, which often paves way for cost and performance bottlenecks for the servers at the central position. On the contrary, in blockchain based systems, a transaction can be conducted between any two peers (P2P) without the need for central agency authentication. Blockchain can help to alleviate performance constraints at the central server and drastically lower server expenses (including development and operating costs).

Persistent: It is very challenging to tamper with the network's transactions since each one must be verified and logged in blocks that are distributed throughout the whole network. Each transmitted block would also undergo transaction verification and validation by other nodes. Therefore, any manipulation might be immediately found.

Anonymous: With a uniquely generated address, any user may interface with the blockchain network. A user might also create many addresses to protect their identity. There is no longer a single entity in charge of protecting user privacy. With the help of this method, the transactions recorded on the blockchain are kept somewhat private. Be aware that owing to an inherent restriction, blockchain cannot ensure full privacy protection.

Auditable: Because every transaction on the blockchain is validated and documented with a timestamp, users can quickly audit and monitor the history of records by getting access to any dispersed network node. Each transaction on the Bitcoin blockchain may be iteratively connected to previous transactions. It enhances the data recorded in the blockchain's transparency and traceability.

19.4 Challenges Faced by Blockchain Technology

Though blockchain technology has a great deal of promise for developing the next generation of the digital infrastructure, there are a variety of technical difficulties to overcome. To begin, scalability is a huge issue. For present, a bitcoin block can only be 1 MB in size, and a block is mined every 10 minutes or so. As a result, the Bitcoin network can only handle 7 transactions per second, rendering it unsuitable for high-frequency trading. Bigger blocks, on the other hand, need more storage space and travel more slowly over the network. Users will want to keep such a large blockchain running, which will eventually lead to centralization. As a result, balancing security and block size has grown problematic.

Moreover, selfish mining strategies have been proved to let miners to make more money than is fair to them. Miners conceal their extracted blocks in order to gain more cash in the future. Blockchain development is limited by the likelihood of many branches. As a result, certain solutions must be presented in order to overcome this issue.

19.4.1   Blockchain and Smart Contracts

Blockchain systems, which are decentralized, distributed networks that enable the generation and execution of smart contracts, are where smart contracts are commonly deployed. A blockchain is a decentralized digital ledger that is used by a network of computers to record transactions. A block is created for each transaction and added to a chain of blocks (hence the name "blockchain"). By doing this, a permanent, unalterable record of every network transaction is produced. The usage of a blockchain for smart contracts offers a number of significant advantages. First, because the parameters of the agreement are recorded on a public, decentralized ledger that cannot be changed, it assures the transparency and immutability of the contract. Second, it enables process automation and contract execution without the need for middlemen, which can lower transaction costs and boost efficiency. Finally, because there is no one point of control that can be exploited, the decentralized structure of the blockchain makes it immune to fraud or manipulation. Overall, the integration of smart contracts and blockchain technology provides a potent tool for automating complicated procedures and effectively, transparently, and securely enforcing the terms of contracts [6].

19.4.2   Smart Contracts

The key component of blockchain technology, the smart contract, has proven crucial in converting the bitcoin framework into a trust structure that supports a wide range of decentralized applications. A smart contract is a standalone code fragment that shares similarities with classes in object-oriented programs in terms of structure. It is a deployable piece of code containing information and capabilities. Functions are specifically used for message verification, validation, and message recording. An application's rules and regulations may be digitally facilitated, verified, validated, and enforced using a smart contract, which is executable code on the blockchain. Without the involvement of other parties, smart contracts enable legitimate transactions. These transactions may be monitored and are irrevocable [7].

In the actual world, a contract includes terms like requirements, laws, standards that must be followed, conditions, backup plans, and objects with provenance like dates and signatures. In a blockchain environment, a smart contract executes the contract rules for resolving a decentralized issue. Considering that it serves as both a rules engine and a gatekeeper, it seems sensible that the architecture of a smart contract must be well thought out.

19.4.3 Actions of a Smart Contract

The soul concept of a blockchain application is the smart contract. It serves as the equivalent of the human brain's operational logic layer for the verification and validation of application-specific circumstances, among other essential tasks, which are listed below:

- It simplifies the development of rules asset transfer in a decentralized network and paves way the declaration of rules for activities on the blockchain.
- It includes functions that may be called by accounts of participants or smart contracts via messages or function calls.
- It serves as the software-based intermediary for decentralized applications related to blockchain.
- These messages and their input parameters, coupled with extra information like the sender's address and timestamp, result in transactions that are recorded in the blockchain.
- The blockchain gains programmability and intelligence by having the parameters for its functions specified in the smart contracts [8, 9].
- Thus, a smart contract is unquestionably a key element of the decentralized blockchain application given all these essential characteristics.

19.5 The Use of Smart Contracts in Decentralized Autonomous Organizations

A decentralized autonomous organization, or DAO, is a blockchain-based system that enables individuals to coordinate and govern themselves through a set of self-executing rules placed on a public blockchain. There is a great wealth of literature in organization theory on different types of decentralized organizations. However, the term "decentralized autonomous organization" (DAO) did not initially appear until the

1990s, when it was used to characterize nonviolent decentralized action in the counter-globalization social movement or multiagent systems in an internet-of-things (IoT) context [10]. However, the previous idea of a Decentralized Autonomous Corporation (DAC), which was introduced a few years after the invention of Bitcoin, is where the present definition of DAOs originates (bitcoin). Early bitcoin enthusiasts used the terms "decentralized" and "distributed" autonomous corporations interchangeably in online forums and chats to refer to the DAC idea. DACs were referred to as a new kind of corporate governance that paid dividends to shareholders via tokenized tradable shares. Such organizations were defined as "open-source software dispersed across the computers of their stakeholders," "incorruptible," operating "without any human intervention," and having bylaws that were "publicly auditable." By simply "purchasing stock in the firm or being compensated in such stock for services rendered to the company," anybody might, in accordance with this definition, become a stakeholder in a DAC. Owners of DAC stocks would thereby be eligible for "a portion of its earnings, involvement in its growth, and/or a say in how it is run" [11].

19.5.1   Decentralized Applications

Decentralized applications (DApps) are applications that are built on the blockchain with the facilitation of smart contracts. DApps can be made for financial websites, gaming apps, social media, etc. Decentralized Apps help to provide the blockchain technology at the user level (application level).

Ethereum: Ethereum is a cryptocurrency and blockchain framework which allows the developer to create decentralized applications by running programmable code using the EVM (Ethereum Virtual Machine). As of the writing of this work, Ethereum is the most widely used blockchain technology for running smart contacts and DApps.

Solidity: Solidity is the most popular programming language used for writing smart contracts that run on Ethereum. Solidity is a Turing-complete and object-oriented programming language. It was developed by Christian Reitwiessner, Alex Beregszaszi, and several initial contributors to Ethereum. The first stable release of Solidity dates back to March of 2018 [12].

The following is the code snippet for a basic program written in Solidity language, that can increment or decrement a stored variable: '*count*'.

```
// SPDX-License-Identifier: MIT
pragma solidity ^0.8.13;

contract Counter {
    uint public count;

    // Function to get the current count
    function get() public view returns (uint) {
        return count;

    }

    // Function to increment the count by 1
    function inc() public {
        count += 1;

    }

    // Function to decrement the count by 1
    function dec() public {
    // This function will fail if count – 0
    count -= 1;
    }
    }
```

19.6   Smart Contracts: An Overview

A smart contract, which is executable code that runs on the blockchain, may be used to facilitate, carry out, and enforce the terms of an agreement. The basic purpose of a smart contract is to automatically carry out the terms of an agreement once the requirements are met. As a result, smart contracts promise to have lower transaction costs than traditional systems that require a trustworthy third party to enforce and carry out an agreement's provisions. Szabo developed the notion of smart contracts in 1994. Nevertheless, the notion did not become a reality until the introduction of blockchain technology. A smart contract is a mechanism that distributes digital assets to all or some of the involved parties when arbitrary pre-established parameters are met [13, 14].

In the literature, a smart contract has been defined in a wide variety of ways. According to some authors, smart contract code and smart legal contract are the two categories into which all definitions fall. Code that is saved, validated, and executed on a blockchain is referred to as smart contract code. The blockchain's properties and the programming language used to represent the contract determine completely how powerful this smart contract is. A code that completes or replaces legal contracts is referred to as a smart contract. Legal, political, and business institutions—rather than technology—are what give this smart contract its functionality. The first definition—smart contract code—will be the primary subject of this investigation [15]. A smart contract has an account balance, private storage, and executable code. Its state is determined by the storage and the contract balance. The status of the contract is updated and kept on the blockchain each time it is utilized.

Each contract will be given a 20-byte unique address. The contract code cannot be altered once it has been posted into the blockchain. Users only need to send a transaction to a contract's address in order to run it. To reach a consensus on its result, this transaction will then be carried out by each consensus node (also known as a miner) on the network. The state of the contract will then be updated as necessary. Depending on the transaction it gets, the contract may be able to send/receive messages, money from users or other contracts, keep money in its account balance, read/write to its private storage, or even create other contracts. Deterministic and nondeterministic smart contracts are the two different forms of these contracts. A deterministic smart contract is one that, when it is executed, does not need any input from a third party (from outside the blockchain). A smart contract that relies on data feeds or oracles from a third party is said to be nondeterministic. Consider a contract that needs to operate and is dependent on the current weather data, which is not present on the blockchain [16].

19.7   Smart Contract Platforms

Smart contracts may be developed and deployed using various blockchain technologies like as Ethereum, bitcoin, and NXT. Several platforms offer unique features for establishing smart contracts. Several platforms allow the use of high-level programming languages to create smart contracts. The authors discuss smart contracts in depth in Miller *et al.* [17].

19.8   Applications of Blockchain Technology

Today, blockchain is being used in many applications, the concept was stated usually for finance applications like Bitcoin but now its use has been shifted towards non-finance applications also.

Many details applications of blockchain can be found in, and a few essential decentralized partitions have been explained here:

A. BLOCKCHAIN FOR VALIDATING ARTIFICIAL INTELLIGENCE (AI) DECISIONS

Artificial intelligence and Blockchain end up being a solid mix, boosting pretty much every area in which they are applied. From food production network coordination and medical care record sharing to promoting incomes and monetary security, these apparatuses can be incorporated to refresh anything. AI and blockchain incorporation influence numerous territories, including security AI and blockchain, which will give a twofold shield against digital assaults [18].

Through an enormous dataset, AI can successfully mine and fabricate more current situations and find patterns dependent on information conduct (refer to Figure 19.1). Blockchain permits to wipe out of bugs and phoney informational collections effectively. On a decentralized blockchain foundation, new classifiers and examples created by AI can be checked and their legitimacy confirmed. In any buyer confronting network, for example, retail exchanges, this can be utilized. Information got from clients through the blockchain framework can be utilized by AI to create promoting computerization [19]. For validating AI decisions using Blockchain we can go with a retail company, e.g., which can be used to develop market trends from the sales transaction. As seen in Figure 19.1 above, each sales transaction will be reported in the infrastructure of the Blockchain based on the four events:

(a)   Transaction event—all single sales transactions are registered in the blockchain

(b)   Transaction validation—the validity of customer credentials will be carried out, e.g., creditworthiness, authentication, repeat sale.

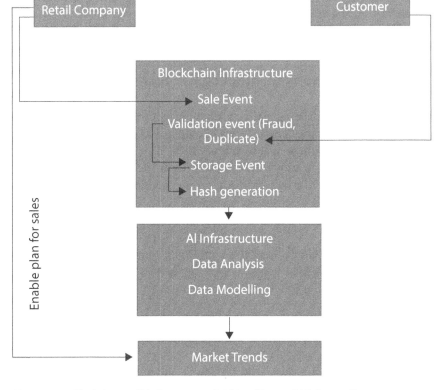

Figure 19.1 Blockchain validations on artificial intelligence (AI) for retail.

   (c)   Chain block storage—the successfully validated record will be stored in the blockchain in this situation.

   (d)   Hash generation—to identify the record in the block uniquely, any effective record will be created with a hash.

The retail company introduced an AI infrastructure to enable the retail company to use the genuine ledge red data (blockchain data) effectively for analysis. This AI infrastructure allows services, such as data analysis, data modelling, and complex algorithms to be designed to support business needs and as an output to provide Market trends. Due to the authenticity of the blockchain data, which is enhanced by the business algorithms within artificial intelligence, this market trend is very similar to the real business situation. As a result, the consumer trend can be considered very authentic and can be used as input to forecast future sales, allowing the retail business to plan future sales effectively [20]. We may infer from the above that blockchain and artificial intelligence technology brings successful business dynamics to help retail companies better manage their sales.

B. MACHINE LEARNING-BASED KNOWLEDGE EXTRACTION TECHNIQUES COLLECTED FROM SMART PLATFORMS

Information extraction is the advancement of data from organized (social information base, XML) and unstructured (text, archives, pictures) sources. The ensuing consensus should be in a machine-recognizable and machine-interpretable arrangement, and information should be passed on in a manner that empowers deriving. The key principles, while effective like data extraction or Natural Language Processing (NLP) and ETL (data conveyance focus) [21], are that the eventual outcome of extraction goes past the headway of composed information or the change into a social outline. It incorporates either the reuse of current coordinated information (reuse of identifiers or ontologies) or the advancement of a piece subject to source data. As of now, a resource description framework (RDF) extraction language from social databases is standardized by the RDB2RDF W3C clustering. To arrange ways to deal with this subject, the accompanying measures can be utilized (some of their account just for extraction from social information bases [22]: Source–Language, Relational Databases, XML, and CSV to secure data sources.

(a)   Exposition—How to make the information extracted transparent (ontological text, semantic database)? How is it possible to put it into question?

(b)   Synchronization—Is the information extraction strategy performed once to make a dump, or is the outcome adjusted to the source? Static or dynamic by the same token. Changes composed back to the outcome are (bidirectional).

(c)   Automation—how much extraction is helped/computerized. Manual, GUI, self-loader, programmed.

(d)   Includes area philosophy—a prior metaphysics is important to plan it. Either planning or construction is hence made from the source (ontology learning).

The objective is to characterize pertinent primary as well as transient examples ("information") in the information that are regularly disguised in discretionarily high-dimensional spaces where it is not accessible by people [23]. ML is as of now the quickest developing specialized territory, with numerous application areas, for example, smart well-being, keen processing plant (Industry 4.0), and so on, with numerous ordinary use cases, for example, proposal frameworks, discourse acknowledgement, self-governing driving, and so on, in importance making, in foundation mindfulness, and in dynamic under vulnerability, are the extraordinary challenges. This present reality is loaded with vulnerability and probabilistic information, and man-made brainpower and factual learning are colossally impacted by probabilistic deduction. The opposite likelihood allows unknowns to be inferred, data to be learned and forecast to help in decision making. Effective, useful and functional solutions for the discovery of knowledge and extraction of knowledge involve increasingly complex datasets. Some of the smart platforms' extractions of information are;

- **Knowledge extraction and text and data mining:** This category focuses on three areas: the extraction from documents of information elements such as named persons, relationships, and events; the construction of analytical tools for automated candidate evaluation, performance assessment mining, training suggestions, mining survey responses, and human capital assessment; and the construction of fraud and cash instruments.
- **Knowledge representation and reasoning:** The focus of this team is on learning and reasoning for complex automation tasks, such as question-answering and problem-solving for specific domains using organized knowledge graphs. The techniques used range from hierarchical Bayesian modelling and probabilistic graphic models to probabilistic logic, sampling of Monte Carlo and Natural Language Processing (NLP). The aim is to dramatically increase the reliability and effectiveness of business operations [24].
- **Ontology learning (OL):** Philosophy learning is the mechanized or self-loader production of metaphysics, including the extraction of the related space terms from a natural language text. Since it is amazing work escalated and tedious to physically make ontologies, there is an extraordinary motivating force to computerize the cycle.
- **Ontology-based information extraction (OBIE):** Philosophy-based data extraction is a sub-field of data extraction that controls the way toward extricating data from common language messages utilized in metaphysics.

The OBIE framework utilizes conventional strategies for the extraction of data to depict implications, examples, and connections of the ontologies utilized in the content that will be coordinated into metaphysics after the technique. Hence, the information ontologies comprise the data model to be gotten.

- **Semantic annotation (SA):** During semantic clarification, natural language text is improved with metadata (oftentimes described in RDFa) that should make the semantics of contained words sensible by the system. In this cycle, which is generally self-loader, data are taken out as an association is outlined between lexical terms and ontological thoughts, for example. Data on the perception of a word in the readied setting is then learned and the significance of the substance is then established on machine-recognizable data with the ability to draw determinations. Semantic clarification is normally part of the going with two subtasks: phrasing extraction and object interface.

- **Language annotation/natural language processing (NLP):** The biggest extent (about 80%) of the data contained in business records is put away in natural language and is in this way unstructured. Since unstructured information is a test for information extraction, further developed procedures are required, which will in general create more awful outcomes contrasted with organized information as a rule. The potential for an enormous procurement of removed data, notwithstanding, could adjust the expanded unpredictability and the diminished effectiveness of extraction. Normal roots of language are perceived in the accompanying as wellsprings of data, where the information is given in an unstructured way as plain content. On the off chance that the given content is likewise implanted in an increased report (for example, an HTML record), the increased components are normally separated consequently by the frameworks referenced previously. One or a few NLP devices might be important to perform semantic comment as a prehandling venture for the extraction of data. Generally, singular modules expand on apparatus explicit info and yield designs in an NLP work process; however, normalized designs have been presented with regard to information extraction to speak to phonetic comments.

Typical NLP assignments applicable to the extraction of information include

(a) Part-of-speech labeling (POS).
(b) Lemmatization (LEMMA) or stemming (STEM).
(c) Disambiguation of the set of terms (identified with semantic explanation beneath).
(d) Named object acknowledgement (additionally, observe IE beneath).
(e) Syntactic parsing, regularly receiving syntactic conditions.
(f) Shallow syntactic parsing (CHUNK): lumping yields, if execution is an issue, a basic extraction of ostensible and different expressions.
(g) Resolution by anaphora resolution (see the co-reference goal in IE beneath, yet observed here as the undertaking to make joins between printed specifies as opposed to between the notice of a substance and a theoretical portrayal of the element).
(h) Semantic naming of positions (identified with connection extraction; not to be mistaken for semantic comment as depicted beneath).
(i) Debate parsing (relations between various sentences, infrequently utilized in true applications).

In NLP, such information is ordinarily spoken to in TSV designs, frequently alluded to as CoNLL designs (CSV designs with TAB as separators). For data extraction work, RDF sees on such information have been made as per the accompanying network norms:

(a) Format for NLP Interchange (for frequent types of annotation).
(b) Annotation from the internet (often used for entity linking).
(c) CoNLL-RDF-RDF (for annotations originally represented in TSV formats).
(d) Include other platform-specific formats.
(e) The LAPPS interchange format (LIF, used in the LAPPS Grid).
(f) Format for Annotation of NLP (used in the News Reader workflow management system).

19.9   Future Data Storage Issues in Blockchain and Its Solution

Although blockchain is on the ascent, current stockpiling structures are not by any means the only innovation that strains it. The current putting away cut-off points are in addition attempted by Artificial Intelligence (AI), and especially the Internet of Things (IoT). It is expected that by 2025, there will be more than 40 billion related gadgets, all of which will pass on gigantic proportions of information and sometime later require administrators, clustering and recovery. Related contraptions all have their effect in making putting away interest, getting together with client personalization applications and the developing need to share information across business lines. Affiliations wanting to dispatch new information-driven applications face a load of time, exertion and engineering to have new information bases today. It pushes towards a more extravagant, more information-focused (and information-substantial) method of working against a worldwide foundation of significant information penetrates from concentrated server farms. It is a stressing blend: business reliance on data that prompts amazingly a lot of it being put away in problematic incorporated information bases, making peril on a scale once in a while observed previously. The usage of decentralized applications dependent on blockchain innovation is likewise causing new issues as they can trade huge amounts of information that should be prepared and directed [25–32].

Decentralized networks, with highlights that satisfy the down-to-earth needs of putting away huge information volumes, can assemble the best parts of blockchain advancement. As the name proposes, decentralized capacity works by dispersing the information through a network of hubs likewise to the circulated record advancement for the blockchain. An exceptionally unified single framework and cloud-based information bases are as of now accessible, which makes them a reference point for programmers hoping to strike. They likewise have obvious purposes of weakness if, for instance, a controlling organization's foundation is upset because of a force blackout. Interestingly, decentralized capacity doesn't confront these issues since it utilizes geologically dispersed hubs, either territorially or worldwide. Any assault or disappointment won't have an overwhelming effect at a solitary stage, since different hubs will keep on running in different sections. These additionally offers the benefits of making decentralized breaking point uncommonly flexible, as customers can doubtlessly get to a business focal point of cutoff suppliers and high cutoff, as the intensity of the affiliation gives better uptime. While decentralized cutoff shows two or three of the fundamental highlights of the blockchain, we truly need to reevaluate how information is dealt with on the blockchain. Since blockchain has been over-trouble with trades, it has expected to look for responses to the adaptability question. It is simply not possible to store a great deal of blockchain data.

As a solution to the above-discussed problem, swarming and sharding can be used here. Two key corresponding advancements address these issues. The first of these is sharding, *where information* bases are passed along legitimate lines. These shards are gathered away and got in a decentralized amassing model by a decentralized application utilizing a specific package key. Additionally, as the blockchain utilizes a middle point affiliation, decentralized cut-off utilizes huge parties of focus to store and regulate information. The multitude impact decreases dormancy and improves speed by recovering information equally from the closest and quickest hubs, much as downpours do. For current information stockpiling suppliers, the system in the hubs and multitudes is not run by a solitary individual, most essentially. They are claimed by and worked by people. Data-storing customers will be given the benefits of buying from inside and outside one-of-a-kind business focal points of providers, instead of the current oligopoly that faces them today. New players will enter the market and the enthusiasm for how information is dealt with will be improved. This will require a gigantic premium in a market that is hazard reluctant. In any case, it will in like way be driven by more wide business objectives that complement the task and decentralized utilization of blockchain. While it will require some venture to transform into a portrayed level-headed, a more secure, capable and adaptable plan is offered by decentralized data storing in a data-hungry course of action.

Blockchain for Validating Artificial Intelligence (AI) Decisions is discussed in section 19.3. Further section 19.4 presents Machine Learning-based Knowledge Extraction Techniques collected from several Smart Platforms or computing environments.

19.10   Conclusion

This work has discussed several possible uses of blockchain in detail and proves how blockchain has changed the life of human beings and made them comfortable and reliable life to live. Through blockchain, data can be kept secure, and also can be transferred securely over public, private and hybrid try work. We have not heard a single case of attack over blockchain over a public based blockchain network. Yes, an attack is possible over a privately based blockchain network (especially when no of users in a private network is very less). On another side, blockchain based decentralized applications have increased nowadays, especially today smart contact is being used in many financial and nonfinancial to keep data secure forever. Hence, we invite all future researchers who are working towards blockchain and smart contracts to solve some real problems for society through this innovative concept of distributed ledger technology.

References

1. Deshmukh, A., Sreenath, N., Tyagi, A.K., Eswara Abhichandan, U.V., Blockchain enabled cyber security: A comprehensive survey. *2022 International Conference on Computer Communication and Informatics (ICCCI)*, pp. 1–6, 2022.
2. Tyagi, A. K., Chapter 2 - Decentralized everything: Practical use of blockchain technology in future applications, in: *Distributed Computing to Blockchain*, Rajiv Pandey, Sam Goundar, Shahnaz Fatima (Eds.), pp. 19–38, Academic Press, 2023, ISBN 9780323961462, https://doi.org/10.1016/B978-0-323-96146-2.00010-3.
3. Cruz, J.P., Kaji, Y., Yanai, N., RBAC-SC: Role-based access control using smart contract. *IEEE Access*, 6, 12240–12251, 2018.
4. Panarello, A. *et al.*, Blockchain and IoT integration: A systematic survey. *Sensors*, 18, 8, 2575, 2018.
5. Jabbar, K. and Bjørn, P., Growing the blockchain information infrastructure. *Proceedings of the 2017 CHI Conference on Human Factors in Computing Systems*, 2017.
6. Wang, S. *et al.*, Blockchain-enabled smart contracts: Architecture, applications, and future trends. *IEEE Trans. Syst. Man Cybern. Syst.*, 49, 11, 2266–2277, 2019.
7. Staples, M., Chen, S., Falamaki, S., Ponomarev, A., Rimba, P., Tran, A.B., Weber, I., Xu, X., Zhu, J., *Risks and opportunities for systems using blockchain and smart contracts*, Data61, CSIRO, Sydney, 2017.
8. Hewa, T.M., Hu, Y., Liyanage, M., Kanhare, S.S., Ylianttila, M., Survey on blockchain-based smart contracts: Technical aspects and future research. *IEEE Access*, 9, 87643–87662, 2021.
9. Mohanta, B.K., Panda, S.S., Jena, D., An overview of smart contract and use cases in blockchain technology, in: *2018 9th International Conference on Computing, Communication and Networking Technologies (ICCCNT)*, IEEE, pp. 1–4, 2018.
10. Deshmukh, A., Patil, D., Tyagi, A.K., Arumugam, S.S., Arumugam, Recent trends on blockchain for internet of things based applications: Open issues and future trends, in: *Proceedings of the 2022 Fourteenth International*

Conference on Contemporary Computing (IC3-2022), Association for Computing Machinery, New York, NY, USA, pp. 484–492, 2022, https://doi.org/10.1145/3549206.3549289.

11. Hewa, T.M., Hu, Y., Liyanage, M., Kanhare, S.S., Ylianttila, M., Survey on blockchain-based smart contracts: Technical aspects and future research. IEEE Access, 9, 87643–87662, 2021.

12. Tyagi, A.K., Chandrasekaran, S., Sreenath, N., Blockchain technology: A new technology for creating distributed and trusted computing environment. 2022 International Conference on Applied Artificial Intelligence and Computing (ICAAIC), pp. 1348–1354, 2022.

13. Bailis, P., Narayanan, A., Miller, A., Han, S., Communications of the ACM, 60, 5, 48–51, May 2017, Available at: https://dl.acm.org/doi/pdf/10.1145/3028687.3043967.

14. Yang, W. et al., Smart-contract enabled decentralized knowledge fusion for blockchain-based conversation system. Expert Syst. Appl., 203, 117089, 2022.

15. Ahmadisheykhsarmast, S. and Sonmez, R., A smart contract system for security of payment of construction contracts. Autom. Constr., 120, 103401, 2020.

16. Wang, S., Ouyang, L., Yuan, Y., Ni, X., Han, X., Wang, F.Y., Blockchain-enabled smart contracts: Architecture, applications, and future trends. IEEE Trans. Syst. Man Cybern. Syst., 49, 11, 2266–2277, 2019.

17. Miller, A., Cai, Z., Jha, S., Smart contracts and opportunities for formal methods, in: Leveraging Applications of Formal Methods, Margaria, T., Steffen, B. (eds.), Verification and Validation. Industrial Practice. ISoLA 2018. Lecture Notes in Computer Science, 11247. Springer, Cham, 2018. https://doi.org/10.1007/978-3-030-03427-6_22

18. Deshmukh, A. et al., Applications of distributed ledger (Blockchain) technology in e-healthcare, in: The Internet of Medical Things (IoMT) and Telemedicine Frameworks and Applications, pp. 248–261, IGI Global, 2023. Available at https://www.igi-global.com/chapter/applications-of-distributed-ledger-blockchain-technology-in-e-healthcare/313079.

19. Tasatanattakool, P. and Techapanupreeda, C., Blockchain: Challenges and applications, in: 2018 International Conference on Information Networking (ICOIN), IEEE, pp. 473–475, 2018.

20. Dillenberger, D.N., Novotny, P., Zhang, Q., Jayachandran, P., Gupta, H., Hans, S., Verma, D. et al., Blockchain analytics and artificial intelligence. IBM J. Res. Dev., 63, 2/3, 5–1, 2019.

21. McEwan, R., Melton, G.B., Knoll, B.C., Wang, Y., Hultman, G., Dale, J.L., Meyer, T., Pakhomov, S.V., NLP-PIER: A scalable natural language processing, indexing, and searching architecture for clinical notes. AMIA Summits Transl. Sci. Proc., 2016, 150, 2016.

22. Monteiro, E., Righi, R., Kunst, R., da Costa, C., Singh, D., Combining natural language processing and blockchain for smart contract generation in the

BLOCKCHAIN-EMPOWERED DECENTRALIZED APPLICATIONS 501

accounting and legal field, in: *International Conference on Intelligent Human Computer Interaction*, Springer, Cham, pp. 307–321, 2021.

23. Shahbazi, Z. and Byun, Y.C., Blockchain-based event detection and trust verification using natural language processing and machine learning. *IEEE Access*, 10, 5790–5800, 2021.

24. Kumar, A., A broad survey on AI integration in blockchain: A forward-looking approach, in: *Proceedings of the National Conference on Recent Trends of Engineering & Technologies,* (RTET-2022) Ramgovind Group of Colleges, Koderma, Jharkhand, India, pp. 5–7, 2022, October.

25. Androulaki, E., Barger, A., Bortnikov, V., Cachin, C., Christidis, K., De Caro, A., Enyeart, D., Ferris, C., Laventman, G., Manevich, Y., Muralidharan, S., Murthy, C., Nguyen, B., Sethi, M., Singh, G., Smith, K., Sorniotti, A., Stathakopoulou, C., Vukolić, M., Cocco, S.W., Yellick, J., Hyperledger fabric: A distributed operating system for permissioned blockchains, in: *Proceedings of the 13th European Conference on Computer Systems (EuroSys'18),* vol. Article 30, p. 15, ACM, New York, NY, 2018.

26. Tyagi, A.K., Aswathy, S.U., Aghila, G., Sreenath, N., AARIN: Affordable, accurate, reliable and innovative mechanism to protect a medical cyber-physical system using blockchain technology. *IJIN*, 2, 175–183, October 2021.

27. Nair, M.M., Tyagi, A.K., Sreenath, N., The future with industry 4.0 at the core of society 5.0: Open issues, future opportunities and challenges. *2021 International Conference on Computer Communication and Informatics (ICCCI)*, pp. 1–7, 2021.

28. Tyagi, A.K., Fernandez, T.F., Mishra, S., Kumari, S., Intelligent automation systems at the core of industry 4.0, in: *Intelligent Systems Design and Applications,* ISDA 2020, Advances in Intelligent Systems and Computing, vol. 1351, A. Abraham, V. Piuri, N. Gandhi, P. Siarry, A. Kaklauskas, A. Madureira (Eds.), Springer, Cham, 2021, https://doi.org/10.1007/978-3-030-71187-0_1.

29. Tyagi, A.K. and Nair, M.M., Preserving privacy using distributed ledger technology in intelligent transportation system, in: *Proceedings of the 2022 Fourteenth International Conference on Contemporary Computing (IC3-2022)*, Association for Computing Machinery, New York, NY, USA, pp. 582–590, 2022, https://doi.org/10.1145/3549206.3549306.

30. Deshmukh, A., Patil, D., Tyagi, A.K., Arumugam, S.S., Arumugam, Recent trends on blockchain for internet of things based applications: Open issues and future trends, in: *Proceedings of the 2022 Fourteenth International Conference on Contemporary Computing (IC3-2022)*, Association for Computing Machinery, New York, NY, USA, pp. 484–492, 2022, https://doi.org/10.1145/3549206.3549289.

31. Nair, M.M. and Tyagi, A.K., Preserving privacy using blockchain technology in autonomous vehicles, in: *Proceedings of International Conference on Network Security and Blockchain Technology. ICNSBT 2021. Lecture Notes in Networks and Systems*, vol. 481, D. Giri, J.K. Mandal, K. Sakurai, D. De (Eds.), Springer, Singapore, 2022, https://doi.org/10.1007/978-981-19-3182-6_19.

32. Mishra, S. and Tyagi, A.K., Intrusion detection in Internet of Things (IoTs) based applications using blockchain technology. *2019 Third International Conference on I-SMAC (IoT in Social, Mobile, Analytics and Cloud) (I-SMAC)*, pp. 123–128, 2019.

Privacy of Data, Privacy Laws, and Privacy by Design

Elanur Özmen[1,2] and Aswani Kumar Cherukuri[1*]

[1]School of Information Technology and Engineering Vellore Institute of Technology, Vellore, India
[2]Department of Computer Engineering Kocaeli University, Kocaeli, Türkiye

Abstract

Resolving privacy issues is crucial for protecting fundamental human rights, mitigating risks, and maintaining trust in digital technologies and services. This article examines privacy issues and how they can be resolved. It explores privacy issues across three different categories: privacy problems concerning the data itself, privacy issues related to communication, and privacy issues arising from calculated data. It then examines privacy laws that have been implemented to address or mitigate these problems. Additionally, several methods for implementing privacy in data, such as k-anonymity, l-diversity, and t-closeness, are discussed. Finally, the article looks at how privacy can be incorporated into application design.

Keywords: Data privacy, privacy laws, privacy by design, sensitive data, the General Data Protection Regulation (GDPR)

20.1   Introduction

Personal data have actually existed since the beginning of humanity, as it consists of information that is based on the human being, belonging to and determining the human being. But it was not seen as a legal area and a legal value that needed to be protected. However, the development of information technologies, the extensive utilization of the internet and the increase in information exchange opportunities, especially with the development

_____

*Corresponding author: cherukuri@acm.org

Amit Kumar Tyagi (ed.) Privacy Preservation of Genomic and Medical Data, (503–528) © 2024 Scrivener Publishing LLC

of communication networks, started to create threats of different nature on individuals and their data. The idea that lies at the root of the threats is that the information belonging to individuals is passed into the hands of third parties who do not have the right to access this information, and that this information is processed by third parties in accordance with the law or in violation of the law. Thus, it is possible to access and process all kinds of information that will help determine the personal life of individuals, including information about their private life. Due to these dangers emerging today, the problems related to the protection of personal data have been better understood and studies have been started in this direction [13, 19].

Data protection refers to a range of techniques and protocols that can be implemented to ensure the security, accessibility, and accuracy of data. It is crucial for any organization that deals with sensitive data to have a data protection strategy in place. A well-crafted plan can prevent the loss, theft, or damage of data, and decrease the repercussions of a security incident or catastrophe. Data protection is especially relevant when it comes to personal health information (PHI) and personally identifiable information (PII). By safeguarding data, companies can avoid data breaches and mitigate harm to their reputation [3, 17].

In our data-driven world, privacy laws are gaining more significance. GDPR is one of the most notable and extensive privacy laws, which came into effect in the European Union (EU) in 2018. It offers strict guidelines for collecting, processing, and storing personal data, as well as granting individuals greater authority over their data. In the United States, two significant privacy laws are the California Consumer Privacy Act (CCPA) and the Children's Online Privacy Protection Act (COPPA). On the other hand, COPPA is specifically focused on safeguarding the privacy of children under the age of 13 who use online services. These and other privacy laws around the world play a vital role in safeguarding individuals' privacy and ensuring that their personal data are used responsibly [10, 11].

There are many different methods to protect data. Some of these are backup, having firewall, encryption, authentication and authorization. In this article, we discuss the concepts of k-anonymity, l-diversity, and t-closeness, which are important in maintaining privacy in large datasets. While k-anonymity ensures that the identity of individuals is protected, l-diversity and t-closeness ensure that sensitive information cannot be inferred from the dataset. Taken together, these concepts form a robust framework for safeguarding the confidentiality of individuals' data while also enabling valuable analysis of extensive datasets.

Ensuring data privacy can be achieved not only by trying to protect an existing system, but also by designing the system in a safe way from the start. Ann Cavoukian's seven basic principles introduced an approach to privacy through design, specifically highlighting the principle of "Privacy Embedded into Design." This concept is known as "Privacy by Design Resolution" [12].

The major contributions of this research are as follow,

- Privacy issues were extensively examined under three different headings: (1) data privacy, (2) communication privacy, and (3) computation privacy.
- Privacy laws were examined in detail.
- Three privacy models (k-anonymity, l-diversity, t-closeness) that are effective in solving privacy problems were examined.
- Approaches for incorporating privacy into design were presented.

The rest of this article is organized in the following manner. Section 20.2 about privacy issues, followed by Section 20.3 privacy laws. Section 20.4 presents three privacy models. Section 20.5 explains how to incorporate privacy into the design.

20.2 Privacy Issues

Sensitive Data

Sensitive data are a type of information that is not intended to be publicly accessible. Some databases contain only sensitive data while others contain only public data. The two types can be easily handled through access controls applied to the entire database. The challenge arises when the database contains both sensitive and non-sensitive information. In such cases, there may be different levels of sensitivity, such as in a university database where information on students' names and dorms are less sensitive while details on financial aid, drug use, and parking fines are more sensitive. Access to such data may be granted to varying degrees depending on the user's authorization level. It is important to consider not only the data elements themselves but also their context and meaning as knowledge of their existence may itself be sensitive. For example, in Table 20.1, information that may be in a university's database is given. Name and dormitory are the

Table 20.1 Example database.

Name	Gender	Race	Aid	Fines	Drugs	Dorm
Alex	M	C	6000	30	1	Yellow
Cedric	M	B	0	0	0	Blue

least sensitive; most vulnerable are financial aid, parking tickets, and drug use; That is, many have access to the name, some have access to race and gender, and access to financial aid, parking tickets, and drug use is relatively low.

- The value itself can be sensitive: some values can reveal sensitive information, like the location of defense missiles.
- Sensitive source: data obtained from a confidential source, such as an informant, may require confidentiality to protect the source's identity.
- Declared sensitive: data can be designated as sensitive by the owner or administrator, such as classified military data or anonymous art donors.
- Sensitive attribute or record: an entire record or attribute within a database may be considered sensitive, such as a personnel database's salary attribute or a record of a classified space mission.
- Sensitivity in relation to other information: certain data may become confidential or private when combined with other pieces of information, such as longitude coordinates of a secret gold mine being relatively unimportant alone, but in conjunction with latitude coordinates pinpointing the location of the mine [14].

20.2.1 Privacy Issues in Data

As the volume of data being generated, stored, and shared increases, the likelihood of encountering data privacy issues also increases. As a result, each new piece of data should be considered a potential vulnerability in their privacy policy.

20.2.1.1   Exact Data

The most severe form of data disclosure is when the complete value of a sensitive data element is revealed. This can happen in a situation where the user is aware that they are requesting sensitive data, or they may be unaware that they are requesting public data that contains sensitive information. In some cases, an unintentional mistake by the database administrator can also result in the transmission of sensitive data to the user.

20.2.1.2   Bounds

A precision value x is between the limits of K and L. By doing a binary search, the user first looks at K <= x <= L and then looks at K <= x <= L/2 to find the value of x he is looking for. On the other hand, disclosing more than a certain amount of the budget for sports scholarships or the number of CIA agents, could be a serious breach of security. But imposing limits is a frequently used technique to display sensitive information in a secure manner. For instance, a teacher might explain that the highest mark on the exam is 88 and the loPink is 12. The person who gets 85 may know that they got a good grade compared to the class, but the individual grades of the students are not disclosed.

20.2.1.3   Negative Result

Negative queries can be used to access sensitive data. For example, knowing that a person's criminal record is different from 0 indicates that that person has a criminal record. The distinction between 30 and 31 is not as precise as the distinction between 0 and 1. It can be important to know that a value is not 0.

20.2.1.4   Existence of Attributes

The mere existence of data can be considered sensitive information, irrespective of the actual content. For instance, an employer may want to keep it private that they monitor their employees' entry and exit times. In such a scenario, accessing the file containing the input and output time data would be a violation of sensitive data.

20.2.1.5   Direct Inference

Direct inference is a type of inference or deduction made by an attacker or unauthorized party based on the information they have gained access to. It involves drawing conclusions based on the information that is directly available, without necessarily needing to combine it with other information or make any additional inferences.

For instance, if an attacker can access to a database that contains a list of usernames and corresponding passwords, they may be able to directly infer the passwords for some users if they are stored in plaintext or encrypted in a way that can be easily cracked. Direct inference attacks can be dangerous because they can often lead to immediate access to sensitive information or resources, without the attacker needing to engage in more complex attacks.

20.2.1.6   Direct Attack

To perform a direct attack, a user aims to obtain information about sensitive attributes by making queries that retrieve only a few records. The most effective way to do this is to create a highly specific query that matches only one data item.

If someone writes a query with a drug value other than 0, they can directly see who is using the drug. For example List NAME where Gender=F $\wedge$ DRUGS!=0. But the DBMS may not allow this query because one of the sensitive fields is searched directly in this query.

20.2.1.7   Tracking Devices

Electronic devices that we always have with us also send and receive data. Cell phones constantly search for a nearby tower, GPS navigators both receive and send location data of devices. While these technologies are used for good purposes, they record our movements throughout the day. The challenge with metadata is that it is not readily apparent to the owner but is well-organized and readily available to anyone who seeks to utilize it. While it would be desirable to implement suitable access controls for this delicate geospatial data, many products and applications lack adequate security measures. As a result, data monitoring can transpire without the user or owner's awareness.

20.2.1.8   Storage Security Breach

The concept of storage privacy is centered on the idea of securing stored data from any unauthorized access or manipulation. It involves ensuring that only the data owner and authorized parties can access the data. However, the challenge lies in preventing unauthorized access to the stored data. In the case of locally stored data, physical access control could be a viable option. However, merely connecting the computer to a network is not sufficient, as hackers can still gain remote access to the data. Conversely, if the data are stored in the cloud, physical access control is not feasible, leaving the data susceptible to possible breaches. In addition to physical access control, other measures such as encryption and access controls can be employed to enhance storage privacy. Encryption involves converting data into an unreadable format that requires a secret key to decrypt. Access controls limit who can access data based on their identity, authorization level, and other parameters.

20.2.2   Privacy Issues in Communication

20.2.2.1   Aggregation

To tackle the challenge of aggregation, it is necessary for the database management system to monitor the outcomes received by each user and shield any outcomes that may result in a more precise conclusion. However, addressing this issue is not an easy task, as it can also occur beyond the system. For instance, if the security policy allows access to either the latitude or longitude of a particular location, but not both, individuals could obtain one piece of information each and communicate with one another to piece together the missing information.

20.2.2.2   Authentication

The process of user authentication is a crucial security measure in computer systems, as it establishes a secure link between users and principals who have access to confidential information or privileged actions. User authentication is the first step in accessing remote services or facilities and controlling access. Robust authentication can also protect privacy by ensuring that only authorized parties, such as data subjects, can access private information.

However, there are privacy concerns associated with user authentication. For instance, a passive network observer may monitor users' authentication sessions during network authentication protocols, making it possible to identify or track them. Furthermore, users may inadvertently authenticate to the wrong service controlled by a malicious entity, which could result in their identity being compromised (in phishing attacks) and possibly their credentials. Finally, a successful authentication can lead to the establishment and maintenance of a session between two endpoints, which could be intercepted by a passive observer to infer the identities of the communicating parties.

20.2.2.3 Privacy of Private Conversations

In order to guarantee privacy and confidentiality, contemporary cryptographic methods should be utilized to encode all communication between users or between a user and a service, as most physical network connections do not offer reliable assurances of confidentiality and privacy. With the growing use of wireless local networks and the difficulty of physically securing large area networks against comprehensive monitoring, encryption has become a critical component. All user communications, including sensitive user input or personal information, should be encrypted. Even accessing publicly available resources should be encrypted to prevent snoopers from deducing users' browsing behaviors, building user profiles, analyzing service use, or extracting identifiers for potential tracking purposes.

20.2.2.4 Communications Anonymity and Pseudonymity

To safeguard communication content, end-to-end encryption is often utilized, but this doesn't shield the meta-data from third-party exposure. Meta-data pertains to details regarding the communication, such as the time and frequency of messages, duration of sessions, identification of network endpoints and their location, and additional information. Meta-data leakage can severely impact privacy. For instance, discovering that a journalist is conversing with someone in a government agency may compromise their status as a journalistic source, even if the message details are not accessible. Similarly, continuous searching for information on a specific cancer may reveal a health problem. By analyzing mobile phone location logs, WiFi/IP addresses, or other meta-data, these relationships can be identified even if the individuals involved have not communicated directly [12].

20.2.3 Privacy Issues in Computations

In order to protect individuals' identities, organizations often conceal their personal information such as names, addresses, or other identifying features. Instead, they publish only general statistics such as totals or averages.

However, even with seemingly anonymous statistical metrics, an indirect attack can still be used to extract individual data. Such attacks aim to reach a certain conclusion based on statistical results.

20.2.3.1   Total

The addition attack tries to extract a specific value from the existing total. In Table 20.3, with the data obtained from Table 20.2, student aids were collected on the basis of gender and dormitory. From this painting that seems innocent at first, it is learned that no woman living in Gray receives help. This approach often leads to negative results.

Gender distribution by dormitories is given in Table 20.4. This table is harmless on its own, but combined with Table 20.3, shows that the 2 men in yellow and pink received financial aid of $6000 and $4000. Their names can be seen from the non-sensitive name–dorm scheme.

20.2.3.2   Mean

In cases where the attacker can manipulate the subject population, the arithmetic mean or average can lead to exact disclosure. Consider the scenario where a hacker gains access to a company's confidential data, such as employee salaries. Using this information, they can easily calculate the average salary of all employees and the company, except for the president's salary.

Table 20.2 Sample database with sensitive and non-sensitive data.

Name	Gender	Race	Aid	Fines	Drugs	Dorm
Alex	M	C	6000	30	1	Yellow
Cedric	M	B	0	0	0	Blue
Rosa	F	A	3000	20	0	Pink
Jack	M	C	4000	0	3	Pink
Amy	F	A	0	10	2	Blue
Lina	F	B	5000	10	2	Yellow
Terry	M	C	2000	0	2	Blue
Robin	F	C	0	0	1	Pink
Beck	F	C	2000	95	1	Yellow

Table 20.3 Table showing total result.

Gender	Yellow	Blue	Pink	Total
M	6000	2000	4000	12000
F	7000	0	3000	10000
Total	13000	2000	7000	22000

With these data, the hacker can then estimate the salary of the president with relative ease.

20.2.3.3   Tracker Attacks

A database can be tricked into revealing specific data through a tracker attack, which involves using additional queries that produce small results. By adding extra records to two different queries, the desired data can be located while canceling out the unwanted results. The technique involves using intelligent padding of two queries, where n-1 elements are requested instead of just one element, given that there are n values in the database. This approach can be used to retrieve a single desired element, such as determining the number of white women residing in Yellow Hall.

$$\text{count }((\text{Gender}=F) \wedge (\text{RACE}=C) \wedge (\text{DORM}=\text{Yellow}))$$

There may be a situation where a database management system is checking a database for a particular query and the response is 1. However, because a record significantly affects the result of the query, the database management system may decide to restrict it [14].

20.3   Privacy Laws and Regulations

Data Protection Authority (DPA) is a regulatory body that is responsible for enforcing data protection laws and regulations in a specific jurisdiction.

Table 20.4 Table showing counts.

Gender	Yellow	Blue	Pink	Total
M	1	2	1	4
F	2	1	2	5
Total	3	3	3	9

DPAs are established by national or regional governments to ensure that organizations comply with the relevant data protection laws [15].

The primary role of a DPA is to protect individuals' personal data and privacy rights. This involves educating individuals and organizations about their rights and obligations under data protection laws, investigating complaints from individuals or groups about violations of data protection laws, and conducting audits and inspections of organizations to ensure fit with data protection laws. DPAs also have the power to impose sanctions or penalties on organizations that violate data protection laws, such as fines, injunctions, or administrative orders.

DPAs are crucial for promoting trust and confidence in digital technologies and services. By enforcing data protection laws, DPAs help to prevent the misuse of personal data and ensure that individuals' privacy rights are respected.

In summary, Data Protection Authorities are regulatory bodies that enforce data protection laws and regulations in a specific jurisdiction. They play a crucial role in protecting individuals' personal data and privacy rights and promoting trust and confidence in digital technologies and services [4, 5].

20.3.1   General Data Protection Regulation

General Data Protection Regulation (GDPR) is a significant development in data privacy laws. Widely regarded as the most rigorous legislation on privacy and security globally, it was created by the EU but applies to any organization that targets individuals in the EU or collects data about them, regardless of their location. Enforced from May 25, 2018, GDPR imposes substantial fines for violations of privacy and security standards, with some reaching tens of millions of euros. The impact of GDPR is evident in the growing number of countries adopting similar privacy frameworks, such as CPRA, CDPA, and CPPA.

GDPR applies to entities that process personal data within or outside the EU if they sell goods to the EU or operate within it. The definition of processing is broad and covers any use of data, including collection, storage, retrieval, modification, and destruction. GDPR is applicable to both data controllers, who decide the purpose and manner of processing data, and data processors, who are external parties that carry out data processing on behalf of the controller.

In accordance with Article 4 of the GDPR, personal data are defined as "any information relating to an identified or identifiable natural person." This definition necessitates the implementation of appropriate security measures by most organizations to safeguard the data of their employees, customers, and partners. The scope of personal data under GDPR is broader than before, encompassing any information that could indirectly identify individuals, such as identification numbers, biometric data, resumes and employment information, CCTV footage, etc.

The global convergence data privacy standards and laws report recognizes GDPR as a landmark in data privacy regulations and identifies its key principles. The conditions specified under European data protection law include several measures, such as granting administrative sanctions and fines to data protection authorities (DPAs), giving individuals the right to object to processing based on the controller's or public interest, requiring organizations to inform DPAs and data subjects of any data breaches, imposing stricter approval requirements, broadening the definition of sensitive data to include biometric and/or genetic data, and mandating organizations that process personal data to appoint data protection officers.

Key responsibilities under the GDPR

- European data protection law mandates that personal data can only be processed under particular circumstances. These include obtaining unambiguous consent from the individual whose data are being processed, processing that is necessary for the performance of a contract, compliance with a legal obligation, protection of vital interests of the data subject, performing a task carried out in the public interest, or processing for the purposes of legitimate interests pursued by the data processing entity, provided that such interests do not override the fundamental rights and freedoms of the data subject [12].

- Within the legal context, obtaining consent is crucial for the legitimate handling of personal identifiable information belonging to individuals. To ensure the validity of consent, individuals must explicitly express their intentions about the processing of their data in a specific, informed, and transparent way. Failing to meet these requirements renders the consent declaration invalid. Thus, transparency is crucial for obtaining consent. Additionally, individuals retain the right to withdraw their consent, which remains valid for future use.

- In the realm of equitable handling of data, it is important that data collected for a particular intention is not utilized for other purposes that are incompatible. The intention behind data collection must be legitimate and clearly articulated beforehand.

- Only the necessary personal information required for the specific aim should be processed. During the gather and further processing stages, personal data should be minimized or avoided as much as possible. Once personal data are no longer essential for the intended aim, it should be deleted or effectively anonymized.

- To ensure a fair data proccesing, it is important for all relevant parties to have access to sufficient information about the collection and use of personal data. This includes an understanding of the risks associated with processing and the measures that can be taken to control it. Being transparent is crucial to ensure that individuals can effectively exercise their rights, data controllers can evaluate processors, and data protection authorities can oversee compliance with their obligations.

- Individuals have the right to access and correct their personal data, and the right to block and delete their personal data in certain circumstances. They also have the right to withdraw their consent for future use. These rights must be reinforced in a way that enables individuals to effectively and easily exercise them.

- In GDPR, protecting information is a priority and involves ensuring the confidentiality, integrity, availability, and security of data. Achieving these objectives is crucial for privacy and data protection, and requires measures to prevent unauthorized access, processing, manipulation, loss, destruction, and damage to data. Accuracy of data is also important, and organizations need to establish appropriate technical and organizational processes to handle data effectively and enable individuals to exercise their rights.

- In addition, accountability is a key concept that involves ensuring and demonstrating compliance with privacy and data protection principles and legal requirements. This requires clear responsibilities, internal and external auditing, and control of all data processing. Some organizations employ Data Protection Officers to conduct internal audits and handle complaints. A data protection impact assessment is a way to demonstrate compliance. Independent

Data Protection Authorities serve as supervisory bodies at the national level to monitor and control accountability.

20.3.2   California Privacy Rights Act

The shift in California's privacy legislation began with the introduction of the CCPA in June 2018, which was implemented on January 1, 2020. The CCPA grants California residents the right to know the types of personal data that companies collect and allows them to object to the sale of their data to third parties. On November 3, 2020, the California Privacy Rights Act (CPRA) was passed by California voters as a ballot measure, bringing about significant changes to the CCPA. The CPRA updates, revises, and broadens certain regulations and provisions, thereby expanding the rights of Californian consumers.

In terms of coverage, the CPRA) supersedes the CCPA. Specifically, the CPRA applies to any for-profit business that handles personal information of California residents, provided that it meets one or more of the following criteria:

- earns an annual gross revenue of $25 million or more
- collects personal data from 100,000 or more California residents, households, or devices annually
- derives at least half of its annual revenue by selling or sharing personal information of California residents.

The meaning of personal data is defined broadly and is consistent with the definition in the CCPA. It encompasses information that can directly or indirectly identify or be linked to an individual or household. The definition of personal information includes unique identifiers, which are commonly used for marketing purposes. These identifiers include persistent identifiers such as device identifiers, internet protocol addresses, and mobile advertising identifiers, among others. This implies that, like the GDPR, online tracking cookies and similar technologies are subject to regulation.

The CPRA created a new classification of personal information, known as SPI, which mandates additional security measures for organizations and provides consumers with the ability to restrict the usage of their SPI. More details on the content of SPI can be found in Piwik PRO [9].

The CPRA entails certain crucial responsibilities that organizations must undertake. These include:

- Conducting an extensive review of your data processes and practices.
- Ensuring that all third-party data sources are in compliance with the CPRA.
- Developing an effective and efficient system for handling consumer requests regarding their personal data.
- Regularly updating your data privacy policy to remain compliant with the CPRA.

20.3.3   Virginia Consumer Data Protection Act

Virginia became the second state after California to implement a comprehensive data privacy law on March 2, 2021, when the Consumer Data Protection Act (CDPA) was approved. Residents of Virginia now have more say over how businesses use and sell personal data. As a "withdrawal law," the CDPA requires consumers to take specific steps to object to the acquisition of their data.

The core principles of the CDPA determine its extent. The legislation defines a "consumer" as "a natural person who is a resident of the Commonwealth of Virginia acting only in an individual or household context," which means that the law does not cover employee data. Additionally, according to the CDPA, the term "sales of personal information" refers specifically to the exchange of personal data for monetary compensation between the controller and a third party. This means that sharing personal data for non-monetary benefits or purposes is not considered a sale of personal information under the law.

The CDPA provides a definition of personal data as any data that either directly or indirectly refers to a specific individual, making it possible to identify or link them to that information. The CDPA does not offer a precise definition of what qualifies as "reasonably linkable" data. Therefore, any data that can identify an individual, including online identifiers like user IDs or cookies, falls under the purview of the law.

The CDPA has exceptions to the definition of personal data. Employee data are one of the exclusions, as is unidentified data that cannot be used to identify an individual. Public information, which is widely accessible to the public, is also not considered personal data under the CDPA.

According to the CDPA, publicly available data refers to any information that has been legitimately made accessible through media by the individual or by a third party to whom the individual has revealed such information. This implies that information disclosed through social media profiles may be considered public under the CDPA.

The CDPA has introduced the concept of sensitive data, which encompasses personal information that can potentially identify an individual, such as their race or ethnicity, mental or physical health diagnosis, religious beliefs, genderual orientation, citizenship or immigration status, genetic or biometric data, personal information of a child, and precise geolocation data.

The CDPA requires businesses to take on various responsibilities to ensure the security of consumers' sensitive data. One important obligation is to respect consumer rights, which includes obtaining active consent from users before processing sensitive information. In such instances, organizations are required to offer consent mechanisms that are comparable to those mandated by the GDPR. Additionally, businesses should describe their data processing methods in their privacy policies, limit the usage and collection of data, apply technical security measures to protect data, and perform data protection assessments. Finally, organizations are advised to sign data processing agreements with any third party that processes data on their behalf.

20.3.4   Other Privacy Laws

There are many other privacy laws in the world, although only three of them are examined in detail in this article. For example, New Zealand Privacy Act, Canada's Consumer Privacy Protection Act (CPPA), German Telecommunications and Telemedia Data Protection Act (TTDSG), and so forth.

20.4   Techniques for Enforcing Privacy

20.4.1   K-Anonymity

K-anonymity is a widely used privacy model and anonymization method that safeguards the confidentiality of individuals in a dataset. The notion of k-anonymity was introduced in 2002 by Latanya Sweeney as a means of preventing the disclosure of identities in public data releases.

To achieve anonymity in a dataset, k-anonymity involves grouping together records that have the same quasi-identifiers, which could include characteristics like age, gender, or ZIP code. Quasi-identifiers are attributes that, when combined, could identify an individual in a dataset. By clustering records with matching quasi-identifiers, k-anonymity guarantees that each group contains a minimum of k-1 other records along with the one being anonymized. This signifies that every record is identical to at least k-1 other records within the same group, making them indistinguishable from one another.

The selection of the value of k is determined by the intended level of privacy and data utility. While a larger value of k can offer enhanced privacy protection, it may result in decreased data utility. Conversely, a smaller value of k preserves more data utility but may provide weaker privacy protection.

To implement k-anonymity, sensitive attributes in the dataset are either removed or generalized within each group of records. Generalization involves replacing specific values of the sensitive attribute with more general categories. For example, a specific age value might be replaced with a range of ages, such as "20–30." The desired degree of privacy and data utility also determines the extent of generalization to be applied.

K-anonymity has been widely used in various applications, such as healthcare, finance, and census data. It is a well-established and effective technique for privacy protection in many scenarios. However, it also has its limitations, such as the potential for attribute disclosure through background knowledge attacks and the difficulty in choosing an appropriate value of k and degree of generalization [7, 16, 18].

20.4.2   L-Diversity

In order to protect sensitive information in datasets, a privacy model called L-diversity is utilized. Its purpose is to prevent the identification of individuals based on their attributes present in the data. Machanavajjhala et al first introduced the concept of L-diversity in 2007.

The L-diversity model recognizes that removing direct identifiers, like names and social security numbers, alone is insufficient to ensure privacy in many cases. Adversaries may still use other attributes present in the dataset to infer SPI. For instance, if a dataset contains medical records, an adversary might utilize a combination of age, gender, and zip code to identify a patient.

To address this issue, L-diversity mandates that each group in the dataset contains at minimum L distinct sensitive values. A group is defined as a collection of records that share the same quasi-identifiers, which are characteristics that are not direct identifiers but can be employed to link records. In a medical dataset, for example, the quasi-identifiers might include age, gender, and zip code.

To achieve L-diversity, a dataset is partitioned into groups based on their quasi-identifiers, and each group is required to have at least L distinct sensitive values. A sensitive value is considered distinct if it represents at most a fraction of 1/L of the records in the group. For instance, if L is set to 10, a group of 100 records must have at least 10 distinct sensitive values, each representing at most 10% of the records in the group.

K-diversity is a useful tool for protecting privacy in datasets, but it has some limitations. For example, it does not prevent background knowledge attacks, where an adversary uses external knowledge to identify individuals. Additionally, L-diversity may not be effective if the dataset has low diversity, meaning that many records have the same values for the quasi-identifiers and sensitive attributes. Nevertheless, L-diversity remains a valuable technique for protecting privacy in datasets, particularly when combined with other privacy-preserving techniques [6].

20.4.3   T-Closeness

T-closeness is a privacy model and anonymization technique that extends k-anonymity to address the issue of attribute disclosure. It was introduced by Li et al in 2007 as a way to protect the privacy of sensitive attributes while preserving data benefit.

In the context of preserving privacy in datasets, T-closeness is a model that ensures the distribution of sensitive data in a group of records is similar to the distribution of these attributes in the overall dataset. The goal is to prevent adversaries from identifying individuals based on their sensitive attributes. The T-closeness approach entails grouping records with identical quasi-identifiers, such as age, gender, and ZIP code, evaluating the distribution of sensitive data in each group, and comparing it with the distribution in the entire dataset, utilizing a distance metric to ascertain that the two distributions are not significantly different. The distance metric is employed to measure the extent of dissimilarity between the distributions.

If the distance metric surpasses a predetermined threshold, the values of sensitive attributes within the group are altered to align them more closely with the overall distribution. The modification can take different forms, depending on the type of sensitive attribute. For example, numerical attributes can be rounded to a certain number of significant digits, while categorical attributes can be replaced with more general categories.

One of the challenges in implementing t-closeness is choosing an appropriate distance metric and threshold. The distance metric should be able to capture the differences between distributions while avoiding false positives. The threshold should be set carefully to balance privacy and data utility.

T-closeness has been shown to provide better privacy protection than k-anonymity in certain scenarios, such as when sensitive attributes have a skewed distribution or when there are few distinct values of the sensitive attributes. However, t-closeness is not a silver bullet and has its own limitations, such as the potential loss of utility and the risk of attribute disclosure through background knowledge attacks [8].

20.5 Privacy by Design

Privacy by Design (PbD) is a comprehensive approach to designing and building systems, products, and services with a primary focus on protecting individuals' privacy and personal data from the very beginning. The concept of PbD was initially introduced by Ann Cavoukian, the former Information and Privacy Commissioner of Ontario, Canada, in the 1990s and has now gained broad acceptance as a methodology for ensuring privacy protection.

The PbD framework operates based on seven essential principles that direct the development and design of products, systems, and services, with the aim of ensuring the safeguarding of individuals' privacy and personal information:

Proactive, not reactive; preventive, not remedial: Privacy protection should be incorporated from the beginning of the design process, not added as a response to a problem.

Privacy as the default setting: Personal data should be automatically protected, and individuals should not have to take additional steps to protect their data.

Privacy embedded into design: Privacy should be an essential aspect of the design process and not a feature that is added later.

Full functionality - positive-sum, not zero-sum: Privacy and functionality should be viewed as complementary objectives, not competing goals.

End-to-end security - full lifecycle protection: Privacy protection should be ensured throughout the entire lifecycle of the system, product, or service, from the collection of personal data to its deletion.

Visibility and transparency - keep it open: Individuals should be informed in a clear and easily understandable way about how their personal data are collected, used, and shared.

Respect for user privacy - keep it user-centric: The privacy needs and preferences of individuals should be respected and incorporated into the design of the system, product, or service.

Implementing the PbD framework requires a holistic approach that involves multiple stakeholders, including designers, developers, data controllers, and data subjects. The PbD approach can help organizations build trust with their users, improve their brand reputation, and avoid legal and financial penalties for privacy violations.

Overall, PbD is a comprehensive and proactive approach to privacy protection that promotes privacy as a fundamental human right and an essential element of responsible innovation [1].

How can we enforce privacy in the design?

In today's digital age, privacy is a critical concern for individuals and organizations alike. Designing an application with privacy in mind is essential to protect users' personal data and privacy rights. PbD is a principle that emphasizes the importance of privacy considerations throughout the entire software development process.

To enforce privacy while designing an application, developers should consider the following:

Collect only necessary data: Collecting too much data increases the risk of data breaches and compromises user privacy. Developers should limit data collection to only what is necessary for the application to function.

Use privacy-preserving technologies: Developers should use privacy-enhancing technologies such as encryption, anonymization, and pseudonymization to protect user data.

Provide Transparent Privacy Policies: Ensuring that users receive unambiguous and succinct details about the methods of collecting, using, and distributing their personal data is crucial. Achieving this can be accomplished by creating a transparent privacy policy that clearly outlines the data collection and processing procedures of the application.

Conduct Privacy Impact Assessments (PIA): PIAs can help identify privacy risks and recommend privacy-enhancing measures. PIAs should be conducted throughout the development lifecycle, from the design phase to the post-deployment phase.

Train employees: Developers and employees should be trained on privacy best practices and policies to ensure that they understand the significance of privacy and how to protect user data.

Monitor compliance: Regular monitoring and auditing of the application's data handling practices can ensure that it is complying with privacy laws and regulations.

In summary, enforcing privacy while designing an application requires a holistic approach that considers privacy throughout the entire software development life cycle. Developers should collect only necessary data, use privacy-preserving technologies, implement privacy policies and controls, conduct privacy impact assessments, train employees, and monitor compliance. By following these principles, developers can create applications that protect users' personal data and privacy rights.

Deloitte has created a collection of criteria and controls that companies can utilize to appraise and enhance their privacy measures. Additionally, the company provides a certification program for organizations that satisfy the requisite privacy standards.

In order to become certified in Privacy by Design, companies are required to undergo an evaluation conducted by Deloitte, during which the organization's product, service or offering is evaluated against the 7 Foundational Principles of PbD. This assessment is conducted by Deloitte's privacy and security professionals who evaluate the company's privacy practices in relation to internationally recognized privacy principles, regulations, and best practices.

The steps to certification for implementing PbD are as follows:

Step 1: Initial Assessment
To begin the process, the initial step involves an evaluation by Deloitte, where their experts in security and privacy will scrutinize your product, service, or proposal, against the principles of Privacy by Design (PbD) and appraise your privacy practices based on globally recognized privacy principles, regulations, and best practices.

Step 2: Privacy Criteria and Controls Assessment
The next step is the Privacy Criteria and Controls Assessment, where Deloitte will evaluate your organization's privacy practices based on 30 measurable privacy criteria and 107 sample privacy controls. The assessment will utilize a distinct scorecard system that aligns with each of the PbD principles.

Step 3: Certification
Upon successful completion of the initial assessment and privacy criteria and controls assessment, your organization will receive a privacy certification from Ryerson University. This certification indicates that your organization has met the necessary privacy criteria and has implemented PbD principles effectively.

By following these three steps, your organization can demonstrate its commitment to protecting privacy and earn the trust of customers and stakeholders [2, 20].

20.6 Conclusion

Privacy is a fundamental human right that is essential for personal autonomy, dignity, and freedom. The importance of privacy has become increasingly relevant in today's digital age, where large amounts of private data are collected, processed, and shared.

Privacy is critical in protecting individuals from discrimination, identity theft, and other forms of harm. It also enables individuals to control how their private information is used and shared, promoting transparency and accountability in data processing [21].

Moreover, privacy is essential for building trust between individuals and organizations. Businesses and other entities that prioritize privacy and implement appropriate safeguards can establish themselves as trustworthy partners, fostering positive relationships and long-term loyalty.

With the continuous expansion and intricacy of data, it is imperative that people and institutions give priority to privacy and implement necessary actions to safeguard confidential data. This includes incorporating privacy-by-design principles into data processing systems and adopting a proactive approach to data protection.

The right to privacy is an essential human entitlement that is crucial in enhancing individual independence, self-respect, and liberty. By prioritizing privacy and implementing appropriate safeguards, individuals and organizations can establish trust, promote accountability, and safeguard sensitive information.

Privacy laws play a critical role in protecting the privacy rights of individuals, regulating data processing activities, promoting trust and confidence, and facilitating international data transfers. It is essential for individuals and organizations to be aware of their privacy rights and obligations under these laws and to take appropriate measures to protect personal data.

K-anonymity, l-diversity, and t-closeness techniques are effective tools for addressing privacy concerns and protecting sensitive information. By incorporating these methods, data can be anonymized and diversified, minimizing the risk of re-identification and privacy breachs.

It is crucial for organizations to prioritize privacy and adopt a proactive approach to data protection. The implementation of these models, along with PbD practices, can not only help to prevent legal and financial consequences resulting from privacy breaches but also foster trust and confidence among users.

As the volume of data being collected and processed continues to grow, organizations must remain vigilant in their efforts to safeguard sensitive information. By utilizing these models, they can help mitigate privacy risks and protect the privacy rights of individuals.

These models offer practical solutions for addressing privacy challenges and should be considered essential components of any comprehensive data protection strategy.

PbD is essential in today's digital age, where large amounts of personal data are collected and processed. By incorporating privacy considerations into the design and development process, organizations can minimize privacy risks and build trust with their customers.

PbD promotes transparency and accountability in data processing. It encourages organizations to be upfront about how they gather, use, and share private data, and to provide individuals with meaningful choices about how their data are processed.

PbD is also consistent with privacy regulations such as the GDPR and other international data protection frameworks. By implementing privacy by design principles, organizations can ensure that they comply with these regulations and avoid potential legal and financial consequences.

PbD is a proactive approach to data protection that emphasizes privacy from the very beginning of the design process. By implementing privacy by design principles, organizations can minimize privacy risks, build trust with their customers, and promote transparency and accountability in data processing.

In conclusion, the use of k-anonymity, l-diversity, and t-closeness models can help to mitigate privacy risks and protect sensitive information. These methods work by anonymizing data and adding diversity to datasets, thereby reducing the risk of re-identification and privacy breaches.

By implementing these models and adopting a PbD approach, organizations can build trust with their users by demonstrating a commitment to protecting their privacy. This not only helps to prevent legal and financial consequences resulting from privacy breaches but also helps to establish a positive reputation and build consumer confidence.

It is imperative for organizations to acknowledge the significance of privacy and take necessary steps to safeguard sensitive information. As the volume of data being collected and processed continues to rise, it is vital to prioritize privacy and establish appropriate measures to ensure its protection. Organizations can address privacy concerns and safeguard users' privacy rights by adopting a PbD approach and implementing models like k-anonymity, l-diversity, and t-closeness [22, 23].

References

1. Cavoukian, A., Privacy by design: The 7 foundational principles. Information and Privacy Commissioner of Ontario, 2011.
2. Deloitte. Privacy by design. Retrieved from https://www2.deloitte.com/content/dam/Deloitte/ca/Documents/risk/ca-en-ers-privacy-by-design-brochure.PDF.
3. European Union Agency for Fundamental Rights, *Handbook on European Data Protection Law: Edition 2018*. Publications Office of the European Union, 2018.
4. European Union, General data protection regulation (GDPR). *Official Journal of the European Union (OJEU)*, 2016.
5. California Legislative Information. California consumer privacy act of 2018, 2018.
6. Machanavajjhala, A., Kifer, D., Gehrke, J., Venkitasubramaniam, M., L-diversity: Privacy beyond k-anonymity, in: *Proceedings of the 22nd International Conference on Data Engineering*, IEEE, pp. 24–24, 2007.
7. Sweeney, L., k-anonymity: A model for protecting privacy. *Int. J. Uncertain. Fuzziness Knowledge-Based Syst.*, 10, 5, 557–570, 2002.
8. Li, N., Li, T., Venkatasubramanian, S., t-Closeness: Privacy beyond k-anonymity and l-diversity, in: *IEEE 23rd International Conference on Data Engineering*, IEEE, pp. 106–115, 2007.
9. Piwik PRO. Privacy laws around the globe – An overview. Wrocław, Poland: Piwik PRO, 2021, February 9.
10. Federal Trade Commission. Children's online privacy protection act (COPPA). (Year unavailable). Retrieved from https://www.ftc.gov/enforcement/rules/rulemaking-regulatory-reform-proceedings/childrens-online-privacy-protection-rule.
11. European Commission. General data protection regulation (GDPR). 2018. Retrieved from https://ec.europa.eu/info/law/law-topic/data-protection_en.
12. European Union Agency for Cybersecurity (ENISA). Privacy and data protection by design: From policy to engineering. 2014. Retrieved from https://www.enisa.europa.eu/publications/privacy-and-data-protection-by-design.
13. Cloudian, *Data protection and privacy: 7 ways to protect user data*, Cloudian, 2021, March 25, https://cloudian.com/guides/data-protection/data-protection-and-privacy-7-ways-to-protect-user-data/.
14. Pfleeger, C.P., Pfleeger, S.L., Margulies, J. Security in computing. Prentice Hall: United States. 2015.
15. RedScan. GDPR summary - what you need to know. (Year unavailable). Retrieved from https://www.redscan.com/services/gdpr/summary/.
16. Satori Cyber. How K-anonymity preserves data privacy. (2022, February 22). Retrieved from https://satoricyber.com/data-masking/how-k-anonymity-preserves-data-privacy/.

17. Global Internet Liberty Campaign. Privacy survey introduction. (Year unavailable). Retrieved from https://gilc.org/privacy/survey/intro.html.

18. Samarati, P. and Sweeney, L. Protecting privacy when disclosing information: K-anonymity and its enforcement through generalization and suppression. Technical Report SRI-CSL-98-04. SRI International, Computer Science Laboratory. 1998.

19. DataGrail. Data privacy issues: Definition, types & examples. (2021, January 13). Retrieved from https://www.datagrail.io/blog/data-privacy/data-privacy-issues/#:~:text=Malicious%20third%20parties%20may%20infiltrate,reputational%20damage%2C%20and%20regulatory%20fines.   DataGrail: United States.

20. O'Connor, D., *Privacy by design framework*, Smashing Magazine, 2017, July 18, https://www.smashingmagazine.com/2017/07/privacy-by-design-framework/.

21. Incogniton, *Top data privacy issues you need to know in 2021*, Incogniton, 2021, January 20, https://incogniton.com/top-data-privacy-issues/.

22. Preethi, G. and Cherukuri, A.K., Privacy preserving hu's moments in encrypted domain, in: *Intelligent Systems Design and Applications. ISDA 2017,* Advances in Intelligent Systems and Computing, vol. 736, A. Abraham, P. Muhuri, A. Muda, N. Gandhi (Eds.), Springer, Cham, 2018, https://doi.org/10.1007/978-3-319-76348-4_32.

23. Thaseen, S., Cherukuri, A.K., Kopparapu, A., Velu, G., Cross-border e-commerce security issues and protections, in: *Cross-Border E-Commerce Marketing and Management*, M. Hoque & R. Bashaw (Eds.), pp. 98–119, Hershey, PA: IGI Global, 2021. Retrieved from https://doi.org/10.4018/978-1-7998-5823-2.ch005.

Index

Printed and bound by CPI Group (UK) Ltd, Croydon, CR0 4YY